Professional Site Server 3.0 Commerce Edition

Marco Tabini

with additional material by

Andreas Wallberg
Steven Livingstone
Jarrod Marshall
Gene Wenning

Wrox Press Ltd. ®

Professional Site Server 3.0 Commerce Edition

Published by Wrox Press Ltd
Arden House, 1102 Warwick Road, Acock's Green, Birmingham B27 6BH, UK
Printed in USA
ISBN 1-861002-50-5

Trademark Acknowledgements

Wrox has endeavored to provide trademark information about all the companies and products mentioned in this book by the appropriate use of capitals. However, Wrox cannot guarantee the accuracy of this information.

Credits

Author
Marco Tabini

Additional Material by
Andreas Wallberg
Steven Livingstone
Jarrod Marshall
Gene Wenning

Editors
Paul Cooper
Claire Fletcher
Soheb Siddiqi

Managing Editor
Joanna Mason

Development Editor
Sarah Bowers

Project Manager
Sophie Edwards

Index
Diane Brenner

Technical Reviewers
Mike Drips
Steve Eden
Scott Haley
Stephen Howard
Timothy Huckaby
Ron Landers
Stephen Leonard
Mark Oswald
Rob Ryan
Gopalakrishnan Sreeraman
Mark Stringer
Andreas Wallberg
Peter Watt
John Wooton

Design/Layout
Tom Bartlett
Mark Burdett
Jonathan Jones

Figures/Illustrations
William Fallon
Jonathan Jones

Cover Design
Chris Morris

About the Author

Marco Tabini is co-founder and CTO of Inisoft Corporation, a company based in Toronto, Canada that researches and develops next-generation Internet platforms. Marco likes to spend his spare time, when he has any, with his wife Emanuela and their two cats, Point and Click.

Dedication

To Emanuela

Acknowledgements

Writing a book is truly an interesting task. I use the word "interesting" because there isn't quite a term that fits well, and "writish" doesn't exist in the dictionary. Looking back at the past few months, I can only recognize that I couldn't have gotten by without the help of so many people, that including a complete list would merely be a way to trick myself into sleeping comfortably at night.

The people at Wrox, who helped me put together the book from its inception to the very end, have been extraordinarily patient, understanding, helpful...even here, someone should invent an adjective designed to fit perfectly. Maybe I'll use "Wroxy". In particular, a big word of thanks goes to Anthea Elston and Jeremy Beacock, the managing editors, who helped start and continue the project respectively, Joanna Mason and Sophie Edwards, who kept it alive, and, mostly, to Paul Cooper, Claire Fletcher and Soheb Siddiqi who made the translation from "Tabinese" to English possible.

Naturally, I'm sure that you are not particularly eager to see members of my family listed in great number here. They do, however, and I feel obliged to be fair to everyone. After all, if it weren't for them, I probably would have never had a chance to get this far. The biggest hug goes to my wife, Emanuela, for she has been near me any time I needed her. Without her, just about any electronic appliance – let alone the darn computers – in my house would at some point been thrown out of the balcony. My parents, Orlando and Paola, also helped me from their outpost in my native Italy. I know you're my biggest fans! And, why not, a little thank-you note also to the cats who live with us, Point and Click, for trying to keep me company during the invariably long nights – and nearly sabotaging the project at least a couple of times in the process (I should point out that when we chose a name for them we *weren't* thinking about computers, but who would believe me?).

Finally, a number of people have helped me discover and learn about Site Server – to them, thanks for giving me the opportunity. I hope I put it to good use.

Additional Material

Andreas Wallberg

Andreas Wallberg is a software consultant, trainer and developer, who lives in Örebro, Sweden. When he's not breaking his legs on his in-lines or on the ski-slopes, he's working at Information Highway, creating innovative web solutions. He would like to make the following acknowledgements:

I would like to thank my mother and father for the great support they've given me, my friends for forcing me to socialize even if I have much to do, and all my colleagues at work for the wonderful creative and inspirational environment.

Steven Livingstone

Steven Livingstone is based in Glasgow, Scotland and specializes in developing distributed web applications for business, as well as the creation of Electronic Commerce stores using Site Server and XML. He also maintains the citix.com and deltabiz.com web sites. He enjoys trying to learn other languages, travel and sport, especially watching Celtic (when they win). He would like to make the following acknowledgements:

I would like to thank everyone I know for the patience they have shown while I was writing and my cat Rambo for the important code changes she made whilst constantly walking over the keyboard. I would also like to dedicate my section of the book to my Grandma and my late Grandad, Daniel O'Sullivan, who have always been an inspiration to me. I can be contacted at `ceo@citix.com`.

Jarrod Marshall

Jarrod Marshall is a consultant for G.A. Sullivan, a company focused on custom application development. His main responsibility is consulting on e-commerce projects using ASP, Microsoft Site Server and Windows NT systems. He would like to make the following acknowledgements:

I would especially like to thank the team at Wrox for their help, not to mention the following, to whom I am most indebted: Jerry Marshall, Peggy Marshall, Greg Sullivan, Tom Klein, Alan Stuart, Michael Barnes, and Sean Leahey. Thank you.

Gene Wenning

Gene Wenning is a Managing Consultant with Breakaway Solutions in Philadelphia, Pennsylvania where he provides project and technical leadership for consulting engagements in Electronic Commerce application design and development. Currently, he is working on turning Breakaway's E-Commerce-in-a-box service-offering into a product through the use of Microsoft's Internet technologies.

Previously, he worked for twelve years at Lockheed-Martin where he gained experience supporting the full lifecycle of large-scale information systems. Specific lifecycle experience includes: concept generation, requirements development, requirements analysis, design, development, test, delivery, and operations and maintenance support.

He has an undergraduate degree in Aerospace Engineering from The Pennsylvania State University and masters degree in Mechanical Engineering from Villanova University.

He would like to thank Stephen Howard for introducing him to the opportunity of participation within the Wrox technical community.

Table of Contents

Chapter 2: System Requirements and Capacity Planning   31

Chapter 3: Installing and Administering MS Commerce Server　45

Chapter 4: Examining the Sample Stores　63

Chapter 5: Creating a New Commerce Server Store 97

Chapter 6: The Basic Store 127

Chapter 7: Security Considerations   149

Chapter 8: The Database Structure

Chapter 9: Using the Commerce Server Objects

Chapter 10: Using the Order Processing Pipeline · 255

Chapter 11: Technical Analysis of the Sample Store   329

Chapter 12: Business-to-Business E-Commerce 381

Chapter 13: The Microsoft Wallet and Buy Now   **439**

Chapter 14: Writing Pipeline Components   **465**

Case Study 1: How to Run Commerce Server in Batch Mode Using VB6   535

Case Study 2: Report Emporium 563

Introduction

"The wonderful world of the Internet is before us." I think this is still true, even though some people want us to believe that it *was* before us, and it's now increasingly difficult to get into it. What these people seem to forget is that the software industry is – so much more today than twenty years ago – open to escalation by a few people who are willing to close themselves in a garage and come out with the next great idea.

In the past five years, the World Wide Web has made an amazing number of (mostly) young entrepreneurs rich beyond their imagination. Sure, they were all pioneers and visionaries, but the great thing about computers and the Internet is that they are fields evolving so rapidly that one can be sure some part of them is always in its infancy, waiting for the next Andy Groove, Steve Wozniak or Ian Sinclair to open the garage door and take over the world.

Electronic commerce is certainly one of the portions of the Internet that show the most promise these days. It's sad, as I mentioned before, that so many individuals think how everything that was to be discovered, everything that had to be thought of in terms of commerce done through the Internet is already out there. My humble opinion is that there is still so much more to do, so many opportunities to make a change in the way people think of it.

The real advantage that today's aspirants to the throne of the world's filthiest rich (yes, of course there is much more to it…) have is that they can take advantage of numerous tools and technologies that help them lay the foundation of their success story without having to start from scratch. This may seem a trivial detail, but it's like the difference between having an engineer build your dream home and building it yourself. No matter how smart you are, the engineer has years of experience and will actually succeed at building the house, far more rapidly than you could. What's more, since the engineer already knows how to build a house, you can concentrate on turning it into your *dream* house – once the basics are taken care of, you can unleash your creativity and build something new and exciting.

Say Hello to Site Server

The tool that is at the very center of this book, Microsoft Site Server, Commerce Edition (SSCE) is something similar to a team of engineers for building advanced websites. It can be helpful in taking care of just about any area of your online creation – from managing content to delivering advertisements. Unfortunately, the teams of engineers that Microsoft has entrapped between the two sides of the Site Server CD do not really talk well to each other, and need a little help. On the other hand, integration between the various products in Site Server – even though not an easy task – is feasible and well worth the time it takes to accomplish the mission.

Professional Site Server 3.0, Commerce Edition deals with a very specific portion of the entire Site Server package – Commerce Server. As you can imagine, Commerce Server deals primarily with electronic commerce in its many shapes and forms. Its function is essentially to provide developers and site architects with a solid foundation on which cutting-edge applications can be built.

Commerce Server is a *platform*, as opposed to an *application*, and it has been designed with the goal of extensibility in mind. Since the entire package is based on COM and ASP, you can easily tap into it, expand its functionality, or even separate one of its portions from the main body and take advantage of what it, in particular, has to offer. In the hands of a well-trained developer, Site Server can do miracles as demonstrated by the Barnes and Noble and Dell online stores.

What Do You Need To Use This Book?

Naturally, Site Server does not stand on its own: it is based on several other successful Microsoft platforms. If you intend to use it and take advantage of this book, you will first of all need to install Windows NT 4.0 and Internet Information Server 4.0. These are obviously required so that you can run the ASP and COM code on which Commerce Server is based.

In addition, you will need a database system in which Commerce Server will store all the data that it needs to handle – such as product and customer information. Even though Commerce Server is compatible with several products, in most cases during the book we will focus on the usage of Microsoft SQL Server, which probably represents the most common choice for everyone. As you probably know, SQL Server is in a sort of "transition" between two major versions – 6.5 and 7.0. The latter has undoubtedly many advantages, and features many new technologies, but SSCE was developed at a time when SQL Server 6.5 was the only system available, and therefore the original package works well with it. Nonetheless, it would unrealistic to expect everyone to stick with an older version of the product, and therefore we'll make the appropriate distinctions whenever appropriate.

From a point of view of knowledge, it would be of help to have a firm handle on ASP development using VBScript before you start learning about Site Server. It would be beyond the scope of this book to provide a complete tutorial on these technologies, but it could be interesting to check out these two books, published by Wrox Press, that can help you:

> **Beginning Active Server Pages 2.0. ISBN 1-861001-3-47**
> **Professional Active Server Pages 2.0. ISBN 1-861001-2-66**

Some portions of the book also require at least some knowledge of either Visual Basic or Visual C++ (naturally, knowing both is fine as well!), but don't worry: you don't need to know these two languages if you want to use Commerce Server. They are employed only when certain advanced features – extensibility in particular – want to be taken advantage of.

What Does This Book Cover?

Here comes the interesting question: how should you read this book? Well, I hate to be obvious, but the first answer that comes to mind is, start from the first page and work your way to the last. By this I don't necessarily mean that the Shakespearian quality of my writing will keep you glued to these pages for hours, but rather that the book was designed to work as a continuous flow of ideas that takes you from the basic concepts of electronic commerce down to the grittiest details of SSCE's internals.

It's also true, however, that you don't need to read the entire book if you're only interested in learning about *certain* aspects of Commerce Server, and therefore I have divided it into four parts.

Part I is dedicated to "making sure everyone is on the same page". There is so much talk about electronic commerce that it sometimes difficult to really tell whether what we hear is always true or not, or what the actual meaning of an expression we might use is. Thus, in this first section of the book we spend some time finding out what electronic commerce is, and how it works. We also introduce SSCE in more detail, and discuss how it is installed and deployed to best suit a variety of scenarios.

Part II deals with Commerce Server from an "administrative" point of view, explaining how it is used and how it works without actually going into the code. The reason why I have separated the "whys", represented by this section, from the "hows", which are part of the next one, is that it's sometimes difficult to see the big picture while hundreds of line of code are being dumped on you at the turn of every page. Part II is probably the least technical section of the book, but it delivers a grand tour of Commerce Server by showing how it works and how it is used in detail.

Part III is where we finally get into the code. Just about anything you need to know in order to use Commerce Server from a developer's viewpoint is in this section: we analyze the structure of all the databases used by the system, the COM objects it provides, and the special technologies it includes. In particular, we'll talk quite a bit about pipelines – a great new technology that makes it possible to easily streamline complex business processes. We'll also discuss *business-to-business* electronic commerce, a specialty that is quite different from traditional "retail" electronic commerce and features its own sets of rules.

Finally, Part IV is where we talk about how Commerce Server can be expanded and optimized. If you're interested in just making Site Server work and create an online presence with it, and don't want to bother with the Visual Basic or Visual C++ stuff, then the only portion of this section that you will be interested in is Chapter 16, which illustrates a few possible techniques to improve the performance of a store created using Commerce Server.

Also provided are three case studies, which give you a more complete picture of Commerce Server and its applications.

The first case study, *How to Run Commerce Server in Batch Mode Using VB6*, gives you a batch processing template to use in your projects. It walks you through creating the template, showing you how it works and then showing you the benefits it can bring to Commerce Server's order processing capability.

The second Case Study, *Report Emporium,* focuses on the less-traditional idea of selling soft goods to customers. It goes through the setting up of a store, including all the background workings, to build a store to deliver documents electronically. This is a break away from the 'norm', where customers expect to buy physical goods.

The final Case Study, *The Wine Store,* walks through the implementation of a store that extends the basic Commerce Server functionality in several ways. It tackles intelligent cross-selling, promotions, special offers, and variable delivery charges, incorporating them into a sophisticated online wine-buying experience.

Once you've gone through a first read of the book, it should be relatively easy to use it as a reference. In particular, Chapter 9 gives you a complete and detailed rundown of all the COM objects available in a Commerce Server environment – we even look at a few "undocumented" objects that officially do not exist! Naturally, there is nothing secretive about them (the reason why they aren't in the documentation is that Microsoft felt they weren't part of Commerce Server's core functionality and simply decided they didn't want to support them), but some of them can prove to be quite useful, or quite disastrous in the wrong hands, and therefore you should be aware of them.

In the end, the goal of *Professional Site Server 3.0, Commerce Edition* is to give you a pleasant and informative reading experience about Commerce Server. If you, like me, think that Site Server is a great product, then I hope this book will serve you well.

Who Is This Book For?

In short, this book is for everyone who has a reason to use Commerce Server. The approach that I have tried to take in writing it has been to try and satisfy the need to learn about electronic commerce and SSCE from many points of view, and not merely by explaining how code should be written. I have always thought that being a developer means a lot more than being a "code cruncher" – understanding the business foundation of a problem is just as important as being able to write the perfect script or program.

Thus, program managers, architects and project leaders will find the book just as interesting as developers will, since the solutions to most of the problems presented are based on business perception, as I think should be the case in a well-oiled development team, applied to the creation of a complete software system.

Conventions

We have used a number of different styles of text and layout in the book to help differentiate between the different kinds of information. Here are examples of the styles we use and an explanation of what they mean:

Advice, hints, and background information comes indented and italicized, like this.

> **Important information comes in boxes like this.**

Bullets are also indented, and appear with a little box marking each new bullet point, like this:

- **Important Words** are in a bold type font

- Words that appear on the screen in menus like the <u>F</u>ile or <u>W</u>indow are in a similar font to the one that you see on screen

- Keys that you press on the keyboard, like *Ctrl* and *Enter*, are in italics

- Code has several fonts. If it's a word that we're talking about in the text, for example when discussing the `For...Next` loop, it's in a fixed width font. If it's a block of code that you can type in as a program and run, then it's also in a gray box:

```
Set oCars = CreateObject("WCCCars.Cars")
Set recCars = oCars.GetAll(RegistryRestore("Showroom", "Not Set"))
```

- Sometimes you'll see code in a mixture of styles, like this:

```
If IsMissing(ConnectionString) Then
varConn = RegistryRestore("Showroom", "Not Set")
Else
varConn = ConnectionString
End If
```

The code with a white background is code we've already looked at and that we don't wish to examine further.

These formats are designed to make sure that you know what it is you're looking at. We hope they make life easier.

Tell Us What You Think

We've worked hard on this book to make it useful. We've tried to understand what you're willing to exchange your hard-earned money for, and we've tried to make the book live up to your expectations.

Please let us know what you think about this book. Tell us what we did wrong, and what we did right. This isn't just marketing flannel: we really do huddle around the e-mail to find out what you think. If you don't believe it, then send us a note. We'll answer, and we'll take whatever you say on board for future editions. The easiest way is to use e-mail:

feedback@wrox.com

You can also find more details about Wrox Press on our Web site. There, you'll find the code from our latest books, sneak previews of forthcoming titles, and information about the authors and editors. You can order Wrox titles directly from the site, or find out where your nearest local bookstore with Wrox titles is located.

Customer Support

If you find a mistake, please have a look at the errata page for this book on our Web site first. If you can't find an answer there, tell us about the problem and we'll do everything we can to answer promptly! Just send us an e-mail:

```
support@wrox.com
```

or view the information on our Web site:

```
http://www.wrox.com/Consumer/Contacts.asp
```

What is Microsoft Site Server, Commerce Edition?

Curiosity is only vanity. Most frequently we wish not to know, but to talk. We would not take a sea voyage for the sole pleasure of seeing without hope of ever telling.
– Blaise Pascal, *Pensées*

There is little doubt that the Internet is the latest trend in worldwide business investment. Shares of Amazon.com, a company that is still losing money after several years of being in the business of selling books, are trading at levels that are comparable with Microsoft's – and well beyond those of giants like General Electric or Citicorp.

When you think about it, the most attractive business opportunity of all is **Electronic Commerce** (EC). It encompasses every industry imaginable, bringing new opportunities and unexpected benefits to all of them. Online banking saves money and time both for the customer and for the bank (and considering the courtesy of some branch clerks, it *really* is a blessing!); online shopping is convenient and – finally – secure to a point where a little common sense virtually eliminates any possibility of fraud; the electronic distribution of goods, although still somewhat hurt by bandwidth problems, is an emerging industry that promises us that we'll soon be able to instantly receive everything from music to movies to registered mail.

For those people who want to be on the successful side of this amazing chapter of human history – those who want to make things happen and profit from the opportunities offered by the Internet – other trends have to be identified. Questions like "Will the PC architecture win?", "What will be the future of EC?" and "Will I have to reboot Windows 2000 every time I sneeze, as I do now with NT 4?" must be answered. In brief, we must choose the right tools with which EC solutions will be developed. We cannot afford to repeat the same mistakes that developers made in the Fifties, Sixties and Seventies, when they thought that two digits for the year *were* enough. Granted, they are enjoying a lot of business now, but there are those who think that the entire Western world will collapse because of that small judgmental miscalculation and, in the true spirit of the American way of life, are preparing for endless legal litigation.

This book will guide you through **Microsoft Commerce Server 3.0**, Microsoft's own EC platform based on the Windows NT operating system, and several other Microsoft technologies that we'll explore in the following chapters. Now, whether you like Microsoft or not, I'm sure that we can all agree on the fact that the Windows platform has matured considerably since it was first introduced and is becoming a growing presence in many enterprise environments. Realistically, it would be improper to believe that NT can handle everything from computer animation to space travel. After all, can you imagine a dialog box with words like "Welcome to Microsoft Space Shuttle. This Wizard will guide you through the launch procedure of your ship. To begin, please enter your thirteen-digit CD key below." ?

If there's one thing that suits NT well, however, it's the Internet. Microsoft has come up with some really interesting technologies and products: Internet Information Server, Active Server Pages, Transaction Server, and the operating system itself is finally becoming stable enough to support high usage traffic and complex operations. Compare that to any other server technology, combined with the ease-of-use and affordability that only Windows' graphical interface can give, and you'll end up with a very long-lasting platform to build your future on.

What Does This Chapter Talk About?

The goal of Chapter 1 is to get you acquainted with what we will be working with through the rest of the book. This is what we will be talking about:

- ❑ What is Electronic Commerce?
  We'll begin with a quick look at what the term Electronic Commerce means. As you'll find out, it's not just counting beans and selling books.

- ❑ A brief history of Microsoft's EC technologies
  How did Microsoft Commerce Server come into existence? The mystery behind an incredibly fast entry into the market is revealed!

- ❑ Microsoft Site Server
  As we'll discover in this section, Commerce Server does not come alone. We'll explore Microsoft Site Server 3.0, an incredibly complete package for Internet and Intranet development.

- ❑ Microsoft Commerce Server
  At last, we'll take a look at what the real McCoy has to offer. This section takes you for a tour of Commerce Server's major features and characteristics.

- ❑ Commerce Server in action
  The last section of this chapter will take us on the Web, where we'll examine some real-life EC sites created using Commerce Server and what they have to offer.

What is Electronic Commerce?

When television was in its infancy, TV shows were simply radio programs that also featured the images of their characters. Being such a novel medium, most people had not yet realized what could be done with it. Slowly, as the confidence and interest in televised programs grew, more and more ideas that were only applicable to this new medium began to blossom: TV shows; mini-series; ads that were based more on visual stimulus than on the spoken presentation of a product – they were all created with television.

Mankind never seems to learn from its mistakes, or maybe just needs time to adapt to new things, and the same happened with the Internet. Web pages looked like bad magazine scans in the beginning, then they slowly evolved to include concepts and technology that are only pertinent to the Net. Indeed, we are still in the process of creating new concepts that work well online; to this very day, advertising has not found a definitive place in the online world, and as more and more Internet companies move toward a free-for-all model, the push to develop new promotional technologies is as strong as ever.

When asked about EC, many people react in the same way; they point at Amazon.com, or Egghead.com – all successful examples of the reaching power of the Internet, but also all mere transpositions of the traditional concept of trade. If you think that doing commerce online means simply receiving credit card numbers and shipping physical goods to your customers, you will never get past the radio programs. Let's instead jump to digital TV directly and examine some of the alternative aspects of EC that are beginning to take form.

Digital Delivery of Goods

Imagine buying a software program and having it delivered to your door the next day. Exciting idea, isn't it – you don't have to move from your home or office, and the software is there after only one day. If you live outside North America, chances are that you will also save some money compared to what you would have spent at your local store.

Now, imagine buying a program and having it delivered to your computer *right away*. Sure, this is quite a wild idea these days – even downloading a small piece of software can prove to be a challenge over a dial-up connection, especially if your ISP's connectivity isn't much better than yours. So much for the $9.99 unlimited-access special offer, huh?

Still, technology is becoming available that will make the delivery of digital goods through the Internet possible. ISDN lines are more and more widely available, while cable modems and ADSL are finding their way inside many homes with an amazing speed – in all senses. Indeed, certain portions of the online market are ready for digital delivery today; most businesses have access to the Internet, and a significant part of them have T1 or better connections that make large downloads acceptable. Some EC providers have not overlooked this detail: Microsoft has recently begun to deliver the contents of its gigantic Developer Network (MSDN) library – a collection of all the enterprise, office and developer software published by the company – through a members-only site.

If you think about it, MSDN is the perfect example of an EC site that breaks all the rules of traditional commerce: there are no physical goods delivered, and the customer doesn't pay for every thing that he or she downloads, but rather disburses an annual subscription fee. Naturally, because not all businesses can afford to download gigabytes of software, the online library is only a support tool for the actual CD-ROM distribution that reaches all members regardless of their Internet connection speed, often late (especially when compared to the online version) and sometimes in pieces, thanks to the gentle touch of some postal workers. I wouldn't be surprised if Microsoft soon introduce an online-only subscription; cheaper because the costs associated with printing and distributing all those CDs will be gone, and more convenient because people living in remote areas will finally know that a new version of Visual Studio is available *before* the next one comes out.

Service Rendering

A not-so-remote possibility is also that you will not be paying the owners of the EC site to give you anything at all, either electronically or physically. Perhaps you will be paying them to provide you with a service.

For example, raise your hand if you regularly backup your hard drive. Well, I see that some things never change. If you *did* backup your machine, you would have probably noticed how easy it is to overwrite floppy disks or backup tapes containing two years of research with the latest version of Solitaire. Not to mention what could happen in the event of some natural disaster, like earthquakes or floods. But hey, who are we kidding? You probably would not be around to notice anyway.

Some companies – being in the business of making backups for those who love Solitaire a little too much – *have* noticed this and are beginning to provide backup services through the Internet. After all, if you can accept the fact that digital encryption works, the Net ends up being an ideal solution for backups: your service provider can be hundreds of miles away from you (hopefully not in a seismic risk zone) and will probably store his tape devices in fireproof containers and well away from card game lovers.

Another well-known example of companies providing services through electronic commerce is that of online securities brokers. In this case, the two obvious advantages that bringing their business onto the Internet gives these companies are the practically limitless availability of their systems (no more waiting on hold for a human broker to become available while your hot stock falters away) and significantly lower costs caused by the reduced human interaction. What's more, the fact that even the big players have finally decided to move online is a clear sign that electronic commerce is becoming more and more secure – remember, these people buy and sell *money*: security is not an option for them.

Software Licensing

It often happens that one needs to use a software package only for a short period of time. Students preparing their thesis may need access to specialized programs that cost thousands of dollars. Pinball game enthusiasts easily grow tired of playing the same table over and over again and don't want to spend money to buy a piece of software that they will soon stop using.

The problem with buying a CD at the store is, of course, that you *have* to buy it. There is no try-before-you-buy or pay-as-you-play. No, there is a pay, buy, and keep it. Of course, the store will give you a refund, but only if you haven't opened it or if the postal workers mentioned in a previous section delivered it. So, if you bought a game that you don't like, there's no escape, and your hard-earned money is now in somebody else's pockets.

Some companies, aware of this kind of problem, have begun using the Internet as a medium for licensing software. "Enabled" applications, as they are often called, connect to the Internet, where the user can purchase *usage time*; that is, the ability to use the software for a limited amount of time. Once the initial period has expired, the user has the option of purchasing additional time, sometimes at a reduced price.

Limited-time software licensing is not exactly a new concept. Shareware has been around for quite a while now, although it often had to either rely on the honesty of the user (as if the average one had any respect for software development) or stop working abruptly after the trial period ended. Software unlocking via phone or fax has also been available for long time; however, due to the high cost associated with maintaining call center staff, it has only been justified for high-end packages. Even these, though, can benefit enormously from the use of the Internet as their licensing method, not only because the call center can be virtually eliminated, but also because anybody who ever bought license-via-fax software knows that there *has* to be a better way to input a license code than to copy ten lines of garbled text from a barely readable piece of thermal paper.

Business-to-Business EC

All the scenarios that we have examined so far, from the traditional selling of physical goods to electronic software licensing, have one thing in common: their recipients are end users. There is, however, a different type of commerce where there is a business at both ends of the rope, which is called **business-to-business** (b2b) commerce.

A typical example of b2b commerce is represented by corporate procurement. If you work for a medium to large-size company, chances are that the organization that you belong to will purchase all of its office supplies from a single distributor. Most probably, you will also have to fill out a ridiculous amount of paperwork and obtain permission from the Pope in order to buy a stapler.

If your company has an Intranet site, however, it could include a corporate procurement section where ordering the stapler would become as simple as clicking your mouse. As your organization is wired, your boss will receive an e-mail asking permission on your behalf to purchase the stapler. If he or she approves it, your order will be automatically sent to the supplier, which will in turn bill the company's account electronically at the end of the month. If all goes well, you could be happily shooting staples at your neighbors in a few days without going through too much trouble.

More examples can be found – suppliers of parts to manufacturers, accounting consultants, and so on – but a few things remain the same. Amount of paper moved around: none. Number of people required to handle the paperwork: none. Possibility of error: only that your boss finds out what you *really* needed the stapler for.

There are many analysts who think that business-to-business electronic commerce will be the Next Big Thing. Their consideration is a rather simple one: by far the largest parts of all transactions are already performed by business partners. This becomes evident if you consider that even before it reaches the retail market, any given product usually goes through several sets of hands: from the manufacturer to the national distributor, then from there to the regional distribution center and on to the retailer, who finally sells it to the end-customer. Just in this one example, for one business-to-consumer operation, three additional business-to-business transactions took place.

When two different business partners talk to each other, there are many parameters to take into account, particularly if you consider that the two companies will most likely use completely different computer systems internally.

A Brief History of Microsoft's EC Technologies

Until 1996 Microsoft did not have any EC technology at all. In that year, the software giant acquired a small company based in San Mateo, California, by the name of e-Shop Inc., which specialized in EC software. At the time, Microsoft had already initiated an internal development effort to create an online commerce tool, but they probably figured that it was more time effective to acquire an external company. After all, don't forget that Microsoft entered the Internet scene late and had to get up to speed with the rest of the industry as quickly as possible.

e-Shop's on-line commerce software was then integrated into Microsoft Merchant Server 1.0, the precursor of Commerce Server. Merchant Server already offered some of the aspects that would become characteristic of Commerce Server later on, but it had much more limited expansion capabilities. Merchant Server 1.0 was unveiled by Mr. Gates himself during his keynote speech at the 1996 Site Builder Conference, and became available on the market in December of that year.

Microsoft sold licenses to install Merchant Server for a whopping $15,000 each. If you think that's perhaps a tad too much so must have many others, because when Microsoft Commerce Server 2.0 was introduced in 1997 its licensing price dropped dramatically to $5,000. Commerce Server 2.0 was also part of a larger package, known as Site Server, Enterprise Edition, that offered a wider range of services aimed both at Intranet and Internet development. We'll take a look at what Site Server has to offer later on in this chapter.

Commerce Server 2.0 represented a significant improvement over Merchant Server. For one thing, support for the Component Object Model (COM), the technology on which ActiveX controls are based, was heavily introduced into the solution, fundamentally for a matter of better integration with Active Server Pages. To this day, all the components used by an online store created with Site Server, Commerce Edition are in fact COM objects. Commerce Server 2.0 still maintained backwards compatibility with components that were part of Merchant Server – especially those designed to handle order processing.

Commerce Server 2.0 also offered a more open integration with multiple database systems than Merchant Server, although it still carried some design features that where designed to "hide" the database from the developer in its predecessor. One of these is the use of *data marshalling*, which we'll examine in Chapter 8.

Commerce Server 3.0, the most current version of the software and also the topic of this book, was introduced early in 1998. It features support for Internet Information Server (IIS) 4.0 and the most recent Microsoft technologies, such as Microsoft Transaction Server (MTS). It also provides a more flexible order processing structure that overcomes many – albeit not all – of Commerce Server 2.0's limitations.

Like its predecessor, Commerce Server 3.0 is also part of a larger package, known as Site Server 3.0, Commerce Edition. The licensing structure has been changed again, although its cost ends up being very close to that of Commerce Server 2.0.

Microsoft Site Server

Site Server is a comprehensive software product designed to address several areas of Internet and Intranet development, including publishing, data replication, content staging, membership, content personalization, traffic analysis, advertising and, of course, electronic commerce.

Site Server comes in two flavors: the standard edition, known simply as Microsoft Site Server, and the EC edition, known as Microsoft Site Server, Commerce Edition. The only difference between the two editions (besides the price) is the presence of Commerce Server and the Ad Server, which we'll see later in this chapter.

> For more information about Microsoft Site Server, you can visit its homepage on the Microsoft web site at http://www.microsoft.com/siteserver.

Content Authoring

Site Server includes the popular Microsoft FrontPage and Microsoft Visual Interdev web site development tools, and provides several *starter sites* that can be used as starting points for creating a web site in a significantly shorter time span than if the developer was starting from scratch. The most significant features, however, are in content management and deployment.

Content Management

Most web sites have areas whose content changes very often. Whenever a change has to be made, even though the format usually stays the same, it is always necessary for somebody knowledgeable in HTML to edit the code of a page in order to insert the new content.

Site Server introduces content management features that make it possible to separate the display format of any given page from its content. This, in turn, makes it possible to base certain pages, or even an entire site, on templates whose content is determined by non-technical people through submission of HTML forms to the web server.

Content Deployment

There are two important rules in web development – rules that most developers have learnt from their own mistakes. First, never – ever – make a change on a live web page, unless of course it has a bug in it (but, then again, you shouldn't have put it online without testing it in the first place). Second, always plan for capacity; often just one server is not enough.

Site Server addresses these two issues by providing tools for the deployment of content in stages and across multiple servers. Therefore, it becomes possible to preview the contents of a page on a *staging server* before it goes online. This makes it possible to trap bugs and format imperfections before they become visible to the public. At the same time, it is also possible to concurrently deploy the content from one single staging server to one or more deployment servers without any human intervention, making capacity planning significantly easier.

Content Delivery

Continuously updating the content of a web site is only part of the recipe for Internet success. Web site owners must also make sure that their users are able to easily find the content that they are looking for. Often, the best way to do this is by analyzing the users' behavior on the site and presenting the most interesting content to them directly. Site Server makes this possible with **Search**, and **Personalization and Membership**.

Search

Those of you familiar with Microsoft Index Server know that indexing and searching are not easy tasks – even to administer. Luckily, Site Server provides several features that make the creation of powerful search tools easier. These include the ability to handle several document formats at once (with the possibility of creating custom filters for the formats that are not directly supported), enhanced security, the possibility of searching databases, directory trees and Exchange directories with a single query and, last but not least, native support for the SQL language.

Additionally, Site Server Search can be instructed to automatically crawl entire web sites using a fault tolerant approach to prevent crashes when the web server reports unusual responses.

Personalization and Membership

A good way to prevent "information overload" on your users is to ask them what they want to see and then deliver only content that is pertinent to their answers. Site Server Membership provides a distributed approach to user data collection by supporting the Internet-standard Lightweight Directory Access Protocol (LDAP). The latter, which will also be at the core of the Windows 2000 Active Directory technology, is an extremely fast and lightweight protocol that makes it possible to store information about a site's user base in a structured fashion. This information can then be used to deliver content that is tailored to a specific user profile through Site Server Personalization.

> If you want to learn more about Site Server Personalization & Membership, check out *Professional Site Server 3.0 Personalization and Membership* by Robert Howard, published by Wrox Press (ISBN 1-861001-94-0).

Content Push

Push technologies, that is the action of delivering content to a user without him or her requesting it explicitly, has not turned out to be a successful industry. The Active Channels, introduced as a prominent feature of Internet Explorer 4.0, met a lackluster response and are less evident in IE5, to the point that the channel bar is now hidden by default.

Still, there are some areas in which Push technology can be helpful. For example, Intranet applications can benefit from it for the timely distribution of material within an organization, such as memos. Online stores can use them to reach their customers. Microsoft is also pushing (if you'll excuse the choice of words) this technology as the preferred way of delivering content to a Windows CE device.

Site Server provides native support for Push, providing Active Channel server software, support for Internet Multicasting technology, and automatic update of the content to be pushed through *Agents* that crawl web sites or directories in search of changes in their content. In addition, channels can be used not only to deliver content but also software, making the update of programs significantly easier.

Analysis

Being able to determine if your web site is in good shape and what your visitors like about it is very important. Contrary to other media, where the only way to know the users' preferences is to conduct expensive market research or polls, every user that visits your web site leaves a trail of information, stored in your server logs. Of course, because an entry in the log files looks like this:

        14:01:16 127.0.0.1 GET /iishelp/common/coua.css 200

it is not a good idea to analyze the server logs by hand even if you are trying to emulate Lee Majors' character in the Bionic Man.

Luckily, Site Server helps us out by means of the **Site Server Analysis** tool, which automates the analysis of server logs and stores them in a way that makes the production of reports easy and efficient. Several types of reports can be generated using Site Server Analysis; they include usage statistics, server capacity, referring sites, and, in conjunction with Personalization & Membership, user profiles.

The only big problem with Site Server Analysis is usability. It is sometimes quite difficult to import very large log files into it – especially if you're trying your luck integrating it with Personalization & Membership or with the Ad Server (which we'll see later in this chapter).

Content Analysis

All web site administrators should be extremely interested in maintaining their sites in perfect shape. Do all the pages function correctly? Are there any missing images? How about broken external and internal links?

If you run a large web site these questions can be very difficult to answer. You certainly cannot go through thousands and thousands of pages and look at them individually in search for missing images or broken links, especially because it is very easy to get sidetracked by clicking on a link and then following it instead of continuing the analysis of the original page.

Site Server's **Content Analyzer** provides an easier way to examine your web site by crawling inside it and detecting broken links, missing images and problems with pages. The result is a neat report, stored in an HTML file, which contains all of your little no-nos spelled out with ruthless precision. Understandably, the analysis of a complex or large site can take up to several hours (if your machine can take it), but the result is certainly worth the wait.

Internet Advertising

Selling advertisements has probably been the first commercial activity carried out on the Internet. Yet, until not long ago it was quite difficult to set up a viable solution for delivering banner ads without having to change the content of a site's pages continuously. Moreover, advertisers are beginning to be more and more demanding, knowing the unique customer relationship that can be created through the Internet thanks to the interactivity it offers, and are beginning to request that their ads be delivered only to accurately targeted groups of users.

Advertisement servers have been available for a while on the market now – the most widely known is published by NetGravity, Inc. – but they are often too expensive for the quantity of advertisements that the typical site can handle. The only alternative so far has been selling the site's advertising space to an ad agency that groups several sites together (and so can usually justify the cost of an advertisement server!).

Site Server, Commerce Edition comes with an advertising server called **Ad Server**, a set of ASP applications that make it possible to deliver ads over the Internet. In addition to traditional GIF or JPG banner ads, Ad Server also supports HTML ads, in which the ad itself is not an image but rather a chunk of HTML code that is inserted in the page, as well as NetShow data streams or Enliven ads. Enliven is a promising technology – currently limited by the scarce availability of bandwidth – that makes it possible to deliver complex interactive ads to a web browser.

> *For more information about the Enliven technology, visit* `http://www.enliven.com`.

Ad Server is certainly a viable alternative to more expensive advertisement server software, as it provides the ability to target ads, as well as to limit the number of times that a user can see a given ad during the same user session, a technique often referred to as *exposure limit*. It also offers the possibility of programming ads for automatic inclusion and exclusion in the rotation schedule, and can be easily expanded by providing alternative methods of targeting ads. Its only major drawbacks are the difficulty of delivering more than one ad in the same page (the only solution is to set the exposure limit for the ad to 1 and then reset the user's history every time he or she requests a new page) and the fact that it's impossible to change the algorithm that decides which ads have to be delivered.

Microsoft Commerce Server 3.0

Of all the wonderful things that Site Server has to offer, we still have to talk about the most important one (at least for this book): electronic commerce – represented, of course, by Commerce Server.

Once installed on a Windows NT Server machine, Commerce Server provides the essential tools for the creation, maintenance and expansion of one or more EC sites.

Because Commerce Server is fundamentally based on Active Server Pages technology, most of its functionality is provided by ASP components that fall within four main categories:

- ❑ Input/output and content delivery
  These components facilitate the delivery of content to the user by providing functions that address issues typically connected to the operations of an EC site. For example, the Page component, examined in Chapter 9, makes it possible to display currency values according to different locales.

- ❑ Order handling and processing
  The ability to collect information about and process an order is probably the single most important aspect of designing an EC site. Commerce Server provides a structured – and yet expandable – approach to collecting all the data required to store an order through the Dictionary object (Chapter 9) and a systematic approach to order processing through the Order Processing Pipeline (OPP). The latter, in particular, is of extreme importance; therefore, Chapter 10 is entirely dedicated to it.

❏ Order storage
Storing an order in a database can be quite a challenge, because it is very difficult to determine a priori the quantity – or the nature – of the information that is contained in it. Commerce Server deploys a technique known as data marshalling to solve this problem in a very elegant way. More about database storage in general, and data marshalling in particular, in Chapter 8.

❏ Business-to-business functionality
As we mentioned above, business-to-business transactions entail particular considerations and require specialized tools that can be difficult to build from scratch. Luckily, Commerce Server includes a dedicated type of pipeline, called the Commerce Interchange Pipeline (CIP), that was specifically designed to handle business-to-business communications; we'll talk about it in Chapter 12.

User Interaction

For the most part, users interact with Commerce Server through a web interface of some sort; there are basically three levels of user access:

❏ End user
The end users interact with the storefront of a Commerce Server site: they browse through the catalog of available products and (hopefully) buy them.

❏ Store administrator
The store administrator accesses the backend of a Commerce Server site to modify the way it behaves. This includes, for example, accessing the database of products, setting the shipping rates, and so on. The store administrator also queries the backend to learn about the shopping habits of the site's visitors and to obtain reports on many other aspects of the site.

❏ Server administrator
Once installed on a machine, Commerce Server makes it possible to create a virtually unlimited number of EC sites on it (at least as long as your memory, CPU and hard drive space hold, and you meet all the required licensing requirements). If the server belongs to an ISP who is reselling hosting space, each of the sites might belong to different owners. Therefore, it is necessary that a separate interface be present for the server administrator to control all the stores as a whole.

> For more information about Site Server licensing rules, you can visit the Microsoft website at this URL:
> http://www.microsoft.com/siteserver/commerce/ProductInfo/Pricing.htm

The Commerce Server Storefront Philosophy

We are all used to walking into a supermarket, grabbing a shopping cart, strolling around in the various aisles and finally ending up at the cashier with our wallet open. On the web we are not really entering anything, let alone grabbing the cart, so some decisions have to be made as to how an online store really works. This is really tricky, because, as we saw earlier, EC sites can do a whole different number of things.

Some Basic Concepts

No matter what an EC site does, there are three concepts that are always applicable:

Every store always sells something

As we mentioned earlier in the chapter, not all the EC sites will be selling physical goods. Therefore, the concept of product as we know it from our real-life experience has to be expanded to include those goods that are not physical – like electronic documents – or that are not goods at all, but services – as is the case with our backup company – or even software licenses.

The user must choose one or more products to buy

In a similar way to what happens in traditional supermarkets, online shoppers are given a repository, known as a **shopping basket**, to hold the product or products that they have chosen to buy.

Although the two concepts are strikingly similar, there are some differences that are not immediately obvious. For one thing, if we want to buy more items of a product, or if we want to drop the product from our shopping cart altogether, we are used – well, at least most of us are – to having to go back to the aisle where we picked the product up and either put some back on the shelf or pick up some more. On the Internet, however, this concept doesn't apply because we are not really picking up or dropping anything – what we're really saying is that we'd be interested in buying n items of a certain product.

Similarly, we are used to the fact that, once we pick something up from the shelves, nobody else can pick up the same item. Please note that I said the same item, not the same product. If for example, we were buying a numbered copy of this book signed by the author (a real rarity, thank God) and I picked up copy number 127, nobody else would be able to pick up the same copy.

Well, this doesn't apply to Internet shopping, because all the user is doing is going through the aisles and writing down what he or she would like to buy. Now ask yourselves why it's called a shopping basket!

Finally, I'd like to draw your attention to one more peculiarity of Internet shopping. When leaving a real store, we can't really take the contents of the basket with us unless we are paying for them. Sure, we can try, but I don't think that the owner of the store will be too happy, and you don't really like to see all those people in blue suits wearing badges knocking at your door, do you?

Again, Internet shopping works differently, because our customers are not taking anything with them unless they actually buy it. Also, because we live in a world where programming a VCR with more than one button is considered a branch of subatomic physics, the customers will expect us to remember what their shopping cart contained when they leave our site and then come back.

A transaction that assigns the products to the user is always executed

Even if your customers are not going to pay directly for the products that they buy from our site, there still has to be a process by means of which they are going to be assigned the products they're asking for. This process must include at least the following steps:

1. Determine the availability of the products and, optionally mark the ones that are not available now for future delivery to the customer.

2. Collect all the significant information about the products. Because the nature of a product often changes over time, it is important to store a "snapshot" of it for future reference.

3. Determine the price of every single product in the order. This includes applying any special offers and discounts that might be pertinent.

4. Determine how much it will cost to deliver the products to the customer. This includes both shipping and handling charges, if applicable.

5. Determine if any taxes have to be paid by the customer.

6. Determine if the customer can pay for the total of the order and charge him or her.

7. Update the site's inventory, if applicable.

8. Save the information collected up to this point in some storage medium for later retrieval.

9. Initiate the delivery process.

Keep in mind that, although all of these steps cause some action to be taken, they can all be skipped, with exception of 2 and 8, by simply causing one or more steps to simply do nothing. This technique is known as *defaulting*.

The Storefront Execution Flow

In order for an EC site to work properly, it is necessary that all its elements interact in a logical fashion. In particular, certain steps must be followed by the user when placing an order on the site.

The user must decide to buy something

This means that the "virtual aisles" of the site must be readily available, and that information regarding each and every product must be easily accessible. Users must also be able to add items to their shopping basket, as well as remove them or alter their number.

The site must collect ship-to information

For those cases in which the goods must be delivered to an address different from the one specified in the bill-to information – if the purchase is a gift, for example – additional shipping information must be specified. This data will also be used to determine what the shipping and tax costs will be.

The site must collect bill-to information

In order to be able to charge users for their purchases, the site must know their addresses and payment information (that is, credit card numbers).

The order must be processed

Once all the appropriate information has been collected and its completeness has been verified, the site must apply whatever rules have been specified by its developer for processing an order, such as verify that a credit card number is correct and that the card contains enough funds to cover the order's cost, make sure that all the goods requested are available, and so on. If an error is encountered at this stage, the order will not go through.

Clearly, the site must be able to respond to these errors by helping the customer solve them. After all, let's not forget that the ultimate goal of the site is to generate income by selling goods to the customers; if they are unable to understand how the site works, the goal is not achieved. For example, this error message:

```
ASP Error 0x00234029

Invalid use of null: VerifyCCNumber()

xt_orderform_purchase.asp, line 45
```

will leave most users puzzled – and those who actually know ASP amused; either way, neither of them will purchase anything from your site. If the error message was instead presented as follows:

```
The credit card number that you have specified does not seem to be correct.
Please return to the payment page and try inserting the number again.
```

your customers will be able to understand what they should do in order to successfully complete the order.

The user must be notified of a successful purchase

Imagine calling a travel agency and asking for a flight ticket. The customer representative on the other end of the phone line asks you all your personal details, including your credit card number, then hangs up. No "thank you", no "your ticket will be in your mailbox in three days", no nothing. How do you know that your order went through? Most likely, you would call the agency back and ask what happened.

The same concept applies to the customers of a store, especially considering that they will not be dealing with a human being. Therefore, the final step of the purchase process must be a confirmation page that explains to the user how the purchases were successful and perhaps adds other details, such as the estimated time of delivery, an order number and so on.

It is important to keep in mind that it is sometimes possible, and appropriate, to change the order in which these steps are executed, or even skip some of them altogether. For example, a members-only site might ask the users to identify themselves as they enter the site; at that point, the bill-to information might be immediately available. At the same time, if your site is used to sell services, you might not need to present the users with a shopping basket at all *even though your store will maintain one internally.*

The Commerce Server Storefront Structure

Let's now take a quick look at how Commerce Server implements the concepts examined so far in this section. Although we will explore the Commerce Server storefront more in detail in Chapter 6, it is important that we acquire some bearings on how a Commerce Server site works. Let's begin by taking a look at the figure below; it shows a slightly simplified flowchart of how the storefront works:

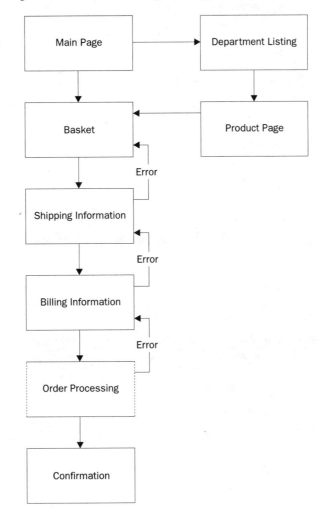

The Main Page

As you can imagine, the main page is the entry point into the store. It is also the central landmark of the whole site. As such, it contains general information about the store, such as its name, as well as links to the available departments (that's what Commerce Server calls the virtual aisles of a site) and to the basket.

The basket exists for two reasons. First of all, as we said, the Main Page is the focal point of the whole store. Users will most likely end up there quite often; therefore, it makes sense to provide a link to the basket, from where the purchase process is initiated. At the same time, because the contents of the basket themselves are preserved between one user session and another, the link gives returning customers a shortcut to purchase what they already have in their basket.

The Department List

Clicking on one of the departments displayed by the Main Page takes the user to the Department List page, which contains a list of available products for the selected department. Each product listing links to the appropriate Product Page.

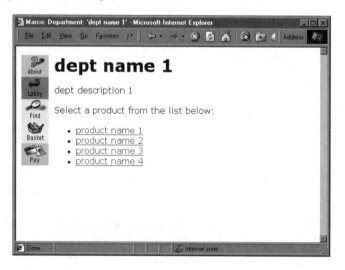

The Product Page

This page contains information that is specific to one single product, such as description, price, whether or not the product is on sale, and so on. From this page, it is possible to add a product to the basket by clicking the appropriate link; by default, the item is stored in the basket with a quantity of 1.

The Basket

The Basket page is fundamentally a list of all the products that the user has decided to put aside for purchasing. It contains links for removing a product from the basket and links to the Shipping Information page – the first step in the purchase process.

It is possible to alter the number of items for a specific product in the basket by simply editing the quantity text box and clicking on Update Basket; setting a quantity of 0 corresponds to clicking on the Remove Product link – it removes the product from the basket. It is therefore possible to delete more than one item at the same time by setting the quantity boxes to 0 and then clicking on Update Basket.

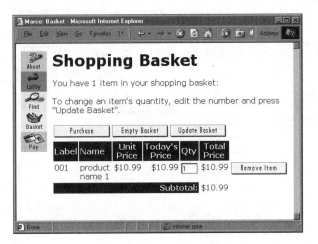

The Shipping Information Page

Clicking on Purchase from the basket causes the purchase process to begin. The first step consists of entering the ship-to information. This must be done before the bill-to information is given because the site needs to know what the destination of the goods will be in order to be able to calculate shipping costs and present the users with a complete order detail and total before they enter their payment information.

By default, Commerce Server supports the Microsoft Wallet, an information collection system that we will examine further in Chapter 13. For those browsers that do not support the Wallet – or for those users who do not want to use it – Commerce Server also provides standard HTML forms, in which all the required information can be entered.

The Billing Information Page

This page displays a complete and detailed view of the order, including any shipping costs and tax fees and collects the bill-to information. As with the Shipping Page, by default the Billing Information Page uses the Microsoft Wallet to collect the bill-to information. Again, however, it is possible to use standard HTML forms if needed.

The Order Processing Page

Although this page is not normally visible to the user, it is an important step of the purchase process. Its goal is to process all the information collected so far and to determine whether it is sufficient to successfully complete the order. This is accomplished by applying all the rules that the site's developers have specified while programming Commerce Server.

The Order Processing Page becomes visible to the user only if it finds that the information collected is not satisfactory; in this case, it prints out a number of error messages, usually aimed at explaining what the user should do in order to successfully complete the purchase process.

If the order is successful this page transparently redirects the user's browser to the Confirmation Page.

The Confirmation Page

If the Order Processing Page determines that all the information collected by the site during the purchase process is sufficient to successfully complete the order, it redirects the user to this page.

The Confirmation Page contains a message explaining to the user that the order was successfully accepted, providing the user with a **reference number** that can be used to identify the order. The latter can be useful, for example, if something goes wrong and the user needs to initiate a correspondence with the site's owner.

Adapting the Storefront to Different EC Models

As you may have noticed, the storefront provided by Commerce Server follows closely the concept of a store that is commonly accepted in the real world. This does not prevent us from adapting it to other EC models, though.

For example, if the site delivers digital goods, the ship-to information can simply consist of an e-mail address; at the same time, if the site is not shipping anything at all – but provides services, for example – the Shipping Information page can be skipped altogether.

As Commerce Server is based on some well-established Microsoft Technologies – namely IIS, ASP and SQL – the process of customizing a store to the owner's needs is relatively straightforward, as we'll see from Chapter 9 onwards.

> Always remember that the goal of Commerce Server is to provide a *platform*, not a product. Therefore, by default a Commerce Server site provides solid foundations on which to build your own site; this means that, unless your needs are very basic, you will not be able to use Commerce Server to create and operate a complete store out-of-the-box.

Commerce Server In Action

Before reviewing all the topics that we have discussed in this chapter, let's take a look at a real-life example of what can be done using Commerce Server. After all, there is no better demonstration of how good a product is than seeing it in action!

Softmania

Softmania is an online store developed and run by Internet Frontier, Inc. (iFront), a company based in Toronto, which is a wholly-owned subsidiary of Microforum Inc. Softmania sells software of all kind, and ships throughout the world using DHL Express Delivery as well as standard mail.

Softmania is a typical example of how Commerce Server can be expanded. In addition to the basic features provided by Commerce Server, which we have seen briefly earlier in this chapter, Softmania offers numerous additional functional elements, such as a reward program, support for shipments from multiple warehouses, a credit card fraud prevention system, and many other enhancements.

The basic idea here is that, while Commerce Server offers you a solid and systematically organized base to work on, you will always be able to add your own functionality on top of it. Alternatively, you can buy a package that expands the functionality of Commerce Server, such as the iFront ECS (tm), which was used to develop Softmania, and deploy that to create your site.

For more information about Softmania, you can visit `http://www.softmania.com`.
IFront can be reached at `http://www.ifront.com`.

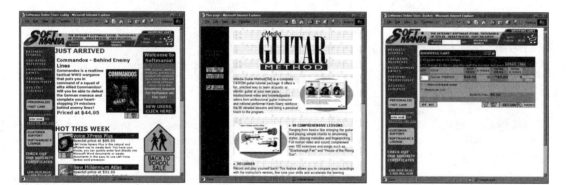

Summary

In this chapter, we took a look at the various types of EC, including those that transcend the ordinary concept of 'store' that we are used to in the real world. In particular, we identified these EC models:

- ❑ **Digital delivery of goods**
  In this scenario, the "products" that an EC site delivers to its customers are digital in nature, such as files or software products.

- ❑ **Service rendering**
  This type of EC site does not deliver any product at all – its intended goal is to sell services.

- ❑ **Software licensing**
  The EC site is used to grant the customers the possibility of running a software program following certain rules (For example, 30 days licenses, and so on).

- ❑ **Business-to-business EC**
  In this type of EC module, businesses are at both ends of the site; a typical example is corporate procurement, where a company purchases goods directly from another company, even though the individual orders originate from individual employees.

We also examined what the key elements of an EC site are, how they interact with each other, and how they can be metaphorically linked to real-life concepts that we are used to.

Finally, we met Microsoft Site Server and its EC portion, Microsoft Commerce Server 3.0. We examined the technologies on which they are based and we took a look at how Commerce Server implements all the concepts that we discussed previously.

System Requirements and Capacity Planning

You can never plan the future by the past
– Edmund Burke, *letter (1781)*

The brief history of the Internet is disseminated with tales of "traffic indigestions" – sites that were not designed to handle a sudden surge of popularity were crushed under the weight of the traffic. Although this is an issue that is thought of as a "happy problem" when a site is designed, it can rapidly turn into a nightmare when it presents itself to an unaware store owner, because it not only causes opportunity losses, but true losses as well, since many customers will be driven away.

Knowing the exact requirements of the software our store runs on, as well as how much traffic a particular installation will be able to withstand, are therefore invaluable tools that will help us when we need to plan for the overall capacity of our system. In particular, we should put ourselves in the position of being able to quickly add more machines to our server pool when the necessity to do so arises.

Clearly, when we most need to be quick, the last thing we want to happen is to find that we forgot to apply a particular Service Pack to our OS; this will make our new machine operate improperly or not at all, making us waste more time when we are frantically trying to do things quickly. The best way to avoid this scenario is to create and maintain an "emergency procedure" that contains all the steps required to create a new installation of your store – in the right order!

Another important element of planning for the capacity of our system is determining how we will present the various machines our store runs on to the public. As we'll see later on in the book, there are a number of special considerations that should be made if we run a "server pool" where a customer could be redirected to any of two or more computers. If we start off with a single machine, we will also have to consider this issue as soon as another computer is needed, and it's *much* better to plan ahead in this case.

What Does This Chapter Talk About?

This chapter has two goals: first, to explore the system requirements needed to run Site Server, Commerce Edition (SSCE) and second, to understand how much performance can be expected from a single computer running our store and how we can plan for the future safely. These are the topics we'll be talking about:

❑ **System requirements**
In this section, we'll explore what we need to install SSCE onto our machine. We'll also prepare a pre–setup sequence of operations that should prepare our computer for the actual installation of SSCE, which we'll tackle in the next chapter.

❑ **Capacity planning**
Next, we'll look into what can be expected from of a single installation of an SSCE store, and how we can do benchmarking measurements for our own store. We'll also talk about possible clustering techniques and introduce a tool that will let us pack and redistribute our store across multiple machines in a breeze.

System Requirements

There are a number of software packages that must be installed onto our computer before we will be able to successfully complete an installation of SSCE. Thanks to the marvels of Service Packs there are also a few steps that have to be taken *after* the setup process!

Our Machines

To start off, let's talk about our configuration. Generally speaking, there will be two major software packages that we will need in order for our store to work: Site Server and a database system of some kind. SSCE supports three DBMSs: Microsoft Access, Microsoft SQL Server, and Oracle products. For reasons that we shall explain later on in the book, we should not use Access unless we expect our store to consistently have very little traffic. Should we decide to go with Access and then need to switch to a more powerful system, we will have to make radical changes to our store's code, something that can't be done quickly in the best of cases. In addition, choosing Access will bring other problems – for example, the Ad Server only runs on SQL Server.

Regardless of whether we decide to go with SQL Server or Oracle, we may decide to install the store and the DBMS on the same machine or on two separate computers. There are good reasons for both configurations, since in the first case we will be able to reduce our hardware budget – a particularly good point if we don't expect much traffic – while in the second case our performance will probably improve, at least in high–traffic situations.

If our expansion plans include the use of more than one web server, however, it's a good idea to be ready to move the DBMS onto a more powerful dedicated machine. In fact, all the instances of SSCE that we will install will have to share the same database. While we will easily be able to spread HTTP traffic load across more than one computer, our DBMS will have to remain on a single machine unless we make at least a few changes to our code or decide to use clustering. Thus, it makes sense that it be stored on a dedicated server in the first place. We might also want to consider using a separate server if we make use of the Membership and Personalization services of SSCE – our user base will build up easily and we will otherwise run the risk of clogging our server very rapidly.

Keep in mind that this is a decision that we do not have to make immediately, since moving a database from one machine to another is a relatively easy operation in any case. However, we should plan for the possibility that our DBMS might become the bottleneck in the overall configuration and be prepared to move it onto a machine of an appropriate specification.

Windows NT

MS Commerce Server, as with the rest of Site Server, requires Windows NT Server 4.0 to run. The first step when we are preparing a new machine for setting up SSCE should be to install a clean version of NT. Although this is not a strict requirement, starting from scratch will give us the opportunity of choosing only the options that we really need.

For example, if we are running a very small operation, and plan to only need one computer for everything, then our domain server will also be the computer on which our store will run. On the other hand, if we have higher capabilities (and deeper pockets), it might be wiser to use a separate machine. In this case, it's a good idea to install NT as a standalone server, with as few services running as we can manage.

Doing so will not only improve our computer's overall performance, but help protect us from outside intrusions. In fact, we should keep in mind that the server on which our store is running is, in the end, our window to the world *and vice versa*, which means that there's a good possibility that whoever will try to hack into our network will start from this machine. Now, in consideration of the fact that the more complex things are, the more difficult they are to handle, keeping our installation as simple as possible will make it easier to protect our data from hackers.

The other good reason for not installing NT in domain master or backup modes is that we will be able to isolate our computer from the rest of our network as a security measure. Clearly, we couldn't do the same if our store was running on the master domain controller that we use on our internal network, since our network will stop working properly; besides, Site Server won't work properly on a computer that is set up as a Backup domain controller. This is as explained in Microsoft's Knowledge Base article #Q184760, which can be found at

http://support.microsoft.com/support/kb/articles/q184/7/60.asp.

We'll talk more about this issue in Chapter 7, when we tackle a few security considerations.

One important consideration is that your hard drive should be in NTFS format, rather than FAT. I will explain more about this in Chapter 3 when we are actually going to install SSCE.

Service Packs

One important matter we must keep in mind when installing NT is that we will need to apply at least one service pack. SSCE requires that NT Service Pack 3 be installed on the machine when we run Site Server's setup program. However, the most up–to–date service pack available for the OS is Service Pack 5, which contains a number of patches and updates that were not available when Site Server was released.

As a result, even if we decide to install SP5, we will need to install **only** SP3 before setting up SSCE, which will create the minimum conditions required for it to run. SP5 can be applied after all the software has been installed to patch any outdated files that might have been installed by Site Server. Installing the Service Packs will also get rid of many security holes in NT and IIS.

You can download and find more information about Windows NT Service Pack 5 on the Microsoft web site at http://www.microsoft.com/windowsnt

Option Pack 4

Since an online store is essentially a web application, we will need to have the appropriate web services installed before we run SSCE's setup program. As a matter of fact, Option Pack 4 is distributed together with the Site Server package, and the setup program for SSCE will let us install it automatically as part of its procedure. However, I have found it better to install the Option Pack before running the setup for Site Server; this will give a greater degree of freedom over our installation choices.

As you may know, Option Pack 4 does not simply contain the HTTP portion of Microsoft Internet Information Server 4.0 but a number of other components as well, some of which we can elect not to install. In general, we should only install the elements of the Option Pack that are strictly suitable for our needs. For example, we should not install the FTP server if we are not going to need FTP access to the computer; the same goes for the SMTP service (which we might however want to keep if we're planning to send confirmation e–mails to our customers and we do not have our own mail server).

Generally speaking, the only essential components of the Option Pack that we will need to be able to run MS Commerce Server are IIS (which also forces installation of the Transaction Server), and the Data Access Components (also known as MDAC), which will make it possible for our store to communicate with our DBMS. We may also decide to install the FrontPage extensions, particularly if we need to edit our store's files using web–editing software, such as Microsoft FrontPage or Visual Interdev 6.0. There are a number of security considerations that involve the FrontPage extensions; therefore we should only install them onto a development machine and never in a production environment.

> We must make sure that we do not change any default IIS settings before installing Site Server. Also, we should not install Site Server Commerce Edition, Proxy Server 2.0 or Exchange Server on the same machine, because the latter two can change several IIS settings that can make our machine insecure.

Internet Explorer

Most of the configuration operations for Site Server Commerce Edition, and MS Commerce Server in particular, are performed through a web browser, and the HTML code that ships with Site Server has been optimized to work with Internet Explorer 4, which is therefore required for the installation.

Once again, the Site Server setup program will install a copy of IE4 for us, but that will be outdated, since several Service Packs are now available for the browser as well. It's a good idea to install a newer version of the browser before installing SSCE, therefore, but we must make sure that we do not install anything more recent than IE4 SP1, because SSCE will only install properly with that version of IE. This may mean that you have to uninstall your current version of IE and reinstall IE4 with SP1.

After the installation process for SSCE has been completed, we can proceed to apply a more recent Service Pack to our copy of IE, or even install version 5.0, if we want to.

The Database

The installation procedure for our DBMS depends on the product that we are using. If SQL Server is our choice, then we must make sure we install it onto a machine that has Service Pack 4 installed. If we're working with SQL Server 6.0, we should consider upgrading to version 6.5; if we are already using the latter, we must make sure that we install the most recent SQL Server Service Pack. If we're planning to use version 7 of SQL Server, we will be required to apply Service Pack 2 to our installation of Site Server; however, it is recommended that SQL Server 7 and Site Server 3 do not reside on the same machine – this is quite unreasonable for a small business, and I believe it is possible for them to live together if our machine has a great deal of RAM: we'll talk more about SQL Server in the next chapter.

In order to properly set up a store, we will need to create a database device and a schema that will contain our data. We must make sure that we create a database device that will be large enough for our needs (we can always increase its size, but you just *know* it's going to happen during the night, over a weekend, when you have taken that hard–earned vacation...!). If we are using SQL Server 7, we can set it to automatically grow the size of the database for us as needed; we must not forget to leave enough space for the log database, which is used by SQL Server to hold transaction data: it tends to grow very quickly, especially if our store is serving a lot of customers, and when it becomes full, the server will return an error.

> *For more information about Microsoft SQL Server Service Packs, visit the Microsoft website at* http://www.microsoft.com/sql.

Data Access Components

A particular discussion should be made about the Microsoft Data Access Components (MDAC), which are optionally installed by the NT Option Pack, SQL Server and Visual Studio 97 or 6.0, as well as a number of other products

> *The table at* http://www.microsoft.com/data/MDAC21info/MDACinstQ.htm *may be of some assistance.*

If we are installing any of this software onto a machine that will host Site Server, we should not install version 2.1 of MDAC, as it is not compatible with the version of the Active Directory Services Interfaces (used by Personalization and Membership) shipped with Site Server (ADSI 2.0) or Site Server itself.

To make things safer, we should first install Site Server, and only at that point run the MDAC setup, assuming that we absolutely need to install it (more information can be found at the previous URL). If we're installing Visual Studio, we will not be given the choice of whether to set up MDAC – the setup program will do it in all cases. Therefore, we should try to avoid installing Visual Studio on a machine running Site Server.

> **Microsoft SQL Server 7.0 includes MDAC 2.1 as a mandatory install; if we intend to use SQL7, we should install it on a separate machine. Otherwise, we will need to perform the workaround described in Microsoft's Knowledge Base article #Q216709.**
>
> **http://support.microsoft.com/support/kb/articles/q216/7/09.asp**

For More Information

Microsoft products tend to change very rapidly, in response to new additions and bugs that are found. As a result, it's somewhat difficult to stay on top of every possible configuration that one should be aware of. Luckily, Microsoft publishes an installation guide for Site Server that is continuously kept up–to–date. You can find it on their web site at the following URL:

http://www.microsoft.com/support/siteserver/install_ss3.asp

Capacity Planning

Before we can proceed with the installation of Site Server, we still have to plan for how our system as a whole will be configured. In order to do that, however, it's appropriate to have a good idea of how much performance we can expect out of a store that runs on SSCE.

Performance Benchmarking

A while back, Microsoft published a white paper that explained how working around several bottlenecks in the software could boost the performance of an SSCE store, as it comes out of the box. This white paper also contained a few benchmarking measurements of a store developed using Site Server, which are extremely valuable during the capacity planning phase. We'll talk more about this topic in Chapter 16, once we have a firm hold on how MS Commerce Server works internally.

A Good Starting Point

The benchmarking tests that we will be doing on our site will be useful for knowing at what point we will be required to add more machines, and how much traffic each computer will be able to handle. However, we will only be able to perform these tests *after* we have installed MS Commerce Server and created the store.

What we need, therefore, is a good starting point from which to build the first machine that we will use for benchmarking. With computer hardware being so inexpensive today, we should focus on three areas in particular:

❑ **Processing power**: the store can be quite an intensive application in terms of resource requirements. If our computer doesn't feature a processor (or several processors) powerful enough, the performance of our store will decrease.

❑ **RAM**: for SQL Server in particular, RAM is much more important than hard drive space or even processing power – at least to a certain degree.

❑ **Redundancy**: no matter how powerful our computer is, if we do not have any redundancy systems in place of any kind (for example: backups, database connection, web server failure or machine failure) and our hard drive fails, our store will stop working!

In general, the performance white paper mentioned above recommends that the minimum starting system be composed of one or two machines, one dedicated to running the store and the other to hosting the database server. The suggested configuration calls for a Pentium Pro CPU for both machines, with 128MB of RAM for the former and 512MB for the latter.

While memory requirements work well today as well, you should keep in mind that the white paper was in mid–1998, and several processor enhancements have become available since then. These days, the minimum machine that we should consider buying contains a single Pentium II Processor with a 400 MHz clock and 100MHz–ready RAM. This will ensure good performance without excessive disbursements.

Multi–Processor Machines

A possible way to improve the performance of a store without adding other computers is to increase the number of processors in a server. Keep in mind, however, that this will only work to a certain point, and adding one more processor will not be as performance enhancing as adding another machine.

Due to the limitations in the database usage that we mentioned in the previous section, however, adding more processors to the machine that hosts our DBMS is a possibility that we should keep in mind – therefore, it makes a lot of sense to buy a machine capable of supporting additional processors for that purpose. We should, however, keep in mind that adding one processor to our computer is not the same as adding a whole different computer! Due to the way that multi–processing works, every processor has to share the same internal environment – bus communications, peripherals, network cards, hard drives and memory, for example – with its counterparts, and therefore its performance will be limited by these factors.

Environmental Variables That Will Affect Your Capacity

There are a number of things that must be taken into consideration when measuring the performance of a store. First of all, completing a purchase is usually much more resource–intensive than browsing the rest of the store, since there are particular tasks that are only carried out when a customer buys something, such as contacting a credit card processor to obtain payment authorization, dispatching the order to our suppliers, and so on.

Another important element is the complexity of the store itself. As we'll see later on in the book, many online stores feature certain techniques aimed at improving the chance that a user will be turned into a customer. These include, for example, store promotions, cross–selling and historical predictions (discussed in Chapter 9), which are all very greedy of computing power. Several other aspects of our store, such as the number of pages that shoppers go through on average during a session, as well as the complexity of our ASP code are all variables that we should keep in mind. The use of other parts of the Site Server package, such as Search, Content Management, Personalization and Membership and the Ad Server, will also affect the overall performance of our store.

Finally, on the database side, the more complex our data schemas are, the more they will put a strain on our server's ability to return datasets promptly. In particular, our use of indexes should be very careful: if employed appropriately, they will help speed up the data retrieval process, but they also tend to eat up a lot of RAM, and should only be utilized when needed.

Clustering and Farming

When one machine is not enough to keep up with the performance requirements of our store, we should consider implementing some clustering or farming techniques. Both techniques make it possible to increase our overall system performance by adding more machines to it, but in two very different ways.

Clustering is a technique that makes it possible for two or more machines to share each other's resources and offer them to the rest of the world as if they belonged to a single computer. Thus, two clustered machines will essentially behave as a single unit whose power is slightly less than the sum of its components.

Farming, on the other hand, provides a way for a user to access several machines through one common entry point. For example, when we go to the Microsoft web site we are actually hitting on different servers, even though the URL on our browser's address bar remains as www.microsoft.com.

Clustering Database Servers

Incidentally, although we can use both techniques in our store, we will only be able to utilize each of them for a particular case. We cannot, in fact, create a farm of database servers, although they can be clustered; similarly, it is recommended that we do not cluster the web servers, which can however be part of a farm.

One way to use more than one machine to handle our data is to use the clustering capabilities of Microsoft Cluster Server, which is part of Windows NT Server 4.0 Enterprise Edition and SQL Server 6.5 Enterprise Edition. Needless to say, the "Enterprise" part of the name requires us to pay a higher price!

The Cluster Server has a few limitations, in particular the fact that we cannot cluster more than two servers at the same time (at least in version 1.0). Nevertheless, even this can be more than enough if our two servers are very powerful. We should decide early on whether we want to support clustering, because we will have to buy the Enterprise Edition of both products.

> **If you want to know more about clustering, I recommend reading 'Enterprise Application Architecture' by Joseph Moniz, published by Wrox Press: ISBN number 1-861002-58-0.**

Web Farming

In a web farm, the users access a web site through a common entry point, which is often offered by a dedicated router that then dispatches the HTTP request to a specific member server according to internal rules that are set into it. It's important that we do not confuse this router with a proxy server, which provides the opposite functionality. The figure below shows how this technology works.

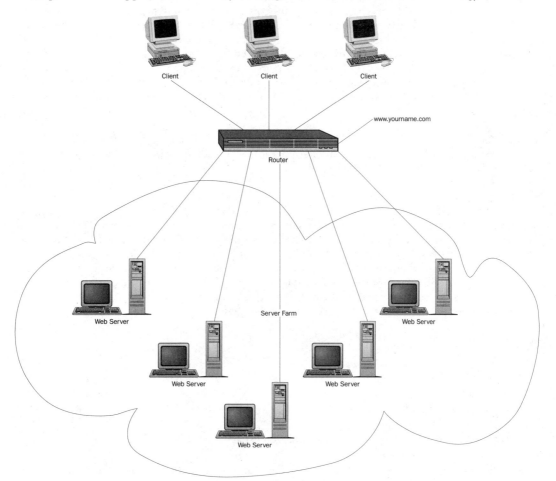

Essentially, there are two types of web farms:

❑   In **random access farms**, the load of web service is equally balanced throughout all the members of the farm. Thus, there is no way to tell whether a user currently visiting Server A when accessing a page will then receive the next from Server B or Server C.

❑   With **sticky IP farms**, on the other hand, the load balancing is done on the user session rather than on the individual page access. Therefore, users are always guaranteed to go back to the same server for as long as their user session lasts.

Normally, IIS web sites cannot reside in a random access farm if they make use of the Session object; to better understand why this happens, we'll have to analyze how it works. As you probably know, Session Objects are essentially a collection of data where information about a particular user visiting the site is stored.

The difficult part of handling this data comes with the fact that the HTTP protocol is essentially stateless (meaning that the server "forgets" what happens between one page and the other) which means that it's impossible for the web server to recognize whether two page requests come from the same user. As such, IIS needs to use some kind of trick to be able to associate the data set stored in the Session object to the right user, even when he or she leaves a page and then requests a new one. The approach that it uses consists of sending a 'cookie' to the client, which contains a unique identifier for the session object in which the user's information is stored. When the next page is accessed, the server retrieves that cookie and is therefore able to link the user to his or her session data once again.

The problem with this approach is that the data stored in the Session object is kept locally in the RAM (or paging file) of the web server where the user opens the first page and is not accessible to any other member of the farm. In the random access configuration, however, the next page request could be directed to *any* server, and therefore there's a good chance that the session data will be lost.

Luckily, as we'll see later on in the book, MS Commerce Server does not make any use of session variables in its stores, to the point that this feature is turned off by default when we create a new store. MS Commerce Server maintains the state by storing the session data in the store's database – accessible to all the servers in the farm – and either sends cookies to the client browser or – if the latter refuses or doesn't support them –passes the unique identifier of the session to the URL query string. Using the database to store session data not only makes it possible to easily use a random access server farm, but also has the added advantage that the information can be persisted indefinitely and presented to the user when he or she comes back.

Farming With NT

The Enterprise Edition of Windows NT Server 4.0 can be used to create a farm of as many as 32 different servers by downloading and installing a component called Windows NT Load Balancing Service (load balancing is another term for server farming). This add–on to NT Enterprise Server is free to download from the Microsoft web site found at the following URL:

http://www.microsoft.com/ntserver/all/downloads.asp#windowsNTServerFeatures

Naturally, we will *still* have to own one copy of the Enterprise Edition of the OS for each server that we want to include in the farm.

Being Ready For Expansion

Before moving on to the next chapter, in which we'll tackle the actual installation and administration of SSCE, it's a good idea to spend a few pages discussing what can be done to be prepared when a sudden surge of usage traffic hits our servers.

At the end of 1995, when Windows 95 came out and people all over the world started getting onto the Internet *en masse*, the Microsoft web site was still sort of an experiment in its infancy. The fact that the IT team hadn't planned for the surge of users who suddenly started hitting the site to download patches (and probably just to find out what this Internet was all about) caused a lot of discomfort and headaches on both ends of the wire: while technicians scrambled to provide the amount of computing power required to keep up with usage, the visitors were often unable to get to the site in a timely manner.

After that episode, the server pool that is used to run the Microsoft web site has been designed to always work at half of its capacity, thus providing enough spare power to cover any reasonably imaginable usage spike. You can find out all about this in an interesting article that was published in June of 1997 in the Microsoft TechNet suite; the article can be viewed online at the following URL:

http://technet.microsoft.com

Scaling Your Needs

Though looking at the Microsoft web site as a successful implementation of a good capacity planning policy (at least after the first try!) is certainly a good idea, it's also probably true that we will not have the same needs in terms of traffic. Therefore, we should plan to meet at least twice the expected normal traffic to our site, allowing us to meet unusually high demands whilst giving us enough time to understand if the traffic surge happened in response to an event that is limited in time or if it simply represents the natural evolution of our site.

As setting up a new copy of our store can be a complex procedure, we should write it down – start with a new computer with no software (including NT) installed on it and write down a list of the software we install, in what order and what should be expected from each step. We should store this recipe together with our capacity plans and keep it handy for any emergency situation!

SSCE installs a useful utility, called **Commerce Site Packager**, that makes it possible to compress a complete copy of a store and reproduce it on a different computer. While this is useful if we're going to be putting copies of the store onto the different computers of a web farm as we add them, we could also use any other compression utility, such as WinZip. The figure here shows the Site Packager's main screen.

Keeping Up to Date

It's important that we periodically review our capacity forecasts to make sure that we're on track and that everything is performing appropriately. If we keep copies of our store packed, we must endeavor to keep them up-to-date (it's hardly conceivable that the store will stay the same for a long time). The same should apply to our software installation procedure, which should be revised as new hardware or software (*including* the various service packs) becomes available.

Summary

Having explored the two important parts pre-setup operations, we are now ready to install a new copy of Site Server and start playing with it. Of all the concepts that we introduced in this book, there are two that are particularly important: first of all, it's essential to make sure that the procedures we have in place for installing all the software needed to set up our store on a new machines are accurate and up-to-date.

Secondly, our system should be geared towards the kind of traffic that we are expected to handle – and we have seen how what that really means is that it should be able to handle spikes of twice as much traffic as we can imagine. Clustering and farming are two very important techniques that can significantly improve our store's performance, but planning is an absolute must if we want to implement them in a painless manner.

Installing and Administering MS Commerce Server

A good start makes for half the job
– Popular saying

In Chapter 2, we discussed in-depth how to prepare our server (or server farm, depending on what our expectations of growth are) for installing Site Server, and it's now time to move on to actually installing the software itself.

As we mentioned earlier in Chapter 1, there are two versions of Site Server on the market. The first one – that shall be called "plain" Site Server to avoid confusion – was originally intended mainly as an Intranet tool, although it contains a lot of technology that can be invaluable for a web site as well. The second one, called Site Server Commerce Edition (SSCE), includes all the tools available in its counterpart, *plus* Commerce Server and Ad Server, which are the topics of this book.

Thus, if we're holding in our hand a copy of SSCE, we're ready to start. If we only have a copy of the plain Site Server, we'll have to obtain an upgrade or buy a copy of SSCE, or we will not be able to install and use Commerce Server.

> **If you are interested in the Commerce Edition of Site Server 3.0, but not quite ready to buy a copy yet, you can download the evaluation version of MS Commerce Server from the Microsoft website at** http://www.microsoft.com/siteserver/commerce. **This is a full-featured copy of the software package that will keep you running for 90 days.**

SSCE comes in the usual Microsoft-look box (it's an unfortunate choice that all Microsoft products look so similar, so we never know if we're picking from the shelf a copy of NT or something else!) which contains a set of three CDs plus a Quick Start Guide (the actual documentation is in electronic format on the CD itself, reflecting a typical trend in MS products). Two of the CDs are to setup Site Server (the first contains the plain version, while the second contains MS Commerce Server and the Ad Server). The third one contains a number of products, including the Windows NT 4.0 Server Option Pack, which we have already examined, Internet Information Server 4.0 and Transaction Server 2.0. These should be installed before moving on to SSCE installation, although the setup program for SSCE will remind us to do so if we haven't.

What Does This Chapter Talk About?

Chapter 3 functions as a logical continuation of Chapter 2, and therefore we will discuss how SSCE is installed and set up. Since we are particularly interested in the electronic commerce portion of the product, we will focus on the installation of MS Commerce Server and Ad Server rather than the entire package, discussing only those sections that are relevant to these two products. In addition, we'll also take a look at how SSCE is administered either using the Microsoft Management Console (MMC) or the administration web site that it creates during setup.

Thus, this chapter will be divided into three parts:

❑ **Installing Site Server**
This section will briefly outline how the plain Site Server should be installed in order for MS Commerce Server to work properly. As we'll find out, this is a necessary step in the installation of the Commerce Edition CD.

❑ **Installing the Commerce Edition**
Next, we'll look at the installation procedure for the second CD of the MS Commerce Server set, which contains Commerce Server and the Ad Server, covering all the possible setup options.

❑ **Administering SSCE**
Finally, we'll take a look at how SSCE is administered using either the MMC or a portion of a special administration web site that is created when we install SSCE.

Installing Site Server

If our computer has been set up with the *CD Autoplay* feature of NT 4.0, inserting the first CD in the MS Commerce Server set will cause its setup program to start automatically. Otherwise, we will have to manually open the CD and run the `setup.exe` in the CD's root folder (we must make sure that we run that one and not one of the setup programs nested in one of its folders).

> **If you're installing MS Commerce Server from a network share point, make sure that there are no spaces in the shared folder's name.**

In either case, you will end up looking at something similar to the screenshot here. As we can see, there are a number of options available at this point. However, the only one we are interested in at this point is the possibility of installing the server. If we click on Server Installation, the actual setup program will launch.

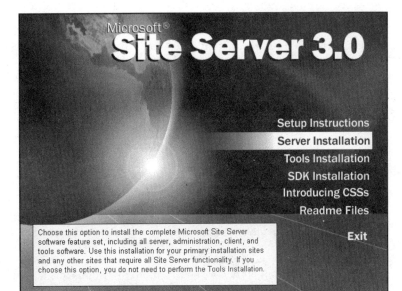

The Setup Process

As installation order is so critical with this product, I will again refer you to http://support.microsoft.com/support/siteserver/install_ss3.asp for the most up-to-date installation information.

The first operation attempted by the setup program aims at determining whether our computer meets the minimum requirements needed to run SSCE and that all the recommended components are installed. When necessary, the program will advise us as to the status of our machine by showing a dialog box similar to the one that we can see in the figure opposite:

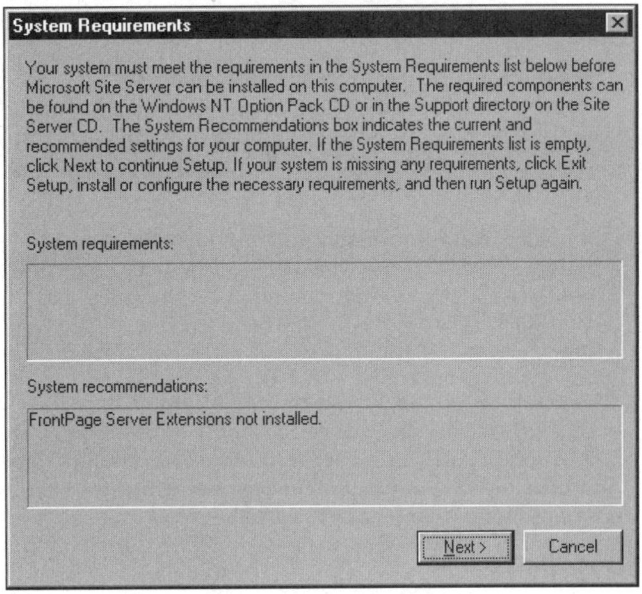

In my case, the machine I was installing the software onto didn't have the FrontPage Extensions installed, which, although not part of the requirements, are very useful when we are developing a new site, as they allow our store to interact directly with Microsoft tools such as InterDev or FrontPage. However, if we are installing SSCE onto a machine that will be accessed by the public, it's a good idea not to install the Extensions at all, as they can become a security concern, because they effectively let an external machine access the files on the server.

If we have forgotten to install something that is part of SSCE's requirements, the setup application won't let us continue until we go back and install them.

Site Server Components

The next step in the setup process consists of choosing the Site Server components that we want to install on the machine. Although we will not discuss any of these options in detail, as they would be off-topic for our book (because this book's primary concern is Site Server 3.0 Commerce Edition, and not the plain Site Server), we'll spend a few words on the Analysis component, which will be useful even if we only decide to use the electronic commerce part of SSCE.

> **If you do want more information on what components are included with plain Site Server, point your browser to:**
> http://support.microsoft.com/support/kb/articles/Q165/2/41.ASP **or read**
> **"Professional Site Server 3.0", published by Wrox Press, ISBN number: 1-861002-69-6**

Analysis includes a set of tools that can be used for two purposes:

❑ analyzing the structure of a web site, identifying broken links, circular references between pages and other inefficiencies in the code, such as pages that take too long to download

❑ examining the data that is collected by a web site, such as usage patterns, ad delivery schedules, and purchase information, analyzing it and producing reports in a variety of formats

The portion of Analysis that is used to analyze the contents of a web site and their structure (which is actually an enhanced version of the old application called **Site Analyst** that Microsoft also distributes freely as part of the NT Option Pack 4) is obviously something that we only want to install on a development machine, as it will only take up hard drive space on a production machine that is accessible to the public.

Similarly, we will probably want to dedicate a separate machine to the data examination and report building features, onto which we'll be able to copy all the data logs from the individual web servers and perform any analysis operations. Also, since a database is required for this portion of the Analysis tool, we will be required to make a choice between using Microsoft Access and SQL Server here.

Generally speaking, all the considerations that we have made about the differences between Access and SQL Server are valid here as well – except, of course that we really won't have to write any SQL code to use Analysis – but the correct choice really depends on the amount of traffic that we expect our site to have and the frequency with which we will need to pull reports out of the system. SQL Server is, once again, a better choice if only for the sheer amount of data that it can handle when compared to its desktop-sized cousin. Even though SQL Server is quite expensive – and we may have reservations as to the usefulness of spending that kind of money on an application that carries out single tasks for a single-user environment – it should be our choice if we intend to use the analysis tools for large amounts of data or for P&M logs.

> Analysis is a very resource-intensive application. Unless the computer we run it on is powerful enough and we need to pull reports on a regular basis (for example, daily), its throughput will not be able to keep up with the data flow (that is, reports will take longer to produce than the data to accumulate). If we are using SQL Server and reports take a long time to generate, we should consider adopting a separate machine – with *plenty* of RAM available – on which to move the database.

Completing the Installation

Once we have made our choice of components to install, the setup program will copy all the files onto the hard drive and folder that we select. Before this, however, the setup program requires us to configure our user accounts. Keep in mind that we should change the default destination if the hard drive that we select already contains a folder that begins with the word Microsoft – this is just a simple measure to prevent other important files being wiped out.

At the end of the installation, we will be required to restart our computer.

A useful resource to consult at this point can be found at:

www.teched99.com/slides/10-305.ppt

Installing the Commerce Edition

Once we're up and running again, we can start installing Commerce Server and the Ad Server. To do so, insert the second CD-ROM into the drive; once again, if we don't have CD Autoplay enabled, we will need to launch the setup application manually in the same way as we did before.

The welcome screen is very similar to the one we encountered earlier, although the options available are fewer (and different).

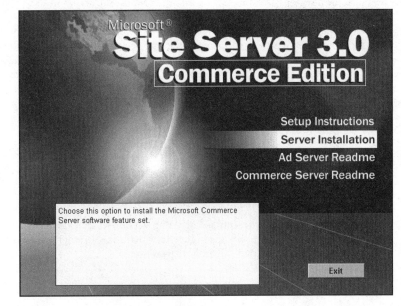

We may want to check out the setup instructions, as well as the two `readme` files, which contain a certain amount of interesting information and things that we should be aware of before we proceed with the installation (which has already been covered for the most part in the previous chapter).

System Requirements Analysis

One very important aspect of SSCE is that, contrary to what happens with its plain counterpart, it **requires** the destination hard drive to be in the NTFS format. If our hard drive isn't in the NTFS format, or if we didn't install the plain Site Server, the setup program will stop. However, if we do not meet the other minimum requirements for running SSCE (including Option and Service Packs), we will not be required to install them manually: the setup program will automatically ask us to insert the Option Pack CD and will run the appropriate installation application.

> **More information about the NTFS format can be found in the following article:**
> http://www.microsoft.com/SYSPRO/deploy/fat.htm

MS Commerce Server Components

Next, we will be required to select the components that we want to install. The setup program will automatically install the "core" files that are required by MS Commerce Server to operate properly, but we will still have our say as to what other optional modules we want copied onto our machine.

The Sample Stores

MS Commerce Server includes a number of sample stores whose goal is to illustrate the functionality that is provided by Site Server as a whole. Whether we will want to install these components onto our machine or not depends once again on what we intend its main use to be.

For example, we should not normally need to install them on a server that will only be used as a production site, since they will simply take up space and provide hackers with possible entry points into our system. At the same time, if our server will be mainly dedicated to development activities, it might be useful to install the sample stores: even if we don't need them as a tutorial, the techniques used by their developers might turn out to be useful and show us, especially if we are new to MS Commerce Server, the different ways in which an online store can operate.

Here's a brief description of each sample store, in order of complexity:

❑ **Clocktower**
The simplest store included in the MS Commerce Server package, Clocktower illustrates MS Commerce Server's basic functionality and provides a fully functional shop of unusual clocks.

❑ **Volcano Coffee**
Volcano coffee represents a stepped-up version of Clocktower (with a different theme), and incorporates several advanced functions that MS Commerce Server can provide, such as dynamic product attributes and customer registration.

Most people learn the commerce product from this sample site; because of that, a completely new volcano coffee sample site has been developed, called Volcano Coffee Turbo, which is free to download from the Microsoft site. It's also included in the commerce resource kit and more information can be found at

http://technet.microsoft.com/cdonline/content/complete/internet/server/sitesrv/commerce/tools/vc turbo.htm

❑ **Microsoft Press**
Microsoft Press presents essentially the same level of complexity as Volcano Coffee, although different techniques are used to present the user with products sold by the store. In addition, MSPress provides an interesting application of the promotional functionality offered by MS Commerce Server.

❑ **Trey Research**
The goal of this sample store is to demonstrate how the various components of Site Server can be integrated together to provide a superior set of functionality. Trey Research is a fictional market research firm that sells access to online reports to registered members.

> **In order to be able to successfully install and use the Trey Research sample store, we will need to have installed the Personalization and Membership component of the plain Site Server and set up a membership server and mapped it to our installation website. More information can be found in "Site Server: Personalization and Membership" by Rob Howard, published by Wrox Press: ISBN number 1-861001-9-40**

❑ **Microsoft Market**
Finally, Microsoft Market is the only sample store that integrates any business-to-business functionality. A reproduction of a real Intranet tool available to Microsoft employees, it illustrates how MS Commerce Server can be used to streamline the process of corporate procurement.

We'll discuss all the sample stores in the next chapter, with the exception of Microsoft Market, which we'll examine in Chapter 12 together with the business-to-business functionality of MS Commerce Server.

It's important to understand that we do not have to make a choice as to whether we need to install any of the sample stores right away: we can run the setup program at any time and install (or uninstall) each sample store separately. However, if we decide to uninstall one of them, remember that any changes we have made to its code will be lost.

The Ad Server

The other product that is an integral part of MS Commerce Server is the **Ad Server**, which can be used to deliver Internet ads in a variety of formats, using an ASP application appropriately designed. We should install this item if we intend to deliver ads either for ourselves or for a third party.

Two components make up the Ad Server: the core functionality (marked as Ad Server in the setup program) and the Ad Manager, which provides a user-friendly management interface for the user. It's difficult to understand why these two options are offered, since the Ad Manager is required in order to be able to set the Ad Server to deliver ads properly. Therefore, in most cases we will choose to either install both components or none.

The Commerce Server SDK

The last optional component of the MS Commerce Server setup is the Commerce Server Software Development Kit, which the setup program simply refers to as **SDK**. This contains a number of tools that are useful to the developer seeking to extend the functionality offered by MS Commerce Server by writing their own addition to either the pipeline technology (described in Chapters 11, 12 and 14) or the Microsoft Wallet (discussed in Chapters 13 and 15).

Clearly, we only need to install the SDK on our machine if we are going to use it as a development server, because it would waste space on a production computer. Also, the SDK is only useful if we expect to extend the functionality of MS Commerce Server as was just mentioned.

The Setup Process

If we have chosen to install any of the sample stores or the Ad Server, the setup application will ask us to name a database DSN for each of these components to use (see figure below). Make sure that the DSN works and that the database user referenced by it has the appropriate privileges to create objects in the database *before* installing MS Commerce Server, otherwise the setup process won't complete successfully.

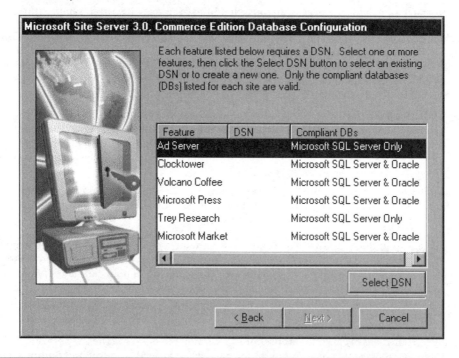

If you are not running setup for the first time (that is, you want to add or remove a component) and the program asks you to specify a DSN, do *not* click on the Back button or the application will automatically assume that you have selected the default choice.

The File Copy Process

The setup procedure will continue with the process that copies all the files from the CD or network location to our hard drive. All the appropriate services (that is, IIS and Transaction Server) are stopped before the copy operation starts and restarted after it ends.

It's not uncommon to encounter a problem of some kind during the setup process – the installation program has to interact with so many other programs and services that it's easy to find an unfavorable situation at some point. In particular, this happens if we have not rebooted our machine after installing one of the pre-requisite software packages, in which case the copy process will be unable to overwrite or register a .DLL.

In most cases, rebooting the machine and restarting the setup program will do the trick. However, if we still encounter problems, we must begin with identifying the exact file that is giving us problems (setup will usually tell us its pathname), and try to understand what is wrong with it. Often, setup will be unable to overwrite a .DLL because some other service or application is using it; we must make sure that we have closed all other programs and stopped any services that are not directly required by SSCE. These services are easily found in the services list: they are all prefixed with "Site Server" – we can always start the services again once the setup process is complete.

Site Server Service Packs

There are now two Service Packs that are available for SSCE. The first one fixes some bugs that are in the original release, and provides updates mostly aimed at the plain version of Site Server. The second one, on the other hand, is intended to fix several compatibility issues with SQL Server 7.0 that plague both Personalization and Membership and MS Commerce Server. If we are looking at using the new version of Microsoft's DBMS, we should definitely consider installing this Service Pack and reading the documentation.

A third SP is also on the way, which will enable Site Server 3.0 stores to be upgraded to Windows 2000 and includes faster and more robust versions of some of the commerce objects. Although the release date for this Service Pack has not been set, it's probably reasonable to think that a beta will be available by the time Windows 2000 hits the market.

Administering MS Commerce Server

The entire Site Server package is administered by either using the Microsoft Management Console (MMC) 1.0 snap-in that is automatically installed by the setup process, or through the section of the server's default web site that this creates.

The latter will generally be our preferred choice, not only because it makes remote administration of the whole server much easier, but also because it provides a much richer set of functions than its MMC counterpart. At the same time, the fact that it might be accessible from the outside can constitute a big risk that should be accurately taken care of through the implementation of a good security policy (we'll talk more about this in Chapter 7).

MMC Administration

In order to access the MMC snap-in that is distributed with SSCE, we will need to click on the **Site Server Service Admin (MMC)** link in the **Start | Programs | Microsoft Site Server | Administration** menu. This, in turn, will launch the MMC and show us a window similar to the one we can see here. As can be seen, on the left side of the screen each portion of Site Server has its own tree of icons that can expand or collapse, which shows all the appropriate entries for that particular component.

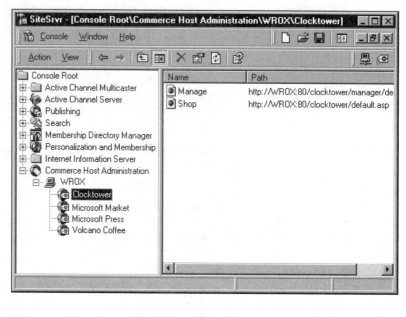

The portion dedicated to MS Commerce Server, called **Commerce Host Administration**, features an entry for each store that currently resides on the server.

If a popup dialog box appears the first time you run the MMC that asks you which server should be opened, enter your machine's name.

The main portion of the screen shows the address of the public and administration entry points into the store. However, as the screenshot here shows clearly, from the MMC it is only possible to open or close the store (two simple operations that we will discuss later in Chapter 6) and to reload the IIS application associated with it.

We can also click on the Properties menu entry, which will show a property page for the store we have selected. As we can see in this screenshot, there are several aspects of the store that we can manage through this interface:

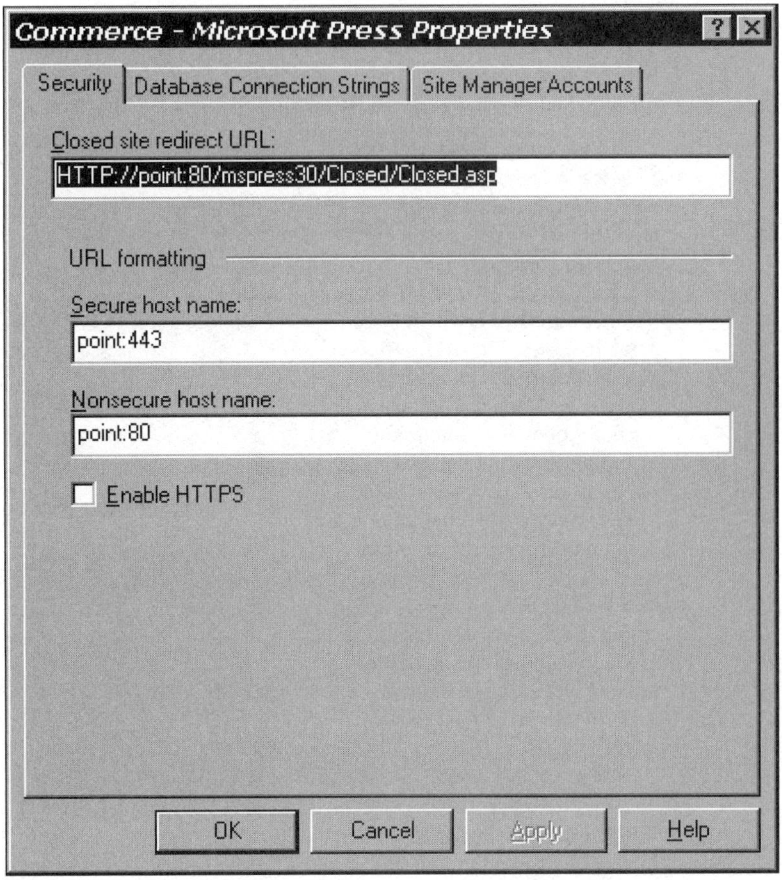

Commerce - Microsoft Press Properties   [?] [X]

Security | Database Connection Strings | Site Manager Accounts

Closed site redirect URL:

HTTP://point:80/mspress30/Closed/Closed.asp

URL formatting

Secure host name:

point:443

Nonsecure host name:

point:80

☐ Enable HTTPS

[OK]   [Cancel]   [Apply]   [Help]

❑ **Closed site redirect URL**
   This entry defines the URL users are redirected to when the store is "closed" – that is, temporarily inactive. Although we will discuss store status more in detail in Chapter 6, in general a store is closed when maintenance needs to be performed on its pages. As a result, users are redirected to a different URL that, for example, explains why the store is closed and reminds them to come back again later.

❑ **Secure host name**
   This represents the hostname and port (for example: www.wrox.com) that the store will use for all HTTPS transactions. The code for an MS Commerce Server store features a series of functions that make it possible to centralize the definition of the hostnames that are used throughout the site, thus making it easier to change hostnames consistently with a single operation.

❑ **Non-secure host name**
   Similarly, this property defines the hostname that should be used for non-HTTPS activity, which includes most of the store navigation, with the exception of the areas in which sensitive information is exchanged, such as the basket, shipping, payment and confirmation pages.

❑ **Enable HTTPS**

This box enables the site developer to stop using the https:// prefix (substituting it with a normal http://) when accessing pages that should be secure. This is particularly useful in the development phase, when the digital certificates required for HTTPS access are not usually handy.

❑ **Database connection strings**

This section, shown in this screenshot, is used to define all the OLE-DB/ODBC database connection strings that the store will use. Usually, we will need to use the same DSN (which is actually inserted for us by the system when we create a new store, as we'll see in Chapter 5) for both the management and shopping entry points. However, once the store has been created, the Site Server documentation recommends changing the DSN used by the "shopper" as they only require limited access to the store's database tables: changing the DSN will provide an added layer of security.

Commerce - Microsoft Press Properties

Security | Database Connection Strings | Site Manager Accounts

Shopper connection strings

Default connection string

`DSN=LocalServer;UID=sa;PWD=;`

Edit... | Connection Map...

Manager connection strings

Default connection string

`DSN=LocalServer;UID=sa;PWD=;`

Edit... | Connection Map...

OK | Cancel | Apply | Help

❑ **Site Manager accounts**

Finally, we can define the Windows NT accounts that will have access to the management portion of the store in the next panel. This list of users is obviously very important, as people who access the management interface have a lot of control over the store's contents (including user information).

Creating a New Store

If we right-click on the icon that represents our computer in the MS Commerce Server tree and select the New/Commerce Site Foundation..., we will be able to start the process that leads to the creation of a new store, which we'll examine in Chapter 5.

Website Administration

A similar set of functionality is available through the administration website created by the SSCE setup program, which can be accessed through the following URL:

http://your_host/siteserver

where *your_host* is the name or hostname of the machine we are working on. As we can see, there is a much wider array of functionality available through this interface, most notably access to the documentation and the samples that ship with SSCE (with the exclusion of the sample stores, which are instead accessed through the administration section).

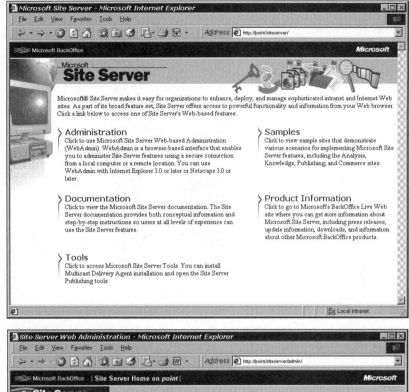

Clicking on the Administration link leads to a page (shown here) from which we can access the individual administration interface for the entire family of SSCE components, including MS Commerce Server (whose section also includes the Ad Server).

The Commerce Host Administration is really a composite of three elements: a *Getting Started* guide, the server administration tools and the entire SSCE documentation, which is obviously very useful if we're going to work with the code (we'll spend a few more words on how to navigate the documentation later on in this section).

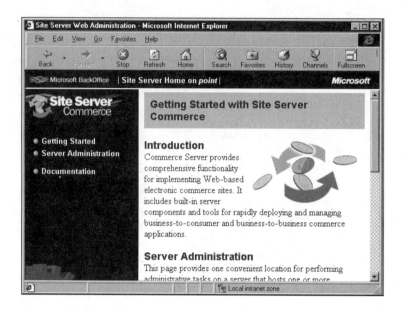

Server Administration

The figure below illustrates the WWW server administration tools for SSCE. As we can see, the look is quite different from the MMC snap-in (a simple consequence of the different design needs of the two systems), but the list of available options is essentially unchanged. Any store in the list can be deleted, opened, closed, shopped, managed and reloaded, with the same results that we saw when we were looking at the MMC.

Similarly, selecting a site and then clicking on the Properties... tab of that site will lead to a set of web pages (the first of which is visible below) that perform the same task carried out by the Property page in the MMC.

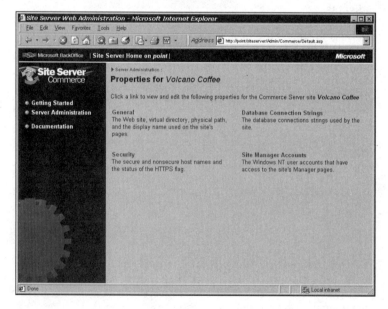

The controls that are used to show a list of all the stores installed on the machine, among other things, are actually Java applets controlled by scripts inside the HTML code for the pages. They seem to be a little unstable and often stop working or show no entries when there should obviously be at least one. In these cases, the best possible solution is to try and reload the page we're on: however, bearing in mind that it is a web page, there is little we can do if the Java applets will not load!

If that doesn't work, we can try to reboot our system and start from the beginning the task that we were carrying out. Although this can be annoying, it is a small price to pay knowing that it will give our machine a fresh start – after all, something had to be wrong in the first place, right?

Sadly, not even the three-finger salute (some kind of insider joke that stands for the *CTRL-ALT-DELETE* that was required to reboot a PC before NT came along and decided that it would henceforth be used to *log on* to the computer) can help us in certain cases when there is actual corruption somewhere in the installation of SSCE. Should this be our case, we may have to reinstall Site Server and possibly reapply several service packs before the administration website will start working again. Unfortunately, even this is sometimes not enough, and we will be forced to go back to a clean machine and start all over again from the very beginning. We can also take a look at the Microsoft Knowledge Base, which contains a number of tips and otherwise useful articles on Site Server.

> Go to http://support.microsoft.com/search/, **select Site Server from the top drop-down list and then enter the topic you wish to find out about.**

So, Why is HTML Better Anyway?

Since the functionality offered up to this point by the administration web site is essentially the same as that provided by the MMC snap-in, and in consideration of the fact that the former can misbehave much more easily, you may be wondering why we should rather use the HTML Site Server Administration.

We have already introduced the matter of convenience, which can be very important, particularly if we have to manage several machines, especially if at least some of them are not physically accessible to us. The same – to be fair – is also true of the MMC, with which we can connect to an arbitrary number of computers, but it's much easier to get through to a remote computer using the standard HTTP protocol of the website rather than the MMC's own, particularly if a firewall is involved.

In addition, it's important to understand that the functionality we have uncovered so far is only part of what the website has to offer. In fact, through it we will also be able to create and administer new stores – all functions that cannot be performed through the MMC.

The Documentation

As promised, let's take a quick look at the documentation that comes with SSCE. First of all, there are two versions available: the online, searchable HTML pages, and several Microsoft Word documents that can be found in the Docs\WordDocs folder of the installation CD-ROM. There is also Win help, available on the machine on which we installed SSCE.

Although we can certainly print out the Word documents and use them as a reference, the HTML version is so much easier to operate and more powerful (particularly thanks to the search function) that we will probably end up using it all the time. We can access the documentation through the series of steps that we saw earlier, or by typing the following URL directly into our browser's address bar:

> http://*your_host*/siteserver/docs/default_com.htm

Even though it's not difficult to memorize, it pays off to create a link to it on our desktop or add it to our Favorites/Bookmarks. As we can see in the screenshot below, the documentation pages are divided into two sections: the left part of the screen is used for navigational purposes, while the right part displays content to the user.

If we know what we're looking for in the documents, we will find it easier to use the interactive Java navigation tool available in the Contents section; the Index can be used when we know the word we need to find but have no idea as to where it could be located. The only problem with these two tools is that they load quite slowly, since the Java applets need to be filled with information about the entire documentation set every time. The Search section, on the other hand, offers the maximum flexibility, since it essentially behaves like a search engine. However, it may be time-consuming to go through all the results returned by it, and we may prefer the Index, particularly if we have a good idea of what we are looking for.

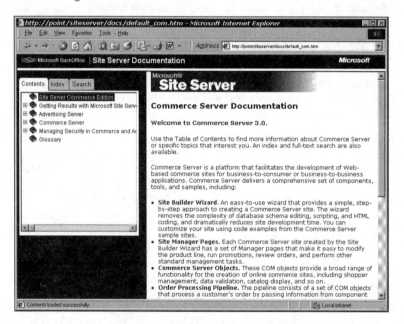

As an alternative to the web-based documentation tool, you can also use its Win32 counterpart. We can start it by double clicking the \docs\com.chm file in our Site Server installation directory.

Summary

As we have seen in this chapter, installing and administering SSCE is not a particularly difficult task, as long as we have performed all the preparation steps properly and are willing to accept the fact that the complexity of this product can sometimes lead to a few little accidents.

If we encounter any problems, the best places to look for solutions are the documentation, the Microsoft Knowledge Base, and the section of the Microsoft website dedicated to SSCE. We could also try the search capability at www.15seconds.com for more information. Often, we will discover that our problems are largely caused by conflicts between the different pieces of software installed on our computer, or by the fact that we forgot to apply all the packs in the appropriate order.

The preparation lists available from Microsoft that we mentioned in Chapter 2 are of great use even at this stage, since installation issues can arise at any moment. Of course, if everything goes wrong and we just cannot get the application to work, there is always the option of starting from the very beginning with a clean machine - however disheartening that may seem after all our hard work and effort!

Finally, it's a good idea to become very accustomed to the way the web administration interfaces work, since we will need to be able to navigate them quickly when we need to fix a problem with one of our stores. As we said in the last section of the chapter, this approach to server administration is very convenient and should be our preferred method of managing our installation of SSCE.

Examining the Sample Stores

Setting too good an example is a kind of slander
seldom forgiven
—*Benjamin Franklin*, Poor Richard's Almanac

It is often very difficult to learn to do something simply by reading a manual. Think of driving, for example: after months of reading that small booklet full of symbols and questions like "is it appropriate to run over a pedestrian if she is crossing the road outside a zebra?", you will tend to think that you're really ready to tame the four-wheeled monster.

Your father, who will most likely be providing the aforementioned vehicle, will probably disagree – as his father did before him – knowing that the lifespan of his beloved car will be reduced by about 50% in two weeks. After realizing that getting the car in first gear is not exactly like "press the clutch, shift the gear stick into the position marked '1' and release the clutch", you will end up learning more about how to really drive watching your dad than what all the books in this world can teach.

Indeed, it takes a while to become a good driver – sometimes a very long while – and the only way to get there is with hands-on experience. Still, a book is a very important resource for learning how to do something; for example, you certainly can't learn what a STOP sign means by missing it!

Hands-on experience is also useful because it often gives us new ideas and it helps us find creative solutions to seemingly unsolvable problems: Galileo discovered the laws that regulate the movement of a pendulum by watching a chandelier oscillate during a storm; Newton – apparently – first thought about the laws of gravity when an apple fell on his head (one wonders if something heavier would have given birth to even grander discoveries!).

For an EC site developer, hands-on experience comes primarily by watching carefully what's out there – not to imitate, but to innovate. By understanding fully what SSCE has to offer, we will be able to master and expand its features into better online stores.

What Does This Chapter Talk About?

After having learnt how to install SSCE and plan for its deployment, Chapter 4 will take us for a grand tour of the **sample stores** offered by it.

❑ **Browsing the sample stores**
We'll start with a crash course in Internet shopping, including a couple of tips on how to make the most of our customer experience.

❑ **Clocktower**
Our first stop is the Clocktower store, the simplest sample store available in SSCE. Clocktower illustrates the basic features offered by SSCE, providing a very straightforward shopping experience that perfectly shows how the principles discussed in Chapter 1 can be applied in a real-life situation.

❑ **Volcano Coffee**
This sample store, which sells – you guessed it – coffee, offers a more sophisticated shopping experience, providing advanced functions such as product search, customer registration and one-click purchasing. We will examine Volcano Coffee in a great deal of detail because it's the closest sample to a real-life EC storefront, and also because the SSCE team has recently released a version of it 'on steroids' that provides improved performance.

❑ **The Microsoft Press Store**
Based on the real-life MSPress store, this sample focuses mainly on making the customer experience as enjoyable as possible by providing a number of user-friendly features like cross-selling. In brief, we will also examine how important it is that an EC site be easy to use for its customers.

❑ **Trey Research – a different kind of store**
To this point, I have mentioned more than once how SSCE is principally aimed at an EC model that is very similar to our traditional concept of commerce. However, it is also possible to customize and expand it to fit different models; the Trey Research sample demonstrates how an SSCE site can be used to handle subscription-based services; it also shows how it can be integrated with other Site Server components, such as Personalization and Membership.

Browsing the Sample Stores

In order to be able to use the sample stores, we must first install them. We saw how to do this in Chapter 3. Once installed, the samples are accessible as normal websites on our SSCE server, each of them with its own URL.

A Crash Course in Internet Shopping

We will be examining the sample stores mainly from an architectural point of view – this is a book about programming, after all. However, it is also important that, when looking at the sample stores, we consider the features that they have to offer from the point of view of the end user; this will help us understand what is worth implementing in our solution.

It is clear that what online shoppers want most is **convenience**. A good price is also important (and beyond the scope of this book), but people who buy online are looking for an easy way to get what they want. Therefore, our store must be easy to reach, fast, and reliable. It must delicately push the customers toward making a purchase without being intrusive, and it must make it really easy for them to get to the confirmation screen.

Cross-Selling

A good way to gently attract customers toward making a purchase is cross-selling, which is the action of correlating several items based on common attributes.

For example, if we are looking at a game in an online store, it may be reasonable to presume that we might be interested in other games as well. This way, the possibility of turning a user into a customer increases significantly.

There are fundamentally three types of cross-selling:

❑ **Complementary cross-selling**
This type of cross-selling is mainly used to offer to the customer products that are somehow related to those that he or she is already examining. For example, if we're looking at a board game, the store might display a list of other board games available. Or, at a fast-food restaurant, we may be offered French fries if we buy a hamburger.

❑ **Historical cross-selling**
The analysis of historical data can prove to be an important marketing tool. For example, if we are buying a book on Commerce Server at our favorite online store, we might be informed that other people who bought the book also bought books on SQL and ASP programming. Perhaps, we didn't think that those tomes would have been useful, but now that we have been informed we might decide to buy them as well.
Thus, by analyzing the historical purchase data, the store has been able to offer us a number of choices that have been made by other people who, because they bought the same book, possibly fit our profile. Of course, if we were looking for a recipe book, this isn't going to help (in this case, personalized content comes into play; we'll examine it a little further on in the chapter).

❑ **Upselling**
Another very common form of cross-selling, also known as upselling, consists of providing products similar in nature to the ones that the user is looking at, but having additional features that increase the cost of the order. Going back to our fast-food example, the clerk could ask us to "megasize" our drink for just a few more pennies. The cost of the additional beverage for the restaurant is minimal, and chances are that we won't even drink all that pop, but the idea of "getting more" for a small additional fee is usually very inviting to the customer.

The only big problem of cross-selling is that it is often based on assumptions made a priori or based on statistical information that has not been gathered directly from the single user. Going back to the example made a few lines back, if I end up looking at a product by mistake in a store that simply offers cross-selling features, the selection range that is offered to me is completely outside my personal interests, and the possibility of turning me into a customer is considerably reduced.

Personalized Content

A good way of making cross-selling more effective is to derive it from a profile that fits the single user instead of the entire audience of a store. In this scenario, the content that is delivered to the user becomes personalized to his or her own preferences and behavior, therefore presenting an extremely targeted range of choices.

The delivery of personalized content happens in two phases. During the first phase, relevant information regarding the user's preferences is collected and analyzed, whenever needed, then specific content whose nature fits the preferences is delivered to the user.

The collection of information about what a user likes or doesn't like can be done in one of two ways:

❑ **Explicit personalization**
The user is explicitly asked by the store to specify what their preferences are. This can be done through simple questions, wizards or fill-out forms.

❑ **Implicit personalization**
In this scenario, the store carefully analyzes the actions that the user performs and calculates a profile based on a number of rules. For example, if a user consistently looks at black shirts, it might be reasonable to infer that he or she is a) interested in shirts and b) mainly interested in black shirts. Please note that there is a difference between the two statements. In fact, if the user were buying a pair of pants or a skirt, then the store might decide to offer a shirt, because of what has been inferred by the user's past behavior. A black shirt, however, might not be the correct choice, perhaps because black doesn't go well with the color of the trousers or the skirt. Therefore, it is important to make this kind of distinction when collecting user information.

At first glance, implicit personalization might look like a more preferable choice for an online store than explicit personalization, because the users are not requested to actually spend the time needed to specify their preferences. On the other hand, people don't usually like the fact that things are done "behind their back", and the action of collecting user information about somebody without them consciously knowing about it might have a big-brother connotation that we want to avoid.

In my experience, the best solution is to carefully mix the two possibilities, giving the users the possibility of having their say as to what the store should show them, while still collecting information about their behavior to create a more complete profile of them; giving them the possibility of turning implicit personalization off might also be a good idea, especially considering that in some countries the law prohibits the collection of information about a person without his or her explicit consent.

One thing that you must be very careful about when using personalization, regardless of the system that you are using, is to avoid creating circularity in the delivery of content. For example, in a store you would normally collect implicit information about a user when he or she looks at a specific product – such as assigning a certain value to a variable (for example, looking at skirt causes the "skirt value" to be increased by 1 point).

Whenever personalized information has to be delivered, you will rely on those values to decide what exactly has to be displayed; in this case, a high skirt value might cause a list of skirts available from the store to be shown. At this point, it becomes important that, if the user chooses to see one of the skirts from that list, the skirt value is not increased again. Doing so would cause the personalization process to "feed" itself, because the range of selections from which the user can choose is narrowed down arbitrarily. This would result in the store displaying more and more information about skirts, with the risk of missing the other interests of the user.

Purchasing from the Sample Stores

Almost all the sample stores that we'll see in this chapter offer the possibility of buying products using a credit card. Don't reach into your pocket just yet! Even though the fact that we will not be actually buying anything from any real store (relax, Microsoft is not receiving your information!) might make it reasonable to use our own credit cards for the examples, it is always better to be cautious – after all, other people might have access to the store. Here are a few sample numbers that you can use; some of them, for example those with the long series of 1s, can be found in SSCE's documentation. Personally, however, I find them quite difficult to enter because it is hard to count so many repetitive digits; therefore, I'm providing a second VISA test number that can be easier to type in:

Card type	Test number
VISA	4111 1111 1111 1111
	4000 1307 1535 4079
MasterCard	5111 1111 1111 1118
American Express	3111 1111 1111 1117
Discover	6111 1111 1111 1116

> **These are "test" credit card numbers; they do not correspond to real credit card accounts. Therefore, you should not use them in real-life situations!**

The Clocktower Sample

It's a good idea to look at the sample sites offered by SSCE, starting with the simplest one of them: Clocktower. This is a fictitious online store that sells clocks; its feature set is extremely limited, allowing it to give a clear overview of the basic EC functionality offered by SSCE.

To open the Clocktower store – assuming that you have correctly installed it during the setup of SSCE – simply point your browser to the following address:

    http://your_host/clocktower

where *your_host* is the hostname of your server (which could be a numeric IP, DNS entry or NetBIOS name). You should see something very similar to what is described in the next section.

The Main Page

As you may have already noticed, the main page of Clocktower resembles closely the one described in Chapter 1, and contains three main sections (shown in the figure below):

❏ **The header**
  The top part of the page contains a number of elements that are targeted at catching the attention of the user while providing the means of accessing important functionality features at the click of a button.
  The **store branding logo** reminds the user that he or she is visiting the Clocktower site. Branding is a very important aspect of a website, as it helps build a consistent relationship between a site and its users.
  The **store navigation links**, on the other hand, provide quick access to critical sections to the site: the Lobby (the main page), the Basket, the User Information page (from which the purchasing process can be initiated faster than from the basket – in Clocktower, this is represented by the 'Pay' icon) and the About page, which provides some details regarding the store itself.

❏ **The Department list**
  As Clocktower is a simple store that does not contain many products, its main goal is to give the user immediate access to its catalog. Therefore, it provides a list of all the categories of products available in the site.
  This division is necessary because, even if the number of products available is small, it gives the user the possibility of immediately narrowing down the number of choices that they will be presented with. In a larger store this technique might not work as well because, for example, the main departments are so generic in nature that it is necessary to sub-categorize them; this way, the user has to go through several steps – often too many – before reaching the desired level of detail.

❏ **The footer**
  The bottom part of the screen includes information that brings a feeling of closure to the page. In most cases, this includes information regarding copyrights, how to reach the customer support department through the phone or mail, and so on. In this case, it also includes the store's motto, which is sometimes part of the header because it catches the user's attention.

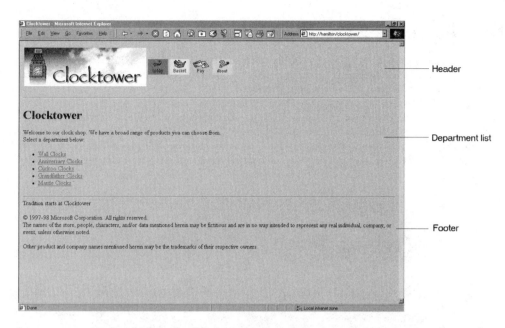

Header

Department list

Footer

It may seem a little odd that the header contains a link to the main page, considering that we *are* on the main page. As a matter of fact, the header and footer sections are contained in files that are included by every page in the store; this accomplishes several practical goals. For one thing, the look and feel of the store will remain consistent throughout the entire shopping experience; therefore there is no risk that the users might be confused by changes in the layout. Also, because many elements that are common to all the pages do not have to be hard-coded in each page, the files used to generate them become smaller and easier to maintain. As a matter of fact, any given ASP file in the store will end up looking like this:

```
<!--#include file="i_header.asp"-->
```

　　[page body]

```
<!--#include file="i_footer.asp"-->
```

A number of tags that would normally appear in an HTML file, such as `<HTML>`, `<HEAD>` `<TITLE>` and `<BODY>` are stored in the include file `i_header.asp` and do not need to be repeated in the page. Similarly, the include file `i_footer.asp` will contain the `</BODY>` and `</HTML>` tags.

SSCE capitalizes on the advantages that come with the use of include files by using them extensively. I encourage you to do the same in all your sites, as long as you remember that every time the server processes a file inclusion command, it must open a new file, read its content, insert it into the page and then close the file. Needless to say, all this wastes precious computing cycles, and you can actually run the risk that your site be slowed down by an overload of include files.

Another interesting trait of Clocktower is the fact that it has been intentionally designed to be fast and compatible with a wide range of browsers. If we resize our browser window, we see that the page will promptly adapt to the new boundaries and we will have no difficulty in browsing the store, no matter whether we are using the latest version of Internet Explorer or a text-based browser like Lynx.

The About Page

As we mentioned above, the About page is simply used to display some useful information about the store. Unfortunately, as it is a fictitious store, there is very little information to display about Clocktower – as you can see from the first figure below.

In a real-life store, this page is often expanded into an entire section that offers customer support-related information and functions (including how to reach live customer representatives), Frequently Asked Question pages, store policies, procedures for returning merchandise purchased through the store, and so on. The customer support page in Softmania, the second figure below, gives a better example of this.

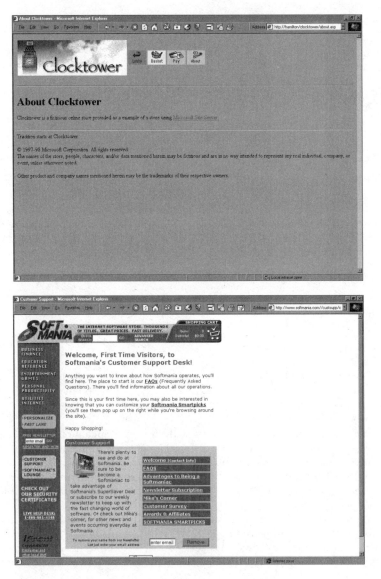

Browsing the Departments

Departments can be compared to the aisles of a real store – or the way we want to group and present our products logically. The page that offers us more information regarding one of Clocktower's departments is not very different from the main page. The only difference is that the central part of the page is dedicated to showing each product available from the selected department.

In a real-life store, it might also be appropriate to offer a little more information about our products. The goal here is to give the users enough data to understand if a product is what they are looking for while at the same time preventing "information overload" by delivering too much information about every item. It might also be a good idea to provide a link to add the product to the basket directly, without having to go through the product page; this will make it easier for the user to buy a product that he or she knows about already.

The Product Page

Clicking on one of the products displayed in the department listing page brings the user to a page that contains more information about a specific item.

Because this page focuses on a single product, its contents contain a lot of details: the name of the product, a picture of it, its current price, and a brief description of its main features. This page also includes a link that can be used to add the product to the shopping basket.

As we have mentioned in the previous chapters, the entire store's catalog is based on a database; therefore, each of the pages that somehow refer to the products (in our case the main page, the department listing page and the product page) have to be designed to function as **templates** for the pages that are actually displayed.

This is not usually a difficult task to perform, even though it might "flatten" the look of the site and make it quite boring. Therefore, it's a good idea to always think about a way of customizing the layout of the store to fit with the unique features of a single product.

For example, a software store that sells games might program the product page to change the text font to a Gothic-like typeface when the product being displayed belongs to the fantasy genre. The best solution, however, is to provide support for hard-coded pages within your layout; my team implemented this concept in Softmania; the result can be seen here.

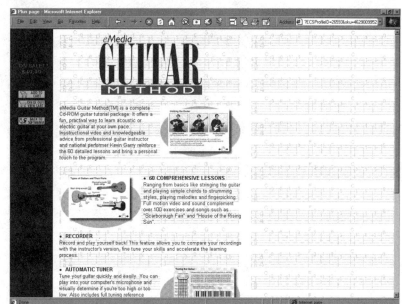

The Basket

Let's now add something to the basket. We can do so by clicking on the **Add to Basket** button that can be found on a product page.

As you can see from the figure below, and as we have mentioned before, an item is added to the basket with a default quantity of 1. This is because it is often reasonable to believe that the users will not need to buy more than one item of a single product at any one time. If our store deals with merchandise that is often sold in batches of more than one unit (for example, if we're selling something by weight), then it might make more sense to give the users the possibility of specifying how many units they want to add to their baskets. We'll talk more about this in Chapter 10.

Using the basket is – relatively speaking – very straightforward. If you want to change the quantity for a specific item, you may do so by editing the text box marked **Qty** and then clicking on **Update Basket**. To remove an item from your basket, click on the **Remove Item** button; to remove more than one item at the same time, set their quantities to 0 and click on **Update Basket** again.

When you are ready to begin the ordering process, just click on **Purchase**. This will take you to the User Information page.

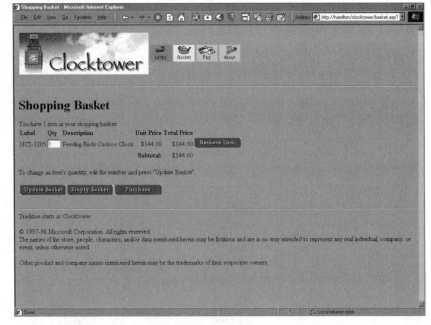

The User Information Page

The User Information page, or Address Form (by default) is a pretty large HTML document – so large that the picture below only shows its central portion. This is because, by design, Clocktower allows its customer to specify both the ship-to and the bill-to information in a single page.

In a simple store like Clocktower this makes sense because it helps make the whole shopping experience concise and simple; this is important, because the site doesn't have much to offer. In a more complex EC site, however, we could opt to use a two-step system like the one that we outlined in Chapter 1, which is less confusing for the customer.

Another important aspect of this page is that it assumes that the customer lives in the United States (there is no mention of a country in either the shipping or billing information). This is fine as long as it is clear that the store can only sell to the US – by design. Never forget that, because of the global nature of the Internet, your users might be coming from other countries and they won't be able to shop from a site like this.

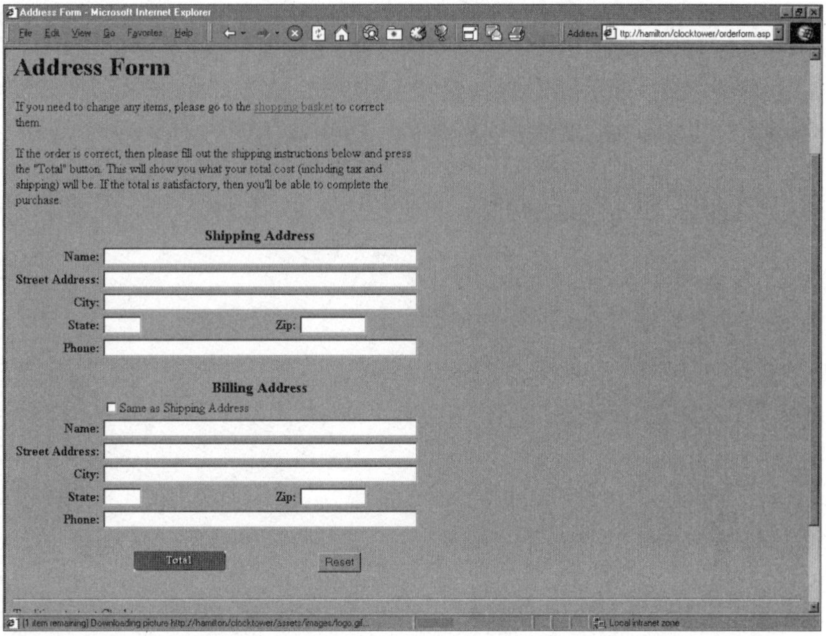

The Purchase Verification Page

Clicking on Total from the User Information page brings us to the Purchase Verification page. This page displays a short recap of all the costs associated with the order and asks the customer to enter his or her credit card information if the order comes to a satisfactory total.

This page is on a simple HTTP connection, which only happens because we are looking at a sample store. Normally, the User Information and the Purchase Verification pages, as well as the confirmation page that we'll see in a moment, should be sent out of the Web server through an SSL-protected connection. We'll talk more about this in Chapter 7.

Once all the appropriate information has been entered (we must enter one of the test credit card numbers specified earlier), the user will click on the Purchase button in order to complete the order. This, in turn, will call the order-processing page which, as we mentioned in Chapter 1, is invisible to the user unless an error occurs.

The order processing page will analyze all the information collected from the user and determine whether it is satisfactory to complete the order or not. If it is, it redirects the customer's browser to the confirmation page, otherwise an error is printed out and the user is sent back to fix it.

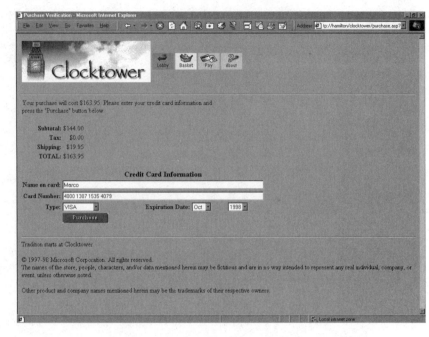

Note that the ordering process only verifies that the credit card number the user provides is valid from a mathematical point of view: that is, it runs a checksum on the number to see whether it satisfies criteria specified by that credit card provider. In order to make sure that it actually belongs to a real credit account, you will need to integrate it with a third-party credit card processing software. More about this in Chapter 13.

The Confirmation Page

The next figure shows the confirmation page. As you can see, the store puts a lot of effort into telling the user that his or her purchase was successfully completed. We mentioned how important it is to do so in Chapter 1.

You might also want to note that an order number is displayed as well. This might be helpful when the customer needs to reference their order in their correspondence with the store's customer support representative. We will see in Chapter 6 how this number is useful to the customer support representative.

The order number issued by Clocktower – which is also the one that SSCE produces by default – is *a little* difficult for the user to write down (let's not even consider the possibility that he or she wants to *memorize* it!). We will discover the reason behind this in Chapter 9.

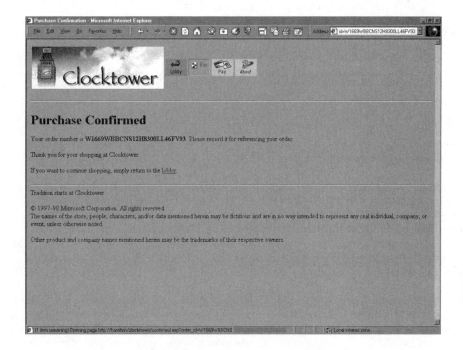

Volcano Coffee

I am sure that you didn't miss how simple the Clocktower sample store is. Still, it offers a complete range of EC services that can indeed be used in a real-life scenario. The good thing, as we'll see in the next chapter, is that creating a store like Clocktower takes approximately fifteen minutes! Of course, you will have to apply your own design to the site, but all the functionality is provided directly by SSCE through a couple of wizards.

Let's now move on to the more complex Volcano Coffee (VC) site, a site that trades in blends and paraphernalia dedicated to caffeine lovers. It also demonstrates the use of a number of interesting techniques, including user registration, cross-selling, the use of variable attributes for the products, and advanced search features.

To access the VC store, type the following URL into your browser:

    http://your_host/vc30

where *your_host* is the address of your web server.

The Main Page

You should now see something similar to the figure below. As you may notice, this main page is very different from the one that we saw in Clocktower. As the store is more complex, the page functions almost exclusively as a welcome page that tells us a little about the store and provides a couple of links for entering it.

Another interesting feature here is that there is no way to browse the store anonymously. The users must identify themselves *before* being able to access the site's functionality. This approach presents a number of advantages and disadvantages.

For one thing, the way the site interacts with the user can be easily customized on a per-user basis, and this feature can be deployed to deliver content that is extremely targeted to fit a user's profile. At the same time, many users will be reluctant to visit the site because they have to give up personal information to do so. After all, don't forget that most of the navigation on the Internet is still done on an anonymous basis – and for many of us that's what makes Internet shopping better than going to the local mall: no annoying salespeople and the ability to look at everything the store has to offer, knowing that the site's owner is unaware of who we are.

In many cases, you will find that providing the possibility of registering with your EC site as an optional feature is a better solution. The users will expect some kind of added value for giving up their anonymity – and you should provide some – but everybody should be able to look at what your store has to offer. As an alternative, you can always offer the opportunity to register as part of the purchase process; in this case, the advantages are clear to the user, who has decided to give away his or her identity anyway, because the registration will make future purchases much easier.

Registering with Volcano Coffee

Because we are new users, we must click on the register now link on the main page. This brings us to the registration page that you can see in the next figure.

As you can see, the site asks us some basic information about ourselves, including our e-mail address (which will later be used as a username when re-entering the site) and a password (which will help the site make sure that it's really us and not somebody else using our address).

> Using the user's e-mail address as a username is usually a good idea, because the user himself only has to remember his or her password, and e-mail addresses are unique, just as usernames have to be unique. As the address is often a piece of public information, however, you have to provide some extra layer of security, such as requiring a minimum length for the password, and so on. This will help prevent somebody who knows the address from gaining unauthorized access to the user's information.

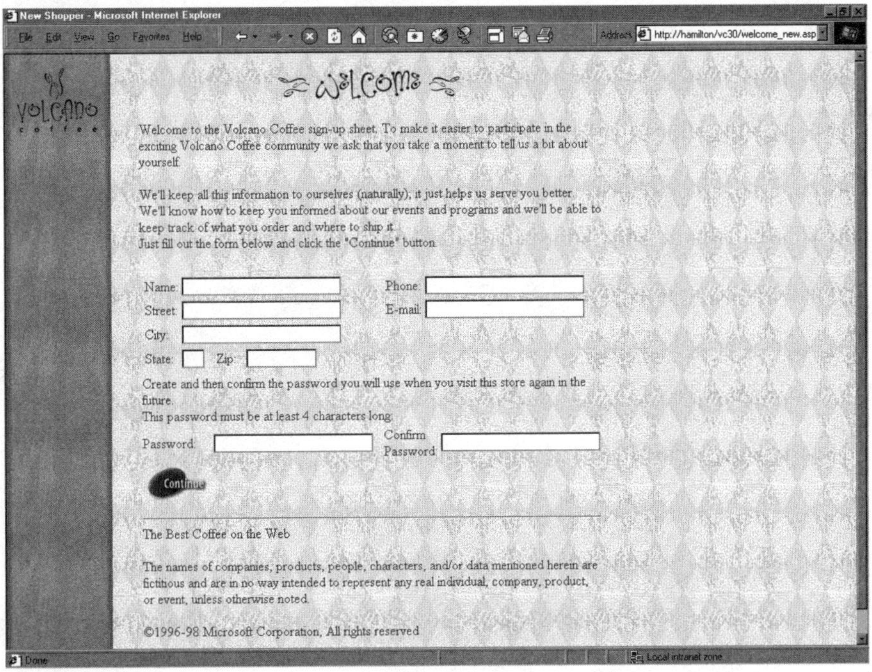

Using the User's Information

I would like to point your attention to two interesting sentences that can be found on the site:

> We'll keep all this information to ourselves (naturally); it just helps us serve you better.

And:

> We'll know how to keep you informed about our events and programs and we'll be able to keep track of what you order and where to ship it.

An EC site, at one point or the other, collects user information, so we must decide what to do with it – and we should tell the user. In the case of VC, the store registration page does take the time to explain that the information collected from the user will never be resold to third parties and that it will be used to send promotional material.

In a real-life store, if we were going to use the user's address to send promotional information, we would also have to provide a way for the user to choose not to receive it. This is a legal requirement for snail "junk" mail, and it will soon become one for e-mail solicitation as well.

The Welcome Page

After registering, the first page that is displayed by the VC site gives us more information regarding the history of the store's founders. This itself is not very interesting – particularly considering the fact that the store does not *really* exist – but it gives us a better idea of how VC is structured. For one thing, this store tries to deliver a more complete online experience than the straight get-in-and-buy approach that Clocktower uses.

The goal is to make the potential customer feel more comfortable and transmit the warm and fuzzy feeling typical of a coffee shop (unless you're there fighting for the last donut at 8 in the morning!).

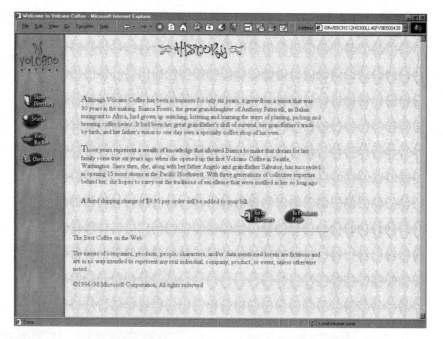

The welcome page also gives us access to the two different ways of browsing VC's catalog:

❑ **Store directory**
The store directory allows us to select a category and then browse its products one by one.

❑ **Product listing**
The product listing gives us immediate access to any product in the store.

Again, remember that if your store has a vast catalog, the product listing concept will not work unless you use a paging technique: for example, "now displaying products 61-70 of 1500" – you certainly can't load thousands of products into a single web page! Most online stores simply divide up the number of elements that they have to display and show them one page at a time – very much like search engines do when a request brings up many different results.

Returning to Volcano Coffee

Users returning to the VC store will want to click on the enter the store link from the main page. This will take them to the login page shown below.

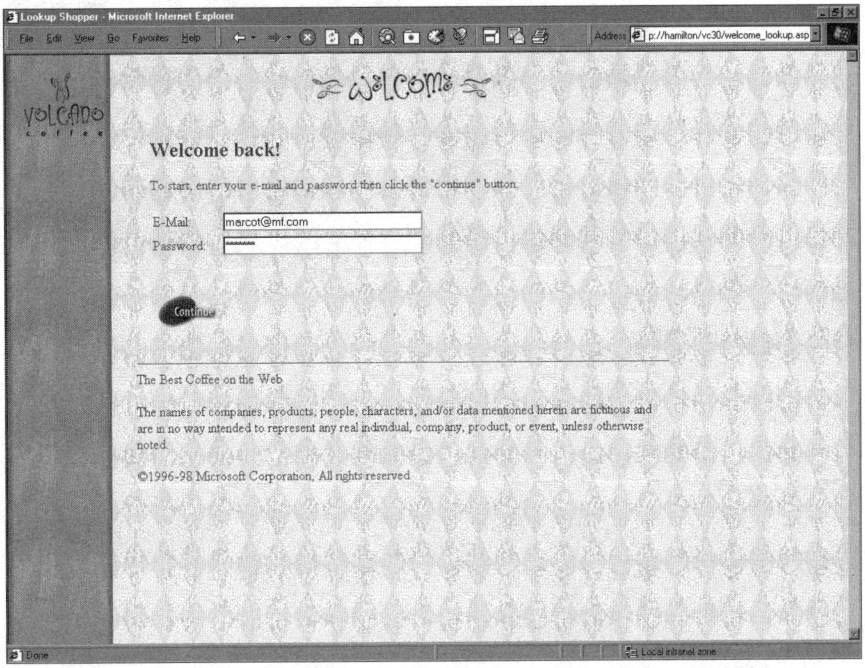

> **Always remember that all pages used to exchange customer information should be protected by an SSL connection. See Chapter 7 for more information.**

Clicking on Continue, after entering our e-mail address or password, takes us to the welcome page again. As you can see, coming back into the store after registering is a lot easier and certainly more convenient. A good idea in this case is to give our users a slightly different feedback when they enter the store; this will add more convenience (from a user satisfaction point of view, at least) to the fact that they have registered. For example, the StorageTek REX registration web site delivers a very personalized message when users come back to renew their license, as we can see overleaf.

Note how the store remembers the contents of our basket when we return. As we mentioned in Chapter 1, this is a very important feature for an online store.

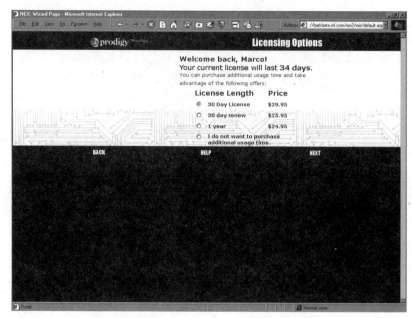

Browsing the Store

Let's now take a quick look at how the VC store can be browsed. We will find that VC delivers a higher degree of sophistication than Clocktower, mainly to make the user experience more varied.

The Store Directory

As we can see from the adjacent figure, the store directory presents the user with a list of all the available product categories. Clicking one of the categories brings the user directly to a page that describes the first product available in it. Note that on this page the user can choose the quantity of items to be purchased *before* adding a product to the basket.

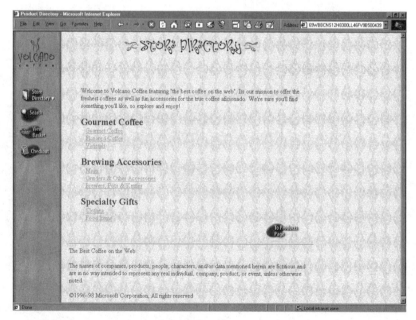

At the top of this page, the Next Item and Previous Item icons make it possible for the user to navigate through all the products in the selected category. Even though the idea in itself is very good – after all, the concept behind the store directory is as close to browsing through a supermarket aisle as it gets – this is a very inefficient method of presenting our product catalog to the users. Most likely, we will want to show a number of products at a time and *then* let the user get into a description page for a specific item.

The Product Listing

This page shows a complete list of all the products available in the store, grouped by category. Clicking on a specific product brings the user to its specific page.

Again, this approach to delivering access to the store's product catalog only works if your store has very few items. VC only has 26 items, and already the users have to scroll down their browser window quite a bit to access the whole listing.

Search

What do you do when you are in a store and you can't find the item you're looking for? Well, if you're extremely shy, you will probably just leave – after all, it's the owners' fault if they can't deploy their products properly. If you're *really* interested in finding something, however, you will most likely ask one of the clerks.

There is nothing to be shy about in an EC site, therefore the ability to search for an item is extremely important. VC offers a very simple search function that attempts to match the user's input to the name of one or more products in the database. Typically, this kind of search function is based on a simple SQL query similar to this one:

```
Select * from product_table where product_name like '%' + search_spec + '%'
```

where `search_spec` is the user's input. Clearly, the possibilities offered by this approach are very limited; not only is the search limited to the product's name (ignoring other characteristics like color, price, and so forth) but it does not adapt to certain aspects of natural languages. Searching for "mug", for example, will find all the products whose name contains the words "mug" and "mugs", but searching for "mugs" will not obtain the same result, as the user might expect.

A better solution for performing searches is the creation of "advanced" search pages that are still based on SQL queries but offer a wider variety of options, or even use the search functionality provided by Site Server that we discussed in Chapter 1.

Supporting Different Product Attributes

Although many stores on the Internet specialize in selling one type of product only, some of them are moving on to providing a wider catalog.

As a result, it becomes difficult to handle hundreds of products that are inherently different: for example, a computer's attributes include processor model and speed, hard disk capacity and amount of RAM installed, whereas none of these will be interesting for a car (unless you have an Auto-PC installed, of course!).

Even with its small size, our VC store sells items of a varied nature: coffee, coffee machines and clothing all have different characteristics. In fact, if we go to a product page for the "Volcano T-Shirt", shown in the figure here, you will see that the site asks us what color and size we'd like to buy – which doesn't happen when we're trying to buy a bag of coffee. We'll see how this works in detail in Chapter 11.

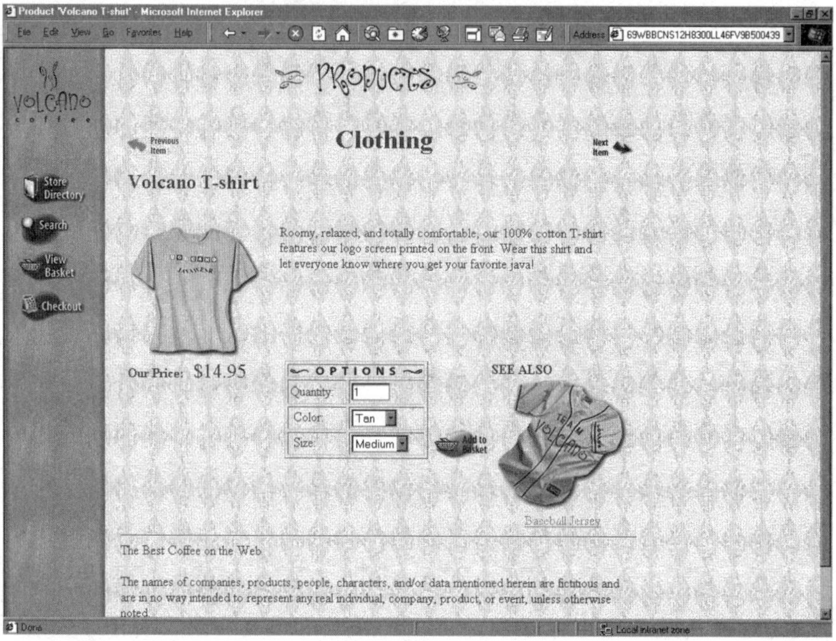

Buying from Volcano Coffee

The purchase process implemented by VC is very similar to the one that we saw in Clocktower. The only significant difference is the use of the **Microsoft Wallet** (see the next figure).

The Wallet is a browser plug-in that can be used to safely store personal information, including addresses and credit card numbers. As the information is encrypted and protected by a password, multiple users can share the same Wallet on a single computer.

The Wallet supports both Netscape 3.x and 4.x browsers, as well as Internet Explorer 3.x, 4.x and 5.x browsers. However, because Navigator and Explorer use two different standards for plug-ins (notably, IE uses ActiveX controls, which are not supported by Navigator), it is critical that the web server where our EC site is be able to properly recognize the type of browser that the user has. It would be unfortunate, to say the least, if we were to send out the code for Navigator to an IE browser!

One of the most interesting features of the Wallet is the ability to support an arbitrary number of payment systems. Out of the box (or out of the Net, if you prefer), it is compatible with the major credit cards – VISA, MasterCard, American Express and Discover – but it can also be extended to work with private labels, such as department store or gas bar charge cards. We will look at ways to expand the Wallet in Chapter 15.

Unfortunately, not all of our customers will want to use the Wallet, either because their browser doesn't support it or because they do not have it pre-installed (it became a standard component of IE only with version 4) and are not willing to download it. In this case, VC provides the Click here if you have problems with the Wallet link, which points to a normal HTML form.

Naturally, Microsoft wants us to use the Wallet: therefore the previous link is in the smallest font possible and, quite frankly, is hard to see in the page at first. In a real-life store, we would probably want to provide the HTML forms as a standard payment method and then offer those customers who have the Wallet, and know how to use it, the opportunity of navigating to a page that uses it.

This will ensure that we address the most generic scenario first (the user *does not* have the Wallet), thus making it easier and more convenient for customers to buy from our site.

The Buy Now Wizard

As we have seen earlier in the book, one of the main goals of an EC site is to target its content as much as possible. This is even more true in the case of advertising – if you are running banner ads on a third-party site, it would be a lot better if you were able to advertise specific products instead of your site in general. The difference would be akin to saying "Here, we have this wonderful product and it only costs this much" instead of "Come down to the store and take a look around", the first offer being a much more focused proposition.

Moreover, if you're running banner ads on another site, the owners of that site would rather not have their users leave to enter your store, and might be willing to offer you some kind of incentive, such as a lower rate, if you adopt a solution that will allow the users to stay.

SSCE implements a technology called **Buy Now**, that makes it possible for a user to purchase one or more products from an EC site without leaving the site he or she is currently in. What's even better, there is no need for special software to do this: clicking on a Buy Now ad simply opens a new window that collects all the user's information and then closes itself when the purchase process is completed.

To take a look at how Buy Now works, all we have to do is point our browser to this location:

http://*your_host*/vc30/manager

where, as usual, *your_host* is the address of your web server. You should see a page similar to the one shown here. This is the **Store Manager**, which is the interface that is used to administer the store. We will not talk about the Store Manager until Chapter 7, but I would like to draw your attention to the Try our Buy Now section of the page. This contains a banner ad that points directly to the storefront and implements the Buy Now feature of SSCE.

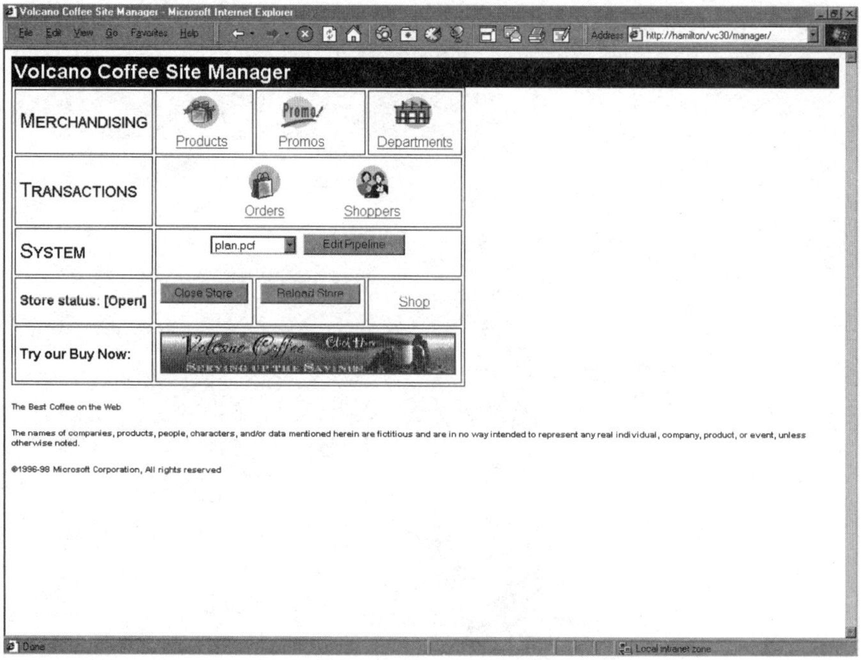

It is important to understand that normally you would not find this banner in the Store Manager, but rather on a third-party site, or even within your own store. In the case of VC, the SSCE team decided to put the banner here to better give the idea that it doesn't necessarily have to be in the storefront. After all, it's just a demo!

Clicking on the banner brings up a new window, visible in the figure below, that initiates the purchase process for the Kona brand of coffee. All we have to do is specify the number of coffee bags that we want to buy and click on the Next button. This brings us to the Shipping page, which again contains the Wallet by default, albeit this time in a slightly different form. The reason behind this is that first of all this is a "compressed" version of the shipping page that should appear more compact than the normal one, and also that it's reasonable to expect that the user might want to ship the product to a different address than the default address.

After having selected a ship-to address, the store shows us a detailed breakdown of the order's cost and asks us to provide our credit card information. Once we have done so, our order is processed and a confirmation page is displayed. Clicking on Finish closes our Buy Now window and lets us continue with our online browsing on the original site.

As you can see, the speed of a Buy Now wizard is astounding – we were only three mouse clicks away from purchasing something, without having to spend any more time looking for it in the store. Clearly, the big disadvantage here is in the fact that there is no user retention: customers come, buy, and leave. For this reason, it isn't a good idea to base an entire online advertising campaign on Buy Now ads; it is also very important to display a very strong store branding when Buy Now is used – this will ensure that your customers will at least remember what store they bought from!

The Microsoft Press Sample Store

Amazon.com wannabes, here is your chance to get a quick start toward your goal. The next sample store that we will be visiting sells books, and has been inspired by the real Microsoft Press (MSPress from now on) site that you can find at http://mspress.microsoft.com.

MSPress offers a more complex approach to guiding the user through the product catalog. In fact, while the number of products carried by VC was still small enough to be listed in a page, this is not the case anymore: MSPress carries over 100 titles (though this is still far less than a real-life store!).

Our small bookstore also provides the historical cross-selling functionality that we described earlier in this chapter. Data regarding previous purchases (fictitious ones in this case) is analyzed to deliver complementary offers to the user.

Navigating the Store

The MSPress sample can be found at:

http://*your_host*/mspress30/

where, as usual, *your_host* is the name of your SSCE server.

Contrary to Volcano Coffee, MSPress does not require its users to register prior to entering the store. As mentioned earlier, this is a better approach because it allows the customers to browse anonymously through all the products available. Users are still required to register, however, as soon as they express the intention to purchase something by adding a product to their basket.

The purchase process in MSPress is exactly the same as VC, with the exception that the MSPress store does not support the Buy Now feature.

Browsing the Product Catalog

There are four ways of searching for a title in MSPress, each corresponding to a different technique of catalog browsing.

Chunking

If we click on View by title the site displays a list of all the titles available, as shown in the adjacent figure. This page is similar to the product listing in VC, with the exception that the products are divided into pages (this technique is called **list chunking**). Clicking on the '<' and '>' buttons moves us back or forward one page, while the '<<' and '>>' buttons move us to the beginning and final page of the listing respectively.

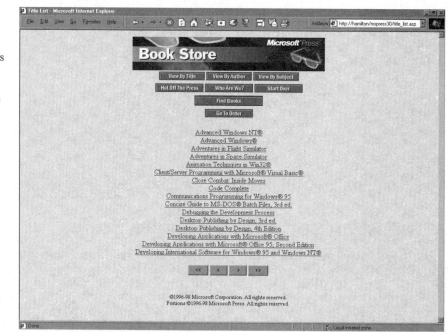

This is a great way of displaying any product listing in the store, because it adapts easily to any number of results. In a real life example, however, you will want to provide a slightly less cluttered page that contains fewer entries and more details about each product.

The navigation method itself could certainly be refined, by providing the opportunity to jump directly to any given page in the result set (possibly already knowing what is on the page) and providing a page count for easier reference.

Cached Queries

If our site is going to use some data – such as the result set of a SQL query – in a consistent fashion throughout our site, it makes sense to cache that information in memory so that it will be faster to retrieve. Naturally, we will have to make sure that the data is small enough not to affect the performance of the site as a whole and that the result set doesn't vary in response to external parameters (in which case the data would continuously change and there would no point in caching it!).

MSPress uses this technique to display a page that contains all the books available, grouped by their authors; as we can see below, the result is quite long (it doesn't fit in the browser window, and it sums up to about 13 and a half screens!) but still acceptable if we're not on a slow connection. A better solution would be to give to the user the possibility of picking a letter and only display those authors whose last name starts with that letter.

The best way to cache information that must be shared by all the instances (or sessions) of a web site in IIS4 is to use the **Application** object, which fundamentally acts as a collection of variant variables, able to handle anything from numbers to objects. Ideally, data such as a result set should itself be stored in a collection object, which in turn should be stored in the Application object.

> For more information about the Application object and the ASP object model, check out **Beginning Active Server Pages 2.0** published by Wrox Press (ISBN 1-861001-34-7) or **Professional Active Server Pages 2.0**, published by Wrox Press (ISBN 1-861001-26-6)

The only problem is that the Application object cannot contain ActiveX controls created using the Apartment threading model. This, by default, rules out the `Scripting.Dictionary` object, which – you guessed it – uses exactly that threading model. Luckily, SSCE provides us with a number of objects that can help us solve this problem; we'll talk about them in Chapter 9.

For the moment, let's assume that we have our own component, called `My.Collection`, which behaves like a collection and uses a free-threaded model, therefore being compatible with the Application object. An easy way to cache the result set of a query in the Application object could be the following:

```
' Database objects, used to retrieve the information

Set cConn = Server.CreateObject (''ADODB.Connection'')
cConn.Open MyConnectionString

Set rsRecordset = Server.CreateObject (''ADODB.Recordset'')
rsRecordset.Open ''select name from authors_table'', cConn,
                 adOpenForwardOnly,  adLockReadOnly

' Here's our collection object

Set cOurCollection = Server.CreateObject (''My.Collection'')

' Retrieve all the available rows from the recordset

While Not rsRecordset.EOF
      cOurCollection.Add (rsRecordset (''Name''))

      rsRecordset.MoveNext
Wend

' Now, store the collection in the Application object

Set Application (''AuthorsList'') = cOurCollection

' Close the database objects

rsRecordset.Close
Set rsRecordset = Nothing

cConn.Close
Set cConn = Nothing
```

There is one major setback when using this technique: if you make a change to the table from which the result set originated, this change will not be reflected in the cached data until the ASP application is restarted. This happens either when the web server is stopped and then restarted, or when the `global.asa` file is modified. Naturally, you can always change the cached data at the same time as the database; generally speaking, however, you should only use this technique if your data is not going to change too often.

Drill-down Navigation

Another commonly used technique for navigating an EC site is **drill-down navigation**. This consists of guiding the user through a process that progressively narrows the scope of the data presented to him or her, until a single product is chosen.

In MSPress, you start the drill-down process by clicking on the View by subject hot image. The resulting page shows a list of available subjects; clicking on one of them, in turn, shows a list of available books for that subject. Finally, clicking on one of the results brings up a specific page.

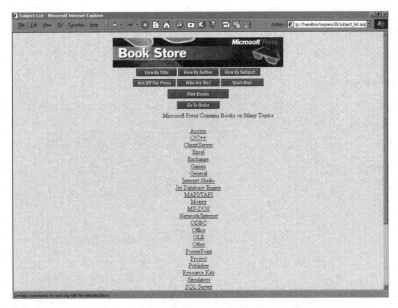

You probably have a similar approach to finding objects in your local library. The Dewey Decimal System, which is the most widely used categorization system worldwide, assigns a decimal number to each topic. Each digit in the number represents a category whose scope narrows from left to right. So, for example, in the number 599.8846, 5 means "Natural Science and Mathematics", 9 is "zoology", the second 9 stands for "mammals", 8 for "primates", the second 8 for "apes", 4 stands for "great apes" and 6 for "gorillas". If you were looking for gorillas, therefore, you would just start from the broadest category available (in this case "Natural Sciences and Mathematics") and you would proceed down to the narrowest one ("gorillas"), ending up with a list of available books from which you would choose a specific tome.

Advanced Search

As we mentioned above, the search capabilities of Volcano Coffee were quite limited. MSPress offers a slightly more advanced search page, which is shown below.

Even though the user is now able to control a higher number of parameters to better narrow down the search to a useful set of results, MSPress still suffers from the same problems connected with the fact that SQL does not understand the construction of natural languages (the "mug" and "mugs" issue).

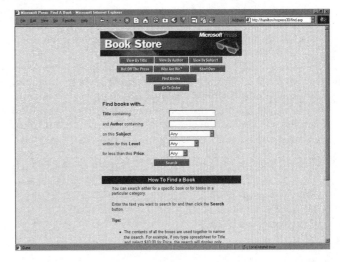

Historical Cross-selling

If we add a book to our basket – yes, we *will* have to register again, even if we have registered with VC – we'll see a page similar to the one below. It's a pretty big basket page, but what really interests us is the text at the bottom.

Other customers may have bought the same book as us and also ordered a number of related titles at the same time, making up one order; these orders may be the source of the titles that the store is suggesting we may be interested in. This is a very powerful selling point (used by a number of successful stores), and we'll see how to implement it in Chapter 9.

Trey Research – a *Different* Kind of Store

All the stores that we have examined so far have shared a common trait – they all sell physical goods. So, is this all that can be done with SSCE? Of course not! Keep in mind that, when SSCE was published, the audience of developers it was targeted towards had to cope with a growing business request for new stores, similar to amazon.com, to be opened.

Therefore, that's the area where SSCE focuses particularly, even though, because it has been conceived as a platform and not as an application, its features can be easily leveraged to deliver different kinds of stores. The real problem we will encounter if we try to write our own "unusual" EC site is in the fact that the documentation and the sample stores will not help us a great deal. Thus, we will have to use our imagination, which is not that difficult once we come to realize that almost all the EC sites can be reduced to the simple browse-basket-purchase metaphor.

The Trey Research sample store provides a glimpse of what can really be done with SSCE, and how it can be integrated with the other functionality offered by Site Server. To access it, type this URL into your browser:

http://*your_host*:5293/tr/

As in all the other examples, *your_host* is the address of our web server on which the sample stores are installed. This time, however, we are opening the site in a particular way: that number in the URL is a *port number*. A port is a concept specific to TCP/IP that is simply used to subdivide all the resources available on a single machine connected to a network. For example, the HTTP protocol normally uses port 80, while the FTP protocol uses port 21. However, it is not mandatory to use a particular port for a particular protocol; therefore, the URL syntax allows for the specification of an alternate port on which the browser should look for the resources that have been requested.

In our case, we are looking for the tr directory on port 5293 of your_host using the HTTP protocol. Normally, it wouldn't be necessary to tell the browser that it should be looking for an HTTP service but, because 5293 is *not* the standard port for the protocol we are looking for, we must add the http:// at the beginning, or the browser will not know what to look for and will pop up an error.

Naturally, all this still doesn't explain *why* we have to use a different port number. The reason lies in the fact that Trey Research uses a component of Site Server called **Personalization and Membership**, which we already mentioned in Chapter 1. In this case, the membership functionality of the component is used to grant or deny access to specific portions of the site, and it needs to be installed on a different instance of our IIS 4 server in order not to interfere with the other sites. Therefore, during the installation process, the SSCE setup program created a new site on port 5293 and installed the Trey Research sample on it.

What Does Trey Research Do?

Trey Research is a fictitious company that sells analyst reports online. The store requires the user to register and then pay for a subscription to a set of reports that he or she can then read and download.

> **You must have installed Site Server Personalization & Membership as part of your Site Server setup in order to be able to view the Trey Research sample store.**

Even though the site doesn't sell physical goods, it still maintains the usual concept of the "basket"; in this case, our customers will add their subscriptions to it, then go through the purchase process and, finally, be able to view the reports that they purchased.

Once we have entered the site, we will see the screen shown here. From here, if we are registered users, we can directly access our account or visit the reports offered by the site.

Registering with the Site

A site that requires registration before being able to access its content is not new to us – we have seen an example of this approach already. In the case of Trey Research, however, this paradigm *does* work well, because what we are looking at is a subscription service, and as such the site owner needs to know who is accessing the site in order to regulate the access to its content.

Still, Trey Research requires *all* its users to identify themselves, even though they might not be (or become) customers at all. In a real life example, you might want to divide the site into two parts: one for public access, that features the possibility of browsing and "previewing" the content without actually having complete access to it, and one accessible only to those users who have registered and purchased a subscription.

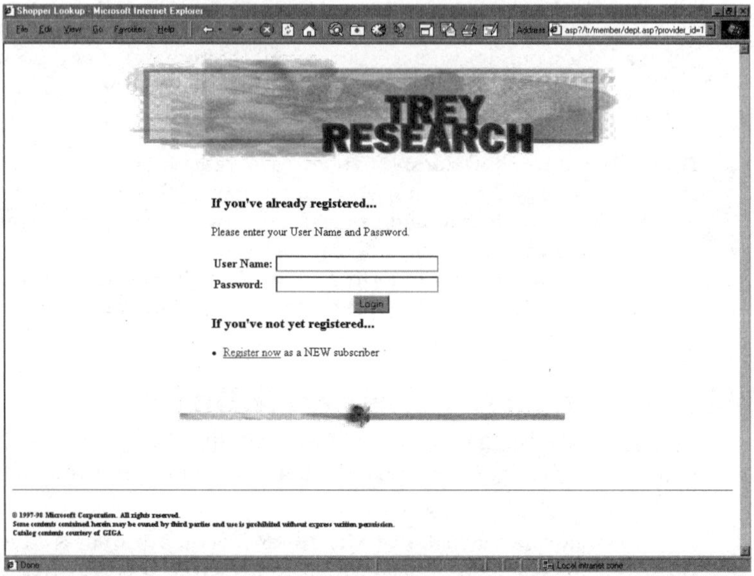

Once we click on any of the links on the main page, we will end up in a page that will ask us for our login information (as shown above). As we are new users, we should click on Register Now and end up in the page shown here. After entering all our information, we will be taken back to the main page.

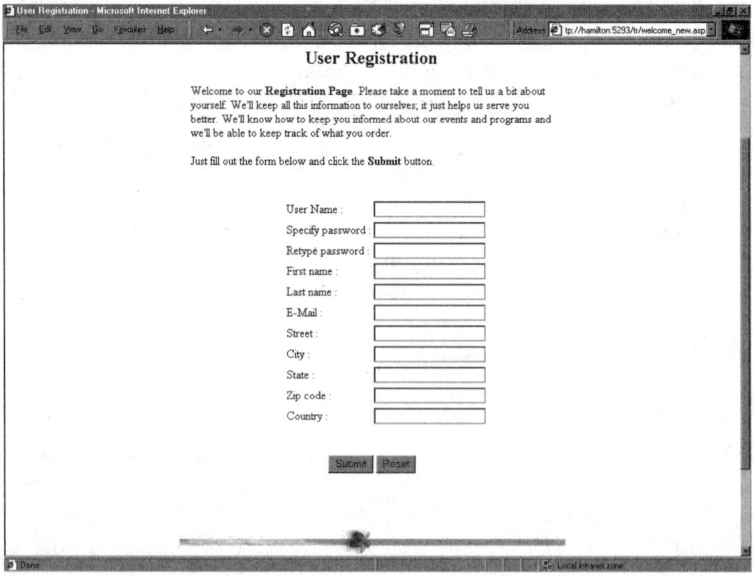

As we are now using Personalization & Membership, the information that the store collects from us doesn't simply end up in a database; rather, it's stored in a specialized structure known as the **Membership Directory**. In the membership directory, all the data is organized as a series of *attributes* of a personal account, or *membership*, and can be easily retrieved and distributed across several machines. Personalization & Membership supports an Internet standard, known as Lightweight Directory Access Protocol (LDAP), which can be used for accessing a hierarchical structure (such as a directory), or a collection of attributes across a TCP/IP network.

The possibilities here are significantly greater than what can be done if the information is simply stored in a database. For example, user information could be shared across several stores, thus making the process of having to register with each one of them superfluous. At the same time, the same piece of information can be correlated across several users to generate interesting usage reports.

> For more information about Personalization & Membership, check out Robert Howard's **Professional Site Server 3.0 Personalization and Membership**, published by Wrox Press (ISBN 1-861001-94-0).

Navigating the Site

After registering, we are finally able to browse the site. As you can see from the following figures, the site divides the available reports into categories. Access to the individual reports of each category is only granted if the user has subscribed to the category. Several options are available, based on the length of the subscription.

Once we have decided on a subscription option, we can add it to our basket, and then proceed to the purchasing process. As Trey Research doesn't really have to ship us anything, there isn't a page asking us for a shipping address. As we mentioned in Chapter 1, however, this doesn't mean that the step that takes care of the shipping calculations doesn't exist at all, but rather that it *defaults* to not doing anything.

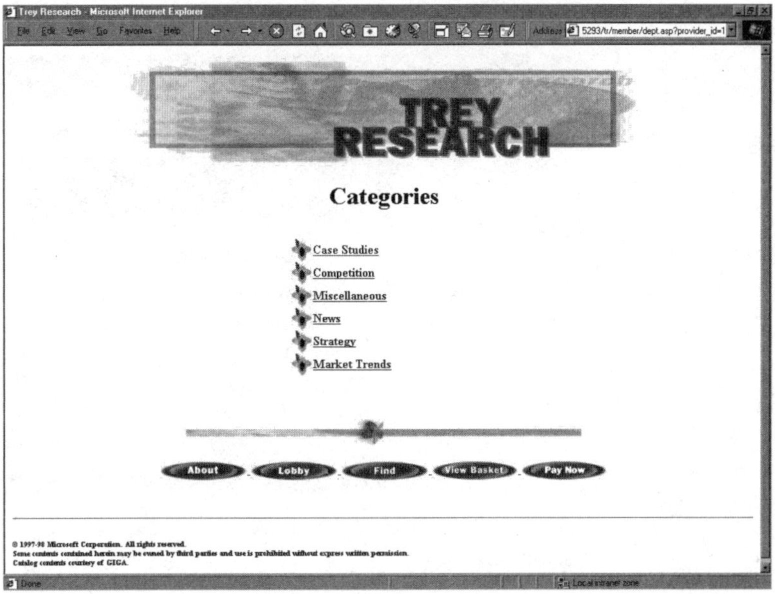

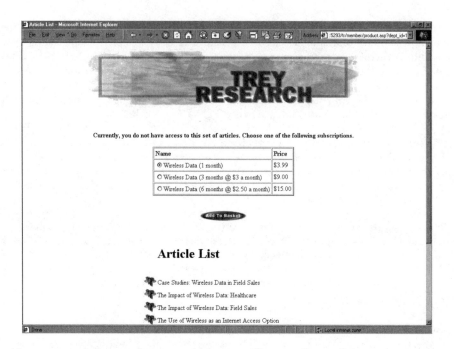

If we are able to successfully complete our purchase, we'll get to the confirmation page shown below. As you can see, the store provides us with a link to a list of categories we have subscribed to. This is very useful, because it might be difficult in the future to remember exactly what we purchased in the past.

Going back to the category we subscribed to before, you can now see that the reports available are linked to the actual documents, which we can view for as long as our subscription lasts.

Membership is, unfortunately, a very complex topic, as you may discover if the Trey Research doesn't work properly (which is quite possible) and you try to fix it yourself. The next version of SSCE will hopefully contain a more developer-friendly technology, as Microsoft will certainly capitalize on the recent acquisition of Firefly Technologies, a company specializing in the development of personalized content delivery tools.

Summary

In this chapter, we have had a chance to get more acquainted with what can be done with SSCE. We started by examining what some of the important elements of an electronic commerce site are:

❑ **Cross-selling**
   The ability to present the user with a wider array of choices based on what he or she clicks on is a very important technique for improving our site's chances of selling its goods.

❑ **Personalized content**
   To further enhance the user's shopping experience, we can tailor the site to his or her preferences, thus displaying only the information that he or she can reasonably be presumed to be interested in.

One of the most important concepts that we discussed is how SSCE can be used in a variety of scenarios, from the creation of a simple store like Clocktower, to the development of a complete online EC site, such as the Microsoft Press Store.

We also examined how Commerce Server can be integrated with other Site Server technologies: the Trey Research site uses the Personalization and Membership feature to collect information from the users and organize it. This can be a much better approach than using a database, because the data can be shared across several servers through the use of LDAP, and because it can be used to profile users by generating the appropriate reports. We also mentioned, however, that Personalization and Membership is a very complex technology; therefore, it should only be used when there is a real necessity for it.

As we go further in the book, I recommend that you frequently go back to the sample stores and see how the concepts that we will progressively unveil can be applied. After all, there is no better explanation than an example!

Creating a New Commerce Server Store

Nothing can be created out of nothing.
– Lucretius, De rerum naturae

As we are about to discover in the next few chapters, MS Commerce Server provides all the infrastructural elements that are required to develop and operate a complete EC site. This includes not only those components that are unique to MS Commerce Server, but also the combination of functionality that is provided by NT for security and network access, IIS for web serving, and so on.

In the old days, when the term Integrated Development Environment (IDE) had not yet been used, and developers wrote their code with a simple text editor, this would have been more than enough. All the functionality that we need is there – let's just start from a blank folder, design our application (thinking of all the possible problems) and build the EC site from the ground up.

Sure enough, this can be done with MS Commerce Server, too. The point is – is it worth it? Once we've done a bit of research on EC, we'll find out that pretty much all the possible scenarios can be reduced to the "shopping basket" metaphor with little or no variation, with the exception of business-to-business sites, which, as we'll see in Chapter 12, follow a different model.

So, the answer to the question is no – there really isn't any good reason why we would want to develop our own EC site by starting from nothing. After all, nothing can be created out of nothing.

The Commerce Server Site Creation Wizards

There are two ways for us to create our own EC site using Commerce Server. The most obvious one consists of copying one of the sample stores that are provided with Commerce Server that we have seen in Chapter 4. Each one of them provides a starting point for addressing a very specific type of EC site, and their code is explained in the documentation provided together with the product.

There are a number of reasons why we will not usually end up using the sample stores, however. First of all, they were not designed to be used as foundation blocks, so their code is intended to solve one specific problem and nothing else. This means that we might eventually encounter one situation in which we need to provide some functionality that the code is simply not flexible enough to provide. The ultimate risk is that we will end up rewriting a lot of the scripts just because of this. Moreover, because these stores are samples, they represent a "finished product" that forces the navigation down a very specific path. This might be a problem if we're seeking to provide a different experience – we can end up developing a copy of the sample store that just "looks different", with little or no improvement.

All these situations are very likely to happen, particularly if we think that the sample stores are, as their name might suggest to the most imaginative among us, *samples*. Therefore, they do not necessarily provide a range of functionality that is wide enough for a real-life site, and there is a good chance that we will have to expand them when we are writing our own application.

The best way to create a new store is to use the site creation Wizards provided by MS Commerce Server. I'm sure that everybody is familiar with Wizards – fundamentally, they are a process that executes a task based on a set of answers given by the user to specific questions. The questions are also asked on a series of pages, that can be moved through by the use of the 'Back' and 'Next' buttons. For example, if we want to create a new Memo in Microsoft Word, we can use the Memo Wizard, which will ask us questions like "what style should the memo be in?" and "who is the recipient of the memo", to then produce a memo document that will conform to our specifications.

Two Wizards are provided together with MS Commerce Server: the **Site Foundation Wizard** and the **Site Builder Wizard**.

What Does This Chapter Talk About?

First of all, we'll spend a few words trying to figure out why there are two wizards. After all, there is only one task to be accomplished! Naturally, there is a good explanation, and we'll see what it is.

Right after that, we'll concentrate on the two wizards and what they can be used for:

❑ **The Site Foundation Wizard**
As its name suggests, this Wizard can be used to create a new "site foundation" – the minimum structures and settings that are required by Commerce Server to know that our site *is there*.

❑ **The Site Builder Wizard**
Once a site foundation has been created, the Site Builder Wizard can be used to create a site that can be used as the building block of any EC application.

Why Two Wizards?

As we just mentioned, a very good question that we could be asking ourselves is why there are two wizards when the ultimate task is only one – to create a new store?

The point here is that the site foundation is as close to starting from scratch as we can get. Commerce Server needs all the structures and settings that are created as part of the Site Foundation Wizard in order to be aware of the existence of any given store on the server. If these are not there, we will not be able to administer the site from the Commerce Host Administrator.

Therefore, if we want to write a store starting from the ground up, all we have to do is run the Site Foundation Wizard and then begin writing our code. Additionally, we can run the Site Builder Wizard and create a higher-level foundation that can be used as a starting point to create our own application.

The Site Foundation Wizard

In order to create a new site foundation, we will have to go to the Commerce Host Administration (HTML version) using the URL http://*your-server*/siteserver/admin/commerce, select Server Administration and then click on the Create... button.

Alternately, you can launch this wizard through the MMC by right clicking on the appropriate computer under the Commerce Host Administration folder, and then selecting New | Commerce Site Foundation:

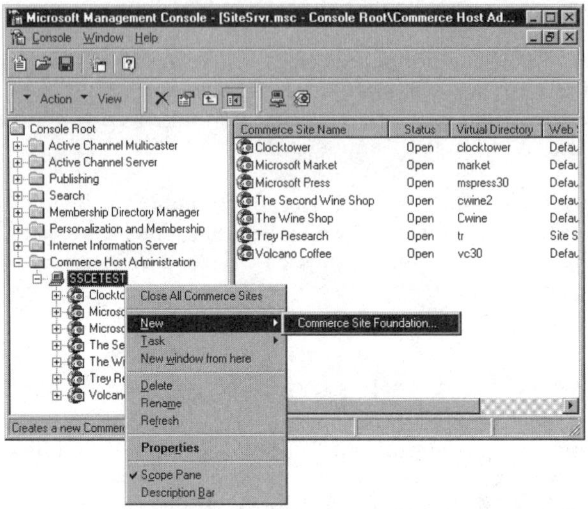

This will cause the first page of the Site Foundation Wizard to be opened.

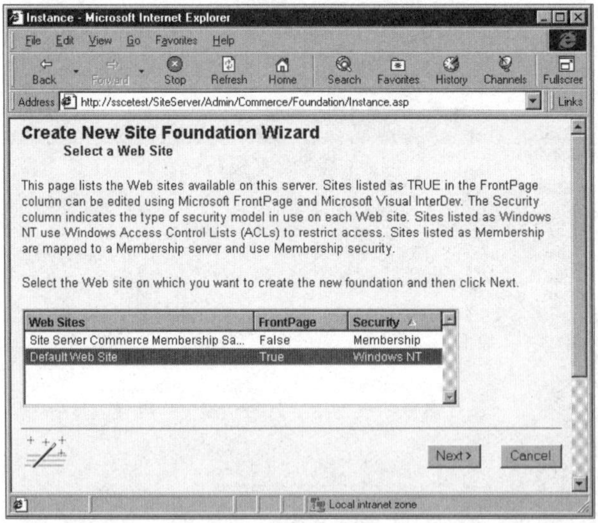

Because the Site Foundation Wizard (SFW) is entirely web-based, we will need to pay attention to the time that we let pass between one step and the next. Because the Wizard uses the Session object to store the information that it collects from us, waiting for too long (usually longer than 20 minutes) will cause our session to expire and all the data we entered to that point to be lost. Attempting to access the next page of the Wizard after the session is expired will cause the browser to reload the Commerce Host Administrator's main page.

Creating a DSN

Even before we can start the SFW, we
must create a datasource (DSN) that our
store will use to access its database. The
exact procedure for creating a DSN is
slightly different depending on which
DBMS you are creating it for, and also on
what version of ODBC you are using to
create it. In all cases, the procedure starts
by going to the Control Panel and
double-clicking the **ODBC Data Sources**
icon. This brings up a dialog box similar
to the one shown here.

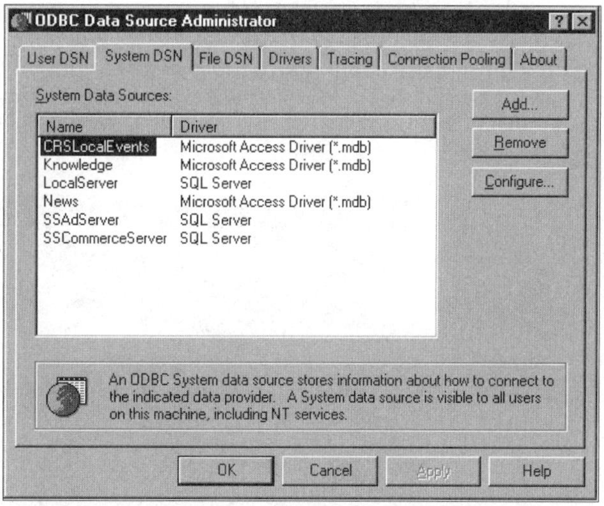

Commerce Server can only work with
System data sources, which are available
system-wide to all the processes and users
on the computer. To create a new DSN,
click on the **System** tab, and then on the
Add button. Next, you will have to
choose the appropriate driver for the
DBMS that you will be using. If you
select SQL Server, and you have a fairly
new version of the ODBC driver for this
platform, you will be presented with
something similar to what you can see
here.

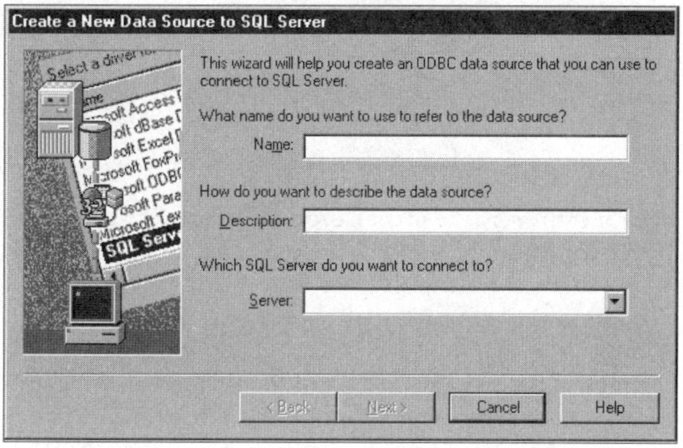

This is the first step of a wizard that will guide us through the creation of the DSN. As you can see,
here we must simply specify a name for a DSN, as well as a description for it and the address of the
Server to which we want to connect. The name of the DSN should not contain any spaces – this is an
identifier that you will use programmatically from your code to uniquely identify the DSN. The
server address must also be formulated using the appropriate convention for the communication
protocol that you will be using to communicate with your DBMS; for example, if you are using
TCP/IP, then the name should be a valid DNS entry or numeric IP; if you're using named pipes, then
it should be the UNC name of the server, and so on.

The next step, shown below, asks us to specify login information for the newly created DSN. As you can see, there are two fundamental options as to what authentication method we can use to connect to our database, and your choice here should really depend on how your server is set up. In either case, you can instruct the wizard to automatically connect to the database using the username and password that you provide and retrieve certain settings that need to be configured as part of the DSN setup. Even if you don't need to perform this operation, entering setup data here will help you confirm that your DSN works properly – if the wizard can't connect to retrieve the information it needs, then something is definitely wrong!

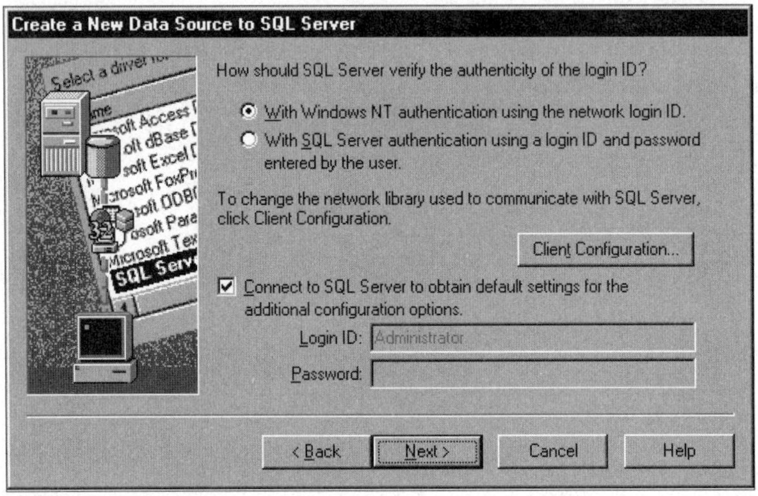

From this screen, it is also possible to alter the client configuration. This will let you determine what network library – and therefore what network protocol – is used to connect to the database, and how the connection should take place. For a SQL Server DSN, Named Pipes and TCP/IP are the fastest communication protocols.

Finally, the next two steps of the wizard allow you to alter several settings (that will normally be automatically downloaded by the wizard if you allow it to connect to the server). The only thing to which you should pay attention here is the Create temporary procedures... setting, which instructs the ODBC driver to translate your queries into temporary SQL stored procedures whenever you run them. The logic behind this is that stored procedures are faster than simple queries once they have been compiled by the server; as a result, by creating a temporary stored procedure for your statements, the driver will be able to speed up the execution of a query if you run it more than once. However, this process is inefficient if you never – or almost never – run the same exact query more than once. In a store, most database access operations are different from each other, and, therefore, the use of this setting is not recommended.

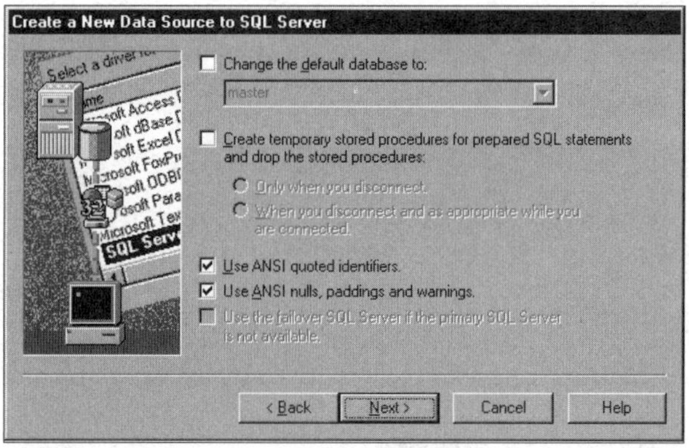

When you are done with the step-by-step process, the wizard gives you a chance to test your DSN. Keep in mind that, unless you have specified the appropriate authentication method and a valid username and password early in the wizard, your DSN will not test properly. It should be pointed out, however, that you do not necessarily need to specify the username and password in the wizard, as they will be indicated again in your connection string.

The Wizard Step-by-Step

Having set up our DSN, we can now return to the Site Foundation Wizard and begin creating our store.

Step 1: Selecting an IIS application for our store

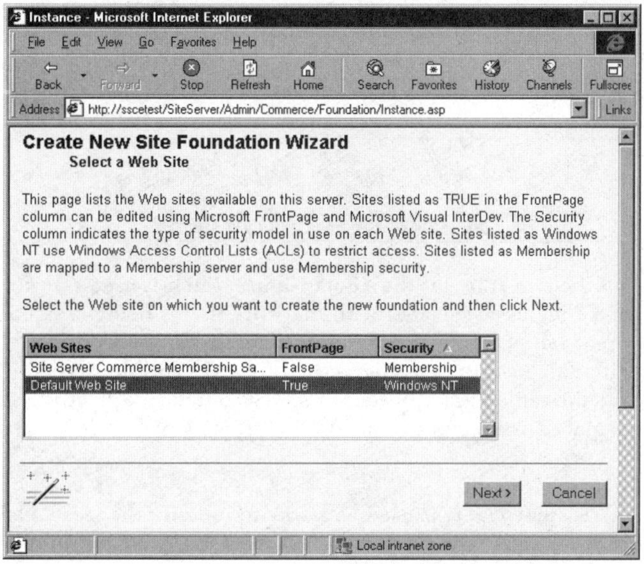

As we see, the first step consists of selecting the IIS web site where we want our store to reside. Always keep in mind that a Commerce Server site must be placed in a virtual folder of an existing site – this is the only way for Commerce Server to be aware of the fact that the site is there.

> **If we want our site to appear in the root folder of a web site (that is, http://www.wrox.com rather than http://www.wrox.com/store), we will first have to create the store in a virtual directory, then manually configure the IIS application's root to point to that folder.**

Once we have chosen a web site where to create our store, we can click on Next to continue.

Step 2: Choosing a name for our store

In order to complete the next step, we will have to choose a name for our site. As we can see here, there are actually *two* names that have to be chosen.

The more important of the two is by far the **Short Name**, which is used internally as "code" to identify all the elements that are associated with the store that is being created. For example, all the database tables that are used by the store will be prefixed by the short name (that is, if the short name is sam, then the product table could be called sam_product), and the virtual directory where the site will be stored will have the same name. Because of the use that is typically made of it, the Short Name cannot contain spaces or special characters. It can, however, contain underscores, if we really need them.

On the other hand, the **Display Name** is used as a way to identify the store when human intervention is required. Generally speaking, it should be much more descriptive than the Short Name, because it should appear meaningful, for example, to a site administrator who wants to modify the settings for the site.

Although a 12-character maximum is forced on the length of the Short Name field, it's a *very* good idea to keep it as short as possible – no more than two or three characters. Just think of the places in which we are likely to use this name: URLs (if our users have to access the store through a virtual directory path, `http://www.wrox.com/ws` is much easier to type in than `http://www.wrox.com/thewroxstore`, although both names fit in the text editing form); database tables (sure, let's face it, we'll have a lot of fun with a long name when we are writing code...), and so on.

Also, keep in mind that the Short Name should be unique across our entire server – and therefore not only to the IIS site where we are creating the store. The small list box on the right side, labeled **Reserved**, should list all the Short Names that have already been used on the web site. If it doesn't, then either we don't have any other stores installed or something has gone awry with the Commerce Server settings and the Wizard is not able to retrieve a list of reserved names. Sadly, that was what happened to me at the first try, so I had to guess a Short Name that had not been used already. Oh well, I just had to reboot...

They're all part of the same family

Besides the obvious naming issues, there is a particularly good reason why Commerce Server adopts this dual-name approach for designating stores. In fact, even though almost all the database structures used by all Commerce Server stores are the same, their names are always different for each store. This means, for example, that if we have two stores A and B, their product tables will be called A_product and B_product respectively.

If we think of it, this leaves us with an impressive amount of freedom – we could have both stores work off the same database, which will save us space and overhead when the stores are still small enough not to draw too much traffic, and then move each one of them off to its own database when the stores grow in popularity over time. This level of flexibility would not be possible if we were forced to store all the information for all the stores in the same database structure.

Step 3: Providing a physical location for our store

The next step lets us specify the physical location of our store. Although this can be anywhere on our computer (or on our network), Commerce Server actually suggests the best possible location for it, which is in a subfolder of the site's root directory that has the same name as the store's Short Name.

Using the default location is a good idea because it helps us group our store with the data that belongs to the site on which it will be installed. However, you should take some caution here regarding the security of your site. It can be a bad idea to use the default location because your files will be stored under wwwroot, which is one of the first places that an attempted intrusion could occur on your system.

Step 4: Choosing a datasource

What good is a store without its database? Step 4 lets us choose a datasource where all the data used by our store will be saved. As you can see, we can choose from all the system datasources that are available on our machine; in this case there are a few Microsoft Access ones, and a SQL Server one called Test that we are actually going to use. Together with the datasource, we must also specify a valid username and password to access the data itself.

Although a more complete overview of the database structures used by Commerce Server stores will not come until Chapter 8, let me spend a few words on how we should choose a database for our store. Access is not a good choice for a production server unless we expect our traffic – and the load on the database – to be extremely small. As we know, Access has been designed as a desktop database system, and does not well adapt to client-server scenarios in which multiple data access may occur at the same time. SQL Server (MSSQL from now on), on the other hand, represents a solid choice because it has been designed exactly for that purpose (and, may I add, Microsoft has done a great job with it!).

Obviously, the natural choice would be to use Access when we are prototyping our store, and then move to MSSQL when we are ready to go into production. Unfortunately, the problem here is that the syntax used by Access for SQL queries is slightly different from the one used by MSSQL, and therefore our store won't work when we make the move to a production environment, unless we change all our queries to work with MSSQL.

Also, we should place a lot of consideration on the account that we will use for accessing the database. In the example that we see in these pages, you will notice that I chose sa, the system administrator account. This may be a good choice in a prototyping environment – this account gives us a lot of freedom and lets us concentrate on *real* problems rather on why we can't execute a stored procedure.

Things change significantly, however, in a production environment, where, if we keep on using sa, we will actually let *all* the users of our store access the database with the maximum access level possible. Since this practice is the equivalent of giving everybody the keys to your server room with a complimentary administrative login, we should never *ever* do that. Take the time to have one of your IT people create a login that is only going to have access to the right structures and use it (for more information on what the right structures are, check out Chapter 9).

Step 5: Select an NT administrative account

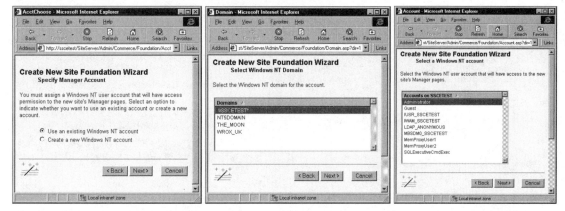

The next step allows us to select or create an NT account for accessing the site's administrative interface. Even though it's a legitimate choice to create a new account from the Wizard, the best place to carry out this task is the right Windows NT administration tool, which gives us a wider array of functionality.

Another word of caution should be used here. Whatever your choice, we don't want to create an account that has too much power over the system or the network as a whole, since there is always the remote possibility that somebody will be able to intercept the password when we will be logging in. Even though we will most likely access the site's administrative functionality through an SSL-protected connection, the risk is even higher if we need to turn off the use of NT authentication because we want to access the site using browsers other than Internet Explorer.

The best idea here is to create a new account that is local to the machine, give it only limited permissions on the store and force a change of the password on a regular basis (for example, two weeks). Because the entire regulation of access rights is delegated to NT security, we can also create a group, as well as other user accounts and grant them the proper permissions manually.

Step 6: Creating the foundation

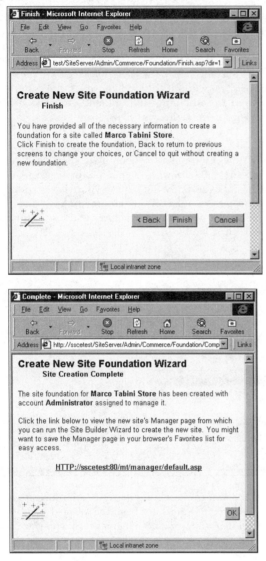

Well, that's it! We have now specified all the information that is required in order to create a site foundation. After choosing the NT account, the Wizard will ask us if we're really sure that we want to continue. This would be a great moment to review our information...if only the Wizard would let us do that. Unfortunately, all we get is what we see in the adjacent screenshot, so if we want to review the information we have entered we must go back screen by screen (luckily, the Wizard will retain the information, so we won't have to type it in again).

If we click on the Finish button, our cursor will turn into an hourglass, our hard drive will hum noisily for a while and, if everything goes well, we will see the page here. If we get an error, the best technique is to return to the confirmation page using our browser's back button and try again. If we keep on having trouble try the magic solution – reboot. If even that doesn't help, we will most likely have to reinstall Site Server Commerce Edition on our machine.

What Does Really Happen?

Let's now take a look at what was physically created on the server while we were waiting.

The screenshot above shows a directory listing for the root folder of my store; as we can see, the folder's name is the same as the Short Name we chose for the site (although we could have chosen a different one in Step 3 earlier).

The only two files that we will find in there are global.asa, which contains all the initialization parameters for the virtual folder and takes care of setting up whatever global entities are needed by the store to work, and default.asp, which in its current state only tells the user that our store will soon be available for them to browse.

The Assets folder contains nothing and is simply the part of the recommended structure for a Commerce Server store that is supposed to contain all the data files, like images, sounds, animations, and so on. The Closed folder contains the files that should be displayed when the store is closed (see Chapter 3 for an explanation on opening and closing a store), whereas the Config folder contains all the settings for the store.

Finally, the Manager folder contains only a handful of files and folders that are needed to hold more configuration information and provide the functionality needed to launch the Site Builder Wizard.

This is all that there is to it. As we can see, a site foundation is extremely simple, and at the same time is a powerful starting point for our store, because it provides us with a well thought out structure and many of the global parameters that we will need, which we'll find in the global.asa file. As we said, we could use this to start our own project from scratch if we really think that either the sample stores (or the starter store that is created by the Site Builder Wizard) cannot be modified easily enough. Even though I don't personally think that we will ever find ourselves in such a situation, and therefore this possibility is not directly covered in this book, we will find enough information here to start our own project if we need to. The best way to do so is to learn as much as we can about the data structures and components used by Commerce Server (Chapters 9 and 10) and the way they are implemented in the starter store (Chapters 6, 7, 11 and 12).

The Site Builder Wizard

Now that a site foundation has been created, we can proceed and actually have the Site Builder Wizard (SBW) create a *store* for us. The goal here is to end up with a site that provides the groundwork from which we can build our own solution without having to reinvent the wheel every time.

Unlike the Site Foundation Wizard that can be launched from either the MMC or the HTML version of the Commerce Host Administration tool, the SBW can only be launched from a site's management interface. As we mentioned before, each Commerce Server store provides a special section (usually protected by a password) that can be accessed to manage certain aspects of the site.

There are three ways to access the management interface of a newly created store. The easiest one – assuming that we will want to run the SBW right after creating the store's foundation, which is not mandatory – is to click on the link that the Foundation Wizard provides at the end of its execution (http://sscetest:80/mt/manager/default.asp in the second screenshot of Step 6 above).

If we happened to close our browser window without going to the management interface, don't despair! We can still get there in one of two ways. The quickest way is to open another browser window and type in the same URL that the Foundation Wizard was providing; even if we don't remember it, there is an easy way to compose it:

> http://*your_site*/*short_name*/manager/default.asp

where *your_site* is the address of the site where our store resides (sscetest in our example before), and *short_name* is the short name of the store.

What Can I Expect From the Site Builder Wizard?

We have already seen the very short answer to this question: a basic store that we can expand to suit our needs. Before we move on to check out the Wizard step-by-step, let's see some of the features that we can expect to configure with it:

- ❑ **Product attributes**
  We'll be able to specify whether the products in our store have pre-defined – or *static* – attributes and which attributes are different from product to product – otherwise called *dynamic* attributes. For example, if the store was selling merchandise as diverse as mugs and shirts, we'd have to define different attributes for each of them, like color and size for the shirts and design for the mugs. Commerce Server lets us do this by defining a set of attributes and then assigning them to the products individually.

- ❑ **Supported payment methods**
  Commerce Server provides all the functionality needed to validate credit card numbers in the basic store. All we'll have to do is specify which credit cards the store should accept and the Wizard will do the rest for us.

- ❑ **Site structure**
  A very important part of a store are its aisles, or departments – the way we group and present products logically. Commerce Server lets us create a store with single-level or multi-level departments. The latter structure lets us organize departments hierarchically, to further organize the products. For example, we can have a department dedicated to clothing and then a series of sub-departments, each of them dedicated to specific types of clothes like shirts, pants, coats, and so on.

❑ **Order tracking**

A very neat feature of online stores is their level of interaction with the customers: they are always open (unless our server goes down), and they let customers perform numerous tasks without the need for annoying customer service phone calls. One of these tasks is checking the status of an order online – whether the order has been accepted, shipped, is on hold, and so on.

❑ **Shipping/Handling and Taxes**

One of the peskiest tasks in setting up an online store is taking care of all the fees related to tax collection, shipping and handling. Although Commerce Server does not offer a fix-all solution, the SBW will help us establish some rules for handling the basic needs linked to these charges.

The Wizard Step-by-Step

Once we get into the store's management interface, we should see something similar to the figure above. As you have probably already figured out by yourself, all we have to do in order to start the SBW is to click on the Start the <u>Commerce Site Builder Wizard</u> link – not that we can do much else, can we?

Step 1: Getting started

As we can see above, the first step is simply a welcome screen. Nothing major here, apart from a warning that the SBW will overwrite any files that are already in the store's folders and therefore any manual changes that we might have made to a previous incarnation of the site will be lost. This includes ASP scripts, pipeline configuration files, and any other files that have been customized.

Although it is possible to run the SBW on the same store as many times as we want, that's something that we will generally do only if we made some mistake during the first execution and we want to fix it so we have the best possible starter store to work on. If we plan the needs of our stores carefully enough, we should never need to run the SBW once we have made significant changes to another starter store.

Step 2: Choosing a site type

Step 2 asks us to choose a site type. As we can see, and as we have mentioned before, we have the choice of either creating a copy of a sample store – which will be re-branded according to our settings – or start from a generic store.

I've said this earlier, and I'll say it again. Starting from a sample store might look like a good idea – after all they have been developed with a specific idea in mind – but we might find ourselves having to make significant changes to the site just because we wanted to make a seemingly simple modification to the site's architecture. So, unless we want a simple store that will look very much like the sample store we choose (at least from an architectural point of view), I strongly recommend that we start from a custom site, which is what we'll do here.

Step 3: Specifying our store's contact information

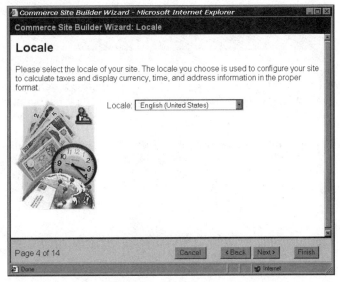

The next step allows us to specify some contact information for the store. This includes a contact address, phone and fax numbers, e-mail address and a brief description of what our store does. In the next chapter, we'll see how this information is transferred into a special section of the site that hands out information regarding the store to our customers.

For the moment, keep in mind that if we are going to make extensive modifications to the starter site, we will want to create a separate customer support section that contains not only contact information, but also store policies, special offers, and so on. Therefore, whatever the starter store has to offer from this point of view will be of little help unless we are aiming at launching a very simple store.

Step 4: Selecting a locale

Next, we'll select a locale for the store. The locale is used to determine how a number of features of the store will behave, like the way numbers are displayed, what currency symbol should be used, and how taxes should be applied to our customers. Contrary to what we might think, however, the locale does not determine the language that will be used; no matter what our choice, the store's text will always be in English.

As we can see in this figure, we can only choose one locale for our store. This means that if we want, for example, to serve customers both from the US and, say, Italy, providing the best possible locale-related functionality, we will have to manually develop a dual system that supports both locales.

Taxes, on the other hand, present a different problem. In fact, while every other aspect of the locale depends on who our audience is, the way taxes are applied depends on where *we* are. If we are located in the US, we must charge taxes according to the US rules, no matter where we are shipping our merchandise. Since changing the locale for all the display-related functionality (number formatting, currency symbols, and so on) is a trivial task, as we will see in Chapters 10 and 11, I recommend that we make our selection here based on the taxation system that we will want to use.

Step 5:Choosing a site style

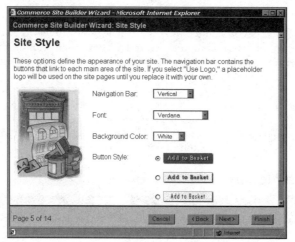

This screenshot shows Step 5 of the SBW, which asks us to select a style for the store that we are going to create. While the Button Style choice is almost always meaningless, since we will most likely change the buttons to reflect the style of our own store, getting the other settings right will save us a lot of customization work.

The Navigation Bar style, which can be set to either vertical or horizontal, will determine how certain elements of our site will be placed across each page. Most sites these days have settled on vertical sidebars, usually on the left side of the screen (which is where the SBW will put it for us). Horizontal navigation bars, located at the top of a page, are less used but equally viable.

The Font setting can be used to establish the font face that will be used throughout the whole site. We should stick to a font that is part of the basic package for all browsers. This includes Arial (sans serif proportional), Times New Roman (serif proportional) and Courier (serif mono-spaced). Unfortunately, all these fonts have their share of problems: Arial and Times New Roman are not easy to read, especially at small sizes, while Courier is not very elegant because it's mono-spaced (each character occupies the same horizontal space). In my opinion, the best compromise between elegance and readability is Verdana, but version 3 browsers do not support this unless users manually install it on the client machines. However, on earlier browsers or machines on which the font is not installed, Verdana degrades to a graceful Times New Roman, which makes it a good choice anyway.

Finally, the Background color setting is pretty much straightforward. Again, choosing the right color here will save us a lot of customization work once our store has been created.

Step 6: Promotions

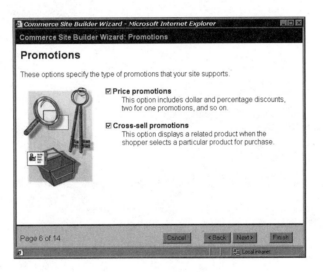

Step 6 lets us specify whether we want our store to include the necessary functionality to handle price and cross-selling promotions.

Price promotions are very popular in everyday life, and they are often presented as *buy x for y* offers: buy two shirts and get a pair of trousers for 40% off, and all the similar combinations. Taking care of them inside a store is a potentially tricky business, as there might be a lot of possible combinations to take into account. Commerce Server provides all the structures and functionality needed to manage a wide variety of promotions, and including it into our store, even if we are not going to use it right away, will definitely save a lot of development time; thus, check both the boxes. When we look at the management interface, we will discuss price promotions in detail.

Cross-sell promotions are becoming more and more typical in online stores. They represent the typical "pitch" of a salesperson who "suggests" complementary products to his or her customers. It's like entering a store, looking for a pair of roller blades and hearing the salesperson say how nice they would look with that pair of kneepads. Commerce Server supports two kinds of cross-selling: direct and historical. Direct cross-selling promotions – the ones we turn on through the SBW – work by manually specifying affinity rules among products. The store takes care of displaying complementary merchandise when, for example, a certain product is added to the basket.

Historical cross-selling works instead by comparing the shopping habits of the current user to a database of data collected from other customers throughout time, and then proposing what appear to be complimentary entries to those in the user's basket. Commerce Server provides this type of cross-selling functionality – which is sometimes presented as customers who bought product x also bought products y and z through the `Predictor` component – which we'll discuss in Chapter 10.

Step 7: Features

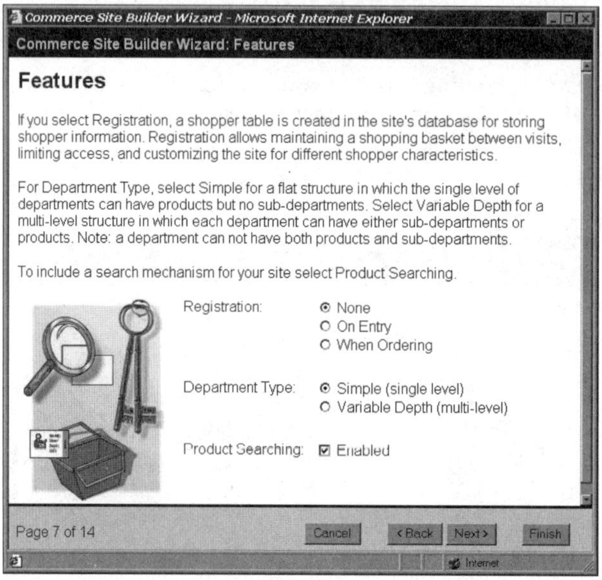

The next step is shown above. In this screen we are given the chance of choosing when, if at all, our customers are to register, if we want single-level or multi-level departments, and if we want product searching to be enabled on the site.

Generally speaking, as we have already mentioned in the previous chapters, we will not want our customers to register *before* they enter our site unless it is absolutely necessary (for example, if we are operating a subscription service). The idea here is that people like the anonymity that only Internet shopping can give them, and asking them who they are does not exactly take this fact into account. On the other hand, we might want to ask our users to register before they can buy, which would allow repeat customers to only have to type in their e-mail, password and credit card information in order to make a purchase. Unfortunately, most people won't like not having a choice, so our only viable solution is really to implement a registration system by ourselves, maybe integrating it with the Personalization & Membership functionality provided by Site Server.

The department structure settings are a selection that must be made according to our own needs. 'Simple' allows one level of departments with all products under each respective department, whereas 'Variable' allows multiple levels of both products and departments. For a simple store, organizing our products in a hierarchical structure might be a little overkill and end up confusing our audience, while for a larger store it will actually help them find their way through the merchandise better.

Product searching, *en fin*, is something that all but the simplest store should have. Unless our store has fewer than ten products, or it simply incorporates the EC functionality to provide some alternative kind of service, we should turn this option on.

Steps 8 and 9: Product attributes

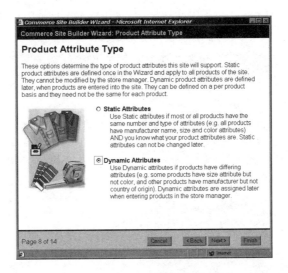

Steps 8 and 9 regulate what is, in my opinion, the most difficult feature to modify manually after the SBW has been run: product attributes. I'm sure that everybody understands what a product attribute is – we'll describe it as a unique characteristic of the product. For example, a shirt might have attributes like Color and Size, while a software title might have something like Format and Platform.

From the point of view of product attributes, we can find ourselves in two situations. If the products we sell are homogeneous enough to be grouped under a single category, we will only need one set of well-defined attributes, which will never change (**static attributes**). If, on the other hand, we sell a very heterogeneous mix of merchandise, then we will need to specify different attributes for each product (**dynamic attributes**).

If we select Static Attributes the next screen will look similar to the one below. As we can see, we can specify right here all the attributes that our products will have.

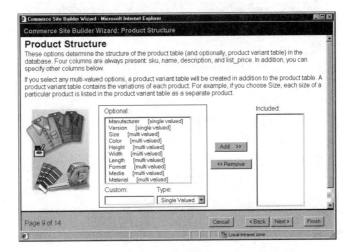

It's a good idea to sort out all the attributes we need at this stage, because the SBW will create all the necessary structures and interface elements to administer them through the management pages. If we need to add new attributes after the SBW has been run, we will have to do all this work by ourselves.

If our choice in the first screen was Dynamic Attributes, we'll be taken to this screen:

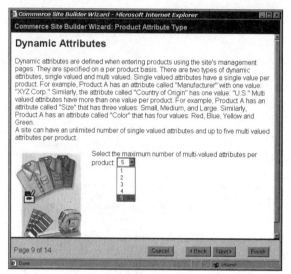

In this case, the Commerce Server engine lets our store handle up to 5 different attributes for each product. All the possible variations of a product are organized into **product families**, and the price and product id (known as 'Stock Keeping Unit', **SKU**, in Commerce Server) become dependent on the individual combinations of the attributes' values. For example, a large blue shirt will have an SKU of 123 and a price of $15.99, while an extra large white one will have an SKU of 124 and a price of $19.99. However, both shirts belong to the same product family, that is, they are variations of the same product.

Step 10: Shipping and handling

As part of the next step, we will have to specify any shipping and handling charges. As we can see, the Wizard lets us specify a number of different shipping methods (Overnight and 2nd day in this example), but the total amount of the shipping fee is calculated on a per-order basis only. If we need to use another computation method (for example, an amount for each item in the basket), we are on our own. Luckily, creating our own shipping calculation system is not enormously complicated.

No matter what our shipping needs, it's a good idea to set up all our shipping methods here, even if we can't use the functionality provided by MS Commerce Server, because the SBW will create the entire infrastructure necessary to handle it (like web pages, and so on). Getting it right will save us a lot of development time later.

Step 11: Taxes

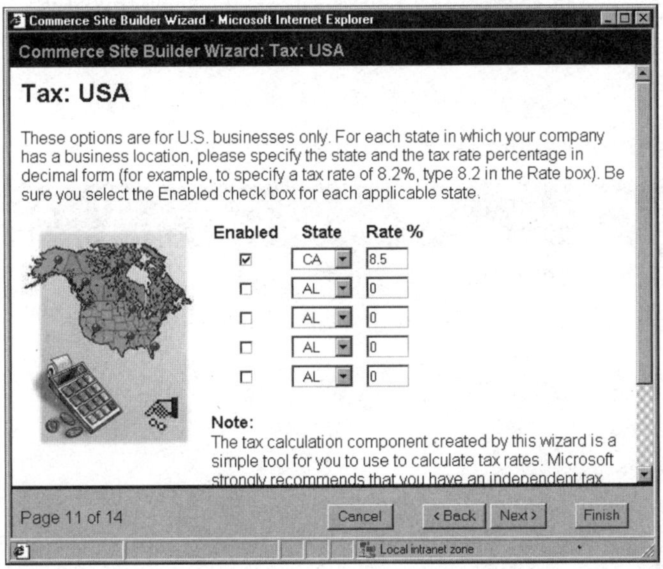

No store is a store unless it makes us pay taxes, I guess, so Step 11 asks us to specify the tax rates. While the screenshot above is specific to the US locale, what we will actually see will effectively depend on the choice we have made back in Step 4. If we selected Canada as our locale, for example, we will be asked to insert a value for the Goods and Services Tax (GST) and a value for the Provincial Sales Tax (PST) for each province. In the UK we would need to specify the value of the Value Added Tax (VAT). Since in the US taxes work differently, here all we have to do is specify a rate for each of the states where we will be charging taxes.

As I'm writing this chapter, the Euro has just become a reality in Europe, or at least in parts of it. Since Site Server 3 came out a while before this happened, it doesn't have any direct support for any new European taxation system that will arise from that (support for the Euro is provided indirectly through the operating system with the installation of the Euro hotfix available from Microsoft).

The documentation that comes with Commerce Server states that the tax rate calculation functionality provided with the software is for demonstration purposes only, and should never be used in a real-life environment, where a more complete taxation package should be integrated instead. From my personal experience, we can just go ahead and use the standard Commerce Server features if our tax needs are simple enough. For example, if we only have one physical location, say, in New York, we will only need to charge New York state residents the local sales tax rate, whereas all other customers will enjoy tax-free shopping (although foreign shoppers will have to pay customs dues).

As soon as our situation gets a little more complicated, however, things become really pesky. For example, if we have other physical locations (like subsidiaries, for example), we will have to charge the appropriate sales taxes for those states where our locations are. The best solution in these cases is to consult with a tax specialist (just take a look at the Yellow Pages, they thrive in our tax-ridden society!) and make our choice according to his or her recommendations. After all, never forget that taxes are the offspring of politicians' minds, and as such their relationship with simplicity is, in the best of cases, dubious!

Step 12: Choosing our payment methods

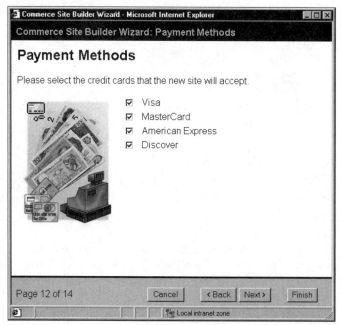

As we mentioned at the beginning of this section, Commerce Server comes with the built-in capability of verifying credit card numbers. All we have to do is specify what credit card brands our store will accept, and this step lets us choose from four different types.

It is important to understand the difference between verifying the validity of a credit card number and actually charging money to it. Commerce Server will let us make sure that a number provided by a customer satisfies the verification algorithm (known as the *Luhn* or *Mod 10 Check Digit Algorithm*) that is used to create the card numbers. This algorithm calculates the last digit of a credit card number based on the value of the other digits as follows:

1) Starting with the rightmost digit (excluding the last one, which is a check digit, and is not part of the actual account number) and moving left, multiply all the digits in odd positions by two, then sum up the resulting digits. For example: 6*2 = 12 = 1 + 2 = 3.
2) Sum the resulting digits to the remaining digits (including the check digit).
3) If the resulting sum modulus 10 results in a value of 0, the credit card number is valid.

Let's for example apply the Mod 10 algorithm to one of the credit card numbers that we saw in Chapter 4, like 4000 1307 1535 4079:

First, we multiply all the odd digits (starting from the rightmost account digit – 7 in this example) by two:

9
$7 * 2 = 14 = 1 + 4 = $ **5**
0
$4 * 2 = $ **8**

5
$3 * 2 = $ **6**
5
$1 * 2 = $ **2**

7
$0 * 2 = $ **0**
3
$1 * 2 = $ **2**

0
$0 * 2 = $ **0**
0
$4 * 2 = $ **8**

Let's now sum all the digits together:

$9 + 5 + 0 + 8 + 5 + 6 + 5 + 2 + 7 + 0 + 3 + 2 + 0 + 0 + 0 + 8 = 60 \bmod 10 = $ **0**

which means that the credit card number is valid. Naturally, you can reverse the algorithm to create your own credit card numbers (that's how I got the numbers in the first place), but I won't make it easy for you – you'll have to reverse the algorithm by yourself!

Now, how much does this algorithm tell us about the owner of the credit card or his spending limits? My fake credit card number passed the test, but I won't be able to make any money out of it! Credit card authorization has to be performed using a specialized service. There are a number of providers that will offer to authorize the credit card purchases made on our site through the Internet. In general, we should only choose an established provider that will not overcharge us, but offer a reliable and safe service.

Step 13: Order tracking settings

The final step before we decide what should be created by the Wizard allows us to determine whether users on our site will be able to review their past purchase history. As we saw above, this is a very important part of online shopping and we should really let our users take advantage of it – it will save us a lot of undesired phone calls that even our customers won't like to make.

However, as we are going to see in the next chapter, we will probably have some work to do over the functionality provided by Commerce Server in order to provide some added security for our customers.

Step 14: Telling the Wizard what to do

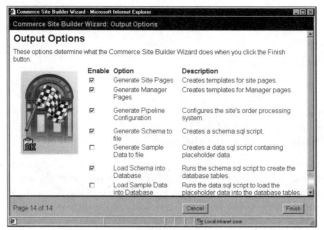

The last step of the Wizard allows us to specify what exactly we want the SBW to do for us. For a new store, we would generally want to check every box, with the exception of those related to sample data. These generate and load mock data into our database that we can use to test our store; unless we don't have any real data to work with at the beginning, we shouldn't bother checking these boxes – we'll have to enter actual information at some point, so why not do it right away?

Again, this would be a perfect spot for us to review our decisions. Unfortunately, the SBW shows a striking consistency with the Foundation Wizard in that it doesn't show us what our choices have been, so we'll have to go back step-by-step and make sure we didn't make any mistakes. As mentioned before, we can run the Wizard as many times as we want, but it's better to get it right the first time.

After we have clicked on the Finish button, the Wizard will start to create files and structures for us. Contrary to what happens with the Foundation Wizard, we will actually be able to see what's going on, step by step.

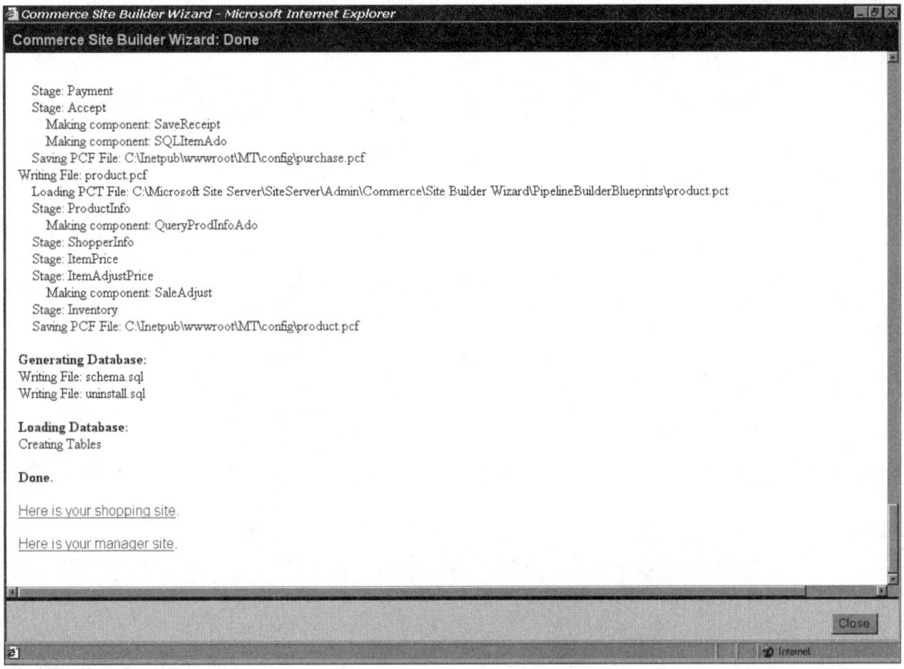

The two links that appear at the end of the Wizard execution now point to our starter store, which is ready to run!

Summary

This chapter gave us an overview of the tools Commerce Server has to offer to make the creation of a new site simple. We took a look at the Site Foundation Wizard, which builds the very basic structures needed by Commerce Server to be aware of the existence of a store, then moved on to the Site Builder Wizard, which actually creates a starter store that we can use to create our own sites.

As you may have imagined, there are only a few cases in which you will end up using the SFW alone. Unless the structure of your store is so different from that of the basic store created by the SBW, you will most likely want to run the latter and avoid starting from scratch. In most cases, however, you should be able to adapt the starter store to your needs, particularly if you become very familiar with it (we'll take care of that in the next few chapters!) and if you keep in mind that the overall structure of an online store does not really change much, even if you're not dealing with physical goods, as we saw earlier on in the book.

The next few chapters will be dedicated to a closer look at what the starter store has to offer, both on the storefront and the management side.

The Basic Store

Drive thy business, or it will drive thee.
–Benjamin Franklin, *Poor Richard's Almanac*

As we said in the previous chapter, the store that is created by the Site Builder Wizard should only be considered a starting point from which we can build our own customized online presence. Essentially, the big advantage of creating our stores using the SBW is that it provides us with a well-thought-out platform on which we can build. If we had to start from scratch, we'd probably have to figure out our own architecture, as well as design the execution flow of the site and fix all the bugs that would inevitably appear in the code.

While this is a perfectly acceptable situation – after all, that's how others got started in the first place – it might not be feasible in today's very competitive marketplace, since by the time we had everything ready with our store there's a good chance that the technologies and techniques we used would already be outdated.

Naturally, the SBW does not provide a complete solution for every possible case – as a matter of fact, it hits the mark only for a very narrow range of online stores – but it can be easily adapted to function as the building block of most systems. This means that investing a little money in MS Commerce Server can significantly affect the cost, efficiency and quality of our final product.

The anatomy of the **starter store** that we'll end up with once the SBW has been run successfully can vary significantly depending on the choices that we made during the running of the Wizard. This concept applies both to the storefront and to the management pages, since the latter will have to be able to properly handle whatever happens in the former.

As you can imagine, it is very important to be familiar with the way the store works in any of the possible variants that are generated by the SBW. This means not only understanding the technical structure and design of the site – which we'll examine in Chapter 11 – but also how the users of both the storefront and the management interface interact with the site.

What Does This Chapter Talk About?

During this chapter, we'll focus on how a newly created store is designed, and how it flows from a user's point of view. As mentioned earlier, we'll look at both the storefront *and* the management pages, in particular examining how they change in response to the various choices that can be made during the SBW's execution:

❑   **The Storefront**
First of all, we'll take a look at how the public portion of the site works. As we'll see, the actual shopping experience varies greatly, depending in particular on whether the store supports dynamic attributes, user registration and promotions.

❑   **The Management Interface**
Next, we'll move on to examine how the store is administered through the restricted–access area of the Store Manager, and we'll find out that the same elements that influence the structure of the storefront have a great bearing on the management interface.

The Storefront

When we have completed running the SBW, we can get to the storefront by either clicking on the "Click here to shop this site" or by typing the following URL into our web browser:

http://*your_host*/*store_name*

In my case, the store I've created is called mt and resides on a server called FOCA, therefore, I'll type the following URL into my browser:

http://foca/mt

which will lead us to the site's entry point.

Basic Structure of the Storefront

The basic structure of a starter store is very similar to the one we presented in Chapter 1, although a few differences can be introduced by our selections in the SBW. In general, the storefront can be divided into four areas:

Store entry point
This is the first set of pages that are shown to the client. In most stores, the entry point will correspond to the main page, although several other pages can be involved if the site requires its users to register when they first enter it.

Catalog browsing

The goal of this section is to allow users to find the product or products they are interested in by using a variety of tools, such as search functionality, promotions, cross-selling, or by just looking around the store's virtual aisles.

Purchase process

These pages take care of guiding the user through all the steps needed to complete a purchase, essentially collecting and processing the information that the user passes along.

Customer support

This section is used to perform several tasks that are usually performed by human customer service representatives, such as providing information about the store, keeping the customer up-to-date with the status of their orders, and so on.

Changing our Store's Appearance

If you have navigated a little bit around our store already, you will have noticed that, from the main page of the management pages, it is possible to run the SBW again. As you may imagine, doing so will let us change the structure of our site any way we want – if, for any reason, we were not happy with our site and wanted to run the SBW again, it's a good idea to do so *before* we start customizing the site because the SBW will overwrite any changes we have applied to the store's ASP pages.

> We need to close our store in order to run the Site Builder Wizard. We will need to open the store again if we want to start browsing it after the SBW's execution.

Entering the Site

The site's entry point – which is not always the store's main page, as we might think – can be very different, depending on what choice we made with respect to user registration during the execution of the SBW. If we selected to have our user register when they enter the site, opening the store will cause a page similar to the one here to appear.

As we can see, the two options here are to either enter a user's login information or to register as a new customer for the store. If this is our choice, then we will be taken to the page shown here, whose goal is obviously to collect the appropriate information about the customer, either using the Microsoft Wallet (which we introduced in Chapter 1 and will examine in detail in Chapter 13) or through a normal HTML form for those browsers that do not support the Wallet.

We have already discussed the merits of customer registration briefly in the past chapters. The real problem with requiring customer registration at the entry point is that it forces our shoppers to give up their identities even before they get into the site, which is something unlikely to make them happy.

At the same time, user identification might be useful, or even necessary, in several instances. For example, if we are building a store for a members-only club or something of the sort, we will indeed need to know who the shopper is before letting him or her in. This happens, particularly in corporate procurement business-to-business sites, where the customer's identity is often used not only to regulate access, but also to determine the availability and price of the products. In Chapter 12, when we talk about business-to-business EC, we'll encounter the Microsoft Market store, which uses this approach.

The Main Page

The next figure shows the main page of the site, which, as we can see, does not differ much from what we have seen in Chapter 1. The department names have been automatically inserted by the SBW as a result of the fact that I checked the appropriate box, **Load sample data in the database**, in the last page.

There are two major variable elements in this page, and they are both represented by a link at the bottom. The first one is the Shopper Update Page, which only appears if we have chosen to have some kind of user registration in our store. The other is the Order History Page, which will appear if we instructed the SBW to create a store that would show the user's order history.

One interesting characteristic of the main page – which also appears in the rest of the site – is the fact that in the navigation area all the links are active no matter what page we are visiting. For example, the fact that the Lobby image still links to the main page even when the browser is already on it can be confusing to our customers. In Chapter 11, we'll discuss how to change this behavior.

Modifying a User's Properties

The Shopper Update Page is essentially a copy of the page that is used initially to sign up a new user, with the exception that the Wallet is not used in this case. As we can see here, there is the possibility of changing one's password (by typing the old one first), as well as any other piece of information.

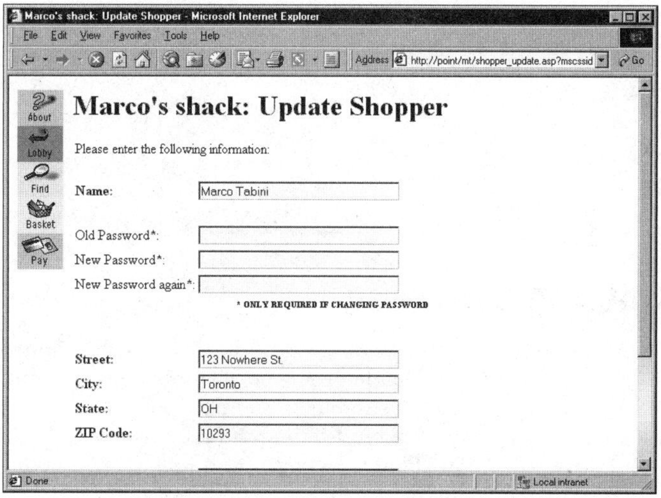

The Order History

The order history section of the store, which should actually be considered part of the customer support section, displays a list of all the purchases successfully completed by the user. In my case, as shown below, I only have one order on file.

It should be pointed out that the order history page contains a lot of personal information – as we'll see later on in the book, you could even add credit card data to it if you wanted. Therefore, it would be advisable to make the user access it through a secure HTTPS connection, even though by default the store itself doesn't do so.

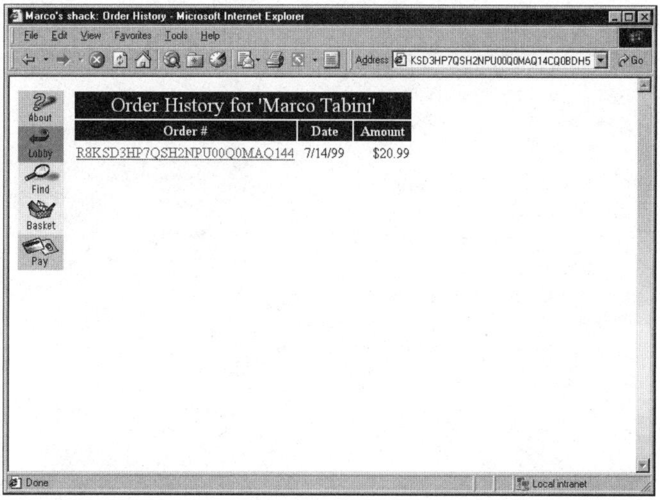

Clicking on the order's number brings up a detailed description of it, containing the address it was shipped to, the billing information and a complete breakdown of what was purchased (also shown).

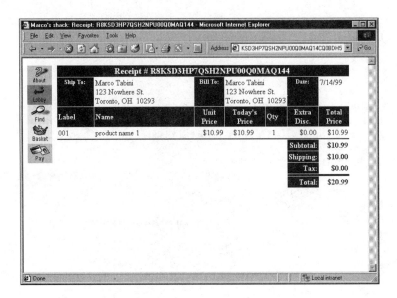

Catalog Browsing

As mentioned earlier, there are several ways for the shopper of an MS Commerce Server store to look through the available products. The most obvious method is to simply click on one of the departments that are available in the main page, and then look at the products they contain. Another possibility is to use the built-in search functionality to find a particular product (or group of products) in the catalog. Finally, the users can also jump to a specific item through promotional links, such as those that are supplied by the cross-selling system.

Product Pages

If we click on one of the department links in the store's main page, we will end up on a page that lists all the products in that category, unless we have chosen to have multi-level departments in which case we will have to choose a sub-department before getting to the products. Similarly, selecting a particular product brings up a page that provides more information about it, shown in the figure here.

Here, there there are a number of differences between what we saw in Chapter 1 and what can happen in a starter store. First of all, if we have chosen to support cross-selling promotions, we will see at the bottom of the page a list of all the products that are related to the one currently being displayed. This is clearly visible in the above figure, but it would not be there if we had not chosen to have cross-selling promotions running on our site.

Similarly, things will look different if we have chosen to support dynamic attributes. As we can see in the next figure, the user can now choose between any of the possible values for each of the product's dynamic attributes, which will let him or her select a particular variant of that item, the validity of which will be checked when it is added to the Basket.

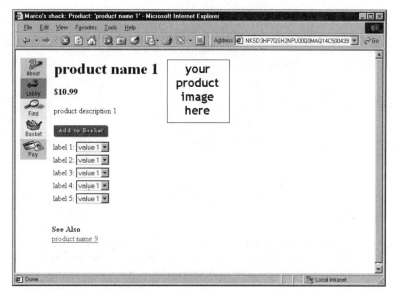

Search Functionality

Even though MS Commerce Server includes a very advanced and powerful search technology, the only functionality aimed at letting the user find particular products implemented in the starter store consists of a simple keyword-based search page. As we can see from the figure here, this is essentially the same search page that we saw in Chapter 1.

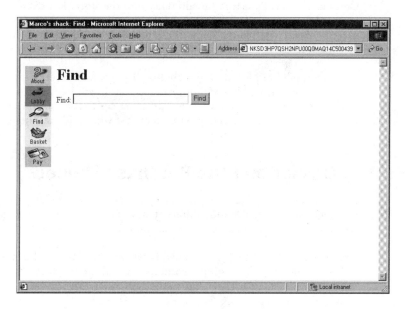

Unless our store contains only a very limited number of products, this is probably the first area of the site that we will be thinking about when we talk about improvements. As you can probably imagine, this simple page works by executing a query that contains an SQL LIKE statement against the product database, and then returning the result set in the form of a list – something similar to this:

```
<%
    ' qr contains the search parameters requested by the user

    Set db = Server.CreateObject ("ADODB.Connection")
    Set rs = db.Execute ("select * from products where name like "%" & qr & "%")

    If rs.EOF Then
%>
        No products found
<%
    Else
        While Not rs.EOF
%>
            <A HREF="product.asp&SKU=<% = rs ("SKU") %>"><% = rs ("Name") %></A><br>
<%
            rs.MoveNext
        Wend
    End If

    rs.Close
%>
```

Even though the code inside the actual store pages is slightly different – as we'll see in Chapter 9, SSCE provides a number of built-in structures that will help us make this entire procedure a little easier – the basic concept remains the same.

There is, therefore, a lot of room for improvement even if we are not thinking of integrating MS Commerce Server's search functionality into the store. For example, we could provide extra parameters for reducing the scope of the query, by extending the where clause to include other search criteria, such as the department or product category in which the user expects the product to be found, its price range, the date when, or after which, it was added to the database, and so on.

Moreover, the built-in find functionality displays all the results in a continuous list. Again, this works well if we only have a handful of products, but it will become confusing to the users and difficult to download for those who have a slow Internet connection as our catalog grows in size. Therefore, it's a good idea to provide a pagination system that will divide all the data into smaller chunks (for example: 10 records per page).

The Basket and the Purchase Process

The structure of the basket remains essentially unchanged, regardless of what choices we make when we create our store. The only differentiation takes place when dynamic attributes are chosen, in which case the exact characteristics of the variant chosen by the customers are accurately spelled out.

As we can see from the figure below, however, this doesn't alter the overall design of the basket page, which still functions as a simple container for all the products that the user is interested in and eventually wants to purchase.

Shipping and Payment Pages

The shipping and payment pages that come with the starter store are not particularly different to those that we saw in Chapter 1. In both cases, the Microsoft Wallet is used as the default data collection method, although normal HTML forms are also available. We have quickly looked at how this may not be the best arrangement for the store, since those users who do not have the Wallet installed on their computer – or whose browser does not support it – will have trouble entering their information. We'll talk about this more in detail in Chapter 13.

It's also interesting to notice that if we selected 'user registration upon entry' when we were creating the store, the HTML forms will be pre-populated with user registration information. Similarly, if we chose instead to have our customers sign up once they decide to purchase something from our store, they will be asked to either log in or register before they start the purchase process, and their data trail will automatically be used to fill out the HTML forms.

Data Validation Functionality

It's important to keep in mind that the store performs several checks to verify that all the data that has been input is correct straight after the user exits the shipping page *and* the payment page. These checks ensure that the user will not be allowed to continue with the purchase process if the information he or she entered was somehow incorrect.

If an error of any kind occurs, the system informs the user and instructs him or her to go back to the previous page to correct the error. MS Commerce Server does not provide any kind of logging for errors that occur at this point.

> As we'll see in Chapter 10, the Order Processing Pipeline can actually be instructed to log its activity to a text file. However, the log files produced in this way are very bulky and only useful for debugging purposes in a controlled environment; using them on a live server will rapidly fill up your hard drive and slow down your server.

Therefore it will be impossible for us to tell whether the errors themselves will have been caused by the user or by our store misbehaving in some way, even when this doesn't have anything to do with our code. For example, if we're out of stock of some item and instruct the store to refuse orders unless we can ship the merchandise immediately, the users will still receive a polite error from the store and be invited to try again. However, they will not be able to fix the error – unless they are willing to buy some other product – and we won't receive any notification of the problem.

The Purchase Process

In addition to the checks that we have just described, between the payment and confirmation page the store automatically performs the final steps of purchase processing and determines whether the order can be successfully completed. If this is the case, an order ID is generated, and the appropriate information is stored.

Once again, if an error is found, the system advises the user appropriately; similar to what was happening before, the store will not be able to distinguish between user-generated errors and problems that originated inside the store's code. Therefore, it is advisable to consider implementing some kind of monitoring mechanism whose only purpose would be to inform the store administrators that something is wrong. There are a number of packages available on the market that perform this duty, and some of them are quite sophisticated, to the point where they will call you on the telephone to notify you that something is wrong.

The Confirmation Page

In a similar way to the basket page, the confirmation page is not significantly affected by the settings in the SBW. The figure here shows what the page looks like when support for keeping a user's order history is turned on. The order ID becomes a link to the order detail page.

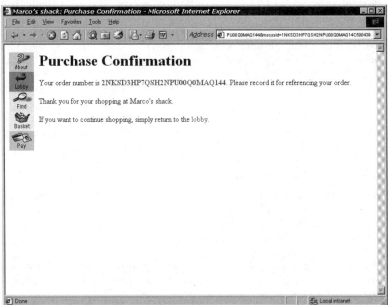

Customer Support Pages

The customer support section of the starter store only contains one page, which is used to provide the user with some basic contact information about the site, and is just really a placeholder for a much larger set of pages; a good reason why this section only contains such basic functionality may be that the amount of information that each store discloses to its users varies greatly.

Certainly, this is one of the areas of the site that will require a lot of changes, although most of the time we will not need to write a significant amount of code for it. Keep in mind that our customers will use the customer support pages as a reference point when they are in need of additional information about our store; therefore, it is very important that we concentrate on making it as comprehensive as possible. Doing so will accomplish two goals: first, we will be able to convey to our users the feeling that behind the virtual façade of our web site there is a real organization that is eager to help them; second, since the most commonly requested information will be available through the web, we will have to respond directly to fewer customer inquiries.

The Management Interface

One of the things that we have already mentioned in the previous chapters is that the management interface's role is much more functional than aesthetic. This means that its design is significantly simpler than that of the storefront, and it was conceived to make the life of the administrators easier rather than please the eye. However, simpler does not mean less user-friendly: since most of the tasks that are carried out through the store manager are security conscious in their nature, this section of the site contains pages that load quickly in the browser window where navigation elements are always at the user's fingertips.

The Main Page

Contrary to what happened with the storefront, the main page of the management interface always corresponds to the entry point. As we can see in this figure, it contains links to a number of different options, which are divided into three major sections.

Merchandising functions deal primarily with the product catalog and all the data that is associated with it, such as departments and promotions. Links in the Transactions section are used to manage the database of orders and shoppers. Finally, the System section is employed to regulate the behavior of the store in areas like the purchase process, availability of the storefront and the structure of the site itself.

One of the biggest problems with the design of the main page is that once we get access to it, we also automatically gain the right to use every section in the management interface. Clearly, this can be a problem, especially if we are expecting several people to visit this section of the store for different reasons. For example, we do not want one of the operators in the warehouse to be able to see the same kind of information that our CEO sees.

Unfortunately, in the starter store there is no support for granting separate access levels to the individual users. The simplest solution to this problem consists of regulating the access to the individual sections – or even pages – of the interface. However, this is – and remains – a manual task that cannot be easily automated; if we expect that users of the interface themselves will need to change user permissions on a regular basis, we can devise our own access control system – or, even better, we can use Site Server's Personalization & Membership server.

Merchandising Functions

The management interface provides three merchandising functions. The two links, Departments and Products, are used to access the databases that contain information about the product catalog, while Promotions, which is only available if we have chosen to support promotions in our store, makes it possible to manage price and cross-sell promotions that are running in the store.

Departments

Clicking on the Departments button will take us to a page similar to the one shown here, which, as we can see, contains a list of all the departments in the store. You will also notice that this page contains a list of navigational links both at the top *and* at the bottom – the reason why they're repeated is that if the page was longer than this and we would be looking at its end, it would be easier to simply use the links at the bottom than those at the top.

The rest of the page shows an interface that we'll find replicated across the entire site (as a matter of fact, many pages are shared by different functions within the Manager). The Add New Department link allows us to add a new department; by clicking on it, we'll be taken to the page shown in the next figure, which asks us for a department ID (unique to the store and used to identify the department in the database), a name and a description. The name and description will be used in the storefront's pages.

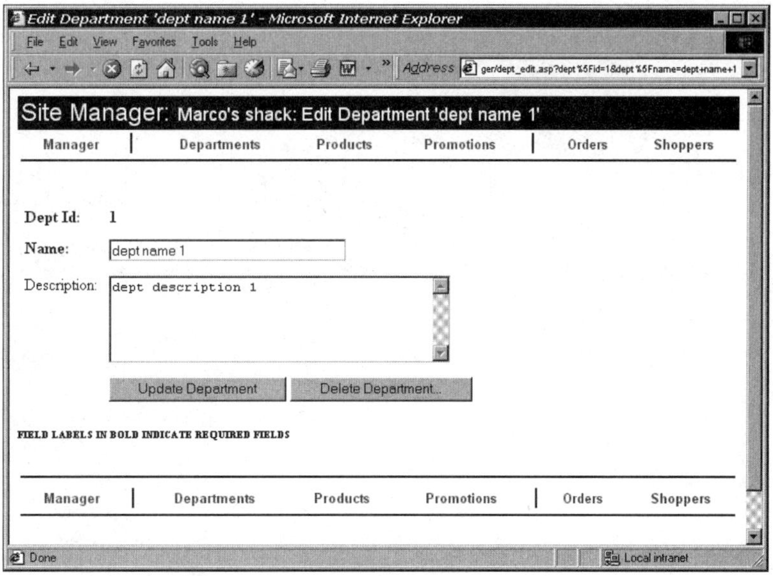

Editing departments is equally easy – all we need to do is click on a name and edit the data. You will notice that we are not allowed to edit the department ID; this is because that number is used as the primary key in the department table and therefore cannot be changed, as the system won't be able to recognize the correct record for that department.

Variable-Depth Departments

If we chose to have variable-depth departments in our store when we first launched the SBW, the procedure for editing existing departments and adding new ones will be slightly different to allow for the fact that these are arranged in a different way. As we can see from the figure here, the list now contains a "parent department ID", which identifies the relationships between each department and the others.

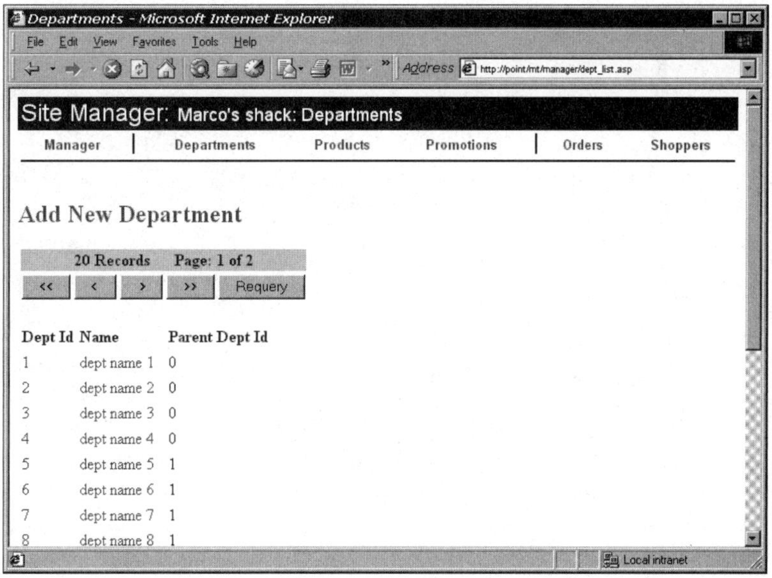

139

A department can't contain both sub-departments and products. Thus, you can only add products to "leaf" departments that do not have any sub-departments under them.

Products

The product interface, shown here, works in a similar way to its counterpart that deals with departments when we have static attributes; the only significant difference is in the fact that there are many more fields to fill out here.

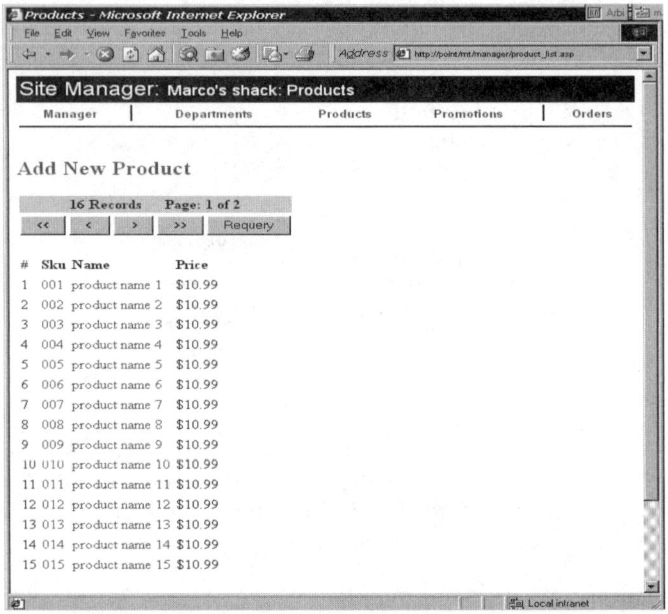

The fields used to create or edit a product are all very straightforward, but a few words should be said about the Sale fields (the last three fields) and the department list. As you can imagine, the sale fields are used to determine whether a product is on sale. It is possible to specify a start and an end date for the sale, and a sale price. The system will automatically apply the sale price to all purchases during the specified time (we'll talk more about this in Chapter 10). The department list, on the other hand, makes it possible to associate a product with one or more departments – pressing *Ctrl* while clicking on any department will alternately add or remove it from the list of linked departments.

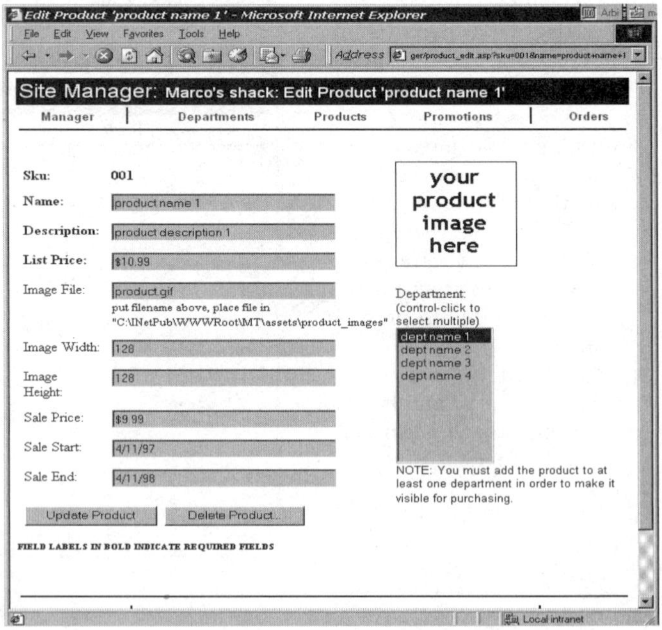

Handling Dynamic Attributes

If our site supports dynamic attributes, adding new products – and editing existing ones – works in a slightly different way. First of all, products are grouped into *product families*, which represent a group of *variants* that are generally considered as being variations of the same fundamental item. This concept is somewhat similar to thinking of a car model (the product family) and all the possible combinations of its different characteristics (for example: colour, engine size, and so on): a blue Jaguar is no less a Jaguar than a red one.

Most of the product attributes that we have seen previously are still present, but are assigned to the product family; as we can see from the next figure, the editing of a product (which is in no way different from adding a new one) becomes a three-step process: first, we can specify those attributes that belong to the entire family. In step 2, also shown below, we are asked to specify what the dynamic attributes for the family are. These, in turn, will be used in the third and final step for specifying an arbitrary number of variants.

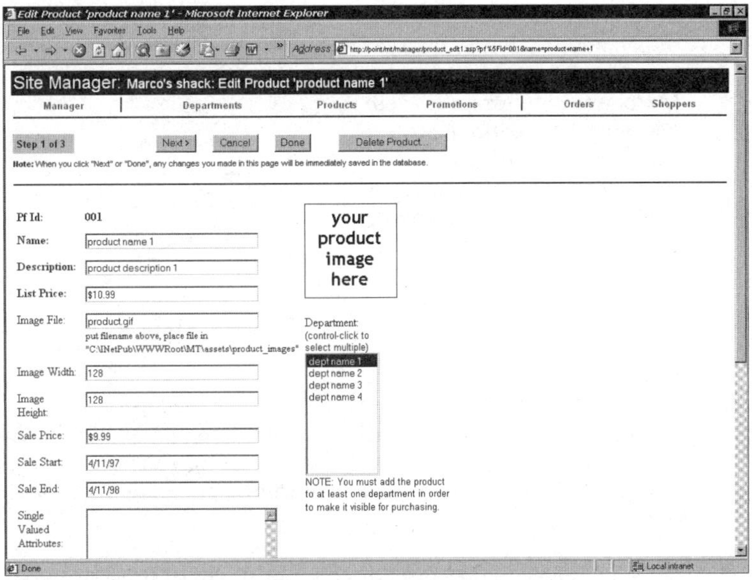

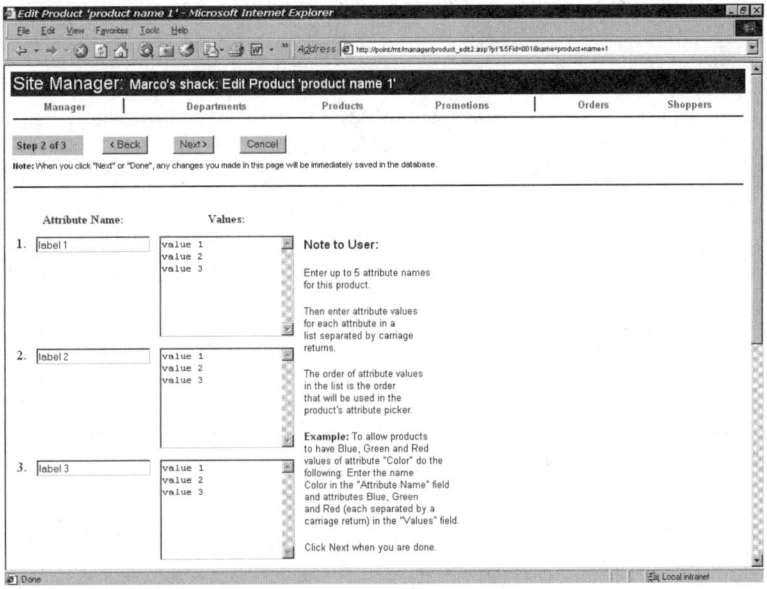

As we'll see later on in Chapter 11, the possible combinations of five different attributes – especially considering that we can assign as many values as we want to them – can be astronomical. Luckily, we do not need to create a new variant for each combination, so we can limit our additions to the variants that we really need.

Promotions

The promotional functionality of the store, which is only available if we chose to support any kind of promotions during the store's creation, is located in the **Merchandising** group as well. As we can see here, there are two categories of marketing promotions that we can set up: price promotions and cross-selling promotions.

A Marketer's Dream: Price Promotions

If you've had a chance to work with marketing people in the course of your career, you will know how difficult they tend to get. Their idea of "special offers" can take on the most convoluted forms, and they will always expect us to promptly generate the code that will make these "Promotional Frankensteins" come to life.

MS Commerce Server provides a set of standard price promotions that can save our life. As a matter of fact, out-of-the-box it is possible to generate three different types of promotions:

❑ **buy x get y at z% off**
This kind of promotion gives the customer a discount on one item if another one is also purchased. The discount is expressed in percentage points. Obviously, the promotion can also be expressed as buy x and get x at z% off, which means that a product can be discounted depending on the quantity purchased (for example: buy two cans of beans and only pay for the second one would correspond to a 50% discount).

❑ **buy x get y at $z off**
This promotion is exactly the same as the previous one, except that the discount is expressed as a dollar amount.

❑ **buy 2x for the price of 1**
The third possible type of promotion is a variation of the first one; if the customer buys two (or a multiple of two) items of the same product, he or she will receive each second item for free. As you have probably already imagined, this is the same as offering a 100% discount on a product if the same product is present twice in the basket.

With a little thought, it's easy to see how all the three built-in promotions are really all variations of the same operation. In fact, if, after adding a promotion, we click on the **Advanced Attributes** link, we will always be presented with the same page, visible in the figure here. This screen makes it possible to modify the parameters of the offer with a higher degree of freedom than by using the pre-determined entry screens that we just saw.

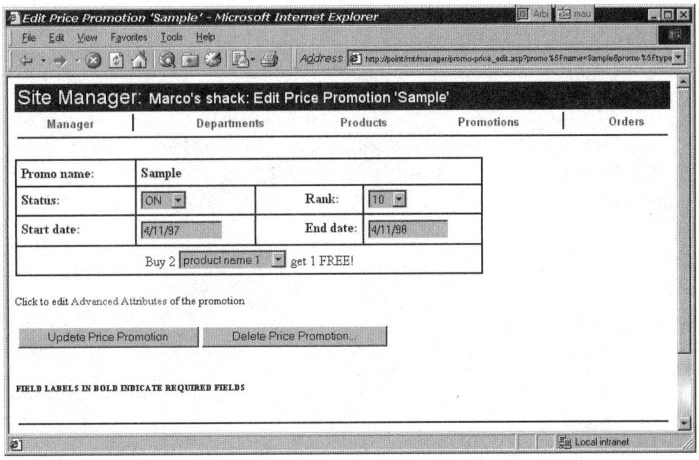

An important element of a promotion is its **rank**, which expresses its importance or – in other words – the order in which it will be applied to the orders. The need for the rank derives from the fact that two or more promotions might be in conflict with each other and, because only one promotion can be safely applied to any given product (with the goal of preventing paradoxical scenarios from happening), the promotion engine must be able to decide which one is applied in every specific case. The lower the ranking, the higher the priority that a promotion has on the others (that is, a promotion with rank 10 will take precedence over another one with rank 20, and so on).

Cross-selling Promotions

As we mentioned in earlier chapters, cross-selling is an important part of a site's interface with the user. MS Commerce Server supports cross-selling promotions through the management interface, as shown in the next figure. As we can see, the system is very simple, and it practically allows the store manager to associate products one to each other. Once we have added a new promotion, it appears on the web site in the product information page as a complementary product suggestion.

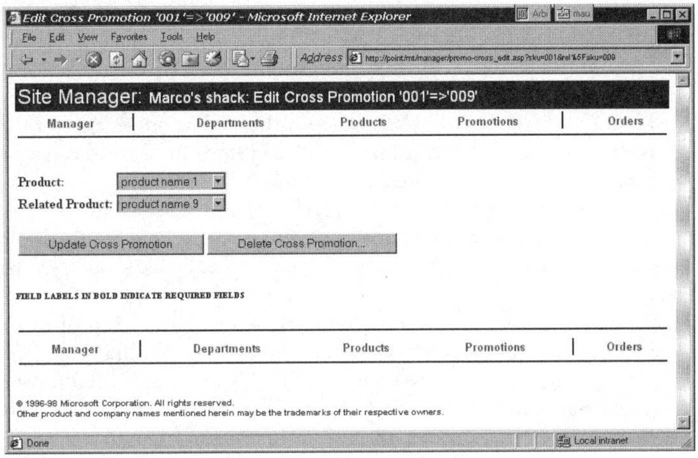

While this cross-selling system allows us to handle both cross-selling and up-selling (we'd just have to add promotions between a product and its accessories, for example), it easily becomes awkward if we have a large database of products, and is unable to handle historical cross-selling (although MS Commerce Server provides this kind of functionality through the `Predictor` component that we'll see in Chapter 9).

Transactions

In the picture of the Store Manager's home page that we saw earlier in this chapter, the Transactions section contains two different links. Orders, as we can imagine, can be used to view all the purchases that were successful, as well as run a few simple reports on them. Shoppers, on the other hand, can be used to view a list of all the registered users that our store has. Naturally, this link will not be available unless we have instructed the SBW to create a store that supports customer registration.

Orders

Clicking on the Orders button brings us to a list of several possible choices. The All Orders link will take us to a list of all the orders currently in the store's database, sorted according to their order ID. If we choose to view orders divided either by month, year or product, we will be shown a non-editable list of orders similar to the one here. It may be argued that the information shown here is not particularly relevant – when we will be looking for a particular order neither the order ID nor the shopper ID is probably going to be of any help in our search.

In Chapter 11, we'll look at how this section works and how the listing can be changed.

If you click on the All Orders from the orders main screen, the Manager will show a list of all the orders that have been placed on the system in chronological order. Clicking on an order ID brings up a page with more detailed information on the order. As we can see, shipping and billing information are provided, as well as a complete breakdown of the items that were purchased. You will probably find annoying the fact that no credit card information is being displayed, but I can assure you that it's there and can be retrieved easily, as we shall see – once more – in Chapter 11.

However, what's really missing here is a link to a line-of-business system. Naturally, there is a reason for this: it's impossible to write a generic sample that will be able to interface successfully with all the possible line-of-business systems. Therefore, the MS Commerce Server team thought that they would provide an interface suitable for a store that doesn't have a real system designed to handle and dispatch orders, and left the implementation of such a system to the site's developer. Luckily, MS Commerce Server includes a wide range of functionality for business-to-business transactions, which we'll see in Chapter 12.

Shoppers

The structure of the Shoppers section is essentially identical to the one that we just saw, except, of course, that the nature of the data changes. As we can see from the figure below, the information shown in the list in this case is a little more useful than the one that appears in the Orders section, although we will still have a hard time trying to find a particular user if he or she has a very common name, in which case a few more fields are needed (for example, city of residence, e–mail address, and so on).

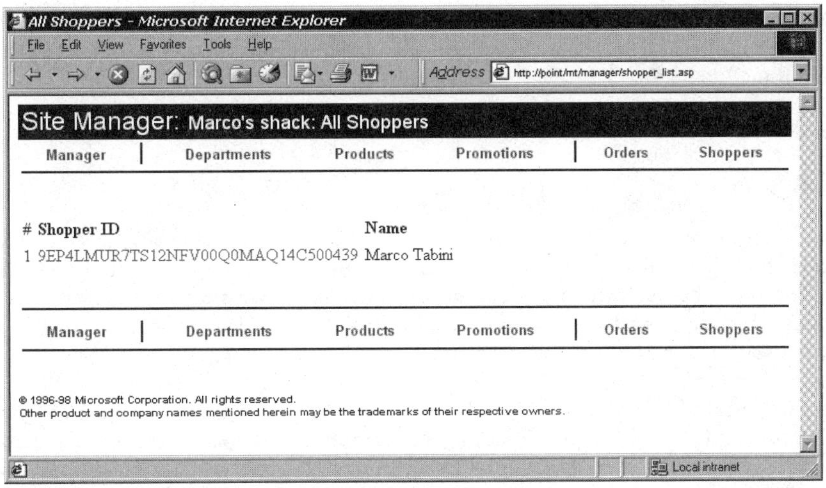

System

The system functions that are provided by our sample store are very basic (as is the store itself). The first part allows us to edit the pipeline files, which, as we'll see in Chapter 10, are used to configure the Order Processing Pipeline and manage the handling of orders.

Site Wizards

Next, we can jump to the storefront (using the Shop Site button), close the site and force IIS to reload the store's `global.asa` file, which resets the entire ASP application. We've already taken a good look at the Site Builder Wizard, but we still have to talk a little bit about the Promotions Wizard (PW), which can be used to add promotional capabilities to a store after it has been created.

The PW consists simply of two steps that have been taken straight from the SBW – one that asks us for the kind of promotions that we want to run in our store and the other that applies the required changes to the site's code. The rationale behind this Wizard is that it has a smaller impact on the files that make up the store, and therefore will "cause less damage" when run on a store on which a certain amount of customization has already been applied.

Opening and Closing the Store

Let's talk for a moment about the closing and opening operations. The concept that they control is quite simple, as you have probably already figured out: when major updates, or redesign changes, are required, the store can be temporarily "closed" so that users cannot browse through it or make purchases. A closed store will usually display only an informational page, or be restricted to the non-commerce related functionality. In any case, displaying this kind of interface is much better than taking the site down!

How does MS Commerce Server handle a "closed" store? As we'll see in Chapter 11, when we will be discussing the technical structure of a site, the user is redirected to an entirely different set of ASP pages when the Close Store button is clicked on.

Summary

As we have seen in this chapter, the structure of a newly created store can vary greatly, and this demonstrates how flexible a tool the SBW really is, considering the range of choices that it allows us to make while building our own site. Becoming very familiar with how the both the storefront and the management interface work is very important, because it will allow us to plan for the customizations that we will apply better and more effectively.

The easiest way to understand the code is to first understand the store from a user's perspective, whether the user belongs to the public-at-large or is part of our own organization. This useful exercise will help us to understand what goes on behind the scenes once we start examining the code.

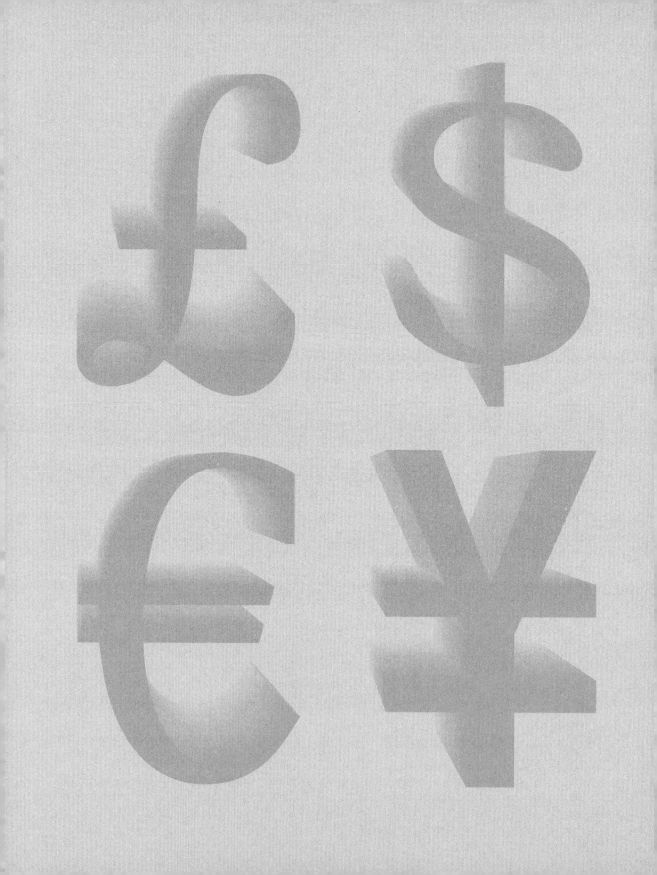

Security Considerations

Blah blah, blah blah blah.
– **Arsenic**

While security is an everyday concern for essentially all online sites – and for stores in particular – it always seems to be neglected in some way, with new breaches becoming public every day and probably many others that are not disclosed. What many people in the IT business do not realize is that security should be considered an *ongoing* problem and therefore be kept under constant surveillance.

The well-known saying among Internet professionals is that the only way to have a completely secure computer is not to buy one. Should you already own one, the next best available solution is to never turn it on. One could extend this concept a little further and say that, if you really have to own a computer and keep it on, it shouldn't be on the Internet.

If we think about it, there isn't anything particularly funny about this statement: the applications that run on computers today, from the operating system to the ASP script, are becoming more complex as every new version comes out, with the result that it is increasingly easy to poke holes into them and take advantage of their weaknesses to breach the overall system security.

Thus, we should make a point of budgeting a slice of our expenses for setting up the appropriate security on our systems. Doing so can be reasonably easy and relatively inexpensive, particularly if we compare it to the costs that a security breach can have through theft, damage and lost lawsuits.

An interesting point to remember is that our own code is but the tip of the iceberg: numerous other applications, whose quality we essentially have no control over whatsoever, will run on our servers, each with their bugs and weaknesses that eventually some malicious user will find and exploit. As security is such a cat-and-mouse game, with software vendors scrambling to patch and fix any holes found in their products by hackers, we should always be on top of the situation, ready to take the appropriate action when a problem arises.

What Does This Chapter Talk About?

The goal of this chapter is to illustrate just a few of the possible security considerations that we should keep in mind when designing our online store with MS Commerce Server. We'll tackle the topic from three points of view:

❑ **Computer configuration**
First of all, we'll examine what NT itself has to offer in terms of the possibility of securing a computer from outside intrusion. We'll also take a look at what *opportunities* it provides to hackers who are not just there to shop from our sites.

❑ **Network configuration**
Next, we'll see how our network can be configured to minimize the possible points of entry into our overall system. As we'll see, this doesn't necessarily correspond to minimizing the risk of an attack, but rather maximizes our chance of plugging all the holes.

❑ **Site configuration**
Finally, we'll talk about how our site should be configured to reduce the possibility that somebody with nothing but a browser will be able to break into our system.

Exactly What are We Trying to Secure?

When planning for our site's security, we should divide the elements that we are trying to protect into at least two levels: *important* and *critical*. In the end, in fact, it's not the server, or our code, or even the look of our sites that we are really protecting – the real reason why we're taking so much care in making sure nobody can get to them is that we're trying to protect our data.

Customer information, product catalogs, credit card numbers and sales figures should all fall into the critical level, because their theft can cause immediate and long lasting losses from many points of view – legal, financial *and* customer satisfaction. Other items, such as the appearance or availability of our service, should belong to the important level, not because they're less relevant, but because they can be fixed without excessive cost.

To give an example, if somebody is able to get into our HTML code and defaces our main page, we can quickly revert to a backed-up version (we *will* be keeping backups, right?) and, if we're lucky, maybe even get a little publicity out of it. If, however, somebody can get into our database because the database connections used by it can be read in the ASP code and the database is happily responding to queries coming from any address, we'll soon be in real trouble.

Items in the important list are not to be left out of our concerns for the safety of our system, but should be taken care of once the critical list has been safely dealt with.

Internal Security

One thing that we won't discuss, although it's just as important as any of the topics in this chapter, is *internal* security; that is how much our system is protected from someone who has access to it. When it's one of our own employees who gets to the data by misusing his or her password privileges, it doesn't matter how many firewalls we have put on our network in order to protect it. For this reason, it is worth looking into a reputable ISP to host our site, just to eliminate any doubts or risks we can think of.

There have also been cases of employees releasing confidential information by mistake, which made it possible for malicious users to break into online stores. In the end, the best protection that we can have against these problems is to establish very strict guidelines that all our employees (including ourselves!) will have to follow.

From this point of view, it helps to have a rigid security and confidentiality policy that all employees must adhere to. It's important to understand that the term "all employees" does include *everyone* in our organization – from the janitorial department all the way up to the executives. As anybody who has worked in an organization with more than two employees will know, the involvement of senior executives is crucial to the success of any initiative, from the next generation of products to the company picnic.

This rings particularly true if we consider that the higher the position, the more damage can be done with one's credentials: for example, if we were to grant our CEO's account administrator access on all the systems and he or she adopts a two-character password, we can understand that it will be remarkably easy for a hacker to break into our system. At the same rate, if all employees are required to follow a specific procedure when accessing the server room and a high-placed executive leaves the door open, he or she shouldn't be allowed to hide behind "executive ignorance" of the procedures. In other words, no one is above the Laws of Security that the organization establishes, and so the only successful security and privacy policies start right at the top.

Computer Configuration

Placing a PC with a freshly installed copy of Windows NT onto the Internet without doing any security configurations has been described as the equivalent of technical suicide. This is not to say that NT is necessarily an insecure operating system but rather that, out of the box, it comes with many "user–friendly" functions turned on that can be exploited by malicious users. While the reason for this is probably that it makes the OS easier to use for the inexperienced computer user, it's certainly something that we should keep in mind when planning to put our store online.

Users and Passwords

As we'll see in later chapters, we may decide to physically separate our web server from the Internet-at-large by using a firewall. Even if this is the case (firewalls can be very expensive, particularly if we're performing a small startup), we should keep in mind that since there are no completely secure protective devices, a particularly skilled hacker could get around our firewall and have an opportunity to log on remotely to our server using normal NetBIOS services, very much the same way we do when we open a computer through the Network Neighborhood icon on our desktop.

NetBIOS

Many people seem to be surprised by the fact that it is possible to break into a computer from the Internet this way. If we want to test this ourselves, we can try to hook up a PC directly to the Internet, activate NetBIOS over TCP/IP (which is pretty much the standard way to configure our computers these days) and note the computer's numeric IP address.

Next, we move to a PC that does not reside on our network; for example, if we connect to the Internet at home using an ISP, we can use that for our test. Since the machine we have at home is not on our own internal network at work, we would expect to be unable to access the other computer that we set up on the Internet, right? Try the following: go to the Start menu, then click on Run and type the following:

\\our_IP

where our_IP is the numeric IP address of our machine at work. If we have NetBIOS installed on the machine at home, after a while we will be asked for a username and password: entering the correct login information for a user defined on that machine will actually allow us inside the computer and let us browse happily through the folders. Depending on how permissions have been set up, we might even be able to read and write files!

Users and Permissions

While it's possible to simply disconnect the NetBIOS service from our network, as we'll see later on in this section, the first task at hand should be to revise the logins that we have activated on our computer. The first thing that a hacker who has gained access to our computer's NetBIOS interface will try to do is use the Administrator login to enter into it.

Sounds strange? Well it shouldn't; since Administrator is a login created by default when we install NT, there's a good chance that it will not have been deleted or modified manually: the hacker will only have to guess its password, half of his or her job having already been inadvertently done by us. Thus, we should not only make sure that we immediately rename the Administrator username, but also that we do not use any particularly obvious usernames in general.

Passwords

Passwords should also be of concern to us. Bear in mind, however, that if we want a password protected shop, we will have to code the requirements manually; things such as minimum length, alphanumerical check, check for special characters and so on. The simplest way to crack a password is to use a "brute-force" approach, which consists of simply iterating through all the possible combinations, starting from one letter passwords and continuing until the password is eventually found.

There is a simple way to protect our computers from this problem: firstly, we should require a minimum length for all the passwords on our system. The number of iterations required to find a password by brute-force is directly proportional to the power of the number of characters available to form a password. Assuming that a password can be created using the entire Roman alphabet (both upper and lowercase), digits, and 33 symbols (for example, the asterisk, brackets, and so on), each character in it will have a total of 95 possible values.

If, on average, the hacker's brute force program will need to go through 50 per cent of the possible iterations in order to break a password, the number of iterations required for the breach to be successful can be expressed by this formula:

$$I(n) = \frac{95^n}{2}$$

where *n* is the number of characters in your password. It's easy to see how a very low number of iterations are required to break short passwords: for 2 characters, just over 4,500 tries will, in most cases, do the trick. Keep in mind that the attempts are being made by a program, and not by a human, resulting in many thousands of iterations being performed every minute. However, the iteration count increments exponentially, so for a password just 7 characters long the number of iterations will soar to 34,916,864,804,687, making it very difficult even for a program to crack a password in a short time.

It's important to understand that all these assumptions are only valid if the characters in our passwords are equally distributed across the possible range of values that they can have. Another common technique for cracking a password consists of using a set of common words – taken, for example, from a dictionary – and simple variations thereof. Thus, while a brute-force approach will approximately take the same time cracking the password `apple` and the password `a$3c*`, the former will be easily defeated by a program that uses all the words from a dictionary.

Expiration Dates and System Policies

A brute-force program can eventually crack even a long password that does not contain any common words – it's just a matter of time. A good way to protect our data from this problem is to require users to change their password regularly (for example: every week, or every month).

All this, and more, can be achieved by setting the **Account Policies**, which are accessible from the Policies menu in NT's User Manager. As we can see from the screenshot below, there are quite a few parameters that we can set:

❑ **Maximum password age**
This is the maximum number of days allowed when we indicate that a password has a fixed expiration date.

❑ **Minimum password age**
Similarly, this is the minimum number of days to which we must set the expiration date of a password.

❑ **Minimum password length**
This is the minimum number of characters to which a password can be set.

❑ **Password uniqueness**
This parameter determines whether a user will be able to reuse the same password once he or she is asked to change it because it has expired. We can also choose to have NT remember a certain number of passwords previously used and make sure that the user does not use one of the passwords in that list.

❑ **Account lockout**
Finally, this section makes it possible to determine whether a user will be locked out of the system if he or she fails to log on after a certain number of attempts. This is another important tool in the fight against password crackers. As we can see, we can also determine a time after which the number of bad attempts recorded is reset to zero, as well as how long a user remains locked out once the maximum number of attempts is reached.

> We must be careful about how we set the policies for the interactive user used by IIS
> to access the information for a website. We can certainly set its password to expire,
> but it will not be able to choose a new password by itself! Thus, if we do not change
> the password ourselves, our users will not be able to access our site anymore!

Permissions

Another important element of NT security that we should keep under careful consideration is access
permissions. These include not only determining who has access to what on our computer's hard
drive, but also what kind of access they have.

When we install IIS on our computer, the latter will create a new user account, which is by default
called IUSR_our_machine, where our_machine is the name of our computer. This is the user
under whose alias people accessing our site anonymously will actually be reading and writing data to
and from the hard disk.

Clearly, this fact makes it an optimal target for hackers, who will be trying to break into the computer using that login. Therefore, we should not only change its username and make sure that it has a password long enough, but also ensure that the interactive user only has access to the resources appropriate to their role and is not given access to the entire machine. We should make sure that we explicitly exclude the interactive user from the access list of all the directories that do not belong to our website.

In addition, we should carefully assign read/write and execute permissions to the interactive user. As a rule, unless we will be using ISAPI filters and DLLs, we should never grant NT execution permissions to the interactive user. Similarly, when configuring IIS, we shouldn't grant execute permissions on any virtual folder.

For more information, see
`http://msdn.microsoft.com/library/partbook/mts/html/handlinganonymoususers.htm`

Who Will Control the Controllers?

One question that we should be asking ourselves at this point is: how effective are the built-in checks provided by NT for password security? As we can expect, they do have limitations, particularly in consideration that there is no way for a program to counter human stupidity at its finest. For example, even if we force the user not to reuse the same password for, say three times, they can still change it three times in a row and reinstate their old password without the operating system being able to detect the problem!

So, does this mean that NT's password policies are ineffective and useless? No – it simply means that they can only provide a certain amount of functionality and that we should be aware of their limitations. Most of the problems that we will have with users trying to work around our password policies will be caused by unawareness of the reasons why they have been established in the first place, rather than maliciousness. Therefore, we should not only rely on them, but also take the time to educate our users as to why certain rules are in place.

Closing our System to the Outside

Ultimately, the best way to defend our system from many intrusions will be to block all its TCP/IP ports except those that are strictly necessary to conduct HTTP transactions. This will prevent anyone (including ourselves!) from entering the machine using NetBIOS or any other service. Another good idea is to shutdown all the services that are not required by our system, which will improve its overall performance by freeing the CPU of useless tasks.

In order to control what ports are available on our machine, we need to access the Network settings from the Control Panel. We can also do this by right clicking on the **Network Neighborhood** icon on our desktop. If we go to the **Protocols** pane, click on the **TCP/IP** protocol and then on the **Properties** button, we should end up in a screen similar to the one shown here, which contains all the TCP/IP settings for our system.

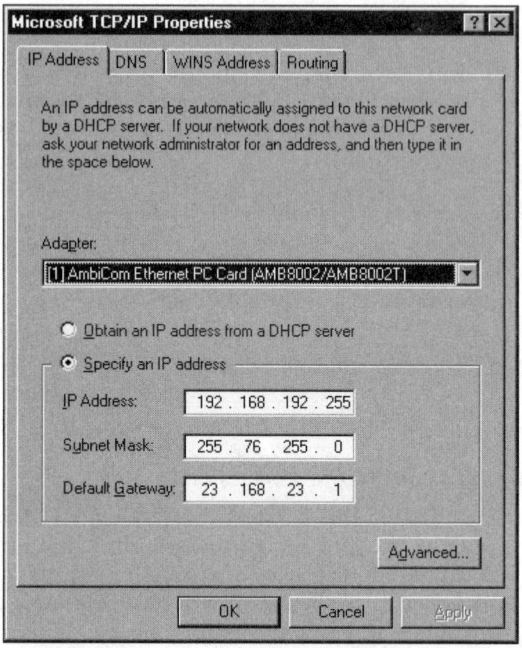

Clicking on the **Advanced** button brings up yet another dialog box, as shown here, from which we can control – among other things – the security settings. Selecting the **Enable Security** checkbox will activate NT's advanced packet filtering system, which can be configured by clicking on the **Configure** button.

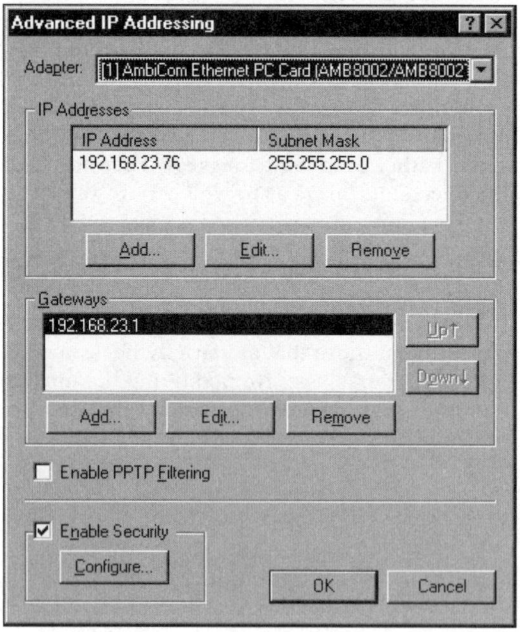

This in turn will bring up the dialog box shown here, which will allow us to select which ports will be available to the outside world. In the example visible here, only ports 80 and 443, used by the HTTP and HTTPS protocols respectively, are active.

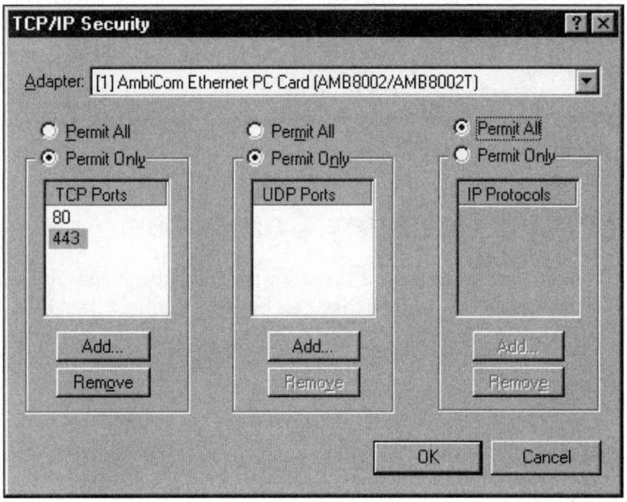

Keeping up with NT

No matter how good we are at setting the security properties of our installation of NT, all our labor will be fruitless if a hacker can exploit a security hole that is built into any of the software packages that we are using – from NT to IIS to MS Commerce Server.

Thus, it's very important that we keep track of any new bugs and problems that are found, reported and fixed by the IT community. There are several good resources that we should periodically check for new information. One of them is the Microsoft website, on which the company publishes security information and patches for any possible security holes found in all of its products. The security section of Microsoft's site can be found at this URL:

http://www.microsoft.com/security

In particular, a checklist of security measures to be taken when installing a web server using Microsoft technologies is published at the following address:

http://www.microsoft.com/security/products/iis/CheckList.asp

Another good source of information is the well-known NTBugTraq, maintained by Russ Cooper, which regularly publishes up-to-date information on exploits, holes and other NT news. The good thing about this site, and its related mailing list, is that it is maintained by a person independent from Microsoft who cares primarily about the safety of IT systems. You can find more information about NTBugTraq at the following URL:

http://www.ntbugtraq.com

Network Configuration

It's now time to talk a little bit about how our network can be configured to minimize the risk of security breaches. A good way to start is to look at how it's possible to simply place our servers in a configuration that can inexpensively save us a lot of headaches.

Using a Gateway Computer

It's easy to understand how the probability of leaving a security hole uncovered depends on the number of computers that can be potentially attacked from the outside. At the same time, a high number of computers are harder to monitor for potential intrusions than a smaller one.

Therefore, we should consider the possibility of arranging our network so that a minimum number of computers possible are directly accessible from the outside, while every other machine is physically separated from the Internet. As an example, in a typical configuration all the computers reside on the same network, which also makes them all accessible from the Internet, as we can see here:

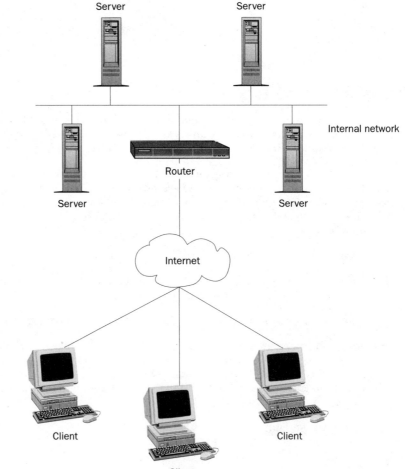

This is a configuration that we should try to avoid, if possible, because so many computers are exposed to the outside world that it can be rather difficult to keep track of what's happening to each one of them. Even if we have a firewall, something that we will be briefly discussing below, it's a good idea to try and rearrange our network so that only what's strictly necessary is exposed.

Generally speaking, in an online store the only computers that should be accessible from the Internet are the web servers. In fact, there is no reason why a database server should be on the Internet, for example. The best solution in this case is to simply add one more network interface card to the web server, making sure that IP-forwarding is disabled, and use that for internal communications only, leaving the other as the only open channel to the world.

This way, we will be able to focus exclusively on the web server (or servers, if we have more than one), and at the same time make sure that our data is protected at least from the most direct of possible attacks.

Installing a Firewall

A popular security device that is widely used these days is a *firewall*. A firewall is simply a device – or software program – that regulates the way traffic comes in and goes out of a network. Typically, this includes not only determining on which ports inbound and outbound traffic is allowed, but also whether specific IP addresses are allowed to perform certain operations.

Even though many people seem to think of firewalls as black boxes with a bunch of cables hanging out of them, it should be noted that a software product performs the actual firewalling operation. Whether that's inside a dedicated appliance (the black box mentioned above) or on a common PC running any given operating system is purely a strategic decision.

In fact, both configurations have their advantages and disadvantages. If we purchase one of the many firewall packages available for NT or several flavors of UNIX, we will probably enjoy lower costs, but we'll have to tweak the OS itself so that all of the security holes are properly patched. Similarly, a "black box" appliance will be significantly more expensive – and we won't be able to use it for anything else as we would a normal computer – but it will require less maintenance, since it will run on its own custom-designed firmware that is less prone to security problems.

Many firewall appliances will also fill the role of a router, thus giving us the opportunity to kill two birds with one stone. A few models also support the possibility of implementing "sticky" IPs, which, as we have seen in Chapter 2, can be useful if we are running a server farm.

A firewall can be a good investment, particularly if our site experiences a lot of popularity and therefore becomes a good candidate for a hacking attempt. At the same time, however, it can also be quite a big expense for a startup; for a smaller operation, we might want to consider a good network design, such as the one we discussed above, combined with a well-tweaked NT configuration that blocks out all the known security holes in the OS.

Site Configuration

For the final part of this chapter, let's talk a little bit about how the site itself can be set up so that we can minimize the possibility that somebody will be able to break into it. A properly configured and designed site should be part of our overall security strategy, because the configuration can be exploited as a security hole in itself.

In fact, since the site itself will need to access the database in order to work properly, it's easy to understand how breaking into the former will make it possible to get to the latter.

Writing Smart Code

Historically, most of the security holes that have been found in IIS have made it possible for unauthorized people to view the source of ASP scripts instead of their result. Examples of these bugs are the "dot" security hole, which afflicted IIS 3.0, and the '::$DATA' bug in IIS 4.0 (and earlier).

The former was very easy to exploit: all we needed to do was to append a dot at the end of the filename of an ASP script and the server would have returned its source instead of executing it. This was a simple consequence of the fact that NT considers only the last substring of a filename after a dot as its extension. Thus, for example, DEFAULT.ASP has a '.ASP' extension, while DEFAULT.ASP. has a null extension because the last digit is the one considered by the OS as the extension delimiter. Thus, the web server thinks that this file should be simply outputted to the browser and not interpreted as a script.

As for the '::$DATA' bug, it has to do with how NTFS accesses files. The result of appending the '::$DATA' suffix to a web page address is that the page's exact contents are dumped rather than being passed through IIS's execution filter. Thus, calling DEFAULT.ASP::$DATA will show us the script's source code.

While we will be protected from both these holes if we install the latest NT Service Pack, there is a good chance that sooner or later someone will find other issues and exploit them on our site before we can take any protective action. Therefore, we should be ready for these scenarios by proofing our code so that even if somebody is able to read it, they won't be able to take advantage of the information contained in it.

A good starting point is making sure that no sensitive information, such as usernames and passwords, are stored in clear inside the scripts. In particular, we should not store any database connection strings in them, and we should also avoid storing any queries in the files that are directly accessed by the users.

For example, let's consider the case in which an ODBC connection string is stored inside an ASP script. Obviously, as we just said, this poses a security threat because anybody who can read the file where the script resides can also discover a lot of sensitive information about our database server. If we were, for example, to store the connection string as a text file that is not directly accessible from the web site, we would solve the problem, because even if someone could get read access to the script, they still wouldn't be able to access the text file that contains the connection string, and therefore our data would be safe:

```
<%
        ' Read the connection string from a text file on disk
        ' Note: the text file must be in a folder that is NOT directly
        ' accessible from the web site

        Set fs = Server.CreateObject ("Scripting.FileSystemObject")
        Set f = fs.OpenTextFile ("c:\protected\dsn.txt")
        sOdbcConnStr = f.ReadLine
        f.Close
        Set f = Nothing
        Set fs = Nothing
%>
```

It's important, however, that we keep in mind a simple fact: this is not a catch-all solution. In fact, it *will* protect our database connection string from unauthorized access as long as all the hacker can do is gain *read* access to the script. If he or she can also modify it, then this approach will not protect us from an intrusion – all the hacker will have to do is modify the script to something like this:

```
<%
    ' Read the connection string from a text file on disk
    ' Note: the text file must be in a folder that is NOT directly
    ' accessible from the web site

    Set fs = Server.CreateObject ("Scripting.FileSystemObject")
    Set f = fs.OpenTextFile ("c:\protected\dsn.txt")
    sOdbcConnStr = f.ReadLine
    Response.Write sOdbcConnStr
    f.Close
    Set f = Nothing
    Set fs = Nothing
%>
```

The page will neatly print out the connection string to any browser whenever it's invoked. Once again, this doesn't mean that we shouldn't bother protecting our sensitive data using a technique similar to the one just illustrated, but rather that this will not protect us from all possible intrusion attempts. Since most security holes, however, only involve unauthorized read access, a simple trick like this should cover us most of the time.

Using the Appropriate Security

Protecting our data is also a matter of choosing the right login information to access all the various resources. We have already talked about usernames and passwords in general, and the interactive user in particular. Another important element is the user account that we will use to access our database server. Many times, the system administrator's account (SA) is used to access the database during the development phase and, in the end, this same approach makes its way into the production code.

Unfortunately, the same discussion that applies to NT's Administrator user is valid for the DBMS as well, for example in SQL Server. SA is an easy username to guess – virtually everybody who has ever used a database will know about it – and once again the hacker will only have to find out its password (which hopefully we will not have left empty as it is by default).

Moreover, we should be careful to set the proper permissions for the user account that we use to access the database. For example, not all the information from an order needs to be read by the site – we wouldn't normally need to show a customer his or her credit card number or other sensitive information. Similarly, the site's user should not have access to any table that is not strictly necessary for it to operate properly. This means no write access to tables not used by the storefront, and no access at all to databases other than the one specifically used by the store. One way to limit access is to create database views for each role – in this way, each user will only be able to see what they need to see, and their access will be limited to this restricted set of information.

If we are hosting more than one store on the same computer, we should also consider using a different user for each store. This will ensure that, should one of the stores be broken into, the data belonging to the others will be relatively safer than if we were using a single user for all the sites.

SSL Connections

Secure HTTP connections can be significantly slower than normal HTTP communications on both the clients and the server, since all the data has to be encrypted at one end and decrypted at the other. Alas, it's very important to use HTTPS whenever any kind of sensitive information is exchanged. In the storefront, this includes every page in the purchase process beyond the basket (although by default even that is secure in the starter store).

For the backend, HTTPS connections should be enforced all the way through. If we can, we should enforce 128-bit connections for all users of the Store Manager – the data at stake is simply too important to accept anything less secure. Unfortunately, we can't do the same in the storefront, since most users still download 40-bit versions of their browsers, some because they are forced to by U.S. export regulations, the others because they just probably do not know that they have to go through a special process in order to get 128-bit browsers Whoever visits the management interface, however, should be authorized by the store owner, and therefore it's certainly easier to enforce the use of a secure browser.

More About the Backend

One of the characteristics of the Store Manager that we already noticed in Chapter 5 is the fact that everybody who has access to the Store Manager also has access to all the information contained in it.

As we mentioned, this may not be the best approach to conduct business for at least a couple of reasons: firstly, having access to portions of the site that are not directly related to his or her specific area of competency gives any of our employees a higher possibility of causing unintentional damage. Secondly, indiscriminate access to all the data makes it difficult to protect sensitive information from unauthorized use.

It's a good idea, therefore, to consider the possibility of implementing some kind of access level system that will prevent users from accessing data they are not meant to manipulate. A simple way of doing so is, first of all, to make sure that each user has his or her own account on the web server. Next, we can divide all the users into groups as appropriate (for example, warehouse, finance, credit, sales, and so on) and assign the appropriate access permissions to the individual files in the store.

> Keep in mind that setting account permissions through NT security for each user is something that should only be done for administrative accounts (the people who will access the Store Manager). Doing the same with your actual users will be very difficult, particularly because it's hard to manage NT security programmatically. You should use P&M instead for this type of application.

A Few Resources

Finally, this should not be considered *the* guide to system security. There are numerous publications, both in print and online, that can be useful in helping to establish a security strategy.

Before moving on to the next chapter, it's a good idea to list a few resources that can help you with administering your security. We have already mentioned both the security section of the Microsoft website and the NTBugTraq mailing list, which are two very important sources of information about security.

It's also worth taking a look at the Site Server documentation, which contains an entire book on security, and at the Site Server WWW site (http://www.microsoft.com/siteserver). A number of books on NT security also exist in print – a simple search on Amazon.com will return over thirty titles. It's difficult to recommend a clear winner here, since most books analyze particular aspects of the topic, and there's never anything to be missed about it. Perhaps, the best starting point is *Microsoft Windows NT 4.0 Security, Audit, and Control (Microsoft Technical Reference)*, published by Microsoft Press.

Summary

The goal of this chapter was to provide a glimpse of how important having a complete security strategy is for an online store. It's *essential* that this strategy be ongoing and periodically revised to make sure that it is up-to-date with the latest developments in the technologies we use. We should also make sure that our IT team stays on top of any new security bulletins that are released concerning the products we use.

Another important piece of information that we should have learned from this chapter is the fact that our approach to security must encompass all the possible angles from which our system can be attacked and broken into by a malicious hacker. This includes not only our network, but also the way we configure IIS and all the other software we use, and especially how we develop our own store.

The Database Structure

If you'll excuse my pathetic attempt at poetry, a store without its data is like an empty shell: in fact, although the IIS scripts provide a window on the world, it's our database that provides us with the means to remember who our customers are and what they bought (among other things).

Now that you know why literature isn't part of my day job (rest assured, it isn't my hobby either), you'll agree that the database plays a crucial role in making a store work well. Our SSCE sites will have a very important dynamic component to them, which will revolve around the information that will be stored in our DBMS. Therefore, we will only be able to fully understand how the starter stores created by the Store Builder Wizard (SBW) work if we first familiarize ourselves with how the database has been designed and works.

What Does This Chapter Talk About?

In this chapter, our goal will be to examine the structure of the database used by a starter store. Although we will have to account for the differences caused by the choices made while executing the Wizard, we'll divide the database information into three groups:

❏   **User information**
    The first portion of the chapter will deal with how the system handles user data, including information about what is stored in the shopping basket and introducing the shopper table. We'll discover how MS Commerce Server solves the problem of storing information of a varying nature in a database by using a technique known as *data marshalling*.

❑ **Product information**
Next, we'll move on to the structures that are used to store information about what the store sells, including the organization of products in departments. We'll also examine what happens when a store supports dynamic attributes.

❑ **Promotions and historical records**
The final part of this chapter will illustrate how promotions and historical records, such as receipts for successfully completed purchases, are stored.

A Bit Of Background

Before we delve into the depths of database organization, it's a good idea to give ourselves a few basic pointers on how SSCE treats the database. As you may have gathered from what we have said so far, virtually all the elements of the store that are prone to periodic change are stored in one or more tables.

It's important that we choose our DBMS carefully; as we mentioned before, Site Server itself supports Microsoft Access, Microsoft SQL Server and Oracle SQL products. Because all three systems have their own "quirks", our first decision will in most cases be final.

In particular, Microsoft Access is not compatible with the SQL-92 standard, and supports a slightly different version of the SQL language than its two counterparts. Choosing Access is probably the worst choice we can make, unless our store is going to have very limited traffic, because it was designed as a desktop DBMS and not as a network system able to handle a large number of users at the same time. Therefore, in all but the most basic cases, we will eventually have to switch to a more powerful DBMS, and we'll run into a lot of problems because Access' SQL dialect does not work on any of its counterparts.

Oracle and Microsoft SQL Server products have their differences as well. For example, the ODBC driver for SQL Server supports the `RecordCount` property of the `ADODB.Recordset` component (at least under certain conditions), but the one for Oracle doesn't. As a result, we'll have to count the number of records in our result sets in a different way depending on what DBMS we are using.

Sharing The Same Database Among Different Stores

It's plausible to expect that more than one store will share the same database device, for example because of space constraints. Keep in mind that I'm not referring to the same set of data – that being another problem altogether – but simply to using a database with the same schema as a container for different set of tables, one for each store.

Since the SBW generates all of the tables used by the starter store, they generally have the same basic name (`products`, `departments`, and so on), which would seem to make it impossible for more than one store to reside in the same database. To solve this problem, MS Commerce Server assumes a simple convention: the short name of the store is used as a prefix for each table. Suppose, for example, that the SBW has to create a table for a store whose short name is `mt`. If the table would normally be called `promotions`, the particular instance running in that store would be called `mt_promotions`.

In this way, an arbitrary number of stores can share the same database – naturally, as long as our DBMS holds (this means that this won't prevent the database device from filling up, etc.).

User Information

There are two sets of data that must be maintained about the user: his or her personal information (name, address, and so on), and the contents of his or her basket. The problem with both of these is that it's difficult to predict exactly what the nature of the data will be – a prime requisite for creating a SQL Server table!

In fact, there is a good chance that we will want to collect very different information depending on who the user is and what he or she does in the store. For example, we may want to add a note concerning the fact that a customer has the bad habit of returning the merchandise he or she purchases a little too often, or that he or she is entitled to a special discount on the next order, and so on.

Data Marshalling

If SSCE were to depend only on the functionality offered by SQL Server, it would be very difficult to provide the flexibility necessary to make the store handle the situations that we have just outlined (which are just a small subset of all the possible scenarios). When we create a SQL Server table, we are expected to know in advance what every piece of information that we will store in it will be like, how long it will be, and so on.

The solution to this problem that the SSCE team came up with consists of creating a sort of "superfield" that can contain an almost arbitrary amount of information of any kind. The field is created using the "binary" format of SQL Server, and therefore only appears as a meaningless sequence of bytes to the DBMS. Internally, however, MS Commerce Server is able to encode and decode that field into a set of data using a technique known as **data marshalling**.

Tricking SQL

Data marshalling is not a new concept. In fact, it originates from the need to exchange information between two environments that cannot communicate directly. For example, data must be marshaled when two COM objects residing in different threads need to "view" each other's data, or when certain information needs to be exchanged between two DCOM components running on different machines.

When MS Commerce Server needs to write a set of dynamic data into a marshaled field, it starts by collecting all the information that needs to be stored, and then proceeds to compress it. Finally, it renders it as a sequence of bytes and saves it into the database table. As a result, marshaled fields are meaningless for human beings, as well as for the DBMS. As an example, here's what one might look like:

```
DDS15AS63D51S4D8W5A5S33DA2S
```

This doesn't obviously yield any meaning for any of us, but MS Commerce Server is able to "un-marshal" it into the appropriate number of individual data elements that can be used inside the store.

What Can Be Stored In A Marshaled Field?

During the marshalling process, the appropriate MS Commerce Server object gathers all the necessary information and stores it in the database. In the un-marshalling phase, the opposite happens: MS Commerce Server analyzes the binary field and re-builds the data one piece at a time.

To be honest, this is not an accurate rendition of what happens in reality. If it were, the possibilities of marshalling would be very limited, since MS Commerce Server would need to know how each and every data element that it stores could be saved and reconstructed properly. If MS Commerce Server were dealing with objects (and it is), this would also be at odds with the very principles of object-oriented programming, since an object should be able to construct and deconstruct itself, but not be able to construct and deconstruct another object.

To allow for the maximum flexibility possible, MS Commerce Server requires any object that can be marshaled to support a particular set of standard COM interfaces, which are called to construct and deconstruct objects during the marshalling and un-marshalling processes respectively. As a result, a marshaled field can truly contain *any* kind of data, from simple numeric values to entire objects.

But, There's A Catch. Well, More Than One

Sounds complex? It sure is. The big problem with data marshalling is that it is very slow. Since a store needs to manipulate user information very frequently, the use of marshalling will significantly reduce the performance of our site, forcing us to buy additional equipment much earlier than we really need.

The *really* big problem with marshalling is that it essentially prevents SQL Server from doing what it does best: organizing data. In fact, since the DBMS won't be able to understand the information in its marshaled form, you will not be able to execute even simple queries on it. As a result, the only way to find a particular data element is to search each record individually by un-marshalling and examining it. The fact that data marshalling is not exactly fast doesn't help, either.

The marshalling problem is widely recognized but, since the technique is used in the starter store, it cannot be solved without making significant changes – and several compromises – to the site's code. Therefore, we will dedicate the whole of Chapter 16 to making our MS Commerce Server store marshalling-free. As we'll see, the conversion process is slow and somewhat painful, with the additional problem that we will have to do it all over again every time we create a new starter store, since the Wizard will continue to generate sites that use marshalling.

The Basket Table

After all this discussion on marshaled fields, it is now time to look at the actual information that is stored in our database. If we have not chosen to have any user registration in our store, all the user information is kept in a single table, called `basket`, whose structure is extremely simple:

Name	Datatype	Length	Notes	Description
Shopper_id	Char	32	Not nullable Primary Key	The unique ID of the shopper whose basket is being stored.
Date_changed	DateTime	N/A	Not nullable	The last time the basket's values were changed.
Marshaled_basket	Binary	16	Not nullable	The marshaled basket contents.

MS Commerce Server generates the unique ID of the shopper internally, while date_changed is automatically updated every time that the basket is accessed. As a result, we can use it to determine when a record is too old to keep and delete it to avoid making our database too cluttered with useless data.

Additional User Information

If our store doesn't support user logon at any stage of the shopping experience, the basket table will be the only location where customer information is stored: along with the pieces of information stored in the marshaled basket, MS Commerce Server will also save data such as the ship-to and bill-to addresses.

If, however, we choose to let our customers log on to the site either upon entry or when a purchase is made, another table is created in the database called shopper. The latter contains all the information that is gathered from the users at the time of registration, such as their personal information, username and password:

Name	Datatype	Length	Notes	Description
Shopper_id	Char	32	Not nullable Primary Key	The unique ID of the shopper whose basket is being stored.
Date_created	DateTime	N/A	Not nullable	Date and time when the record was created.
Name	Varchar	100	Nullable	User's name
Password	Varchar	100	Nullable	Password (can be empty)
Street	Varchar	100	Nullable	Address
City	Varchar	100	Nullable	Town
State	Varchar	100	Nullable	State or province
Zip	Varchar	100	Nullable	ZIP
Country	Varchar	100	Nullable	Country
Phone	Varchar	100	Nullable	Phone number
E-mail	Varchar	100	Not nullable Uniquely indexed	E-mail. Also used as login username.

As you can see, this table leaves plenty of room for everything. In particular, you will notice that a few fields, such as the ZIP code and phone number, are *definitely* oversized, and it wouldn't hurt to make them the appropriate length. The e-mail field is also used as the customer's username for login purposes. This makes it easier for the users to remember at least part of their login.

Also, it's interesting to note that there is no direct SQL Server relation between shopper and basket, although MS Commerce Server will take care of synchronizing the two tables by means of the Shopper_id field.

Product Information

Products and departments are stored using a slightly more complicated structure to allow for the possibility that one product might belong to more than one department, and that products might have multiple attributes. We'll start from the simplest case, in which products only have static attributes.

Fixed Attributes

The figure below shows a simple Entity-Relationship (ER) diagram of the three tables that are used to store product information when only static attributes are supported. As we can see, the product information is stored entirely in the product table, while all the departments reside in the dept table. The dept_prod table, on the other hand, functions as a link between the two tables, providing a way to determine which products belong to any given department.

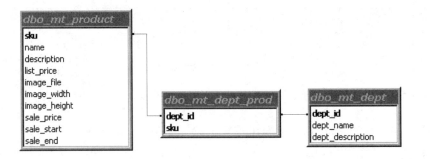

Product Information

The actual nature of the data stored in the product table will depend greatly on what fields we chose to include in the database during the execution of the SBW (corresponding to the product attributes we were asked to choose). Assuming that we chose none – or static attributes – this will be the basic structure of the table:

Name	Datatype	Length	Notes	Description
SKU	Varchar	100	Not nullable Primary Key	The unique ID of each product.
Name	Varchar	255	Nullable	Name of the product.
Description	Varchar	255	Nullable	Description of the product.
List_price	Int	N/A	Nullable	The price that is normally applied to the product, when it is not on sale and before any discounts.
Image_file	Varchar	255	Nullable	URL of the file that contains a product-related image (for example a box shot or screenshot).
Image_width	Int	N/A	Nullable	The width of the image, in pixels.
Image_height	Int	N/A	Nullable	The height of the image, in pixels.
Sale_price	Int	N/A	Nullable	The price that is applied to the product when the current system date falls between `Sale_start` and `Sale_end`.
Sale_start	Datetime	N/A	Nullable	Start of product sale. After this date, and before `Sale_end`, the `Sale_price` is applied to the product.
Sale_end	Datetime	N/A	Nullable	End of the sale.

There are a number of considerations to be made here. First of all, notice that all the prices in this table are stored as integer values, rather than floating-point or currency data as one would normally expect. This is actually a small trick to save storage space and make calculations inside the store's code faster.

In general, we will not need to use all the precision that a floating-point variable would be able to give to store currency data. In fact, we will rarely need more than two decimal digits of precision, and we are definitely unlikely to need extremely large numbers (for example greater than 100,000,000). Thus, all currency values are stored by multiplying them by 100 and saving only the integer part. For example, 104.32 becomes 10432, and so on. From a mathematical point of view, this changes very little, as long as the store remembers to divide all values it displays by one hundred; from a computational perspective, however, integer calculations are much faster than their floating-point counterparts; in addition, integer values are smaller and take up less database space.

An important consequence of using this technique is the actual range of values that is available for use. Normally, a four-byte unsigned integer variable can hold any value between 0 and 4,294,967,295; since we are multiplying everything by one hundred; however, the maximum integer value that MS Commerce Server can handle is 42,949,672.95 – more than enough for your everyday store!

Another feature worthy of further examination is the group of sale-related fields. As you may have already understood, the price that is normally applied to a particular product, stored in `list_price`, is overridden when the current date is between the datetime values expressed by `sale_start` and `sale_end`. However, during normal operations, both these values are in fact used as pure date values, in the sense that they do not contain any time information.

Therefore, both the start and end dates refer to the midnight of a particular date. This, in turn, causes the total time period to be effectively one day shorter than one would expect; for example, if the end date is July 15, the sale will actually end at 11:59:59 PM on July 14, since the next second will be 00:00:00 of July 15, which is greater than or equal to the value stored in the `sale_end` field.

Finally, we notice that a maximum of 255 characters have been allocated for the purpose of storing a product description. From personal experience, this often turns out not to be enough, especially if we are looking at storing HTML tags together with the description.

If we are using SQL Server as our DBMS, it's a good idea to think about converting this field to the Text type, which will let us store up to roughly 2MB of data. However, we need to be very careful as to how we use these fields, because the server engine will allocate the text field in pages 2KB long (8KB for SQL 7.0). This means that each text field that is not null will occupy at least 2KB or 8KB, *even if we only store a single character in it!* The good news, on the other hand, is that a null field will only occupy 16 bytes.

Departments

The `dept` table only contains four fields, whose purpose is easy to understand:

Name	Datatype	Length	Notes	Description
Dept_id	Int	4	Not nullable Primary Key	The unique ID of the department.
Dept_name	Varchar	255	Nullable	Name of the department.
Dept_description	Varchar	255	Nullable	Description of the department.
Parent_id	Int	N/A	Nullable	If multi-level departments were chosen, then this field indicates the parent of this department.

A very important characteristic of this table is the fact that the `dept_id` field is not automatically generated, but rather chosen by the user, as is the case with the **pf_id** field in the product table. It might be a good idea to implement some kind of automatic numbering for it, which will make the life of people who have to maintain the data stored in this table a little easier. If we are using SQL Server, it's a good idea to insert a default value into the table declaration. We can do so using something similar to the following:

```
Alter table dept add default identity (1,1) for dept_id
```

This will cause the `dept_id` field to be automatically set to a value that starts from one and increases by one once every new record is added.

Linking Products To Departments

You might be wondering what the need is for the `dept_prod` table – after all, a simple foreign reference on the product table would have taken care of the problem of linking products to departments. Well, the problem is that it might be necessary to link one product to more than one department, and it would be difficult to do so using that technique.

Therefore, MS Commerce Server adopts a slightly different approach to the problem: a separate table holds all the references between one product and the departments it belongs to:

Name	Datatype	Length	Notes	Description
Dept_id	Int	N/A	Not nullable Primary Key	ID of a department. This field references the `dept_id` field in the `dept` table
Sku	Varchar	255	Not nullable Primary Key	SKU of the product that must be associated with the department. This field references the `sku` field in the `product` table.

As we can see, both fields in this table are used to generate a primary key, ensuring that the same product cannot be assigned to a particular department more than once. Also, referential integrity is used to make sure that all the fields identify valid SKUs and department IDs. This resolves a many-to-many relationship between the two tables and creates a one-to-many on both sides, which is the correct logical way of resolving the cardinality.

Dynamic Attributes

If we choose dynamic attributes for our store, the situation gets a little more complicated, and additional tables start to pop up like daisies. First of all, let's try to understand how things work when dynamic attributes are supported.

Dynamic attributes come in two flavors: single- and multi-value. The former ones represent defined characteristics of the product, such as its manufacturer, while the latter ones can assume a value that the user chooses from a pre-defined list. By default, MS Commerce Server supports an arbitrary number of single-value attributes and up to five different multi-value attributes for each product.

Clearly, when an attribute assumes a different value, a different SKU must be used to compensate for the fact that the product's characteristics have changed. For example, a "black" coffee cup will have a different SKU from a "red" one. Therefore, the concept of product is expanded into that of **product family**, whose various configurations are called **variants**.

While each variant has its own SKU, other general characteristics of the product, such as prices, descriptions and sales information, are stored at the family level. Similarly, it is the family that is linked to a particular department, and not its individual variants. The figure below shows an ER diagram of the six tables that take care of product data when dynamic attributes are implemented. Since we have already had a chance to examine `dept` and `product`, we'll focus on the remaining three.

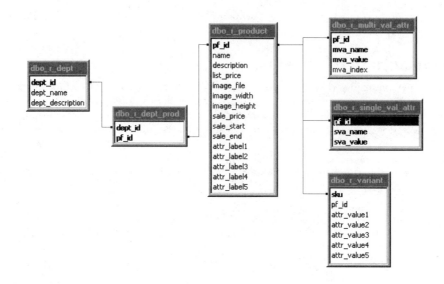

Attribute Definition

Single-value attributes are defined in the `single_val_attr` table. As we can see, this table only contains three fields:

Name	Datatype	Length	Notes	Description
Pf_id	Varchar	100	Not nullable Primary Key	The ID of the family to which this attribute belongs. This field references the `pf_id` field in the `product` table below.
Sva_name	Varchar	100	Not nullable Primary Key	Name of the attribute.
Sva_value	Varchar	100	Not nullable Primary Key	Value of the attribute.

In a similar way to what happens for the `dept_prod` table, all three fields are used to form a primary key for the table, which makes sure that the same attribute can never be defined more than once for a particular product. Also, you can notice that there is no numeric attribute ID; as we'll see in a moment, the attribute system uses the names of the attributes themselves as a key ID (keep in mind that the primary key in this table consists of the combination of all three fields, so it is possible for an attribute that has a particular name – such as Manufacturer – to be added for more than one product family.

Multi-valued Attributes

This works well for single-value attributes, and actually saves space since an additional ID field would have taken out an extra four bytes for each attribute. However, it represents quite a waste of database space in the case of their multi-valued cousins. These are stored in the `multi_val_attr` as a list of records that contain all the possible values that the attribute can hold, from which the user will eventually choose one in particular:

Name	Datatype	Length	Notes	Description
Pf_id	Varchar	100	Not nullable Primary Key	The ID of the family to which this attribute belongs. This field references the `pf_id` field in the `product` table below.
Mva_name	Varchar	100	Not nullable Primary Key	Name of the attribute.
Mva_value	Varchar	100	Not nullable Primary Key	Value of the attribute.
Mva_index	Int	N/A	Nullable	The position of this attribute value when it is shown to the user.

To better understand how multi-valued attributes work, let's look at a simple example. Suppose that our store had a product family, called *coffee cups*, whose ID is 75 and that has a multi-valued attribute called *color* that can assume the following values:

ID	Value
0	Red
1	Green
2	Blue

In the database, it will show up as follows:

Pf_id	Mva_name	Mva_value	Mva_index
75	Color	Red	0
75	Color	Green	1
75	Color	Blue	2

The `mva_index` field does not have any particular meaning for the DBMS, to the point that it can be null. The store's logic uses it to determine in what order the possible attribute values should be presented to the user.

Product Families

The `product` table contains the elements common to all the variants of a product family. As we have mentioned above, and as we can see in the following table, this also includes price and sale information:

Name	Datatype	Length	Notes	Description
Pf_id	Varchar	100	Not nullable Primary Key	The unique ID of each product family.
Name	Varchar	255	Nullable	Name of the product.
Description	Varchar	255	Nullable	Description of the product.
List_price	Int	N/A	Nullable	The price that is normally applied to the product, when it is not on sale and before any discounts.
Image_file	Varchar	255	Nullable	URL of the file that contains a product-related image (for example a box shot or screenshot).
Image_width	Int	N/A	Nullable	The width of the image, in pixels.
Image_height	Int	N/A	Nullable	The height of the image, in pixels.
Sale_price	Int	N/A	Nullable	The price that is applied to the product when the current system date falls between `Sale_start` and `Sale_end`.
Sale_start	Datetime	N/A	Nullable	Start of product sale. After this date, and before `Sale_end`, the `Sale_price` is applied of the product.
Sale_end	Datetime	N/A	Nullable	End of the sale.
Attr_label1	Varchar	100	Nullable	Name of the first dynamic attribute
Attr_label2	Varchar	100	Nullable	Name of the second dynamic attribute
Attr_label5	Varchar	100	Nullable	Name of the third dynamic attribute
Attr_label4	Varchar	100	Nullable	Name of the fourth dynamic attribute
Attr_label5	Varchar	100	Nullable	Name of the fifth dynamic attribute

One could argue – with good reason – that often the values of the attributes also determine the price of the merchandise (think for example of the size of jewelry), and therefore that the price data shouldn't be here. In that case, all you would need to do would be to move these values from this table to the `variant` table (which we'll examine in a few moments) and modify the store so that it would read them from the right place.

The five fields called `attr_label1` through `attr_label5` are the reason why the maximum number of dynamic attributes supported by MS Commerce Server is 5. Each of them represents the name of a dynamic attribute that the product family owns, unless it is null, in which case the code in the store ignores it.

If you need more than five dynamic attributes – an unusual but very possible scenario – you can simply decide to add one or more fields in this table. Naturally, you will also have to modify the code in `product.asp` in the store so that it will recognize the additional fields you have inserted. Another possibility would be to use a system similar to the one that MS Commerce Server employs to link products and departments: just add one more table that references the primary key elements of both `product` and `multi_val_attr`.

Variants

Finally, let's take a look at how an individual SKU is stored in the `variant` table:

Name	Datatype	Length	Notes	Description
Sku	Varchar	100	Not nullable Primary Key	The SKU of the product variant.
Pf_id	Varchar	100	Not Nullable	ID of the product family this variant belongs to. This field references pf_id in the product table.
Attr_value1	Varchar	100	Nullable	Value of the first attribute that identifies the variant.
Attr_value2	Varchar	100	Nullable	Value of the second attribute that identifies the variant.
Attr_value3	Varchar	100	Nullable	Value of the third attribute that identifies the variant.
Attr_value4	Varchar	100	Nullable	Value of the fourth attribute that identifies the variant.
Attr_value5	Varchar	100	Nullable	Value of the fifth attribute that identifies the variant.

The basic idea in this case is that each record in the `variant` table matches a particular combination of the possible values of each attribute for a given product family, which in turn corresponds to a given SKU. Clearly, if we change the way `product` works in order to increase (or decrease) the number of multi-value dynamic attributes supported by the system, we will also make similar changes in this table.

Promotions And Historical Records

There are only a few more tables to take a look at before we have covered the entire database structure of a store. The first two are used to save information about the promotions that are run by the store. Keep in mind that we are not talking about simple sale promotions, whose data is stored directly in the product (or product family) table, but rather of the more complex price and cross-promotions that can be set from the Promotions menu in the Store Manager. The third one is used by the store to save a complete detail of all the orders that have been successfully completed.

Price Promotions

Price promotions are entirely handled by a few pipeline objects that we will examine in the next chapter. Therefore, the promo_price table functions purely as a storage device for the information that is fed to that object. Since we have not yet discussed the ItemPromo component, we won't go too much into detail about this table here – there'll be more information on price promotions in Chapter 10, where we talk about the Order Processing Pipeline.

One aspect of price promotions that we will focus a little more on is how the promotions are prioritized for use. As we have seen in Chapter 6, when an administrator enters a new price promotion in the Store Manager, he or she is asked to enter a 'rank' value that expresses the precedence that will be enjoyed by it – the lower the rank, the higher the priority.

It's important to understand that this ranking system is a bit artificial, in that the pipeline component that takes care of price promotions does not know anything about it. It's the code inside the store that provides support for this feature through the rank field in the promo_price table.

Rank is an integer field in which the ranking value specified by the user is stored. When the store needs to extract the information from the database that will be fed to the ItemPromo component, it does so by running a query similar to the following:

```
Select * from promo_price order by rank
```

As we can see, the order by clause forces SQL to sort the price promotion records according to the value of the rank field and will return them in ascending order.

Cross-selling Promotions

Cross-selling promotions are much simpler in nature than price promotions, and they do not make use of any special object provided by MS Commerce Server. In fact, the promo_cross table has only two fields, and in a way it works very similarly to dept_prod, which we saw above:

Name	Datatype	Length	Notes	Description
Sku	Varchar	100	Not nullable Primary Key	SKU of the main product. This field references Sku in the product table.
Rel_sku	Varchar	100	Not Nullable Primary Key	SKU of the related product. This field references Sku in the product table.

Each record in this table represents a single association between two products in the database; referential integrity is employed to ensure that the two fields point to a product that really exists in the appropriate table. As was the case with `dept_prod`, both fields are used here to form a primary key, thus ensuring that, while a product can be associated with any other product in the database, the same association cannot appear more than once.

Receipts And Receipt Items

Finally, the only two tables that we haven't discussed yet are `receipts` and `receipt_item`. The first one is used to store a complete detail of all the orders that go through the purchase process successfully. Essentially, it contains a marshaled copy of the user's basket that contains all the products in the order plus all the information that was collected during the purchase process, such as addresses and telephone numbers:

Name	Datatype	Length	Notes	Description
Order_id	Char	26	Primary Key	The unique ID of the order (generated internally by MS Commerce Server during the purchase process)
Shopper_id	Char	32	Not nullable	The unique ID of the shopper this order belongs to. Used for displaying a user's purchase history.
Total	Int	N/A	Nullable	The total final cost of the order.
Status	Int	N/A	Nullable	The order's status.
Date_entered	Datetime	N/A	Nullable	The date when the order was entered.
Date_changed	Datetime	N/A	Nullable	The date when the order was last modified
Marshaled_receipt	Image	N/A	Nullable	The order's marshaled receipt.

While the purpose of all the fields in this table is quite straightforward, it should be pointed out that the `status` field is not used anywhere in the store that MS Commerce Server creates when we run the SBW. The best possible explanation (at least, the best one that I can come up with) is that this is some kind of "suggestion" to implement some kind of status tracking system, even though MS Commerce Server does not support anything of the sort by default.

Generally speaking, the status field will be useful to determine at what stage of the post-purchase fulfillment process it is. Orders that have just been posted will start with a value of zero, meaning something similar to "received", and then move on into whatever chain of events you have in place, going through different statuses, such as "checked", "backordered", and so on. Usually, all orders will come to a stop when they reach the status that corresponds to "shipped", although you might also want to track when users return their merchandise.

A Faster Way To Access Receipt Information

As proof of the fact that marshalling is a slow and painful process, the starter store maintains a copy of some order information in a separate table, so that SQL queries can be run against it. This data is stored in the `receipt_item` table:

Name	Datatype	Length	Notes	Description
Order_id	Char	26	Not Nullable Primary Key	The unique ID of the order, as generated internally by MS Commerce Server.
Row_id	Int	N/A	Not Nullable Primary Key	The ordinal position of this product in the user's basket.
Sku	Varchar	100	Nullable	The SKU of the product.
Quantity	Int	N/A	Not nullable	The quantity of items purchased.
Adjusted_price	Int	N/A	Not nullable	The total price paid for all these items.

`Receipt_item` is organized as a collection of all the individual products purchased by all customers. Therefore, in order to extract the products that are part of a specific order, one will have to extract the individual items from the table. MS Commerce Server uses `receipt_item` essentially for statistical purposes in the Store Manager.

Summary

There are a number of things that we have covered in detail in this chapter. Probably the most significant one (aside from the database structure itself) is the concept of marshalling. It's important that we have this concept very clear in our minds, as this won't be the last we hear of it. As mentioned earlier, we'll go about trying to get rid of it in Chapter 16.

Another important feature that we examined is how MS Commerce Server handles dynamic attributes. As we have seen, the techniques used are quite interesting, although the limit of five attributes may be a little tight for our needs. One thing that we should keep well in mind when we are designing a dynamic-attribute system is that its complexity – at least from a product management point of view – increases exponentially, and I mean that in the most literal of senses: a product family with two multi-value attributes, each with two possible values, has only four variants. Move that up to three attributes with three possible values and the number of variants soars to 27. Five attributes with five values each gives us a total of 3,125 possible variants!

While this aspect of dynamic attributes doesn't really bother us from a code perspective, it will create nightmares for the people who are supposed to work with the Store Manager, since they will have to handle so many possible combinations. If the number of possible variants becomes too many, it's a good idea to reconsider our need for multi-valued dynamic attributes, and try to cut their usage a bit wherever possible.

Using the
Commerce Server Objects

*All a computer does is tell a consistent
story: a consistent truth or, if the
programmer's guesses are unlikely, a
consistent fiction.*
– Paul A. Samuelson, in Newsweek

In the past chapters, I have presented SSCE as a collection of COM components, database structures and code. Well, we have seen how the database works – although we'll talk more about it in Chapter 11 – and, before we can go on to the code itself, we must learn what the components do.

At the core of SSCE, a set of COM components provides a wide range of functionality, from formatting operations to the complete management of the whole purchase process. These components are automatically installed as part of the installation of Site Server – unless of course you're unlucky and SSCE's setup program is unable to register the appropriate DLLs (which is quite possible, especially if your server is performing other tasks). If that happens, well, reinstalling SSCE is just about your only option; disabling all your services and disconnecting your server from the network might also help.

What Does This Chapter Talk About?

Chapter 9 describes in detail all the Commerce Objects provided by SSCE and their functionality. We'll take a look at each individual component and find out what it has to offer and how we can use it in our EC sites.

- ❑ **How to use the Commerce Components**
  No, you don't have to know the whole Object Oriented Programming thing and a couple of languages to use ASP components in VBScript. This section offers a crash course to refresh your memory.

- ❑ **The Commerce Server Objects**
  In this section, we'll go through all the components available. Each component is closely examined and every function that it provides is discussed, together with its uses and, when appropriate, a few good examples.

- ❑ **The role of Microsoft Transaction Server**
  Some of SSCE's Commerce Components make extensive use of the Microsoft Transaction Server (MTS). In this section we'll discover what it is, what it does, and how it can benefit EC applications.

- ❑ **Undocumented Commerce Server Objects**
  Finally, we'll take a look at a couple of components that, according to the documentation of Commerce Server, do not even exist! These are mainly used for administrative purposes by the code that is part, among other things, of the Wizards and the web-based pipeline editor, but can come in handy also for use in your very own stores.

How to use the Commerce Components

This is not a book about ASP programming. You should know this, especially if you have read the title before buying it. On the contrary, I assume that you already have a quite extensive knowledge of ASP programming, at least enough to develop a good dynamic web site. After all, SSCE is an advanced product, and it is reasonable to believe that whoever wants to develop an EC application using it has the appropriate knowledge in the first place.

Even the best minds, however, tend to forget things, as all my acquaintances who owe me money know! At the same rate, it is always a good idea to make sure that everybody starts from the same concepts (or, at least, gives the same meaning to certain words), so to avoid useless misunderstandings.

Therefore, this portion of the chapter will try to refresh your memory on how to use ASP components from within VBScript. If what you read here is new for you, I strongly recommend that you read a good ASP programming book before proceeding. VBScript is a powerful and easy-to-learn language – one more reason to learn it well!

> **If you're looking for a good ASP book, check out Professional ASP 2.0, published by Wrox Press (ISBN 1-861001-26-6)**

What Are ASP Components?

A few years ago (almost twenty, to say the truth), a gentleman by the name of Alan Kay wrote a language known as *SmallTalk*. The big deal about this language, which is still widely used today, was that instead of focusing on the actions that had to be accomplished, like all the other languages did at the time, this one focused on the logic and the data themselves.

Let's make an example. If you were programming in a structured language, such as C, you would write a program following the logic that it has to somehow *act* on its data, for example, by multiplying the values of two variables and storing the result in a third variable:

```
C ← A x B
```

The same program, written in an object-oriented language such as C++, uses a completely different approach. In fact, the data itself becomes "smarter", and able to handle itself. Therefore, you would create an entity, or **class**, and call it Number. Then, you would create three instances, or **objects**, of Number, tell the first two to assume a given value, then tell the third one to assume a value that is equal to the product of the first two.

```
Create Class Number
[ define all the properties of Number here]

Create Number A, B, C

A.AssignValue (10)
B.AssignValue (20)
C.AssignMultiplicationResult (A, B)
```

Although this might seem the worst example that anyone could ever make (it takes five lines of OOP code to do what one line of normal code does – and I was giving you the *simplified* version!), there are some interesting considerations to be made here.

First of all, our plain code. For my language, the symbol 'x' has a specific meaning – we are assuming it's a multiplication, but it could in fact be just about anything. This also mean that A and B must be of a very specific type (assuming the operation requires them to be homogeneous). So, my language certainly knows that 3 x 4 = 12. But, does it know what (4+2i) * (2+1i) makes? Even worse, does it know that those are imaginary numbers *at all*?

Let's now take a look at the second example. As you can see, in this case we let the objects themselves do all the arithmetic (so to speak). The notation Object.Member means "a reference to Member inside Object". The term "member" is used to identify any function or parameter inside an object. Does the code know what happens inside the object? No. Even more important, does it care? No! A, B and C can be everything – integer numbers, imaginary numbers, matrices, bricks, automobiles. As long as C knows how to handle A and B inside its AssignMultiplicationValue member, we are set.

There are some very interesting aspects of OOP. The one that's most relevant to us is the fact that any class, together with its functionality, can be taken as it is and moved on to another project and, assuming all the support functionality is present, still work. This *is* a very relevant concept if you think of how useful it is sometimes to be able to reuse code, or even to just "plug and play" somebody else's code into your application without ending up spending more time trying to make it fit than you would have needed to write the code yourself in the first place.

For a number of years, OOP effectively failed to deliver this fundamental promise. There were two main reasons – at least in my opinion – why this happened. The first was in the fact that the operating systems, at least until the advent of Windows 95 and NT 3.5, were not adapted too well to OOP, and any attempt to make them look like they were in fact designed to use this technique were a little too cumbersome to be effective. The second, and I know I will regret saying this because you can find out my e-mail address with relative ease, is that the most diffused object-oriented language, C++, does not adapt well to the concept of creating reusable code, mainly because it inherits a syntax that can be easily cryptic from its ancestor, C. This is not necessarily a design flaw of C or C++, but rather a consequence of the fact that these are low-level languages that have been conceived to leave a very high degree of freedom to the programmer, and therefore code written using them tends to be very complex.

To confirm what I just said (I hope you did get this far and did not rush to your e-mail program to send me a flame!), it took the diffusion of object-oriented Visual Basic to make OOP a favorite concept with the masses. VB is a simple enough language, very strict and extremely ordered, that makes it more difficult to write "contortionisms" than C++. Together with the COM (Component Object Module) technology, developed by Microsoft, VB really delivers on the promise of being able to consistently reuse code, to the point that writing a VB program has become more an exercise of properly gluing together the right pieces and adding some smart logic than writing every single piece of code from scratch.

ASP components are special COM components that have been developed to work with Microsoft's Active Server Pages platform. They follow special rules and expose a certain number of members in order to take advantage of the advanced features offered by ASP.

How Do I Use the Commerce Components?

With very few exceptions, before using an ASP component, you must create an instance of it. This is done using the `Server.CreateObject` method. `Server` is a **built-in** object that is automatically created and provided to the script by ASP itself.

```
Server.CreateObject (ObjectStringID)
```

ObjectStringID is a string that identifies a particular component. Each component is given a unique string that can be used to identify it. This string is made of three parts:

Class.Name.Version

Where:

❑ **Class** is the name of the group of objects to which the component belongs. For example, all the Commerce Components belong to the class **Commerce**.

❑ **Name** is the name of the component itself, such as **Page**.

❑ **Version** can be used to refer to a specific version of the component, for example, **1**.

The `Version` portion of the string can be omitted; in this case, the default version of the object, generally the most recent one, will be created.

Once an object has been created, it has to be assigned to an object variable. VBScript has a special way in which an object is assigned to an object variable: know that a variable should be treated as an object variable. The keyword **Set** must be used whenever an object is assigned to an object variable.

```
Set MyObject = Server.CreateObject ("Commerce.Page")
```

The object variable can then be used to refer to specific members of the component:

```
MyObject.Procedure (var)
a = MyObject.Function (var1, var2)
b = MyObject.Parameter
```

Destroying Objects

Destroying objects is something that is usually not necessary in an ASP script – the interpreter does it for you once your script has finished running. It might happen, though, that you need to destroy an object within your code. This is done by "disassociating" your object variables from their objects. This is done by assigning them the value **Nothing**:

```
Set MyObject = Nothing
```

It is important, though, that you understand that this operation does not directly destroy the object. In fact, if the object has been assigned to another variable, it will exist until you disassociate the other variable as well. This happens because the interpreter only destroys an object when no variable refers to it anymore.

The Commerce Server Objects

It's now time to take a look at each individual Commerce Server Object in detail. For each component, we will take a look at what its intended use is, how it is created and each of its members. We will also present a few examples whenever a particular concept needs further explanation.

This chapter only talks about those components that belong to version 3.0 of SSCE. The object set also includes several legacy components inherited from version 2.0, but, because it makes no sense to use them if you are developing a version 3.0 Store, we will not go through them.

> If you are interested in the legacy Commerce Server Objects that ship with SSCE, check out the documentation at
> http://*your_host*/siteserver/docs/default_com.htm – look under **Commerce Server Component Reference.**

In general, it is possible to divide the components into four categories:

- ❑ Configuration components
  These components can be used to read or alter the configuration of the store (and its site). Some of them also offer a number of functions that are not related to EC in particular, but can be useful during the development of an EC site.

- ❑ Storage components
  These components are used to store data in several ways, such as in a database table or in a file.

- ❑ User Interface components
  These components are used to validate the user's input, or to alter the data while preparing it for output, for example to adapt it for a particular locale.

- ❑ Pipeline components
  These components are used to manage all the pipeline-related operations, such as handling the purchase process. We won't examine the pipeline in detail until Chapter 14, so we will only talk briefly about these components here.

Configuration Components

SSCE includes a number of components that can be used to either read or write the configuration of a particular EC store or of the corresponding IIS4 web site. In this category, we will also include a component that makes it easier to read text or binary information from a server-side file.

The AdminFile Component

Those of you who have had to use ASP to output a binary file, such as an image, for example, know that it isn't that easy. The `Scripting.FileSystemObject` that comes with ASP has a limitation in the fact that it can only read text files, which are handled internally using the Unicode standard (2 bytes for each characters) and can't be used to output binary data. Most people – those who don't have SSCE, at least – end up writing their own components to handle this kind of data.

Luckily, SSCE comes with the **Commerce.AdminFile** component that can be used to read information from a server-side binary or text file. AdminFile has only two methods: `ReadFromBinaryFile` and `ReadFromFile`.

ReadFromBinaryFile

This function is used to read the contents of a binary file. The whole file is read into an array of bytes that can be outputted directly using the `Response.BinaryWrite` function.

- ❑ **Syntax:**
  AdminFile.ReadFromBinaryFile (*sFilename*)

- ❑ **Parameters:**
  sFilename   The complete pathname of the file

As we mentioned above, this function can be useful if you want to either examine (or alter) the contents of a binary file, or if you want to output them to the user's browser. In this latter case, you will have to do a little more than just using the `Response.Write` command; let's take a look at the following example, which loads and outputs a GIF:

```
<%
' Turn on error checking
On Error Resume Next

' Declare some vars
Dim afAdminFileObject
Dim bFile

' Create AdminFiles object
Set afAdminFileObject = Server.CreateObject ("Commerce.AdminFile")

' Load file into memory
bFile = afAdminFileObject.ReadFromBinaryFile ("C:\myfile.gif")

' Now, tell the browser that it will be receiving a GIF
Response.ContentType = "image/gif"

' Finally, output the file
Response.BinaryWrite (bFile)

' Handle errors
If Err.Number <> 0 Then
    Response.ContentType = "text/html"
%>
    <HTML><HEAD><TITLE>Error!</TITLE></HEAD>
    <BODY><B>Unable to load image file!</B></BODY>
    </HTML>
<%
End If
%>
```

It is important that you use the ContentType member of the Response object in order to let the browser know that what it's about to receive is an image and not plain text (or HTML, which is the same thing) like it expects by default. At the same rate, the use of BinaryWrite ensures that all the eight bits that make a byte are sent to the client in ASCII, or text, mode: in fact, the system will only transmit the lowest seven bits of the byte – with disastrous consequences in our case.

There are a number of ways in which ReadFromBinaryFile can be of use. The most typical is the scenario in which your EC site is selling digital goods. Since you must perform some kind of authentication in order to make sure that the user who is attempting to download a file is in fact authorized to do so, you cannot just give the users direct access to the file via a URL, like for example:

http://*your_host*/downloads/file.zip

This approach will either give all the users indiscriminate access to the file or turn into a security nightmare if you were to try and manage the access list for it dynamically. Instead, you could write a simple ASP script, similar to the one of the example that we saw above but with some authentication checking functionality, that would only output the file if the user is actually authorized to download it.

ReadFromFile

The other member provided by `AdminFiles` is `ReadFromFile`. This function is very similar to `ReadFromBinaryFile`, with the exception that it returns the contents of a file as a text string. Therefore, it cannot be used to read binary files, and its functionality is somehow redundant, considering that the same effect can be obtained using the `Scripting.FileSystemObject` component that ships with ASP.

- ❑ **Syntax:**
  AdminFile.ReadFromFile (*sFilename*)

- ❑ **Parameters:**
  sFilename   The complete pathname of the file

It's obvious, however, that `ReadFromFile` is much easier to use (just one call) than to create an instance of `FileSystemObject`, open a text file, read the file's contents and then, finally, close the file.

The AdminWebServer Component

While `AdminFile` is more of a "server-side access" component, **Commerce.AdminWebServer** can be used to access a few specific parameters relating to the configuration of Internet Information Server. Although IIS already provides a set of ASP components that can be used to fully administer a web server, `AdminWebServer` has been designed with an eye to the specific needs of SSCE.

> **For more information about the IIS configuration objects, visit MSDN online at http://msdn.microsoft.com.**

`AdminWebServer` only has three methods: `GetWebSites`, `GetWebSiteProperties` and `GetCommerceSites`.

GetWebSites

This method can be used to enumerate all the instances of IIS (web sites) that are available on the server.

- ❑ **Syntax:**
  AdminWebServer.GetWebSites()

- ❑ **Parameters:**
  None

The result of a call to `GetWebSites` is an array of numbers that contains an entry for each instance of IIS installed on the computer. These numbers can be used as parameters to several functions, such as `GetWebSiteProperties` and other methods belonging to the `AdminSite` component (see below).

> **The default web site's instance number is 1.**

In order to retrieve the dimension and lower bound of the array, you can use VBScript's LBound and UBound functions, as you can see in the following example.

```
<%
    ' Dim some variables
    Dim awsAdminObject
    Dim nIISInstances
    Dim i

    ' Create instance of AdminWebServer
    Set awsAdminObject = Server.CreateObject ("Commerce.AdminWebServer")

    ' Retrieve array of IIS instances
    nIISInstances = awsAdminObject.GetWebSites

    ' Output instances
    For i = LBound (nIISInstances) to UBound (nIISInstances)
        Response.Write nIISInstances (i) & "<BR>"
    Next

    ' Destroy objects

    Set awsAdminObject = Nothing
%>
```

GetWebSiteProperties

Once the number of an IIS instance is known, it is possible to retrieve several of its properties using the GetWebSiteProperties method:

❑ **Syntax:**
AdminWebServer.GetWebSiteProperties (*iInstance*)

❑ **Parameters:**
iInstance   The number of the IIS instance whose properties have to be retrieved

The result of GetWebSiteProperties is an object, called **Commerce.Dictionary**, which we'll see in a little while. For the moment, all you need to know is that it works like a list and that you can access its members by name:

```
Set dProperties = AdminWebServer.GetWebSiteProperties (1)

' This prints the virtual root's path of the first IIS instance
Response.Write dProperties ("VrPath")
```

A word of caution if you want to use GetWebSiteProperties: if you try to call it from a web site with anonymous access, you will get the following message:

Commerce.AdminWebServer.1 error '80070005'

Access is denied.

/clocktower/book/enumwebsiteproperties.asp, line 4

This happens because, being logged in as the IIS anonymous user (by default called IIS_USRMachineName, where MachineName is your server's NetBIOS name), you do not have access to the configuration parameters for IIS. If you think of it, this is an absolutely obvious security feature, but it tends to take you by surprise when you are trying to make your script work. If you really want to use GetWebSiteProperties, you should do it from a web site or virtual directory where you can login as a member of the administrative group for IIS. To do this, simply change the permissions for the folder (or even for a single file) to be limited to the administrative group (remember to remove – but not exclude – both the Everyone group and the IIS_USRMachineName user from the access list).

The GetCommerceSites method

As we have seen in Chapter 5, the creation of a new EC site only requires a reserved virtual directory on any specific instance of IIS. This means, of course, that each IIS web site can contain any number of SSCE stores. The GetCommerceSites method provides a way to enumerate all the SSCE stores that are installed in a specific instance of IIS.

❑ **Syntax:**
AdminWebServer.GetCommerceSites (*iInstance*)

❑ **Parameters:**
iInstance   The number of the IIS instance for which the installed SSCE stores must be retrieved

The value of iInstance can be retrieved using GetWebSites(). Similar to that function, GetCommerceSites returns an array that contains all the SSCE sites installed on the IIS instance specified.

The AdminSite Component

While AdminFile is more of a "server-side access" component, the **Commerce.AdminSite** can be used to access the configuration of a SSCE site. As it can be used for a variety of functions, including creating new EC sites and deleting existing ones, it certainly is a powerful tool – in particular if you want to develop your own site creation tools. This might happen, for example, if you are an ISP reselling SSCE-based hosting to your clients: in this case you will not want to give them access to all the functionality provided by the administration system that is provided by SSCE, but you can rather develop a simpler set of functions whose scope is limited to what you want them to be able to do.

How to Use the AdminSite Component

There are fundamentally two ways of using the AdminSite component. You can use it to create a new IIS site or SSCE store: for this you will need to use the Create method. You can also delete an existing site using the Delete method. On the other hand, you can use it to access an existing site and access or modify its properties through the Initialize or InitializeFromMDPath functions.

Once an instance of AdminSite has been initialized, you can edit the properties of the site it refers to; this is done in a three-step process using the ReadDefaultProperties or ReadManagerProperties to read the site's properties. You can then modify them by accessing their values through the **Dictionary** object (which we describe in the section dedicate to storage components), and save your changes using WriteDefaultProperties or WriteManagerProperties.

The Create Method

We have seen in Chapter 5 that creating a new SSCE store usually involves the use of the MMC or the Web administration tools. However, it is also possible to create a new store programmatically, through the `Create` method of the `AdminSite` component:

- ❑ **Syntax:**
  AdminSite.Create (*iServerInstance*, *sVirtualDirectory*, *sPhysicalPath*, *bIsApplication*, *bIsCommerceSite*)

- ❑ **Parameters:**

iServerInstance	The number of the IIS instance in which the SSCE store will be created
sVirtualDirectory	The name of the virtual directory where you want the site installed. Also the short name of the store.
sPhysicalPath	The physical path where you want the store to be created
bIsApplication	`True` if an IIS application should be created, `False` otherwise
bIsCommerceSite	`True` if the directory support for an SSCE store should be created, and if the site should be marked for administration through SSCE. `False` otherwise.

The value of *iServerInstance* can be retrieved using the `GetWebSites` method of the `AdminWebSite` component; you can also specify 1 for the default website. The value of *bIsApplication* should be `True` for all those cases where you want to use ASP within the site you are creating – and this *definitely* includes SSCE stores!

It is important to understand that `Create` does **not** perform the same functions as the Site Builder Wizard, but it rather provides the basic tool for creating a store foundation that will have to be populated appropriately. If you set *bIsCommerceSite* to `True`, `Create` will create the /Config folder and its subfolders.

The Initialize Method

As mentioned above, we need to initialize an instance of `AdminSite` before we can use it to retrieve a store's configuration parameters. This can be done through the `Initialize` method:

- ❑ **Syntax:**
  AdminSite.Initialize (*iInstance*, *sVirtualDirectory*)

- ❑ **Parameters:**

iInstance	The number of the IIS instance to be referenced by the object
sVirtualDirectory	The virtual directory (store) to be referenced by the object

`Initialize` is, typically, the first call that should be made when using the `AdminSite` component. You should always make sure that you have administrative privileges when accessing a site's properties (we discussed how to do this while we were looking at the `AdminWebSite` component); if you don't, you will be denied access to the IIS information metabase.

The Delete Method

Once you have initialized an instance of `AdminSite` with a reference to a specific web site, you can use the `Delete` method to remove the latter from the IIS metabase:

- ❑ **Syntax:**
  AdminSite.Delete()

- ❑ **Parameters:**
  None

Always remember that `Delete` only removes the IIS metabase entries (that is, the information that is stored inside IIS's own registry), but it doesn't delete the site's files and folders.

The InitializeFromMDPath Method

An alternative way to initialize an instance of `AdminSite` is using the `InitializeFromMDPath` method, which uses a Metabase path to create a reference to a site that can then be used by `AdminSite`'s functions.

A Metabase path for an IIS site has the following format:

/machine/W3SVC/instance/virtualfolder

where *machine* is the server's NetBIOS name, *instance* is the IIS site's instance number and *folder* is the virtual directory where the SSCE store is.

- ❑ **Syntax:**
  AdminSite.InitializeFromMDPath (*sMetabasePath*)

- ❑ **Parameters:**
  sMetabasePath   The IIS Metabase path to be used for referencing an SSCE site

The obvious advantage that `InitializeFromMDPath` has when compared to `Initialize` is that you are able to specify the machine where you want to read the information from. On the other hand, you can only access SSCE sites that are at the virtual directory level (as opposed to in a sub-directory thereof).

> *You can use the value "LM" to indicate that the server you want to connect to is your local machine.*

The ReadDefaultProperties Method

When you have initialized an instance of `AdminSite` to reference the site of your choice, you will want to access its properties. This can be done using the `ReadDefaultProperties` method:

- ❑ **Syntax:**
  AdminSite.ReadDefaultProperties()

- ❑ **Parameters:**
  None

`ReadDefaultProperties` returns a `Commerce.Dictionary` object. While we will examine this object in detail further on in the chapter, all we need to know about it to use it here is that it can be used to store **name/value pairs**. From this point of view it works in a similar way to a collection, in that we can assign values to it as follows:

```
Set dDictionary = Server.CreateObject ("Commerce.Dictionary")
dDictionary ("MyName") = "MyValue"
```

Dictionaries can contain any type of information – including other objects. The value of a name/value pair can be retrieved as follows:

```
sMyVar = dDictionary ("MyName")
```

Naturally, if you are storing or retrieving an object, you will have to use the `Set` keyword:

```
Set dDictionary ("MyName") = oMyObject
Set oMyObject = dDictionary ("MyName")
```

The dictionary returned by `ReadDefaultProperties` is a particular collection of data, known as the **Site Dictionary**, which contains relevant information about a SSCE site. This information is stored in and retrieved from the **/config/site.csc** file (using a method of the `FileDocument` component that we'll see later on).

The Site Dictionary contains a number of name/value pairs that can be used to change several settings of the store:

CloseRedirectURL	The URL to where the user is redirected when the store is closed
ConnectionStringMap	A `Dictionary` object that contains all the ADO/ODBC connection strings that are available to the site
DefaultConnectionString	The default connection string used by the site
DisableHTTPS	0 if the pages that are marked as secure on the site should indeed be called using the **https://** URL prefix. A value of 1 causes those pages to be called using a standard **http://** prefix – extremely useful for testing purposes. See the `Page` object for more information.
DisplayName	The long name of the store, which is displayed prominently in several locations, including the Store Manager.
NonsecureHostName	The name of the host that should be used when building non-secure URLs (see the `Page` component `PageURL` and `PageSURL` methods below)
SecureHostName	The name of the host that should be used when building secure URLs
Status	The current status of the store. Can assume the values of "Open", "Closed" and "Invalid".

The WriteDefaultProperties Method

If you need to make any changes to the configuration data stored in the Site Dictionary, you will also have to save it back to the `site.csc` file. To do so, you will have to use the `WriteDefaultProperties` method of `AdminSite`:

❏ **Syntax:**
AdminSite.WriteDefaultProperties(*dSiteDictionary*)

❏ **Parameters:**
dSiteDictionary   A variable that contains the Site Dictionary for the site the instance of `AdminSite` points to

Using ReadDefaultProperties and WriteDefaultProperties

The `ReadDefaultProperties`/`WriteDefaultProperties` is an easy combination of functions to use. All you have to do, in substance, is to create an `AdminSite` object, reference it to an existing SSCE site (or create a new one), then call `ReadDefaultProperties` to retrieve the Site Dictionary. Once you have made all your changes, you simply write the dictionary back to the `site.csc` file using `WriteDefaultProperties`.

The following example illustrates what we just said: a store's Site Dictionary is loaded and its contents are displayed. The store's Display Name is then changed, and the Site Dictionary is saved back to disk using `WriteDefaultProperties`.

```
<%@ Language=VBScript %>
<HTML>
<HEAD>
</HEAD>
<BODY>

<%
    ' Create and initialize an instance of AdminSite

    set asAdminSite = Server.CreateObject ("Commerce.AdminSite")
    asAdminSite.Initialize 1, "ClockTower"

    ' Load the site dictionary

    set dSiteDictionary = asAdminSite.ReadDefaultProperties

    ' Dump all the properties

    For Each Property in dSiteDictionary
        If Not IsObject (dSiteDictionary (Property)) Then
            Response.Write Property & " = " & dSiteDictionary (Property) & _
            "<BR>"
        Else
%>
            <TABLE>
                <TR>
```

```
                    <TD>
                        <% = Property %> =
                    </TD>
                    <TD>
    <%

                    For Each SubProperty in dSiteDictionary (Property)
                        Response.Write (SubProperty) & "<BR>"
                    Next
    %>
                    </TD>
                </tr>
            </table>
    <%
        End If
    Next

    ' Change the display name of the store

    dSiteDictionary ("DisplayName") = "The New ClockTower!"

    ' Save the modified Site Dictionary

    asAdminSite.WriteDefaultProperties (dSiteDictionary)

    ' Unreference all objects

    set dSiteDictionary = Nothing
    set asAdminSite = Nothing
    %>

    </BODY>
    </HTML>
```

There are a couple of things that are worth taking a look at here: first of all, the `For Each - Next` loop that dumps all the properties that are included in the `Dictionary` object – as you can see there is a condition before printing out the value of the property that checks to see if the property itself is an object. The necessity of this approach is twofold: as we saw above, the `Dictionary` object can also contain other objects, of any kind; at the same time, we cannot print out these objects directly, because doing so would generate a VBScript error.

In this specific case, we are just assuming that if we find an object, then it is going to be a collection of some kind, and therefore we attempt to iterate through its properties. It is important to understand that we are making this assumption because we know that, under normal circumstances, the only object that we'll find is `ConnectionStringMap`, and *that* is a `Dictionary` object. This assumption might not always be correct, however, and therefore we must be very careful as to how we handle `Dictionary` objects.

Once you have run the script shown previously, you can go to the Clocktower Store Manager (assuming that Clocktower is installed in the /ClockTower virtual directory of the default IIS site) to see that it has indeed altered the Display Name for the store.

The ReadManagerProperties and WriteManagerProperties Methods

Similar to the Site Dictionary, which is stored in the storefront, the manager has its own configuration file, which is stored in the `/manager/config/site.csc` file. This configuration file only contains the `DefaultConnectionString` and `ConnectionStringMap` properties, and can be accessed by using the `ReadManagerProperties` and `WriteManagerProperties` methods:

❑   **Syntax:**
    AdminSite.ReadManagerProperties()

❑   **Parameters:**
    None

Similar to `ReadDefaultProperties`, `ReadManagerProperties` returns a `Dictionary` object that contains all the configuration parameters.

❑   **Syntax:**
    AdminSite.WriteManagerProperties (*dDictionary*)

❑   **Parameters:**
    DDictionary   The `Dictionary` object containing all the parameters to be stored
                              in the configuration file.

Opening and Closing a Store

Through an instance of the `AdminSite` component, we can also open and close a SSCE store – as well as learning whether it is open or closed. This is done through the `Status` property:

❑   **Syntax:**
    Public Property AdminSite.Status

❑   **Parameters:**
    None

`Status` accepts and returns Boolean values, indicating whether the store referenced by the `AdminSite` object is open (`True`), or closed (`False`). Assigning a value to this property causes the store to be opened or closed, and the value of the status parameter in the Site Dictionary to be set accordingly.

Keep in mind that whenever you change the value of `Status`, SSCE has to change a few files in your store. If the user you are currently logged on as doesn't have permission to access those files, (or if the files are marked as read-only), you might not be able to open or close a store.

The Version Property

As we have mentioned – probably more than once – before, SSCE is able to handle stores that have been created using version 2.0 of the software. We also mentioned that we were not going to explore that possibility in this book, but because it *is* a possibility, being able to distinguish between v2 and v3 stores might be useful at times.

This can be done through the `Version` property:

- **Syntax:**
  Public Property AdminSite.Version

- **Parameters:**
  None

`Version` returns an integer value – 2 if the store referenced by the `AdminSite` object has been created using the previous version of SSCE, 3 otherwise.

The Directory Property

This property can be used to determine the physical path where the currently selected SSCE site is stored.

- **Syntax:**
  Public Property AdminSite.Directory

- **Parameters:**
  None

The return value here is a string that contains the fully qualified path to the folder where the site is stored. As IIS supports UNC paths, we must be prepared to handle non-local paths (that is, in the `\\machine\folder\` format).

The IsValidName Method

At times, you might want to know whether a certain store really exists in an instance of IIS. This can be done using the `IsValidName` method, which determines whether a store name (a) is valid from a syntax point of view and (b) is not already in use:

- **Syntax:**
  AdminSite.IsValidName (*sSiteName, iInstance*)

- **Parameters:**
  SSiteName   The short name (or virtual directory name) of the SSCE store
  IInstance   The numeric instance of IIS where the SSCE site is found

`IsValidName` returns a Boolean value – `False` if the parameters passed match an existing store, and `True` otherwise.

Reloading a Store

It is often necessary to cause the store to "reload" itself (which corresponds to resetting and reloading the IIS application it runs on), for example when the contents of an object that is created in `global.asa` has to change. In those cases, you can use the `Reload` method:

- **Syntax:**
  AdminSite.Reload

- **Parameters:**
  None

Storage Components

A very important aspect of electronic commerce is the ability to properly store all the information that comes from the user. SSCE provides a variety of objects that can be used for this purpose – and for a lot more.

The SimpleList Component

As the name suggests, SimpleList is an array of Variants that supports enumeration. This means that we can add values to it, and then either retrieve a specific value using a numeric index or iterate through all the values, one at a time.

The Add Method

The Add method can be used to add a new value to a SimpleList object:

❑ **Syntax:**
SimpleList.Add (*Value*)

❑ **Parameters:**
Value   The value or object to be added to the SimpleList object

Keep in mind that, because SimpleList is, fundamentally, an array of Variants, you can add any kind of data to it, including objects.

The Delete Method

You'll agree with me that it doesn't really take psychic powers to guess what this method does! You can use it to delete any value from the SimpleList object.

❑ **Syntax:**
SimpleList.Delete (*iIndex*)

❑ **Parameters:**
iIndex   The zero-based index of the item to be deleted from the object

An error occurs if the value of *iIndex* is greater than the number of objects stored in the object minus one.

The Count Property

You can use this property to know how many items are included in the SimpleList object:

❑ **Syntax:**
SimpleList.Count

❑ **Parameters:**
None

Count returns an integer value corresponding to the number of objects in the SimpleList object.

Using SimpleList

SimpleList is used through a two-step process. First of all, you will load all your values into it; then, you will want to access them either individually or through enumeration. The following example loads some strings into a SimpleList object and then uses both methods to print them out.

```
<%@ Language=VBScript %>
<HTML>
<HEAD>
</HEAD>
<BODY>

<%
    ' Create the SimpleList object
    set slSimpleList = Server.CreateObject ("Commerce.SimpleList")

    ' Load some string values into it
    slSimpleList.Add "Unable to print entire file. Your monitor is too short."
    slSimpleList.Add "Hard disk full. Feed less."
    slSimpleList.Add "Do you want to abort? "
    slSimpleList.Add "Click on 'Yes' if you do, otherwise click on 'No'."
    slSimpleList.Add "Windows detected. Do you want to format your hard drive?"

    ' Now, print out the number of items in the SimpleList
    Response.Write "The SimpleList object contains " & slSimpleList.Count & "
objects.<P>"

    ' Print one random value

    iRndValue = int (rnd * slSimpleList.Count)
    Response.Write "Value number " & iRndValue & " is: " & slSimpleList (iRndValue)
& "<BR>"

    ' Finally enumerate through and print out all values

    Response.Write "<P><B>Printing all values:</B><BR>"

    For Each Value in slSimpleList
        Response.Write Value & "<BR>"
    Next
%>

</BODY>
</HTML>
```

The Dictionary Component

Together with `SimpleList`, the `Dictionary` component represents the basic foundations of most of the storage requirements of SSCE. Therefore, we will analyze it in great detail throughout the book – this is essential in order to understand how a SSCE store works under-the-hood.

As we saw briefly earlier in the chapter, a `Dictionary` object fundamentally behaves like a collection of name/value pairs. Those of you who are familiar with ASP development might have heard of a component called **Scripting.Dictionary**. Similar to the `Dictionary` object provided by SSCE, `Scripting.Dictionary` is a name/value collection that can be used to store an arbitrary number of items.

However, the fundamental difference between `Scripting.Dictionary` and `Commerce.Dictionary` is in the fact that, while the former has been created using an *apartment* threading model, the latter has been written using both the apartment and the free-threaded model. If you are not familiar with these terms, don't worry – you don't need to know them to use SSCE. They are simply two ways of expressing how a component behaves in a multi-tasking environment.

Apartment-threaded components share one single thread for all their implementations. A different set of parameters is created for each instance, so that if two different calls are made to the component at the same time they do not interfere with each other. Components that have been written to support both the apartment- and the free-threading models can instead be used in those scenarios in which each instance of the component needs to run in its own processing thread (the `Session` object works like this, for example), therefore providing more speed and a higher degree of flexibility.

Moreover, the `Commerce.Dictionary` component can be used in combination with other SSCE storage components to save the information it contains to either a database or a structured storage file. And, because the values it accepts are Variants, you can basically use it to save anything, including objects.

Another very interesting aspect of `Commerce.Dictionary` objects – in terms of convenience – is that whenever a name/value pair is added to them, its *name* part becomes a property of the object itself. The following example illustrates this:

```
<%
    Set dDictionary = Server.CreateObject ("Commerce.Dictionary")

    dDictionary.MyName = "MyValue"
%>
```

As you can see, whenever we want to reference a name/value pair, all we have to do is add the name part after the dot, which is really more convenient (and easier to read) than having to use an explicit method or brackets.

Preventing Values From Being Saved – the Prefix Property

When you store a dictionary object either to a database or to a file (we will see how to do so later on in this chapter), you might want to prevent some name/value pairs from being saved. This can be accomplished using the `Prefix` property:

❑ **Syntax:**
Public Property Dictionary.Prefix

❑ **Parameters:**
None

`Prefix` is used to specify a string prefix that prevents a specific name/value pair from being saved when it is found as the beginning of its name part. For example, the pipeline components in SSCE use the _cc_ prefix to prevent credit card information (such as the _cc_number pair) from being stored in a database.

The Count Property

Similar to the `SimpleList` component, `Dictionary` allows us to retrieve the number of name/value pairs stored in it by using the `Count` property:

❑ **Syntax:**
Public Property Dictionary.Count

❑ **Parameters:**
None

`Count` returns an integer value that corresponds to the number of name/value pairs that are in the `Dictionary` object.

The Value Method

As we have seen before, a `Dictionary` object exposes its name/value pairs as properties that can be accessed directly by using the name portion of the pair as a method of the `Dictionary` object.

There are instances in which this approach doesn't work; for example, if the name of the pair that you want to retrieve has to be built dynamically at runtime, the method described above does not work. In this case, you will want to use the `Value` property:

❑ **Syntax:**
Public Property Dictionary.Value (sName)

❑ **Parameters:**
sName   The name of the name/value pair to be retrieved or set

Keep in mind that `Value` is the default property for the `Dictionary` component, and therefore it doesn't have to be explicitly called to access a name/value pair stored in a `Dictionary` object:

```
dDictionary.Value ("MyName")
```

is the same as:

```
dDictionary ("MyName")
```

Iterating Through a Dictionary Object's Collection

As the `Dictionary` component behaves like a collection, we can iterate through its contents one at a time using the VBScript `For Each - Next` construct. However, because just about anything can be stored in a `Dictionary` object, we must be very cautious in how we treat the data that we get during each cycle.

In particular, we must provide the right code to handle the case in which the value part of a name/value pair is an object. In this case, we must use the `Set` keyword if we are assigning the value to another variable, or create a special case if what we're doing is dumping the `Dictionary` object to the client browser.

SSCE Implementations of Dictionary and SimpleList

As we mentioned earlier, `Dictionary` and `SimpleList` are two building blocks of SSCE – they are used pervasively throughout a store's front-end and back-end interfaces.

In particular, SSCE takes advantage of the fact that (almost) anything can be stored inside a `Dictionary` object, including `SimpleList` and other `Dictionary` objects. We saw an example of this when we were looking at the Site Dictionary, which contains another `Dictionary` object under the name of `ConnectionStringMap`.

Other implementations of the `Dictionary` object within SSCE include `QueryMap` and `PipeContext`. We'll take a look at the former in Chapter 11, while the second one will be worth a look when we'll be talking about the Pipeline later on.

The FileDocument Component

While we were discussing the `AdminSite` object earlier in the chapter, we came across the `ReadDefaultProperties` and `WriteDefaultProperties` methods, which can be used to load the Site Dictionary from a file or store it to the same file.

Clearly, being able to do the same with *any* `Dictionary` object would be a definite advantage – you could store a number of data elements for various uses, such as configuration information, and so on. Luckily, SSCE provides the `FileDocument` component to read or write *any* persistable object to disk.

Now, of course, you should be aware of what persistable means. When you create an object and store information in it, it is considered persistable if it is autonomously able to save and retrieve that information in a structured format. Thus, for example, when you load name/value pairs into a `Dictionary` object, it is possible for another object to "persist" them – retrieve them from the `Dictionary` and store them somewhere else. When the data is then loaded back into another instance of `Dictionary`, you can expect that object to behave exactly like its predecessor.

Persisting Objects

There are two methods that you need to use to persist objects. They are `WriteToFile` and `ReadFromFile`:

- ❑ **Syntax:**
  FileDocument.WriteToFile (sFileName, sEntryName, oObject)

- ❑ **Parameters:**

sFileName	The fully qualified path of the file from where the object must be persisted.
sEntryName	The name of the entry corresponding to the position within the file where the object is stored.
oObject	The object to be persisted

- ❑ **Syntax:**
  FileDocument.ReadFromFile (*sFileName, sEntryName*)

- ❑ **Parameters:**

sFileName	The fully qualified path of the file from where the object must be retrieved.
sEntryName	The name of the entry corresponding to the position within the file where the object is stored.

Each structured file is composed of one or more objects, each one of which can be given a name as long as 31 characters. When you write an object to a file, that file doesn't necessarily need to exist – `WriteToFile` will create it for you, or it will add your object's data to an existing file.

As `ReadFromFile` creates the objects that it retrieves, they can only have page scope. This means that they are intended to exist only within the page, and are usually treated as apartment-threaded objects. As we mentioned before, however, apartment-threaded objects do not do well in an environment in which multiple calls to them might be made at the same time.

Such is the case with `Session`-wide and `Application`-wide objects, which are intended to be used throughout a user session or an ASP application respectively. These objects can only be created using the `<OBJECT>` tag in the `global.asa` file, and therefore `WriteToFile` cannot be used to persist them.

At the same rate, it would be very difficult to create a persistance method that would be able to handle all objects. In fact, persistable objects support special COM interfaces that allow them to retrieve their data only as part of the creation process; therefore, this system cannot be used when retrieving data that should be stored in an object that already exists (as would be the case with trying to load an application-wide object, which must be created *prior* to any use). The only feasible method is to manually load each value into the object, but this requires a different approach for every possible object – a real stretch even for the SSCE team!

Application-wide objects, if properly implemented, are extremely efficient, however. Therefore, `FileDocument` does provide a method that makes it possible to retrieve values into an object that already exists. It's called `ReadDictionaryFromFile` and – you guessed it – only works with `Dictionary` objects:

- ❑ **Syntax:**
  FileDocument.ReadDictionaryFromFile (*sFileName*, *sEntryName*, *dDictionary*)

- ❑ **Parameters:**

sFileName	The fully qualified path of the file from where the object must be retrieved
sEntryName	The name of the entry corresponding to the position within the file where the object is stored.
dDictionary	The `Dictionary` object the data has to be read into

As we just mentioned, `ReadDictionaryFromFile` cannot rely on the traditional persistence mechanism, and therefore manually loads each name/value pair into the `Dictionary` object. This also means that, because `ReadDictionaryFromFile` does not create the object itself, if any other data is loaded in the object, it will remain there.

The following example illustrates the use of `FileDocument`. First, we will load the Site Dictionary from disk, change once again the store's `DisplayName` property and then store it back to disk. We are not using `ReadDictionaryFromFile` here – we'll see how it works in Chapter 11, when we'll examine the `global.asa` file of the SSCE storefront. The Site Dictionary is stored in the /config/site.csc file in any SSCE site, under the `IISProperties` entry.

```
<%@ Language=VBScript %>
<%
    ' Create the FileDocument object
    Set fdFileDocument = Server.CreateObject ("Commerce.FileDocument")

    ' Load the Site Dictionary
    ' It is located in the /config/site.csc file
    Set dDictionary = fdFileDocument.ReadFromFile(Server.MapPath _
                    ("/clocktower/config") & "\site.csc", "IISProperties")

    ' Change the store's display name--again!
    dDictionary ("DisplayName") = "The alternative Clocktower!"

    ' Now, save it to disk
    fdFileDocument.WriteToFile(Server.MapPath("/clocktower/config") & _
                    "\site.csc", "IISProperties", dDictionary)
%>
```

Once again, you can test out the result of this script by looking at Clocktower's Store Manager. Remember that, in order for the changes to take effect, you will need to reload the site. We'll see why this is necessary in Chapter 11.

The OrderForm Component

Let's examine now a very specialized storage component. `OrderForm` can be used to store order-related information in an ordered manner. To its core, an `OrderForm` object corresponds to a specific implementation of the `Dictionary` object containing a set of name/value pairs, some of which are other `Dictionary` or `SimpleList` objects:

Items	A `SimpleList` of `Dictionary` objects, one for each item that is part of the order.
Shopper_ID	The unique identifier for the shopper
ship_to_name	The name portion of the ship-to address
ship_to_street	The street portion of the ship-to address. Includes street number and apartment number
ship_to_city	City portion of the ship-to address
ship_to_state	The state (or province) portion of the ship-to address
ship_to_zip	The ZIP or Postal Code portion of the ship-to address
ship_to_country	The 3-letter ISO country code portion of the ship-to address
ship_to_phone	Phone portion of the ship-to address
bill_to_name	The name portion of the bill-to address
bill_to_street	Street portion of the bill-to address. Includes the street and any apartment numbers
bill_to_city	City portion of the bill-to address
bill_to_state	State (or province) portion of the bill-to address
bill_to_zip	ZIP or Postal Code portion of the bill-to address
bill_to_country	3-letter ISO country code portion of the bill-to address
bill_to_phone	Phone number portion of the bill-to address
_Basket_Errors	A `SimpleList` object containing a set of strings, corresponding to all errors that have occurred during the basket preparation phase of the purchase process
_Purchase_Errors	A `SimpleList` object containing a set of strings, corresponding to all errors that have happened during the purchase process
cc_name	The name that appears on the credit card to be used to pay for the order

Table continued on the following page

cc_type	The type of the credit card to be used to pay for the order
_cc_number	The number of the credit card to be used to pay for the order
_cc_expmonth	The credit card expiration date's month portion
_cc_expyear	The credit card expiration date's year portion
Order_id	The unique identifier that has been assigned to the order. Becomes available only if the order has been successfully processed
_total_total	The total cost for the whole order. Includes shipping, handling and taxes
_oadjust_subtotal	The cost of all the items in the OrderForm as calculated after the global order adjustments
Shipping_method	The code of the shipping method that should be used to ship the order. Used to calculate the shipping costs
_shipping_total	The total shipping cost included in the order total
_tax_total	The total amount of tax calculated for the order
_handling_total	The total handling cost included in the order total
_tax_included	The amount of tax included in the order total
_verify_with	A Dictionary object that contains the fields that must be checked when verifying that the contents of an order have not been altered during the order process. Used by the Page component (see below)
_payment_auth_code	The authorization code for the payment. Returned by financial institution whenever a transaction is completed

As you can see, there are quite a few values stored here. While some of them will only make sense in Chapter 10, after we talk about the Order Processing Pipeline, let's take a closer look at certain interesting ones.

❑ **The Items SimpleList**
   This collection is used to store relevant information about each item in the user's shopping basket. Each of the SimpleList's members is a Dictionary object that typically contains the following information:

SKU	The SKU number for this item
Quantity	Number of items in the basket
Name	Name of the item
list_price	The price of the object when it was added to the basket
_product_name	Name of the product as it appears in the product database
_product_dept_id	Department number of the product as it appears in the database
_product_image_file	Pointer to the image file for the product, as it appears in the database
_product_image_height	Height of the image file for the product, as it appears in the database
_product_manufacturer	Manufacturer as it appears in the database
_product_image_width	Width of the image file for the product as it appears in the database
_product_list_price	Price of the item as listed in the product database
_product_sku	SKU of the product as listed in the database
_product_description	Description of the product as it appears in the database
_n_unadjusted	Number of items available to the user (without any adjustments). This value is initially set to the same value as Quantity and then used when calculating the number of available items (inventory check)
_oadjust_adjustedprice	The total price for all the items of this product after having been adjusted taking into consideration the order as a whole (for example, applying special cross-selling discounts, and so on)
_iadjust_regularprice	The normal price of the item. Normally set to the value of `list_price`
_iadjust_currentprice	The price of all the items of this product after having been modified keeping into consideration the single item (for example, after having applied quantity discounts)
placed_price	The final price that has been calculated for the single item, keeping into account only the single product.
_oadjust_discount	The discount that was applied to this product when the order was considered as a whole
_tax_total	The total tax calculated for the item
_tax_included	The tax actually included in the final calculation of the order's total

Pairs whose name part is preceded by a `_product_` prefix are extracted directly from the database by certain pipeline components.

❏ **The shopper ID**
   Each shopper who visits the site is assigned a unique identifier that is then used by SSCE for various tracking purposes, including associating basket records and orders with individual shoppers. The shopper ID is actually a Global Unique Identifier – a number that is guaranteed to be unique among all the computers in the world. Of course, you do understand that to create a number that is globally unique, one needs a lot of digits – 128 bits to be accurate – and therefore that's why the order id is so long.

   The choice of using a GUID was made because it is an easy way to encompass all the possible database technologies, even those that don't support, for example, automatic numbering. If you know that you will be using a specific type of database server, for example, you can choose to create a different numbering system (you can also use triggers for the purpose).

❏ **Ship-to and bill-to addresses**
   The addresses stored in the `OrderForm` component are broken down into their main elements. If you are doing business on the Internet, you will probably lament the absence of an e-mail address. I usually add that under the ship_to_email and bill_to_email names (remember, the `OrderForm` is fundamentally a `Dictionary` object, so anything can be added to it). We'll see how that can be handled in the next chapter.

   Notably, the "state" and "ZIP" portions of the address look like they are specific to the United States. The truth of the matter is, because these are all `Variants`, they can be set to anything, and therefore will work with anything you want. Whenever you create a store and set it to a specific locale in the Store Builder Wizard, however, SSCE might create alternative entries in the `OrderForm`; in the specific example of Canadian stores, the values ship_to_postalcode and ship_to_province are added – this is more for an aesthetic than practical reason.

   Also, note that the country portion of both addresses is stored using the 3-letter ISO country code. This is an internationally recognized system that assigns a 3-letter code to each country. Thus, for example, The United States has been assigned the code USA, while Canada is CAN, and Italy is ITA. These are also the same codes that you will see in the Olympic Games broadcasts besides each athlete's name. This book contains a complete list of them in Appendix C.

❏ **Basket and Purchase errors**
   As we have seen while visiting the storefront, there are two moments during the purchase process when we can get errors (or simple communications) from SSCE. One is while looking at the basket, and the other is after clicking on Purchase in the payment screen. These two moments correspond to two different parts of the purchase process from a technical point of view, as well, and they generate two different sets of error messages, which are stored in the _Basket_Errors and _Purchase_Errors SimpleList objects.

❏ **The order ID**
   Whenever an order has been successfully completed and has to be stored, a unique order id (or order number) is generated by SSCE. This is the very long string that we see in the confirmation screen – and that the user is supposed to write down for future reference! The same string is used when storing the order to a database as its primary key, as we saw in the previous chapter.

   Similar to the shopper ID, the order ID is generated from a GUID. As it's so long, it's difficult to remember for the user; we'll look at how to get rid of it in Chapter 15.

You have probably noticed that there are several values, both in the OrderForm itself and in the Items collection, that begin with an underscore ("_"). SSCE sets the Prefix value accordingly so that those values are not saved when the OrderForm Dictionary is saved to the database for temporary storage.

Most of these values, however, are of significant importance when the order has been completed. Therefore, SSCE resets the Prefix property to an empty string so that when the order is completed and saved to its final storage medium, all the values contained in it are saved.

Adding Your Own Values to the OrderForm

Keep in mind that the OrderForm is fundamentally a Dictionary object. This means that you can add your own values to it, being very careful with the way you name them (remember, those starting with an underscore are *not* saved to the database). SSCE will not only let you use as many pairs as you want, but will also save them to the order database for you!

Adding Products to the OrderForm

The whole goal of the game in an online EC site – at least if you want to make money out of it – is to get your customer to buy something. Clearly, however, they can't really do so if you don't let them, either knowingly or not, add products to their baskets.

While you could in principle add a product to the basket by simply creating a new Dictionary object and its appropriate entries in the Items dictionary of the OrderForm component, the latter provides a method that does the trick for you:

- ❏ **Syntax:**
  OrderForm.AddItem (*sSKU, iQuantity, iPrice*)

- ❏ **Parameters:**

sSKU	The SKU of the product that has to be added to the OrderForm
iQuantity	The number of items to be added to the order
iPrice	The list price for the individual item, expressed in the base monetary unit of the default currency for the store

AddItem will add the product to the Items collection and set the appropriate pairs. In addition, it will return the Dictionary that was created as its result.

Clearing the OrderForm

There are two methods to clear the contents of an OrderForm object. The first one, ClearItems, cleans up the Items dictionary – this corresponds to emptying one's basket – while ClearOrderForm deletes all the values in the object.

- ❏ **Syntax:**
  OrderForm.ClearItems()

- ❏ **Parameters:**
  None

- ❏ **Syntax:**
  OrderForm.ClearOrderForm ()

- ❏ **Parameters:**
  None

211

The DBStorage Component

In the previous chapter, we introduced the concept of data marshalling. As you have seen, marshaled data is not really human-friendly – quite the contrary.

It is obvious, therefore, that a special component is needed to read and write data in that format. Such functionality is provided by DBStorage, which can marshal Dictionary, SimpleList and OrderForm objects directly to a database table. If you remember, the marshaled_basket column in the *store*_order table is a text-type field, which limits the amount of data that can be saved through DBStorage to about 2 GB for a Microsoft SQL 6.5 database. Sure enough, that should be sufficient for all uses!

Initializing a DBStorage Component

Before being able to use a DBStorage component, you will need to initialize it. This will make sure that it is connected to a database and that it knows what data to look for and where. The InitStorage method takes care of this for us:

❑ **Syntax:**
DBStorage.InitStorage (*sConnectionString, sTable, sKey, sProgID, sMarshalColumn, sDateChanged*)

❑ **Parameters:**

sConnectionString	The connection string that should be used to connect to the database.
sTable	The name of the table that contains the marshaled information
sKey	The name of the column that is used as a key for the table
sProgID	The name of the object that has been stored in the table (that is: "Commerce.Dictionary" or "Commerce.OrderForm")
sMarshalColumn	The name of the column that contains the marshaled information. If this parameter is not specified, then DBStorage only maps existing fields to entries in the OrderForm or in the Dictionary that is passed to it.
sDateChanged	Name of a datetime-type column that should be set whenever a row in the database is changed

By default, a DBStorage object will try to map the individual fields inside a record to the entries of the same name in the Dictionary or OrderForm object that is associated with it (or created by it, when a reading operation is performed). If you specify a value for the sMarshalColumn parameter, then all the information in the Dictionary or OrderForm object will be marshaled to the column by that name.

The sKey parameter, on the other hand, is used to specify a field that should be searched upon when looking for a specific record. This field must contain unique values. Finally, sProgID is used to tell DBStorage which component has been (or should be) saved in the table. The valid values are "Commerce.Dictionary" and "Commerce.OrderForm".

Let's now make an example. In Chapter 8, we saw that the typical order database table (*store*_order) contains the following fields:

```
order_id
marshaled_order
shopper_id
date_changed
```

We also learned that order_id is a unique identifier for the order, shopper_id is the unique identifier for the shopper, marshaled_order contains the marshaled order information (that we now know to be stored in an OrderForm object) and date_changed is a datetime-type field that contains the timestamp corresponding to the latest change to a particular row.

Let's now see how a DBStorage object can be initialized to access this table:

```
Set dbsDBStorage = Server.CreateObject("Commerce.DBStorage")

dbsDBStorage.InitStorage(dSiteDictionary.DefaultConnectionString, "store_order", _
    "order_id", "Commerce.OrderForm", "marshalled_order", "date_changed")
```

As you can see, here we are using the order_id field as the value for sKey. Because we said earlier that the order ID is a unique value that is assigned to each order, we can use it to retrieve an individual order.

It's important to understand that, when we write to the database, all the fields in the table will be automatically filled by DBStorage. The values for order_id and shopper_id, in particular, are mapped directly by the component from the pairs in the OrderForm.

Reading From the Database

Reading data from the database into an object is a relatively easy operation. If the data you are looking for can be accessed through the default value for sKey that you specified when calling InitStorage, and if you know that key to be unique, then you can use the GetData method:

- ❑ **Syntax:**
  DBStorage.GetData (*oReserved*, sKey)

- ❑ **Parameters:**
oReserved	Should be Null. Included for compatibility with previous versions of SSCE
sKey	The value for the default key that identifies the object that is being searched for in the database

In our example, GetData will look in the database for all the records that contain the value that we pass in the order_id column. As we now that value to be unique, we can also assume that only one record will be found; therefore, as a result, the DBStorage object will only return one OrderForm object.

If, by any chance, the object were to find more than one record, then `GetData` would return Null (unfortunately, the same happens if `GetData` is unsuccessful in finding any records). If we are indeed looking at this possibility, we should consider using `LookupMultipleData`:

❑ **Syntax:**
   DBStorage.LookupMultipleData (*oReserved, sColumns, Values*)

❑ **Parameters:**

oReserved	Should be Null. Included for compatibility with older versions of SSCE.
sColumns	An array containing the names of the columns that should be used as keys
Values	An array containing the values that should be searched for

As you can see, this method is significantly more complex than `GetData`. The `sColumns` and `Values` arrays must have the same upper and lower bounds (they must, therefore, have the same size); they are used by `LookupMultipleData` to create a select statement that looks like:

```
Select * from sTable where sColumns (1) = Values (1) and sColumns (2) = Values
(2)...
```

Of course, this is the simplified version, but the idea here is that `LookupMultipleData` will try to match every member of the `sColumns` array with the corresponding entry in the `Values` array to build a search query. If the lower and upper bounds of the two arrays do not correspond, or if no records are found, then `LookupMultipleData` returns Null; otherwise, the method returns a `SimpleList` object that contains as many `OrderForm` or `Dictionary` objects as the number of records found.

Going back to our example, we could use `LookupMultipleData` as a method to retrieve all the orders for a single customer:

```
dim sColumns (1), sValues (1)

sColumns (1) = "shopper_id"
sValues (1) = "3EFAVJSLAIJDEOO3JFLIFJJE32F23"

Set slResult = dbsDBStorage.LookupMultipleData (Null, sColumns, sValues)
```

Finally, `DBStorage` offers one more function that acts just like `LookupMultipleData`, with the difference that it only returns one row:

❑ **Syntax:**
   DBStorage.LookupData (*oReserved, sColumn, Value*)

❑ **Parameters:**

OReserved	Should be Null. Included for compatibility with older versions of SSCE.
Scolumn	Name of the column to be used as key
Values	Value that should be searched for

Writing to the Database

When writing an object to the database, you could be either creating a new record, or updating an existing one. In either case, DBStorage has the right method for you!

If you are storing a Dictionary or OrderForm object in the database for the first time, you should use the InsertData method:

❑ **Syntax:**
DBStorage.InsertData (*oReserved*, *Data*)

❑ **Parameters:**

oReserved	Should be Null. Included for compatibility with older versions of SSCE.
Data	The object that should be saved. Must be the same type of object as specified in the sProgID parameter of InitStorage

Keep in mind that InsertData automatically maps certain values to the corresponding fields in the database – this should include the values that you intend to use as keys.

If you need to update a record that already exists, you would typically read the object from the database first, make modifications to it, and then call the CommitData method:

❑ **Syntax:**
DBStorage.CommitData (*oReserved*, *Data*)

❑ **Parameters:**

OReserved	Should be Null. Included for compatibility with older versions of SSCE.
Data	The object that should be saved. Must be the same type of object as specified in the sProgID parameter of InitStorage

Deleting Data from the Database

You can delete data from a DBStorage database table in one of two ways. If your goal is to simply empty the contents of the marshaled object, without actually eliminating the database record where it sits, then you should use DeleteData:

❑ **Syntax:**
DBStorage.DeleteData (*oReserved*, *Data*)

❑ **Parameters:**

oReserved	Should be Null. Included for compatibility with older versions of SSCE.
Data	The object that should be deleted. Must be the same type of object as specified in the sProgID parameter of InitStorage

DeleteData will look for the correct record in the database, then load the corresponding object into memory. The pairs in the object that have corresponding pairs in the object passed as a value of the Data parameter are subsequently deleted and, finally, the object is written back to the database.

This method is useful when deleting a whole record is not convenient; for example, when a user purchases something, his or her basket should be *emptied*, and not *deleted* – simply removing the product information from the `Items` collection is a more efficient solution.

For those cases in which you *really* want to get rid of a whole record, however, there is the `DeleteDataKey` method, which gets rid of an entire row by specifying a value to search for in the key column for the object:

❑ **Syntax:**
DBStorage.DeleteDataKey (*oReserved, Value*)

❑ **Parameters:**

oReserved	Should be Null. Included for compatibility with older versions of SSCE
Value	The Value in the key for the object that identifies the row to be deleted

Mapping Values Between a DBStorage-Compatible Object and the Database

Let's suppose for a moment that you want to map certain values for which you are using different names in the `OrderForm` or `Dictionary` object than in the database. As `DBStorage` by default only maps fields that have the same name on both ends of the rope, you will have to use the `Mapping` property:

❑ **Syntax:**
Public Property DBStorage.Mapping (*sObjectField*)

❑ **Parameters:**

sObjectField	The name part of the name/value pair in the object passed to `DBStorage` that has to be mapped

All you have to do is assign the name of the field in the database table that has to be mapped to `Mapping`, specifying which name/value pair you want to map to it as the value of the `sObjectField` parameter. For example, the following line of code tells a `DBStorage` component that the field ShipToName in the database table maps to the **ship_to_name** in an `OrderForm` object:

```
dbsDBStorage.Mapping ("ship_to_name") = "ShipToName"
```

Should You Use DBStorage?

In the previous chapter, we mentioned how data marshaling is an expensive operation in terms of computational burden. At the same time, if all the data is marshaled to the database, performing searches on that database becomes a nightmare – you have to load each record, decode it and check for the value or the values you are looking for manually until you find what you are looking for. Even if you let `DBStorage` do the job for you, the procedure won't change much.

Thus, if you're serious about developing fast and reliable sites using SSCE, you will end up having to discard the `DBStorage` component. This is not just a quirk of my oversized ego talking here – the SSCE team itself has declared the `DBStorage` an outlaw in their white paper on improving the performance of SSCE sites, which we'll examine in Chapter 16.

> You can find the white paper on improving SSCE's performance at
> http://www.microsoft.com/siteserver/commerce/DeployAdmin/VolcanoCoffee.htm

User Interface Components

The components that we will look at next are either dedicated to handling the input and output of data to and from the user, or to transforming the information stored in the database according to certain rules.

The DataFunctions Component

The goal of the `DataFunctions` component is to solve two classic problems that Internet developers – and in particular EC site developers – face continuously. First, the need to localize currency values, numbers, dates and so on to a specific locale. Second, the necessity of validating that user input (or values that end up in the database, for example) falls within certain ranges.

The first problem in particular deserves considerable attention. Windows NT – being, after all an internationally recognized operating system – does support formatting rules for several locales, including 13 different versions of the Arabic language and 6 of the English language among others. The problem is that the operating system allows you to only set one locale at a time, and all the formatting functions provided by Windows use that locale by default. The only way to change it is to actually write a `DLL` that encapsulates all the relevant OS functionality; luckily, the SSCE team has done it for us!

Choosing the Right Locale

According to the latest version of the MSDN library in my possession (the one distributed with Visual Studio 6.0), Windows supports a total of 107 locales. I thought that I would save you from listing them all – I have included them in the `i_Locales.asp` include file that you can download freely from the Wrox web site.

It is important to understand that a locale is not only tied to a specific language, but also to the conventions that people from a specific country or ethnic group share. For example, when considering the difference between Canada and the UK, although the languages are slightly different, what really matters to us is, for example, the fact that Canadians use dollars as their currency, whereas people from the UK use pounds.

To instruct a `DataFunctions` object to work with a specific locale, you can set the `Locale` property:

❑ **Syntax:**
Public Property DataFunctions.Locale

❑ **Parameters:**
None

For example, the following chunk of code creates a `DataFunctions` object and then uses the `i_locales.asp` file to set its locale to the identifier for Italy:

```
<!--#Include file="i_Locales.asp"-->

<%
    Set dfDataFunctions = Server.CreateObject ("Commerce.DataFunctions")
    dfDataFunctions.Locale = lItalianStandard
%>
```

Converting Values

`DataFunctions` provides a set of methods for converting a string to a specific data type. In general, all these methods follow the same principle: they return a value of the specified type if they are able to convert the string; otherwise, they return Null.

We can divide the conversion methods into two groups. The date and time methods convert a string that either contains a date, or a time, or a combination of the two to a `Date` or `DateTime` variant:

- ❑ **Syntax:**
  DataFunctions.ConvertDateString (*sDate*, *iLocale*)

- ❑ **Parameters:**
sDate	A string containing a valid date expression for the locale used
iLocale	The locale to be used. If this parameter is not specified, then the method uses the default locale specified for the object

- ❑ **Syntax:**
  DataFunctions.ConvertTimeString (*sTime*, *iLocale*)

- ❑ **Parameters:**
sTime	A string containing a valid time expression for the locale used
iLocale	The locale to be used. If this parameter is not specified, then the method uses the default locale specified for the object

- ❑ **Syntax:**
  DataFunctions.ConvertDateTimeString (*sDateTime*, *iLocale*)

- ❑ **Parameters:**
sDateTime	A string containing a valid date and time expression for the locale used
iLocale	The locale to be used. If this parameter is not specified, then the method uses the default locale specified for the object

All these conversion functions should work fine – with a couple of exceptions. When converting values that are formatted according to the locales for Latvia and Bulgaria, it might be possible that the conversion methods return Null even if the formatting is correct. In that case, you will have to remove the final portion of the date string that is used as a "postfix" to the date itself.

The other group of conversion functions that can be used is dedicated to converting numbers. The three methods in this category can convert integers, floating-point numbers and currency values:

❑ **Syntax:**
DataFunctions.ConvertIntegerString (*sInteger*, *iLocale*)

❑ **Parameters:**

sInteger	A string containing a valid integer for the locale used
iLocale	The locale to be used. If this parameter is not specified, then the method uses the default locale specified for the object

❑ **Syntax:**
DataFunctions.ConvertFloatString (*sFloat*, *iLocale*)

❑ **Parameters:**

sFloat	A string containing a valid floating-point number expression for the locale used
iLocale	The locale to be used. If this parameter is not specified, then the method uses the default locale specified for the object

❑ **Syntax:**
DataFunctions.ConvertMoneyStringToNumber (*sMoney*, *iLocale*)

❑ **Parameters:**

sMoney	A string containing a valid currency-value expression for the locale used
iLocale	The locale to be used. If this parameter is not specified, then the method uses the default locale specified for the object

Formatting Values

While the conversion methods can be used to validate the conversion from the user's input to a common format, whether you are in China or in the U.S., formatting methods perform the opposite operation and can be used to convert values from common format to their string representation for a specific locale.

Once again, we can divide them into two groups – date functions and number/currency functions. The date formatting methods act on `Date` and `DateTime` values and return strings:

❑ **Syntax:**
DataFunctions.Date (*dDate*, *iLocale*)

❑ **Parameters:**

dDate	A valid Date expression
iLocale	The locale to be used. If this parameter is not specified, then the method uses the default locale specified for the object

❑ **Syntax:**
DataFunctions.Time (*tTime*, *iLocale*)

❑ **Parameters:**

tTime	A valid Time expression
iLocale	The locale to be used. If this parameter is not specified, then the method uses the default locale specified for the object

❑ **Syntax:**
DataFunctions.DateTime (*dDateTime*, *iLocale*)

❑ **Parameters:**

dDateTime	A valid DateTime expression
iLocale	The locale to be used. If this parameter is not specified, then the method uses the default locale specified for the object

On the other hand, the number/money functions act on integers, floating-point numbers and currency values:

❑ **Syntax:**
DataFunctions.Number (*iNumber*, *iLocale*)

❑ **Parameters:**

iNumber	A valid Integer or Long expression
iLocale	The locale to be used. If this parameter is not specified, then the method uses the default locale specified for the object

❑ **Syntax:**
DataFunctions.Float (*fNumber*, *iLocale*)

❑ **Parameters:**

fNumber	A valid Float expression
iLocale	The locale to be used. If this parameter is not specified, then the method uses the default locale specified for the object

❑ **Syntax:**
DataFunctions.Money (*mNumber*, *iLocale*)

❑ **Parameters:**

mNumber	A valid Currency expression
iLocale	The locale to be used. If this parameter is not specified, then the method uses the default locale specified for the object

Keep in mind that both the currency conversion and formatting methods do not use the standard OLE type for currency values that is used by Visual Basic, but rather the one that is used by SSCE to store currency values in the database. As a result, all the values are in the base monetary unit for the selected locale: this means cents for the dollar.

The Naked String

Don't you hate when you ask for a credit card number and the user types in something like:

```
  "      4000 13071535      4079       "
```

I have my own personal opinion of those people, which really isn't suitable for a G-rated book! Luckily for us, DataFunctions provides the CleanString method that helps us a little bit in solving this problem:

❏ **Syntax:**
DataFunctions.CleanString (*sString, iMinLength, iMaxLength, bStripWhiteSpaces, bStripReturn, iCase, iLocale*)

❏ **Parameters:**

SString	The string that has to be "cleaned"
IMinLength	The minimum length of the string
IMaxLength	The maximum length of the string
bStripWhiteSpaces	True if CleanString should remove all the white spaces characters in the string
bStripReturn	True if CleanString should remove all the CR+LF pairs – which are inserted when you press on the *Return* button – from the string
Icase	Controls how the case of the string is modified. If its value is 0, then no modification is made; if it is 1, then the entire string is converted to uppercase; if it is 2, then the entire string is converted to lowercase
ILocale	The locale to be used. If this parameter is not specified, then the method uses the default locale specified for the object

CleanString returns the value of sString modified according to the instructions given. You could even call it the Naked String.

Validation Methods

To conclude our exploration of planet DataFunctions, let's take a look at its validation methods. These can be used to make sure that the user input falls within certain acceptable ranges. You will usually use them in combination with the conversion methods – first, you convert the strings to a recognizable value, then you will check for its accuracy.

There are three validation functions offered by DataFunctions – one for integer values, one for floating-point values and one for Date or DateTime values. Keep in mind that, once converted, a currency value becomes an integer, too.

❏ **Syntax:**
DataFunctions.ValidateNumber (*iNumber, iMinimumValue, iMaximumValue*)

❏ **Parameters:**

INumber	A valid Integer expression
iMinimumValue	The minimum valid value for the expression
iMaximumValue	The maximum valid value for the expression

❑ **Syntax:**
DataFunctions.ValidateFloat (*fNumber*, *fMinimumValue*, *fMaximumValue*)

❑ **Parameters:**

FNumber	A valid `Float` expression
fMinimumValue	The minimum valid value for the expression
fMaximumValue	The maximum valid value for the expression

❑ **Syntax:**
DataFunctions.ValidateDateTime (*dtDateTime*, *dtMinimumValue*, *dtMaximumValue*)

❑ **Parameters:**

dtDateTime	A valid `DateTime` expression
fMinimumValue	The minimum valid value for the expression
fMaximumValue	The maximum valid value for the expression

All these functions return `True` if the value passed falls within the specified range and is of the right type, `False` otherwise.

The MessageManager Component

Another problem connected with the localization of a store is the display of error or communication messages in different languages. Although English is a language that is universally recognized, this doesn't mean that all of your customers will understand it; therefore, you should be able to display the same message in the language chosen by the user.

SSCE lets you do this through the `MessageManager` component, which is essentially a collection of named strings. `MessageManager` is used throughout the basic site created by SSCE, and especially in the Order Processing Pipeline to produce error messages related to the ordering process. However, you are free (and encouraged, if I may say so) to use it anywhere in the site, as we'll see in the next chapter.

Selecting a Language

Before you can use a `MessageManager` object, you need to specify what language or languages it will use. This is done through the `AddLanguage` method:

❑ **Syntax:**
MessageManager.AddLanguage (*sLanguageName*, *iLocale*)

❑ **Parameters:**

sLanguageName	An arbitrarily selected string that contains a unique identifier for the language (for example: "Canada", "USA", "Italy", and so on)
ILocale	The locale identifier for the language

You will need a call to `AddLanguage` for every language that you want the system to use. The locale identifier is a number picked from the list that we saw earlier on in the chapter while we talked about the `DataFunctions` component.

Even though you will only need the value of sLanguageName to identify a particular language for your calls to MessageManager, the *iLocale* parameter is just as important – you can use it, for example, to know what locale you should be using in your calls to DataFunctions for the language that is being used to print out messages. Quite convenient, don't you think?

You can also instruct the MessageManager object to use a default language. This will make it easier for you to write code, as you won't have to specify a language every time you will be asking for a message. To specify a default language, use the DefaultLanguage property:

❑ **Syntax:**
Public Property MessageManager.DefaultLanguage

❑ **Parameters:**
None

All you have to do is assign to it a string that corresponds to the identifiers for the language you want to use by default. Remember that the identifiers are compared using a case-sensitive algorithm, thus "usa" is different from "Usa" or "USA".

Retrieving Information

There are two pieces of information that you can retrieve from a MessageManager: a message and a locale identifier. As we mentioned earlier, you would typically need the latter for your localized calls to a DataFunctions objects; you can get it by calling GetLocale:

❑ **Syntax:**
MessageManager.GetLocale (*sLanguageName*)

❑ **Parameters:**
sLanguageName   Optional. The string corresponding to the language that MessageManager should return the locale identifier for.

You can feed this method's output directly to any method of a DataFunctions object.

As for the messages, you will have to add them before you can retrieve them! This is done through the AddMessage method:

❑ **Syntax:**
MessageManager.AddMessage (*sMessageName, sMessage, sLanguageName*)

❑ **Parameters:**
sMessageName   A string that will be associated
sMessage   The message itself
sLanguageName   The language identifier string for the chosen language. If you
      don't specify this value, MessageManager will use the default
      language specified for the object

As you may have already noticed, the `MessageManager` behaves like a collection object that only accepts string name/value pairs. You can use the `GetMessage` method to retrieve a specific message:

❑ **Syntax:**
MessageManager.GetMessage (*sMessageName, sLanguageName*)

❑ **Parameters:**

sMessageName	A string that will be associated
sLanguageName	The language identifier string for the chosen language. If you don't specify this value, `MessageManager` will use the default language specified for the object

`GetMessage` returns a string that corresponds to the name specified in *sMessageName*.

Messages used by SSCE

We mentioned above that `MessageManager` messages are most often used during the order process to report errors to the user. SSCE defines a few of these messages by default, as we will see in the next chapter. Here's a list of them:

MessageName	Message type
pur_badplacedprice	The price of an item in the basket does not correspond to the price in the database
pur_badhandling	The handling cost for the order cannot be computed
pur_badpayment	The payment authorization code has not been set
pur_badshipping	The shipping cost for the order cannot be computed
pur_badsku	The SKU of an item does not correspond to an existing product in the database
pur_badtax	The tax for the order cannot be computed
pur_badverify	The data in the `OrderForm` has been modified and the user must review the order before being able to continue
pur_noitems	There are no items in the order
pur_out_of_stock	At least one of the items in the order is out of stock

I'm sure that most of these values explain themselves. Perhaps the only one you will want to know about is pur_badverify, which happens when the data included in the order changes during the purchase process in a way that might affect the nature of the order itself. This includes, for example, a change in the price of one of the items (for good or, especially, for bad), and so on. Always keep in mind that, once they have entered their credit card number, your customers will expect to pay exactly what they last saw on their screen. Therefore, you must notify them *before* you charge their credit cards, or you'll receive some nasty calls!

The StandardSManager Component

While we were discussing the `OrderForm` object, we encountered a very important parameter called **ShopperID**. This parameter is used to identify a customer during his or her visit, or in subsequent visits, and particular care must be taken in making sure that it is absolutely unique within your store.

SSCE stores can handle Shopper IDs through the `StandardSManager` component, which takes care of generating, storing and retrieving those pieces of information. The storage and retrieval can be done using one (or both) of two methods: through a cookie and through the URL request parameters.

You are probably already familiar with cookies. A cookie is a small piece of information that is sent to the browser. The browser retains it for a period that varies from the duration of the user session to an indefinite amount of time, and returns it upon request (as long as the requesting server belongs to an authorized domain).

As you can see, cookies are pretty safe but, due to a mix of misleading media coverage and several bugs that have afflicted the major browsers, they are not very popular among the general public. Many people, concerned with the safety of their information – and not knowing any better – turn off their browser's support for cookies, making a user retention system based only on those useless.

As for the URL query string parameters, you have certainly seen – and used – those in the past. Let's for example consider the following URL:

http://store.wrox.com/default.asp?shopperid=REW241OIJ212OIJAFDI244J

Clearly, this URL opens the page `default.asp` on the HTTP server at the address store.wrox.com. This leaves us with the portion after the question mark, which is a *parameter* that we can retrieve using the `Request` intrinsic object. This works fine, even if the user's browser has been instructed to refuse cookies. However, it will be impossible to remember who our shoppers are when they return to the site, because their Shopper IDs will be lost (usually, the entrance point to the site is some easy-to-remember address, such as www.wrox.com).

Those of you who know ASP better might be asking themselves why the shopper ID is not stored in the `Session` intrinsic ASP object. Well, the reason is twofold. First of all, because the HTTP protocol is stateless (that is, it forgets who its clients are between one connection and the next one), `Session` variables have to be cookie-based. This makes the `Session` object an inconsistent storage medium, which will not work for those customers who have their browser set to refuse cookies. In addition, the information collected into the `Session` object is stored in the server machine's own memory; this makes it impossible to use the `Session` object in a scenario where more than one server is used to respond to the same address (this configuration is known as "clustering").

The system used by SSCE stores all the information in a database, while the Shopper ID can be easily retrieved through the URL query string parameters or through the use of cookies, both of which are methods suitable for any clustering configuration (as long, of course, as all the HTTP servers have access to the database that contains the user information).

Initializing StandardSManager Objects

In order to save system resources, you will want to make the `StandardSManager` object that you will use in your own store an Application-wide object (SSCE does this for us when we create a store, as we'll see in the next chapter). In addition, other SSCE components will expect to find a `StandardSManager` object in the `Application` object, under the **MSCSShopperManager** key – which makes for a *compelling* reason to create the object in the `global.asa` file of your store.

In order to initialize the object, you must call the `InitManager` method, which takes care of telling the object what store it's working for and what method should be used to store (and retrieve) the shopper IDs:

❑   **Syntax:**
    StandardSManager.InitManager (*sStoreName, sMode*)

❑   **Parameters:**

sStoreName	The short name of the store. Can be retrieved from the Site Dictionary
sMode	Instructs the object as to how shopper IDs should be stored and retrieved.

The *sMode* parameter can assume one of the following values:

cookie	The shopper IDs are written to and read from the cookies.
url	The shopper IDs are written to and read from the URL query string
cookieurl	The shopper IDs are written both to the URL query string and to the browser's cookies. When reading, the object attempts to retrieve shopper ID first from the cookies, then, if unsuccessful, from the URL query string
urlcookie	The shopper IDs are written both to the URL query string and to the browser's cookies. When reading, the object attempts to retrieve shopper ID first from the URL query string, then, if unsuccessful, from the browser's cookies

Creating, Reading and Writing Shopper IDs

To create a shopper ID, you can use the `CreateShopperID` method:

❑   **Syntax:**
    StandardSManager.CreateShopperID()

❑   **Parameters:**
    None

`CreateShopperID` returns a string that can be used to identify the current user in a unique manner. Keep in mind that you should not attempt to retrieve the shopper ID on your own – SSCE already provides all the functions you need.

Although `StandardSManager` provides a set of functions that you can use to read and store shopper IDs, you should use the functions provided by the `Page` component, which we will see in the next section.

The Page Component

One of the most ubiquitous components provided by SSCE is `Page`, which handles several HTTP- and HTML-related functions. These include, for example, requesting data from the URL query string, reading and saving shopper IDs, and creating HTML form objects.

Handling Shopper IDs

`Page` offers two functions that can be used to read and write shopper IDs respectively. `GetShopperID` retrieves a shopper ID according to the rules established when initializing the site's `StandardSManager` object:

❑   **Syntax:**
   Page.GetShopperID()

❑   **Parameters:**
   None

At the same rate, the `PutShopperID` stores a shopper ID created by `StandardSManager`:

❑   **Syntax:**
   Page.PutShopperID (*sShopperID*)

❑   **Parameters:**
   sShopperID   The shopper ID that must be stored

The `Page` component stores and retrieves information either to the browser's cookies, or into the URL query string, or in both. The name of the parameter or cookie in which these are stored is specified by a variable stored in the `Application` intrinsic ASP object under the name MSCSIDURLKey. By default, SSCE sets this value to "mscssiteid".

In order to be able to read and write Shopper IDs, a `Page` object needs to be able to locate the `StandardSManager` object for a particular store. As we mentioned before, the latter must be stored in the `Application` object under the name MSCSShopperManager.

Creating HTML Form Elements

Forms are the most-used interactive elements of HTML. They allow the server to collect and elaborate upon information from the user in an easy and intuitive fashion. However, writing forms is rated among the least interesting parts of HTML development (at least by me!)

Although it can't do miracles, the `Page` object can facilitate the creation of checkboxes, radio buttons and drop-down lists. Let's consider checkboxes and radio buttons first; when declaring a checkbox, you will write some code similar to the following:

```
<INPUT TYPE=checkbox NAME="Check1" VALUE="Yes">
```

Obviously, this line of code will only cause the browser to draw a checkbox that is always unchecked. Often, however, you will want to write a checkbox that is checked or unchecked depending on the value of a particular value; in that case, this could be your code:

```
<INPUT TYPE=checkbox NAME="Check1" VALUE="Yes"
    <% If Check1 = True then %>checked<% end if %>>
```

Try writing that ten times, and you will appreciate the practicality of the `Page.Check` method:

❑ **Syntax:**
Page.Check (*bValue*)

❑ **Parameters:**
bValue   A Boolean value. `True` if the checkbox should be checked,
                             `False` otherwise

`Check` returns the string value "CHECKED" if the Boolean condition expressed by *bValue* is `True`. Here is an example:

```
<% Set pPage = Server.CreateObject ("Commerce.Page") %>

<INPUT TYPE=checkbox NAME="Check1" VALUE="Yes" <% = pPage.Check (Check1 = True)
%>>
```

At the same rate, creating drop-down listboxes can be a painful experience, especially if you want to select the default value. For example, consider this piece of code:

```
<SELECT NAME="Select1">
    <OPTION VALUE="Option 1" <% if Option = "Option 1" then %>SELECTED<% end if
%>>Option 1
    <OPTION VALUE="Option 2" <% if Option = "Option 2" then %>SELECTED<% end if
%>>Option 2
    <OPTION VALUE="Option 3" <% if Option = "Option 3" then %>SELECTED<% end if
%>>Option 3
    <OPTION VALUE="Option 4" <% if Option = "Option 4" then %>SELECTED<% end if
%>>Option 4
    <OPTION VALUE="Option 5" <% if Option = "Option 5" then %>SELECTED<% end if
%>>Option 5
</SELECT>
```

As you can imagine, it takes a while to write this code, and the result is not elegant at all. Luckily, the `Page.Option` method can be used to take care of the part that determines whether a particular option should be selected:

❑ **Syntax:**
Page.Option (*Value1, Value2*)

❑ **Parameters:**
Value1   Any value. This value will appear in the HTML that is
                             generated, in the `VALUE=` field
Value2   Any value of the same type as *Value1*. This is the variable
                             that is checked to determine the current value.

This method returns the string "**SELECTED**" if `Value1` equals `Value2`. Going back to our piece of code:

```
<SELECT NAME="Select1">
    <% = Page.Option (Option, "Option 1") %>Option 1
    <% = Page.Option (Option, "Option 2") %>Option 2
    <% = Page.Option (Option, "Option 3") %>Option 3
    <% = Page.Option (Option, "Option 4") %>Option 4
    <% = Page.Option (Option, "Option 5") %>Option 5
</SELECT>
```

Retrieving Information From the URL Query String

As you will be using forms to collect information from the user, you will also have to retrieve the values stored inside the forms' elements from the query string or from the HTTP parameters. As you probably know, the `Request` ASP intrinsic object provides a few methods that can be used for this purpose. Their main disadvantage, however, is in the fact that they do not provide validation, whereas the `Page` component provides several values that can be used to retrieve, and at the same time validate, information from the query string or HTTP parameters.

There are a total of eight `Request` methods in the `Page` component:

❑ **Syntax:**
Page.RequestDate (*sParameterName, dDefaultValue, dLowDate, dHighDate, iLocale*)

Page.RequestDateTime (*sParameterName, dtDefaultValue, dtLowDateTime, dtHighDateTime, iLocale*)

Page.RequestDefault (*sParameterName, sDefaultValue*)

Page.RequestFloat (*sParameterName, fDefaultValue, fLowValue, fHighValue, iLocale*)

Page.RequestRequestMoneyAsNumber (*sParameterName, iDefaultValue, iLowValue, iHighValue, iLocale*)

Page.RequestNumber (*sParameterName, iDefaultValue, iLowValue, iHighValue, iLocale*)

Page.RequestString (*sParameterName, sDefaultValue, iMinLength, iMaxLength, bStripWhiteSpaces, bStripReturn, iCase, iLocale*)

Page.RequestTime (*sParameterName, tDefaultValue, tLowValue, tHighValue, iLocale*)

□ **Parameters:**

sParameterName	The name of the URL query string parameter or HTTP parameter to be retrieved (input field on a form). The method will look for the parameter first in the URL query string, and then in the HTTP parameters
dDefaultValue	A valid date expression to be used as the default value if the parameter specified does not exist or if it contains no value. If no value is specified for **dDefaultValue** and the parameter doesn't exist or contains no value, then `RequestDate` returns Null.
dLowDate	A valid date expression to be used as the lower limit for the validation check
dHighDate	A valid date expression to be used as the upper limit for the validation check
iLocale	A locale identifier. If no value is specified, then the validation method will use the default locale specified for the store's `DataFunctions` object
dtDefaultValue	A valid `datetime` expression to be used as the default value if the parameter specified does not exist or if it contains no value. If no value is specified for **dtDefaultValue** and the parameter doesn't exist or contains no value, then `RequestDateTime` returns Null.
dtLowDateTime	A valid `datetime` expression to be used as the lower limit for the validation check
dtHighDateTime	A valid `datetime` expression to be used as the upper limit for the validation check
sDefaultValue	The default string to be returned if the parameter specified does not exist or if it contains no value. If no value is specified and the parameter doesn't exist or contains no value, then `RequestDefault` and `RequestString` return Null
fDefaultValue	A valid float expression to be used as the default value if the parameter specified does not exist or if it contains no value. If no value is specified for **fDefaultValue** and the parameter doesn't exist or contains no value, then `RequestFloat` returns Null.
fLowValue	A valid `float` expression to be used as the lower limit for the validation check
fHighValue	A valid `float` expression to be used as the upper limit for the validation check
iDefaultValue	The default integer value to be returned if the parameter specified does not exist or if it contains no value. If no value is specified and the parameter doesn't exist or contains no value, then `RequestMoneyAsNumber` and `RequestInteger` return Null

iLowValue	A valid `integer` expression to be used as the lower limit for the validation check
iHighValue	A valid `integer` expression to be used as the upper limit for the validation check
iMinLength	The minimum length of the string
iMaxLength	The maximum length of the string
bStripWhiteSpaces	`True` if white spaces should be eliminated (stripped) from the string. `False` otherwise
bStripReturn	`True` if return characters should be eliminated from the string. `False` otherwise
iCase	1 if the string should be converted to uppercase, 2 if it should be converted to lowercase. 0 causes no modification to be made to the case of the string
tDefaultValue	The default `time` value to be returned if the parameter specified does not exist or if it contains no value. If no value is specified and the parameter doesn't exist or contains no value, then `RequestTime` returns Null
tLowValue	A valid `time` expression to be used as the lower limit for the validation check
tHighValue	A valid `time` expression to be used as the upper limit for the validation check

All these methods return Null if the values retrieved by them do not satisfy the conditions expressed by their lower and upper limits. I am sure that almost all the methods are self-explanatory, perhaps with the exception of `RequestDefault`, which corresponds to the simple call to the `Request` object to retrieve a string value without any validation.

Keep in mind that all these functions rely on the fact that a `DataFunction` object has been created in the store's `global.asa` and stored in the `Application` object under the name MSCSDataFunctions. SSCE does this by default when a new store is created, and you should maintain this convention in your own customized stores if you intend to use the `Page` component.

Creating URLs

Putting together a URL can be a tricky task – parameters have to be taken into consideration, the correct protocol has to be used, and so forth. The `Page` component provides several methods that come to our help.

First of all, let's see how we can affect the way that URLs are composed. Most often, we will want to establish whether we want to really use a secure channel, which requires the https:// prefix, while we are testing our stores. In fact, to be able to use secure communications, we have to obtain a security certificate from a certificate authority, which requires time and money, and is usually just about the last thing we do before going live.

At the same time, we cannot ignore the fact that, if we hard-coded the normal http:// prefix everywhere, we might forget to change some of its occurrences when we later go live, with the risk of leaving pages that contain sensitive information unprotected. The solution to this problem is to use a global function – stored in a file included by all the pages of our store – that encapsulates the functionality of the SURLPrefix method or of the SURL method:

❑ **Syntax:**
Public Property Page.SURLPrefix

❑ **Parameters:**
None

❑ **Syntax:**
Page.SURL (*sFileName, Parameters...*)

❑ **Parameters:**
sFileName	The name of the file that the URL should point to
Parameters	A set of name/value pairs that will form the URL query string

The result of SURLPrefix and SURL varies depending on the value of the **DisableHTTPS** value stored in the Site Dictionary. If that is 1, then the prefix used to create the URL will be a simple http://, otherwise the Page component will assume that the communication should be secure and the https:// prefix should be used.

While SURLPrefix only returns the secure host name for the server where the site is on (for example: https://www.wrox.com), the SURL method makes it possible to compose entire URLs very easily. This is done by specifying a set of name/value pairs after the name of the file that the URL should point to. For example, consider this call made within the Clocktower store on a computer called Hamilton:

```
pPage.SURL ("default.asp", "par1", "1", "par2", "2", "par3", "3")
```

It will cause the following output to be returned (assuming that the **DisableHTTPS** value is 0):

https://Hamilton/clocktower/default.asp?par1=1&par2=2&par3=3

If the StandardSManager object for the store has been set to store the shopper ID into the URL, SURL (and all the other URL building functions of the Page component) will automatically append the shopper ID to the URL:

https://Hamilton/clocktower/default.asp?mscsshopperid=D3T2APFZFJIEO23D9D2P3&par1=1&par2=2&par3=3

If you need to create a plain URL, which will not be affected by the value of the **DisableHTTPS** parameter, you can use the URLPrefix and URL methods – the same considerations above apply to them as well.

It is also possible to create only parts of an URL; this can be useful in those situations where the URL and SURL methods cannot be used. To create the part of a query string that contains all the parameters, for example, you can use the URLArgs methods:

❑ **Syntax:**
Page.URLArgs (*Parameters*...)

❑ **Parameters:**
Parameters   A set of name/value pairs that will form the URL query
string

The parameter list is built the same way as for the URL and SURL methods, only this time the shopper ID is never attached to the generated string. For example:

```
pPage.URLArgs ("par1", "1", "par2", "2", "par3", "3")
```

always returns:

par1=1&par2=2&par3=3

regardless of how the StandardSManager object for the site has been set. If you are interested in retrieving the shopper ID as well, you can use the URLShopperArgs method, which has exactly the same syntax as URLArgs. A call similar to the one above to URLShopperArgs, assuming that the StandardSManager object for the site has been set to store the shopper ID in the URL query string, will return the following:

mscsshopperid=D3T2APFZFJIEO23D9D2P3&par1=1&par2=2&par3=3

Finally, it might be useful to retrieve also the name of the virtual directory where the site's files are stored – this is essential if we want to build URLs that point to our own store! The VirtualDirectory property comes to our help:

❑ **Syntax:**
Public Property Page.VirtualDirectory

❑ **Parameters:**
None

As you might have imagined, VirtualDirectory returns the name of the virtual directory where the site is stored (for example: clocktower).

What You See is What You Pay?

As we have mentioned more than once throughout the book, in the next chapter we will be talking about the Order Processing pipeline. As its use pervades Site Server so deeply, however, we are often forced to reference it even if we haven't talked about it yet.

Even the Page object ties with it, by providing a set of functions that can be used to make sure that certain information stored in an OrderForm does not change between, for example, the payment page and the confirmation page.

You will probably be asking yourselves, how can the user change values in the basket without knowing it? Well, to quote a very interesting character from a Star Trek movie, "You think in such three-dimensional terms!" Don't forget that while the user is visiting the store using a browser, he or she could get to the payment page and, before making a purchase, open another browser and maybe add something to his or her basket, thus modifying the grand total of the order.

If the user clicks on the purchase button in the first browser, he or she will be under the impression that the old grand total will be charged to his or her credit card – a very wrong impression, because the total has now changed. As you can imagine, big trouble can arise from this problem, and it is both for the user's protections and for yours that the Page component provides a simple mechanism for verifying that the information in the OrderForm has not changed between any two pages.

The mechanism works by storing certain values taken from the OrderForm while the first page (that is: payment) is being created. The values are outputted in a set of HIDDEN HTML form tags and passed along to the second page through a GET or POST action. The second page picks them up and compares them against the new values in the processed OrderForm. If any change is detected, the Order Processing pipeline generates an error, and the store responds by returning to the first page and prompting the user to review his or her basket.

The HIDDEN tags are generated by the VerifyWith method:

- **Syntax:**
  Page.VerifyWith (Orderform, Arguments...)

- **Parameters:**

Orderform	The OrderForm object where the values have to extracted from
Arguments	One or more strings that contain the names of all the pairs that have to be extracted from the OrderForm object

Typically, the values that you will want to check against are the grand total of the order (for obvious reasons) and a value from the shipping address that will make it possible to determine if the shipping costs have changed, or if the current shipping method is available at all to the recipient of the order. In general, this means either the ship-to ZIP code or the ship-to state (or country). For example:

```
pPage.VerifyWith (MSCSOrderForm, "ship_to_zip", "_total_total")
```

will produce the following output:

```
<INPUT TYPE="HIDDEN" NAME="ship_to_zip" VALUE="90211">
<INPUT TYPE="HIDDEN" NAME="_total_total" VALUE="10320">
```

which means that the total value of the order is $103.20 and the ZIP code of the order's recipient is 90211.

VerifyWith can only be used with integer, floating-point and string variants. It will not work if you try to use it with date values or objects, even if the latter support property bags.

When you get to the second page, where you want to check that your information has not indeed been changed, you will have to move the information back into the OrderForm. This is done through the ProcessVerifyWith method of the Page component:

- ❑ **Syntax:**
  Page.ProcessVerifyWith (Orderform)

- ❑ **Parameters:**
  Orderform   The OrderForm object that contains the values that the form
  values will be compared with.

ProcessVerifyWith proceeds to write all the values into the _verify_with dictionary object inside the pipeline (which, because its name starts with an underscore character, will not be saved by the DBStorage component). These values are subsequently verified against the values in the OrderForm during pipeline processing. We'll take a look at how that happens in Chapter 10.

Encoding Functions

You are all probably familiar with the encoding functions that are provided by ASP, like Server.URLEncode. The Page component offers similar functions that perform a little better than their ASP counterparts.

The HTMLEncode method, for example, can be used to convert plain strings into HTML code. This is useful, especially when the string contains "dangerous" characters, like quotation marks, that can be misinterpreted by an HTML renderer.

- ❑ **Syntax:**
  Page.HTMLEncode (sString)

- ❑ **Parameters:**
  sString   A string value that contains the text to be converted

The only difference between Page.HTMLEncode and the ASP-intrinsic Server.HTMLEncode is in the fact that the former returns an empty string if *sString* is NULL, whereas the latter simply fails. It's not like we can't live without the method provided by SSCE, but it saves a lot of error handling!

To encode strings into text that can be used as part of a URL (generally in query parameters), we can use the Page. URLEncode method, which converts characters that are difficult to digest for a web server into healthier escape sequences:

- ❑ **Syntax:**
  Page.URLEncode (sString)

- ❑ **Parameters:**
  SString   A string value containing the text to be converted

Similar to HTMLEncode, URLEncode acts exactly as its ASP counterpart; the only difference, once again, is in the way the two methods handle NULL values.

Other Properties Provided by the Page Component

Before we bid our farewell to the `Page` component, it is time to take a look at another two of its properties that can be of interest. *SiteRoot*, as its name suggests, contains the name of the root folder where your store is located.

Context, on the other hand, contains the ASP context for the current page. The context contains interface pointers to all the intrinsic ASP objects, such as `Request`, `Server` and `Response`, and is something that you wouldn't use under normal circumstances. Some SSCE components, however (most notably, the ever present pipelines!) need to have a pointer to them in order for them to work properly.

Using the Predictor Component

In Chapter 4, we discussed briefly the possibility of making the shopping experience more profitable (for the owner of the EC site, that is) by providing cross-selling and up-selling functionality. SSCE provides the functionality needed for these services through the `Predictor` component.

`Predictor` works by comparing information regarding the user's "purchasing interests" – collected, for example, from the user's basket and navigation patterns – with a knowledge base of information collected from previous purchases made from the store itself. The result of this comparison is a set of "product recommendations" that the store can make to the user in order to complement the contents of his or her basket. Online bookstore Amazon.com has offered this feature for a while under the guise of the "People who bought this book also bought..." section of their product pages.

The first step in using the `Predictor` component is collecting the purchasing history information. This is a very essential step, because in the beginning `Predictor` won't be able to predict much due to the fact that it won't have any historic information to compare the user's data against.

Historical information is collected by adding rows to a database table that contains, as a minimum, the following columns:

- ❑ Shopper ID
- ❑ SKU
- ❑ Quantity

You can also choose to add a "date entered" field, which will let you delete obsolete entries. There is no special name that you are supposed to give to the table, although the MSPress sample, which features `Predictor` functionality, calls it mspress30_predictor_data.

Information regarding purchases is added to the table at the end of the purchasing process through – you guessed it – the Order Processing pipeline. It's a little early to talk about it, so we'll defer explanations to Chapter 10.

Initializing a Predictor Object

Generally, you will create a `Predictor` object as part of the ASP application initialization process. On initialization, the object will have to analyze the historical data in order to create a prediction knowledge base in memory (which is faster to access than data stored in a database table); because of this, you will only want one copy of it running in your store, which is available to all the users.

The `InitPredictor` method can be used to initialize a `Predictor` object:

❏ **Syntax:**
Predictor.InitPredictor (sDSN, sTable, sUserColumn, sSKUColumn, sQuantityColumn, iMaxMemory)

❏ **Parameters:**

sDSN	The name of the datasource to be used to access the table holding the historical purchase information
sTable	The name of the database table that contains the historical purchase information
sUserColumn	The name of the column that contains the user ID
sSKUColumn	The name of the column that contains the SKU
sQuantityColumn	The name of the column that contains the quantity of items purchased
iMaxMemory	The maximum memory in kilobytes that can be allocated by the `Predictor` component.

The data analysis that is performed at the beginning works by substantially merging all the products purchased, grouped by SKU, until either the whole knowledge base is complete or the maximum memory specified by the *iMaxMemory* parameter is reached. This should be no less than 1,000KB (approximately one MB), but the SSCE documentation recommends a size of at least 4MB.

If `InitPredictor` runs out of memory, it gives priority to the merged baskets that contain a higher variety of items, in order to ensure that the predictions will cover as many combinations as possible.

Predicting User Purchases

Once our `Predictor` object has been initialized, we can use it to make predictions. The first thing that we must do is to extract all the relevant information from the user's basket and store it in a `SimpleList` object containing one `Dictionary` object for each product. These `Dictionary` objects, in turn, should contain one entry called "SKU" and another one called "Quantity" – their values are obvious.

The method that returns predictions is called `GetPredictions`:

❑ **Syntax:**
Predictor.GetPredictions (sItems, iMaxPredictions, fPopularItemFilter, iRequiredMatches)

❑ **Parameters:**

SItems	The `SimpleList` object containing the user's purchasing interests
iMaxPredictions	The maximum number of predictions that should be returned by `GetPredictions`
fPopularItemFilter	A floating-point number between 0 and 1 that expresses the possibility that "popular" items could be removed (filtered) from the list of predictions. 0 means that no filtering should be done, while 1 means that popular items will be filtered out.
iRequiredMatches	The minimum number of baskets that a prediction must be matched with in order to be considered valid and returned by `GetPredictions`

There are two parameters here that deserve special attention. One is *fPopularItemFilter*, which can be used to decide whether certain items, which are very popular (that is, have been often bought by the shoppers in the knowledge base), should be included in predictions. The rationale behind this is that if these items are so popular, it is perhaps reasonable to assume that users are very familiar with them and therefore it makes very little sense to advertise them. Therefore, if you want to provide more focused prediction, set this parameter closer to 1, whereas if you want to emphasize the prediction of popular items, you should set it closer to 0.

The *iRequiredMatches* parameter, instead, determines how "certain" `GetPredictions` must be, before establishing that a prediction is realistic. This is done by measuring the number of occurrences in which the combination of products used to create the prediction is found. If this number is less than the value of *iRequiredMatches*, then the prediction is discarded. According to the SSCE documentation, you should use a value between 4 and 6 if your historical database contains a decent amount of information. Using a lower number will cause the predictions to be inconsistent, and could lead to actually duplicating the contents of a single user's basket (a wasps nest for privacy issues!), while a higher number might impair the functionality of `GetPredictions`, because it would make returning a prediction too difficult.

`GetPredictions` returns a `SimpleList` object that contains a `Dictionary` object for each prediction generated. Each `Dictionary` object contains the following name/value pairs:

❑ **SKU**
This is the SKU for the suggested item.

❑ **Weight**
Indicates the number of items that the user is likely to purchase. It can also be used to identify the level preference that the `Predictor` object believes the user will have in purchasing the item.

❑ **MatchSupport**
Indicates the number of merged baskets that were used to return the prediction. This value could be used to indicate the confidence level that `GetPredictions` had in returning a given prediction, but in this version it is set to the same value for all the predictions returned.

Extending the Predictor Component

With a little imagination, it is possible to extend the functionality of the `Predictor` component to other areas of work. After all, what is a SKU if not a unique key into a table? And what is a quantity if not a weight for a specific entry?

All these considerations can be used to make `Predictor` an all-purpose prediction engine. All you have to do is build a table with your own information, find something that might correspond to the required values (SKU – the primary key, quantity and user ID) and pass it along to a `Predictor` object.

For example, let's assume that we want to return a list of links that the user might want to click based on previous experience. We will have to build a historical data table similar to the following (we use a unique string to identify each link):

Name	Type	Description
ID	Varchar	The ID of the link
Count	INT	The number of times that the link was clicked by the user
SessionID	Varchar	A unique identifier for the user session

Instead of having to deal with SKUs, quantities and user IDs, we will consider only the link ID, the number of times that it was visited during any given session and a unique identifier for a user session. Keep in mind that it makes very little sense to tie the statistical sampling to a user, because of the nature of the data being collected. What matters to us is knowing which links were clicked during any given visit and for how many times, not by whom.

The session ID can be generated by using for example, a SQL trigger, or by means of a similar technique. It is not a good idea to use IIS sessions (they are tied to a single machine and will not work in a clustered environment); you will have to manually determine when a session ends. For example, you could carry the session ID along as a URL query string parameter, which will be lost when the user exits the site and then re-enters it by typing the URL manually.

Similarly, statistical information could be collected by adding a special parameter to the query string and trapping it through an include file that is included by all the pages in the store.

To initialize our `Predictor` object, we could use the following call to `InitPredictor`, which maps `ID` to the `SKU` column, `Count` to the `Quantity` column and `SessionID` to the `UserID` column:

```
Predictor.InitPredictor MSCSSite.DefaultConnection, "link_data", "SessionID",
"ID", "Count"
```

Once in the store, we can use the `GetPredictions` method to retrieve links that we can show, assuming that we have collected the count of all the links for the current users in the `LinkStats` `SimpleList` object, as described above, and that we have defined the maximum number of predictions to be returned in the `iMaxPredictions` local variable:

```
Set Predictions = Predictor.GetPredictions (LinkStats, iMaxPredictions, 0, 4)
```

As you can see, we set the value of *fPopularItemFilter* to 0 here because what we really want to do is to emphasize popular links and not assume that the users will know about them.

The `SimpleList` object returned by `GetPredictions` can be used to determine what links should be used (the ID will be stored in the SKU name/value pair) and how they should be sorted (using the Weight name/value pair, in descending order).

Resetting the Knowledge Base

If you are aiming pretty high in terms of uptime for your web servers, and you want to use the `Predictor` component, you will encounter a pretty serious problem – your historical data knowledge base will get obsolete.

To prevent this from happening, you will need to periodically re-initialize the `Predictor` object that is stored in your `Application` intrinsic ASP object. Even though no "re-initialize" method is provided, the correct way to do this is *not* to restart your machine, nor to delete the object in the `Application` and create a new one. Doing so will prevent the creation of an Application-wide object which will end up being slightly slower than the one that was created in the `Application_OnStart` event handler found in your store's `global.asa` file. Instead, you should just call `InitPredictor` again from a page that can only be called from the store manager (to prevent users from continuously re-initializing your knowledge base).

> As the initialization operation might take time, it's a good idea to lock the `Application` object (using the `Lock` and `Unlock` methods) to prevent other users from accessing the `Predictor` object while it's being re-initialized. Doing so will also temporarily stop everybody from using the store, but it will also save you a lot of headaches!

Pipeline Components

As we mentioned above, the components that belong to these classes are used to manage Order Processing pipelines. Generally speaking, therefore, they all share the same goal: to load a pipeline (from disk or from a memory cache) and to execute it.

Pipelines are a very important part of SSCE, and there is good reason to believe that they will become even more so as new versions of the software package become available. Chapter 10 addresses them in detail. For the moment, let's take a brief look at what objects are available for manipulating them.

The MtsPipeline and MtsTxPipeline Components

Due to the nature of their actions, pipelines support the Microsoft Transaction Server (MTS) interfaces. MTS is a system that supports *transactions*; a transaction is defined as a group of actions that can be successfully reverted (or **rolled back**, as the correct terminology goes) at any time during their execution. Rollback operations usually take place in response to a condition of failure, such as an error.

SSCE provides two components to handle pipelines, and they are both "MTS-aware". `MtsPipeline`, even though it is registered with MTS, does not support transactions. This means that the actions taken inside it cannot be rolled back even if an error occurs.

There is a good reason for this behavior, and it will become even more apparent as we visit the store's front-end. `MtsPipeline` is used in those instances in which the ability to roll back a transaction is of no importance – namely when products are being passed through the pipeline only with the goal of finding out the total price of an order but without actually meaning to complete the order transaction. In this case, no data is modified by the execution of the pipeline, and therefore there is no need to roll back anything. As maintaining a transaction causes a certain overhead, fundamentally due to the fact that each data access has to be logged in order for MTS to be able to revert its effects, this approach improves the overall performance of the system.

On the other hand, the `MtsTxPipeline` component fully supports transactions and should only be used when you are sure that the pipeline execution *is* going to modify some data (for example, when the user wants to complete a purchase). If you set this difference aside, the two components offer exactly the same functionality through the same methods.

Loading and Executing Pipelines

As we'll see in a few chapters, pipelines are stored in files of a special type known as "PCF format". In order to be executed in an `MtsPipeline` or `MtsTxPipeline` object, they must first be loaded using the `LoadPipe` method:

❑ **Syntax:**
MtsPipeline.LoadPipe (sPath)
MtsTxPipeline.LoadPipe (sPath)

❑ **Parameters:**
sPath   The qualified path of the pipeline file

When loading a pipeline file, you must make sure that the file pointed to by *sPath* can be properly accessed by the NTLM account currently impersonated by IIS (in the storefront, this will typically be the anonymous `IUSR_` account).

Once a pipeline has been loaded into an `MtsPipeline` or `MtsTxPipeline` object, it can be executed using the `Execute` method:

❑ **Syntax:**
MtsPipeline.Execute (iMode, Orderform, PipeContext, iReserved)
MtsTxPipeline.Execute (iMode, Orderform, PipeContext, iReserved)

❑ **Parameters:**

iMode	Not used (included only for backwards compatibility). Should be set to 1.
Orderform	The `OrderForm` object containing the data that has to be processed by the pipeline
PipeContext	A dictionary that contains the pipeline's "context", that is, a set of environmental variables that are needed by the pipeline's code. This usually includes the default DSN (for connecting to the database), the store's message manager (for outputting error messages), and so on.
iReserved	Should be set to 0.

`Execute` returns one of the following values:

1. the execution was successful

2. logical errors occurred in the pipeline (that is, the pipeline was unable to calculate shipping rates because the ship-to address is incomplete)

3. a failure occurred in the pipeline (that is, the database was unreachable, and so on)

Logging Pipeline Activity

The only way to debug what goes on inside a pipeline is to log its activity. As we will see in Chapter 14, the log files generated by pipeline execution are also very difficult to follow, but we'll also review a couple of "rules of thumb" that will help you through them.

For the moment, all you need to know is that pipeline execution can be logged by calling the `SetLogFile` method:

❏ **Syntax:**
   MtsPipeline.SetLogFile (sPath)
   MtsTxPipeline.SetLogFile (sPath)

❏ **Parameters:**
   sPath   The fully qualified path of the log file

Always keep in mind that the NT account impersonated by IIS must have write access to the log file or the execution of the pipeline will result in an access error.

Micropipes

So far, we have depicted a pipeline as a way of performing very high-level functions, such as "process order". However, SSCE introduces a kind of pipeline, called **micropipes**, that can be programmed to perform a smaller set of simple functions, such as "calculate shipping costs only".

Micropipes are not used in the standard SSCE store, therefore we will defer their exploration to the by now (in)famous Chapter 10.

Caching Pipelines

As pipeline-handling components are not application-scoped, they are created every time their pipelines must be executed. This also means that pipelines must be read from disk every single time – an operation that is potentially very costly in terms of system resources.

Luckily, SSCE provides the functionality needed to cache pipelines in memory through the `ConfigurationCacheHelper` component, which is able to save the configuration of any pipeline object and then reload the same configuration at any other time. Clearly, you must create a `ConfigurationCacheHelper` with application scope in order to be able to retain the cached data across all your pages.

The first step in using ConfigurationCacheHelper objects is in saving the configuration status of a pipeline in the cache. This is done through the SaveToCache method after a pipeline has been loaded and stored in the pipeline object:

❑ **Syntax:**
ConfigurationCacheHelper.SaveToCache (Pipeline)

❑ **Parameters:**

Pipeline   The pipeline object (usually an instance of either MtsPipeline or MtsTxPipeline) whose configuration has to be saved

The SaveToCache method returns a unique token that can later be used to configure another pipeline object through the LoadFromCache method:

❑ **Syntax:**
ConfigurationCacheHelper.LoadFromCache (Pipeline, Token)

❑ **Parameters:**

Pipeline   The pipeline object (usually an instance of either MtsPipeline or MtsTxPipeline) whose configuration has to be retrieved

Token   A token returned by SaveToCache that is used to uniquely identify a specific pipeline configuration

Cached entries, finally, can be deleted through the DeleteCacheEntry method, whose syntax is defined below:

❑ **Syntax:**
ConfigurationCacheHelper.DeleteCacheEntry (Pipeline, Token)

❑ **Parameters:**

Pipeline   The pipeline object (usually an instance of either MtsPipeline or MtsTxPipeline) whose cache entry has to be deleted

Token   A token returned by SaveToCache that is used to uniquely identify a specific pipeline configuration

Programming Considerations for Cached Pipelines

There is one important consideration to be kept in mind when using the ConfigurationCacheHelper component. As you won't be loading your pipelines from a file anymore, any changes that you make to the configuration files that physically reside on your server's disk drive will not be reflected in the store until you somehow forcefully clear the configuration cache.

The best way to overcome this problem is to write a page that deletes all the cached configurations and reloads them all from disk (remember to lock the access to the Application object while you are doing this!). It's also a good idea to periodically schedule a refresh of the cache – for example by using the NT system scheduler to launch a browser window that points to the refresh page – just in case you forget to update your cache manually.

Undocumented Commerce Server Objects

In a perfect world, information should be readily available whenever we need it and for anything we might want to know. Naturally, we don't live in a perfect world and every once in a while we stumble on something that we didn't know existed. To some people, that is the starting point of a paranoid research of hidden truths and conspiracy, while others are simply curious and try to find out as much as they can about it. I prefer to fall into the second category, if not for any other reason, then just because I like to keep a positive attitude – and also because I know that often there are good reasons why not everything is immediately known and well-documented.

As with many other software programs, SSCE has a number of features that are not publicly spelled out in the product's documentation. There are several reasons why this may happen: these features are not an integral part of SSCE's functionality and therefore Microsoft didn't think it would have been necessary to document them; or, simply, they didn't want to support them, and therefore decided not to make them public knowledge. As you can see, in neither of these cases are we being kept unaware of things because a mysterious race of aliens will soon be taking over our beloved planet!

Undocumented features do not remain so forever, as a lot of people find it interesting to learn as much as they can about a product and eventually stumble on some of the little "Easter eggs" that are scattered within it. Site Server is obviously at a disadvantage from this point of view, since it is entirely based on COM and ASP, two technologies that are renowned for their transparency. As a result, finding hidden features is not at all difficult, if one is willing to look in the right place.

A good starting point is the code that is used to run the Store Builder Wizard and the Win32-based pipeline editor (which we'll see later on in the book). If any undocumented objects are shipped with SSCE, chances are they will be used in there (otherwise, they would be pretty useless, wouldn't they?). Another good idea is to take a look in the Registry and try to extract a list of all the COM components that start with the `Commerce` prefix. If you undertake a little investigation, you'll find out that there are quite a few more objects than those listed in the documentation.

In this last section of the chapter, we'll run through some of the undocumented objects that can be found in SSCE (who knows, there might be more…). It should be noted that, as this functionality is undocumented, what is written below is the result of some empirical testing and a lot of research. Since Microsoft is not supporting these components, you should carefully consider whether the fact that they will be helpful for your system would counterbalance the fact that if you run into trouble with them it might be difficult to find help.

AdminSecurity

The `Commerce.AdminSecurity` object is designed to give access to the security features of Windows NT. As such, it makes reading and writing permissions and audit settings possible, and also gives secure access to many NT resources, such as the Registry, metabases and the filesystem.

`AdminSecurity` is mostly used in the SFW and SBW for securing the site so that the correct permissions are applied to its files and Registry entries. The following is a list of members with a brief explanation:

Method	Description
AddAudit	Adds a parameter to the audit list
AddPermission	Adds a permission
Audit	(Property) Represents an audit member or list
DelAudit	Deletes an audit parameter from the list
DelPermission	Deletes a permission
Group	(Property) Represents a group of user accounts
Owner	(Property) Represents the owner of an object
Permission	(Property) Represents a permission
ReadSecurityDirectory	Reads the security attributes of a Directory
ReadSecurityFile	Reads the security attributes of a file
ReadSecurityMetabase	Reads the security attributes of a metabase
ReadSecurityRegistry	Reads the security attributes of a Registry key
WriteSecurityDirectory	Writes the security attributes of a directory
WriteSecurityFile	Writes the security attributes of a file
WriteSecurityMetabase	Writes the security attributes of a metabase
WriteSecurityRegistry	Writes the security attributes of a Registry key

The functionality of AdminSecurity revolves around its four properties, which represent all the security attributes of an NT object. These can be set by either reading the properties of an existing object by using one of the ReadSecurity methods, or by adding and removing attributes as appropriate. Once the correct combination of attributes has been set, they can be written as required using one of the WriteSecurity methods.

AdminFiles

AdminFiles provides a lot of functionality that, for the most part, complements that found in the Scripting.FileSystemObject component. As such, you will find it very interesting and useful in your programs, and I must say that this is by far the easiest of the undocumented components to use. Here's a list of what it can do:

Method	Description
Attributes	Returns the attributes of a file or directory (for example, whether it's read-only, and so on).
CopyFile	Copies a file
CreateDirectory	Creates a new directory

Table continued on the following page

Method	Description
CreateTempFile	Determines a unique name for a temporary file and creates it
DeleteDirectory	Deletes a directory
ExecuteProgram	Executes a program
ExecuteProgramNOUI	Executes a program without user display (useful for unattended server side execution)
Exists	Determines whether an object (for example: a file or a directory) exists
FileTimeCreated	Returns the time and date when a file was created
FileTimeLastAccessed	Returns the time and date when a file was last accessed
FileTimeLastWritten	Returns the time and date when a file was last written to
GetDirectories	Returns an array containing a list of subfolders within a specified directory
GetFiles	Returns an array containing a list of folders in a given directory
IsNTFS	Determines whether a volume (logical drive) is formatted using NTFS or not.
ReadFromBinaryFile	Reads the contents of a binary file.
ReadFromFile	Reads the contents of a text file
Rename	Renames a file
RegisterServer	Registers a COM server (that is a DLL)
Touch	"Touches" a file, simulating a change in it (the time and date when the file was last changed are modified). Used to force IIS to reload a site by simulating a change in global.asa
UnRegisterServer	Un-registers a COM server (for example: a DLL)
WriteToBinaryFile	Writes to a binary file
WriteToFile	Writes to a text file

If you think of it, AdminFiles opens a lot of possibilities with regards to what you can do with your store now. The possibility of registering COM objects or executing programs from within your scripts alone is a big plus for a lot of applications, such as printing, initiating serial communications, and so on.

AdminRegistry

`AdminFiles` being able to access the Registry from within an ASP script is at the same time important and difficult. For example, it could be possible to use the Registry to store certain data that you do not want to make visible in the scripts (for example: special passwords, etc.); even though you can also use the site configuration to save this information, it's always good to have an alternative. `AdminRegistry` offers a wide range of functionality to access the Registry, although it doesn't let you *create* new keys:

Method	Description
DeleteKey	Deletes a key, all its subkeys and their values
DeleteValue	Deletes a specific value from a key
ExistsKey	Determines whether a specific key exists
ExistsValue	Determines whether a specific value exists
GetSubkeys	Returns an array containing all the subkeys of a given key
GetSubvalues	Returns an array containing all the values within a specific key
GetValue	Gets a specific value
SetValue	Sets or creates a specific value

AdminDB

The goal of the `AdminDB` component, which is mainly used in the SFW to create and verify DSNs, is to give access to the OLE-DB and ODBC administrative functionality on the server where Commerce Server resides. `AdminDB` works similarly to `AdminSecurity`: a group of attributes are used to set all the parameters of a DSN, which can then be written to the server.

Method	Description
CreateSystemDSN	Creates a system DSN
DatabaseName	(Property) Represents the name of the database to which a DSN refers
DBMSName	(Property) Name of the server on which the database resides
DBType	(Property) Type of database (for example: SQL Server, Access, and so on).
DriverName	(Property) Name of the driver that the DSN will use
ExecuteScript	Executes a SQL script stored in a database (they can be found in your store under the Config/SQL folder, and they have a .sql extension)

Table continued on the following page

Method	Description
GetAllSystemDSNs	Returns all the system DSNs on the server
GetDrivers	Returns a list of all the available drivers
GetSystemDSNs	Returns the system DSNs that point to a specific server
IsConnectValid	Returns TRUE if the system can successfully connect to a DSN
Version	(Property) The version of the driver to be used for the DSN

AdminIIS

If you thought that the functionality provided by the AdminWebServer component was not particularly exciting, then you'll love AdminIIS, because it gives you a lot more control over virtual directories. This component, in particular, is used in the SFW when it's necessary to lookup a list of the virtual folders on a server and create the virtual directory where a new store will reside.

Method	Description
AddVirtualRoot	Adds a new virtual root to the current hostname
CommitChanges	Commits any changes made to the hostname. Must be called once all changes are made or IIS won't refresh
DeleteVirtualRoot	Deletes a virtual folder
DeleteVirtualRootsInDirectory	Deletes all the virtual folders that point to a certain location
Exists	Determines whether a virtual folder exists
GetVersion	Returns the version of IIS
GetVirtualRoots	Returns an array containing a list of all the virtual folders residing on the current host
Hostname	Sets/retrieves the name of the current host

AdminLanManager

This component gives you complete control over the structure and configuration of your domain (or, if you do not have a domain, of your workgroup). With it, you can retrieve a list of all the users that sit on a particular computer, determine whether a domain exists or is accessible, create new users, or add users to a group. Used in conjunction with `AdminSecurity`, it provides the perfect tool for remote administration!

Method	Description
AddUserToGroup	Adds the current user to a particular group
CreateGroup	Creates a new group
CreateUser	Creates a new user
DeleteGroup	Deletes a group
DeleteUser	Deletes a user
DeleteUsersFromGroup	Deletes all the users from a given group
DomainExists	Determines whether a domain exists
GetBackupDomainControllers	Returns an array containing a list of all the backup domain controllers on a given domain
GetCurrentComputer	Returns the UNC name of the computer where the component resides
GetCurrentUser	Returns the current user
GetDomainController	Returns the UNC name of the domain controller for the domain where the current server
GetDomainForServer	Returns the name of the domain for a particular server
GetDomainForUser	Returns the name of the domain for the current user
GetDomains	Returns an array containing a list of all the domains accessible from the current server
GetGroups	Returns an array containing a list of the groups on the current domain
GetGroupsForUser	Returns an array containing a list of the groups to which the current user belongs
GetLocalDomain	Returns the domain in which the current server resides
GetServers	Returns an array containing a list of all the servers on the current domain

Table continued on the following page

Method	Description
GetTrustedDomains	Returns an array containing a list of all the trusted domains for the current domain
GetUsers	Returns an array containing a list of the users for the current domain
GetUsersInGroup	Returns an array containing a list of the users for a particular group
GroupExists	Determines whether a group exists on the current domain
Server	(Property) The current server
User	(Property) The current user
UserExists	Determines whether a user exists given his or her username
UserInGroup	Determines whether a user is in a particular group

PageGen

There's no doubt (at least in my mind) that the VBScript engine is too powerful to be used only in ASP pages. The truth is, there are so many other things that could be done with it if it only were possible...and it is! One of the undocumented objects in Commerce Server is called PageGen, and it is able to correctly interpret and execute an entire VBScript script. The SBW uses it to generate the pages of the starter store based on a set of templates that it keeps in the installation folder.

In order not to interfere with any *normal* ASP code that might be stored in the template that has to be generated, the commands that should be interpreted by PageGen are identified by the delimiters <%% and %%>, which use two percent signs rather than the one normally used by ASP. The code inside these special delimiters is just plain and simple VBScript – you can even create objects and run them within it!

> The syntax and context used by PageGen are the same used by the CreatePO pipeline component, which is described in Chapter 10.

PageGen has only one method, GenPageText, which is used to load and run the script, and which returns the compiled template as a string.

PipeManager

The last component that we'll look at is called `PipeManager`, and it can be used to access – and alter – the internal structure of a pipeline configuration file. The SBW uses this component to generate the pipelines for a newly created store, while the Win32-based editor, which we'll see in Chapter 10, uses it to access and modify an existing pipeline configuration file.

Here's a list of all the methods of this component:

Method	Description
CreateComponent	Creates a new instance of a pipeline component
CreateComponentFromStream	Creates a new instance of a pipeline component and loads its configuration from an OLE stream
CreateStage	Creates a new stage
CreateStageFromStream	Creates a new stage and loads its components and configuration from an OLE stream
CreateStreamFromComponent	Creates an OLE stream that contains the configuration of a component
CreateStreamFromStage	Creates an OLE stream that contains the components of a stage and their configuration
DeleteComponent	Deletes a component
DeleteStage	Deletes a stage
GetComponent	Retrieves a component
GetComponentName	Retrieves the name (label) of a component
GetComponentPage	Retrieves the property pages of a component
GetComponentsByStageAffinity	Gets a list of the components that show affinity with a particular stage
GetStage	Retrieves a particular stage
Load	Loads a pipeline configuration file from disk
MoveComponent	Moves a component within the current pipeline configuration file
MoveStage	Moves a stage within the current pipeline configuration file
Save	Saves the current pipeline configuration file to disk

A Final Cautionary Note

As you have undoubtedly noticed, there's quite a bit of damage that can be done with the undocumented objects of Site Server. What many developers do not realize is that these objects are sitting on your server and *can* be used by anyone who is running ASP code on it. Under normal circumstances, this won't be much of a problem, since your developers will be the ones putting their hands on the code.

However, if you are running a multi-host machine on which several customers are hosting their own Site Server-based solution, the potential for each of your customers to write code that can access someone else's data is very much there. Not all is lost, however – as long as you are aware of the problem and do something about it. In a well-controlled environment, in which all the appropriate permissions have been set, the undocumented components won't be able to cause much damage.

Since each of your customers will access their own sites using a separate unique account (at least hopefully!), the easiest way to prevent them from accessing the undocumented objects is to deny their account read and execute access to the DLLs that contain them. These are stored in the \bin folder of your Site Server installation, and for the most part the undocumented objects are stored in separate DLLs to the other Commerce Server objects. These are:

❑   MSCSAdmin.dll

❑   MSCSPageGen.dll

❑   PipeConfig.dll

In addition, you should make sure that each store is properly protected from unauthorized access by verifying that the NT security permissions are set correctly, and that each user only has access to the correct data.

Summary

Wow! Chapter 9 was really a big chunk to digest, eh? The goal of this chapter was to give you all the tools you need to understand the inner working of a SSCE store, which is what we will be discussing in the next two chapters.

To recapitulate briefly, we identified four different types of commerce objects and we discussed each one of them in detail. The only items that we skipped briefly were those related to the order processing pipelines, which deserve much more detail and will be dug into in Chapter 10.

I also gave you some insight into the undocumented components within SSCE - however, use these with caution!

Using the Order Processing Pipeline

Thinking is the hardest work there is, which is the probable reason why so few engage in it.
– Henry Ford

Many processes in real life can only take place if a carefully ordered approach is taken in carrying them out. It's impossible, for example, to start making a car by installing the door lock if the door itself isn't already in place – which, in turn, requires a frame to have been built, and so on.

These tasks are usually performed using a technique known as *pipeline*, which was invented at the end of the 19th century and largely perfected by Henry Ford, founder of the Ford Motor Company, whose concept is essentially the same as that used today to build everything from trucks in a factory to a sandwich at the fast food store around the corner.

The structure of a pipeline is necessarily rigid – in the sense that its stages and their boundaries are well defined, as are the actions that have be undertaken at each step – but can allow for certain variable elements to be introduced. In a car factory, for example, custom orders, such as colors and special gears, are handled through a "branch" of the main pipeline that is, in effect a pipeline of its own.

The rigidity of a pipeline ensures that a particular process is always executed the same way. This also means that, if you start the same pipeline under the same initial conditions, you should expect the same result at the end of its execution. As a result, pipelines are an excellent tool for carrying out repetitive tasks through a specific sequence of individual actions.

What Does This Chapter Talk About?

As you might have guessed, this chapter talks about the pipeline technology in Site Server, focusing in particular on the Order Processing Pipeline, which, as we have mentioned earlier, takes on the task of providing a rigorously ordered approach to the checkout stage of a retail online store. Since the discussion of pipelines has been quite vague to this point, we will also examine the technology itself and look at how it is used from within an ASP script; we'll leave a description of the practical use of pipeline to Chapter 11, where we will explore the actual code of the starter store created by the Store Builder Wizard.

The chapter is divided into four parts:

- **Why pipelines?**
  This section will tackle the topic of pipelines a little more in detail, explaining how they work, how they are used in the stores, and why the pipeline technology has been invented in the first place.

- **Using pipelines**
  In this section, we'll learn how to use pipelines in our stores. First, we'll take a look at the pipeline editing technologies that are provided by Commerce Server. Then, we'll delve into the details of how pipelines can be executed from within your own scripts.

- **The Order Processing Pipeline**
  Next, we'll talk about the OPP. We'll examine its structure and the way it is used; we'll also take a look at the built-in components that Commerce Server has to offer.

- **Small is beautiful: micropipes**
  Micropipes are a particular kind of pipelines that can contain only one component. As we shall see in this section, they can be used to execute a single pipeline component without having to go through the entire overhead caused by executing a standard pipeline.

Why Pipelines?

Until now, I have been pretty vague as to what a pipeline really is. As a matter of fact, I have limited its description to something similar to "a systematic approach to order processing" and the likes.

The truth is, the concept of pipelines in Commerce Server is in no way different from its corresponding concept in the traditional industry of, for example, car making. The reason why a car is built in a pipeline is that the process works well only if a set of steps are taken in a specific order: you can't install the window glass until the body has been painted, or wire the lights before they have been screwed in!

Before Henry Ford came onboard, the concept of pipeline was very different from what it is today: the car stayed in one place, while the workers moved. This means, for example, that workers had to take all their instruments with them and move from car to car. The need to continuously move around was perceived a waste of time by Ford, who was always looking for a way to make his model T cheaper to produce, and therefore to sell.

In a bid to improve the process, he made the cars move and his employees stand still at their workstations. As a result, cars were built faster and the correct chain of events was always respected, because the car had to physically move through all the right steps before getting to a particular point.

Microsoft Site Server Commerce Pipelines

A Commerce Server pipeline is a software framework in which one or more stages are linked together, forming a business process. These stages could be validating the users credit card values, shipping address and calculating a correct shipping charge based on different properties of the ordered items. It could also be a completely different process, like encrypting, signing and sending EDI files over the HTTP protocol.

Below is an illustration of the principles of a pipeline. Every stage of the pipeline can have one or more pipeline components (COM objects). These components can be modified to fit a specific stores requirements, components can be added or removed, and even stages could be added and removed.

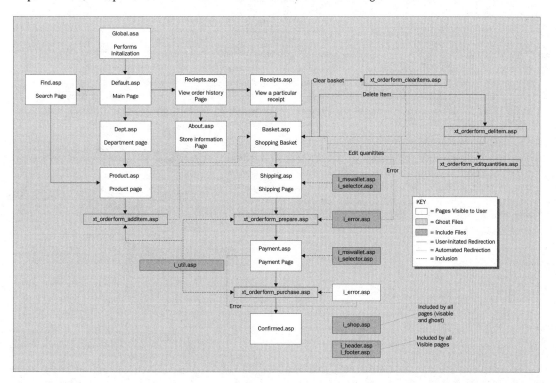

A `Dictionary` object is run through each stage and their respective pipeline components. For each pipeline component, different values are calculated and added to the Dictionary sequentially, so components in one stage may depend on the presence of values added by other objects earlier in the process. The number of stages, and which components they each have attached are stored in files called pipeline templates, with the extension `.pct`.

In order to implement both business-to-consumer and business-to-business sites, Commerce Server includes seven basic types of pipelines, accessible as pipeline templates (pct files) in the Win32 Pipeline Editor.

Template Name	Description
`CorpPurchaseSubmit.pct`	Corporate purchasing pipeline, 2 stages
`CorpPurchasingPlan.pct`	Corporate purchasing pipeline, 14 stages
`plan.pct`	Order Processing Pipeline (OPP), 14 stages
`product.pct`	Order Processing Pipeline (OPP), 5 stages
`purchase.pct`	Order Processing Pipeline (OPP), 3 stages
`receive.pct`	Commerce Interchange Receive Pipeline (CIP), 7 stages
`transmit.pct`	Commerce Interchange Transmit Pipeline (CIP), 6 stages

You will use these pipeline templates as a foundation when you create your own pipelines. The newly created pipelines will get the extension .pcf, for "pipeline file". When you use the Site Builder Wizard to create a new store, all the Order Processing Pipeline (OPP) files (`plan.pcf`, `product.pcf` and `purchase.pcf`) will be generated and stored in the `Config` directory of your store. They will have different sets of pipeline components, depending on what options you chose in the Site Builder Wizard.

The product pipeline computes the price of an individual product and the plan pipeline computes the total amount of an order. Finally, the purchase pipeline accepts an order for purchase and processes the payment. You can edit these pipeline files in the Win32 Pipeline Editor, a tool that comes with Commerce Server:

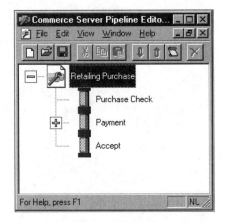

This is the pipeline based on the pipeline template file `purchase.pcf`. It consists of three stages called **Purchase Check**, **Payment** and **Accept**, and each of these stages has zero or more pipeline components attached. This particular pipeline is run when the user has selected the items to buy, entered all the ship-to, bill-to and credit card information and clicks the purchase button. If any of these pipeline components generates an error, the purchase is not carried through and the user is notified about the problem so it can be dealt with. This could, for example, occur if there was something missing from the credit card.

Using Pipelines

We will now describe how to actually use these pipelines. We will go through the process of creating a pipeline using the pipeline editor and then programatically call the pipeline with the required supporting objects. Before we can get into how pipelines are run, however, we'll have to talk extensively about how they are *created* in the first place.

Creating Pipelines

Commerce Server provides two different editors for creating and managing pipelines. One is Win32-based, and can only be run from a machine on which (a) the pipeline configuration file is reachable and (b) all the required components are installed. The other is entirely web-based, and can be run from just about anywhere the Commerce Server is reachable through the network.

In choosing one editor or the other, you should mainly take into consideration their convenience versus their capabilities. In general, the Win32-based editor provides a wider array of functionality, including the possibility of creating your own pipeline templates, in which the names and order of the stages are not necessarily those pre-determined by Commerce Server's standard pipelines. On the other hand, the web-based editor gives you the convenience of being able to edit your pipelines from just about anywhere: all you need is a web browser and the appropriate credentials to access your store's management pages.

The Web-Based Editor

We'll start from the web-based editor, which you will most likely use a lot when you do not have direct access to your server, or if you do not have Site Server installed on your local computer. The figure below shows the editor's main screen for a plan pipeline, which is reached by clicking on the **Edit Pipeline** button of the Store Manager's main page. As you can see, Microsoft is taking the metaphor of the pipeline pretty seriously!

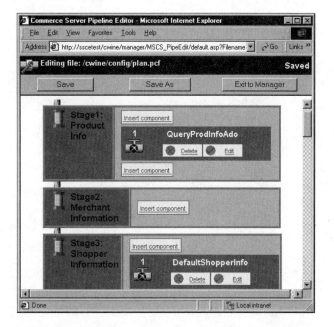

The editor is very easy to use. The section at the top, which is enclosed in a frame so that it remains visible even as you scroll down the pipeline, is used to perform activities such as saving the pipeline with the same or a different filename, or going back to the Store Manager's main page. It's interesting to notice that the **Save** and **Save As** button do not cause the browser to navigate back to the Manager's main page, so you will have to click on **Exit to Manager** *after* you have saved your pipelines anyway. If you forget to save, a message will notify you that continuing to the main page will cause all the changes that you have made to be lost. You can verify whether your pipeline's changes have already been saved by looking at the upper right corner of the screen, which will read **Not Saved** in bright red if you have not yet saved your edited configuration file.

By default, the editor is only able to load and display the pipeline files that belong to a specific store. Even if you decide to use the Save As function, you will still only be able to save the files within your store's virtual folder. This is not a limitation, but rather an obvious security measure. In fact, since this editor can be executed without having physical access to the server, it's reasonable to expect that the person using it might only have access to his or her own store's virtual root, and should not be allowed to reach any other file in the system: this is the case, in particular, of an ISP who is re-selling Site Server functionality on its servers. Therefore, allowing somebody to save their configuration files anywhere on the hard drive might lead to disastrous consequences (such as the owner of one store overwriting somebody else's pipelines!).

Editing and Deleting a Component

You can edit a component that is already in the pipeline by clicking on its Edit link (each component is represented by a green box within a stage with an icon of what looks like a hydraulic valve). Doing so will take you to a page lets you specify the properties of the component that you have selected. For example, the screenshot here shows the property page for an instance of QueryProdInfoADO.

As you can see, you can also specify a *label* for the component that will be displayed in the editor's main screen. The value of the label field bears no importance in how the pipeline or the components are executed, but it can be used to make the role of each component in the pipeline easier to understand.

To delete a component, go to the editor's main screen and click on the Delete link that appears beside the component. The editor will not ask you for a confirmation before deleting the component, and there is no undo functionality, so make sure that you know what you're doing!

Inserting a New Component

To insert a new component, click on any Insert Component box. As you may have noticed from the previous pictures, the link appears twice for each stage. This lets you decide whether you want your component to be added at the beginning or at the end of a stage.

Clicking on the Insert Component link takes you to another page that lists all the components that show affinity with your stage. You can also select the component that you want to add from a list of all the components that are available on the server.

> **Although you can add any component to any stage regardless of the affinity rules, you should be careful in adding a component to a stage it doesn't show affinity for. In many cases, the component might require that certain values be set in the pipeline's data dictionary, and those values might only be set in or before the component for which it shows affinity.**

Once you've added a component, you can elect to move it around in the stage by using the small arrows that are on its right side in the editor's main page.

How Does the Editor Work?

As you may have understood, the editor is simply an ASP application that has been designed to handle configuration files through an undocumented Commerce Server object called Commerce.PipeManager, which is also used at the end of the Site Builder Wizard to create the pipeline configuration files for a store, and has the ability of loading and manipulating configuration files.

When a store is first created, Commerce Server adds a virtual folder to it called `Commerce Server_PipeEdit`, which points to the following location:

`Commerce ServerRoot\SiteServer\Admin\Commerce\PipeLine Configuration`

where `Commerce ServerRoot` is the installation directory of your copy of Site Server, Commerce Edition. This folder contains the pipeline editor's source files.

The Win32-based Editor

Working with the Win32 pipeline editor is a somewhat speedier process, and the functionality that it provides is in many ways superior to that offered by the web-based editor, although the latter is obviously more convenient. Naturally, you do not necessarily need to be on the server in order to edit a pipeline configuration file, but you will need to have all the pipeline components installed on your workstation in order for the program to work properly outside a server environment.

If you are using a machine on which Site Server is installed, you may run the editor by selecting Programs | Microsoft Site Server | Commerce | Pipeline Editor from the Start menu. Doing so will cause the editor to load and its interface, shown below, to be displayed on your monitor.

As you can see, the basic look of the editor is a little different from that of its web-based counterpart, with the inclusion of the Win32 common elements (such as menus, buttons, and so on) that you obviously couldn't have in your browser window. The first big difference that you will notice, however, is in the fact that this editor does not load any pipeline configuration file by default. As a matter of fact, you even have the choice of creating a new pipeline from scratch! The relevant `.pcf` files for your particular site can be found in the `Config` folder for that site.

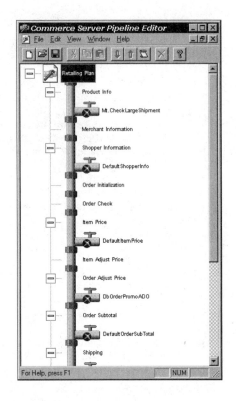

Editing or Deleting a Component

To edit a component that sits already in the pipeline, all you have to do is double click on it. The editor will display a dialog box with several tabbed panels. Their actual number varies, depending on how many property pages each component has, but in general you will see any combination of the following:

❑ **Property pages**
Each property page (components rarely have more than one) contains the configurable properties for the component. The title of the tab for this panel is decided by the component's developer, and therefore varies considerably from component to component. For example, the figure here shows the property page for an instance of `QueryProdInfoADO`.

❑ **Component properties**
This panel, not to be confused with the property pages, is always present for all components, and provides basic information about them. This includes the label, the COM Class ID, the COM Program ID and a description. Both the label and the description can be modified to better explain what a component does and how it has been configured.

Component Properties	☒

Query Prod Info (ADO) | **Component Properties** | Values Read and Written

Label:
QueryProdInfoAdo

Class ID:
{5AD58957-68F1-11D0-A689-00C04FD658FF}

Program ID:
Commerce.QueryProdInfoADO.1

Description:

[OK] [Cancel] [Apply] [Help]

❑ **Values Read/Written**
This optional panel contains a list of all the values that the component reads and writes to the data dictionary, and reads from the pipeline's context.

Component Properties	☒

Query Prod Info (ADO) | Component Properties | **Values Read and Written**

Values Read:
item.sku
item.dept_id

Values Written:
[optional]item._product_*
[optional]item.delete

Context Values Read:
[optional]DefaultConnectionString
[optional]ConnectionStringMap
[optional]QueryMap

[OK] [Cancel] [Apply] [Help]

Deleting a component is a very easy operation: just select the component by clicking on it with your mouse, then either select Delete from the Edit menu, or press the *DEL* key on your keyboard. Contrary to what happens with the web-based editor, the Win32 editor will ask you for a confirmation before proceeding, but will not provide any undo functionality once you've taken your decision.

Inserting a New Component

To insert a new component in your pipeline, you can right click on either an existing component or on a stage. In the first case, the resulting popup menu will give you the possibility of adding a component before or after the existing one, while in the second case you will be simply adding a component to the beginning of the stage you selected.

In both cases, the editor will display a dialog box that will list all the components available for the stage you are currently in. As before, you can also select your component from a list of all the components available on the server. Naturally, the same caveats apply!

The Expert Mode

Wouldn't it be nice if you could create your own pipelines? As we have mentioned more than once in this chapter, such a possibility exists, and it is only available when you use the Win32 editor in *Expert Mode*, also known as Enhanced Mode. When the editor is running in such a state, it is possible to add, move and delete entire stages, as well as deciding what the end-of-stage logic does. As you can imagine, the possibilities are almost limitless, so let's get started!

In order for the pipeline editor to run in Expert Mode, you need to start it from the command line. To do so, click on <u>R</u>un from the Start menu, and then type in the following:

```
"SiteServer Root\bin\pipeeditor.exe" /e
```

where `SiteServer Root` is the installation folder of your copy of Site Server (for example, in my case, its value would be `C:\Microsoft Site Server`). Make sure that you include the quotation marks in your command line.

At first glance, the editor in Expert Mode looks exactly the same as it does normally. As soon as you either create a new pipeline or open an existing one, however, things start taking on a different image, as you can see below. The first difference that you will probably notice when opening an existing Plan pipeline is the presence of certain components that were not there before. They all start with Required... and are designed to handle the end-of-stage logic.

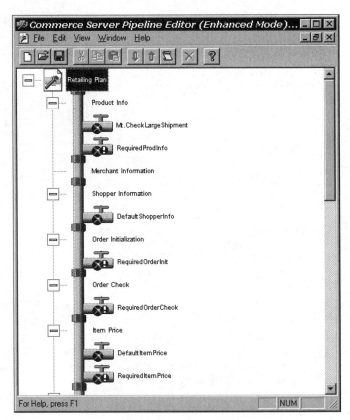

If you try to delete one of these components, you will notice that the editor doesn't complain much more than usual and will actually let you take the components out. After all, that's what the Expert Mode is all about: giving you more freedom in choosing what goes in and out of a pipeline. If you now try to access the properties for any component, and select the **Component Properties** tab, you will notice the presence of an apparently innocuous checkbox that reads **Required**. If you select that box, the component will be marked as required, and the editor will simply not show it in the pipeline when run in normal mode.

Another very interesting feature of Expert Mode is the ability of doing to stages what you would normally do to components only: moving them around, adding new ones, or deleting existing ones. To move a stage from its current position, right-click on it and select either **Move Up** or **Move Down**. To insert a new stage, click on an existing stage and select **Insert Stage**, then **Before** or **After**, if available. To delete an existing stage, simply select it and press the *DEL* key on your keyboard. It's that simple.

When you add stages, you will notice by right clicking on them that you can change their label and add a comment. In addition, the editor generates (and lets you change) a GUID for the stage, which will be used to determine what components have affinity to it (we'll talk more about how components are assigned to stages later on in this chapter). Finally, you can specify the minimum execution mode in which a stage will run (as specified by the pipeline objects that we'll examine shortly), as well as the maximum error level that a stage will be able to tolerate. If the error level returned by any of the components at any point in the stage goes beyond that level, the pipeline execution will stop immediately.

You will notice that a few properties are available also for the pipeline as a whole by right clicking on it and selecting **Properties** (the pipeline is identified by the first icon that appears in the editing window). As you can see, along with the usual label and description fields, there is a drop-down list that reads **Transaction Compatibility**, which can be used to determine whether the pipeline requires a transacted environment, is transaction-neutral or that it can be run in an environment that does not require a transaction. We'll talk more about pipelines and transactions in the next section.

We will later take on the daunting task of creating a pipeline from scratch, using the Empty pipeline template. To create a new pipeline based on the Empty template, all you have to do is simply select `Empty.pce` from the dialog box that the editor displays when you click on **File | New**. Speaking of which, wouldn't it be nice if you could create your own pipeline template and then make it available through the **File | New** mechanism? To do so, all you need is to copy the configuration file that contains your template to the following location:

SiteServer Root\bin\Templates

where, as usual, *SiteServer Root* is the installation folder for your copy of Site Server, Commerce Edition.

> It's worth noting that the Expert Mode does not bear its name by mistake. Shuffling stages around requires a certain amount of planning, and can lead to disastrous consequences for the stability of your pipeline (and of your psyche, as well). Therefore, before starting to play with the Expert Mode, you should make a backup of every pipeline that you intend to modify.

Creating the Supporting Objects

Each pipeline requires two supporting objects in order to run properly:

❑ **The context**
The context is a Dictionary object that is initialized to contain a number of "environment" objects required by the pipeline at execution time. This includes ASP intrinsic objects, connection strings, query strings, the shopper manager object and so on.

❑ **The data dictionary**
The data dictionary is either an OrderForm object (for OPP pipelines) or a Dictionary object (for CIP pipelines), and contains the data that the pipeline is supposed to manipulate.

Clearly, both the context and the data dictionary must be created before the execution of the pipeline can happen. Generally speaking, you can elect to create the context only once, for example in the Application_OnStart method of the global.asa file, and then store it in the Application object, while, naturally, the data dictionary will probably vary every time a pipeline is executed.

Creating the Context Object

As we just said, the context object is a Dictionary object, and it should contain whatever values the components in your pipeline require to run. By default, a basic Commerce Server store creates a dictionary that contains the following Name/Value pairs:

Object Name	Description
MessageManager	An instance of Commerce.MessageManager that is generally created in the store's global.asa file, which contains all the possible error messages for the pipeline's components.
DataFunctions	An instance of Commerce.DataFunctions, usually created and initialized in the store's global.asa file.

Object Name	Description
QueryMap	An instance of Commerce.Dictionary, usually created and initialized in global.asa, which contains a list of all the SQL queries used by the store.
ConnectionStringMap	A Dictionary object that contains a list of the connection strings available to the store
SiteName	The display name of the store
DefaultConnectionString	The default connection string to be used by the store
Language	The default language/locale used by the store (must be defined in the MessageManager object)

You can obviously add whatever objects or other values you like to the context dictionary, including the ASP intrinsic objects (which are not by default available to the pipeline components). For example, if you need to read the user's cookies from within the pipeline, you can add the Request object to the context as follows:

```
Set objContext = Server.CreateObject ("Commerce.Dictionary")
Set objContext.Request = Request
```

Creating the Data Dictionary

The data dictionary is also a Commerce.Dictionary Object, usually the Commerce.OrderForm object that is an implementation of the Dictionary. The data dictionary holds the data we want our pipeline to work with, and each stage and their respective pipeline components are expecting certain values to exist at a certain given time. One such object is the Items SimpleList object, which is used extensively throughout the Order processing pipelines since it does contain all the items the user has in their basket.

For OPP pipelines, the creation of the data dictionary is a process that most of the time spans the entire site. In fact, the OrderForm is used from when the user first enters the store until when he or she either leaves or makes a purchase to hold all of his or her personal information and basket contents. For a CIP, the data dictionary is usually created right before the pipeline's execution, and loaded with whatever values are needed.

Pipeline Objects

Pipelines are executed by using specialized objects provided by Commerce Server. There is no difference between the way an OPP and a CIP are executed, except, naturally, the fact that in one case the data dictionary is a Dictionary object, while in the other, it is an OrderForm object. As such, the procedure for loading and executing a CIP and OPP is exactly the same.

The reason why Commerce Server provides two different objects for loading and executing a pipeline is one of convenience. Since the introduction of the Microsoft Transaction Server, many Microsoft products have been developed to be fully transaction-friendly, and Site Server is no exception – the pipeline is an excellent candidate for the benefits that transactions bring along.

As we'll see in the next chapter, however, pipelines are used pervasively throughout the Commerce Server store, and their role is almost never to perform tasks that it makes sense to make part of a transaction. As a matter of fact, the only time when you will really need transactions is when a customer purchases something (and, in fact, the Purchase pipeline is automatically marked as "transaction required"). For all the other instances, using transactions would only add a useless overhead and therefore limit the capacity of your site.

MtsPipeline

The `MtsPipeline` object is used to load and execute pipelines that do not require transactions. The first operation that you must take care of is to actually load the pipeline from its configuration file. This is accomplished by calling the `LoadPipe` method:

- ❑ **Syntax:**
  `MtsPipeline.LoadPipe(sPath)`

- ❑ **Parameters:**
  sPath   The complete pathname of the pipeline configuration file

This method will attempt to retrieve and load the pipeline configuration file that you specify, giving you the opportunity to modify the behavior of your pipelines any way you want. If the file cannot be found or is not accessible, you can expect a runtime error. This might happen, for example, if there were permission problems while attempting to open the pipeline file. However, you can also expect problems if the pipeline file you are trying to load has been marked for transacted execution (more about that later) – in that case, since `MtsPipeline` does not support transactions in any way, you will not be able to execute the pipeline.

Assuming that everything went fine with your call to `LoadPipe`, you can attempt to execute the pipeline using the `Execute` method:

- ❑ **Syntax:**
  `MtsPipeline.Execute(lMode, MainDictionary, PipeContext, lReserved)`

- ❑ **Parameters:**

lMode	The mode in which the pipeline must be executed (1 under normal conditions)
MainDictionary	The pipeline's main dictionary
PipeContext	The pipeline's context
lReserved	Reserved value, must be zero

The `lMode` parameter is implemented mainly for legacy reasons (in Site Server 2, only one pipeline per store could be used – and therefore it was necessary to differentiate between Plan and Purchase pipeline by stuffing all the components in a single pipeline and marking them with an "execution mode". The pipeline was then executed with a specific mode, which prevented certain components from running). You should never use a value of zero, which will prevent *any* component from running. All the built-in pipelines provided by Commerce Server that we have seen so far are designed to run when `lMode` has a value equal to or greater than one.

Naturally, you can design your own pipelines to run only in specific modes, as we'll see later on in the chapter, but in doing so you will force the pipeline objects to load the entire pipeline configuration file every time even though you might be needing only a handful of components. This will increase your overhead significantly, and will make your store less efficient than if you simply used more than one pipeline file in the first place.

Execute returns a value of type long integer that expresses the level of success of the pipeline's execution. These return values have different meaning:

Return Value	Description
1	corresponds to a successful execution, meaning that all the components were run without any problem
2	a "recoverable" error occurred and, while the pipeline's execution was not entirely successful, it might have continued until the end
3	corresponds to an unrecoverable failure, and means that the pipeline's execution was not successful.

In general, since transactions should be treated as atomic processes (that is, they either happen, or they don't), you should consider the pipeline's execution unsuccessful unless you receive a return value of 1.

Make no misake about it: pipelines are a pesky critter at times. Their biggest problem – the one that will sometimes keep you stuck for hours – is that they are extremely difficult to debug, because you cannot even see the code for most of the components. Luckily (or *unluckily*, if you're the it's-never-enough-for-me type), pipeline objects are able to write all the actions that components perform on the pipeline's main dictionary to a log file. Clearly, this is not something that you would want the objects to do every time (log files tend to be *very* large with time), and therefore you must turn on this behavior by calling the SetLogFile method:

❑ **Syntax:**
   MtsPipeline.SetLogFile(Path)

❑ **Parameters:**
   Path   The pathname of the log file

It's important to make sure that the file chosen can be accessed for writing by the pipeline component – this includes the fact the appropriate permissions are set and that the file is not read-only. Pipeline log files can be quite complex to understand – but only because they usually contain a lot of data and are not very easy to read. We'll take a look at them right after we have talked a bit about how transacted pipelines are run.

> **Always remember to turn off pipeline activity logging before you go to a production environment – either by commenting out the call to SetLogFile or removing it completely. If you don't, your store's performance will suffer, and your hard drive will rapidly run out of space (log files can be *really* big!) .**

MtsTxPipeline

This Commerce Server object can be used to run pipelines that require a transaction-enabled environment. `MtsTxPipeline` supports exactly the same set of methods provided by `MtsPipeline`, with no difference whatsoever in their parameters or return values. However, there are a number of differences that you should keep into account when using either component.

As mentioned above, pipelines that require transactions can only be run using `MtsTxPipeline`. Likewise, if you mark a pipeline as requiring a non-transacted environment, you will not be able to run it unless you use `MtsPipeline`.

`MtsTxPipeline` can use the transaction context of your ASP script, if you create one. If you do not, the object will automatically create one and run the pipeline within it. Due to the stateless nature of web serving, you cannot create an instance of `MtsTxPipeline` in one script (for example, in `global.asa`) and then use it in another, which is something that, in theory, you could do with `MtsPipeline` (although it's not recommended). You will need to create a new instance of the object every time you need to use it.

When you create a transacted pipeline, always remember to use components that support transactions. In particular, you should make sure that all the components that access a database do so through transaction-aware ODBC-compliant COM objects, such as ADO. The same recommendation is valid if you decide to develop your own pipeline components, a topic that we will tackle later on in this chapter.

Caching Pipelines

As you can imagine, the action of loading a pipeline from disk every time that it is run can waste a lot of valuable system resources. Luckily, Commerce Server provides us with the `Commerce.ConfigurationCacheHelper` component, which can be used to cache a pipeline configuration file once it's been loaded from disk.

In order to use this component, you must first create an instance of either `MtsPipeline` or `MtsTxPipeline`, which you will use to load the configuration file that you want to cache. Once the file has been loaded, you can save it into an instance of `ConfigurationCacheHelper` by calling its `SaveToCache` method:

- ❑ **Syntax:**
  `ConfigurationCacheHelper.SaveToCache(Pipeline)`

- ❑ **Parameters:**
  Pipeline An instance of `MtsPipeline` or `MtsTxPipeline` that contains the pipeline configuration file to be cached

`SaveToCache` will return a unique token that you can use to retrieve your pipeline. It's important to understand that the component will not save the pipeline object, but only its configuration. As such, you can use the cached configuration files anywhere in your store, and you should save the unique token in a location that is accessible by all the scripts (that is the Application object). To do so, you need to call the `LoadFromCache` method instead of loading the pipeline configuration file from disk, as you would normally do:

- ❑ **Syntax:**
  `ConfigurationCacheHelper.LoadFromCache(Pipeline, CacheToken)`

❑ **Parameters:**

CacheToken   The unique token returned by `SaveToCache` when the configuration file was
saved to the cache

Pipeline   An instance of `MtsPipeline` or `MtsTxPipeline` that will receive the
configuration file from the cache

Once you've called `LoadFromCache`, your pipeline object is ready to go, without the need to
continuously access the server's hard drive to load the configuration files.

If you have to delete one or more configuration files from the cache, you can do so by calling the
`DeleteFromCache` method:

❑ **Syntax:**
```
ConfigurationCacheHelper.DeleteFromCache(Pipeline, CacheToken)
```

❑ **Parameters:**

CacheToken   The unique token returned by `SaveToCache` when the configuration file was
saved to the cache

Pipeline   An instance of `MtsPipeline` or `MtsTxPipeline` that will receive the
configuration file from the cache

In general, you will initialize an instance of this component in your store's `global.asa` file, so that
the configuration files commonly used will be available to all the pages in your site. If you do so, you
should remember to delete the cache entries when your application ends, so that you will be able to
reclaim all the memory used by them.

Interpreting Pipeline Logfiles

So you've got a pipeline problem, huh? When one of your components isn't working – or is not
properly configured, as it happens in many cases – the best way to solve the problem consists of
looking at the log file that the pipeline objects generate. Always remember that you *have* to turn
logging on every time you execute a pipeline, because the objects do not provide this behavior by
default. At the same rate, as we mentioned earlier, you should always remember to turn logging off as
soon as you stop needing it.

Choosing a Location for the Log File

The first thing that you should do once you decide that you need pipeline logging is to establish a
good location for your log files. Debugging a pipeline is an excruciating process under normal
circumstances, so you shouldn't try to make it even more difficult by placing your logs in a location
that is difficult to reach. Best of all, if you are modifying the site remotely, you should make sure that
the files will be easy to retrieve from where you are.

Therefore, the server's root folder (`C:\`) does not qualify for our good spot contest. The same goes for
the `\Winnt` directory! Depending on what kind of access you have to the hard drive, I recommend
that you create a folder one level below the root and use that exclusively for logging. That way, you
can easily wipe out old log files by simply getting rid of everything that lives in that folder. If you
have created a new directory for this, be sure to give it the proper access rights; the `IUSR_YOURHOST`
user should have change permissions to be able to write the logfile.

Examining the Logfile

Unfortunately for us, Commerce Server does not come with a log file viewer, which means that you'll have to load and examine the logs in a normal editor. I find that Notepad does a really good job from this point of view, at least if you're using the Windows NT version (the one that comes with Windows 9x has the terrible problem of being limited to reading only up to 64kb of data).

```
txpipeline.log - Notepad                                    _ B X
File  Edit  Search  Help
Sink started at 1999/04/26 18:23:56.0857
PIPELINE:++ 1999/04/26 18:23:56.0857  Pipeline Execution st
      7 components in the list (MTS is enabled)
PIPELINE:++ component[0x0] about to be called ProgID: Comme
RootObject:      ReadValue      _Purchase_Errors        UT_
RootObject:      ReadValue      bill_to_name    UT_BSTR Mar
RootObject:      ReadValue      bill_to_street  UT_BSTR 10€
RootObject:      ReadValue      bill_to_city    UT_BSTR Tor
RootObject:      ReadValue      bill_to_state   UT_BSTR ON
RootObject:      ReadValue      bill_to_zip     UT_BSTR M4H
RootObject:      ReadValue      bill_to_country UT_BSTR USA
PIPELINE:-- component [0x0] returned hr: 0x0 in 60 millisec
PIPELINE:++ component[0x1] about to be called ProgID: Comme
RootObject:      ReadValue      _Purchase_Errors        UT_
RootObject:      ReadValue      cc_name UT_BSTR Marco   UT_
RootObject:      ReadValue      cc_type UT_BSTR Visa    UT_
RootObject:      ReadValue      cc_type UT_BSTR Visa    UT_
RootObject:      ReadValue      _cc_number      UT_BSTR 40€
RootObject:      ReadValue      _cc_expmonth    UT_I4   4
RootObject:      ReadValue      _cc_expyear     UT_I4   199
PIPELINE:-- component [0x1] returned hr: 0x0 in 10 millisec
PIPELINE:++ component[0x2] about to be called ProgID: Comme
RootObject:      ReadValue      cc_type UT_BSTR Visa    UT_
RootObject:      ReadValue      _cc_expmonth    UT_I4   4
RootObject:      ReadValue      _cc_expyear     UT_I4   199
RootObject:      ReadValue      _cc_number      UT_BSTR 40€
PIPELINE:-- component [0x2] returned hr: 0x0 in 0 milliseco
PIPELINE:++ component[0x2] about to be called ProgID: Comme
```

You can also use other programs to import the log files. Excel seems to work a lot better than any other, as long as you import the file as a tab-delimited database. However, the spreadsheet program tends to confuse numbers and strings (for example, credit card numbers are taken as numbers, with terrible consequences) and I find the whole process of having to import the file every time a bit annoying (you will too, after the third time that you have to look at a log in a ten-minutes time span).

Once you get past their mass, however, log files are relatively easy to understand. As you can see by looking at one, they start with an entry that records when the pipeline object was first executed:

```
Sink started at 1999/04/26 18:23:56.0857
```

Next, an entry is used to record that the pipeline was executed:

```
PIPELINE:++ 1999/04/26 18:23:56.0857  Pipeline Execution starts (lMode==0x1,
lFlags==0x0)       7 components in the list (MTS is enabled)
```

This line tells us that the mode specified in the Execute method of the originating pipeline object was 1 (lMode in the log), that there are seven components in the pipeline and that the originating object was an instance of MtsTxPipeline, since MTS is enabled. You have probably noticed that the line begins with the text PIPELINE:++, which indicates the beginning of a task. Similarly, the end of a task is indicated by the text PIPELINE:--. In fact, going forward in the log, we notice the following:

RootObject:	ReadValue	_Purchase_Errors	VT_DISPATCH	PV=[0x33bc60]	VT_EMPTY	_empty_
RootObject:	ReadValue	bill_to_name	VT_BSTR	Marco	VT_EMPTY	_empty_
RootObject:	ReadValue	bill_to_street	VT_BSTR	100 Nowhere Fd.	VT_EMPTY	_empty_
RootObject:	ReadValue	bill_to_city	VT_BSTR	Toronto	VT_EMPTY	_empty_
RootObject:	ReadValue	bill_to_state	VT_BSTR	ON	VT_EMPTY	_empty_
RootObject:	WriteValue	_payment_auth_code	VT_NULL	_null_	VT_BSTR	FAITH
RootObject:	ReadValue	bill_to_zip	VT_BSTR	M4H1L3	VT_EMPTY	_empty_
RootObject:	ReadValue	bill_to_country	VT_BSTR	USA	VT_EMPTY	_empty_

```
PIPELINE:++ component[0x0] about to be called ProgID: Commerce.Scriptor.1
PIPELINE:-- component [0x0] returned hr: 0x0 in 60 milliseconds
```

As you can see, this set of entries corresponds to an entire task, that is, the execution of component number 0 in the pipeline, which is an instance of **Scriptor**. The entries within the task correspond to individual accesses that the object does to the data dictionary. They all begin with RootObject: and can express either read or write operations. Read operations include the following information:

❑ **Action type**
   Always ReadValue, indicating that this entry corresponds to a read operation.

❑ **Source Name/Value pair**
   The name of the Name/Value pair that was read from the data dictionary

❑ **Source pair's type**
   The type of data that was read from the data dictionary. Contains one of the possible subtypes of a COM Variant variable.

❑ **Value read**
   The value that was actually read from the data dictionary

❑ **Destination Name/Value pair type**
   The Variant sub-type of the variable that the component passed to the main dictionary to receive the value.

❑ **Destination Name/Value pair value**
   The contents that the destination Name/Value pair had *before* the data dictionary copied the new value into it.

For write operations, the following information is logged:

❑ **Action type**
   Always WriteValue, indicating that this is a write operation.

❑ **Destination Name/Value pair**
The name of the Name/Value pair whose value is being changed.

❑ **Original type**
The Variant sub-type of the Destination Name/Value pair *before* the change.

❑ **Original value**
The value of the Destination Name/Value pair *before* the change.

❑ **New type**
The Variant sub-type of the Destination Name/Value pair *after* the change.

❑ **New value**
The value of the Destination Name/Value pair *after* the change.

At the end of the pipeline, you will find two lines similar to the following:

```
PIPELINE:-- 1999/04/26 18:23:58.0940 Pipeline Execution completed returning
            hr: 0x0  i: 0x7  hrLoop: 0x0  *plErrorLevel: 1 (MTS committed)
Sink stopped at 1999/04/26 18:23:58.0940
```

They indicate that the pipeline has ended its execution (the pipeline itself is considered one task, and therefore has an opening and closing entry, just like the individual components). In particular, you want to take a look at the last few words of the first line, which indicate the error level at the end of the pipeline (1 in this case) and, if you're running an instance of MtsTxPipeline, what happened to the transaction in which the pipeline was running (in this case, it was committed).

What to Look For in a Pipeline Log

When you have a problem the first thing you should be looking for is where the pipeline stopped. If it stopped in response to an error raised by a component, take a look at the values read and written by it. In most cases, the log will be able to tell you what was wrong. For example, if a pipeline stopped its execution because a component wasn't expecting a value to be Null, take a look at what the last value read by it was, and act consequently.

If your pipeline didn't stop in response to a runtime error, then you are probably trying to look at how one or more Name/Value pairs were modified during the pipeline's execution. If your log file is very cluttered, it might be worth going through it and deleting all the read or write entry that do not have anything to do with the pairs you're interested in. This way, you'll end up with a list of all the changes that your pair went through during the pipeline's execution.

Building MyPipe From Scratch

So we know what a pipeline is, and we know where they are stored and how to edit them, but how are they used in the system? We are going to build a pipeline of our own, MyPipe.pcf, from scratch, just to see how it all comes together. The pipeline will only contain one stage and that stage will have one pipeline component, the Scriptor Component. Executing just one pipeline component can be done using the Micro Pipeline, but we will use the normal pipeline to get a better understanding of the pipelines used in a Site Builder Wizard generated store. We will discuss the Micro Pipeline later in this chapter.

As you can see, the Pipeline Editor is started in Enhanced Mode. This will give us the possibility to add and remove stages as we please. The parts we will be using from Commerce Server are:

- ❑ `Commerce.MtsPipeline` component to run the actual pipeline
- ❑ Win32 Pipeline Editor to create the pipeline file `MyPipe.pcf`
- ❑ `Commerce.Dictionary` for data object and Context object
- ❑ `Simplelist` as error list within the data object

Specifying the Functionality of MyPipe

Our component will require the `Request` object in the Pipeline context to be able to retrieve the user agent. It will also require three numerical values named `value1`, `value2` and `value3`, and a `SimpleList` object stored as errors where the `Scriptor` component can insert any errors that occurred. Now that we know what will happen, we create an ASP file to actually execute the pipeline.

Create a Script to Execute MyPipe

We will begin creating an ASP script that will set up the Data and Context objects, initialize and run the pipeline, and print a result.

```
<% Option Explicit %>
<HTML><HEAD><TITLE></TITLE></HEAD><BODY><H1>Execute MyPipe</H1>
<%
   Dim objPipe, lngErrorLevel
   Dim objData, objContext
   Dim strKey, objErrors, strError

   ' creating the data object
   Set objData = Server.CreateObject("Commerce.Dictionary")
   objData.value1 = "100"
   objData.value2 = "200"
   objData.value3 = "300"
```

The first thing we do in the script is create a Commerce Dictionary object to be the carrier of our data through the pipeline. In a Site Builder Wizard generated shop, this object is actually a `Commerce.OrderForm` object, which in turn is an implementation of a Dictionary object. We also add three values to the Dictionary object, and assign them all numeric values.

```
' creating the errors object and adding it to objData
Set objData.errors = Server.CreateObject("Commerce.SimpleList")
```

The next thing to do is to create the `SimpleList` object errors, which we will use within the pipeline for error handling. We simply create the object and add it to our Dictionary object. When using the `OrderForm` object, this would be equivalent to the `_Basket_Errors` and `_Purchase_Errors` values, which are filled with errors whenever there was a problem with the values in the `OrderForm`.

```
Set objContext = Server.CreateObject("Commerce.Dictionary")
Set objContext.Request = Request
```

The third step will be to create another `Commerce.Dictionary` object to serve as a Context object for the pipeline. This is a required parameter by the `Execute` method of the pipeline object, and can contain basically whatever we want. We decide to settle for the ASP Request object so we can retrieve the user agent. Remember – this is just an example to show how it works.

```
Set objPipe = Server.CreateObject("Commerce.MtsPipeline")
Call objPipe.LoadPipe("D:\Inetpub\wwwroot\mypipe.pcf")
lngErrorLevel = objPipe.Execute(1, objData, objContext, 0)
```

Once the Data and Context objects are set up, we proceed to actually create the Pipeline object itself, initialize it with the `LoadPipe` method, and then execute it. The suspicious first and last parameters are there for backwards compatibility, and should be set to the values show above. The return value of the `Execute` method indicates what happened within the pipeline as it was executed:

❑ "1" means the pipeline executed properly.

❑ "2" means there was an error generated by one of the pipeline components to indicate errors caused by the customer. Those errors are described in detail in the errors `SimpleList` in our case, and in `_Basket_Errors` and `_Purchase_Errors` when using the `OrderForm` object.

❑ A return value of "3" would indicate a failure of the pipeline, such as the inability to access the database.

The last type of errors cannot be corrected by the customer, and should be taken care of using `On Error Resume Next`.

```
If lngErrorLevel <> 1 Then
    Response.Write("<BR>The following errors occured:")
    For Each strError In objData.errors
        Response.Write("<BR>" & strError)
    Next
    Response.Write("<hr>")
End If

Response.Write("<BR><B>user_agent:</B> " & objData.user_agent)
Response.Write("<BR><B>value1:</B> " & objData.value1)
Response.Write("<BR><B>value2:</B> " & objData.value2)
Response.Write("<BR><B>value3:</B> " & objData.value3)
Response.Write("<BR><B>total:</B> " & objData.total)
%>
</BODY></HTML>
```

So, we do the check of the return parameter, but leave it to the user to do the `On Error Resume Next` error handling. If any pipeline component generated errors occurred, they are all written out using a loop, and we end the script by printing out the values we added to the Data object, and those values we expected to get in return.

Starting with creating an instance of a `Commerce.MtsPipeline` object, we then proceed to call the `LoadPipe` method of this object. As briefly mentioned in Chapter 9, this will initialize the pipeline with the configuration file, the `.pcf`, from the store's `Config` directory. We will then proceed, if we want, to create a log file for this component. Logging the pipeline execution is something that should only be done when debugging. It is very performance degrading and will fill up your hard disk in a very short time. The pipeline is then executed using the `Execute` method.

Editing the Scriptor Component

When you add a scriptor component to your pipeline, you will get a number of empty functions to begin with, so all you have to do is add your code. We will only deal with the Commerce Server `Execute` method, since this is the one doing the work when the component is used.

```
function MSCSExecute(config, objData , objContext, flags)
    Dim lngResult
    lngResult = 1

    Set ASPRequest = objContext.Request
    objData.user_agent = ASPRequest.ServerVariables("HTTP_USER_AGENT")
```

We use the context object to retrieve the ASP Request object, and assign a new value to the Data object, `user_agent`, which will receive the value of `HTTP_USER_AGENT`. We then do some validation on the values sent to the `OrderForm`. We could also do a check if the values actually existed, and add errors for that – after all this script is depending on these values, but we leave that to the user.

```
    If Not IsNumeric(objData.value1) Then
        objData.Errors.Add("Value1 was not numeric")
        lngResult = 2
    End If

    If Not IsNumeric(objData.value2) Then
        objData.Errors.Add("Value2 was not numeric")
        lngResult = 2
    End If

    If Not IsNumeric(objData.value3) Then
        objData.Errors.Add("Value3 was not numeric")
        lngResult = 2
    End If
```

If all the parameters were correct, the sum of the three values is calculated and added to a new value in the `objData` Dictionary, and if there were any errors we simply assign the total a value of -1. The script is ended with assigning our return value:

- ❑ 1 if everything went okay and

- ❑ 2 if a parameter wasn't numeric.

```
    If lngResult = 1 Then
        objData.total = CInt(objData.value1) + CInt(objData.value2) + _
                        CInt(objData.value3)

    Else
        objData.total = CInt(-1)
    End If

    MSCSExecute = lngResult

End Function
```

Running the script with non-numeric values will generate this:

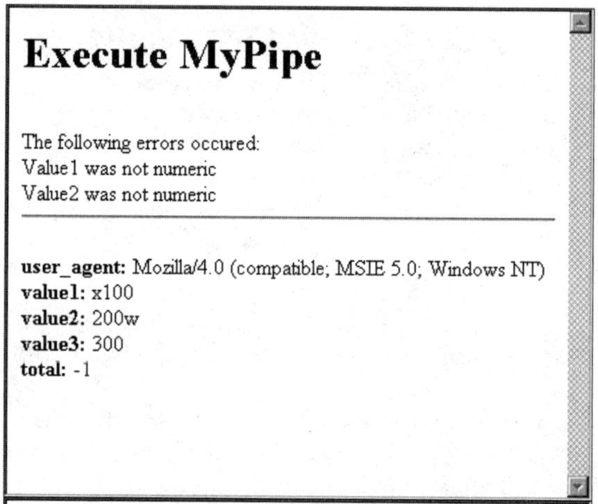

Execute MyPipe

The following errors occured:
Value1 was not numeric
Value2 was not numeric

---

user_agent: Mozilla/4.0 (compatible; MSIE 5.0; Windows NT)
value1: x100
value2: 200w
value3: 300
total: -1

Running the script with numeric values will generate this:

Execute MyPipe

user_agent: Mozilla/4.0 (compatible; MSIE 5.0; Windows NT)
value1: 100
value2: 200
value3: 300
total: 600

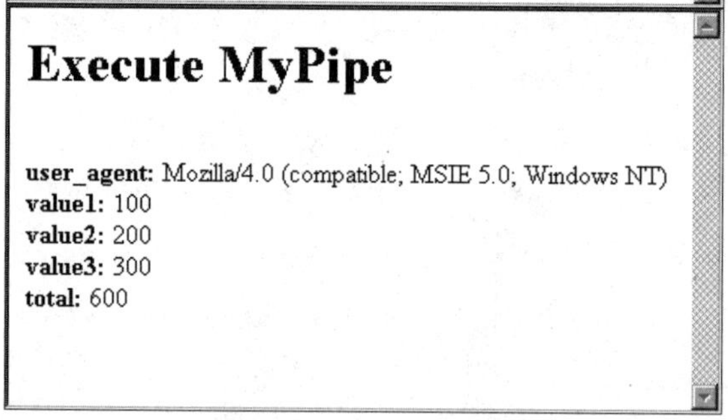

In this example, we used the `Commerce.MtsPipeline` object to execute our pipelines, but there are two other ways to facilitate pipelines in Commerce Server. If you want your pipeline to be executed using a transaction, as is the case in the purchase pipeline, you should go with the `Commerce.MtsTxPipeline`, and if you only want to execute one single pipeline component, you should use the `Commerce.MicroPipe` object.

A Closer Look at the OPP

Commerce Server comes with three pipeline templates with the ordinary store. The Product and Plan pipelines can be executed separately, as is done in a Site Builder Wizard generated store on the `basket.asp` script page, while the Purchase pipeline requires the order form to be run through the plan beforehand.

❑ **Product**
This type of pipeline is used to generate the information that is displayed in the product detail page of a store. It ensures that the data shown is the most up-to-date and accurate, as it applies all the possible discounts and modifiers to an item's base price stored in the database.

❑ **Plan**
The plan pipeline is used to calculate all the information regarding an order without processing it. This makes it possible, among other things, to calculate the true order cost, including shipping and tax fees, and show it to the user *before* he or she makes the final decision on whether to actually complete the purchase.

❑ **Purchase**
Finally, the purchase pipeline is used to complete an order that has already gone through a plan pipeline and is ready to be processed.

In an OPP, the dictionary object that will be run through these pipelines is always represented by an instance of the `Commerce.OrderForm` object, which holds all the data necessary to the completion of an order. In the case of the Product pipeline, the `OrderForm` doesn't necessarily have to hold the entire order, but only the product that you need to determine the information for.

The Product Pipeline

This is the simplest kind of OPP available. As we mentioned above, its goal is to generate the information that is necessary to display in the product information page. As such, its structure is extremely simple, as you can see in the figure shown here, and it only contains five stages:

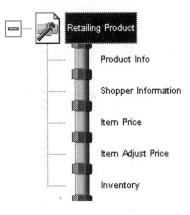

Stage	Description
Product Info	This stage holds components that retrieve information from the database of all the products held in the Items list of the `OrderForm` object. Related components: `QueryProdInfo`, `QueryProdInfoADO`, `RequiredProdInfo` (included)
Shopper Information	The Shopper Information stage adds information about the shopper to the `OrderForm` object. Related components: `DefaultShopperInfo`
Item Price	The goal of this stage is to determine the most current price for each item in the `OrderForm` object. Once the value has been calculated, it has to be stored in the `_iadjust_regularprice` Name/Value pair of each item's dictionary. At the end of the stage, the pipeline makes sure that a value `_iadjust_regularprice` has been set for each item. Related components: `DefaultItemPrice`, `RequiredItemPrice`
Item Adjust Price	This stage is used to determine the actual current price for each item in the `OrderForm`, including any discounts. At the end of the stage, the pipeline verifies that a value for the `_iadjust_currentprice` pair is stored in the dictionary for each item. Related components: `ItemPromo`, `RequiredItemAdjustPrice`, `SaleAdjust`,
Inventory	Finally, this stage is used to determine the availability of each item Related components: `FlagInventory`, `LocalInventory`

As you can see, at the end of its execution the Product pipeline has simply gone through a list of all the items stored in the `OrderForm` object and determine the most current price for each of them. Using this pipeline is a good idea if your goal is to display to each user how much they will be actually paying for a product while they're looking at it. Otherwise, they would normally have to wait until they get to the shopping basket in order to get the final product price.

The Plan Pipeline

If you take a look at the next figure, you will notice that the Product pipeline is really a subset of the Plan pipeline, which is used to determine the complete cost of an order, including shipping and tax fees (when possible). The Plan pipeline is used at least in two different points of an online store: the shopping basket, for which it calculates the order detail and subtotal, and the payment page, for which it calculates the total amount of the order.

The Plan pipeline is also used after the Purchase button is pressed on the payment page to re-calculate the order total and make sure that nothing has changed between when the total was last shown to the user and when he or she actually authorized the purchase. If a difference is found (using the VerifyWith system that we saw in the last chapter), then the pipeline will raise an error and cause the system to return to the payment page and authorize the purchase again.

The complexity of the Plan pipeline is significantly higher than the Product pipeline, and as such it includes several more stages:

Stage	Description
Merchant Information	This stage can be used to set information about the merchant for which the purchase is being made. It is completely optional, and can become useful, for example, if you have modified your system to deal with more than one merchant sharing the same pipeline – the mall structure Related Components: None

Table Continued on Following Page

Stage	Description
Order Initialization	This stage initializes the order information, verifying that the correct quantity for each item (stored in `Item.Quantity`) has been set. At the end of the stage, the built-in checking system performs several clean-up operations, such as assigning an order ID (unless one has already been assigned), setting the `_oadjust_adjustedprice` entry for each Item to `NULL` (which contains the price of each Item in the `OrderForm` adjusted for the quantity of items purchased) and deleting several Name/Value pairs that are to be reset during the execution of the pipeline. Related Components: `RequiredOrderInit`
Order Check	The Order Check stage verifies that the order can be processed. By default, at the end of the stage the checking logic generates an error if the `OrderForm` object contains no items. The goal of any components in this stage should be to either provide further methods of determining the validity of the order (based on the information available at that point) or to attempt and recover from a situation in which the order cannot be processed. Related Components: None
Order Adjust Price	The goal of components in this stage is to determine the final correct price for each item and store it into the `_oadjust_adjustedprice` Name/Value pair in its dictionary. This includes, for example, calculating any order-wide promotions, and so on. At the end of the stage, the pipeline makes sure that the proper Name/Value pairs have been set in the `OrderForm` object. Related Components: `DbOrderPromoDBOrderPromo`, `DbOrderPromoADODBOrderPromoADO`, `RequiredOrderAdjustPrice`
Order Subtotal	The subtotal of the order is calculated here. Typically, this value will be computed by summing together all the `_oadjust_adjustedprice` values and storing the resulting amount in the `OrderForm._oadjust_subtotal` Name/Value pair. The subtotal stored here does not include shipping, handling and taxes, which are calculated later on. The reason why this happens is that those fees are often computed based on the order subtotal, and therefore can only be determined after this stage is complete. In addition, the order subtotal is displayed in the basket, at which point the shipping and tax fees cannot be calculated yet, because the ship-to address is unknown. At the end of this stage's execution the pipeline verifies that a value for `_oadjust_subtotal` has been written to the `OrderForm`. Related Components: `DefaultOrderSubtotal`, `RequiredOrderSubtotal`

Stage	Description
Shipping	Clearly, the shipping stage is used to determine shipping costs for the order. These are, in turn, to be stored in the _shipping_total Name/Value pair of the `OrderForm` object. At the end of the stage, the pipeline makes sure that this value has been set. Related Components: `DefaultShipping`, `FixedShipping`, `LinearShipping`, `TableShipping`, `TableShippingADO`, `RequiredShipping`
Handling	Similarly, this stage takes care of any handling charge that must be added to the order, which should be stored in the _handling_total Name/Value pair. Once again, the pipeline will verify that the value has been set in the `OrderForm`. Related Components: `DefaultHandling`, `FixedHandling`, `LinearHandling`, `TableHandling`, `TableHandlingADO`, `RequiredHandling`
Tax	The final stage before calculating the order's total cost consists of determining the tax fees. Although the pipeline's logic only checks that the components in the Tax stage have calculated tax totals for the order as a whole, it's usually a good idea to keep a per-item value as well. This is especially true if you are going to use the records from your online store directly for accounting purposes and you plan to have different tax rates for different items. In that case, you must be able to determine how much tax was paid and on what items. The components in this stage are expected to set at least two values, _tax_total and _tax_included, respectively used to determine what is the total amount of tax that has to be applied to the order and the amount already included in the order cost. Related Components: `DefaultTax`, `SimpleCanadaTax`, `SimpleJapanTax`, `SimpleUSTax`, `SimpleVATTax`, `RequiredTax`
Order total	This stage takes care of computing the total cost of the order. This is done by summing the order subtotal, shipping, handling and tax fees. In addition, the end-of-stage logic implements the `VerifyWith` algorithm, that determines whether certain information should be shown again to the user because a price has changed somewhere along the pipeline's execution. The total should be stored in the `OrderForm._total_total` Name/Value pair, which is checked at the end of the stage. Related Components: `DefaultTotal`, `RequiredTotal`

The Purchase Pipeline

The goal of the Purchase pipeline is to take an OrderForm object, already processed by the Plan pipeline, and complete the purchase include therein. As such, its structure is extremely simple, as you can see in the following figure, and it only contains three stages:

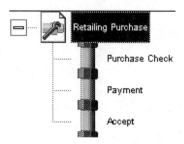

Stage	Description
Purchase check	This stage can be used to verify that an `OrderForm` is ready for the purchase process. This might include making sure that it has indeed gone through the Plan process (i.e. that the order total has been set, and so forth), and that all the required payment information is present. No checks are performed at the end of the stage. Related Components: `ValidateCCNumber`
Payment	The payment stage is where the actual order is processed in the most traditional sense: its goal is to either accept or refuse the order by verifying the customer's ability to pay for it. Any component in this stage should therefore be performing payment-related tasks, such as verifying a user's account status, connecting to an external card authentication and payment processing system . At the end of the stage, the pipeline verifies that the `_payment_auth_code` Name/Value pair is set in the OrderForm. This indicates that the purchase was succesful. Related Components: `DefaultPayment`, `RequiredPayment`
Accept	This final stage takes care of the post-purchase activities, such as updating the inventory, storing the order, sending a confirmation e-mail to the customer, and so on. This stage is entirely optional, and it does not provide any end-of-execution logic. Related Components: `ExecuteProcess`, `MakePO`, `PipeToPipeTransfer`, `POToFile`, `SaveReceipt`, `SendSMTP`, `SQLItem`, `SQLItemADO`, `SQLOrder`, `SQLOrderADO`

Business-to-Business Stores and the OPP

Business-to-business (b2b) electronic commerce is a set of transactions in which businesses, rather than a business and an individual, are at either end of the line. Even if you run a business-to-business store (discussed in full in Chapter 12), you will still need at least part of the functionality provided by the OPP. As a matter of fact, as we have seen while examining the MS Market Store sample, the purchase process is not that different from the one of a business-to-consumer store, although the payment and order submission methods are probably going to be different.

There are two types of business-to-business OPPs: **Corporate Purchase Plan** and **Corporate Purchase Submit**. As you can imagine, they can be compared to the Plan and Purchase pipelines respectively. You can still use the Product pipeline in your business-to-business store, as it does not contain any stages that can be tied either to business-to-consumer or business-to-business electronic commerce.

The Corporate Purchase Plan pipeline, as you can see from the figure below, is exactly the same as the Plan pipeline, although some of the names change because we are now talking about requisitions and buyers rather than orders and shoppers. Keep in mind that, even though we are dealing with a b2b scenario, the order data is still kept in an `OrderForm` object.

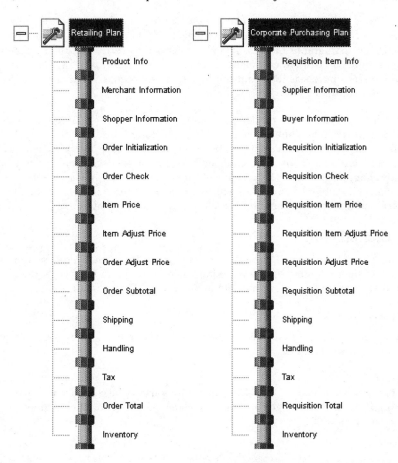

A different discussion must be made for the Corporate Purchase Submit pipeline. In the next diagram, you can see that it only contains two stages – even fewer than the Purchase pipeline! Their goal is to simply make sure that the requisition is valid, which also includes verifying that the buyer is authorized to purchase; if the buyer doesn't have the necessary credentials, then these stages send a request for authorization from the buyer's manager before submitting it to the supplier.

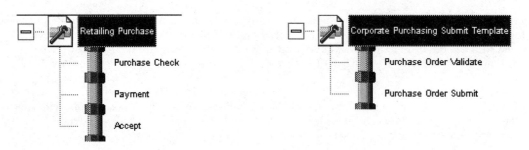

The Purchase Order Validate stage is intended to verify that the order can indeed be completed. This stage is truly a combination of the Purchase Check and Payment stages of the Purchase pipeline that we just saw a few paragraphs back, as it is also intended to verify that the party who is making the requisition has the authority to complete it. Actions that can be taken in this stage include determining the buyer's purchase limit and sending approval requests to a manager if that limit is surpassed, as is done in the MS Market sample store

The Purchase Order Submit stage, on the other hand, is intended for relaying the order to the supplier; naturally, this can be done in many methods, including fax, e-mail, manual transfer and so on. In a purely business-to-business scenario, however, you will most likely have a direct link to your supplier through an interchange of some kind, such as EDI or even a system entirely based on the **Commerce Interchange Pipeline** (CIP), which we'll see later on. In this case, a special pipeline component makes it possible for you to transfer the content of the `OrderForm` to another pipeline (normally a CIP) and launch its execution, which in turn causes an interchange to take place.

Built-in OPP Components

Commerce ServerServer comes with a number of built in components. In this section, we'll take a look at each one of them, divided by the stage they belong to. As we will see, some components are ubiquitous, in that they can be used in more than one stage, or even in all of them.

Elements of a Component

From an OPP-developer point of view, each component is characterized by four elements (with the exclusion of the stage it belongs to):

❑ **Name**
This is obviously the name of the COM object that contains the component. Since in a pipeline each component can also be given a label, the Name should be considered more properly the *type* of the component.

❑ **Properties**
A component's properties represent the data that can be used to determine its behavior. This could include, for example, the name of a table, or the location of a file, and so on. Each component has its own set of properties – or even no properties at all.

❑ **Values read**
This is a list of values that are read from the `OrderForm` object by the component. It's important to understand that this list is generally provided only as a reference point, as a component doesn't have to implement it to function correctly. However, knowing what information a component accesses can be useful when trying to determine what's wrong with a pipeline (and, believe me, that'll happen often enough!).

❏ **Values written**
Similarly, this is a list of the values that the component writes to the pipeline object. Once again, it's only intended as a reference, and a component need not implement it to work properly.

❏ **Context values read**
This is a list of the Name/Value pairs that are accessed by a component from the pipeline's context. What was said for the other lists also applies to this one, and its role becomes important when you're adding a third-party component to your pipelines, because it might require the context to contain some specific values that are not included in it by default. It's important to note that a component is not supposed to *write* anything in the context (although that's possible, because the context is passed as a Dictionary object), because the latter is discarded and re-created every time a pipeline is executed.

The Scriptor Component

Let's start our tour of the OPP components offered by Commerce Server with what is not tied to any specific stage. It's important to understand that, even though all the other components have been designed to work in one or more particular stages, you can also use them anywhere else in the pipeline, as long as the appropriate conditions exist (that is that all the Name/Value pairs that they need to function properly have already been set, and so on).

The first component that we are going to examine is also one of the most versatile, and is called Scriptor. It can be used to run scripts written with any language that is compatible with the Windows Scripting Interface. This includes not only VBScript and JavaScript (or JScript), but also other installable languages such as PerlScript. A neat consequence of the compatibility is the fact that it can interface to COM very easily, provided the scripting language supports it, and therefore it allows us to take advantage of our usual arsenal of components and objects.

Furthermore, there are two advantages if you decide to use VBScript for your scripts. You'll most likely be very familiar with it already, since your ASP scripts work exactly the same way using the same dll, `vbscript.dll`. Secondly, it is a big plus to be able to leverage the existing knowledge of a VBScript or VB programmer to create custom COM components, and then incorporate them into the Commerce Server environment. This then limits the architecture only to your imagination, and the requirements you are trying to satisfy.

Let's start by taking a better look at the component:

Attribute	Description	
Name	Scriptor	
Properties	Scripting Engine	Specifies the scripting engine that will be used to interpret and execute the script. By default, the possible choices include VBScript and JScript.
	Source	Determines whether the script is stored internally within the component, as one of the component's properties, or externally in a file.

Table Continued on Following Page

Attribute	Description	
Properties	Filename	If the source is external, this property contains the path to the file that holds the script text.
	Config	Can be used to set a number of parameters that can be used by the script. This is useful in those cases where you write a generic script that needs configuration settings.
Values Read	Any	
Value Written	Any	
Context Values Read	Any	

When you specify Internal as the source of the script, the latter becomes part of the component's properties and is stored together with them. This means that, when your store loads the pipeline (more on this later on), it will also load the script at the same time. If you choose External, on the other hand, the script will be stored in a separate file and it will have to be loaded separately, causing a potential slowdown, since Windows will have to open another file, read from it, and close it. On the other hand, there are instances in which you might want to store the script in an external file because of other practical reasons, particularly if you are in the development phase and there is the necessity of changing the scripts very often.

In order to work inside a Scriptor component, a script must include the MSCSExecute method defined below:

❑ **Syntax:**
```
Function MSCSExecute(Config, Dictionary, Context, Flags)
```

❑ **Parameters:**
Config	a Dictionary object that contains the configuration data for the component as described below
Dictionary	the dictionary that contains the data to be manipulated by the component (that is, a Commerce.Dictionary object)
Context	a Dictionary object that contains the component's context
Flags	a reserved value

The configuration Dictionary object contains a number of parameters, including those that are specified as part of the component's properties in the Config text box. They are:

Parameter	Description
Script_type	Determines whether the script is internal or external. In the first case, it contains the string value INTERNAL; otherwise, it contains the string value EXTERNAL.
Script_text	Contains the script's entire text when the script_type is set to INTERNAL.

Parameter	Description
Script_name	Contains the fully qualified path to the file that contains the script to execute, when the script_type is set to EXTERNAL.
Engine_prog_id	The name of the scripting engine that is being used to execute this script.

From a practical point of view, I have found that it is very unlikely that a script will be using any of these values, since the scripts are usually written as self-contained entities that either have all the data they need built-in or take it from the dictionary.

The Dictionary parameter is a Dictionary object that contains the data that must be read, manipulated and written by the component. In an OPP, this corresponds to the OrderForm object, from which you can read and write any information regarding the order that is being processed. You should keep in mind a few rules-of-thumb when writing scripts (or pipeline components in general):

1. As we already mentioned, under normal conditions you should never overwrite a value that is already in the pipeline, and you should instead assume that another component before yours has already determined the correct value for that. Naturally, there are a number of exceptions to this, depending, for example, on how your pipeline components are ordered, and on what values you are dealing. You can check to see whether a component has been already written (or exists) in the OrderForm by using the IsNull VBScript function.

2. It is not a good idea to trap an error (using the On Error Resume Next statement) unless you are completely sure that your script will be able to handle it. WSH and the pipeline-handling objects of Commerce Server provide default handling for any run-time errors and will notify the store's ASP script automatically, whereas if you fail to trap an error, but the VBScript engine has been instructed to ignore it, your pipelines will appear to work correctly and your headaches will multiply tenfold (at least). If you want to write any error-handling code, do it in your ASP scripts.

3. Microsoft Transaction Server (MTS) contexts are not available to Scriptor scripts. As a result, you will not be able to create a script that is able to commit or rollback a transaction, although the script itself might run within a transaction context if the pipeline is being run using a transaction-friendly Commerce Server object. We'll discuss the interaction of pipelines with MTS later on in the chapter.

The Context parameter is simply a Dictionary object that contains the set of values and objects that the script can use to perform certain operations. The Context is created by the store as part of the loading and execution of the pipeline (we'll look more into that in the next chapter), and it can contain just about anything, starting from ASP-intrinsic objects (such as Server or Request), ADO recordsets, string and numeral values, and so on.

I should point out that, although the Scriptor component *does* offer a wide variety of possibilities (as a matter of fact, almost just as many as ASP!) it shouldn't be used where complex scripts are needed because of performance reasons. In those cases, Scriptor should only be your starting point, and you should be considering porting the component to Visual Basic (a very simple operation, as we'll see later on) or to Visual C++ if need be.

The MSCSExecute method should return a numeral value that determines whether its execution was successful or not. In A value of 1 means complete success, while a value of 2 corresponds to a status of warning: the script's execution was not successful, but the pipeline can continue running. A value of 3, finally, corresponds to total failure: not only the script's execution was unsuccessful, but the errors encountered were so grave that the entire pipeline should stop running.

In addition to MSCSExecute, a Scriptor script can also implement two additional methods, MSCSOpen and MSCSClose:

❑ **Syntax:**
```
Sub MSCSOpen(Config)
Sub MSCSClose()
```

❑ **Parameters:**
Config   a Dictionary object that contains the configuration data for the component

MSCSOpen is executed before MSCSExecute, thus giving the script a chance to perform any initialization routine before the script is actually run. MSCSClose, on the other hand, gives you a chance to perform any cleanup operations you might need before the script's execution ends.

It's important to understand that, although these three methods are defined and recognized by Scriptor, the script itself is fully functional, which means that you can define your own functions and subroutines, as long as they are called from within one of the three pre-defined methods (you cannot force a Scriptor component to call anything else directly). Thus, while the minimum script contains at least the MSCSExecute method, a particular case can include as many functions, variables and subroutines as you want.

A Polite Way to Raise Errors

Unlike a run-time error, returning a value of 2 or 3 as the result of MSCSExecute's execution does not raise an error that is directly trappable from within an ASP script using the usual method. As a rule, in fact, pipeline components are required to store a description of any error they raise in two dictionaries that are part of the OrderForm object: _basket_errors and _purchase_errors. In principle, all the required error checking, once the pipeline has been executed, can be limited to simply making sure that those two Dictionary objects do not contain any entry (therefore Count = 0).

The _basket_errors collection should be used to indicate errors that are to be trapped by the basket or shipping page. Components in the Plan pipeline should therefore use it, while the components in the Purchase pipeline should use the _purchase_errors Dictionary object.

Components in the Product Info Stage

As we mentioned earlier, the Product Info stage is used to load into the OrderForm object information about individual products in the order.

The QueryProdInfoADO can in fact be used to run a SQL query against each item in the OrderForm:

Attribute	Description		
Name	QueryProdInfoADO		
Properties	Connection String	Specifies the ODBC/OLE-DB connection string to be used when connecting to the database. If no value is given, then the default connection string is extracted from the pipeline's context.	
	Query	Specifies the text of the SQL query that has to be executed. Alternatively, specifies the name of the query within the store's Query Manager	
	Parameter list	Contains a space-separated list of all the Name/Value pairs that will be passed to the query.	
Values Read	None		
Value Written	(Optional) OrderForm.Item._product_*		
	(Optional) OrderForm.Item._delete		
Context Values Read	(Optional) DefaultConnectionString		
	(Optional) ConnectionStringMap		
	(Optional) QueryMap		

* see explanation later

As you can see, this component requires that a certain number of Name/Value pairs be stored in the pipeline's context in order to function properly. In fact, DefaultConnectionString, which contains the store's default ODBC/OLE-DB connection string, and ConnectionStringMap which contains an optional list of all the connection maps that the store can use, are employed by the component to extract a connection string when none is given as part of its properties.

The QueryMap object, which is instead a Dictionary object commonly created in the global.asa file of a store (we'll see more about that in the next chapter), is used as a generic repository for all the queries used by the store. There is a good reason for keeping all the queries in one place: if you change something in your database, you will not have to scan your entire site to find all the places where you need to change your queries! QueryProdInfoADO uses the QueryMap object if the Query property only contains one word – indicating that it should be considered as a pointer within the Dictionary object rather than a SQL query. Naturally, there is the possibility that you might come up with a one-word SQL query: if you're calling a stored procedure. In that case, all you have to do is use the SQL keyword EXEC to make the SQL call two words long!

It's interesting to notice that the QueryMap does not contain straight strings, but rather a collection of Dictionary objects, which, in turn, are supposed to have a Name/Value pair called SQLCommand that contains the query's actual text. The reason for this is probably to offer the possibility of adding more data for each individual query, although I have never seen it actually used, even in the sample stores provided with Commerce Server.

Regardless of whether the query is specified as a property or as part of the QueryMap Dictionary, it is possible to set any number of parameters into it by specifying them into the Parameter List property. At the time of execution, the component will read the query, and then attempt to replace any question mark characters in it with the parameters specified in the Parameter List, one at a time. For example, if the following query is specified:

```
SELECT * FROM product WHERE sku = '?' AND list_price = ?
```

You could use the following as the text for the parameters:

```
Item.SKU Item.list_price
```

As you can see, the individual items extracted in succession by `QueryProdInfoADO` are given the name `Item`. You can also retrieve data from the `OrderForm` by specifying an entry without the `Item.` prefix.

As a result of its execution, this component stores any column from the first row of the query's result set into the `Item`'s own Dictionary within the `OrderForm`, using the prefix `_product_`. Thus, if your query returns a column called `Price`, after the execution of `QueryProdInfoADO` each item in the `OrderForm` object will contain the entry `_product_Price`. It's interesting to notice that, since the parameters set by `QueryProdInfoADO` start with an underscore character (_), they are not saved to disk or database by the `OrderForm`, instead, they are saved to the site's receipt storage when the purchase is finalized.

If, during its execution, `QueryProdInfoADO` is unable to find a product (for example, the query that you specified returns an empty recordset when run using that product's SKU), it sets the Name/Value pair `Item.Delete` to 1. This can be useful to determine if a product in the user's basket is no longer available, in which case they will be deleted by the `RequiredProdInfo` component which is only visible using Expert/Enhanced Editing mode of the Win32 version of the Pipeline Editor. Also, if the `RequiredProdInfo` component deletes any items marked for deletion, the `MessageManager` message `pur_badsku` will be retrieved and added to the `_Basket_Errors`.

The Shopper Information Stage

This stage only contains one component, which is called `DefaultShopperInfo`. Its only task is to load shopper data from the stores Shopper Dictionary object, stored in the pipeline's context, and save these values as properties on the `OrderForm` object prefixed with `_shopper_`.

Attribute	Description
Name	`DefaultShopperInfo`
Properties	None
Values Read	None
Value Written	(Optional) `OrderForm._shopper_*`
Context Values Read	Shopper

If the Shopper dictionary doesn't contain any data, or if it doesn't exist, `DefaultShopperInfo` doesn't perform any operation. Keep in mind that, because a store is not needed to maintain shopper information (and this is indeed very difficult to do, unless you request that your users register in order to make a purchase or enter the site), the use of `DefaultShopperInfo` and the Shopper Information stage is entirely optional.

The Order Initialization Stage

For the Order Initialization stage, there are no specifically dedicated components. The only component that is included is the `RequiredOrderInit` component, which you only will see when editing the pipeline in expert mode.

`RequiredOrderInit` performs a number of cleanup procedures, including:

- ❏ If `OrderForm.order_id` is `Null`, then it creates a new unique order ID, which are GUIDs rendered in base 36 (making it possible to use all the twenty-six letters of the alphabet, and therefore to use fewer digits, to express the number).

- ❏ For each item in the Items `SimpleList`, it sets the Name/Value pair _n_unadjusted (which expresses the number of items of any product shipped to the user before any adjustments) to the value stored in `Item.quantity`, while _oadjust_adjustedprice is set to zero.

- ❏ It sets to `Null` the following values in the OrderForm:

  ```
  _total_total
  _oadjust_subtotal
  _shipping_total
  _tax_total
  _handling_total
  _tax_included
  _payment_auth_code
  ```

The last action ensures that the data in the OrderForm is reset whenever the pipeline is run, so that each component does not mistakenly assume that it had already been set.

Order Check Stage

What we said for the Order Initialization stage applies to the Order Check stage as well. In this case, the end-of-stage logic is provided by the `RequiredOrderCheck`, which simply takes care of verifying that the OrderForm contains at least one item. If it doesn't, the component adds the proper error message in the _purchase_errors collection.

Item Price Stage

The goal of the components in this stage, as we mentioned earlier, is to ensure that the `Item._iadjust_regularprice` Name/Value pair for each item in the OrderForm is set. The _iadjust_ prefix tells us that the price in this pair is calculated taking into account the properties of the individual item rather than the entire order.

`DefaultItemPrice` copies the value of `Item._product_list_price` into `Item._iadjust_regularprice`. As you have probably noticed, `Item._product_list_price` would normally be extracted from the database by the `QueryProdInfoADO` component (incidentally, the standard Commerce Server product table contains a field called `list_price`!). Unless you provide your own price extraction system, you should use `DefaultItemPrice` in all your stores. Always keep in mind that the _iadjust_regularprice value simply represents the normal cost of the product, *before* any modifiers have been applied. Therefore, you do not normally need to perform any calculation in this stage, as all the special offers and promotions are calculated later on.

A built-in component, `RequiredItemPrice`, takes care of validating that each Item of the Item `SimpleList` has a value in _iadjust_regularprice. If there is no value, an error is raised. This could occur if you have removed the `DefaultItemPrice` in your pipeline.

Item Adjust Price Stage

This stage takes care of adjusting the price of each item in the OrderForm so that it accurately reflects any special offers or sale conditions that might be applicable. The resulting adjusted price must be saved in the `Item._iadjust_currentprice` Name/Value pair, which is checked by the end-of-stage logic.

There are two components that are offered by this stage. The simplest one takes care of determining whether a product is on sale and changes its adjusted price accordingly:

Name	SaleAdjust
Properties	None
Values Read	(Optional) `Item._product_sale_start`
	(Optional) `Item._product_sale_end`
	`Item._product_sale_price`
Value Written	`Item._iadjust_currentprice`
Context Values Read	None

`SaleAdjust` works by comparing the current date and time with the period between `Item._product_sale_start` and `Item._product_sale_end` and, if it falls in between the two dates, will copy the value of `Item._product_sale_price` to `Item._iadjust_currentprice`.

As you may have noticed, the sale Name/Value pairs are in the format that we would expect out of the execution of `QueryProductInfoADO`, which means that there should be three fields in your product database called `sale_start`, `sale_end` and `sale_price`. It's important to understand that, because under normal conditions the dates in the database will be registered as of midnight of the days specified, the day stored in `sale_end` will not be included in the sale period. This means that, if you want to create a sale that lasts until April 15, you will have to specify April 16 as its last day.

The other component that can be applied to the Item Adjust Price stage is called `ItemPromo`, and is a somewhat more complex version of `SaleAdjust`, with the difference that it doesn't take the information it needs from the database.

Name	ItemPromo	
Properties	Start Date	Specifies the first date on which the special offer becomes available
	End Date	Specifies the last date on which the special offer is still available
	Condition Order Key	The Name/Value pair on which the condition for the special to be available is checked
	Condition Operator	The logical operator that has to be used to determine if the condition is true
	Condition Value	The right-hand value of the condition
	Discount Type	The type of discount (percent or dollar amount)
	Discount Value	The amount of the discount (must be an integer).

Values Read	`Item._iadjust_regularprice`
	`Item._iadjust_currentprice`
Value Written	`Item._iadjust_currentprice`
Context Values Read	None

Before even starting to consider its properties, `ItemPromo` verifies that the `Item._iadjust_currentprice` Name/Value pair has not already been set by another component. Then, it checks for two conditions to be both true. The first one is the fact that the current date and time falls between Start Date and End Date, which, by the way, can be specified using any common date format (for example 11/02/1999). The same caveat that we mentioned above, due to the fact that dates are considered as of midnight, is valid from `ItemPromo` as well.

The second condition that this component checks for is the following:

```
If Item.[Condition Order Key] [Condition Operator] [Condition Value]
Then
    apply discount
```

As you can see, therefore, the Name/Value pair specified in the *Condition Order Key* property is always taken from the individual item's dictionary and compared to the value specified in *Condition Value* using the *Condition Operator*. For example, if we wanted to apply the discount to the product whose SKU is "123" then we'd set the component up as follows:

```
Condition Order Key:   SKU
Condition Operator:    = or ==
Condition Value:       123
```

It is important to understand that the comparison is case-sensitive, thus a Condition Value of "ABC" is different from "abc". Also, the Condition Operator "=" is equivalent to "==", and "<>" is equivalent to "!=" (as a matter of fact, those among you familiar with both Visual Basic and C – or VBScript and JavaScript – will have recognized that these operators are simply different ways of expressing the same concept in the two languages respectively).

The discount that `ItemPromo` applies can either be a percentage off the product's price, or a fixed amount. There is one important rule to keep in mind:

> **The discount can only be expressed as an integer value. For dollar amounts, it is specified in cents (for example, 100 corresponds to a discount of $1). For percentage values, it is expressed in integer points, and cannot be greater than 100.**

The Order Adjust Stage

While the components in the Item Adjust Price stage affect the items in the `OrderForm` individually, those in the Order Adjust stage calculate changes to their prices based on rules that involve the entire order. This includes, for example, the special offers that we saw in Chapter 2, which can be used to specify offers such as "buy x and get y at z% off", and so on. The price resulting from the calculations – whatever they might be – must be stored in the `Item._oadjust_adjustedprice`, which is checked by the end-of-stage logic. This stage is the last occasion in which the price of the items should be changed, and its results will be used by the next stages as final.

The only built-in component that Commerce Server offers for this stage is `DbOrderPromoADO`:

Name	DBOrderPromoADO	
Properties	Connection String	Specifies the ODBC/OLE-DB connection string to be used when connecting to the database. If no value is given, then the default connection string is extracted from the pipeline's context.
	Query	Specifies the text of the SQL query that has to be executed. Alternatively, specifies the name of the query within the store's Query Manager
Values Read	`Item._iadjust_adjustedprice`	
	(Optional) `Item._product_*`	
	(Optional) `_shopper_*`	
	`Item._n_unadjusted`	
	`Item.quantity`	
Value Written	`Item._oadjust_adjustedprice`	
	`Item._n_unadjusted`	
Context Values Read	(Optional) `DefaultConnectionString`	
	(Optional) `ConnectionStringMap`	
	(Optional) `QueryMap`	

`DbOrderPromoADO` works by applying the promotional information extracted from a database table. A connection to the database is created using either the ODBC/OLE-DB connection string specified in the *Connection String* property, or by using the default connection strings stored in the context if this is left empty. The data is generated by executing the SQL command stored in the *Query* property, which can also be a pointer inside the store's `QueryMap`, similarly to what happened for the `QueryProdInfoADO` component. Here is a sample query:

```
SELECT
    promo_name, date_start, date_end,
    shopper_all, shopper_column, shopper_op, shopper_value,
    cond_all, cond_column, cond_op, cond_value, cond_basis, cond_min,
    award_all, award_column, award_op, award_value, award_max,
    disjoint_cond_award, disc_type, disc_value
```

```
FROM test_promo_price

WHERE active <> 0

ORDER BY promo_rank
```

The columns listed in the query above will be discussed in detail, but before going any further into the details of the component's configuration, let's examine what this component does. Its ultimate goal is to decide whether a particular promotion (taken from the result set extracted by the query) should be applied to any product in the OrderForm. To do so, it takes into consideration the following conditions:

❑ Was the promotion intended to be triggered by this product?

❑ Was the promotion intended to be triggered when this specific user was making a purchase?

❑ Are any of the products affected by the promotion?

❑ Do they satisfy a minimum requirement of price or quantity?

❑ Can the product affected by the promotions also be the one that triggered it?

If the promotion is triggered, then a discount is applied to all the items in the OrderForm that satisfy the conditions. Optionally, the component can be instructed also to verify whether the current date and time fall within a specific period of time during which the promotion is valid.

The amount of data that the component expects the query to return is quite massive – which shouldn't come as a surprise considering the amount of conditions that must be verified – but it's not very complex to understand:

Parameter	Description
cond_column	The individual item's Name/Value pair that must be used as part of the condition that triggers the promotion
cond_op	The logical operator to be used as part of the condition that triggers the promotion (expressed as a string, such as "=" or "<>")
cond_value	The value to be used as the right-side operator of the condition that triggers the promotion
cond_all	An optional integer value that, if set to 1, instructs the component to override the condition that triggers the promotion always trigger the promotion, without checking the condition. If it's equal to 0 (or any other value), the condition will be checked.
award_column	The individual item's Name/Value pair the must be used as part of the condition that determines whether a promotion can be applied to the item.
award_op	The logical operator to be used as part of the condition that determines whether a promotion can be applied to a specific item

Table Continued on Following Page

Parameter	Description
award_value	The value to be used as the right-side operator of the condition that determines whether a promotion can be applied to a specific item
award_all	An optional integer value that, if set to 1, instructs the component to override the condition that determines whether a promotion can be applied to a specific item and force it to apply the promotion to all the items instead. If set to 0 (or any other value), the condition is verified instead.
shopper_column	The OrderForm object's shopper data Name/Value pair that must be used as part of the condition that determines whether a promotion can be triggered by the customer who is currently making the purchase. The pair will be looked for in the OrderForm._shopper_* list.
shopper_op	The logical operator to be used as part of the condition that determines whether a promotion can be triggered by the customer who is currently making the purchase.
shopper_value	The value to be used as the right-side operator of the condition that determines whether a promotion can be triggered by the custmer who is currently making the purchase.
shopper_all	An optional integer value that, if set to 1, instructs the component to ignore the condition that determines whether a promotion can be triggered by the customer who is currently making a purchase and to grant the promotion to all customers.
cond_basis	The type of check that will be made to verify whether an item meets the minimum requirements to trigger a promotion. A value of "P" means a price check, while a value of "Q" means a quantity check
cond_min	The value that represents the minimum requirements for an item to trigger a promotion. Can be expressed either as a price (in cents, only integer numbers allowed) or a quantity.
award_max	The maximum number of products that can be affected by the promotion
disjoint_cond_ award	A numeric value that, if set to 1, indicates that the promotion can be *disjointed*, that is, applied to the same item that triggers it. For example, if a disjointed product X has a "buy one, get one for 50%" promo, the customer will have to buy another product X to get it at 50% off, whereas if the product was not disjointed, the customer would only have to buy one X and then that product would be 50% off.
disc_type	The type of discount that is applied if the promotion is triggered and an item meets the minimum requirements for it. Can be either "%", for a percentage, or "$" for a dollar amount.

Parameter	Description
disc_value	The discount that is applied if the promotion is triggered and an item meets the minimum requirements for it. Can either be a dollar amount expressed in cents (only integer numbers are allowed) or a percentage.
date_start	The first day of the period during which the promotion is valid
date_end	The day after the last day during which the promotion is valid

Fist, the date_start and date_end parameters are used to determine whether the promotion is compared to the current date to see if the promotion is valid. If it was valid – today's date is within the range – the shopper_*, cond_* and award_* fields are used to determine the rules for the promotion. If these conditions are met, the component will perform the adjustment of the prices accordingly setting the _oadjust_adjustedprice value in the OrderForm object.

When you generate a store using the store builder wizard, and you have chosen to use price promotions, you will get the Price Promotion Wizard, which will help you to add Price Promotions to your store. For example, when you first generate the store and choose to insert the sample data, your store will contain a price promotion called Sample. Here are two screenshots on how it appears; the first one shows a buy 2 for the price of one sample, and the second is a buy this and get that for this much % off:

Promo name:	Sample
Description:	Buy 2 '001' for the price of 1!
Status:	ON	Rank:	10
Start date:	4/11/97	End date:	4/11/98
Buy:	2 unit(s) ⊙ Products where: sku ▾ = ▾ 001 ○ Any Products
Get:	1 Unit(s) Same as or Different from Buy ▾ ⊙ Products where: sku ▾ = ▾ 001 ○ Any Products
At:	100 % off ▾

Promo name:	Buy 2 '002' Get '001' at 90% Off
Description:	Buy 2 '002' get 1 '010' at 100% OFF!
Status:	ON	Rank:	10
Start date:	9/27/99	End date:	10/11/99
Buy:	2 unit(s) ⊙ Products where: sku ▾ = ▾ 002 ○ Any Products
Get:	1 Unit(s) Same as or Different from Buy ▾ ⊙ Products where: sku ▾ = ▾ 010 ○ Any Products
At:	100 % off ▾

These `promos` are stored in the database table `price_promo`, and their column values are listed below:

Column Name	Column Values	Column Values
promo_name	Sample	Sample 2
promo_type	3	1
promo_description	Buy 2 '001' for the price of 1!	Buy 2 '002' get 1 '010' at 100% OFF!
promo_rank	10	10
active	1	1
date_start	Apr 11 1997 12:00AM	Sep 27 1999 12:00AM
date_end	Apr 11 1998 12:00AM	Oct 11 1999 12:00AM
shopper_all	1	1
shopper_column	(null)	(null)
shopper_op	(null)	(null)
shopper_value	(null)	(null)
cond_all	0	0
cond_column	_product_sku	_product_sku
cond_op	=	=
cond_value	1	2
cond_basis	Q	Q
cond_min	2	2
award_all	0	0
award_column	_product_sku	_product_sku
award_op	=	=
award_value	1	10
award_max	1	1
disjoint_cond_award	0	0
disc_type	%	%
disc_value	100	100

As you can see, there are some extra columns not discussed, which are used within the Manager. The `promo_name` and `promo_description` are the description of the promotion shown in the list, the `promo_type` is one of four pre-defined promotions – 1 for " Buy x Get y at z% off", 2 for "Buy x Get y at z$ off", 3 for "Buy 2 x for the price of 1" and 100 for any promotions created manually by the manager. If you want to add a pre-defined promotion you will have to edit the manager ASP pages manually. Finally, the `promo_rank` controls the order in which the price promotions should be applied. This can be seen in the query we saw before, where the final `ORDER BY promo_rank` clause will control this.

You should keep in mind that the complexity of the `DBOrderPromoADO` component can take its toll on your server's performance, especially if you implement a large number of special offers in your store and the user is making a large purchase.

Order Subtotal Stage

The goal of the components in this stage is to calculate the order's subtotal and store it in the `OrderForm._oadjust_subtotal` Name/Value pair. The only built-in component provided by Commerce Server for this stage is `DefaultOrderSubTotal`, which simply calculates the sum of all the `Item._oadjust_adjustedprice`.

You won't normally need to add any other component here, unless you need to calculate the order subtotal in a particular way (for example, there has to be a minimum spending, and so on).

Shipping Stage

As you can imagine, the task of the components that reside in this stage is to calculate any shipping costs that are associated with the order. The resulting amount should be stored in the `OrderForm._shipping_total` Name/Value pair, which is checked by the end-of-stage logic.

Commerce Server comes with several built-in components that have been designed to run in the Shipping stage. The simplest one is called `DefaultShipping`, and simply stores the value 0 in the shipping total pair. Clearly, you would use this component only if you are not going to apply any shipping charges to your orders.

The remaining components can be used to calculate shipping costs based on a fixed per-order amount, a per-item fee or a fee schedule stored in a database. In all cases, the determination of the shipping costs is based, at least in part, on the value of the `OrderForm.shipping_method` Name/Value pair, which contains the shipping method selected by the customer for the delivery of his or her order (such as regular mail, express courier, and so on). In a typical Commerce Server starter store, this value is selected in the Shipping page, and is usually equal to a string similar to `"shipping_method_n"`, where n is the number of the entry in the Shipping Method select box. However, you can assign any value you want to the pair, as long as it is consistent through the store *and* the pipeline.

The first component that we'll take a look at is called `FixedShipping`. As you can imagine, it can be used to associate a fixed shipping cost to the order, based on a specific shipping method:

Name	`FixedShipping`	
Properties	Apply when	Specifies the condition which must be satisfied by `OrderForm.shipping_method` in order for the component to apply the specified shipping cost to the order. If it is set to **Always**, then the shipping fee is applied regardless of whether the shipping method has been set. If it contains **Has any value**, then the shipping fee is applied as long as the shipping method pair contains some value (is not null). If it is set to **Equal to Method**, then the fee is applied only if the shipping method pair contains a string that is exactly the same as the value of the method property.
	Method	Contains the string to which the shipping method pair must be compared in order for the discount to apply. The comparison is case-sensitive.
	Cost	The cost of the shipping fee, in cents (only integer values are allowed)
Values Read	`shipping_method`	
Value Written	`_shipping_total`	
Context Values Read	None	

There isn't much to say about this component, except for the fact that you can't have more than one instance of it in the same pipeline with the `Apply When` property set to **Always**. If you do, only the first one will be executed, while the others will be ignored. At the same rate, you should put an instance of `FixedShipping` with the `Apply When` property set to **Always** before any other component, because the latter won't be executed in any case.

A slightly more complex shipping computation system is provided by the `LinearShipping` component, that can be used to calculate the fees based on the multiplication of a fixed rate by one or more values in the OrderForm:

Name	`LinearShipping`	
Properties	Apply When	Specifies the condition that must be satisfied by `OrderForm.shipping_method` in order for the component to apply the specified shipping cost to the order. If it is set to **Always**, then the shipping fee is applied regardless of whether the shipping method has been set. If it contains **Has any value**, then the shipping fee is applied as long as the shipping method pair contains some value (is not `null`). If it is set to **Equal to Method**, then the fee is applied only if the shipping method pair contains a string that is exactly the same as the value of the Method property.

Properties	Method		Contains the string to which the shipping method pair must be compared in order for the discount to apply. The comparison is case-sensitive.
	Basis Item Key		Expresses the key in the OrderForm that is used as a multiplier for calculating the rate. Can be one of the following:
		Order.*fieldname*	A specific Name/Value pair (*fieldname*) from the OrderForm (i.e. `Order._oadjust_subtotal`).
		Sum.*fieldname*	The sum of individual values taken from each item in the OrderForm. For example, specifying `Sum.Quantity` equals to ordering the sum of the Quantity values for all the items. Thus, if you have 3 shirts and 2 ties in your basket, `Sum.Quantity` for your OrderForm is equal to 5.
		Sumq.*fieldname*	Represents the sum of individual values taken from each item in the OrderForm multiplied by the value of the `Quantity` Name/Value pair for each item.
		Count	The total number of **unique** products in the OrderForm (ignoring the quantities).
	Rate		The basic rate that has to be multiplied by the result of the Basis Item Key.
Values Read	(Optional) *		
	(Optional) `Item.*`		
	`shipping_method`		
Value Written	`_shipping_total`		
Context Values Read	None		

The meaning of the `Basis Item Key` can be a little confusing, but all you really have to do in order to understand it better is try to examine the framework in which the component needs to run. When calculating a shipping fee you fundamentally have three scenarios to keep in mind:

❑ **Per-product cost**
The rate is applied to the order based on the amount of unique products purchased, or some other order-wide parameter. This is covered either by the *Count* or the *Order.fieldname* methods.

❑ **Per-item cost**
The rate is multiplied by the number of items, or a similar value. This is covered by the *Sum.fieldname* method.

❑ **Per-linear quantity cost (i.e. weight)**
The multiplier is calculated based on the amount of items time the linear quantity cost for each of them. For example, specifying *Sumq.Weight*, assuming that your `OrderForm` contains an `Item.Weight` Name/Value pair for each product, will cause the Rate to be multiplied by the quantity for each item times its weight:

The third and last component that can be applied to this stage is `TableShippingADO`, which can be used to retrieve the shipping cost for the order based on the information stored in a database.

Name	`TableShippingADO`		
Properties	Apply When	Specifies the condition that must be satisfied by `OrderForm.shipping_method` in order for the component to apply the specified shipping cost to the order. If it is set to **Always**, then the shipping fee is applied regardless of whether the shipping method has been set. If it contains **Has any value**, then the shipping fee is applied as long as the shipping method pair contains some value (is not null). If it is set to **Equal to Method**, then the fee is applied only if the shipping method pair contains a string that is exactly the same as the value of the Method property.	
	Method	Contains the string to which the shipping method pair must be compared in order for the discount to apply. The comparison is case-sensitive.	
	Connection String	The connection string that must be used to connect to the database. If no string is specified, the component looks in the pipeline context for default values.	
	Parameters	Contains a space-separated list of all the parameters that are required by the query in order to return the correct result set. Each parameter can be one of the following:	
	Count	The name of the column in the query's result set that contains the shipping rate.	
		Order.*fieldname*	A specific Name/Value pair (*fieldname*) from the OrderForm (i.e. `Order._oadjust_subtotal`).
		Sum.*fieldname*	The sum of individual values taken from each item in the OrderForm. For example, specifying `Sum.Quantity` equals to ordering the sum of the Quantity values for all the items. Thus, if you have 3 shirts and 2 ties in your basket, `Sum.Quantity` for your OrderForm is equal to 5.

Properties	Count	Sumq.*fieldname*	Represents the sum of individual values taken from each item in the OrderForm multiplied by the value of the `Quantity` Name/Value pair for each item.
		Column	The total number of **unique** products in the `OrderForm` (ignoring the quantities).
Values Read	(Optional) `*`		
	(Optional) `Item.*`		
	(Optional) `Shipping_method`		
Value Written	`_shipping_total`		
Context Values Read	(Optional) `DefaultConnectionString`		
	(Optional) `ConnectionStringMap`		
	(Optional) `QueryMap`		

Once executed, the component starts by verifying that it is compatible with the shipping method currently selected in the `OrderForm`, using the same system that we already illustrated. Next, it prepares the query for execution. This is done in a way similar to the one used for the `QueryProdInfoADO` component: the query text initially contains a series of question marks, which are progressively replaced by the values specified in the *Parameters* property. When the query is ready, the component executes it and then stores the value of the field expressed by the *Column* property in the `OrderForm.Shipping_Total` Name/Value pair.

Keep in mind that only the first row of the query's result set is considered by `TableShippingADO`, and the value of the rate column is stored in the database as it is, without being modified in any way. Therefore, you should create your database table so that it returns the correct amount given all the possible parameters (such as quantity, weight, and so on). Also, the component does not allow you to calculate the shipping costs for each individual item, but only of the order as a whole.

One final note: although you can react to different shipping methods by adding an instance of `TableShippingADO` to the pipeline for each possible value of the `Shipping_method` pair, you can also incorporate this functionality in your query. In that case, all you will need to do is the following:

❑ Start by modifying your database table so that it can calculate the right amount for each shipping method

❑ Change the query so that it passes the shipping method along as a parameter

❑ Add `Order.Shipping_method` to the `Parameters` property

❑ Set the `Apply When` property to **Has any value**.

Keep in mind that you should not set the `Apply When` property to **Always**, because you will most likely need the shipping method pair to have a valid value in order to make a correct computation of the shipping costs.

The Handling Stage

The Components in this stage take care of calculating "handling" fees. These are usually connected to operations such as packing of the products, gift-wrapping, and so on. The built-in components that are provided as part of the Handling stage perform exactly the same functions as the ones in the Shipping stage, to the point that they are based on the OrderForm.Shipping_method Name/Value pair and have very similar names. However, they store their result in the OrderForm.Handling_total Name/Value pair instead.

DefaultHandling – similarly to DefaultShipping – limits itself to storing a value of 0 in the handling total pair. As such, you will normally use it only when your store does not charge any handling fee. FixedHandling performs exactly as FixedShipping, and has the same properties. You will want to use it when you charge a fixed, per-order handling fee.

LinearHandling, which provides the same functionality as LinearShipping, is used instead when the shipping fee is based on values such as weight or quantities. TableHandlingADO, finally, calculates handling costs based on the contents on a database table, exactly in the same way as TableShippingADO.

The Tax Stage

The Tax stage is used – as its name vaguely suggests – to calculate any tax charges for your items. The end-of-stage logic only checks that a value has been stored in the OrderForm._tax_total and OrderForm._tax_included Name/Value pairs, indicating the total amount of tax charged for the order, and the amount of tax that is included in the total cost of the order. Normally, the cost of the order (order subtotal) does not contain any tax amounts, so you will leave OrderForm._tax_included set to 0.

Contrary to what happens for shipping and handling charges, the tax fees are calculated on a per-item basis, because different items might be subject to different tax rates, or none at all. As such, it's also a good idea to store some tax information for each item, so that it will be easier later on to determine how much tax was exactly applied where.

Commerce Server includes several built-in components for this stage, each one designed to provide support for a particular tax model. However, you should always keep in mind that taxes are a very difficult subject to tackle (after all, they are conceived by politicians), and therefore the built-in components might not be able to adequately cover your particular situation. Since miscalculations in how you apply taxes can result in heavy losses (not to mention trouble with the government) it might be a good idea to get in touch with a tax consultant before you decide whether to use the built-in components or a third-party plug-in (there are several that provide a much more complete and up-to-date computation system).

The simplest tax component that Commerce Server provides...doesn't actually calculate any taxes! It's called **DefaultTax** and, similarly to all the other "Default" components that we have seen so far limits itself to setting both OrderForm._tax_total and OrderForm._tax_included to zero. As before, you will want to use this component only if you decide that your store charges no taxes (this is not such an uncommon occurrence in electronic commerce, since most of the individual governments have not caught up with the fact that most of the online sales will take place outside the local area where your business resides).

If you wish to charge sale taxes in the United States, you can use the SimpleUSTax component. As you may know, sale taxes in the US are charged by individual states, and usually apply only to those sales that fall within a state where the company that runs your store has a physical location.

You might have guessed, from the fact that I'm writing a technical book, that the same caveat that applies to the built-in tax components also applies to my "personal" interpretation of how taxes work. As such, you should always seek the advice of a tax consultant before deciding how taxes should be applied to your customers.

Name	`SimpleUSTax`	
Properties	Apply when	Specifies the condition under which the value of the `OrderForm.ship_to_country` Name/Value pair triggers the component's execution. Can be set to **Always**, in which case the component is always executed, **Has any value**, which causes the component to be executed as long as the ship-to country pair has a value (is not null), or **Equal to country**, in which case the value of the pair is compared to the string stored in the *Country* property.
	Country	Contains the string to which the ship-to country pair must be compared if the *Apply When* property is set to **Equal to country**. The comparison is case-sensitive; by default, Commerce Server stores 3-letter ISO country codes in that pair (USA for the US).
	State Rate List	A space-delimited list of state codes and their sales tax rates. Each entry in the list consists of the two-letter state code and the percent value of the rate, separated by a colon (for example California, 5.4% tax = CA:5.4)
Values Read	`Ship_to_state`	
	`Item._oadjust_adjustedprice`	
	`Ship_to_country`	
Value Written	`Item._tax_total`	
	`Item._tax_included`	
	`_tax_total`	
	`_tax_included`	
Context Values Read	None	

Before starting the tax calculation, this component checks whether the right conditions are met. This is decided using a method similar to the one used for the shipping and handling components. You might be wondering why you need to tell the component what country it should apply the tax to (nothing prevents you from entering anything different from USA), since it has been designed to work specifically for the United States. The reason for this is that the component conforms to a tax model that *happens* to be the one used in the States, but that could also be used somewhere else. This will become more evident later on, when we talk about the VAT tax component, which works with the tax methods used in Europe.

For Canadian stores, you might want to use the `SimpleCanadaTax` component, which supports the tax system used in Canada. As you may know, Canadians usually have to pay two sales taxes: the Goods and Services Tax (GST) and the Provincial Sales Tax (PST). Unfortunately, this is not always true, as in some regions the two taxes are incorporated in what is called the Harmonized Sales Tax (HST). `SimpleCanadaTax` can handle both GST and PST, but not HST (at least not as such, as we'll see in a moment):

Name	SimpleCanadaTax	
Properties	Apply when	Specifies the condition under which the value of the `OrderForm.ship_to_country` Name/Value pair triggers the component's execution. Can be set to **Always**, in which case the component is always executed, **Has any value**, which causes the component to be executed as long as the ship-to country pair has a value (is not null), or **Equal to country**, in which case the value of the pair is compared to the string stored in the *Country* property.
	Country	Contains the string to which the ship-to country pair must be compared if the *Apply When* property is set to **Equal to country**. The comparison is case-sensitive; by default, Commerce Server stores 3-letter ISO country codes in that pair (CAN for Canada).
	GST Item Key	The Name/Value pair that contains the GST rate for a certain item.
	PST Item Key	The Name/Value pair that contains the PST rate for a certain item.
	Province List	A space-delimited list of two- or three-letter province codes to which the rates apply.
Values Read	`Item._oadjust_adjustedprice`	
	`Ship_to_state`	
	`Ship_to_country`	
	(Optional) `Item.GSTKey`	
	(Optional) `Item.PSTKey`	
Value Written	`Item._tax_total`	
	`Item._tax_included`	
	`_tax_total`	
	`_tax_included`	
	`_tax_total_gst`	
	`_tax_total_pst`	
Context Values Read	None	

You may be wondering why the GST and PST are not specified as a global parameter, but rather as two Name/Value pairs within each item's dictionary. The reason for this is that Canadians do not pay the same tax rate on every project. There are cases in which only GST is applicable, others – much less frequent – in which the PST is the only tax paid, and cases in which no tax is paid at all (for example: food). As such, it's not possible to apply the same tax rate to all the products – the component gives us the possibility of specifying what the tax rate is for each product. This can be easily done if you add two fields (one for the GST and one for the PST) to your product database and store them in each item's dictionary, for example using the `QueryProdInfoADO` component.

Keep in mind that you do not necessarily need to add two fields with the actual GST and PST rates for each product in the product table – this would pose a problem if the tax rates change. Instead, you can store the rates in a separate table and only provide "links" to them in the product table, then using the query that you pass on to `QueryProdInfoADO` to extract the correct rates.

The problem with the HST is obviously that the component simply doesn't support it. Even though you might be able to work around the issue by using a combination of GST and PST (which is exactly what the HST is), you will still have to provide the necessary logic to recognize the tax as HST and display it as such (which is mandatory).

Japanese stores can use the functionality provided by the `SimpleJapanTax` to apply taxes for that country. This component is the only one that keeps track of the `_tax_included` Name/Value pair, indicating that the price of some items might already be inclusive of any applicable tax fee. When this happens, the component does not recalculate the tax for those items, storing the amount of tax already included in the price in the appropriate Name/Value pair.

Name	`SimpleJapanTax`	
Properties	Apply when	Specifies the condition under which the value of the `OrderForm.ship_to_country` Name/Value pair triggers the component's execution. Can be set to **Always**, in which case the component is always executed, **Has any value**, which causes the component to be executed as long as the ship-to country pair has a value (is not null), or **Equal to country**, in which case the value of the pair is compared to the string stored in the *Country* property.
	Country	Contains the string to which the ship-to country pair must be compared if the *Apply When* property is set to **Equal to country**. The comparison is case-sensitive; by default, Commerce Server stores 3-letter ISO country codes in that pair (JPN for Japan).
	Include Item Key	The Name/Value pair that contains the amount of tax already included in the price for a certain item.
	Rate Item Key	The Name/Value pair that contains the tax rate for a certain item.

Table Continued on Following Page

Values Read	Item._oadjust_adjustedprice
	Ship_to_country
	(Optional) Item.*IncludeItemKey*
	(Optional) Item.*RateItemKey*
Value Written	Item._tax_total
	Item._tax_included
	_tax_total
	_tax_included
Context Values Read	None

SimpleJapanTax works similarly to the Canadian component, in that the included tax and tax rates are extracted on a per-item basis. In this case, however, it is going to be difficult to use the same trick that we used before for the data retrieval, because the amount of tax included in each item will be entirely dependent on the item itself. In addition, you will have to adjust the amount of tax included for each product times the number of items that the customer is buying.

European stores, finally, will be able to compute their sales tax using the SimpleVATTax component:

Name	SimpleVATTax	
Properties	Apply when	Specifies the condition under which the value of the OrderForm.ship_to_country Name/Value pair triggers the component's execution. Can be set to **Always**, in which case the component is always executed, **Has any value**, which causes the component to be executed as long as the ship-to country pair has a value (is not null), or **Equal to country**, in which case the value of the pair is compared to the string stored in the *Country* property.
	Country	Contains the string to which the ship-to country pair must be compared if the *Apply When* property is set to **Equal to country**. The comparison is case-sensitive; by default, Commerce Server stores 3-letter ISO country codes in that pair
	Rate Item Key	The Name/Value pair that contains the tax rate for each individual item in the OrderForm.

Values Read	`Item._oadjust_adjustedprice`
	(Optional) `Item.`*`RateItemKey`*
Value Written	`Item._tax_total`
	`Item._tax_included`
	`Item._tax_vat_item`
	`_tax_total`
	`_tax_included`
Context Values Read	None

This component, too, works in the same way as the last two. If you decide to write your own components for this stage, try to keep in mind that sometimes you must apply tax fees not only to the products, but also to the shipping and handling fees, for example. The built-in components do not do this by default, so you will have to provide the functionality yourselves (a quick Scriptor component will help you out in thiscase as well).

Order Total Stage

After the tax stage, it's time to calculate the total cost of the order. This should be stored in the `OrderForm._total_total`. Commerce Server offers only one component for this stage, called `DefaultTotal`, which simply calculates the sum of the order-wide values calculated to this point (subtotal, shipping, handling and taxes).

Inventory Stage

The inventory stage can be used to check the inventory status of all the items in the OrderForm before the order is sent to the Purchase pipeline. Doing so will ensure that the user will know which products are available immediately and which ones are in backorder. Unfortunately, in order to be able to give a reasonable estimate of the product availability, you will also have to have a direct link to your line-of-business system, which, as we already mentioned, is not always a viable possibility.

Also, most online stores have settled on the standard approach of not charging their customers for backordered items until (or if) these items become available. As you may imagine, having the Inventory stage at the end of the Plan pipeline is not really compatible with this approach, and therefore you will have to be a little creative in how you handle availability-related issues. A possible solution would be to use some Inventory-stage component early in the pipeline, for example in the Product Info stage. This is certainly possible (don't forget that the stage affinity of a component is simply indicative, but not mandatory), although not particularly elegant. As an alternative, you might consider re-organizing the pipeline's stages – thus creating your own pipeline (we'll see how to do that later on in this chapter).

The `LocalInventory` component can be used to determine whether one or more items in the pipeline are out of stock. It works by comparing the quantity for each item to the `Item._product_local_inventory` Name/Value pair, which can for example be loaded by the `QueryProdInfoADO` component that we saw earlier. If the quantity requested for each item is more than what is available, then the components stores the difference in the `Item._inventory_backorder` pair and, optionally, stops the execution of the pipeline so that the user can be notified of the fact that some items are in backorder.

Name	LocalInventory	
Properties	Disallow backorder	Specifies whether the component should stop the pipeline's execution if one or more items are in backorder
Values Read	Item._product_local_inventory	
	Item.Quantity	
	Item.SKU	
Value Written	Item._inventory_backorder	
Context Values Read	None	

An important characteristic of LocalInventory is the fact that it works by SKU, and not by item. This means that, if the same item appears twice in an OrderForm, the component will sum the two quantities and compare *those* to the product availability. A different approach is offered by the FlagInventory component, which limits the inventory availability control to the individual item.

Name	FlagInventory	
Properties	Disallow backorder	Specifies whether the component should stop the pipeline's execution if one or more items are in backorder
Values Read	Item._product_in_stock	
	Item.Quantity	
Value Written	Item._inventory_backorder	
Context Values Read	None	

In this case, the inventory availability should be stored in the Item._product_in_stock Name/Value pair, which could as usual be retrieved by the QueryProdInfoADO component in the Product Infostage.

The third and final component that has affinity with the Inventory stage is called ReduceLocalInventory, and is used to update the inventory information in the product database once an order is completed. As such, that component should not be part of the Plan pipeline, but should rather be included in the Accept stage of the Purchase. We'll talk about it there.

The Purchase check stage

Let's move now on to the Purchase pipeline. Its first stage is Purchase Check, which, as we mentioned earlier, can be used to determine whether all the information in the OrderForm is correct and therefore payment can be applied. It's important to understand that this stage should *not* be used to process a payment, as its goal is exactly to make sure that everything else is ready before proceeding to the Payment stage.

Commerce Server provides only one component that has affinity with this stage, and one that you will probably use very often! Its name is ValidateCCNumber, and it is used to verify that a credit card number is valid.

Name	ValidateCCNumber	
Properties	Apply When	Specifies the condition under which the value of Order._payment_method is verified to determine whether the component should run. It can be set to **Always**, in which case no check is done, **Has any value**, in which case the component runs as long as the pair is set to any value (is not null), or **Equal to method**, in which case the pair's value must be equal to the string stored in the *Method* property
	Method	A string that must be compared against the value of the Order._payment_method Name/Value pair. The comparison is case-sensitive.
Values Read	_cc_number	
	_cc_expmonth	
	_cc_expyear	
	cc_type	
Value Written	(Optional) _Purchase_Errors	
Context Values Read	None	

The component verifies that:

1. The expiration date stored in the OrderForm is set in either the current or a future date, and

2. The credit card number is set to a number that satisfies the algorithm that we described in Chapter 5.

If either of these two checks fail, ValidateCCNumber interrupts the pipeline's execution and stores an error in the OrderForm._Purchase_Errors SimpleList object.

Payment Stage

During the payment stage, components in the pipeline should take care of verifying that the payment information submitted by the customer is satisfactory for completing the order. Typically, this corresponds to connecting to a credit card processor and charging the customer's credit card for the appropriate amount.

Commerce Server doesn't offer any particular component for this stage, its nature being so generic that you will have to integrate your own solution with the pipeline. Many third-party ISVs who develop credit card processing software, however, now offer Site Server 3 plug-ins for their products. These are easy to use; in fact it's usually a matter of just adding the component to the pipeline, setting your custom properties, and away you go. I would expect, as Commerce Server becomes more popular, we'll be seeing more of these vendors supplying such components.

The end-of-stage logic here checks for the existence of the `OrderForm._payment_auth_code` Name/Value pair. If you do not need to insert any third-party component in the stage, for example because you charge credit cards manually, you can use the built-in `DefaultPayment` component, which stores the code "FAITH" in the Name/Value pair.

Accept Stage

The final stage of the OPP handles all the activities that have to take place after an order has been approved by the store. This includes inventory updates, receipt storage, or even business-to-business transactions with your suppliers. Given the wide variety of tasks that can be accomplished in this stage, it's no surprise that Commerce Server includes a number of built-in components that have an attachment with it.

One thing that we have already discussed is the inventory update. In the section dedicated to the Inventory stage, I mentioned the existence of the `ReduceLocalInventory` component, which can be used to update the inventory count in the product database for each item in the OrderForm. Unfortunately, this component has a small – but important – problem: it doesn't support transactions, since it was included for backward compatibility only. The Purchase pipeline should always be run in a transaction-friendly environment, since the operations that it carries out often affect database data (not to mention "Wallet" data when you charge a credit card!) and should therefore be reversible.

The same functionality offered by `ReduceLocalInventory` can however be replicated using a component which both supports transactions and is of a more generic use, and is called `SQLItemADO`.

Name	SQLItemADO	
Properties	Connection String	The connection string that must be used to connect to the database. If no string is specified, the component looks in the pipeline context for default values.
	Query	The SQL query that the component is supposed to executed for each item in the OrderForm. Can either be a straight SQL statement or a pointer to the store's `QueryMap` object.
	Parameter List	A space-delimited list of parameters that have to be passed as part of the query.
Values Read	(Optional) *	
	(Optional) `Item.*`	
Value Written	None	
Context Values Read	(Optional) `DefaultConnectionString`	
	(Optional) `ConnectionStringMap`	
	(Optional) `QueryMap`	

SQLItemADO works by scrolling through the entire list of items in the OrderForm and executing the same query for each one of them. As in other components before this one, the SQL query can contain a number of parameters, marked by question marks in the statement. As usual, the prefix Order. instructs the component to retrieve a parameter's value from the OrderForm, while the prefix Item. indicates that the value should be taken from the individual item. SQLItemADO also recognizes two special parameters:

❏ count – represents the number of products (individual SKUs) in the OrderForm, while

❏ index – corresponds to the index, within the OrderForm's Items collection, of the item being used by the component.

In order to update the inventory count for all the items in the OrderForm, thus imitating the behavior of the ReduceLocalInventory component, you can use a query similar to the following:

```
UPDATE prod_table
SET inventory_field  = inventory_field - ?
WHERE sku_field = ?
```

And pass this parameter list:

```
Item.Quantity Item.SKU
```

This setup will force the component to go through the list of products in the OrderForm and effectively reduce the inventory count for each one of them by the amount set in the Item.Quantity Name/Value pair.

The SQLOrderADO offers a functionality similar to the one provided by SQLItemADO, with the exception that the SQL query is executed only once, and the entire OrderForm is its scope:

Name	SQLOrderADO	
Properties	Connection String	The connection string that must be used to connect to the database. If no string is specified, the component looks in the pipeline context for default values.
	Query	The SQL query that the component is supposed to executed for each item in the OrderForm. Can either be a straight SQL statement or a pointer to the store's QueryMap object.
	Parameter List	A space-delimited list of parameters that have to be passed as part of the query.
	Use Child Object	Specifies whether the order information should be taken from the pipeline's data dictionary or from an object that resides within it.
	Child Object Name	The name of the Name/Value pair within the pipeline's data dictionary that holds the object from which the order information should be taken. Used in conjunction with the *Use Child Object* property.

Table Continued on Following Page

Values Read	(Optional) *
Value Written	None
Context Values Read	(Optional) `DefaultConnectionString`
	(Optional) `ConnectionStringMap`
	(Optional) `QueryMap`

As you can see, the only difference between the two components is the presence here of the concept of "child object". If you were to specify one, SQLOrderADO would try to extract the order information from an object that resides within the pipeline's data dictionary. Now, in an OPP, the data dictionary is the OrderForm itself, and it would make very little sense to have another OrderForm object within the main OrderForm object! As such, you will probably never use this feature. However, this component can also be used in a Commerce Interchange Pipeline (CIP), as we'll see in Chapter 12, in which the order information is not part of the data dictionary, but rather of an OrderForm object that is stored in one of its Name/Value pairs.

SQLOrderADO supports the same types of parameters used by SQLItemADO, with the following exceptions:

- ❑ The Item. prefix is not recognized
- ❑ The Sum.*pair* expression causes the component to calculate the sum of all the *pair* Name/Value pairs for each individual Item in the OrderForm.
- ❑ The same effect is obtained by using the Sumq.*pair* expression, with the difference that the sum is also multiplied by the Item.Quantity value for each item.

Another interesting inhabitant of the Accept stage is called MakePO – Make Purchase Order. Its goal is to transfer the information stored in the pipeline into text format using a user-specified template.

Name	MakePO	
Properties	Template Filename	The complete filename and path of the file that contains the template. Can also be set using the Browse button.
	Script Language for the template	The WSH language that should be used to interpret the code in the template. By default, can either be VBScript or JavaScript
	Output Property Name	The Name of the Name/Value pair where the template's output will be stored.
	Use Child Object	Specifies whether the order information should be taken from the pipeline's data dictionary or from an object that resides within it.
	Child Object Name	The name of the Name/Value pair within the pipeline's data dictionary that holds the object from which the order information should be taken. Used in conjunction with the *Use Child Object* property.

Values Read	(Optional) *
	(Optional) `Item.*`
Value Written	*(Output Property Name)*
Context Values Read	(Optional) `DefaultConnectionString`
	(Optional) `ConnectionStringMap`
	(Optional) `QueryMap`

The template used by `MakePO` is, by all means, similar to an ASP file, in that it can contain both text and scripting code. The main difference is that scripts will be delimited by the symbols `<%%` and `%%>` (rather than the usual `<%` and `%>`)

In addition, the component will make the OrderForm object (either the data dictionary or the child object) an integral part of the template's scripting context, under the name `Items`. The `OrderForm`'s individual Name/Value pair will also be part of the *default* scripting context, which means that you will be able to address them directly without any need for a prefix. So, for example, `Items.Ship_to_country` will be the same as `Ship_to_country`.

Unfortunately, this arrangement comes with one big string attached. In fact, you are probably used to include local variables in your ASP scripts without declaring them – assuming, of course, that you use VBScript. This is generally considered a bad habit by professional developers, and it is a difficult habit to break. It can be damaging if you use it in a template, because any variable that is not declared belongs, by definition, to the default context. In the case of `MakePO`, though, the default context is the `OrderForm`! This means that, if you do not declare *all* your variables using VBScript's `Dim` statement, you will be adding new Name/Value pairs to it.

As an example of what can be done with this component, let's take a look at this simple template, which creates a simple Purchase Order (PO) containing all the items in the `OrderForm` and their quantities. Initially we declare a function called `FormatString` that will help us format the printed text so it will look nice:

```
<%%
Function FormatString(sString, iLength)
    If Len (sString) > iLength - 1 Then
        sString = Left(sString, iLength - 1)
    Else
        FormatString = String(iLength - Len (sString), " ") & sString
    End If
End Function
```

We then move on to declare a number of variables we will use throughout the code. This should always be done when writing ASP scripts, using `Option Explicit`, which unfortunately the Microsoft Team haven't used when they made the templates for the Site Builder Wizard. Here, however, it is very important that you do this as mentioned before.

```
Dim iCounter
Dim sSeparator
Dim arrItemPairs, arrItemPairColumns, arrItemColumnHeaders
Dim iItemPairColumns
Dim nItemCount, iItem, Item
```

The next step will be to create a dynamic array for the columns that will be presented, stored in the array `arrItemPairs`. Then we will use the array `arrItemPairColumns` to tell the script how big each column should be, and the `arrItemColumnHeaders` array will hold the heading text for each column we add.

```
arrItemPairs = Array ("_product_sku", "_product_name", "Quantity")
arrItemPairColumns = Array (10, 20, 5)
arrItemColumnHeaders = Array ("SKU", "Name", "Qty.")
%%>
```

With the double percentage sign we end the scripting part for now, moving to pure print-text in the same way it works using ASP scripting. We print out some static information such as the stores name and address. We then print out the `order_id`, and the `ship-to` and `bill-to` information, stored in our `OrderForm`. We don't have to state the name of the object since it is default; `order_id` will be interpreted as `Items.order_id`.

```
Wroxstore Sample Store
1 Nowhere St.
Elsewhere, MD 14232
USA

Phone:    ++1-416-555-7789
Fax:      ++1-416-555-7788


P U R C H A S E        O R D E R


Order ID:    <%% = order_id %%>

Ship To:
<%% = ship_to_name %%>
<%% = ship_to_street %%>
<%% = ship_to_city %%>, <%% = ship_to_state %%> <%% = ship_to_zip %%>
<%% = ship_to_country %%>

Bill To:
<%% = bill_to_name %%>
<%% = bill_to_street %%>
<%% = bill_to_city %%>, <%% = bill_to_state %%> <%% = bill_to_zip %%>
<%% = bill_to_country %%>
```

Now the time has come to print out the items on the `OrderForm`. This can be confusing at times, considering our OrderForm object contains an Items collection, so to actually get to the `Items` collection `count` property we must do `Items.Items.Count`. First, let us print out the column headers using the stored values in the `arrItemColumnHeaders` array.

```
<%%
For iCounter = 0 to UBound(arrItemColumnHeaders)-1
    PageGen.Print(FormatString (arrItemColumnHeaders (iCounter), _
                              iItemPairColumns (iCounter)) & " ")
    sSeparator = sSeparator & String(iItemPairColumns(iCounter), "-") & " "
Next
PageGen.Print(vbCrLf & sSeparator & vbCrLf)
```

Now it's time for the actual printing of the order rows, and end the script with printing the total values.

```
For Each Item in Items.Items
    For iCounter = 0 to UBound(arrItemColumnHeaders)-1
        PageGen.Print(FormatString(Item.Value(arrItemPairs (iCounter)), _
                              iItemPairColumns (iCounter)))
    Next
    PageGen.Print(vbCrLf)
Next
%%>

Shipping Costs:     <%% = [_shipping_total] %%>
Handling Costs:     <%% = [_handling_total] %%>
Taxes:              <%% = [_tax_total] %%>

T O T A L           <%% = [_total_total] %%>
```

This will print out the internal decimal value for the order, so $10 will end up as 1000. To fix this we would need the Money method from the DataFunctions object, but that is not accessible here, so we will have to add a scriptor component before this one in the pipeline. That scriptor would then calculate the correct values and store them as, for example, the same values only prefixed with _display. The value _total_total would then be _display_total_total, which could be used within the MakePO script. This is done within the MS Market sample application in the script market\config\FormatCurrency.vbs.

It's reasonable to expect that, stored in the OrderForm, the PO will not really do you any good. In most cases, you will want to somehow get it to the outside. This can be done using the POToFile component, which takes care of saving a text string stored on the OrderForm object to a text file:

Name	POToFile	
Properties	Source Field Name	The Name/Value pair that contains the PO's text.
	Destination	The name of the file that will receive the PO. Can be either a specific file (File Name), a file whose pathname is specified in a Name/Value pair in the OrderForm (File named in field) or a temporary file, which is created by the component and whose name is subsequently stored in the specified Name/Value pair (Temporary File, name saved in field).

Table Continued on Following Page

Properties	Append to file instead of overwriting file	Specifies whether the PO text should be appended to an existing file or if the file should be deleted altogether.
Values Read	(Optional) *SourceFieldName*	
Value Written	None	
Context Values Read	None	

Once the PO has been saved to a file, it can be fed to an external program, for example, for sending it over a phone line or to an EDI partner. The ExecuteProcess component can be used to run such a program:

Name	ExecuteProcess	
Properties	Path name of the executable	The complete path name of the program that has to be executed. (The anonymous user that IIS impersonates **must** have execute permission on the file)
	Arguments to the executable	The command-line parameters to the executable. One of the parameters can be the placeholder %1, which will be substituted with the value of the Name/Value pair specified in the *Field Name of substitutable parameter* property
	Field Name of substitutable parameter	Specified the Name/Value pair whose value must be substituted to the placeholder in the *Arguments to the executable* property.
Values Read	(Optional) *SubstitutableParameter*	
Value Written	None	
Context Values Read	None	

This component works by running the executable specified in the properties. Optionally, it is possible to specify a series of command-line parameters that are passed to the program, including one parameter that is taken from the OrderForm.

If you want to send the PO as a receipt to your customer, you could use the SendSMTP component:

Name	SendSMTP	
Properties	From (required)	The email address from which the message is to be sent. For example: wroxstore_order_send@wrox.com
	SMTP Host (required)	The host name or IP-address of the SMTP Server. For example "smtp.yourhost.com".

Properties	Dictionary fields for Email	To (required); Specifies the name of the field in the OrderForm that contains the email address to which the message will be sent.
		CC; Specifies the name of the field that contains the email addresses to which copies of the message are to be sent.
		Subject; Specifies the name of the field that contains the text that will be used as Subject for the email.
		Character Set for Subject; Specifies the character set that will be used for encoding the subject of this message. The dropdown displays the character sets currently installed on the computer.
		Message Body; Specifies the name of the field that contains the message that is to be included in the body of the email message.
	Message Body Contains	These options specify the format of the message:
		MIME header and body: The business data object is already encapsulated in a MIME Header. Use this option if you use EncodeMIME with the Plain Text option to encode the business data object.
		Text body; Specifies that the business data object consists of straight ASCII text.
		Binary body; Specifies that the business data object is a BLOB. The SendSMTP component will Base64-encode it before sending.
Values Read		The values read are those specified on the Send SMTP properties page: To field, CC field, Subject field and Message Body.
Value Written		None
Context Values Read		ReceiptStorage

Even though this appears to be a nice solution, you must remember that for each new order that is produced by your system, the user has to wait for the message to be sent before the receipt page pops up. This would quickly generate a bottleneck in your system.

A better solution would involve having a separate process, such as a Windows Scripting Host (WSH) script executed at delayed intervals using the AT command, loop through the written receipts and generate the receipt information for you. That way neither the end-user nor the web server is troubled with the task to send SMTP messages.

> *There are also some third party ASP components that will allow you to send queued SMTP messages which will also relieve the web server from the task of sending the mail. Check out AspQMail from ServerObjects,* http://www.serverobjects.com *for more information.*

Another important task that can be carried out in the Accept stage is saving the order information to the database. This can also be done in the ASP script once the pipeline has terminated its execution, and in fact, the Commerce Server basic stores act that way. However, the `SaveReceipt` component can be used to store the data in the database as well:

Name	SaveReceipt	
Properties	No save key prefix	Specifies a prefix that is used to identify data in the OrderForm that should *not* be saved to the database.
Values Read	(Optional) *	
	(Optional) Item.*	
Value Written	None	
Context Values Read	ReceiptStorage	

`SaveReceipt` works by using the properly initialized `DBStorage` object that should be present in the pipeline's context in the `ReceiptStorage` Name/Value pair to save all the data in the `OrderForm` to a database. Those Name/Value pairs whose names begin with the string specified in the *No save key prefix* are not saved. For example, specifying _cc_ causes all the credit card related data not to be saved.

Finally, if you are using Site Server to manage business-to-business communications with your suppliers, you will have to transfer a successful purchase to a CIP in order to send a purchase request over to the appropriate partner. You can certainly do so in your ASP scripts by first executing the OPP, then transferring the data over to a Dictionary object and using that to run the CIP, but it might be easier to use the built-in `PipeToPipeTransfer` component, which takes care of loading an existing CIP, transferring the `OrderForm` data over to it, and executing it.

Name	PipeToPipeTransfer	
Properties	Calling pipeline object	Specifies whether the OrderForm data should be taken from the calling pipeline or from a Name/Value pair thereof.
	Receiving pipeline object	Specifies whether the OrderForm data should be passed as the root of the receiving pipeline, or as a child thereof. Also, specifies whether the receiving pipeline is a Dictionary (for the CIP) or an OrderForm (for the OPP).
	Pipeline configuration filename	The pathname of the file that contains the configuration for the receiving pipeline.
	Pipeline type	The type of pipeline object that should be used to create the receiving pipeline.

Values Read	(Optional) *
	(Optional) `Item.*`
Value Written	None
Context Values Read	(Optional) `DefaultConnectionString`
	(Optional) `ConnectionStringMap`
	(Optional) `QueryMap`

As you can see, the component works by creating a new pipeline object (we'll discuss the Commerce Interchange Pipeline objects in detail in Chapter 12), loading its configuration from the specified file, and then copying the contents of the originating pipeline into it. The newly created pipeline is then executed, including any errors reported to the originating pipeline, continuing the processing.

Small is Beautiful: Micropipes

Once you've been working with pipelines for long enough, you'll begin to wonder (a) why there are no branching capabilities in the pipeline technology and (b) how nice it would be to execute a pipeline component without needing to load and execute an entire pipeline.

While there is no immediate solution to the first problem, you can work around the second by creating a custom pipeline that only contains one stage and one component, but that leaves you with a system that wastes a lot of system resources, since the pipeline configuration will have to be loaded every time, and the overhead of running an entire pipeline versus just a component will become apparent, even if you use caching.

Commerce Server, however, includes a component, called `MicroPipe`, which can be used to execute a single pipeline component. `MicroPipe` offers functionality similar to the one provided by the pipeline objects, including activity logging, but doesn't support transactions in any way.

Using the Micropipe Component

The first step in using an instance of this component is to assign a component to execute by calling the `SetComponent` method:

❑ **Syntax:**
```
MicroPipe.SetComponent(Component)
```

❑ **Parameters:**
Component   The component that must be executed

It's important to understand that you *must* create an instance of the component with a call to `Server.CreateObject` before calling `SetComponent` – the instance of the component is what you pass to it:

```
Set mPipe = Server.CreateObject ("Commerce.MicroPipe")
Set obj = Server.CreateObject ("Commerce.FlagInventory.1")

mPipe.SetComponent (obj)
```

> You can find out what the correct Program ID for the built-in components are by looking at their properties in the Win32 editor. For example, the `FlagInventory` component is registered as `Commerce.FlagInventory.1`.

Executing the Component

`MicroPipe` provides an `Execute` method that is in all aspects the same as the one offered by the other pipeline objects:

❏ **Syntax:**
   `MicroPipe.Execute(DataDictionary, Context, Reserved)`

❏ **Parameters:**
   DataDictionary   The pipeline's data dictionary
   Context   The pipeline's context
   Reserved   Reserved long value; must be zero

As for the other pipeline objects, the execution of a `MicroPipe` will return a long integer value of 1 for success, 2 for a recoverable error and 3 for an unrecoverable failure. You can also set the component to log its activities, using the `SetLogFile` method:

❏ **Syntax:**
   `MicroPipe.SetLogFile(sFilename)`

❏ **Parameters:**
   sFilename   The complete path of the log file

> If you wish to run more than one component in the same page using `MicroPipe`, you can do so by reusing the same instance of the component over and over again – you don't need to create a new one every time.

Setting the Component's Properties

The problem here is, of course, that since you are not loading a configuration file for your pipeline, you cannot set the component's properties before you load it as you have done so far. As a matter of fact, if the components you are going to need have been developed in a certain way, you will be able to access their functionality anyway.

In fact, components that are compatible with ASP development (and every component should be, because otherwise it wouldn't be possible to set their properties from within the web-based editor) should expose two methods, called `GetConfigData` and `SetConfigData`. The former returns the configuration parameters for the component in a Dictionary object, while the latter accepts changes to the configuration parameters from a Dictionary object that is passed to it:

❑ **Syntax:**
```
Component.GetConfigData
Component.SetConfigData(ConfigData)
```

❑ **Parameters:**
ConfigData A dictionary object that contains the configuration parameters to be set

Your problem now is that you do not know how each component's parameters are stored in the configuration dictionary, since the individual properties will be saved in Name/Value pairs whose names do not appear anywhere in this book or in Commerce Server's documentation. As a matter of fact, there *is* an easy way to find out what the properties for a given component are – all you have to do is call its `GetConfigData` method and dump the contents of the Dictionary object that you receive in return. For example, the following ASP-script extracts all the properties exposed by the `TableShippingADO` component:

```
<%
    Set objDump = Server.CreateObject ("Commerce.TableShippingADO")

    Set ConfigDictionary = objDump.GetConfigData

    Response.Write "Property count: " & ConfigDictionary.Count & "<BR>"

    For Each PropertyPair in ConfigDictionary
        Response.Write PropertyPair & "<BR>"
    Next
%>
```

Naturally, all you have to do in order to extract the properties of another component is change the class ID in the call to `Server.CreateObject` that appears in the first line of the listing.

Using MicroPipes to Simulate Branching in a Pipeline

If you absolutely need to implement some kind of branching capability inside your pipeline, you can do so by manually converting your configuration file into an ASP script that makes use of the `MicroPipe` component. Such a script would execute each component individually and then implement the branching logic usually with simple VBScript, JavaScript or any other language you might be using.

The result of all this will not be elegant, probably, and it certainly will not be as easy to maintain as a pipeline can be. In most cases, it will also prove to hinder the performance of your store, since `MtsPipeline` and `MtsTxPipeline` act as monolithic objects that run directly in machine language, while your ASP pages must be interpreted and are therefore slower.

An Example

It's difficult to make a truly meaningful example of when using MicroPipes could be a good idea, because in general you will find that the need for branching will often be dictated by the fact that one particular component does not abide by the general "non-interference rule" that prohibits an element of the pipeline from overwriting values that another component has set. Since all the built-in components that ship with Commerce Server follow this rule, you will only encounter this problem when dealing with third-party software.

Another possible instance in which the use of MicroPipes can become necessary is when a particular component must be executed in response to a condition that it was not designed to check for. Let's suppose, for example, that your store needs to save in its internal database only those orders that are shipped to the US, while all others are simply stored in a Purchase Order (PO) that is then manually faxed over the fulfiller in the appropriate country.

A normal pipeline would be unable to handle this situation properly, since both the SaveReceipt and CreatePO components are designed to run always, independently from what the state of the pipeline is (naturally, they will not if a fatal error has occurred). Using a small script that is executed right after the completion of the Purchase pipeline, however, we can in fact decide what component gets to run depending on any condition we like:

```
<%
    ' Global objects

    Dim MicroPipe
```

We create the pipeline context using a predefined function UtilGetPipeContext which is generated by the Site Builder Wizard. We will describe its functionality in detail in Chapter 11.

```
    Set PipeContext = UtilGetPipeContext

    ' Now, create the global instance of Micropipe
    Set MicroPipe = Server.CreateObject ("Commerce.Micropipe")

    ' Uncomment the next line if you want logging
    ' MicroPipe.SetLogFile ("C:\temp\log.txt")

    ' Decide whether we need to make a PO or save the receipt
    If (OrderForm.ship_to_country = "USA") Then

        ' Coming from the States: Save receipt

        ' Create object
        Set Comp = Server.CreateObject ("Commerce.SaveReceipt.1")
        Set Dict = Comp.GetConfigData ()

        Dict.no_save_key_prefix = "_cc"
        Comp.SetConfigData (Dict)

    Else

        ' Coming from outside the USA: make a PO
```

```
        ' Create object
        Set Comp = Server.CreateObject ("Commerce.MakePO.1")
        Set Dict = Comp.GetConfigData()

        Dict.TemplateFileName = "C:\PO.txt"
        Dict.TemplateScriptLanguage = "VBScript"
        Dict.OutPropName = "po_text"
        Dict.ChildObjectName = ""
        Dict.UseChildObject = False

        Comp.SetConfigData()

    End If

    ' Execute Pipeline

    ' Load and execute component
    MicroPipe.SetComponent (Comp)
    MicroPipe.Execute(OrderForm, PipeContext, 0)

    ' Destroy component
    Set Comp = Nothing

%>
```

This script assumes that the OrderForm object has already been loaded and referenced in the OrderForm variable, while the pipeline's context has also been created and stored in PipeContext. As you can see, MicroPipes are easy to employ in your scripts; in this case, we also managed to only limit their use to the bare minimum: in fact, you will be able to still perform the rest of the purchase process using normal pipelines – and you will thus enjoy higher performance and easier maintenance.

Summary

Pipelines are very much an essential part of Commerce Server, and there's probably a good chance that they will gain even more importance as new versions of Site Server see the light, considering the uniqueness that they bring to the entire package.

As we have had a chance to see during this chapter, pipelines offer an interesting approach to order processing, since they not only provide a very ordered environment, but a number of built-in components that can turn out to be extremely useful – and therefore time-saving – when developing a real-life store. In addition, support for transactions makes it possible to execute a pipeline as if it were a unique block of instructions, which is particularly useful during the final order processing (handled by the Purchase pipeline).

Finally, we took a look at MicroPipes, whose role is that of providing a less cumbersome way of executing individual components than by using specially designed configuration files. We also examined how MicroPipes, combined with a cleverly devised ASP script, can be used as a substitute for traditional pipeline execution objects when some level of flow control, or branching, is required. Although this technique can turn out to be very convenient at times – particularly when a very important pipeline component turns out to not have been designed to handle every possible condition that might arise during the pipeline's execution – it also carries several disadvantages and should therefore be used with a good dose of caution.

Technical Analysis of the Sample Store

For knowledge, too, is itself power.
–Francis Bacon, *Meditationes Sacrae*

In the previous chapters, we have looked at the various components that SSCE provides to create, manage and program an online store: Wizards, COM objects, and pipelines. However, it's interesting to notice that, while we examine each part quite in detail, we haven't had a chance to observe and discuss how they all work together. That's what we will be doing in this chapter: we'll start from a newly created store and dissect its inner workings, from the storefront to the management interface.

One of the things that you will undoubtedly notice is that not all of the SSCE functionality is used in a basic store. Most notably, there will be no support for the Commerce Interchange Pipeline (CIP), and you will not see any administration objects anywhere. While it's understandable that a store wouldn't normally need to use any of SSCE's administrative functions, you might find quite odd the fact that the CIP is nowhere to be seen. While there is no official explanation as to why this happens, it's probably reasonable to think that each implementation of the CIP would be so unique that providing a standard pipeline would prove to be very difficult.

What Does This Chapter Talk About?

Throughout the chapter, we will look at the various elements of a store that has been created using the Site Builder Wizard by examining its code. We'll start from the structure of the storefront, and then move on to the manager. Here's a quick breakdown of what we'll discuss:

❑ **The Storefront**
   In the first section of the chapter, we'll look at how the storefront is structured and how it works from a technical point of view; we'll also examine the pipelines that the store creates.

❑ **The Store Manager**
   The second part will instead focus on the management interface. Once again, we'll look at how its code works, and how it can be taken advantage of for expanding the store's functionality.

A Few Notes about the Store

The store that we will be examining in this chapter is called *Wrox Store*, which resides in a virtual directory of the web site called `wroxstore` and has been created by specifying the following settings in the SBW:

❑   Support for price and cross-selling promotions

❑   No user registration is required

❑   Simple (single-level) departments are used

❑   Static product attributes are used

❑   Two attributes added; Size and Color

❑   Product keyword search is enabled

❑   Shipping costs are $10.00 for "overnight" delivery and $8.00 for "2nd day" delivery.

❑   No handling fees

❑   The store does not handle taxes

❑   Only VISA and MasterCard are accepted

❑   Order history is retained for all users.

❑   Use the default output options

By using the same settings, you can easily recreate the same conditions on your own store. This will help you follow this example more closely.

A Quick Look at the Directory Structure

In Chapter 5, during our discussion about the Site Foundation Wizard , we took a look at how the directory structure of a newly created store foundation was organized. After the store generation phase, the SBW adds several files throughout the site, but maintains the directory tree, which is shown in the figure below, essentially intact.

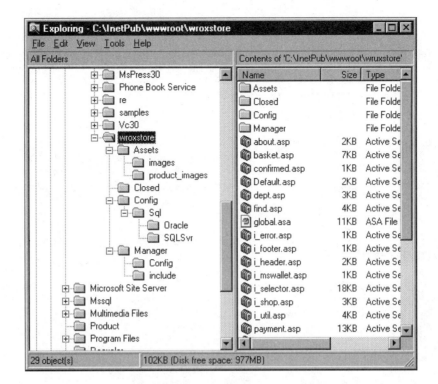

There are five main folders in our site. The root folder contains all the storefront pages and support scripts. The `Assets` subdirectory is instead used for storing "support" data required by the store's pages, such as images and downloads. In principle, this distinction has two main goals. Firstly, this helps in organizing the files, resulting in a more ordered structure that is easier to read. In addition, assuming that all the pages that are in the main folder are scripts, it also makes it possible to separate executable data from data that requires read access. This way, you could – at least in theory – remove read access from the main folder, making sure that `IUSR_SERVERNAME` has execute permissions, to make your site a little more secure. This helps to prevent malicious users from deploying any possible security holes that allow a browser to download the contents of a script rather than executing it (like the famous ':`$DATA`' bug).

> *The :$DATA bug allows malicious users to retrieve the complete ASP source file by appending :$DATA to the end of a requested URL. For example* http://theserver/directory/file.asp:$DATA. *If you want to know more, read knowledge base article Q188806. You can find it at* http://support.microsoft.com/support/kb/articles/Q188/8/06.ASP

All the configuration files used by the store, such as the Site Dictionary and all the pipeline template files, are stored in the `Config` folder; in our case, this directory also contains a copy of the SQL scripts that can be used to recreate the database used by the site, both in their Microsoft SQL Server- and Oracle-specific version. The `Closed` folder contains only one file, `closed.asp`, which is replaced with the `default.asp` file in the root folder when you close the site from the Manager.

Finally, the `Manager` folder contains all the scripts that are required by the store management pages. It's interesting to note that, while the root folder is an IIS application, and therefore has its own `global.asa` file, accessing the Store Manager does not launch a separate application. Therefore, both the Manager and the storefront share the same set of application-level functions that are loaded when the first user accesses the site. Also, the Manager has its own `Config` folder, which contains the `site.csc` file that, among other things, contains the connection string for the Manager part of the site.

> *If you are curious about these Site Dictionary files, you can download* `EditDictionary.asp` *from* http://www.microsoft.com/siteserver/commerce *and use the script to edit the dictionary files and examine what is hidden inside. In addition, it stores its include files in the* `Include` *directory, while they share the same space as the other files in the storefront.*

The Storefront

The execution flow of the storefront, shown in the figure below, is quite complex, even though the root folder of the store contains just twenty-five files. This is simply a consequence of the fact that the entire site was designed with the idea of reusing as much code as possible, thus providing a set of common functionality that could be shared among different files.

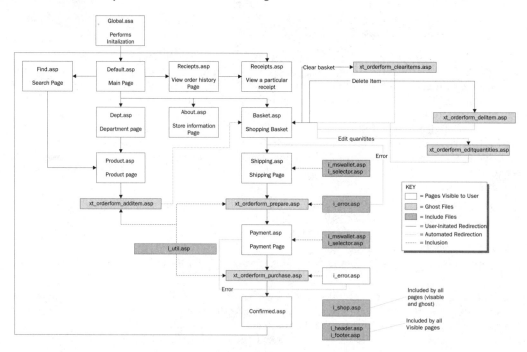

You will also note the presence of a certain number of "ghost" files, whose names begin with the `xt_` prefix. These are called when particular operations have to be performed in response to the user's input, but no output is normally required. Therefore, all they do is perform whatever task they were designed for and simply redirect the browser to the appropriate page. An exception to this behavior happens when these scripts encounter an error; in that case, they *will* output something to the user, indicating the problem and suggesting a possible way to fix it.

Generic Purpose and Initialization Scripts

There are a few scripts whose functionality is taken advantage of by most – or all – of the pages in the site. These include `global.asa`, which is executed upon initialization of the IIS application in which the store resides, and several include files, whose role ranges from helping to maintain a consistent look throughout all the pages of the site to providing a wide array of functions required by most pages in the site.

Global.asa

The initialization script in the `global.asa` is called only once during the application's lifetime, when the first user attempts to access the store and therefore causes its IIS application to be initialized. No code in the file is intended to be executed at the session level, since – as we mentioned earlier in the book – SSCE stores are designed to work without using the Session object and, by default, they turn off support for it inside the IIS metabase.

The Problem with Sessions, and a Solution

While the Session object is undoubtedly very useful in a website, it has a few significant drawbacks, in particular the fact that (a) it is based entirely on cookies and (b) its scope is limited to a single server. This means that, if the user's browser does not support cookies, or if the user has turned them off, then sessions won't work. Similarly, you will not be able to implement your site in a web server farm in which access is strictly random. In fact, any time a new page is requested, the browser can end up on any of the web servers in the farm, which might not be the same that had been accessed previously, and therefore the browser might not be aware of the session that was created on the other machine.

SSCE is able to provide a consistent data storage medium by using an `Orderform` object – available to any script in the site – that is loaded from the `wroxstore_basket` table every time a script starts and then saved back to the database when the script ends. While this may seem quite heavy in terms of performance, it provides a simple solution to the scope problem, since the database will normally be available to all the machines in a server farm.

What about cookies? Well, SSCE *does* use them to persist the shopper ID across different connections, which is in turn used to extract the correct record from `wroxstore_basket`. However, it also provides a system that makes it possible to pass this value across two pages by using the URL query string. While this approach allows the store to serve practically any browser, independently from its configuration, it also has one major drawback in that it cannot be used across different sessions. This means that if the user leaves the site and then comes back, his or her browser will not include the shopper ID in the URL anymore and, as a result, the store will not be able to persist his or her basket.

Global.asa Internals

Generally speaking, `global.asa` takes care of creating several support objects that are later used by most of the scripts in the store. You will notice that all these objects are created using the `<OBJECT>` tag, rather than through a direct call to the `Server.CreateObject` method. This makes them a part of the context of any script in the store, which means that they can be accessed directly using their name.

Moving along through the code in `global.asa`, we encounter the interesting function called `Application_OnStart`. This function is executed on the `OnStart` event of the `Application` object, which is the first time anyone accesses any page within the subdirectory of the site, `wroxstore` in this case. The `Application_OnStart` subroutine is only executed once, and to execute it again you have to edit the file or unload the application in IIS to force IIS to reload it.

```
Sub Application_OnStart
    vRoot = "wroxstore"
```

> **The vRoot parameter, created at the beginning of the application initialization function, contains the virtual folder of the store. If you ever change your store's location, you will need to update this variable accordingly. Similarly, using the root directory value from the Site Dictionary consistently within your scripts will ensure that you will not need extensive changes in case of such a move.**

The Site Dictionary for the store is loaded in the `MSCSSite` object by the `ReadSiteDict` function, which uses an instance of the `Commerce.FileDocument` object to read the dictionary directly from the `'.CSC'` file in the `/config` folder.

A similar treatment is given to the store's instance of `Commerce.StandardSManager`, which is initialized in the `InitShopperManager` function:

```
Function InitShopperManager
    call MSCSShopperManager.InitManager(vRoot, "cookieurl")
    set InitShopperManager = MSCSShopperManager
End Function
```

As you can see, in this case the object is created by selecting the `cookieurl` option, which makes it use cookies to identify the shopper by default.

A global instance of `Commerce.DataFunctions` is also created and stored in the `MSCSDataFunctions` object. While this works well for a store that only serves one particular locale (such as the United States in our case), if you need to support different locales you will need to opt for a different approach, such as creating an instance of `DataFunctions` just-in-time, when needed.

The `InitQueryMap` function is used to create `MSCSQueryMap`, a `Dictionary` object that contains all the SQL queries used by the store.

```
REM -- Create a Query Map and add all queries:
set MSCSQueryMap = InitQueryMap()
```

It's a good idea to add your own queries to this list from within `global.asa`. This will make global updates (such as changes in the names of the tables) centralized and very easy to perform, as opposed to having to scan all the scripts looking for query strings. Each query in the map is represented by a `Dictionary` of its own, which is created by the `AddQuery` function and contains, together with the actual query text, several parameters that can be used to set the ADO objects required to execute the query appropriately.

```
Function AddQuery(SQLCommand)

    ...

    Set query = Server.CreateObject("Commerce.Dictionary")

    query.SQLCommand    = SQLCommand
    query.Timeout       = 0
    query.CommandType   = adCmdText
    query.MaxRows       = 0
    query.CursorType    = adOpenStatic
    query.CursorSize    = 0

    Set AddQuery = query
End Function
```

The constant declarations have been skipped, but, as you can see, a separate `Dictionary` object is created and returned to the caller, where the Query Dictionary is added to the `MSCSQueryMap` Dictionary.

We'll examine two queries, starting with the `dept_by_id`. This one is quite straightforward, as it retrieves information about a department based on `dept_id`, the primary key in the `wroxstore_dept` table.

```
Set MSCSQueryMap.dept_by_id = AddQuery("SELECT dept_id, dept_name,
dept_description FROM wroxstore_dept WHERE dept_id = :1")
```

The `dept_by_id` query is called by retrieving it from the query map, `MSCSQueryMap`, and replacing the parameter value `:1` with the actual value sent to the script in the "`dept_id`" parameter, defined in `dept.asp`:

```
dept_id = mscsPage.RequestNumber("dept_id","0")
sqlText = Replace(MSCSQueryMap.dept_by_id.SQLCommand,":1", dept_id)
Set rsDept = MSCS.Execute (sqlText, nDepts, adCmdText)
```

The query is then executed using the `ADODB.Connection` object named `MSCS` we shall see later on defined in `i_shop.asp`.

The next query is a bit different from the other queries, because it isn't called from any ASP scripts but rather from within the pipeline – from the `QueryProdInfoADO` component. It is the `product_info` query used by the Pipeline Component `QueryProdInfoADO` to retrieve information from the database and insert it into each product in the `OrderForm`. These values are stored in the `OrderForm` object's `Item` collection with a `_product_` prefix, as you have seen in Chapter 9.

```
Set MSCSQueryMap.product_info = AddQuery("SELECT pf.pf_id, pf.name, pf.list_price,
pf.sale_price, pf.sale_start, pf.sale_end, pv.sku, dept.dept_id FROM
wroxstore_product pf, wroxstore_variant pv, wroxstore_dept dept,
wroxstore_dept_prod deptprod WHERE pv.sku = ? and pf.pf_id = pv.pf_id and pf.pf_id
= deptprod.pf_id and dept.dept_id = deptprod.dept_id and dept.dept_id = ?")
```

As you may or may not have noticed, the query parameters are here defined with question marks instead of the previous ":1". This is because it is the way the Pipeline Components handle parameters, as we will discuss in Chapter 14. Adjacent is a screenshot of the properties of the QueryProdInfoADO component in our store:

As you can see, the parameter list consists of `item.sku` and `item.dept_id`, which are assigned to each item as the component loops through the `Items` of the `OrderForm` object.

Finally, `MSCSMessageManager` is a globally available instance of `Commerce.MessageManager` that contains all the error messages that are generated in the store's pipelines. As is the case with `MSCSDataFunctions`, the Message Manager is initialized with a specific locale. However, if you look at how this object works back in Chapter 3, you will remember that it's possible to add more locales and specify the appropriate messages for them as well.

After the `Application_OnStart` subroutine within `global.asa` has been called, the webserver hands out `default.asp`, which is the main entrance to our shop. Since we are not using sessions, the `Session_OnStart` subroutine will not be called. Looking through `global.asa` we see that it includes three other asp-files in the `wroxstore` directory, namely `i_shop.asp`, `i_header.asp` and `i_footer.asp`.

i_shop.asp

All the scripts in the store, regardless of whether they output something or not, include this file, which provides a number of functions that are generically needed by all the other files. First of all, `i_shop.asp` defines the function `this_page`, which makes it easy to find out what script file is being executed. This function is only used within `i_shop.asp`.

Secondly, `i_shop.asp` defines some constants that are required when dealing with ADO. These turn out to be very convenient, as they save you the hassle of having to either re-define them yourself or using their corresponding values, which makes the code harder to read. You might recognize these, as they are a subset of the constants defined in the `adovbs.inc` file that is distributed with ADO, located in \Program files\Common Files\System\ado.

Next, the script verifies that the store is indeed open. If it isn't, then the browser is redirected to the appropriate page, which is defined in the Site Dictionary as `CloseRedirectURL`:

```
REM -- If store is not open then redirect to closed URL
if MSCSSite.Status <> "Open" then
    response.redirect(MSCSSite.CloseRedirectURL)
end if
```

Hunting for the Shopper

Once it is sure that the store is open, the script continues by attempting to retrieve the user's shopper ID, which is then used to retrieve the correct record out of `wroxstore_basket`:

```
REM -- mscs = created on the page; MSCS = created in global.asa
set mscsPage = Server.CreateObject("Commerce.Page")

REM -- Manually create shopper id
mscsShopperID = mscsPage.GetShopperId

REM - Handle shopper
if IsNull(mscsShopperID) then
    mscsShopperID = mscsShopperManager.CreateShopperID()
    mscsPage.PutShopperID(mscsShopperID)
    call Response.Redirect(pageURL("default.asp"))
end if
```

As you can see from this snippet of code, the shopper ID is retrieved from an instance of the `Commerce.Page` object created on the spot. The last part of the code, however, should capture your attention, as it can be potentially dangerous. What it does is pretty clear: if the `Page` object is unable to retrieve a shopper ID, it creates a new one and then uses the `PutShopperID` method to return it to the user. Finally, it redirects the browser to the main page (`Default.asp`), causing the store to start from scratch.

The problem here is that, if you have selected cookies as the method for storing the Shopper ID and the browser does not support or refuses them, the latter will attempt to load `default.asp`, which, however, includes `i_shop.asp`. This, in turn, will still be unable to retrieve and store the shopper ID properly, and will redirect the browser to `default.asp` once again, entering an infinite loop that will make your site inaccessible to the user.

Why is this happening? After all, in `global.asa`, the Shopper Manager was initialized to support cookies *and* URLs; therefore we should expect to see the shopper ID in the URL the second time that the page is loaded. Well, there are two distinct problems here. First of all, as you may remember from Chapter 9, the `Page` object needs to know how the URL query string parameter that contains the shopper ID should be called. This is stored in the `Application` object, under the `MSCSSIDURLKey` key; `global.asa` is the perfect place to set it, right after initializing all the objects:

```
Set Application("MSCSSIDURLKey") = "mscssid"
```

Doing this is not sufficient, however, and you will notice no apparent change in the way the site behaves. To understand the problem, in this case, you need to take a closer look at last line of code of the snippet above, the one that redirects the browser:

```
call Response.Redirect(pageURL("default.asp"))
```

The script obviously expects the pageURL function to append the correct shopperID to the name of the script to which the browser is being redirected. This function is defined at the end of i_shop.asp:

```
function pageURL(pageName)
    pageURL = rootURL & pageName & "?" & emptyArgs
end function
```

pageURL makes use of two variables, rootURL, which is supposed to contain the root URL of the site, and emptyArgs, which will probably contain the shopper ID. In fact, these two variables are declared right at the end of the script:

```
siteRoot    = mscsPage.SiteRoot()
emptyArgs   = mscsPage.URLShopperArgs()
```

While the function is available at the time that the shopper ID is examined and the redirection occurs, the declaration of these variables is scoped together with the script's main code and therefore *has not yet been executed* when the pageURL is called by our snippet! Therefore, pageURL will never be able to attach the shopper ID to the URL.

In order to make the script work properly, we'll have to change the code snippet to declare the proper variables before redirecting the browser:

```
if IsNull(mscsShopperID) then
    mscsShopperID = mscsShopperManager.CreateShopperID()
    mscsPage.PutShopperID(mscsShopperID)

    siteRoot    = mscsPage.SiteRoot()
    emptyArgs   = mscsPage.URLShopperArgs()

    call Response.Redirect(pageURL("default.asp"))
end if
```

If we had chosen the **On Entry Registration** option in the Site Builder Wizard, the generated code would have had a different structure. Instead of directing to the default.asp page, the redirection would go to the shopper_lookup.asp page allowing the user to either log in and verify him-/herself or, if possible, create a new user.

```
mscsShopperID = mscsPage.GetShopperId

REM - Handle shopper
if IsNull(mscsShopperID) then
    if Not this_page("shopper_lookup.asp") and Not this_page("shopper_new.asp")
then
        Response.Redirect(pageURL("shopper_lookup.asp"))
    end if
end if
```

We can see an example of the this_page function discussed earlier. It is used to check if the user already is on the shopper_lookup.asp or the shopper_new.asp page. If this check hadn't been done, we would be redirected back to shopper_lookup.asp and the include code would once again redirect us – we would end up in an eternal redirection loop.

Lifesaving Functions

Let's now take a look at the functions that are declared towards the end of the script. We have already encountered and discussed `pageURL`, which can be used to create a URL that contains all the additional parameters that are required by SSCE. Similarly, `pageSURL` creates a secure URL that behaves the same way. It's interesting to notice that `pageSURL` outputs an HTTPS address only if the `SURLPrefix` name/value pair stored in the Site Dictionary is itself secure. `BaseURL` and `baseSURL`, on the other hand, can be used to create URLs that do not need to include the additional parameters required by SSCE, or when you need to specify those parameters yourself. They can be used to build URLs that must not be used as active links, such as those that point to images.

Using these four functions consistently throughout your store brings at least two significant advantages. Firstly, your store will automatically and consistently adapt to your needs to switch between secure and non-secure URLs, depending on whether you are in a development or production environment. Secondly, you will be able to change the entire store's base address without having to change it throughout the individual pages.

Database à la carte

The last few lines of code in `i_shop.asp` are used to create a database connection and ADO command object – called `MSCS` and `cmdTemp` respectively – that can be used by the page that includes the file:

```
REM -- Create ADO Connection and Command Objects
Set MSCS = Server.CreateObject("ADODB.Connection")
MSCS.Open MSCSSite.DefaultConnectionString
Set cmdTemp = Server.CreateObject("ADODB.Command")
cmdTemp.CommandType = adCmdText
Set cmdTemp.ActiveConnection = MSCS
```

This is quite convenient, since you will not have to rewrite the code to do so in every individual page, and you can indeed use these two directly. On the other hand, it might bring a little overhead if you don't actually need to use the database in all your pages.

i_header.asp and i_footer.asp

These two files are intended to help make the pages in the site consistent. Neither of them includes any code that needs reviewing, although it's worth pointing out that the header, which also prints out the navigation elements that are common to all visible pages, has two minor inconveniences.

First of all, the script is unable to determine what page the user is currently viewing. Therefore, when the browser is displaying, for example, the main page, the Lobby link will still be active, which can prove confusing to the user. It would be better if the script were able to understand that the browser is already on a specific page and consequently remove the corresponding link and, maybe, show a different (perhaps dimmed or grayed) icon. One way to do this is to change the text that displays the links, which currently looks similar to the following:

```
<A HREF="<%= pageURL("about.asp") %>">
    <IMG SRC="<%= "/" & siteRoot %>/manager/MSCS_Images/navbar/btnabout.gif">
</A>
```

All we need to do in order to tell what page we are currently looking at is use the `nowat` function in `I_shop.asp`, which returns `True` if the name of the script currently being processed corresponds to the parameter passed to the function. Thus, a simple `if-then-else` statement does the trick:

```
<% if nowat ("about.asp") then %>
   <IMG SRC="<%= "/" & siteRoot %>/manager/MSCS_Images/navbar/btnaboutblur.gif">
<% else %>
   <A HREF="<%= pageURL("about.asp") %>">
      <IMG SRC="<%= "/" & siteRoot %>/manager/MSCS_Images/navbar/btnabout.gif">
   </A>
<% end if %>
```

You can apply the same technique to all the links in the header include file – all you have to change is the name of the script in the `if-then-else` and the actual HTML code that needs to be displayed in either of the `if-then-else` cases. As you might have noticed, the first link displays an alternative picture, `btnaboutblur.gif`, if the user is currently on this page.

In addition, when linking to the basket page, the script uses the `pageSURL` function, which will produce a secure link in a production environment. This is probably unnecessary, since the basket itself doesn't contain any information that can be deemed strictly confidential. An SSL connection, on the other hand, can be significantly slower than a normal one, and prove inconvenient to the user. Thus, you can change that piece of code to use the `pageURL` function instead.

Store Navigation

The store navigation files (shown here) are not very complicated, since their task is essentially that of producing lists of departments or products. With the exception of `about.asp`, which is essentially a static page, and `xt_orderform_additem.asp`, which is a ghost script, they all follow the same basic execution flow: for example – a particular query is executed with the appropriate parameters and then its results are displayed, unless an error of some sort occurs, in which case the scripts are careful of outputting courteous messages such as "The department you requested is currently unavailable".

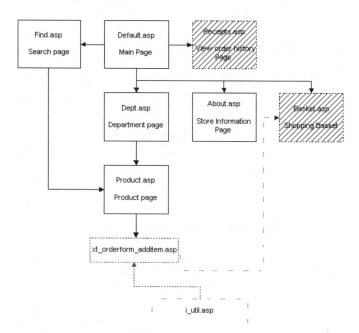

Examining Default.asp

Since the `default.asp` page only displays all the available departments, the executed query does not have any parameters. To optimize the store, this information could be stored in the Application object so that we wouldn't have to do a roundtrip to the database server for each request. Check out how to do this in Chapter 16.

```
sqlText = MSCSQueryMap.depts.SQLCommand
Set rsDepts = MSCS.Execute (sqlText, nDepts, adCmdText)
```

After the query has been executed and the recordset `rsDepts` contains all the departments, a loop prints out an unnumbered list with all the available departments; there is a hypertext link to the `dept.asp` script and the department id we are interested in is used as a parameter.

```
if rsDepts.EOF then
    %>
    <P>
    There are currently no departments available.
<% else %>
    <P>
    Select a department below:

    <UL>
    <%
    set dept_idField = rsDepts("dept_id")
    set dept_nameField = rsDepts("dept_name")
    do while Not rsDepts.EOF
        %>
        <LI><A HREF="<%= baseURL("dept.asp") & mscsPage.URLShopperArgs("dept_id", _
                        dept_idField.value) %>">
            <%= dept_nameField.value %></A>
        <% rsDepts.MoveNext
    loop
    rsDepts.Close
    MSCS.Close
    %>
    </UL>
<% end if %>
<BR>
You can see your order history on the <A HREF="<%= pageURL("receipts.asp")
%>">Order History Page</A>.
```

If we have the `StandardSManager` initialized to `url` or `urlcookie`, the `URLShopperArgs` method on the `Page` object would automatically append our shopper's ID for us, and it would come out like this

```
http://server/wroxstore/dept.asp?dept%5Fid=1&mscssid=EXRGST65AQSH2H5T002
2BCDTW7NGBRJ4
```

After the loop, the objects we have used are closed and a link to the `receipts.asp` file is created for the Order History pages. Surprisingly, the script does not set the used objects to nothing, which is common practice when programming ASP. This should be made right after the `Close` methods are called on the objects:

```
rsDepts.Close
    MSCS.Close
Set rsDepts = Nothing
Set MSCS = Nothing
```

Remember that these objects are created on a per-page basis within the i_shop.asp file, and releasing them by setting them to nothing means that we will take up less resources over time – this is important on a site with many concurrent requests.

Viewing the Products

There are two clicks to actually being able to add a product to our basket. First we need to go through dept.asp to list all the products within one department, and then through product.asp to actually add the product with the attributes we desire to the basket. A quick peek at the database model for this part of the system reveals that to be able to add a product to the OrderForm we need to know the wroxstore_variant.sku value and to get that we need to know what size, pf_id and color the customer requires. So, let's trick the customer into selecting these.

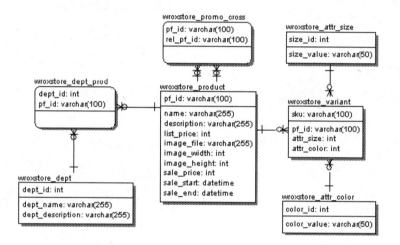

Dept.asp

Our journey towards products in the basket begins with the dept.asp script. This file first executes the dept_by_id query to find out the department name and the department description of the department the customer is interested in. An extra log entry is also written to the IIS log using the Response.AppendLog method to save information for later use with the Usage Analysis Tool (discussed in Professional Site Server 3.0, published by Wrox Press, ISBN number 1-861002-69-6), and to let the manager optimize the department design of the store.

```
Response.AppendToLog "&" & mscsPage.URLArgs("MSS.Request.Category Name",
    dept_name)
```

Provided the requested department exists, the script then executes the `products_by_dept` query to retrieve the list of the actual products.

```
<%
  if dept_exists then
      cmdTemp.CommandText =
Replace(MSCSQueryMap.products_by_dept.SQLCommand,":1",dept_id)
      Set rsProducts = Server.CreateObject("ADODB.Recordset")
      rsProducts.Open cmdTemp, , adOpenStatic, adLockReadOnly

          if rsProducts.EOF then
              products_exist = false
          else
              products_exist = true
          end if
  end if
%>
```

> If you are familiar with ASP and ADO, you might have noticed that there's room for improvement within the generated ASP files. For example, the above query could be using **adForwardOnly** and, while we're at it, only use the **MSCS** instance of the **Connection** object to generate a recordset.

Within the product listing loop, a hyperlink is generated for each new product, linking to the `product.asp` page.

```
<A HREF="<%= baseURL("product.asp") & mscsPage.URLShopperArgs("dept_id" , dept_id, _
          "pf_id", pf_idField.value) %>">
    <%= mscsPage.HTMLEncode(nameField.value) %>
</A>
```

Product.asp

In order to be able to present all the information about a product, the `product.asp` script uses the `product_by_id` query:

```
pf_id = mscsPage.RequestString("pf_id")
quoted_pf_id = "'" & Replace(pf_id,"'","''") & "'"     REM - add quotes

REM -- retrieve product:
sqlText = MSCSQueryMap.product_by_id.SQLCommand
sqlText = Replace(sqlText, ":1", quoted_pf_id)
sqlText = Replace(sqlText, ":2", Request("dept_id"))
cmdTemp.CommandText = sqlText
Set rsProduct = Server.CreateObject("ADODB.Recordset")
rsProduct.Open cmdTemp, , adOpenForwardOnly, adLockReadOnly
```

The two parameters sent from the previous script, `dept.asp`, are inserted into the query, which is then executed. After retrieving the product information and making an extra log-write for the Usage Analysis, a check is done to see if the product is on sale today:

```
REM -- get fields from recordset
sale_price = rsProduct("sale_price").value
sale_start = rsProduct("sale_start").value
sale_end = rsProduct("sale_end").value

REM -- determine if product is on sale:
today = Date
on_sale = DateDiff("d", today, sale_start) <= 0 and DateDiff("d", today, sale_end)
> 0
```

The `on_sale` will contain either `True` or `False` depending on the values in `sale_start` and `sale_end` and the date. After some error checking to see if the product really exists, the actual HTML form is generated, screaming out ON SALE! if the product is on sale.

The second part of the script executes the two queries generated for the attributes size and color; `size_by_family` and `color_by_family`.

```
SELECT DISTINCT size_id, size_value
FROM wroxstore_variant pv, wroxstore_attr_size
WHERE pv.pf_id = :1 and pv.attr_size = wroxstore_attr_size.size_id
```

The query joins the `variant` table with the `attr_size` table to find out what different sizes are defined for the product the customer is interested in (given by the `pf_id` value). These values are then presented as a drop-down, one for each attribute.

The last part of the `product.asp` script executes a query to find out if there are any related products. These are stored in the `wroxstore_promo_cross` table with only a link between the product we are currently viewing and all related products. A check within the loop makes sure we only present 5 products as a maximum.

```
cmdTemp.CommandText = Replace("SELECT prod.pf_id, prod.name, deptprod.dept_id FROM
wroxstore_promo_cross promo_cross, wroxstore_product prod, wroxstore_dept_prod
deptprod WHERE promo_cross.pf_id = :1 AND prod.pf_id = deptprod.pf_id AND
promo_cross.rel_pf_id = prod.pf_id", ":1", quoted_pf_id)

Set rsRelated = Server.CreateObject("ADODB.Recordset")
rsRelated.Open cmdTemp, , adOpenForwardOnly, adLockReadOnly
```

Strangely enough, there is a query already generated in the `global.asa` file named `related_products_with_dept` that is an exact copy of the above, so as a little exercise, why not use that query instead and have all your queries in one place.

Adding Products to the Basket

The customer has decided to add one of our products to the basket, and the script has loaded the hidden form with the values needed; `pf_id` from the product table, `color_id` and `size_id` from `attr_color` and `attr_size` respectively. In order to add this product, the user clicks the button and the whole form is sent to the `xt_orderform_additem.asp` script.

The `xt_orderform_additem.asp` is the first script where we see a reference to the `OrderForm`. Up to this point, in fact, there was no need to access it, since all the information that we needed could be taken directly from the database. In this case, however, the user has expressed the wish to add an item to his or her basket; therefore, we need to access the `OrderForm` in order to perform this task.

This script begins with a large function declaration, which contains the actual code that adds the product to the `OrderForm`. The execution of the script starts after the function declaration when the `OrderForm` is created and retrieved from the database using the `UtilGetOrderFormStorage` function declared in the include file `i_util.asp`.

```
Set mscsOrderFormStorage = UtilGetOrderFormStorage()
```

The `UtilGetOrderFormStorage` function simply creates a `DBStorage` object and initializes it to work against the `wroxstore_basket` table.

```
function UtilGetOrderFormStorage()
    Set orderFormStorage = Server.CreateObject("Commerce.DBStorage")
    Call orderFormStorage.InitStorage(MSCSSite.DefaultConnectionString, _
                        "wroxstore_basket", "shopper_id", "Commerce.OrderForm", _
                        "marshaled_basket", "date_changed")

    Set UtilGetOrderFormStorage = orderFormStorage
end function
```

The `shopper_id` is the unique key for the basket table, `Commerce.OrderForm` is the progid to the COM object we want to store, `marshaled_basket` is the column name and `date_changed` is the column name of the timestamp column.

```
errorStr = ""
success = OrderFormAddItem(mscsOrderFormStorage, mscsShopperID, errorStr)
```

After the `OrderForm` has been initialized, `OrderFormAddItem()` is called to add a product. The parameters are the recently created `OrderFormStorage` object, the `mscsShopperID` that was assigned in `i_shop.asp` and a `ByRef` return value parameter containing error text if there was an error. If there was a success, the customer is redirected to the `basket.asp` page – a bad design decision since we probably want the customer to add more products to the basket.

```
if success then
    call Response.Redirect("basket.asp?" & mscsPage.URLShopperArgs())
else
    call Response.Redirect("product.asp?" &
            mscsPage.URLShopperArgs("pf_id",_ Request("pf_id"),
            "dept_id", Request("dept_id"), "error", errorStr))
end if
```

If there was a failure, we redirect the customer to the product page with a generated error string to be displayed. This error string is generated within the `OrderFormAddItem` function.

Examining the OrderFormAddItem Function

So, what does actually happen in the `OrderFormAddItem` function? First, `UtilGetOrderForm` from the `i_util.asp` include file is called:

```
Set mscsOrderForm = UtilGetOrderForm(mscsOrderFormStorage, created)
```

The `UtilGetOrderForm` first tries to retrieve an `OrderForm` for the `mscsShopperID` using the `GetData` method of the `OrderFormStorage` object. If this fails, a new `OrderForm` is created and assigned to the shopper, and the created flag is set.

```
function UtilGetOrderForm(byRef orderFormStorage, byRef created)

    created = 0
    On Error Resume Next

    Set orderForm = orderFormStorage.GetData(null, mscsShopperID)

    On Error Goto 0

    if IsEmpty(orderForm) then
        set orderForm = Server.CreateObject("Commerce.OrderForm")
        orderForm.shopper_id = mscsShopperID
        created = 1
    end if

    Set UtilGetOrderForm = orderForm

end function
```

Back to `OrderFormAddItem` again, where we now have a valid `OrderForm` for the shopper. The parameters sent to the `xt_orderform_additem.asp` script are retrieved and stored in temporary variables, and the `product_by_attrs` query is executed to retrieve the `list_price`, `name` and `sku` of the product.

```
sku = rsProduct("sku").value
list_price = rsProduct("list_price").value
name = rsProduct("name").value
rsProduct.Close
```

After the retrieval of these values, the `AddItem` method on the `mscsOrderForm` is called using the newly retrieved values as parameters:

```
set item = mscsOrderForm.AddItem(sku, product_qty, list_price)
```

Some extra information is then stored onto the product within the `OrderForm` for easy access, like the department id, the name and the attributes. The last thing that is done in the function is a call to the `UtilPutOrderForm` function declared in `i_util.asp`. This is where the `created` flag is used; if the `OrderForm` was created for the shopper, it will be inserted, otherwise its changes are committed.

```
function UtilPutOrderForm(byRef orderFormStorage, byRef orderForm, byRef created)

    if created = 0 then
        Call orderFormStorage.CommitData(NULL, orderForm)
    else
        Call orderFormStorage.InsertData(NULL, orderForm)
    end if

end function
```

Performing Searches

The search functionality in the store is provided by the find.asp script. As we have already mentioned, the starter store only supports searching against the database with a simple SQL query. The generated script is very rudimentary, only letting the user do a text search of the name column in the product table. There is no support for Boolean operators. The string you type into the search field has to be exactly right in the database, and if you set your database to be case sensitive (which you shouldn't), you must have all the upper and lower case correct too. All this sums up to a pretty useless functionality – still it's better than nothing.

First of all, let's take a look at the query used to perform the search operation. Contrary to most other queries used in the store, this one is not stored in global.asa, but directly in the script:

```
SELECT p.sku, p.name, p.list_price, dp.dept_id
FROM wroxstore_product p, wroxstore_dept_prod dp
WHERE p.name LIKE '%:1%' and p.sku = dp.sku
ORDER BY name
```

As you can see, the query only extracts the necessary fields from a recordset obtain by performing a "loose" search using the LIKE keyword. An interesting technique is used to "filter" the search keywords specified by the user. Since these are used directly inside a LIKE statement, they must not contain certain special characters that SQL would not interpret properly, such as the single quote, which would work as a string terminator, the underscore, and the percent sign, which are used as wildcards.

It is very important to replace these special characters, which would otherwise open up the database to a malicious user that could drop tables, delete rows and so on. This is why it's always very important to have a separate database user with very restricted access to the tables needed.

Find.asp gets rid of all these inconvenient characters in different ways. The single quote is replaced by two single quotes, which SQL will interpret as an individual single quote character rather than a string terminator, while the percent sign and underscore are enclosed within square brackets, which conforms to the LIKE statement's syntax for the specification of an individual character:

```
safeFindSpec =
Replace(Replace(Replace(strFindSpec,"'","''"),"_","[_]"),"%","[%]").
```

The final thing that we will look at in this script is the way that it counts for the number of records in the result set from the query execution:

```
Set rsProductsFindSpec = Server.CreateObject("ADODB.Recordset")
rsProductsFindSpec.Open cmdTemp, , adOpenStatic, adLockReadOnly
nProductsFindSpec = 0

Do While Not rsProductsFindSpec.EOF
    nProductsFindSpec = nProductsFindSpec + 1
    rsProductsFindSpec.MoveNext
Loop
```

As you can see, this is a bit of a "brute force" approach, and can be easily substituted by the use of the `RecordCount` property of the `Recordset` object, as long as the `adOpenKeyset` parameter is used to open the recordset, instead of `adOpenStatic`. Naturally, this will only work if you are using a DBMS that supports the `RecordCount` property, such as SQL Server or Access.

The Basket

`Basket.asp` is arguably one of the most complex scripts in the whole store. Its goal is not only to display the basket's contents, but also to run the `OrderForm` through the Plan Pipeline, and thereby calculate the correct price of the products, as well as the order subtotal. Examining the `basket.asp` script we see that the script starts by setting its own expiration date ten years in the past:

```
<% Response.ExpiresAbsolute=DateAdd("yyyy", -10, Date) %>
```

While this may seem a little weird, it's goal is simply to make sure that no browser or proxy server will ever cache this page, since its contents may change at any time.

The next step consists of updating the information that is stored in the `OrderForm`. This is done by calling the `UtilRunPlan` function, which resides inside `i_util.asp`, which, in turn, ends up executing the store's Plan pipeline.

```
Set mscsOrderForm = UtilRunPlan()
```

`UtilRunPlan` works by executing a number of steps required to create the appropriate environment before it proceeds to run the pipeline. The adjacent figure shows its operation flow.

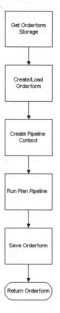

As you can see, the function begins by retrieving the `OrderForm` data, using the `UtilGetOrderFormStorage` and `UtilGetOrderForm` functions that we have already seen before. Next, it retrieves the pipeline's context by calling `UtilGetPipeContext`, which works by instantiating a new `Dictionary` object and storing the appropriate data in it:

```
function UtilGetPipeContext()
    Set pipeContext = Server.CreateObject("Commerce.Dictionary")
    Set pipeContext("MessageManager")        = MSCSMessageManager
    Set pipeContext("DataFunctions")         = MSCSDataFunctions
    Set pipeContext("QueryMap")              = MSCSQueryMap
    Set pipeContext("ConnectionStringMap")   = MSCSSite.ConnectionStringMap
    pipeContext("SiteName")                  = displayName
    pipeContext("DefaultConnectionString")   = MSCSSite.DefaultConnectionString
    pipeContext("Language")                  = "USA"

    Set UtilGetPipeContext = pipeContext
end function
```

If your own pipeline needs additional values stored in the context, this is the place where you would add them to it. You can even add data that is taken from ASP's own context, such as `Server` or `Request`:

```
function UtilGetPipeContext()
    Set pipeContext = Server.CreateObject("Commerce.Dictionary")
    Set pipeContext("MessageManager")        = MSCSMessageManager
    Set pipeContext("DataFunctions")         = MSCSDataFunctions
    Set pipeContext("QueryMap")              = MSCSQueryMap
    Set pipeContext("ConnectionStringMap")   = MSCSSite.ConnectionStringMap

    Set pipeContext ("Server")               = Server
    Set pipeContext ("Request")              = Request

    pipeContext("SiteName")                  = displayName
    pipeContext("DefaultConnectionString")   = MSCSSite.DefaultConnectionString
    pipeContext("Language")                  = "USA"

    Set UtilGetPipeContext = pipeContext
end function
```

Finally, the function calls `UtilRunPipe`, which essentially takes care of creating an instance of `Commerce.MtsPipeline` (thus, the pipeline to be executed doesn't require transactions), loading the pipeline's configuration file, and executing it:

```
function UtilRunPipe(file, orderForm, pipeContext)

    Set pipeline = Server.CreateObject("Commerce.MtsPipeline")

    Call pipeline.LoadPipe(Request.ServerVariables("APPL_PHYSICAL_PATH") & _
    "config\" & file)

    REM Call pipeline.SetLogFile(Request.ServerVariables("APPL_PHYSICAL_PATH") &
    REM "config\pipeline.log")
```

```
        errorLevel = pipeline.Execute(1, orderForm, pipeContext, 0)
        UtilRunPipe = errorLevel

    end function
```

As you can see, the configuration file's path is constructed by mapping the store's `config` directory and adding the filename, which is provided by the caller – in this case, `plan.pcf`. The function also contains a commented line that can be used to instruct the pipeline object to log its activity to a text file of choice. You can uncomment this line if you need to debug your store; just remember to comment it back once you're done, or you will end up with a huge log file eventually.

The pipeline is then executed, that is, the `OrderForm` is sent through the Pipeline defined by the file (usually `plan.pcf` or `util.pcf`), and the return value is assigned the `errorLevel` variable, which is returned to the function caller. The `errorLevel` is letting us know what happened during the execution of the pipeline: 1 means the pipeline was executed successfully, 2 means a pipeline component raised an error in the basket or the purchase error collections. If the returned value was equal to 3, a failure of the pipeline occurred, for example if the database was unreachable.

After the pipeline has been executed, `UtilRunPlan` simply saves the `OrderForm` back to the database using a method similar to what we saw earlier, and returns the data to the basket's script.

Basket Execution

After the customer's `mscsOrderForm` object has been run though the Plan Pipeline, the script creates some local variables for faster access:

```
Set orderFormItems = mscsOrderForm.Items
nOrderFormItems = orderFormItems.Count
Set mscsBasketErrors = mscsOrderForm.[_Basket_Errors]
nBasketErrors = mscsBasketErrors.Count
```

Using these variables, the script determines whether the basket is empty (that is, the number of items in the `OrderForm` is zero), and whether any errors occurred, in which case they are shown to the user:

```
<% if nBasketErrors > 0 then %>
    <TABLE WIDTH="500">
        <% for iError = 0 to nBasketErrors - 1 %>
            <TR><TD><FONT COLOR="#FF0000"><STRONG>
            <%= mscsPage.HTMLEncode(mscsBasketErrors(iError)) %>
            </STRONG></FONT></TD></TR>
        <% next %>
    </TABLE>
```

The basket page itself is built by creating a table and iterating through each item in the `OrderForm`, printing out its SKU (displayed as **Label**), its name, the per-item price, an editable quantity, and the total. In addition, a **Delete Item** link is printed at the end of each line.

Manipulating the Basket

There are three actions that can be taken from the basket page, whose goal is to somehow change its contents: remove an item, change the quantity of one or more items and wipe out the entire order altogether. In the first case, `xt_orderform_delitem.asp` simply loads the `OrderForm`, deletes the items whose number is specified by the `index` URL parameter and stores the `OrderForm` back into the database.

The item quantities are changed all at the same time in the `xt_orderform_editquantities.asp` script, which simply iterates through the Items collection updating the `Quantity` field with the contents of the URL parameters that are passed by the basket page. The actual form that generates these parameters is composed of the individual quantity edit boxes that are shown in `basket.asp`.

Finally, when the user clicks on **Empty Basket**, the browser loads the `xt_orderform_clearitems.asp` script, which simply loads the `OrderForm`, calls its `ClearItems` method and saves it back to the database.

Generally speaking, all the ghost scripts that are used to manipulate the basket's contents contain minimal error checking, and they do not include any code to create the `OrderForm` if it doesn't already exist; clearly, this happens because – at least in theory – a user should never end up running any of them outside a controlled environment, in which (a) the `OrderForm` exists (and, in most cases, must not be empty), and (b) the parameters passed are pre-checked by the basket page.

It's interesting to notice that items are kept track of according to their ordinal position inside the `OrderForm`. For example, here's how the **Delete Item** link is formed:

```
<A HREF="<%= baseSURL("xt_orderform_delitem.asp") &
mscsPage.URLShopperArgs("index", iLineItem) %>"></A>
```

As you can see, this creates a link that calls `xt_orderform_delitem.asp` with a parameter that equals the position of the product in the Items collection, essentially telling it to "delete item number *x*". While this works well in most cases, it can lead to certain problems.

For example, let's assume that the user reaches the basket page, then opens a new browser window and ends up on the same page. This is not an unreasonable scenario, since it's common to use more than one browser window for convenience reasons. Whatever is now done on the first basket page inevitably puts the other one out of sync. In fact, if the user deletes an item from the first page, the second will still list it as available. What's worse, if the user attempts to delete it from the second basket, he or she might end up deleting something else!

A possible solution to this problem could be to use the SKU instead. However, you will also have to change the `xt_orderform_additem.asp` script so that it will be able to recognize whether a particular product has already been added to the basket and change its quantity instead of adding it again if that's the case. This will prevent double entries from showing up in the basket, which, in turn, will avoid annoying problems when manipulating its contents.

Allowing Only One Unique SKU in the Basket

To implement this technique, we'll have to start by changing `xt_orderform_additem.asp` (storefront):

```
bExists = False
REM -- does this item already exist in the orderform?
For Each Item in mscsOrderForm.Items
    If Item.sku = sku Then
        Item.quantity = Item.quantity + product_qty
        bExists = True
    End If
Next
```

The first thing we need to do is to loop through the `Item SimpleList`, to search for our `sku`. If we find the `sku` we increase the quantity and set the `bExists = True`. We then use this flag to skip the inserting part of the script, and jump straight to the part where the whole `OrderForm` is saved.

```
If Not bExists Then
    REM -- add item to order form:
    set item = mscsOrderForm.AddItem(sku, product_qty, list_price)
    item.name = name
    item.list_price = list_price
    item.dept_id = dept_id

    item.pf_id = pf_id
    REM -- adding the attributes to the item allows us to display them in the
basket
    REM -- without needing a query on that page
    sqlText = MSCSQueryMap.product_attrs_by_id.SQLCommand
    sqlText = Replace(sqlText,":1",Request("size_id"))
    sqlText = Replace(sqlText,":2",Request("color_id"))

    cmdTemp.CommandText = sqlText
    Set rsAttr = Server.CreateObject("ADODB.Recordset")
    rsAttr.Open cmdTemp, , adOpenStatic, adLockReadOnly
    item.size_value = rsAttr("size_value").value
    item.color_value = rsAttr("color_value").value

    rsAttr.Close

    MSCS.Close
End If
REM -- commit order form back to storage:
Call UtilPutOrderForm(orderFormStorage, mscsOrderForm, created)
```

Now, that appears to work. The next thing will be to change the delete functionality in the `basket.asp` script so that the `sku` is sent to `xt_orderform_delitem.asp` instead of the index value:

```
    <A HREF="<%= baseSURL("xt_orderform_delitem.asp") &
mscsPage.URLShopperArgs("sku",
            lineItem.sku) %>">
    <IMG SRC="<%= "/" & siteRoot %>/manager/MSCS_Images/buttons/btnremove1.gif"
BORDER="0"
        ALT="Delete item">
    </A>
```

There, now all we need to do to complete this change is to modify `xt_orderform_delitem.asp` to handle the `sku` parameter instead of the index parameter. This is how the function looked before:

```
if mscsOrderForm.Items.Count > 0 then
    index = mscsPage.RequestNumber("index", NULL, 0, mscsOrderForm.Items.Count - 1)
    if Not IsNull(index) then
        call mscsOrderForm.Items.Delete(index)
```

```
            call mscsOrderFormStorage.CommitData(NULL, mscsOrderForm)
        end if
    end if
```

And here are the suggested changes:

```
if mscsOrderForm.Items.Count > 0 then

    sku = mscsPage.RequestString("sku", NULL)
    if Not IsNull(sku) then
        REM -- we need to retrieve the index value for the sku.
        nIndex = 0
        For Each Item in mscsOrderForm.Items

            If sku = Item.sku Then
                call mscsOrderForm.Items.Delete(nIndex)
            End If

            nIndex = nIndex + 1
        Next
        call mscsOrderFormStorage.CommitData(NULL, mscsOrderForm)
    end if

end if
```

The changed script uses the same method for retrieving the `sku` parameter, but has to use the `RequestString` method rather than `RequestNumber`, since the `sku` is, in fact, a string value. If we want to delete just one product from the `OrderForm`, there is no method for this on the `OrderForm` object itself so the solution will be to use the `Delete` method on the Items `SimpleList` within the `OrderForm`. The `Delete` method only accepts the index of the value to be removed so we have to loop through to find all occurrences of the `sku` we want to remove.

The Purchase Process

The purchase process begins when the user clicks on the Purchase button on the basket page, which causes the browser to navigate to `shipping.asp`.

Shipping.asp

This script begins exactly like `basket.asp`, with running the customers `OrderForm` through the Plan Pipeline. There is also the same error detection. Since `shipping.asp` is where the customer is supposed to leave shipping information, this script contains support for showing both the Wallet and traditional HTML forms. Most of the decisions from this point of view are made by the `i_MSWallet.asp` include file, which, in turn, includes `i_selector.asp`.

These two files work by using the `MSWC.BrowserType` component to determine whether the browser is capable of displaying the Wallet. In case of doubt (which, as we have mentioned in the previous chapter, can also be caused by an obsolete `browscap.ini` file), or if the URL parameter `use_form` is 1, HTML forms are used.

Keep in mind that, while the functions in `i_selector.asp` perform most of the decision making process, the actual inclusion of the Wallet is done inside the shipping page by verifying that the browser is able to support it (`i_selector.asp` stores a value of `True` inside the `fMSWltUplevelBrowser` variable in that case) and then passing the appropriate HTML code along to the browser:

```
    <% if fMSWltUplevelBrowser then %>
  ...

        <TD VALIGN="TOP">Ship-To Address:</TD>

        <TD VALIGN="TOP" ALIGN="CENTER">
        <% if fMSWltActiveXBrowser then %>
           <OBJECT
           ID="addrSelector"
           CLASSID="<% = MSWltIEAddrSelectorClassid() %>"
           CODEBASE="<% = MSWltIECodebase() %>"
           HEIGHT="123"
           WIDTH="154"
           >
           </OBJECT>
        <% elseif fMSWltLiveConnectBrowser then %>
           <EMBED
           NAME="addrSelector"
               TYPE="application/x-msaddr"
               PLUGINSPAGE="<%= MSWltNavDwnldURL("plginst.htm") %>"
               VERSION="<%= strMSWltDwnldVer %>"
               HEIGHT="123"
               WIDTH="154"
           >
      <% end if %>
```

The `fMSWltActiveXBrowser` variable is used to determine whether the browser at hand is able to contain ActiveX objects. If it isn't, the script assumes that it must be a Netscape product and acts consequently. In the `<BODY>` tag of the page, you will notice a cryptic line of code:

```
<BODY
    BGCOLOR="#FFFFFF"
    TEXT=    "#000000"
    LINK=    "#FF0000"
    VLINK=   "#FF0000"
    ALINK=   "#FF0000"
    <% if fMSWltUplevelBrowser and CBool(nOrderItems > 0) then
       %>onLoad="<% = MSWltLoadDone(strDownlevelURL) %>"<%
    end if %>
  >
```

As you can see, if the browser is able to display the Wallet, and if the `OrderForm` is not empty, the `MSWltLoadDone` function is called once the page has finished loading. This function, located in `I_selector.asp`, provides specific code for Netscape browsers, which are unable to automatically download and install plug-ins the way Internet Explorer does. Therefore, if the user is running a version of Navigator that supports plug-ins and the Wallet is not installed, this script outputs an elegant box, complete with Load button, that instructs the user to load and install it.

`I_MSWallet.asp` also includes two important settings that you can override and change for your own purposes. The first one is a piece of commented code that can be used to instruct the browser to load the Wallet's installation files from a location different than the standard one (which is usually on the Microsoft.com website). You will need to use this if your store resides on a local Intranet and the users accessing it don't have direct access to the Internet:

```
REM -- For intranets not connected to the internet, override default
REM -- download location here.  For example:
' If LCase(CStr(Request("HTTP_UA_CPU"))) <> "alpha" Then
'   strMSWltIEDwnldLoc  = "/" & siteRoot &
"/manager/MSCS_Images/controls/MSWallet.cab"
' Else
'     strMSWltIEDwnldLoc  = "/" & siteRoot &
"/manager/MSCS_Images/controls/MSWltAlp.cab"
' End If
' strMSWltNavDwnldLoc = "/" & siteRoot & "/manager/MSCS_Images/controls"
```

In this case, if you uncomment the text, it will by default assume that the Wallet's files are stored as `/manager/MSCS_Images/controls/MSWallet.cab`. The virtual folder, `MSCS_Images`, is created by the SBW when it generates the store, and points to the `SiteServer\Admin\Commerce\Images` folder of your Site Server installation. It contains several downloadable files that are required by the administrative Wizards used by SSCE, such as the SBW, the promotions Wizard, and so on.

The other setting that might come in handy is used to determine what payment methods are accepted by the store:

```
REM -- Set wallet control accept credit card types.
strMSWltAcceptedTypes = "visa:clear;mastercard:clear;"
```

We'll talk more in detail about the Microsoft Wallet, including how it works and how it can be used inside your stores, in Chapter 13.

The Missing Country

If you take a look at the HTML-only form, you will notice that there isn't an input box for the ship-to country. In fact, the country is hard-coded on the page:

```
<INPUT TYPE="HIDDEN" NAME="ship_to_country" VALUE="USA">
```

As a result, you will have to remove this tag and add something different if you want your store to support foreign countries. For example, here's a substitute that would let the user choose between the US, Canada and Sweden:

```
<SELECT Name="ship_to_country">
    <OPTION VALUE="USA">USA
    <OPTION VALUE="CAN">Canada
    <OPTION VALUE="SWE">Sweden
</SELECT>
```

Appendix C contains a complete list of all the three-letter ISO country codes, which you will need as values for the `ship_to_country` parameter.

Adding Another Shipping Method

After the `ship_to_country` values, the customer gets to choose one of the shipping methods that was chosen when the code was generated by the SBW. If you try to add another shipping method, for example "Slow steamboat" and assign this new method as `shipping_method_3`, like the code snippet below (remember there are two locations within the `shipping.asp` script you have to add this code), you will most likely run into problems if you do not add the proper functionality to your Plan Pipeline:

```
<SELECT NAME="shipping_method">
    <%= mscsPage.Option("shipping_method_1", mscsOrderForm.shipping_method) %>
    Overnight  
    <%= mscsPage.Option("shipping_method_2", mscsOrderForm.shipping_method) %>
    2nd Day  
    <%= mscsPage.Option("shipping_method_3", mscsOrderForm.shipping_method) %>
    Slow Steamboat  
</SELECT>
```

It is not enough to add another value to the HTML form, as you noticed if you tried to go from the `basket.asp` page to the purchase page after the change above. You might have encountered an error, as I did, exclaiming:

"Wrong number of arguments or invalid property assignment: 'errors.Add' Line: 20. Invalid number of parameters."

The error occurs when then the `ShipTo` validation Scriptor component doesn't recognize our new shipping method and tries to add an error to the `Purchase_Errors` in the `OrderForm`. In the `MSCSExecute` function, there is a check for the shipping methods. To get rid of the error above, you need to change the call to `errors.Add`, replace the comma with a plus sign, and you need to add your new shipping method.

```
function MSCSExecute(config, orderform, context, flags)
    set errors = orderform.[_Purchase_Errors]
    set msg_mgr = context.messagemanager
    result = 1
    if not IsValueValid(orderform.shipping_method) then
        call errors.Add(msg_mgr.GetMessage("val_noshipmethod"))
        result = 2
    else
        select case orderform.shipping_method
            case "shipping_method_1", "shipping_method_2", "shipping_method_3"
            case else
                call errors.Add(msg_mgr.GetMessage("val_shiponeof") + _
    "shipping_method_1" + _
                            "shipping_method_2")
                result = 2
        end select
    end if
```

If you want your new shipping method to have a cost, you must also add another `FixedShipping` component to the Plan pipeline (the `plan.pcf` file in the `config` directory) to support this new method, that can take care of the new value and assign the fee for the Slow Steamboat option: if we say $1, this translates to 100, since all money values in Site Server are stored in cents – if you are using dollars.

xt_orderform_prepare.asp

This ghost script's goal is essentially the storing in the `OrderForm` of the data that the user inputs into the shipping page. Therefore, it works by loading the `OrderForm`, retrieving each individual parameter using the various `Request` methods of the `Page` component, and then storing the purchase information back into the database.

Errors are handled by the `i_error.asp` generic include file, which simply dumps the contents of a `Dictionary` object called `errorList` (created in the `xt_orderform_prepare.asp` script) to the browser and invites the user to click on the back button to correct the problem. The errors are added in clear text within the script, like in this snippet taken from `xt_orderform_prepare.asp` where the `ship_to_name` is retrieved using the `Page` object and a check is made:

```
ship_to_name = mscsPage.RequestString("ship_to_name", null, 1, 100)
    if IsNull(ship_to_name) then
        errorList.Add("Ship to name must be a string between 1 and 100 characters")
    else
        orderForm.ship_to_name = ship_to_name
        orderForm.bill_to_name = orderForm.ship_to_name
    end if
```

The `i_error.asp` include file is also used in `payment.asp`, which is the next step in the purchase chain.

Payment.asp

The payment page starts by running the Plan pipeline once more, this time with the shipping information in the `OrderForm`. Contrary to what happened in the basket, the errors here are looked for in both the `_purchase_errors` and `_basket_errors` collections, since the entire pipeline should now be able to run without any problem.

For the rest, the page behaves similarly to `shipping.asp`, and it either displays the payment interface of the Wallet or the corresponding HTML forms. It's interesting to note that, while the address interface of the Wallet is consistent and can therefore be successfully replaced by a pre-defined HTML form, the same cannot be said of its payment counterpart. You will have to make sure that your store supports the same payment methods both with and without the Wallet, or you may risk losing customers –for example, because their browser doesn't support the Wallet and therefore they can't use the payment method they want. By default, the starter store supports HTML form input only for credit cards.

The VerifyWith Technique

To prevent the `OrderForm` from being tampered with by a malicious customer, the `payment.asp` uses the `VerifyWith` method of the `Page` object to generate a bunch of hidden fields.

```
<% = mscsPage.VerifyWith(mscsOrderForm, "_total_total", "ship_to_zip",
"_tax_total") %>
```

This generated the following HTML code to our client:

```
<!-- VerifyWith for Microsoft Site Server Commerce Edition 3.0 Pipeline -->
<INPUT TYPE=HIDDEN NAME="_VERIFY_WITH" VALUE="_total_total=2298">
<INPUT TYPE=HIDDEN NAME="_VERIFY_WITH" VALUE="ship_to_zip=x">
<INPUT TYPE=HIDDEN NAME="_VERIFY_WITH" VALUE="_tax_total=0">
```

These fields are read by the `ProcessVerifyWith` method of the `Page` object in the `xt_orderform_purchase.asp` script and stored in a `Dictionary` object called _verify_with, which is stored in the `OrderForm` object. The content of the _verify_with `Dictionary` is read when the Purchase pipeline processes the `OrderForm`, and the values are compared to the corresponding values in the `OrderForm` object – in this case _total_total, ship_to_zip and _tax_total.

The pipeline component `RequiredTotal` does the check, and if the values didn't match, an error is generated using the `pur_badverify` constant from the `MessageManager`, declared in `global.asa`:

```
call MSCSMessageManager.AddMessage("pur_badverify", _
    "Changes to the data require your review. Please review and resubmit.")
```

What we said about the ship-to country being hard-coded in the shipping page is valid for the payment page as well. In fact, about halfway down the script, we find the following HTML tag:

```
<INPUT TYPE="HIDDEN" NAME="bill_to_country" VALUE="USA">
```

Once again, if you are planning to let customers from places other than the United States buy from your store, you will have to change this code.

xt_orderform_purchase.asp

This is where the final act of the purchase process takes place. In fact, this script takes care of incorporating the values entered into the payment page into the `OrderForm` and of executing the Purchase pipeline at the same time.

This script calls `OrderFormPurchase`, which in turn goes through a sequence of events we have seen before; the `OrderForm` for the shopper is loaded, and `OrderFormPurchaseArgs` retrieves the purchase information by reading each parameter using the different `Request` methods provided by the `Page` object. The script then calls the `ProcessVerifyWith` method of the `Page` object, which we discussed earlier.

If no errors are encountered while retrieving the HTTP parameters, the function then saves the `OrderForm` back to the database (the pipeline might raise a runtime error, which would otherwise cause all the data to be lost). The Plan pipeline is then run one last time, with the intent of (a) making sure that nothing has changed since the last time it was executed, and that (b) the `OrderForm` data is still all valid.

If the pipeline talk has made you confused, here is a summary of what pipelines the `OrderForm` object is being run through during the different steps of the purchase process. The Plan pipeline is never used in the SBW generated store, since we are using simple queries to retrieve information about the products in the `dept.asp` and `product.asp` scripts.

❑   `basket.asp` – execute Plan pipeline using `UtilRunPlan`

❑   `payment.asp` – executes Plan pipeline using `UtilRunPlan`

❑   `shipping.asp` – executes Plan pipeline using `UtilRunPlan`

❑   `xt_orderform_purchase.asp` – executes Plan pipeline using `UtilRunPipe`, and then the purchase pipeline to finalize the purchase, using `UtilRunTxPipe`

You will notice that, this time, the script uses a different approach to before:

```
REM Set the verify with flags onto the orderform
call mscsPage.ProcessVerifyWith(mscsOrderForm)

REM Create the basic pipe context
set mscsPipeContext = UtilGetPipeContext()

REM Run the plan
errorLevel = UtilRunPipe("plan.pcf", mscsOrderForm, mscsPipeContext)
```

There are at least two reasons why the `UtilRunPlan` function is not used here. First of all, the `OrderForm` data has already been loaded; in addition, the script performs a call to the `ProcessVerifyWith` method of the `Page` component, which we have already discussed earlier. If no errors are returned by the Plan pipeline, the script proceeds to execute the Purchase pipeline to complete the order:

```
if mscsOrderForm.[_Basket_Errors].Count = 0 and _
   mscsOrderForm.[_Purchase_Errors].Count = 0 and errorLevel = 1 then

   REM Create the receipt storage
   Set mscsReceiptStorage = UtilGetReceiptStorage()

   REM Add the receipt storage into the pipe context...
   REM the Save Receipt component uses it
   Set mscsPipeContext.ReceiptStorage = MSCSReceiptStorage

   REM Run the transacted pipe
   errorLevel = UtilRunTxPipe("purchase.pcf", mscsOrderForm, mscsPipeContext)
end if
```

This time, the pipeline is run using the `UtilRunTxPipe` function, which is located inside `I_util.asp` and is essentially identical to `UtilRunPipe`, with the exception that it runs the pipeline in a transacted environment:

```
function UtilRunTxPipe(file, orderForm, pipeContext)
   Set pipeline = Server.CreateObject("Commerce.MtsTxPipeline")
```

```
    Call pipeline.LoadPipe(Request.ServerVariables("APPL_PHYSICAL_PATH") & _
    "config\" & file)
    REM Call pipeline.SetLogFile(Request.ServerVariables("APPL_PHYSICAL_PATH") & _
    REM"config\txpipeline.log")

    errorLevel = pipeline.Execute(1, orderForm, pipeContext, 0)

    UtilRunTxPipe = errorLevel
end function
```

> **You will need to uncomment the call to `SetLogFile` in this function as well if you want to log the Purchase pipeline's activity.**

The Purchase Pipeline

The adjacent figure shows the structure of the Purchase pipeline. As you can see, it's simpler than the Plan pipeline, and the function of all the scripts is pretty straightforward. The one thing that you might want to note is that the `Validate CC Info` script contains a few lines of code that output an error if the credit card is not of a type that is accepted by the store. If you plan to add more credit card types, you will need to modify this script as well.

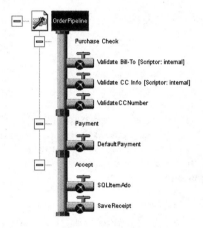

Finally, it's worth noting that, in the accept stage, an instance of `SQLItemADO` is used to store information about the individual products that are part of the order inside the `wroxstore_receipt_item` table. The `SaveReceipt` component, on the other hand, is used to insert the appropriate record, together with a copy of the marshaled basket, into the `wroxstore_receipt` table. It's interesting to note that the properties of `SaveReceipt` are programmed so that the component will not save the credit card information as part of the marshaled basket. If you are processing your credit card online – or if you need to keep them on file – you should change this setting by using an empty string in the **No Save Key Prefix** text box.

`SaveReceipt` requires that an instance of `Commerce.DBStorage` be saved inside the `OrderForm`. This is done in `xt_orderform_purchase.asp` by calling the `UtilGetReceiptStorage` function, which is identical to `UtilGetOrderFormStorage`, with the exception that it instructs its instance of `DBStorage` to access the `wroxstore_receipt` table.

Confirmed.asp

The confirmation page is extremely simple, as it limits its functionality to returning the `order_id` string to the user, and providing a link to `receipt.asp`, which can be used to review his or her order.

It's a good idea here to stop for a moment and talk a little bit about what can be done to substitute a better algorithm for creating unique order IDs than the one provided by SSCE. An easy way to do so is to alter the `wroxstore_receipt` table so that it also includes a numeric integer field that increments by one every time a new record is added to it:

```
ALTER TABLE wroxstore_receipt ADD order_number INT NOT NULL IDENTITY (1,1)
```

This snippet of code starts numbering at one, although you can change that to any number you like. As a matter of fact you would probably want to start with something irregular and large, like 52921.

If I got an order confirmation saying "Thank you for shopping with us, your order reference number is 6", I wouldn't think highly of the store. A higher number on the other hand will lure the customer into a false sense of security that this store has been on the market a while.

Inside `confirmed.asp`, you will also need to change the way the order ID is displayed – but nothing else, since we will still use SSCE's own IDs internally throughout the scripts. Thus, the following portion of the script:

```
Your order number is
<% order_id = mscsPage.HTMLEncode(Request("order_id")) %>

    <A HREF="<% = baseURL("receipt.asp") & mscsPage.URLShopperArgs("order_id", _
    Request("order_id")) %>">
        <STRONG><% = order_id %></STRONG>
    </A>.
```

will have to be changed as follows, with the goal of accessing the database one more time to find out what the "shorter" id assigned to our order is:

```
Your order number is
<%
    ' Retrieve order ID

    Set rs = cmdTemp.Execute(
                    "SELECT order_number FROM wroxstore_receipts WHERE _
                    order_id "& Request("order_id"))
%>
    ' Print it out for the user

    <A HREF="<% = baseURL("receipt.asp") & mscsPage.URLShopperArgs("order_id", _
    Request("order_id")) %>">
        <STRONG><% = rs("order_number") %></STRONG>
    </A>.

<% rs.Close %>
```

As you may notice, we have only changed the text that is actually printed out on the page, while all internal references still use the old "long" `order_id`. If you want to take this a step further, you could add functionality to a query in the Purchase pipeline to write the `order_number` value into the order form and send it as a parameter from `xt_orderform_purchase.asp` instead of the `order_id`.

Order Viewing

The only two pages of the storefront that we haven't yet had a chance to examine are receipts.asp and receipt.asp, accessible from the stores first page, default.asp. Receipts.asp can be used to produce a history of the orders placed by a particular customer, while the latter will provide more detail about a specific order, given its identifier.

Receipts.asp

This script works by executing a query against the wroxstore_receipts table, looking for all the records whose primary key corresponds to the shopper ID of the user. It's important to understand that this page will only work properly if you are using cookies to store the shopper ID, or if you require your customers to login – if you aren't, the shopper ID will be only temporary and it will be changed the next time the user logs in.

By default, receipts.asp still uses the long order IDs provided by SSCE. If you want to use the shorter IDs that we have just examined, you will have first of all to change the receipts_for_shopper query, which will initially be defined in global.asa as follows:

```
SELECT shopper_id, order_id, date_entered, total, status, marshaled_receipt
FROM wroxstore_receipt
WHERE shopper_id = :1
ORDER BY date_entered
```

All you need to do here is simply instruct the query to also retrieve the ID field, which can be done as follows:

```
SELECT order_number, shopper_id, order_id, date_entered, total, status,
marshaled_receipt
FROM wroxstore_receipt
WHERE shopper_id = :1
ORDER BY date_entered
```

Next, we'll have to change the script in receipts.asp so that it will display the correct ID. To do this, we'll modify the following lines:

```
    if Not rsReceipts.EOF then
        set order_idField = rsReceipts("order_id")
        set date_enteredField = rsReceipts("date_entered")
        set totalField = rsReceipts("total")
        do while Not rsReceipts.EOF
            %>
            <TR>
                <TD WIDTH="100" VALIGN="TOP" ALIGN="CENTER">
                    <A HREF="<% = baseURL("receipt.asp") & _
                    mscsPage.URLShopperArgs("order_id", order_idField.value) %>">
                        <% = mscsPage.HTMLEncode(order_idField.value) %> </A>
                </TD>
                <TD WIDTH="100" VALIGN="TOP" ALIGN="CENTER">
                    <% = MSCSDataFunctions.Date(date_enteredField.value) %>
                </TD>
```

```
            <TD WIDTH="100" VALIGN="TOP" ALIGN="RIGHT">
                <% = MSCSDataFunctions.Money(totalField.value) %>
            </TD>
        </TR>
        <%
    rsReceipts.MoveNext
loop
```

into the following:

```
if Not rsReceipts.EOF then
    set order_idField = rsReceipts("order_id")
    set date_enteredField = rsReceipts("date_entered")
    set totalField = rsReceipts("total")
    set idField = rsReceipts("order_number")
    do while Not rsReceipts.EOF
        %>
        <TR>
            <TD WIDTH="100" VALIGN="TOP" ALIGN="CENTER">
                <A HREF="<% = baseURL("receipt.asp") & _
                        mscsPage.URLShopperArgs("order_id",
    order_idField.value) %>">
                    <% = mscsPage.HTMLEncode(idField.value) %>
                </A>
            </TD>
            <TD WIDTH="100" VALIGN="TOP" ALIGN="CENTER">
                <% = MSCSDataFunctions.Date(date_enteredField.value) %>
            </TD>
            <TD WIDTH="100" VALIGN="TOP" ALIGN="RIGHT">
                <% = MSCSDataFunctions.Money(totalField.value) %>
            </TD>
        </TR>
        <% rsReceipts.MoveNext
    loop
```

Receipt.asp

The receipt.asp script presents a complete order, given by the order_id parameter. This script works similarly to the basket, with the only exception that the OrderForm is loaded from the wroxstore_receipt table, rather than from wroxstore_basket. You will also notice that the page includes some more additional information, such as the ship-to and bill-to address. No credit card information is specified – since the pipeline is programmed not to save it – so you will have to manually add it in yourselves if you need to.

The Store Manager

If you take a look at the figure here, you can see that the Manager's folder contains many more files – almost twice as many – than the storefront. As this may lead you to think, its structure is in fact more complex than its counterpart, although a lot of the functionality is repeated across several pages.

```
Exploring - C:\InetPub\wwwroot\wroxstore\Ma...  _ □ ×
File   Edit   View   Tools   Help
Contents of 'C:\InetPub\wwwroot\wroxstore\Manager'

📁 Config                        🗎 promo-cross_edit.asp
📁 include                       🗎 promo-cross_list.asp
🗎 Default.asp                   🗎 promo-cross_new.asp
🗎 dept_delete.asp               🗎 promo-price_delete.asp
🗎 dept_edit.asp                 🗎 promo-price_edit.asp
🗎 dept_list.asp                 🗎 promo-price_list.asp
🗎 dept_new.asp                  🗎 promo-price_new.asp
🗎 order.asp                     🗎 xt_dept_delete.asp
🗎 order_day.asp                 🗎 xt_dept_insert.asp
🗎 order_list.asp                🗎 xt_dept_update.asp
🗎 order_month.asp               🗎 xt_product_delete.asp
🗎 order_product.asp             🗎 xt_product_insert.asp
🗎 order_view.asp                🗎 xt_product_update.asp
🗎 product_delete.asp            🗎 xt_promo-cross_delete.asp
🗎 product_edit.asp              🗎 xt_promo-cross_insert.asp
🗎 product_list.asp              🗎 xt_promo-cross_update.asp
🗎 product_new.asp               🗎 xt_promo-price_delete.asp
🗎 product_view.asp              🗎 xt_promo-price_insert.asp
🗎 promo.asp                     🗎 xt_promo-price_update.asp
🗎 promo-cross_delete.asp        🗎 xt_shopper_delete.asp

40 object(s)              172KB (Disk free space: 977MB)
```

You will also notice that there is no global.asa file in this folder, which means that it doesn't act as a separate application, but leans on the storefront for global object initialization. The Config subdirectory, in this case, contains just the Site Configuration dictionary – no pipelines are required to run the Store Manager. Another difference from the storefront is also that all the include files are stored in a separate directory, called, very fittingly, include.

The Store Manager is the restricted part of the site, which only the persons responsible for maintaining the store should have access to. If you examine the security properties on the Manager subdirectory in your store, you will notice there is no "Everyone" access, but rather the Group Commerce_<store_name>_1 with access to this subdirectory. The user you assigned to manage the store from the Site Builder Wizard will be added to this Windows NT Group and this is the account you should use when you try to access the Manager. If you need more accounts to access the Store Manager, just add them to the Commerce_<store_name>_1 Group.

The Main Page

In the Store Manager, default.asp does not only work as a gateway to the rest of the functionality provided by the other sites, but provides some functionality of its own. In fact, while access to the four main sections is performed by calling the appropriate script, all the administrative functions are taken care of by the Main Page itself.

Tapping Into Global Functionality

Three of the functions performed by the Store Manager – editing pipelines, and launching either the Store Builder Wizard or the Promotions Wizard – are actually taken care of by global code that is provided as part of SSCE but that doesn't appear inside the Manager's folder.

In fact, when the store is generated, the SBW also creates a virtual folder called `MSCS_CommerceSiteBuilderWizard` that points to the location where the files that comprise both the Site Builder Wizard and the Promotion Wizard are physically stored. The pipeline editor, on the other hand, is pointed at by the `MSCS_PipeEdit` virtual folder, which is also created at the end of the store generation process.

Opening, Closing and Reloading the Store

`Default.asp` makes it possible to open and close the store by posting the following HTML form to itself:

```
<FORM METHOD="GET" ACTION="<%= tmplManager %> ">
    <TD ALIGN="CENTER" WIDTH="50%">
        <INPUT TYPE="SUBMIT"
        NAME="Status"
        VALUE=" <%= RevStatus %> Site ">
    </TD>
</FORM>
```

The `RevStatus` variable contains the store's current status, determined using the `GetStatus` function defined in `site_util.asp`, while `tmplManager` is defined in the `mgmt_define.asp` include file. At the beginning of the Main Page, a piece of code examines the URL query string in order to determine whether it contains the `Status` parameter, which, as you can see above, is the name of the submit button in the form.

The value of the `Status` parameter is ignored by the code – all that is needed is its presence, which indicates that the user has clicked on the button that changes the store's status. A call to `ToggleSiteStatus` takes care of opening, or closing, the store as it may be the case:

```
If Request("Status").Count <> 0 then
    ToggleSiteStatus
    Response.redirect Request("URL")
End If
```

A similar technique is used for reloading the store. Once again, a simple form redirects the browser to the Main Page, specifying a parameter – this time called `Reload` – as the name of its submit button:

```
<FORM METHOD="GET" ACTION="<%= tmplManager %>">
    <TD ALIGN="CENTER" WIDTH=50%>
        <INPUT TYPE="SUBMIT"
        NAME="Reload"
        VALUE=" Reload Site ">
    </TD>
</FORM>
```

At the beginning of the file, another snippet of code calls the `ReloadSite` function if the `Reload` parameter is found in the URL query string:

```
If Request("Reload").Count <> 0 then
    ReloadSite
    Response.redirect Request("URL")
End If
```

Logical Structure

As you can see here, four sections within the Manager – Departments, Products, Promotions and Orders – share the same underlying structure; it's easy to guess that they should account for most of the files in the main folder – and they do: *all* the files that are shown in the previous figure, with the exception of `default.asp`, are dedicated to taking care of them. With this in mind, we will concentrate on the Product section, and then show how you can take advantage of this structure to add some new functionality to your store without coding it from scratch.

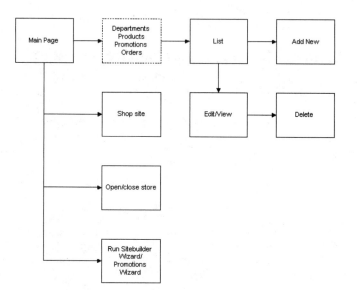

Examining the Product Section

From the starting page, `default.asp`, you access the product management part of the site by clicking on the "Products" button. This will execute the `product_list.asp` script. All the files with the `_list.asp` suffix share the same structure, and use the same include files, listed in the table below.

File Name	Description
include/manager.asp	Included by all Store Manager pages, defines ado constants, and loads and setup the manager site dictionary located in **manager/config/store.scs**
include/site_util.asp	Defines a number of common functions. Included from `manager.asp`
include/mgmt_define.asp	Defines table names and related ASP files for the different sections of the manager

Table Continued on Following Page

File Name	Description
include/mgmt_header.asp	Header file that prints out links to the different parts of the sections in the manager
include/list.asp	A common include file for all list pages, this is the file actually generating the list, based on variables set in the `product_list.asp` file
include/error.asp	Executed upon error. Included from `list.asp`
include/mgmt_footer.asp	Executed upon error. Included from `list.asp`
include/mgmt_footer.asp	Footer file that prints out links to the different parts of the sections in the manager

The `product_list.asp` page itself only contains some basic HTML tags, a function definition of `ShowRow` called from `list.asp`, and some variable definitions:

```
<%  function ShowRow() %>
    <TD VALIGN="TOP"> <% = RowCount %> </TD>
    <TD VALIGN="TOP">
       <A HREF="<% = listElemTemplate & "?" & mscsPage.URLArgs("pf_id", _
       rsList("pf_id").value, "name", rsList("name").value) %>">
       <% = rsList("pf_id").value %> </A>
    </TD>
    <TD VALIGN="TOP">
       <A HREF="<% = listElemTemplate & "?" & mscsPage.URLArgs("pf_id", _
       rsList("pf_id").value, "name", rsList("name").value) %>">
       <%= rsList("name").value %> </A>
    </TD>
    <TD VALIGN="TOP" ALIGN=RIGHT>
    <% if Not IsNull(rsList("list_price").value) then %>
       <%= MSCSDataFunctions.Money(rsList("list_price").value) %><% end if %></TD>
<%  end function
```

`ShowRow` is called within the loop in `list.asp`, printing out each row in the product list. All the different files with the `*_list.asp` suffix must define this function. The `product_list.asp` script then declares some constants, which are used within the included `list.asp` file.

```
listElemTemplate = "product_edit.asp"

listColumns = "<TH ALIGN=""LEFT""> # </TH>" & vbCr & _
              "<TH ALIGN=""LEFT""> Pf Id </TH>" & vbCr & _
              "<TH ALIGN=""LEFT""> Name </TH>" & vbCr & _
              "<TH ALIGN=""LEFT""> Price </TH>" & vbCr

listNoRows = "<I>No products in table</I><P>
   <FONT
      FACE=""Arial, sans-serif""
      COLOR=""#FF0000""
      STYLE=""{font-family: Arial, sans-serif; font-color: red; font-weight: bold;
            font-size: 10pt}""
   >
```

```
    *** IMPORTANT *** You must enter Attributes and Departments before entering new
    products.
    </FONT>"

cmdTemp.CommandText = "SELECT pf_id, name, list_price
                       FROM wroxstore_product
                       ORDER BY pf_id"
```

The `listElemTemplate` holds the name of the script that allows the user to edit the products. If you examine the Manager directory you will see that all the Sections each have a file with an `_edit.asp` suffix. `listColumns` is used in `list.asp` to print out the table headings for the product list, and the `listNoRows` contains the HTML printed when the product table was empty.

Finally the `cmdTemp` instance of `ADODB.Command` is loaded with the query that will retrieve the actual product list from the database. As you can see, only those columns used in the `ShowRow()` function are retrieved as opposed to using `'*'` which will be slower. If you want to add another column, like maybe the `image_file` column, you will only have to do the following changes:

```
<%  function ShowRow() %>
    <TD VALIGN="TOP"> <% = RowCount %> </TD>
    <TD VALIGN="TOP">
        <A HREF="<% = listElemTemplate & "?" & mscsPage.URLArgs("pf_id",
                 rsList("pf_id").value, "name", rsList("name").value) %> ">
          <% = rsList("pf_id").value %>
        </A>
    </TD>
    <TD VALIGN="TOP">
        <A HREF="<% = listElemTemplate & "?" & mscsPage.URLArgs("pf_id",
                 rsList("pf_id").value, "name", rsList("name").value) %> ">
          <%= rsList("name").value %>
        </A>
    </TD>
    <TD VALIGN="TOP" ALIGN=RIGHT>
        <% if Not IsNull(rsList("list_price").value) then %>
        <%= MSCSDataFunctions.Money(rsList("list_price").value) %>
        <% end if %>
    </TD>
    <TD VALIGN="TOP"><%=rsList("image_file")%></TD>
<%  end function
...
:
listElemTemplate = "product_edit.asp"
listColumns = "<TH ALIGN=""LEFT""> # </TH>" & vbCr & _
              "<TH ALIGN=""LEFT""> Pf Id </TH>" & vbCr & _
              "<TH ALIGN=""LEFT""> Name </TH>" & vbCr & _
              "<TH ALIGN=""LEFT""> Price </TH>" & vbCr & _
              "<TH ALIGN=""LEFT""> Image File </TH>" & vbCr

listNoRows = "<I>No products in table</I><P>
    <FONT
       FACE=""Arial, sans-serif""
       COLOR=""#FF0000""
```

```
        STYLE=""{font-family: Arial, sans-serif; font-color: red; font-weight: bold;
            font-size: 10pt}""
    >
    *** IMPORTANT *** You must enter Attributes and Departments before entering new
    products.
    </FONT>"
```

```
cmdTemp.CommandText = "SELECT pf_id, name, list_price,image_file" & _
                "FROM wroxstore2 product ORDER BY pf_id"
```

The final part of `product_list.asp` includes `list.asp`, where all the functionality for creating the paged lists resides. We will now go through all the files that were included in the `product_list.asp` script.

Manager.asp

The manager page is included in all the main files within the Store Manager. The main file includes are `default.asp` and all the files with the suffix `_list.asp`, `_edit.asp`, `_delete.asp`, `_new.asp` and `_view.asp`. The code in `manager.asp` is pretty straightforward. The first line prevents all the Store Manager pages from being cached by the client or by proxies, since their contents are almost exclusively dynamic in nature.

```
<% Response.ExpiresAbsolute=DateAdd("yyyy", -10, Date) %>
```

This code sets the `ExpiresAbsolute` to ten years before today, making sure that the content is expired immediately. Next, the `Commerce.Page` object is instantiated to `mscsPage`. The `Page` object is not used with the `StandardSManager` to maintain state within the Manager pages, since it isn't needed – we already have authentication using Windows NT Challenge/Response and Basic Authentication to protect our pages.

> *See http://www.microsoft.com/NTServer/security/exec/feature/WebSecurity.asp for more details*

Only the money and URL managing methods of the `Page` object are used. `Manager.asp` also defines a couple of ADO constants, and initializes a Dictionary called `mscsManagerSite` to the Site Dictionary for the Manager pages – located in `Manager/config/site.csc`. An ADO Connection object, `MSCS`, and an ADO Command object, `cmdTemp`, are also created and initialized.

Finally, `manager.asp` includes `site_util.asp`, which defines a number of support functions.

Site_util.asp

This script contains a variety of functions, used mainly to carry out clerical operations, such as opening and closing the store and making ample use of the administrative SSCE objects that we saw back in Chapter 9:

Function Name	Description
ReportOnError	Checks if a trappable runtime error has occurred and reports it to the user.
GetSiteObject	Creates an instance of the AdminSite object and initializes it to point to the site where the store resides.
OpenSite	Opens the site by retrieving the Site Object and setting its Status property to True (open).
CloseSite	Same as OpenSite, but sets the Status property to False.
ToggleSiteStatus	Inverts the current status of the site. Thus, if the site was open before the execution of ToggleSiteStatus, it will become closed afterwards, and vice versa.
GetStatus	Returns the status of the site.
ReloadSite	Forces the site to reload by calling the Reload method of the Site object.
GetPCFFiles	Returns a list of the pipeline configuration files stored in the config folder of the storefront.

While most of the code here is straightforward, there are a couple of things worth noticing. Firstly, you will notice that GetStatus returns both the store's current status and its reverse. This is done so that the script in the Main Page can properly display the text in the **Store Status** box and inside the button that alternately opens and closes the store.

Secondly, if you look closely at GetPCFFiles, you will notice that it uses an object of class Commerce.AdminFiles, which we haven't examined. This is one of very few "undocumented" objects in SSCE, and its functionality is very similar to part of what IIS' built-in Scripting.FileSystemObject provides. The GetFiles function used here simply returns an array of strings that corresponds to the files that match the standard DOS specifications passed to it. For example, here is the GetPCFFiles method; it retrieves a list of PCF files in the storefront's config folder.

```
Function GetPCFFiles
    Dim AdminFiles
    Set AdminFiles = Server.CreateObject("Commerce.AdminFiles")

    Dim ConfigDir
    ConfigDir = Request.ServerVariables("APPL_PHYSICAL_PATH") + "\Config"

    GetPCFFiles = AdminFiles.GetFiles(ConfigDir + "\*.pcf")
End Function
```

The GetPCFFiles function is called from the Store Managers default.asp script to display all the pipeline configuration files to open them for editing:

```
PCFFiles = GetPCFFiles
...
```

```
<SELECT NAME="Filename">
    <% For nFile = LBound(PCFfiles,1) To UBound(PCFfiles,1) %>
       <%= mscsPage.Option(PCFfiles(nFile),0) %> <%= PCFfiles(nFile) %> 
    <% next %>
</SELECT>
```

mgmt_define.asp

The mgmt_define.asp include file defines global variables that contain the names of every table required by the Manager. The use of these variables is somewhat inconsistent, since none of the functions within the manager take advantage of them. However, nothing prevents you from using them if you decide to extend or modify the Store Manager:

```
REM    table names:

tableBaskets       = "wroxstore_basket"
tableReceipts      = "wroxstore_receipt"
tableReceiptItems  = "wroxstore_receipt_item"
tableProducts      = "wroxstore_product"
tableDepts         = "wroxstore_dept"
tablePricePromos   = "wroxstore_promo_price"
tableCrossPromos   = "wroxstore_promo_cross"
```

The script is also used to define a few global variables that contain the name of key pages within the Manager, such as the Main Page and the entry points to the four main sections:

```
REM -- template names:

tmplManager = "default.asp"
tmplOrder   = "order.asp"
tmplProduct = "product_list.asp"
tmplDept    = "dept_list.asp"
tmplPromo   = "promo.asp"
```

Finally, it also sets the stdListRange variable, which contains the maximum number of elements that are printed in every page of a list. As we will see later on, all lists are essentially generated by the same script.

```
REM -- appearance:
stdListRange = 15
```

Headers and Footers

Similar to what happens for the storefront, there are two include files – mgmt_header.asp and mgmt_footer.asp – whose goal is to provide a consistent look for all the pages in the Store Manager. In particular, they generate the upper and lower portions of the screen, in which the page's title, a group of links to other significant locations in the Manager and a copyright notice are displayed. The latter is actually stored in a separate include file, called copyright.asp, which is also stored in the include folder.

There is nothing particularly interesting in either the header or footer files, but they, too, present the annoying problem of not recognizing what page the user is looking at. As a result, every page in the Store Manager essentially points to itself! However, this might not be such a big problem in this section of the site, since it's reasonable to expect that its users will be less prone to confusion than the public at large.

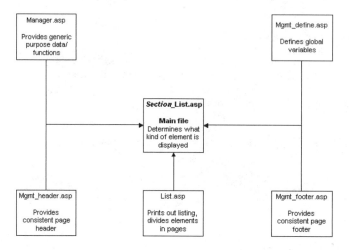

List.asp

The script that takes care of the actual displaying of the product lists starts by initializing a few variables, and then it attempts to determine what page should be displayed, that is, what position it should start outputting records from in the recordset. This is done by looking at the `ListAbsolutePage` URL parameter that it passes to itself when the user goes from page to page:

```
REM -- Get the page we are on
ListAbsolutePage = mscsPage.RequestNumber("ListAbsolutePage")
if IsNull(ListAbsolutePage) then
    ListAbsolutePage = 1
end if
```

As you can see, if the parameter is not present, the script defaults the page number to one. Next, the data is extracted from the database. This is done by first creating a `Recordset` object, and then opening it using the `cmdTemp` instance of `ADODB.Command` created in `manager.asp`:

```
REM -- load recordset
Set rsList = Server.CreateObject("ADODB.Recordset")
rsList.CacheSize = stdListRange

On Error Resume Next

rsList.Open cmdTemp, , adOpenStatic, adLockReadOnly
```

This is where the `cmdTemp` object is used. If you remember, it was assigned a query in the `product_list.asp` script:

```
cmdTemp.CommandText = "SELECT sku, name, list_price FROM wroxstore_product ORDER
BY sku"
```

The script moves on to position the recordset's cursor to the appropriate position, which depends on the value of the `ListAbsolutePage` variable. First, however, it is necessary to calculate the total number of pages in the recordset – this is done using one of two methods, depending on whether the DBMS where the data is stored supports the `RecordCount` property:

```
rsList.PageSize = PageSize
...
if Not rsList.Supports(adApproxPosition) then 'not SQL Server - probably Oracle
    Do While Not rsList.EOF
        RecordCount = RecordCount + 1
        rsList.MoveNext
    Loop

    if Not rsList.BOF then rsList.MoveFirst
    PageCount = Round(RecordCount/PageSize)

    if PageCount < RecordCount/PageSize then PageCount = PageCount + 1
else
    PageCount   = rsList.PageCount
    RecordCount = rsList.RecordCount
end if
```

This explains a little better the "brute force" method that we previously saw while looking at `find.asp` in the storefront, which is required if ADO is unable to determine the number of records in the result set. In this case, both approaches are illustrated, and, since you probably only need one anyway, it's a good idea to delete the code that does not work for your DBMS.

You will also want to notice that the `PageSize` property of the recordset is set to the number of records that should appear on each page. This has the double goal of both making it easier to calculate the total number of pages *and* forcing the recordset to only download the exact number of records for one page each time that new data is fetched from the server.

Next, the cursor is positioned over the appropriate record by looking at whether the page was loaded in response to the fact that the user had requested to view a different page. This is done by checking the `PagingMove` variable, which simply contains the name of the button the user has clicked. This, in turn, is passed as an URL parameter in a posting operation triggered by the buttons themselves using a technique similar to the one that we saw for reloading the store in the Main Page.

For example, let's assume that the user wants to move to the last page of the recordset, and therefore clicks on the '>>' button. The latter is declared as follows:

```
<INPUT TYPE="Button" NAME="list_PagingMove" VALUE=" &gt;&gt; ">
```

When the user clicks on a button, an HTML form is posted to the server with a parameter that contains the current page number, (later stored in the `ListAbsolutePage` variable that we have already seen), and another one whose value changes depending on the button that has been pressed. The latter is retrieved at the beginning of the script and saved in the `PagingMove` variable:

```
PagingMove = mscsPage.RequestString("list_PagingMove", "")
```

The call to the `RequestString` method of the `Page` component causes all the leading and trailing spaces to be removed, so that, in the end, `PagingMove` contains one of four values: '<<', '<', '>' and '>>'. The script traps these values inside a case statement and changes the value of `ListAbsolutePage` accordingly:

```
Select Case PagingMove
    Case "<<"
        ListAbsolutePage = 1
    Case "<"
        ListAbsolutePage = ListAbsolutePage - 1
    Case ">"
        ListAbsolutePage = ListAbsolutePage + 1
    Case ">>"
        ListAbsolutePage = PageCount
    Case Else
End Select
```

Finally, the recordset's cursor is moved to the appropriate position, once again using a different technique depending on whether the underlying DBMS supports absolute movements:

```
if Not rsList.Supports(adApproxPosition) then 'not SQL Server - probably Oracle
    StartRecord = ((ListAbsolutePage - 1) * PageSize)
    For i = 1 to StartRecord
        If rsList.EOF then exit for
            rsList.MoveNext
    Next
else
    rsList.AbsolutePage = ListAbsolutePage
end if
```

One more check is made to make sure that the page does in fact contain at least one recordset, and if that is not the case, the cursor is moved back by one page.

After these preambles, the actual display operation finally begins. First of all, the column headings are displayed by simply outputting the `listColumns` variable, which is defined inside the `section`product_list.asp script. Since the list is outputted in a table, the headings should be included in a set of `<TD>` or `<TH>` tags and, clearly, there should be one heading for each column that the SQL query returns.

```
listColumns = "<TH ALIGN=""LEFT""> # </TH>" & vbCr & _
              "<TH ALIGN=""LEFT""> Sku </TH>" & vbCr & _
              "<TH ALIGN=""LEFT""> Name </TH>" & vbCr & _
              "<TH ALIGN=""LEFT""> Price </TH>" & vbCr
```

Keep in mind that the `vbCr` (a VBScript constant that causes a Carriage Return character to be outputted) that is appended at the end of each row has no particular purpose other than a purely aesthetic one to make the code more readable in the resulting HTML file.

The actual records are outputted one by one through a call to the `ShowRow` function, which, once again, is defined in the main section file. Similar to the contents of `listColumns`, `ShowRow` should output the individual fields separated by the appropriate table tags.

Add a Search Field to Narrow Down Product Lists

If you have a lot of products, it is very tough to try to figure out on which page in the product listing a particular product will show up. To make life easier for the administrator, you can add a search field to the navigation buttons, making it easy to narrow down your product list. First, we need to change the code for the navigation bar in `list.asp`:

```
<% If ListAbsolutePage > 1 Then %>
     <INPUT TYPE="Submit" NAME="list_PagingMove" VALUE="  &lt;&lt;   ">
     <INPUT TYPE="Submit" NAME="list_PagingMove" VALUE="  &lt;     ">
<% Else %>
     <INPUT TYPE="Button" NAME="list_PagingMove" VALUE="  &lt;&lt;   ">
     <INPUT TYPE="Button" NAME="list_PagingMove" VALUE="  &lt;     ">
<% End If %>
<% If ListAbsolutePage < PageCount Then %>
     <INPUT TYPE="Submit" NAME="list_PagingMove" VALUE="   &gt;     ">
     <INPUT TYPE="Submit" NAME="list_PagingMove" VALUE="   &gt;&gt;   ">
<% Else %>
     <INPUT TYPE="Button" NAME="list_PagingMove" VALUE="   &gt;     ">
     <INPUT TYPE="Button" NAME="list_PagingMove" VALUE="   &gt;&gt;   ">
<% End If %>
     <% If pageTitle = "Products" Then %>
     search: <input type="text" name="findspec" VALUE="<%=strFindSpec%>"
size="6">
     <% End If %>
     <INPUT TYPE="Submit" NAME="list_PagingMove" VALUE=" Requery ">
     <INPUT TYPE="Hidden" NAME="ListAbsolutePage" VALUE="<% = ListAbsolutePage
%>">
```

This is how it will appear in your browser:

| 16 Records | Page: 1 of 2 |
| << | < | > | >> | search: | Requery |

We check the `pageTitle` variable, defined in `product_list.asp` to see if we are at the Products page. Now, you could skip this check, but then you would have to change the queries in all the `*_list.asp` pages. For now, we only bother with the `product_list.asp` query, using a similar technique as in `list.asp`.

```
cmdTemp.CommandText = "SELECT pf_id, name, list_price
                       FROM wroxstore_product
                       ORDER BY pf_id"
```

We insert some code to take care of the parameter, findspec, and insert a WHERE clause in the SQL statement. If the parameter was empty, just use the old SQL string, but if there was something in it we do a like check on the pf_id column and the name column of the product table.

```
strFindSpec = Replace(Request("findspec"), "'","''")

If strFindSpec = "" Then
     strSQL = "SELECT pf_id, name, list_price FROM wroxstore_product" & _
             "ORDER BY pf_id"
Else
     strSQL = "SELECT pf_id, name, list_price FROM wroxstore_product"
     strSQL = strSQL & " WHERE pf_id like '%"
     strSQL = strSQL & strFindSpec & "%' or name like '%" & strFindSpec
     strSQL = strSQL & "%' ORDER BY pf_id"
End If

cmdTemp.CommandText = strSQL
```

This is obviously not a daunting task, so you could very easily take this further by including options such as sort order using the ORDER BY ... ASC/DESC clause in the SQL statement. You could also let the user control the amount of records to show at each time, controlled by the PageSize parameter in list.asp. Such functionality would let the user print the whole product list at once, rather than stepping through the products, printing each page.

Editing a Product

As we already mentioned, since each edit and delete operation has to deal with a separate set of information, they are all different from each other, and essentially work by executing the proper queries and showing the correct fields to the user.

These files do share a common structure; they all have one section that takes care of the user interaction, while the database management – adding, deleting and updating – is taken care of in an include file with the prefix xt_; for the product editing, this file is called xt_product_edit.asp. There is a difference from the way the xt_ files were handled in the public store where the user was redirected to the xt_ file, some calculations were made and then redirected to the next page. In the Store Manager, the pages uses post-to-self and includes the xt_ code, which is executed if any changes were made.

Examining product_edit.asp, we discover that it does include the Manager.asp page and the xt_product_update.asp page. The script then proceeds to set a client-side scripting variable called dirty. This flag is set to True whenever the user has edited one or more of the fields, and when the user clicks on one of the links a warning is issued that the changes he or she made are about to be discarded:

```
<A HREF="variant_new.asp?<% = mscsPage.URLArgs("pf_id", rsProduct("pf_id").value)
%>"
     onClick="if (dirty) return confirm('Do you want to add a new variant and lose
             your changes?\nOK = lose changes\nCancel = stay on this page')">
<H2> Add New Variant </H2>
</A></TD>
```

Unfortunately this does not apply to the links generated from the `mgmt_header.asp` and `mgmt_footer.asp` include files. After this, the form itself is created using HTML, and at the end of the page, all the variants for this particular product are being displayed using the listing functionality discussed earlier.

When the user clicks the "Update Product" button, the form is posted to itself and the `xt_product_update.asp` script will be executed.

xt_product_update.asp

The script begins with creating a `SimpleList` object, which will be loaded with all the errors that occurred while retrieving the form values. A check is made against the `Validate` parameter to make sure the user really clicked the "Update Product" button:

```
Set errorList = Server.CreateObject("Commerce.SimpleList")
On Error Resume Next
if Request("Validate").count <> 0 then
```

A query is then declared and executed using Optimistic locking, this will allow editing of the recordset:

```
cmdTemp.CommandText = Replace("SELECT * FROM wroxstore_product WHERE _
pf_id = ?", "?", "'" & Replace(Request("pf_id"),"'","''") & "'")
Set rsExe = Server.CreateObject("ADODB.Recordset")
rsExe.Open cmdTemp, , adOpenStatic, adLockOptimistic
```

The script retrieves all the parameters sent from the form. If an error occurred, explanatory text is added to the error object to be presented later, giving the user the possibility to correct the mistakes. If the value was satisfactory, it is updated in the recordset, using the `Update` method.

```
name = mscsPage.RequestString("name", "", 1, 255)
if IsNull(name) then
    errorList.Add "name must be between 1 and 255 characters"
else
    if name = "" then name = null
    rsExe.Update "name", name
end if
```

Finally, after retrieving and updating all the form values, the script reloads the site and redirects back to the `product_list.asp` script.

```
if errorList.Count = 0 Then
    ReloadSite
    Response.Redirect "product_list.asp"
end if
```

The reload of the site is done to ensure that application scope variables are reloaded when the database information is updated. If you have encountered an "HTTP 1.1 Application Restarting" error while doing an update, it is because the `ReloadSite` function had not finished reloading the site when you were redirected.

One of the recommendations given in the Performance Kit is to store the department list in an application scope dictionary object (see chapter 16). If you choose to implement this recommendation, not reloading the site would cause the changes your store administrators make to the product database only to be visible when the web server is restarted. If you are experiencing this and still want the reload site statement, you could add a small 'do-nothing' loop between the call to the `ReloadSite` and the `Redirect` statement just to waste some time, or if you don't need the site to be reloaded, simply comment out the call to `ReloadSite`.

As we have seen, the structure is similar for these scripts regardless of which section they belong to; all the scripts for maintaining the database - products, promotions, attributes, departments, orders - work by incorporating an `xt_` prefixed script which will be executed if the user did a change, signaled by the `"Validate"` parameter, and an HTML form which gives the user the possibility to edit the fields.

Summary

Throughout this chapter, we've had the chance to understand how the starter store works internally by examining the way it has been written. This comprehension is essential if you are planning to extend or modify the basic site that results from the execution of the Site Builder Wizard. In fact, spending some time trying to figure out the logic behind the code might save you from the "first-timer syndrome" that causes all developers –no matter how experienced – to create a monster the first time they attempt to set up a new store and add a few more features in!

Also, you will have probably noted that there is no business-to-business functionality of any kind in the starter store – we mentioned this at the beginning of the chapter as well. This means that you will have to perform any integration with third-party line-of-business systems yourself – one more reason to know your starter store *very* well.

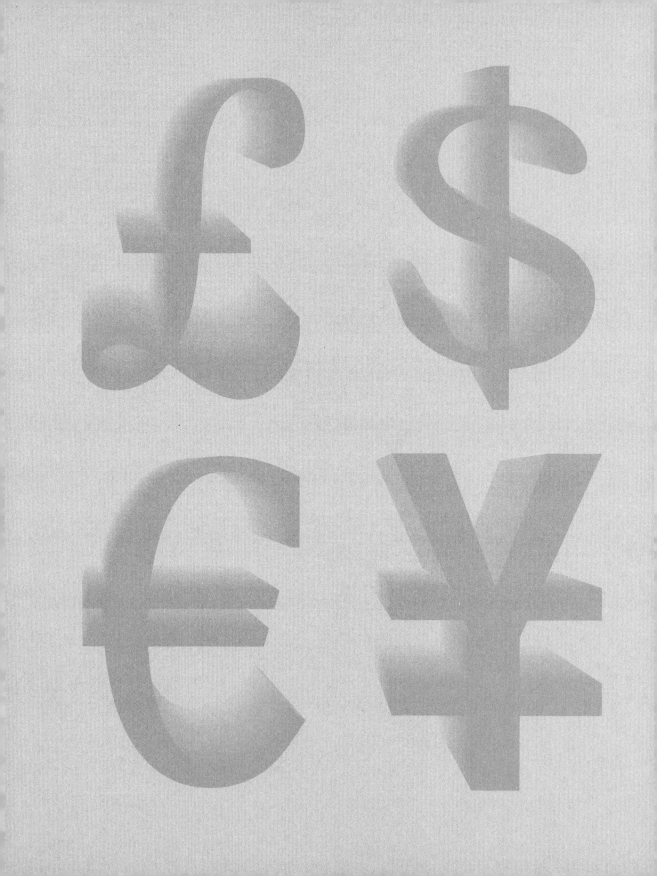

Business-to-Business E-Commerce

Vision is the art of seeing things invisible.
–**Jonathan Swift**, *Thoughts on various subjects*

To this point, we have examined electronic commerce as the interaction between the seller and a buyer. In particular, the transactions that we had in mind had two very particular characteristics:

- ❏ The recipient of the merchandise sold was intended to be its final user (with the exception of gifts, which are paid by someone and delivered to someone else)

- ❏ The customer was paying directly for his or her purchase using a personal payment system, like a credit card

If you think about it, these two assumptions are quite important, and they largely dictate the way electronic commerce transactions should be carried out in their particular scenarios. In fact, just removing the second one opens a number of questions that can't be left unanswered: if customers are not paying directly for their purchases, then they are probably acting on someone else's behalf. It's also possible that this "someone else" might want to control how his or her money is being spent, and should be given the possibility to do so by the store.

Similarly, if the recipient of the merchandise is not its final user, as is the case, for example, with a distributor selling to a store, tracking and automation mechanisms must be put in place so that large shipments can be handled without human intervention and, most importantly, avoiding any losses. As we'll see in this chapter, Commerce Server doesn't provide an out-of-the-box solution to these problems, but it sure offers a good foundation on which complex systems can be built.

What Does This Chapter Talk About?

Both these scenarios fall under what is called **business-to-business electronic commerce** (often condensed to *b2b e-commerce*), that is one or more set of transactions in which businesses, rather than a business and an individual, are at both ends of the line. The same category also includes those cases in which purchases for a company are made by the individuals who are part of it; this, for example, is what usually happens with stationery, which is requested by single employees but paid for and ordered on behalf of them by the company, and is generally referred to as *corporate procurement*.

During this chapter, we will analyze what business-to-business electronic commerce is, how it works, and what Commerce Server has to offer to deal with it:

❑ **A brief introduction to b2b electronic commerce**
In this section, we will introduce business-to-business commerce, trying to understand its most basic concepts and its two main implementations.

❑ **The Microsoft Market sample**
Support for b2b e-commerce in Commerce Server is strong on the technology side, while it somewhat lacks a bit on the application/demonstration aspect. In this section, we will examine *Microsoft Market*, which is the only sample store in the software package that contains b2b functionality.

❑ **The Commerce Interchange Pipeline**
Finally, we will take a good look at the CIP, which, as we mentioned before, is used to handle all b2b operations inside a Commerce Server store.

A Brief Introduction to B2B E-Commerce

We have already mentioned how there are fundamentally two kinds of b2b applications. It's important to understand, however, that the use of b2b-oriented functionality does not exclude the possibility of interaction with a normal retail environment.

As a matter of fact, corporate procurement is essentially a particular form of retailing and, although payment and pricing rules do change, most of the concepts still apply. On the other hand, when a retailer needs to interface to its suppliers, both b2b and traditional retail applications will cohabit the store.

Business-to-business commerce is becoming more and more important, because the Internet provides an easy and inexpensive way to connect different business in an efficient manner. Many financial analysts, in fact, expect b2b to become the largest sector of the overall electronic commerce market, with some experts placing it to as much as 90% of all transactions in the near future.

Corporate Procurement

It would be rather untrue to say that corporate procurement is a concept unique to electronic commerce, or even a new idea for all that matters. If you've ever had the chance of working in a mid-sized organization, you will have probably at some point made use of it, for example when ordering a phone line or stationery.

There are a number of problems connected with letting an employee spend the company's money. On one hand, the company can't obviously let just about anybody purchase anything. On the other, its management will most likely want to try and reduce the costs associated with procurement, which usually is not a revenue-generating activity. Even more important, the company must be able to track the purchases and assign them to the appropriate budget so that they are accurately accounted for.

In a traditional setting – one in which no e-commerce functionality has been introduced – procurement is often a painstaking process of approvals, counter-approvals, and an almost infinite amount of paperwork that has to be continuously filled out, that easily tends to be lost and that generates a number of human errors. When you work for a really big firm, in which a purchase request must go through several hands before it reaches the supplier, you rarely get what you asked for (assuming you get it in the first place).

Internet-based applications can help here in a variety of ways. First of all, they can help make the procurement process as automatic as possible, so that no paperwork has to be filled out and the system itself takes care of routing the data through the appropriate approval channels and assigning the expenses to the correct budget. At the same time, they can provide a direct connection to the supplier, who receives approved requests immediately and fulfills them according to its agreement with the company. As a result, the amount of manpower that is usually required to handle procurements can be redirected towards more productive work, or eliminated altogether.

The Procurement Process

The exact procedure that procurement follows is unique to each company, but in general there are three steps to it.

Request

At first, an employee makes a request for some merchandise to be delivered and charged to his or her department's cost center. In a traditional scenario, this is done by filling out one or more paper forms of some kind. Online, this task can be accomplished by filling out an HTML form or through a dedicated application that connects to the central database and asks the appropriate questions.

Approval

Some companies allow their employees to make purchase within a certain limit without asking for permission of any kind. Often, the "purchase limit" varies depending on seniority and rank and, when it is surpassed, the authorization of the immediate supervisor is required as well. It is quite possible that the purchase goes beyond the supervisor's own limit, and therefore requires approval from two levels of management higher than the employee who originally made the request. In a paper-based world each of these steps means signatures and lost time (not to mention the fact that, if you or the procurement department lose your piece of paper, you're in serious trouble). In addition, this arrangement ends up producing undesirable – or even straight out ridiculous situations: in his latest book, *Business @ The Speed of Thought*, Bill Gates (himself) mentions how he is the only person inside Microsoft who can approve the expenses made by its president, Steve Ballmer. Considering the cost of Gates' own time, you can imagine how expensive that particular approval process can be.

In an online system, the approval process can be taken care of by the system automatically; purchases that do not go beyond the employee's own spending limit are automatically fulfilled, while managerial approval at all levels can be taken care of by means of something as simple as e-mail – which, by the way, beats paperwork when your boss is away from the office.

Transmission

The final act – at least as far as the procurement system is concerned – consists of actually extending the requisition directly to the individual supplier or suppliers. This is usually done through an exchange of several documents, which we will discuss about in the next paragraph. Clearly, an online system can take care of all this automatically, essentially eliminating the possibility of human errors that so much abound when part numbers and SKUs are copied from a piece of paper into a fax, and then from the fax into the supplier's own line-of-business system.

Document Interchanges

The second type of b2b application is designed to handle the way two businesses talk to each other. It's interesting to notice that I do mean *two* businesses in the strictest sense; in fact, even though a particular company might be dealing with one or more other counterparts, b2b transactions always take place between two individual partners, even though they might be part of larger transactions that involve a larger number of entities.

For example, you might want to consider the possibility of a store that sells a product originating from more than one supplier. If a customer makes an order that contains items from Supplier A and Supplier B, the overall transaction obviously includes three partners (the store and the two suppliers). However, the actual communications will only take place between two parties at a time: the store will first call, say, Supplier A and request that its own items be sent over to the customer, and then repeat the same operation with Supplier B. The two suppliers need not – and most often *will* not – know about each other in any way.

It's All About Documents

All businesses communicate by exchanging *documents*, and these are all there really is to a business-to-business system. In fact, **document interchange** is a common practice even in a non-computerized world: a purchase order is sent, the merchandise is shipped (and a shipment manifest is generated), an invoice is issued, and a payment is made. These are all documents that businesses around the world exchange every day. Although they are mostly the same in many aspects, each company has its own way to do business, and therefore requires its documents to be issued, and received, in a particular format.

The EDI Standard

Even before the Internet became a reliable worldwide network, companies around the world had long realized that it was necessary to exchange as many documents as possible by means of electronic transmission. Contrary to what might seem obvious, the ultimate reason for this was not in the cost savings that not using paper would bring, but in the fact that electronic transmission was more accurate, faster and somewhat easier to feed into the individual automation systems that most large companies could already dispose of.

With the goal of making the communication between companies easier to handle, the **Electronic Data Interchange**, or EDI, standard was created. EDI is a rather unusual standard; because it has to deal with many different possible requirements (the automobile industry, for example, needs to exchange different information than, say, dairy product companies), it ends up as a very open-ended and complex set of rules. Furthermore, EDI communications can only take place through dedicated networks that – needless to say – *are* quite expensive to maintain and rent from phone companies.

Nonetheless, EDI has been accepted as a standard by many large companies around the world, which have spent millions of dollars in implementing and maintaining their interchange structure. Smaller companies, for the most part, have been excluded from this possibility by the high costs associated with the EDI business.

As a result, the situation today is that large companies cannot turn to the Internet as an alternative to EDI because they still must justify and recuperate their investment in the older technology. At the same time, smaller companies have a reduced interest in using the Internet because their largest suppliers still rely on EDI.

Receipts

An important advantage of electronic-based interchange systems is the fact that they have the capability of guaranteeing the delivery of the information that is sent through them.

The importance of being able to tell whether important data has been delivered to its intended recipient is paramount to the well being of a business. Registered mail and couriers are often used not only because of their speed, but because it's possible to determine that a package has reached its destination. Conversely, e-mail and fax do not offer the same capability and lead easily to paranoia. After all, an invoice that has not reached its destination can mean a missed payment – with all its hassles on top of a loss of income.

When you are using an electronic system, however, it should be able to generate a receipt for each document that is exchanged, thus advising the sender that its "package" has arrived. At the same rate, a truly functional system should automatically monitor receipts and be prepared to resend a document when it's reasonable to think that it never reached its intended recipient (that is, when a receipt has not arrived after a certain amount of time). This, naturally, also means that the system must be able to tell whether duplicate messages are being sent, because receipts can get lost in the communication line as well.

The Microsoft Market Sample Store

It's now time to take a look at the only b2b sample store supplied with Commerce Server. Its name is *Microsoft Market*, and it is essentially a fictitious representation of a more complex application that Microsoft employees worldwide use to make their own internal requisitions.

Microsoft Market (MSMarket) incorporates both the flavors of b2b e-commerce that we have just described, in that it is an online store that can only be accessed by authorized users who do not directly pay for their purchases and provides a set of document exchange rules for accomplishing various tasks, such as authorizing orders that go beyond the individual's purchase limit or delivering a purchase order directly to a supplier.

Site Structure

Let's start by looking at how the corporate requisition process works. First of all, you should keep in mind that, in the typical scenario, the store is not selling anything directly to its customers, but it's rather acting as a middle tier between the company's employees and its suppliers. This means that, generally speaking, the store must be well aware of the requisition procedure that must be followed for each supplier, as well as what the buying power of each employee is – that is, how much money he or she can spend before authorization from his or her supervisor becomes necessary in order to complete the purchase.

As you can see from the screenshot below, the purchase process for a business-to-business online store is remarkably similar to its retail counterpart, with the exception that, under normal circumstances, users are not allowed to register themselves with the site but must be inserted in the customer database through some alternative method. This happens because the customers will be buying on behalf of the company, and so they should be added to the list of authorized users from the company's own internal employee database. This will also allow whoever is in charge of doing so to set purchase limits for each individual. MSMarket *does* allow users to register, but only because that is a more practical approach for demonstrating how the store works.

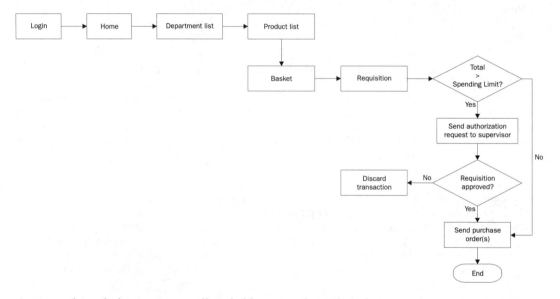

As we go through the store, you will probably notice that MSMarket is much more functionality-oriented than any other store seen before. In particular, no cross-selling or up-selling functionality is being used – the reason being that the customers who visit this store already know what they are going to buy (and certainly, the company doesn't want to promote more purchases than are strictly necessary!).

The result is a slimmer site, in terms of convenience and speed, that works very well in an Intranet scenario. However, there is also the possibility that a business-to-business store might be configured as an *Extranet* application; this would be the case, for example, if each supplier were to provide its own dedicated store for the company's employees. Most considerations, such as the procurement paradigm and purchase limits, would still apply, but this time the store would be run by somebody who actually has an interest in enticing customers to buy more – the supplier. In this scenario, you would probably want to take advantage of cross-selling and up-selling functionality even though you're not selling your products to the whole world.

The real differences between business-to-business and business-to-consumer come into play once the customer clicks on the Purchase button: the order request goes through the process that we have briefly described above. Here's how MSMarket handles it:

❑ **Purchase authorization**
As soon as a purchase is submitted by a customer, its total is calculated and verified against the user's purchase limit. If the total is below the latter, the purchase is automatically sent to the last stage, otherwise an authorization request is sent to the user's supervisor.

❑ **Authorization request**

Whenever an order's total goes beyond the customer's spending limit, the store sends an authorization request to his or her immediate supervisor. This can happen in one of several ways, and can, for example, be initiated with an e-mail that contains, together with the customer's name and the order's detail, a link to a URL where the supervisor can either authorize or reject the order.

❑ **Authorization approval**

At this stage, the supervisor somehow sends a response back to the store either authorizing or rejecting the purchase. Once again, there are several possibilities as to how this can be done; for example, an e-mail can be sent back to the store with the words "accept" or "reject" in a specific spot, or the approval can be submitted through an HTTP post to the store with the appropriate parameters.

❑ **Purchase request submission**

If an order is rejected by a supervisor, the customer is notified (for example, by e-mail) and the order is generally discarded without further possibility of intervention. If the supervisor authorizes it instead, the store proceeds with sending a purchase request out to the appropriate supplier. As we'll see later on in the chapter, this process is technically similar to the one that we just described for authorizing a purchase, and varies from distributor to distributor.

Setting Up The Site

Before being able to use the MSMarket sample properly, we will have to make some adjustments to its setup. In particular, because the site is largely based on e-mail exchanges, we should make sure that the store knows what SMTP server to use when sending messages out to its users.

To do so, we'll have to enter the store's management site at the following URL:

```
http://your_host/market/manager
```

This will take us to the Manager's home page, from which we can click on Configure Email Processes to access the configuration menu. Once here, clicking on Configuration (maildomain) will let us specify the default domain for all the e-mail messages that our site sends to its users, while selecting Configuration (smtphost) will let us type in the hostname of our SMTP mail server. Finally, you will also have to enter a return e-mail account to be used by the store when sending e-mail; you can do so by clicking on Configuration (siteaccount). To make sure that these changes come into effect, you will need to reload the store.

> Once you type in a valid mail domain and SMTP server hostname, be very careful when you create new users for testing purposes within the site. In fact, the store *will* send out e-mail messages to these accounts and, if they correspond to real people, you run the risk of flooding their mailboxes! As a general rule, you should use your own e-mail account for all the aliases that are requested by the store; this will also let you monitor how the site works better.

Navigating the Store

Now that our settings are made, we can proceed with exploring MSMarket and the way it works. The first step in entering the store is either logging in or registering as a new user. Once again, keep in mind that this happens only because this is a sample store – in real-life there normally wouldn't be a way to register with the site from the front-end. This time, the registration process asks questions that better fit the business model that is currently being used: not a ship-to address anymore, but rather a room and building number or name. To access the MSMarket sample store, type in the following URL:

```
http://your_host/market
```

where *your_host* is, as always, the hostname or IP of your server.

It's interesting to notice that the store is not asking us what department we work for – in many large companies each department has its own budget and keeps track of its expenses separately. As we'll see in a moment, this is done later in the purchase process, when we are asked for a cost center code and an account number.

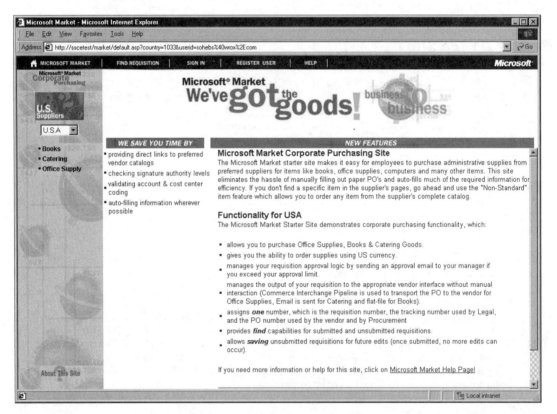

Once we have registered or logged in, we can access the *real* home page, shown above. As you can see, the page's body only contains generic information about the site and the features it provides. What really interests us, though, is the left-side bar, which contains links to the three main areas of the site (international areas are also available, and are treated as different stores altogether). Each of these areas represents a basic category of items, whose products can belong to one or more suppliers.

Finding products is a straightforward process, very similar to the one that we have seen so far for the other stores. As soon as we want to add something to the basket, however, some new information appears to be in the product page. As you can see from the figure below, the store is asking us to choose an account to which the purchase will be charged, and a cost center, which will be responsible for accounting the order. For frequently purchased items, there is also the possibility of specifying an *Internal Order* code.

Once all the items that we want to purchase are added to our basket, we can proceed with the order fulfillment process. The store asks us for some information regarding the purchase that we are about to make, such as when the merchandise is needed by, or (in the case of catering, for example) when our business or lunch will take place and how many people will be participating.

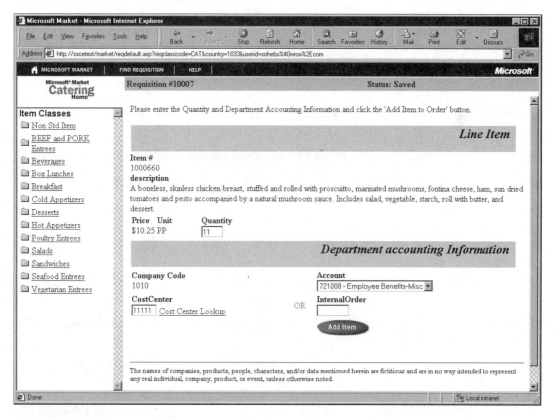

Continuing with the purchase process causes the store to save our purchase request and, if the order's total exceeds our limit, sends an e-mail to our supervisor for approval.

The Approval Process

In our example, it looks like I ordered more food for my event than I can account for. Therefore, my supervisor will receive an e-mail inviting him to review my requisition and either authorize or reject it. In this case, I set myself up as my own supervisor – so that I could better understand what was going on – and I did indeed receive an e-mail from the store, similar to this one:

From: Microsoft Store
To: Marco Tabini
Subject: Requisition # 10005

A requisition is awaiting your approval. To view the details of the requisition click on the link.
http://point:80/market/approveorder.asp?requisitionid=10005&reqclasscode=CAT

Clicking on the link provided by the e-mail brings up the page shown in the figure below, which asks me to verify the contents of the order and either approve or reject it. Clicking on Reject Order causes the requisition to be discarded and the following e-mail message sent back to the requisitioner (myself again):

From: Microsoft Store
To: Marco Tabini
Subject: Requisition # 10005

The requisition has been rejected

If I, on the other hand, decide that my own purchase is worth its money, clicking on Accept Order will initiate the transmission of the necessary purchase orders to the various suppliers (there is only one in this case). In this case, no message will be sent out to the requisitioner.

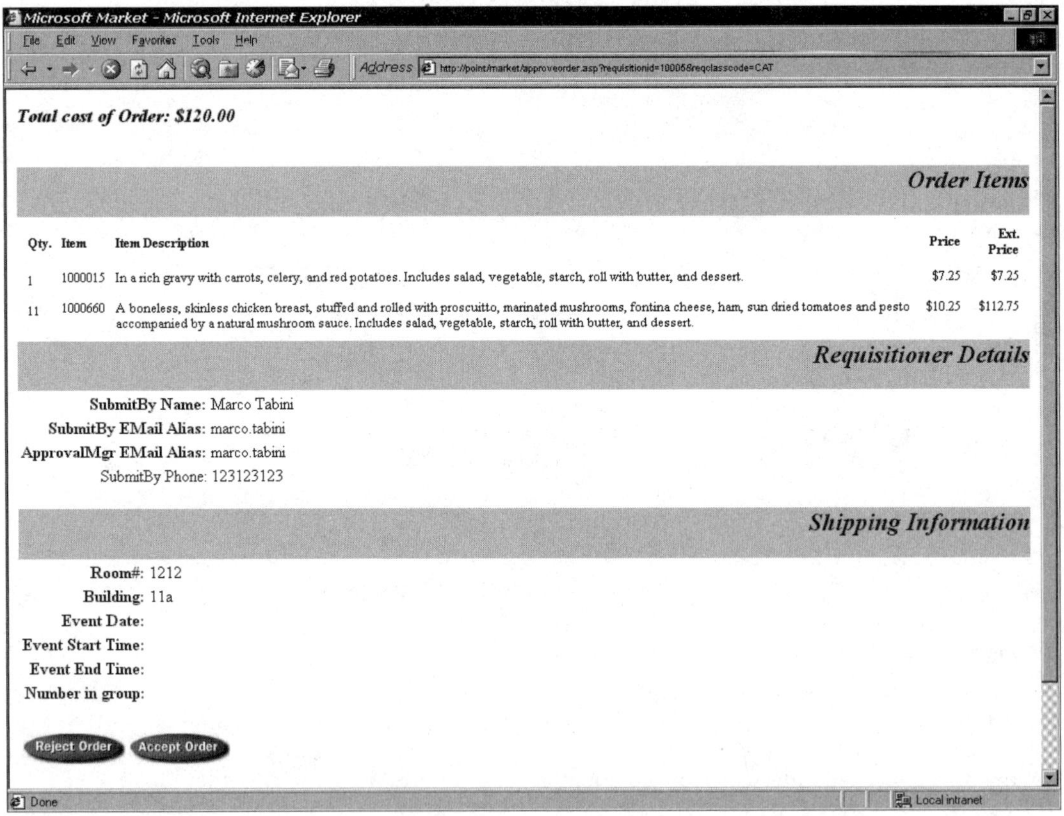

Could it have been Better?

It's a good idea to stop for a moment and reflect on what we have seen so far. The MSMarket sample certainly succeeds at streamlining the requisition and approval process, however there is still room for some improvement. First of all, since the supervisor is going to receive an e-mail message anyway, why not make the most out of it?

For starters, it would have been a good idea if a complete detail of the requisition were included in the message; this would have allowed the supervisor to understand what the requisition was about and how urgent it was without having to start his or her browser and go to the store pages. In addition, the process of authorizing the requisition could have been further improved by providing two different links, one to be used by the supervisor when accepting a requisition and another for rejecting it.

How Does Data Submission Work?

We have seen an example of document exchange in the approval process, in which there was the need to generate and transfer document between the store and the supervisor. A more typical example can be found to pick up right where the process shown in the first figure left off.

In fact, once a purchase has been definitively approved, the store must proceed to somehow open a communication channel with each supplier's line-of-business system and send purchase orders over to them. Ideally, the system should also be able to receive information back from the suppliers – so that it would be able, for example, to track the status of an order or to receive shipment confirmations.

The are three fundamental stages in the submission process; although their exact nature depends on the medium that is being chosen for the transmission of data, they always perform these three tasks:

❑ **Data preparation**
As part of the first step, the data must be prepared for being sent out. This includes calculating and generating all the appropriate fields, and making sure that all the necessary information is available.

❑ **Data mapping**
Data will then have to be formatted in a way that it can be understood by the recipient. This step varies widely depending on the submission medium that is being used, and can consist of generating a flat text file, or creating an e-mail message, and so on.

❑ **Data submission**
Finally, data is sent over to the recipient using the appropriate method. This can include just about anything, from a printout of a purchase order to more advanced methods, such as EDI (which we'll discuss below), e-mail or other Internet protocols.

At the other end of the submission, a line-of-business system must receive the data and perform the same steps in reverse order. This will allow it to "take apart" the document, map the data it contains to the system's internal storage banks and check its validity.

As you have probably noticed, much of the success of this operation depends on the ability of sender and recipient to agree on a common format for the document and on a medium that is available to both systems. This is what EDI is for, although you may decide to create your own document format specifications.

How does Site Server support EDI? Well, it doesn't – not directly, at least. Commerce Server includes a complete interchange system that focuses on the Commerce Interchange Pipeline (CIP), which, similar to the Order Processing Pipeline, offers an ordered approach at exchanging documents between two partners. The CIP doesn't favor any exchange protocol in particular, but rather provides a common framework for any format, *including* EDI.

The good news, therefore, is that if you want to develop a store able to communicate with an EDI-compliant system, you'll be able to do so by adding your own functionality. The bad news is that EDI remains a mostly obscure topic for the uninitiated, and you will have most likely to take advantage of the services offered by a third-party consultant that specializes in traditional interchanges.

If, on the other hand, you are looking at *creating* a new interchange system, you'll be happy to know that the CIP is not only fully self-contained, but also designed to work across the Internet – representing a powerful, and yet significantly less expensive, alternative to EDI. As a matter of fact, once you have established your own document guidelines (that is, what is the format a purchase order, a response, and so on) you will be able to exchange information via e-mail or even HTTP posts.

Remember to Close the Loops

The important thing to remember when designing a business-to-business system is remembering that you should provide a notification system through which the recipient of a message can acknowledge its arrival to the sender. This is particularly important if the correct delivery of the message is vital to the successful completion of a transaction (that is, if your store sends a purchase order that never arrives, then the order will never be completed!)

It's also a good idea to take full advantage of the concept of interchange and implement a two-way communication system. EDI, for example, provides support not only for messages that go from the store to the line-of-business system (therefore from the requisitioner to the supplier), but that also travel in the opposite direction. This become useful, for example, when you want to inform your customers that the merchandise they have ordered has been shipped; in this case, your supplier will send you some form of notification message, which you can use to set the appropriate fields in your order database.

MSMarket's Store Manager Interface

What does the management interface of a business-to-business store look like? As you can see below, it's a little different from that of a normal retail store. In particular, you will notice that, although many concepts are the same, the terms used are unlike anything we have seen so far.

The set of functions on the left side are designed to provide a means to configure several aspects of the store, such as all the e-mail settings, the various locations where employees can be found (including conversion rates for charging customers from foreign countries in their own currency) and the details of the accounts and cost centers that can be used by the users. Each cost center can be assigned to one or more accounts, indicating who can be held accountable for each transaction.

On the right side of the screen, on the other hand, we have access to information about the products that are sold by the store, its customers and a list of requisitions that have been made so far. Products – or **parts** – are organized in **Part Classes**, which in turn are grouped in **Requisition Classes**, which represent the highest-level departments. Requisition classes are linked to account numbers, so that the right account is used to pay for specific products (for example, the Office Stationery account is used to buy office supplies, but not catering).

It's important to understand that, unlike any other store that we have seen so far, MSMarket is designed to work without any human interaction. Users could be entered automatically from the company's employee database, while the store could be retrofitted to interface (through an interchange) with the company's own accounting system in order to provide complete feedback on the requisitions that are made. Finally, even the product database can be automatically updated from each supplier's line-of-business system – using another Interchange, of course!

The Commerce Interchange Pipeline

After so much talking about it, we have finally come to the point where we can talk about the CIP in detail! As mentioned more than once above, its goal is to provide an ordered approach to the exchange of documents between two parties. It's important to understand that, even though the CIP provides the necessary support for both sending and receiving documents, you do not need to have a Site Server site on both ends of an interchange in order to use it, as long as your interchange partner has the ability of understanding the messages you send, and sending you messages you can understand.

As a matter of fact, in most cases you will not be dealing with Site Server sites, as most of your suppliers and partners will probably still use legacy systems, such as IBM AS/400 minicomputers. Naturally, not all your interchange partners will be able to support all the advanced features offered by the CIP, so you will have to be careful about how the documents are exchanged.

Since the CIP is all about sending and receiving documents, there are only two types of pipeline to deal with here:

❑ **Transmit**
The Transmit pipeline is used to – you guessed it – process a set of data into a form that is suitable for transmission to a partner, and then perform all the necessary steps for sending it.

❑ **Receive**
When you're on the other end of the partnership, you can use the Receive pipeline to accept an interchange, verify its integrity, process any requests for receipts, and map it back into a form that can be used by your Site Server application.

In a CIP, the pipeline's dictionary is represented by a `Dictionary` object – not an `OrderForm` as is the case with the OPP.

The Transmit Pipeline

As you can see in the following figure, the transmit pipeline has a very simple structure – six stages in total – but it's very different from the OPP:

Stage	Description
Map	The first stage in the pipeline takes care of converting the data in the Dictionary into a format that is suitable for transmission.
Add Header	This stage's task is to wrap a header around the dictionary data so that the receiving end would know what kind of information it is.
Digitally Sign	One of the advanced features of the CIP is the ability to digitally sign, using a digital certificate, an outgoing exchange. A digital signature (which does *not* encrypt the data) can be used to verify that the data has not been changed along path that takes it from the sender to the receiver.
Encrypt	The Encrypt stage can be used to encrypt the interchange so that, even if it is intercepted before it reaches its intended recipient, unauthorized parties cannot have access to it.
Audit	Components in this stage are used to write data to a database every time that the pipeline runs. This audit information can be used to verify whether a certain transaction took place, when, and so on.
Transport	The final stage of the Transmit pipeline is used to effectively send the interchange to its intended recipient. This can be done in any number of ways, although Commerce Server only offers support for the most commonly used Internet protocols.

As you can see, the procedure here is really to turn the contents of a `Dictionary` object (or some other object that exposes the same functionality, such as an `OrderForm`) into some form that is suitable for the transmission system used in the Transport stage. By default, all the stages work by progressively building the interchange in a Name/Value pair of the pipeline's main dictionary called `working_data`, but you can choose to use some other pair if you need to.

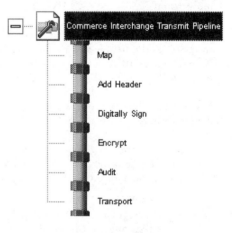

The Receive Pipeline

The Receive pipeline pretty much follows the reverse process of the Transmit pipeline that we just saw, with a couple of exceptions. It's goal, as a matter of fact, is to "deconstruct" an interchange received by the system and turn it into a form that can be used by your application, which – as we shall see in a moment – *doesn't* necessarily need to be an ASP site.

A Receive pipeline is made of the following stages:

Stage	Description
Decrypt	The first step in the pipeline makes it possible to decrypt an interchange (assuming that it has been encrypted in the first place). Keep in mind that you *must* know *a priori* whether the interchange is encrypted, and you cannot rely on a flag in the header, because the header itself will have been encrypted with the rest of the data!
Verify Digital Signature	Next, the interchange's digital signature (again, if present) is verified.
Open Header	In this stage, the interchange's header is open, examined and removed from the interchange. This makes it possible to recognize several parameters that might have been transmitted by the sender.
Generate Receipt	If a receipt has been requested by the sender, the components in this stage can be used to generate and send it, generally using yet another pipeline.
Map	This stage is used to map the data in the interchange to a Commerce Server object (such as a `Dictionary` or an `Orderform`).
Audit	Audit information is once again handled by this stage, which can be used to store a log of all the pipeline's activity into a database (or a log file, if you prefer).
Application Integration	The final stage in the Receive pipeline can be used to transform the data received as part of the interchange into a form that is suitable for the uses of the application that executed the pipeline. In many cases, you will not use this stage unless you want, for example, to store the interchange data in a database, or if you indeed need to transform the data for the use of another application.

It's interesting to note the presence of the last stage, in which the data in the interchange can be transformed for use by another application. Although we will not explore this possibility in detail, it indicates that the pipeline technology can be used by many different programs, and is not limited to electronic commerce and ASP sites.

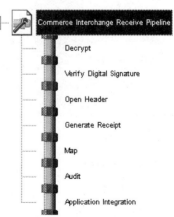

Built-in CIP components

Let's now take a look at the built-in components that Commerce Server provides for use in the CIP. As we'll see, these are far fewer than those offered for the OPP, but several OPP components can be recycled for use in the CIP – we'll mention them as we go through the various stages.

Map Stage (Transmit Pipeline)

As mentioned above, the Map stage is used in the Transmit pipeline to render the data that has to be sent in a format that is suitable for the transmission medium that is going to be used. In many cases, the best format is some sort of organized text, for example a comma-delimited string, or even XML.

Commerce Server provides two built-in components for this stage. One is **MakePO**, which we have already seen in the Accept stage of the OPP. Since it can fundamentally be used to render the OrderForm data in text format, you can also use it to create the body of the interchange, if you need to.

> **Keep in mind that, when dealing with a CIP, the OrderForm is normally placed as a child object inside the pipeline's main dictionary, and not in the main dictionary itself!**

The other component that we are going to examine for this stage is called MapToXML, and can be used to map an entire dictionary into XML format. The main difference between MapToXML and MakePO is that the former automatically maps an entire object, whereas the latter relies on your scripts to do so. In addition, MapToXML is able to persist entire COM objects that are stored inside the dictionary, as long as they support the appropriate COM persistence functionality.

Name	MapToXML	
Properties	Object source key	Specifies the name of the Name/Value pair where the source dictionary is located. The component determines the object type of the dictionary automatically.
	Results XML key	The name of the Name/Value pair that will contain the component's XML output
	Preferred data format	The format that should be used to render the dictionary in XML. If **XML Tags** is selected, then the object is rendered using a series of text-only XML tags, whereas selecting **Encoded Binary** will cause the component to simply encapsulate the object's binary representation within simple XML tags.
Values Read	*ObjectSourceKey*	
Value Written	*ResultsXMLKey*	
Context Values Read	None	

In most cases, you will want to make sure of using the XML Tags format, which renders the entire object using exclusively text – this will be your only solution if you're planning to send data through e-mail or HTTP posts. In addition, you should keep in mind that only persistent COM objects – those that support either the standard `IPersistStreamInit` COM interface, or the Site Server-defined `IPersistXML` interface – will be rendered by the component. Non-persistent objects will simply be ignored.

Finally, it's important to understand that, if you render an object in XML expecting to be able to rebuild the object entirely at the other end of the interchange, you should make sure that all the components you are persisting are installed on the recipient's computer, too.

Add Header Stage

The Add Header stage is used to encapsulate the data that has to be sent over so that the recipient will be able to identify what kind of data it's receiving, where it's coming from, and so on. Commerce Server offers two components for this stage: AddHeader and EncodeMIME.

AddHeader can be used to add a custom header that encapsulates the following information:

- ❑ Unique transaction ID (generated by the component)
- ❑ Receipt request
- ❑ Date and time the request was sent
- ❑ Type of the document
- ❑ Source of the document
- ❑ Destination of the document

The header generated is appended to the data as a series of XML tags, and can be decoded if at the other end of the interchange there is a Receive pipeline properly set up.

Name	AddHeader	
Properties	Input field	Specifies the location of the interchange data within the pipeline's main dictionary. This will usually be the output of `MapToXML`.
	Output field	The name of the Name/Value pair that will contain the component's output. Will normally be the same as *Input field*, but it can be different if you need so.
Values Read	*InputField*	
	`Receipt_requested`	
	`Document_type`	
	`Document_source`	
	`Document_destination`	
	`Txid`	
Value Written	`Txid`	
	OutputField	
Context Values Read	None	

If you are planning to send your data via e-mail or HTTP, you might want to encode it using the `EncodeMIME` component, which turns your interchange data into the Internet-standard MIME format.

Name	EncodeMIME	
Properties	Content Type	Specifies the content type of the MIME-encoded data. The three values allowed by the component (**UN/EDIFACT, ANSI X12 and EDI-Consent**) correspond to three well-known EDI systems in use throughout the world.
	Content Encoding	Specifies the method through which the data itself should be encoded. Can be **Quoted Printable**, which allows only for the use of the standard ASCI character set in the data, or **Base64**, which encodes extended characters and binary values as well.
	Read from field	Specifies the location of the interchange data within the pipeline's main dictionary.
	Write to field	The name of the Name/Value pair that will contain the component's output. Will normally be the same as *Input field*, but it can be different if you need so.
Values Read	*ReadFromField*	
Value Written	*WriteToField*	
Context Values Read	None	

The MIME encoding system is normally used by many Internet applications, such as web browsers and e-mail clients, to exchange data over the network. MIME makes it possible to easily recognize the type of data being transmitted – and therefore invoke the appropriate handler – and properly encodes the information so that it can be sent safely through common Internet systems.

Digitally Sign Stage

Digital signatures are an interesting method of calculating a checksum of a set of data and expressing it in such a way that it cannot be tampered with. Therefore, it can be used to ensure that the data has never been modified since when it was initially signed. This is an important step, especially if you decide to transmit your interchanges over a public network such as the Internet – just think of the damage that a hacker could do!

Two pipeline components have affinity to this stage: `DigitalSig` and `EncodeSMIME`. `DigitalSig` can be used to calculate the digital signature of an interchange and then store it as part of the data that has to be sent over. The digital signature can be calculated using any of the algorithms available on your computer, and either appended to the data as an XML tag or encoded together with the rest of the interchange using the Public Key Cryptography Standard (PKCS).

Name	DigitalSig	
Properties	Signature [and message] in *xxx* format	Specifies how the interchange and the signature should be formatted. It's possible to store both of them in XML format (Signature and Message in XML format) or in the PKCS format (Signature and Message in PKCS7 format). Optionally, it is also possible decide to leave the interchange as-is and simply store the signature in the PKCS format (Signature only in PKCS7 format).
	Input field	Specifies the location of the interchange data within the pipeline's main dictionary.
	Signed output field	The name of the Name/Value pair that will contain the component's output. Will normally be the same as *Input field*, but it can be different if you need so..
	Hash algorithm	Specifies the algorithm used to calculate the digital signature. The actual list of algorithms available changes, depending on the algorithms that are installed on your computer and their strength.
	Hash Algorithm ID Field	The field where the component will store the ID of the algorithm used to calculate the digital signature.
	Signer Certificate(s)	The digital certificate that should be used to sign the data. Using a digital certificate will enable the recipient not only to verify that the data's integrity has not been corrupted, but also who the sender really is.
Values Read	InputField	
Value Written	SignedOutputField	
	HashAlgorithmIDField	
Context Values Read	None	

This component takes advantage of the Microsoft Crypto-API to perform all the signature and formatting functions. The Crypto-API is a standard component of many newer Microsoft applications, such as IIS4, IE4 and higher, and so on. Its most interesting feature is the fact that it only provides a generic encryption, decryption and digital signature interface layer, while the actual functionality is provided by an arbitrary number of plug-ins. Depending on what plug-ins you have installed on your server, you will be able to use different algorithms to encrypt and sign your data.

> In order to use an encryption or signing algorithm, it must be installed *both* on the originating and destination server. If the algorithm is only installed on the originating server, the destination server will not be able to verify the interchange's digital signature or, even worse, to decrypt the interchange in the first place!

The EncodeSMIME component can be used to encrypt and digitally sign the interchange using the Internet-standard SMIME format:

Name	EncodeSMIME	
Properties	Operation	Specifies what kind of action should be carried out by the component:
		❑ Plain Text: forces the component to leave the interchange as it is (no operation)
		❑ Sign: instructs the component to digitally sign the interchange
		❑ Encrypt: causes the interchange to be encrypted.
		❑ Sign and Encrypt: causes the interchange to be both signed and encrypted
	Character set	Specifies the character set to be used in the output. The character set chosen *must* be installed in the system in order for the component to work properly.
	Signature Certificate	The digital certificate that will be used to digitally sign the interchange.
	Encryption Certificate	The digital certificate used to encrypt the interchange.
	Signature Algorithm	Specifies what algorithm to use to digitally sign the interchange. The actual list changes, depending on the algorithms that you have installed on your server.
	Encryption Algorithm	Specifies the algorithm used to encrypt the exchange. As for the *Signature Algorithm* property, the list will only display those algorithms that you have installed on your server.
	Read from field	Specifies the location of the interchange data within the pipeline's main dictionary.
	Write to field	The name of the Name/Value pair that will contain the component's output. Will normally be the same as `ReadFromField`, but it can be different if you need so.
Values Read	`ReadFromField`	
Value Written	`WriteToField`	
Context Values Read	None	

As you can see, the functionality of this component does not *strictly* apply to the Digitally Sign stage, but also to the Encrypt stage, with which, in fact, it shares affinity. Keep in mind that, while you will use your own digital certificate to sign the interchange – thus signaling that you are its originator – you will need to use the recipient's certificate to encrypt it. If you don't, the recipient will not be able to decrypt the message!

As before, if you decide to use this component, you should make sure that the algorithms you choose are installed and properly selected on both ends of the interchange.

Encrypt stage

Two components share affinity with the encrypt stage. One is `EncodeSMIME`, which we just saw. The other is `EncryptPKCS`, and can be used to encrypt the interchange using one of the algorithms supported by the Microsoft Crypto-API.

Name	`EncryptPKCS`	
Properties	Plain text field	Specifies the location of the interchange data within the pipeline's main dictionary.
	Encrypted text field	The name of the Name/Value pair that will contain the component's output. Will normally be the same as *ReadFromField*, but it can be different if you need so.
	Encryption Algorithm	Specifies the algorithm to be used when encrypting the exchange.
	Receiver certificate(s)	Specifies the digital certificate that should be used to encrypt the exchange.
Values Read	*ReadFromField*	
Value Written	*WriteToField*	
Context Values Read	None	

If you are thinking that there is a little redundancy in the functionality provided by the encryption and signing components that we have seen so far, you're right – and you're not. As a matter of fact, `EncodeSMIME` alone performs almost the same tasks as `DigitalSig` and `EncryptPKCS` together, with one important exception: it also formats the data according to the SMIME specifications. Now, this is fine if you are going to send the data through the Internet and your interchange partner is able to handle SMIME. Many legacy systems, however, might be able to handle public-key encryption, but not SMIME, which is a relatively new standard. As such, you will want to use `EncodeSMIME` when sending data through the Internet to another CIP, while `DigitalSig` and `EncryptPKCS` should be used in all the other cases.

Audit Stage (Transmit Pipeline)

As mentioned before, this stage takes care of saving certain information from the dictionary into a database, so that a permanent trace of the pipeline's execution is left behind for future uses. The audit data can become useful, for example, to keep track of what transmissions have been received by your partners. All you have to do is audit the transmission, request a receipt, audit the receipt and cross-relate the database information to verify that an interchange has been received correctly.

The only component provided by Commerce Server for this stage is called – as the most imaginative among you might have already guessed – Audit, and writes an arbitrary number of Name/Value pairs to a user-specified database.

Name	Audit	
Properties	Connection String	Specifies the connection string to be used when connecting to the database. If no string is specified, the default connection string is taken from the pipeline's context.
	Table	The name of the table that will receive audit information.
	Add a field/Fields to record	Specifies a list of Name/Value pairs that will be saved in the database table.
Values Read	(Optional) *	
	Txid	
Value Written	None	
Context Values Read	(Optional) `DefaultConnectionString`	
	(Optional) `ConnectionStringMap`	

In order for Audit to work properly, you will need to make sure that the table contains the appropriate number of fields, and that those fields are named exactly as the Name/Value pairs they will be mapped to. Keep in mind that the component will automatically map the two Name/Value pairs `txid` and `utc_datetime`, which indicate the transaction ID created by the AddHeader component and the Universal Coordinated Time at which Audit was run.

Transport Stage

The last stage of the Transmit pipeline takes care of sending an interchange through the appropriate medium. As mentioned above, Commerce Server only provides built-in components for the most used Internet protocols, such as SMTP, HTTP and DCOM transmissions. If you are going to be dealing with more "traditional" partners, however, you will most likely need to write your own components for communicating with them, because they won't be accessible through the Internet but through some other network, such as DataPAC or EDI.

The `SendSMTP` component can be used to send your interchange using the Simple Mail Transport Protocol, which is used to transmit Internet e-mail:

Name	SendSMTP	
Properties	From	Specifies the identity of the message's sender.
	SMTP Host	Specifies the IP of the SMTP server that will be used to send the message.

Properties	To	The Name/Value pair in the dictionary that contains the e-mail address(es) of the message's recipient(s).
	CC	The Name/Value pair in the dictionary that contains the e-mail address(es) of the carbon-copy message recipients
	Subject	The Name/Value pair that contains the message's subject
	Character set for subject	The character set to be used for encoding the message body.
	Message Body	The Name/Value pair that contains the message body (will generally be the interchange itself)
	Message Body contains	Specifies the format of the message body. If MIME header and body or Text Body are selected, then the component will not perform any further processing, while selecting Binary body causes the component to encode the message using Base64.
Values Read	*To*	
	CC	
	Subject	
	MessageBody	
Value Written	None	
Context Values Read	None	

It's interesting to notice that you can send the e-mail to multiple recipients by separating them using a semicolon. In addition, keep in mind that the use of this component is not limited to the CIP – and to this specific stage. In fact, you can use it in the OPP to send a purchase confirmation (for example, by using the MakePO component to create a receipt), or in the CIP to request supervisory authorization if an order exceeds the customer's purchase limit.

The real problem with using e-mail to send your interchange is that, in most cases, you will not be able to automatically trigger the execution of a Receive pipeline if your partner also runs a Commerce Server site. In fact, the only way to do so is by using a mail server that supports scripting and that will let you execute a process whenever a new message arrives, such as Microsoft Exchange.

A better solution is offered by the SendHTTP component, which can be used to transmit your interchanges using the HTTP protocol, which is normally used by your browser and web servers. In this case, the HTTP POST action will cause the recipient's web server to launch a script, and the automatic execution of a pipeline becomes thus possible.

Name	SendHTTP	
Properties	URL	Specifies the URL that has to be invoked at the recipient's end.
	Field to be posted	The Name/Value pair to be posted as part of the component's operation (normally the pair that contains the interchange).
	As type	Specifies how the data should be posted to the server.
	Store response in field	The Name/Value pair (optional) in which the component will store the remote server's response.
	From Type	Specifies the format in which the response will be transmitted by the remote server.
Values Read	*FieldToBePosted*	
Value Written	(Optional) *StoreResponseInField*	
Context Values Read	None	

You should make sure to examine the response that the remote server sent back, because the component will report connection problems (such as 'server not found', 'unable to connect', and so on), but not HTTP failures.

Finally, the "high-high-tech" way to send your interchanges to another Commerce Server host is by using the SendDCOM built-in component. This will cause an instance of the ReceiveDCOM2.dll (which is built-into Site Server, too) to be created at the recipient's end. ReceiveDCOM2.dll is able to create an instance of a pipeline object, load a pipeline and execute it with the interchange transmitted by the sender.

> **Contrary to any of the solutions that we have looked at so far, this one will really work only if your two Commerce Server stores run at both sides of the exchange!**

Name	SendDCOM	
Properties	Machine name	The name of the receiving machine (can be either a UNC name or an Internet IP).
	From field	The Name/Value pair that contains the interchange.
	To field	The Name/Value pair in which the interchange will be stored in the remote pipeline's main dictionary
	PCF File Name	The name of the remote file that contains the Receive pipeline to be run by ReceiveDCOM2.dll

Properties	Transacted pipe	Specifies whether the remote pipeline should be executed in a transaction-friendly environment.
	MTS Hosted Receive Component	Determines whether the pipeline is instantiated to run in its own address space or as an in-process server with MTS.
Values Read	*FromField*	
Value Written	None	
Context Values Read	None	

Decrypt Stage

It's now time to move on to the Receive pipeline. As you have already seen before, its first stage takes care of decrypting the interchange data (assuming, naturally, that it has been encrypted in the first place). The components in this stage, like most of the components that show affinity to the Receive pipelines, correspond somewhat to similar components in the Transmit pipeline, with the exception, of course, that they perform the opposite tasks.

DecryptPKCS can be used to decrypt an interchange that had been encrypted using the EncryptPKCS component:

Name	DecryptPKCS	
Properties	Encrypted text field	Specifies the location of the interchange data within the pipeline's main dictionary.
	Plain text field	The name of the Name/Value pair that will contain the component's output. Will normally be the same as *Encrypted text field*, but it can be different if you need to.
	Text output	Specifies whether the interchange data should be saved in text rather than binary format. Your choice should depend on whether you had text data to start with.
	Write certificate used for decryption to field	Specifies the name of the Name/Value pair used to store the name of the digital certificate used to decrypt the interchange.
Values Read	*EncryptedTextField*	
Value Written	*PlainTextField*	
	WriteCertificateUsedForDecryptionToField	
Context Values Read	None	

The component is able to automatically determine what digital certificate should be used to decrypt the interchange, as long as that certificate is indeed installed on your computer. If the required certificate is not available, the component will raise an error and cause the pipeline to fail.

If the Transmit pipeline was instructed to use the EncodeSMIME component to encrypt and/or digitally sign the interchange, you can use the DecodeSMIME component in your Receive pipeline in order to decrypt the interchange and verify its digital signature.

Name	DecodeSMIME	
Properties	Read from field	Specifies the location of the interchange data within the pipeline's main dictionary.
	Write to field	The name of the Name/Value pair that will contain the component's output. Will normally be the same as *ReadFromField*, but it can be different if you need so.
	Write signature certificate to field	Specifies the name of the Name/Value pair used to store the name of the certificate used to digitally sign the interchange.
	Write crypt certificate to field	Specifies the name of the Name/Value pair used to store the name of the digital certificate used to decrypt the interchange.
Values Read	ReadFromField	
Value Written	WriteToField	
	WriteSignatureCertificateToField	
	WriteCryptCertificateToField	
	Signature_result	
Context Values Read	None	

This component decodes the contents of the interchange, assuming they have been encoded using the SMIME protocol, and verifies that the digital signature (if present) is valid, storing the verification results in the signature_result Name/Value pair of the main dictionary. If the interchange has been encrypted, it also decrypts it. Once again, you must have the decryption digital certificate installed on your machine in order for the decryption process to work properly. You do not need to have the signature certificate installed, however.

Verify Digital Signature Stage

The DecodeSMIME component can also belong to the next stage in the pipeline, which is dedicated to the verification of the interchange's digital signature. This also happened in the Transmit pipeline with the EncodeSMIME component, mainly because of the fact that SMIME's functionality spans across both stages.

If the sender of the interchange opted *not* to use SMIME to encode the data, but relied on `DigitalSig` to sign it, you can use the `VerifyDigitalSig` component to verify the validity of the signature.

Name	VerifyDigitalSig	
Properties	Verify signature and Message in... format	Specifies the format of the digital signature. Depends on what was selected in the Transmit pipeline for the DigitalSig component
	Message field	The Name/Value pair that will contain the interchange
	Signature	If **Verify Signature Only in PKCS7 Format** was selected, specifies the Name/Value pair that contains the digital signature data.
	Verified Message field	The output field for the component. If both the signature and the message are verified, the component writes the original interchange (without the signature) into this field.
	Text/Binary output	Specifies whether the verified interchange should be written as binary or text data.
	Write certificate used to verify signature to field	Specifies the Name/Value pair where the component will write the name of the certificate used to verify the signature.
Values Read	*MessageField*	
	(Optional) *Signature*	
Value Written	*VerifiedMessageField*	
	WriteCertificateUsedToVerifySignatureToField	
Context Values Read	None	

Open Header stage

This stage takes care of "unwrapping" the interchange and stripping it of its header (assuming it has one). Commerce Server provides a built-in component, called `OpenHeader`, which takes care of mapping the contents of a header created by the `AddHeader` component that can be run in the Add Header stage of a Transmit pipeline.

Name	OpenHeader	
Properties	Input field	Specifies the location of the interchange data within the pipeline's main dictionary.
	Output field	The name of the Name/Value pair that will contain the component's output. Will normally be the same as *Input Field*, but it can be different if you need so.

Table Continued on Following Page

Values Read	InputField	
Value Written	OutputField	
	Txid	
	(Optional) msg_digest	
	(Optional) return_receipt_requested	
	(Optional) document_type	
	(Optional) document_source	
	(Optional) document_destination	
	Send_datetime	
Context Values Read	None	

You are probably already familiar with most of the these fields, since we have examined them as part of the AddHeader component description. Perhaps the one you have not seen yet is msg_digest, which simply represents a "digest" of the interchange – a sort of a "recap" of the message that was sent across by the originator that can be used as the body of a receipt, as we shall see in the next paragraph. The originator sends across also the algorithm with which the digest must be computed by the component.

If the originator used the EncodeMIME to add a header to the interchange, instead, you can use the corresponding DecodeMIME component in the Receive pipeline to unwrap the interchange and store your data (still to be mapped) in the Dictionary object.

Name	DecodeMIME	
Properties	Read from field	Specifies the location of the interchange data within the pipeline's main dictionary.
	Write to field	The name of the Name/Value pair that will contain the component's output. Will normally be the same as ReadFromField, but it can be different if you need.
Values Read	ReadFromField	
Value Written	WriteToField	
Context Values Read	None	

Generate Receipt stage

If the originator of your interchange has requested that a receipt be sent back to it when the recipient processes the message, you will want to include any component that takes care of doing so here. It's interesting to notice that a "receipt" is nothing else than another interchange, and as such will have its own Transmit pipeline and – if another Commerce Server site is at the other end – its own Receive pipeline as well.

In the standard Commerce Server environment, the system will expect a request for a receipt to be stored in the `return_receipt_requested` Name/Value pair, while the receipt itself will be stored in the `receive_msg_digest` pair.

The only built-in component provided for this stage is `GenerateReceipt`, which can be used to launch a Transmit pipeline for sending a receipt back to the originator:

Name	GenerateReceipt	
Properties	Send Receipt PCF Filepath	The path name of the configuration file for the Transmit pipeline to be used for sending the receipt over to the interchange's originator
Values Read	Receipt_requested	
	Txid	
	Receive_Msg_digest	
	Receive_digest_algorithm	
	(Optional) Document_type	
	Receive_datetime	
	(Optional) Document_source	
	(Optional) Document_destination	
Value Written	None	
Context Values Read	None	

`GenerateReceipt` works by creating a new pipeline object, loading the configuration file specified in the *Send Receipt PCF Filepath* and then copying all the values it reads from the originating pipeline into the new pipeline's main dictionary.

> Transmit pipelines for return receipts should *never* include a request for another receipt in their interchange. If they do, you can end up into a loop in which receipts are endlessly exchanged between the two interchange partners. A good way to protect yourselves from this problem is to ignore return receipt requests in your Receive pipelines for receipts.

The Map Stage (Receive Pipeline)

Components in this stage are dedicated to mapping the contents of the interchange – which, by now, should have been decrypted, digitally verified, and stripped of any header – back into the Commerce Server object that originated them (or in the appropriate Commerce Server object if the originator was not using Site Server). The only built-in component provided by Commerce Server is complementary to the `MapToXML` component that can be inserted in the Map stage of a Transmit pipeline.

As you can image, `MapFromXML` is used to turn the contents of an XML interchange into a copy of the Commerce Server object that was originally used to create it.

Name	MapFromXML	
Properties	XML Source key	Specifies the Name/Value pair that contains the XML-mapped interchange, decrypted and stripped of any header or encoding.
	Result Object Key	The name of the Name/Value pair that will contain the component's output.
Values Read	*XMLSourceKey*	
Value Written	*ResultObjectKey*	
Context Values Read	None	

It's important to remember that if the Commerce Server object that was mapped to XML at the origin contains any objects, these will only be presented in `MapFromXML`'s output if the COM components they are instances of are installed on the receiving server.

Audit Stage (Receive Pipeline)

As in the Transmit pipeline, the Audit stage can be used to write a log of the transactions that take place inside a Receive pipeline, normally to a database or to a file.

The Audit component that we saw in the corresponding stage of the Transmit pipeline can be used here as well to save certain elements of the exchange to a database table. If your Receive pipeline has been designed to handle receipts, however, you might want to use the `AuditReceipt` component to update your log information with regards to a specific transaction:

Name	AuditReceipt	
Properties	Input field	Specifies the Name/Value pair that contains the receipt information received by the pipeline.
	Connection String	The connection string to be used to connect to the database. If nothing is specified, the component attempts to retrieve the default connection string from the pipeline's context.
	Table	Specifies the name of the table where the component should write the receipt information.
Values Read	*InputField*.receive_datetime	
	InputField.txid	
	InputField.receive_msg_digest	
	InputField.receive_digest_algorithm	
	InputField.document_type	

Value Written	None
Context Values Read	(Optional) `DefaultConnectionString`
	(Optional) `ConnectionStringMap`

To better understand the basis on which this component works, you should keep in mind that, in a Receive pipeline created to handle receipts, the receipt data *is* the interchange itself. As such, after all the operations of decryption, header management and mapping, you will end up with a dictionary that contains the data that is read by `AuditReceipt`.

The component works by opening a connection to the database and mapping the Name/Value pairs from the receipt data into the fields of the database table that have the corresponding name (which *must* have the same name as the pairs). The `txid` field is used as a primary key. `AuditReceipt` attempts first to create a new record in the database; if that operation fails because of a primary key violation, the component proceeds to update any existing record instead.

To better understand how the whole process of exchanging a complete interchange works, you can take a look at the figure shown here. As you can see, a record in the audit database is created at first when the Transmit pipeline is called, and is *updated* when receipt information is received by the originator – thus making sure that the transmission was entirely successful.

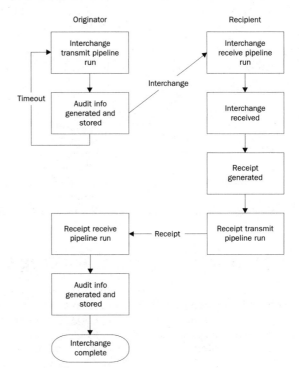

In an interactive environment, you may elect to use a timeout mechanism to determine whether a transmission is successful: if a receipt is not sent back within a certain timeframe, the originator assumes that the recipient did not receive the interchange and sends it again. Naturally, in this case, you will have to make sure that the interchange is marked as a duplicate, so that if the recipient has indeed received the original interchange, but the receipt never made it back to the originator, no duplicates are created by mistake.

Unfortunately, you cannot use timers in ASP applications, and therefore you will have to get a little creative in how you decide to handle this issue. A simple solution is to create a Windows Scripting Host script that simply verifies what transactions are still open and proceeds to re-send the interchanges that have not been acknowledged after the prescribed amount of time. You can schedule the execution of this script by using the Windows NT Task Scheduler (or a similar software).

Application Integration Stage

The final stage in the pipeline, as we mentioned above, is used to transform the data extracted from the interchange so that it can be used in your own application. In most cases, if you are running an ASP application, you will not need to use this stage at all, since the end result of the pipeline will be a dictionary that you can already use in your scripts.

Let's not forget, however, that pipelines are a totally COM-based affair and, as such, you might think of running them from within another type of application, like a Visual Basic or Visual C++ executable. If you consider how much easier pipelines make it to exchange information in an ordered manner, this is not such an unreasonable possibility. In this case, you may want to transform the dictionary data into a form more suitable for your programs in this stage – you could, for example, turn the information into a file (which could be comma or tab delimited), or store it into a database.

Because the scope of this stage is so generic, Commerce Server does not provide any built-in component that has affinity with it, with the exception of SQLOrderADO, which we already described in the previous chapter.

So far we have covered a wide variety of topics, all centered on the concept of business-to-business electronic commerce. The Commerce Interchange Pipeline follows the same basic rules of the OPP, with the fundamental difference that it has been designed with b2b processes in mind. We will now look at the CIP Manager, a valuable asset to any Commerce Server administrator, that provides added functionality in managing b2b commerce. The management of multiple trading partners, their pipelines, and components is, and will become more important over time. This type of communications is only now becoming more prevalent in the industry. As such, maintenance of dealing with many business partners needs to be addressed up front with such a tool.

Introduction to CIP Manager

So you have succeeded in sending a message using the Commerce Interchange Pipeline? Maybe you have sent purchase orders right across the river to the other side, where your vendor is busy sending you the items you request. Maybe you have lured your reseller into the Age Of Interchange, receiving the purchase orders and sending confirmations and catalogue data. Your bosses are thrilled and everything works, making you the smooth operator.

For one week.

Then the C.E.O walks into your office exclaiming: "Great work, but we need to hook up another vendor". So, we start over; coding the CIP's to hook up new business flows. The thrill of doing something you've already done, over and over again, where only the names on the order form have changed.

I say "cheer up, old chap - there is hope!". If you've visited the site server home on Microsoft's web site maybe you will know what I mean.

We will discuss the Commerce Interchange Pipeline Manager (CIPM) add-on that is available, where to get it, what you can do with it and how it will simplify your use of the Commerce Interchange Pipeline configurations in your system. You will get an introduction to the basic functionality and a look at what you can accomplish with the product.

❑ **What is the CIP Manager?**
Initially, we will get into details about the basic functionality of the CIP Manager, discussing some foundational concepts of the design of the CIP Manager.

❑ **Sending and Receiving Documents**
We will delve into deeper details, examining what happens and how everything works together. We will also use a sample scenario to set up a business interchange scenario.

❑ **Installing CIP Manager**
This section will be devoted to the short but intensive process of getting hold of CIP Manager and installing it on your server. We will also discuss the User Interface and describe how the different tasks are performed using the system.

What is the CIP Manager?

The CIP Manager is a Microsoft Management Console (MMC) Snap-in that works with Commerce Interchange Pipelines and provides a data-format and transport protocol independent system for applications to interchange structured business data. CIPM will simplify your management of multiple CIP configurations so you won't have to edit each CIP configuration manually using the Pipeline Editor. This is done by setting up electronic trading relationships between you and the partners you are trading with using easy wizards and dialog boxes to make it easy for you to describe the type of documents you are transferring.

Sending and Receiving Documents

Whenever the CIP Manager sends or receives a document, a Transmit or Receive pipeline is invoked. This is done by gathering information from the settings the user has made within the user interface of the management snap-in, and writing down that information into pipeline files, `.pcf`. Upon request, these pipeline files are then used to transmit the business document. For each different business document type sent to a trading partner there will be a unique Transmit pipeline, and for each different business document type received from a trading partner there will be a unique Receive pipeline, so you can easily imagine the maintenance that is needed to be done when the trading partners and the document types are increasing!

Instead of configuring each of these Pipelines using the Pipeline Editor, CIP Manager will create and manage all the Pipeline configuration files needed for all types of business documents and all trading partners based on information entered with a number of different wizards and property pages. These wizards and property pages represent different entities in the system; such as your organization, trading partners, the type of business documents you send and receive, transmit profiles, certificates and receive locations.

Before we get into the details on installation and using the CIP Manager, we will have to discuss the basic elements that the CIPM is working with:

Business Documents

Any data that is exchanged between trading partners is considered a *Business Document*, such as Purchase Orders, Purchase Order receipts, Invoices, shipping receipts. Within the CIPM, a business Document is represented as a flat file, text or binary, or a business data object. The business data object is an application object used as a data container, programmed using the COM object model. For example, this could be a Commerce Server Dictionary, SimpleList or the by now familiar `OrderForm` object. You can also write your own custom COM objects as long as you implement the demanded COM Interfaces, as described by the API - `IPersistXML`, `IPersistStream` and `IPersistStreamInit`.

Document Profiles

For each different *Business Document* sent and received (Purchase Orders, Invoices, etc.), a *Document Profile* is required. The Document Profile describes the format of the Business Document, and contains the following information:

Interchange identifier	The identification of the organization associated with the document profile.
Certificates	A reference to the digital certificates required for encryption and digital signature.
Business document header type	The format of the document header. CIP Manager supports the following: *CIP XML, ANSI X12, EDIFACT*, and any third-party-supported formats.

Trading Profile

All document profiles for an organization are gathered in an organizations *trading profile*, usually saved as a file with the extension `.tpl`. The trading profile can be published for other trading partners to use. With the CIP Manager, you can export your home trading profile to publish it for other partners. You can also use CIPM to import trading profiles from other partners.

A trading profile, shown in the figure below, contains the following:

Organizational Information	Organization Name
	Home Page URL
	Unique identifier for the organization, such as a Dun & Bradstreet number or a phone number.
	Billing address
	Shipping address
	Contact names

Document profiles	Describes the type of business documents the organization sends and receives.
Certificate information	The names of the certificates to be used to encrypt and digitally sign an outgoing business document
Receive Location	Where the documents are received, such as an URL or an E-mail address. The Receive location is described in the next section.

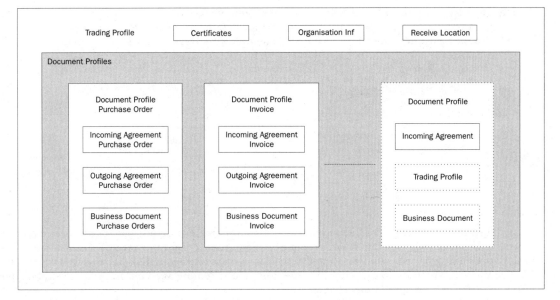

Within the CIP Manager there is a difference between home trading profiles and trading partner profiles. The latter is the trading profile from a partner, either entered manually or imported using the Transmit Profile Wizard. The home trading profile is the own organizations trading profile, which might or might not be public.

Receive Location

Receive Locations are a part of your organizations trading profile. When a partner imports your trading profile, your *receive locations* will appear in their CIP Manager as part of your *transmit profile*.

The receive location specifies the following information:

Transport type	The transport type this receive location accepts. This could for example be Email, HTTP, DCOM
Location	The location where the business document is received. For example a Web address or a mailbox.
Processing method	Describes how the business documents received at the location are processed.

Agreements

An agreement must exist between two trading partners in order to translate and transmit a single business document between them. One agreement must exist for each type of business document that is exchanged between the trading partners. Thus, before an agreement for a business document can be created, a home document profile, as well as the corresponding partner document profile must first be created.

Incoming Agreements

A incoming agreement includes all information needed to generate the receive pipeline for a business document. It requires Home information, Partner information, Home incoming document profile and Partner outgoing document profile, and specifies the following stages of a Receive pipeline:

- ❑ Generate Receipt stage
- ❑ Translation & Deserialization stage
- ❑ Audit Stage
- ❑ Receiving Application Integration stage

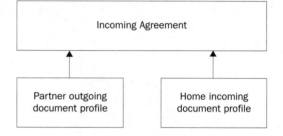

Generate Receipt Stage

As stated earlier, if a receipt has been requested, this stage creates a return receipt business data object. It then proceeds to create a Transmit pipeline in order to send this receipt business data object back to the trading partner that transmitted the business data and requested the receipt. You decide what component you want to use with this stage from the Incoming agreements properties dialog box, which we will describe later in this chapter.

Related Pipeline Components: `GenerateReceipt`

Translation & Deserialization Stage

Translation is the process of converting the data from one business system to another business system, via business documents. The translation could, for example, involve mapping the `order_id` field from one system to the `po_number` field of the other system, and vice versa. The translation is performed by the translation engine component, available from third party software vendors. You can also create your own translation component using the Commerce Server SDK. Translations can be added using the Scriptor component in the Incoming Agreement Properties dialog box, but - in most cases – translation is performed on the sending side rather than on the receiving end.

De-serialization, the opposite of serialization, is when a business data object is converted from a data stream to a data object. Serialization and deserialization are performed by the `MapToXML` and `MapFromXML` components.

Related Pipeline Components: `MapFromXML`

Audit Stage

The Audit stage keeps track of incoming business documents by writing down information into the CIP Manager audit database. The audit database will be discussed later in the chapter. You can set up which audit component to use in the Audit tab on the Home Organization Properties dialog box.

Related Pipeline Components: `Audit`, `AuditReceipt`

Receiving Application Integration Stage

With the application integration, business documents can be transferred to an application after it has been received by a Receive pipeline. The Home Incoming Document properties dialog box is where you can specify which component to use when sending the business document to your application.

Related Pipeline Components: `POtoFile`, `Scriptor`, `SendDCOM` and `SendSMTP`

Outgoing Agreements

The Outgoing Agreement includes all the information necessary to generate the Transmit pipeline in order to send a specific type of business documents to a specific trading partner. It requires a home profile, a partner profile, a home outgoing document profile, a partner incoming document profile and a transmit profile.

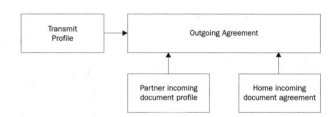

An outgoing agreement defines two of the stages in a Transmit Pipeline; The Outgoing and Serialization stage, and the Add Header stage.

Outgoing Translation and Serialization Stage

This stage matches the translation and deserialization stage we saw in the Incoming Agreements section above. The serialization converts an object, like a business data object, into a data stream that is suitable for transmission. The `MapToXML` performs this task.

Related Pipeline Components: `MapToXML`, `Scriptor`

Add Header Stage

This stage encodes the business data as required. For example, by placing the data within a header that provides additional information about the transmission.

Related Pipeline Components:`AddHeader`, `EncodeMIME`, `Scriptor`

Installing the CIP Manager

Installing the CIP Manager is straight forward, but there is software that needs to be installed before you move on. The CIP Manager itself can be downloaded from the Microsoft Site Server Commerce site.

> **Browse to** `http://www.microsoft.com/siteserver/commerce/` **and click on the link to Commerce Interchange Pipeline Manager. You can then select your language version, and begin to download the software.**

Installation Requirements

Before installing CIP Manager, you will have to make sure you fulfill the requirements. You need to have a machine with the following software installed:

- ❑ **Site Server Commerce 3.0 with Service Pack 2**
  Available at `http://www.microsoft.com/siteserver`.

- ❑ **Internet Explorer 4.01 with Service Pack 2.**
  Available at `http://www.microsoft.com/windows/ie`. You need to install IE 4.01 and the service pack with either the standard installation or the full installation options, since the minimum installation will not be enough to run the CIP Manager.

- ❑ **Microsoft Management Console 1.1**
  The release candidate of the MMC 1.1 is available at
  `http://www.microsoft.com/management/mmc`

The Installation Procedure

Once you are done with the preparations above, you can proceed to installing the CIP manager. The installation process is very straightforward. All you have to do is accept the License Agreement and click on the Complete Install (there is just one installation option) and the product will be installed.

After the installation is completed, the new files will end up in your Site Server Directory under a new directory named `Microsoft Site Server\Bin\CIP Manager`. This is where the MMC Snap-in, all dll's and some default files will reside. The documentation will be placed under the `Microsoft Site Server\SiteServer\Docs` section as a compiled HTML help file; `cipm.chm` and `cipm_sdk.chm`.

Understanding the CIP Manager

When you have installed CIP Manager, you can access it by clicking on the Site Server/Commerce/CIP Manager icon in the Start menu. The user interface of the CIP Manager is a Microsoft Management Console snap-in.

The three icons appearing when you start the CIP Manager is the **CIP Manager task pad**, which we will talk about in the next section.

CIP Manager has a number of wizards that will simplify the configuration of document profiles, agreements and all the other aspects of the CIPM. The wizards are available from the Select Wizard dialog box, which can be accessed once you have defined your home organization. To do this, select Action | New Home Organization... from the menu bar, and fill in the forms as they appear. When you have your Home Organization (CIP Manager only allows one), you can access the Select Wizard dialog box by clicking on its icon in the tool bar. This tool bar will become visible once you click on the CIP Manager(local) icon.

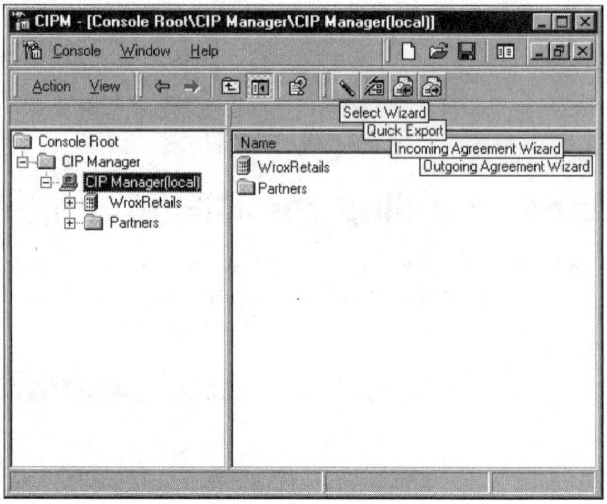

The four icons on the toolbar are: Select Wizard dialog box, Quick Export, Incoming Agreement Wizard and Outgoing Agreement Wizard.

The wizards included with the CIP Manager are:

Wizard Name	What you can do
Home Information Wizard	Create or update information about the home organization.
Home Certificate Wizard	Create certificate request or import a certificate.
Home Document Wizard	Create or update incoming and outgoing home document profile
Receive Location Wizard	Create or update a standard receive location.
Outgoing Agreement Wizard	Create or update an outgoing agreement.
Partner Information Wizard	Create, import or update partner profiles.
Partner Certificate Wizard	Register a partner certificate manually.
Partner Document Profile Wizard	Create or update a partner incoming and outgoing document profile
Transmit Profile Wizard	Manually create or update the transmit profile of a partner.
Export Trading Profile Wizard	Create or update the home organizations published profile.
Incoming Agreement Wizard	Create or update an incoming agreement
Update from profile Wizard	Update a partner profile that was already imported

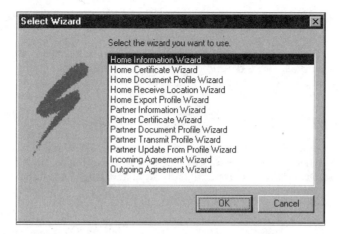

These wizards are accessible by a number of different ways; most can be accessed as mentioned using the Select Wizard dialog box, but also through the Task Pad, or by right clicking the mouse button over an entry in the tree list once you have set up your CIP structures.

The CIP Manager Task Pad

When you first start your CIP Manager, the icons you see is the CIP manager task pad; a graphical interface which will assist you with easy step-by-step instructions for creating incoming and outgoing agreements, as well as setting up your home organization information. The task pad consists of the following icons:

Icon	Description
Export Profile	Create and export a trading profile containing document profiles, certificates and receive locations.
	Wizards involved:
	Home Profile Wizard, Home Certificate Wizard, Home Document Profile Wizard and the Receive Location Wizard
Incoming Agreement Wizard	Configure CIP manager to receive a business document from a trading partner.
	Wizards involved:
	Partner Information Wizard, Home document Profile Wizard, Partner document profile wizard, Receive Location Wizard
Outgoing Agreement Wizard	Configure CIP manager to send a business document to a trading partner.
	Partner Information Wizard, Home document Profile Wizard, Partner document profile wizard. Transmit Profile Wizard.

We will get more familiar with these wizards as we walk you through the process of setting up our sample scenario later in this chapter.

Sending And Receiving Documents

We will now discuss the process of sending and receiving documents using the CIP Manager. This is familiar if you have worked with CIP, and you will notice the great benefit of using the CIP Manager for taking care of your business document traffic.

Sending Documents

In order to send a document from your application, using the CIP Manager, you will use the `Send` method, which will determine which outgoing agreement to use. As we have discussed, the agreement knows how to translate, serialize, encrypt, digitally sign, add a header and how to transport the business document.

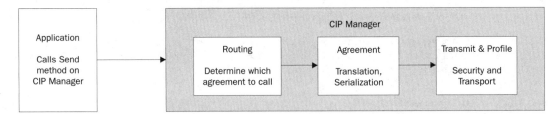

Integrated Application

When the application wants to send something using the CIP Manager, the `Send` method will be called. This method requires the document to be sent, with the interchange identifier for the destination partner and the name of the outgoing document profile as parameters. When the `Send` method is invoked, it will search the CIP Manager database for the outgoing agreement that includes both the specified partner and the corresponding outgoing document profile. With this agreement the `Send` method will then execute the correct Transport pipeline and the business document will be transmitted to the trading partner.

Outgoing Routing

Outgoing routing takes place when the `Send` method uses the document profile and the partner interchange identifier determines which outgoing agreement to use. The interchange identifier, usually a Dun & Bradstreet number or a phone number of the organization, is used to locate the partner in the CIP Manager database.

Transmit Profile

The transmit profile specifies the Outgoing Security Stage and the Transport Stage of a Transmit pipeline.

Outgoing Security Stage

The Outgoing Security Stage supports components that perform digital signature and encryption of the outgoing business document. The `CryptoAPI` encryption methods are supported, including Public Key Cryptography Standard 7 (PKCS7), Secure Multipurpose Internet Mail Extensions (SMIME) and any custom or third-party components.

Related components to this stage:

Component Name	Component Description
DigitalSig	Signs the data in working_data using PKCS7 and a specified certificate
EncodeSMIME	Using S/MIME-encoding to encrypt the working_data entry in the transport dictionary.
EncryptPKCS	Encrypts a business data object using the Public Key Crypto System (PKCS) security standard.

Transport Stage

The transport stage is responsible for sending the byte stream to the destination.

Related Components to this stage:

Component Name	Component Description
SendHTTP	Sends the data using an HTTP post to a script page.
SendSMTP	Converts the data to text and sends it as an SMTP email.
SendDCOM	Sends the data using DCOM to create and execute an MtsTxPipeline or MtsPipeline object on a remote commerce server component.
PipetoPipeTransfer	Initializes and invokes a remote pipeline to receive the transport dictionary from the current pipeline. The control is then returned to the initial pipeline. Fields beginning with underscore are not transferred.

How the Transmit Pipeline is Created

Whenever the CIP manager will send a document, a Transmit pipeline will be created using a predefined pipeline configuration. The pipeline configuration is dependent on the values you have entered for the different entities of your system, like the home organization, the trading profiles, the document profile involved, and so on.

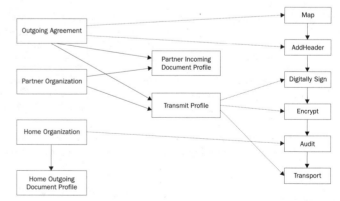

The Map and Add Header stages are configured from the properties of the outgoing agreement. The digitally sign, Encrypt and Transport stages are configured by the properties of the Transmit profile, defined by the Outgoing agreement.

Receiving Documents

When a partner's sending application transmits a business document to your published address using the appropriate protocol, the receiving address, an ASP script (when using HTTP) or a Microsoft Exchange script (when using SMTP) will create an `IMSendRecieve`, `IMSendRecieveTx` or `IMSendRecieveProxy` object and call the `ReceiveStandard` or the `ReceiveCustom` method.

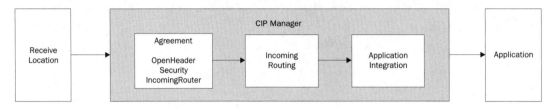

Receive Location

The receive location is the address or mailbox used by your home organizations trading profile. The transport protocol and the address to receive the documents are published within the trading profile for other trading partners to use. The following stages are defined within the receive location profile:

Stage name	Description
Security stage	Specifies how the decryption and the verification of the digital signature will be handled. The actions are performed by the `RecieveStandard` method, and not as one might think, components in the pipeline.
Open Header stage	Defines how the received business document header will be read. The document header type is determined; EDI or CIP XML. from this header is then the source, destination and type of document extracted.
Incoming Router stage	By determining which incoming agreement to use, the business document is routed through the proper pipeline. The incoming agreement is selected based on information retrieved from the header: source, destination, type of business document.
	If the incoming business document is a CIP Manager generated receipt, the `ReceiveStandard` method automatically runs a pipeline which will call MapFromXML and AuditReceipt components.

After the proper routing has been made, the last stage in the receiving process is determined by the application integration stage. This is where any translation and deserialization takes place, as well as application integration.

There are two different receive locations available, Standard and Custom, represented by the `RecieveStandard` and the `ReceiveCustom` methods.

Standard Receive Location

The standard receive location handles incoming business documents automatically. A call to the `RecieveStandard` method will provide the following actions:
decode the business document,
determine document header type and
find appropriate incoming document agreement.

The **incoming agreement** determines which components will be placed in the receiving pipeline when a standard receive location is used.

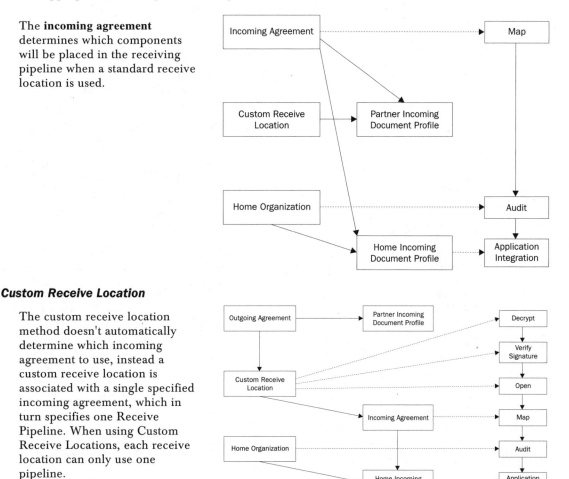

Custom Receive Location

The custom receive location method doesn't automatically determine which incoming agreement to use, instead a custom receive location is associated with a single specified incoming agreement, which in turn specifies one Receive Pipeline. When using Custom Receive Locations, each receive location can only use one pipeline.

The Transport Dictionary

The transport dictionary is a `Commerce.Dictionary` object. The business application will create a transport dictionary whenever it requires to send business documents, adding the business document to the transport dictionary. This transport dictionary is passed as an argument to the `Send` method. The `ReceiveStandard` or the `ReceiveCustom` methods returns a transport dictionary holding the business document received. The transport dictionary may also contain an optional application identifier and a receipt request.

Objects for Sending and Receiving

There are three objects available which provides methods for receiving and sending business documents using the CIP Manager. We will talk more about this when we walk through the sample scenario later.

Object name	Pipeline Created	Usage
IMSendReceiveTX	MtsTxPipeline	Transactions required. Use when the pipeline contains components (GenerateReceipt, PipeToPipeTransfer), or when the send or receive method needs a transaction.
		Methods: SendTx, ReceiveStandard, ReceiveCustom
IMSendReceive	MtsPipeline	Transactions not supported. For example when using a Microsoft Exchange Script.
		Methods: Send , ReceiveStandard, ReceiveCustom
IMSendReceiveProxy	MtsPipeline	Used when the pipeline contains components using Microsoft Exchange Server scripting.
		Methods: Send, ReceiveStandard, ReceiveCustom

Sending

In order to send a document, your sending application must call the Send method of either one of the following objects.

IMSendReceiveProxy.Send

Parameter Name	Parameter Description
InterchangeIdentifierName	This is the name of the interchange identifier used for this transaction. This value, together with the InterchangeIdentifierID will be the unique key identifiing the partner that will receive this business document. A sample value could be "Phone Number".
InterchangeIdentifierID	The identification value; for example "123456790" in the chase of a "Phone Number" InterchangeIdentifierName.
HomeOutgoingDocument	The name of the Home Outgoing Document Profile for the business document being sent.

Parameter Name	Parameter Description
WorkingData	A text string containing the business document.
LoggingType	This parameter is optional and disables or enables logging. A value of 1 means logging is disabled, and a value of 2 means logging is enabled.

IMSendReceiveTx.SendTx() and IMSendReceive.Send()

Parameter Name	Parameter Description
InterchangeIdentifierID	See previous table
HomeOutgoingDocument	See previous table
TransportDictionary	The dictionary containing the business document as an object in the name `object`, or a string in the name `working_data`.
LoggingType	See previous table
PipeContext	A dictionary object that is needed by the Transmit Pipeline.

Receiving

There are two ways to receive an incoming document, The `ReceiveStandard` method and the `ReceiveCustom` method

ReceiveStandard

You can use the `ReceiveStandard` method of your objects, in which case the incoming business data object will used to determine the appropriate incoming document agreement. The matching Receive pipeline is executed based on this information.

```
IMSendReceiveTx.ReceiveStandard(TransportDictionary [, LoggingType]
                                [, PipeContext])
```

Parameter Name	Parameter Description
TransportDictionary	A dictionary holding the received data.
LoggingType	Enable (set to 2) or disable (set to 1) logging. This parameter is optional and is set to 1 by default.
PipeContext	A dictionary that the executed Receive Pipeline requires. parameter is optional.

```
IMSendReceiveProxy.ReceiveStandard(WorkingData [, LoggingType])
```

Parameter Name	Parameter Description
WorkingData	A text string holding the receive business document.
LoggingType	Optional value which enables or disables logging.

ReceiveCustom

If you use the ReceiveCustom method of your objects, the incoming business document will be processed with a Receive Pipeline. The selected Receive Pipline will in this case be controlled by the specified Receive Location – you can only receive one type of business documents for each receiving script with this method:

```
IMSendReceiveTx.ReceiveCustom(ReceiveLocationName,
          TransportDictionary [, LoggingType] [, PipeContext])
```

Parameter Name	Parameter Description
ReceiveLocationName	The name of the Receive Location.
TransportDictionary	A dictionary holding the data that has been received in a name/value-pair named working_data.
LoggingType	Optional value which enables or disables logging.
PipeContext	A dictionary that the executed Receive pipeline requires. parameter is optional.

If you are using the IMSendReceiveProxy object, the data should be supplied in a text string instead

```
IMSendReceiveProxy.ReceiveCustom(ReceiveLocationName, WorkingData [, LoggingType])
```

Parameter Name	Parameter Description
ReceiveLocationName	The name of the Receive Location.
WorkingData	A text string holding the received business document.
LoggingType	Optional value which enables or disables logging.

Business Document Receipts

When a business document is sent, you have the option to require the other end to send you a receipt to validate that everything worked and that the recipient received the business document properly. The receipt does not verify the contents of the document, but merely that it was indeed received. Selecting Receipt requested on the outgoing agreement properties does this. You will also have to setup your receiving end to accept receipts, so you can handle the receipts as they are received.

Auditing

Auditing is the process of logging information on the transmissions that takes place in the CIP Manager. The Audit is done in the Audit stage which is present in both the Transmit pipeline and in the Receive pipeline. The information is logged into the `Audit` Database, which consists of three tables: `IncomingAudit` and `OutgoingAudit` and `AuditReceipt`.

> ***Important* These database tables are not created by default, so this must be done manually**.

Upon installation of the CIP Manager, an SQL installation script was generated for you in the `\\Microsoft Site Server\Bin\CIP Manager` folder called `Audit.sql`. You can run this script from the iSQL/w tool that comes with SQL Server. The Audit component requires Microsoft SQLServer 6.5 or later or Oracle 7, but it does not support Microsoft Access.

Setting up an Audit

The Auditing properties are managed from the Auditing tab on the Home Organization Properties dialog:

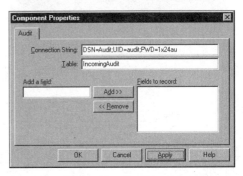

The Audit tab provides us with the possibility to set a component for Incoming, Outgoing and Receipt audit. Upon clicking the Property button for these, we will get the property dialog for the component we have chosen. In the case above, clicking on the Incoming Audit Properties button would give us something similar to what is shown here:

We enter the DSN connection string where we have created the Audit tables, and in this case, since we are creating an Incoming Audit, we specify the Incoming Audit table. We can also choose to add extra fields that we want to audit which will be stored in table columns in our table. These columns must be added manually in the database tables in order to make this work.

The Audit Tables

As mentioned before, the SQL script, `Audit.sql`, will create tables that the component uses. The component relies on these tables, and therefore, some columns in both the `IncomingAudit` and `OutgoingAudit` tables are required:

Required Columns

Column Name	Data type	Description
txid	VARCHAR(255)	Transaction ID. This is the primary key of the `IncomingAudit` and the `OutgoingAudit` tables. A dictionary entry originally written to the transport dictionary by the transmitting application or by the `AddHeader` component.
utc_datetime	DATETIME	The timestamp when the audit component runs.
document_type	VARCHAR(100)	The name of the partner incoming document profile, if the partner uses CIP Manager. If the receiving partner is using EDI, this value is the document type required for their incoming routing.
document_source	VARCHAR(100)	The qualifier and value of the sender's interchange identifier, as XML
document_destination	VARCHAR(100)	The qualifier and value of the receiver's interchange identifier, as XML.
send_datetime	DATETIME	The date and time the `OpenHeader` component is processed. This column is only required in the `IncomingAudit` table.
receipt_requested	VARCHAR(3)	Contains the *Generate receipt* setting on the *General tab* of the *outgoing agreement*. Can be either `Yes` or `No`. This column is only required in the `OutgoingAudit` table.

Optional Columns

These columns are created by default by the `Audit.sql` script, but they are not required. These values are written only if the entries are specified in the Audit component properties **Fields to record** list. Table columns that are not specified will be set to `NULL`. The values correspond to entries in the transport dictionary by the CIP Manager when the business document is sent.

Column Name	Data type	Description
agreement_name	VARCHAR(100)	Outgoing agreement used to send this business document
source_name	VARCHAR(100)	Name of the sending partner.
source_qualifier	VARCHAR(100)	The Interchange identifier qualifier of the sender. This is also included in the `document_source` field.
source_identifier	VARCHAR(100)	Interchange identifier value of the sender. Also included in the document source field.
source_document_identifier	VARCHAR(100)	Name of the outgoing document profile.
destination_name	VARCHAR(100)	The receiving partner's name.
destination_qualifier	VARCHAR(100)	Interchange identifier qualifier of the receiver. Also included in the `document_destination` field.
destination_identifier	VARCHAR(100)	Interchange identifier value of the receiver. Also included in the `document_destination` field.
msg_digest	VARCHAR(100)	Message digest written to the transport dictionary by the `OpenHeader` component. Only created by default in the `IncomingAudit` table.
return_receipt_requested	VARCHAR(100)	Optional entry written to the transport dictionary by the `OpenHeader` component, containing the hash algorithm and the type of receipt document requested. Only created by default in the `IncomingAudit` table.

If you need application specific columns stored in the Audit table, you can do so by adding these columns to the related audit table, as long as it is named exactly like the corresponding entries in the transport dictionary.

Finally, there are some gotchas when working with the Audit component:

❑ Fields to record entries that don't have a corresponding table column will cause the pipeline to return an error. Values end up in the database only if they have a corresponding entry in the Fields to record list on the property page of the Audit component.

❑ Each column in the table must allow null values.

❑ The audit component can't log values containing single-quote characters

Sample Scenario

We will set up a sample scenario using a retailer on the web, WroxRetails, which sells items to their customers online. There is a factory that will receive purchase orders from the WroxRetails online site, and print these orders as they arrive; print-on-demand if you will.

Purchase orders will be sent from the WroxRetails store to the Factory. The Factory will reply with a purchase order acknowledgement that contains information on when the items in the purchase order can be ready for delivery. After the items are manufactured, the shipping receipt will tell the store that the items have been shipped. This information can be used to update information on a secured area as a service to the customers. We will go through the process of setting up CIPM to send Purchase Orders, and leave the PO Acknowledgement and Shipping Receipt as an exercise for the reader.

Sending Purchase Orders to the Factory

First, we want our created orders to be forwarded to our Factory in Chicago. This is the factory where they make their excellent books. To start off, we define our home organization. This can be done by highlighting the CIP Manager entry in the treeview, and clicking on the Action | New Home Organization menu button.

Creating a Home Organization

Enter "WroxRetails" as the Home Organization Name, and leave the URL as default for now. Proceed by clicking Next, and change the Interchange Identifier type to Phone number and enter "11111" as your identifier. There are more options for the Interchange Identifier when using the property pages, accessible by right clicking our home organization entry once we have added it to the CIP Manager.

Accept the default settings for shipping address and billing address, and enter "WroxRetails Primary Contact" as the name of the primary contact and "WroxRetails Secondary Contact" as the name for the secondary contact. Proceed to the verification screen, and complete the process. If you expand the CIP Manager tree in the management console, you will see that we now have a WroxRetails entry there:

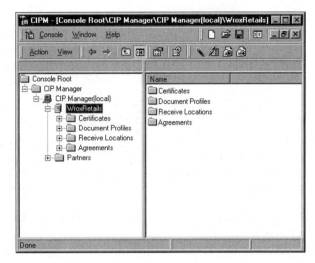

Adding a Trading Partner

Next, we will create a trading partner organization. This can be done by right clicking on the Partners folder, and selecting "New Partner Organization" which will bring up the – you guessed it – Partner Information Wizard. You can use existing Trading Profiles to speed up this process, but since we do not have one for our Factory, we'll create the partner manually.

Let's call the partner "WroxRetails Factory Chicago", and then enter the Partner Interchange Identifier as the phone number "22222". Proceed to accept the default settings for the shipping and billing addresses and enter "Factory Primary Contact" and "Factory Secondary Contact" for the primary and secondary contact, proceed to review your selections and click Finish.

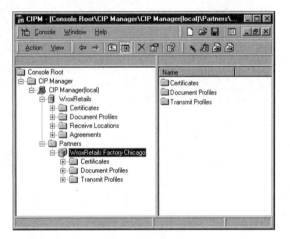

Create an Outgoing Agreement

We need to create an outgoing agreement for the Purchase Orders we will send from the WroxRetails to the WroxRetails Factory. We can do this by selecting the Outgoing Agreement Wizard button on the toolbar.

Set the outgoing agreement name to "Factory Purchase Order", since we will have this agreement define the transport of Purchase Orders between our home organization and the WroxRetails Factory. Proceed by clicking Next, and then accept the "WroxRetails Chicago Factory" as the trading partner to whom you will send this document and click next. Since we don't have any document profiles in our system, we will have to create an outgoing document profile "Purchase Order" and use this for the agreement we are creating.

Adding a Home Outgoing Document Profile

Clicking New will launch the Home Document Profile Wizard, enter the name of the new document profile, "Purchase Order", set it to be CIP XML Document header type, accept the default settings of the Signature Certificate options (none) and you are done. When you have completed the new outgoing document profile, you will get back to the outgoing agreement wizard.

Adding a Trading Partner Incoming Document Profile

Add an incoming document profile with the name "WroxRetails Purchase Order" using CIP XML as the document header type, and leave the Signature Certificate options as they are. Now you can proceed with the Outgoing Agreement Wizard, where we will click Next, ending up on the Trading Profile page. Since we don't have a transmit profile for this agreement, we will have to create one.

Creating a Transmit Profile

Start by giving the new Transmit Profile the name " Purchase Order Transmit" since it will define how the Purchase Orders are transmitted between our home organization and the receiving organization. Proceed to selecting the Transmit method. We will use Transmit to web server, entering the URL of the ASP-script on the receiving side that will accept our Purchase Orders (`http://factoryserver/ReceiveStandard.asp`).

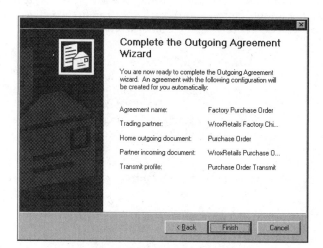

So, now we have created the home outgoing document profile and the trading partner incoming document profile as well as the transmit profile for this agreement.

After the wizard is done, the `Factory Purchase Order.pcf` file is written into the directory `\\Microsoft Site Server\Data\CIP Manager\Pipelines\`. This is the Pipeline that will be executed whenever our home organization application wants to send a purchase order to the WroxRetails Factory. As you can see all the stages and components necessary to perform a successful transmit of the Purchase Order over HTTP to the recipient are there, and we didn't have to edit any pipelines with the pipeline editor. Adding more factories or vendors that will receive purchase orders is not that difficult, and it will not require any modification to the pipeline files.

Sending the Purchase Orders

We have already decided that we will send the orders in CIP XML format using the HTTP Protocol, and that there will be a receiving ASP-script that will inject the purchase orders into the legacy system of the factory to initialize the manufacturing process. The sending script can be just a test script to verify that everything works out, as seen below:

```
Set objSendRec = Server.CreateObject("IMSendReceiveTx")
Set objData = Server.CreateObject("commerce.dictionary")
objData.working_data = "Hello CIPM"
Call objSendRec.Send("Phone Number", "22222", "Purchase Order", objData,2)
```

In a real environment, this would most likely be a step in the final stages of the purchasing process of your Site Server Commerce store, or it could be a scheduled Windows Scripting Host script that scans the order table for new orders, loads the data into an `OrderForm` and sends it off to the user – this approach would increase performance on the web server, since it wouldn't have to take care of the actual transport of the order, and the user won't have to wait for the connection between the web server and the factory receiving end connection.

The code would also be different, and the identifiers and the type of document to be sent would probably be taken from the database for future support of multiple factories and document types.

Receiving the Purchase Orders

The receiving script could be the `ReceiveStandard.asp` script that comes with the Pipeline Manager installation, located in the `\\Microsoft Site server\Bin\CIP Manager\` directory. This script takes incoming requests and stores the data into a `working_data` field on a new `Commerce.Dictionary` object:

```
Set dictTransport = CreateObject("Commerce.Dictionary")
dictTransport.working_data = Request.Form
```

It then proceeds with a possible error check. If you want to enable it you will have to set the `writeOutIncomingDocument` to `True` earlier in the script. This debug uses the `writeOut.WriteOutClass` object; an undocumented object that comes with CIP Manager. It only has one method, `writeOut`, which takes two parameters; the data to be written and the filename where the data should be written to:

```
If writeOutIncomingDocument Then

    Dim writeOut
    Set writeOut = CreateObject("WriteOut.WriteOutClass")

    Dim outputFileName
    outputFileName = "c:\temp\RS_data.txt"   ' Substitute your own file name

    writeOut.WriteOut dictTransport.working_data, outputFileName
    CheckError "writeOut.WriteOut dictTransport.working_data, """ & _
               outputFileName & """"
    Set writeOut     = Nothing

End If
```

Using this undocumented component might not be wise, considering future versions of the product might not support it in its current form. Here is a sample of what the data might look like:

```
MIME-Version: 1.0
Content-Type: text/plain;
       charset="iso-8859-1"
Content-Transfer-Encoding: quoted-printable
Content-ID: <application/ms-cimessage>
X-MimeOLE: Produced By Microsoft MimeOLE V5.00.2014.211

<UTCDATETIME>9/8/99 18:21:52 PM</UTCDATETIME>=0A=
<DOCUMENTDESTINATION><Qualifier>12</Qualifier><Identifier>22222
</Identifier></DOCUMENTDESTINATION>=0A=
<DOCUMENTSOURCE><Qualifier>12</Qualifier><Identifier>11111</Identifier>
</=DOCUMENTSOURCE>=0A=
<DOCUMENTTYPE>WROXRETAILS PURCHASE ORDER</DOCUMENTTYPE>=0A=
<TRANSACTIONID>nfj6lmg00cnh52ncj1tggde9h3</TRANSACTIONID>=0A=
<OBJECTDATA>Hello CIPM</OBJECTDATA>=0A=
```

Next, the script creates an `IMSendReceive` object and uses the `ReceiveStandard` method to inject our dictionary, `dictTransport`, into the CIP Manager.

```
    Dim sendReceive
    Set sendReceive = CreateObject("ImSendReceive")
    CheckError "Set sendReceive = CreateObject(""ImSendReceive"")"

    sendReceive.ReceiveStandard dictTransport, 2
    CheckError "sendReceive.ReceiveStandard dictTransport, 2"

    Set dictTransport = Nothing
    Set sendReceive   = Nothing

    Response.End
```

The script is completed with the `CheckError` subroutine we saw throughout the script. It checks for error, and if there was an error this is logged to the web server log using the `Response.AppendToLog` method.

```
Sub CheckError(statement)
   If Err.Number <> 0 Then

      Response.AppendToLog "Statement          : " _
        & statement & vbCrLf _
        & "  Err.Number        : " & CStr(Err.Number) _
        & vbCrLf _
        & "  Err.Number (Hex) : " & CStr(Hex(Err.Number)) _
        & vbCrLf _
        & "  Err.Description : " & Err.Description & vbCrLf
      Response.Status = L_HTTPReqFailed_Text
      Response.End

   End If
End Sub
```

Once you have all your document profiles, trading agreements in place, it is not a complicated task to add another factory, and you won't have to manage any pipeline configurations, the CIP Manager will do this for you.

Summary

This chapter has covered a wide variety of topics, all centered on the concept of business-to-business electronic commerce. We started by looking at the various kinds of b2b applications that exist, and found out that most processes revolve around the exchange of documents between two parties – which could be either two electronic systems or a human being and one of those.

The MSMarket sample store was our next stop; we examined in detail the only sample b2b application included in Commerce Server, focusing in particular on the way it handles its business processes. In particular, the significance of this sample store is in its ability to give a glimpse of how an automated system can improve the efficiency of the whole procurement procedure, freeing people from the slavery of paperwork and avoiding costs.

We turned to examining the Commerce Interchange Pipeline, with the goal of understanding what Commerce Server can do for our b2b needs. We saw that, essentially, the CIP follows the same basic rules of the OPP, with the fundamental difference that it has been designed with b2b processes in mind.

With business document interchange over the Internet still in its early childhood, we will probably see many different solutions to the problem. It is clear, however, that future business interchange will be based on XML, a far more open and cost-effective technology than the EDI-standards used today. It is my humble opinion that these new business document interchange technologies, together with the rapid adoption of the Internet, will revolutionize business processes of companies around the world.

One of the great benefits is, of course, that the smaller companies that could not justify the cost of an EDI investment, now easily can open up their system both to their end consumers and to their suppliers and vendors. The Commerce Server platform is a good start for opening up your business processes to the wider public. With the rumored upcoming release of BizTalk server – the CIP Manager on steroids, and the release of their website `http://www.biztalk.org`, there is no doubt Microsoft wants a piece of this upcoming megabuck industry. Another interesting site regarding b2b and document interchange is the Open Buying on the Internet Consortium at `http://www.openbuy.org`.

The Microsoft Wallet and Buy Now

Online shopping presents a unique set of challenges for the buyer as much as it does for the seller. In fact, while browsing through an Internet store, many potential customers are looking for a combination of convenience and ease-of-use. Therefore how a store is able to make the shopping experience as straightforward as possible is as important as low prices.

Until recently, the vast majority of people with direct access to the Internet have been characterized by a higher level of education and income. It's therefore reasonable to think that, for most of them, online shopping is a matter of saving time quite more than it is of saving money. Even as time goes on, and more people gain access to the Internet, they will have a preference for those stores that offer a very easy approach to shopping as well as good prices, mainly because it's much easier to hop between different stores online than it is in real life – all we have to do is type a different address and we're there, rather than having to walk two miles to the next mall.

Once the more evident problems of being able to smoothly navigate through the store and proceed through the checkout phase without encountering obscure error messages or incredible waits have been addressed, one of the most annoying drawbacks of shopping online is the necessity of entering one's personal information. I don't know about you, but I personally don't make a point of remembering my credit card numbers and, while I do remember my address – at least most of the time – I hate having to type it every time I make a purchase online.

Internet Explorer 5 includes a feature known as "AutoComplete", which essentially remembers whatever the user types in HTML form single-line text elements and then uses that data to automatically complete the user's input in future uses. This feature, however, has several limitations, like for example the fact that the name of the HTML form element that is being filled is used as a key to the database of entries maintained internally by the browser. As a result, an address typed in a text box called `Addr` will not show up in another form where the name of the input box is `Address`, and so on.

Several stores have taken to allowing their customers to create a "personal profile", which they can access while on the site by means of a username and password. As a matter of fact, we have seen how MS Commerce Server provides this kind of functionality in some of its sample sites, which can also be added to our starter store by appropriately configuring the Site Builder Wizard. However, making this information available, even when protected by the username/password combination, can be risky for the storeowner and when customers move to another site they will have to enter all the information once again.

One other problem that has to do with how easy it is to purchase from a store presents itself when customers access the site through an alternate point of entry, such as an online ad, that identifies a particular product. In this case, the user will most likely want to enter the site specifically to purchase the products that were being advertised and, while it's not a bad idea to let him or her browse through the entire site in order to find those products, they can be easily driven away if this process takes too long. In addition, the organization that sold the ad to the storeowner will probably not be too happy about the fact that the customer has left its site for the store and has been encouraged to stay there – leaving the site with one less visitor.

What Does This Chapter Talk About?

In this chapter, we will be talking about two very interesting features of Commerce Server: the Microsoft Wallet and Buy Now. We already encountered the first feature in Chapter 11, while we were looking at the storefront's code, and we briefly mentioned the second one in Chapter 4 as part of the characteristics of the Volcano Coffee sample store.

Here, we will examine both of them in much greater detail, discussing both how they work from a user's point of view, and how they can be included in our own stores:

❑ **The Microsoft Wallet**
First, we'll tackle the Wallet, explaining how it works from a user's point of view, and how it can be included in our own store. We'll also take a look at the Wallet Webmaster Kit, which is distributed by Microsoft and contains the latest version of the Wallet components.

❑ **Buy Now**
The second portion of the chapter will look into Buy Now. We will reprise the Volcano Coffee sample store and examine the code that is used to implement Buy Now. As we'll find out, there is no magic technology about it, just a clever use of Commerce Server's built-in functionality.

The Microsoft Wallet

The Wallet as we know it to this point is essentially a browser plug-in that makes it possible for us to store our personal information on our own client machines and then release part or all of it to a website that supports it. To enhance privacy and security, a number of measures are put in place to protect the data that we enter into the Wallet, which is always encrypted while on our machine and can only be released with our explicit permission (and, in the case of payment data, by typing in the correct password).

The Wallet's Interfaces

At its core, the Microsoft Wallet is really – surprise, surprise – two COM objects. The first one, called the **Address Selector**, takes care of collecting and releasing personal information such as name and address, while the second one, called the **Payment Selector** takes on the task of collecting payment information.

It's interesting to notice that the information collected by the Payment Selector does not necessarily need to be a credit card number, but can be of other types as well. For example, it can contain account numbers of all kinds, or the data necessary to access a micro-payment system such as CyberCash. As we'll see in Chapter 15, in fact, the Wallet can be expanded in a way that is similar to what is done for pipelines.

Browser Compatibility

Since the Wallet is a browser plug-in, and since each browser treats plug-ins in its own way, there must be a limit of some kind as to the number of browser applications that support it. In fact, Microsoft only distributes a version of the Wallet for Internet Explorer 3.0 and higher, and for Netscape Navigator 3.0 and higher. IE's version, as we can imagine, is an ActiveX object, while Navigator's has been developed using Netscape's own interfaces.

While this combination of browser support covers a large percentage of the Internet's user base, we will not want to exclude anybody from purchasing at our store by forcing them to use the Microsoft Wallet. Similarly, we cannot expect all the people who visit our site using one of the supported browsers to have the plug-in automatically installed. Needless to say, Navigator doesn't come with it, and even Internet Explorer only offers it as an option. Therefore, it's reasonable to assume that a good percentage of our users will have to download and install the Wallet, which can be a long and problematic procedure.

As a rule, therefore, we should consider using the Microsoft Wallet as a secondary information gathering system to be used by those customers who are familiar with it and have the ability to run it on their computers. For all the other customers, we should continue using plain old HTML forms, perhaps with the help of a server-side user profiling system. A notable exception to this rule is a "controlled" environment, in which it is possible to pre-determine the configuration of all the clients that will be accessing the online store, for example an extranet to which only authorized personnel have access.

Using the Wallet

The use of the Wallet is essentially the same, regardless of whether we are running Internet Explorer or Navigator. When we get to the shipping page of the checkout process, we will see something similar to the figure below, naturally assuming that the store supports the Wallet and we have it installed on our machine. This is what the Address Selector interface looks like when we launch it for the first time and no address information has been stored in it.

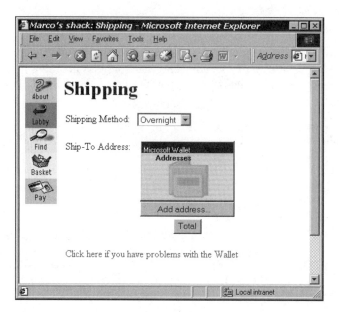

The Address Selector

Clicking on the Add Address... button brings up the dialog box shown here, which simply asks us for a few pieces of information about ourselves (or, more accurately, about the person who should be receiving the merchandise we are ordering). As we can see, it's possible to select an address from the standard Address Book (also available in Outlook and Outlook Express) that all Windows applications share, in which case we won't have to type in all the information.

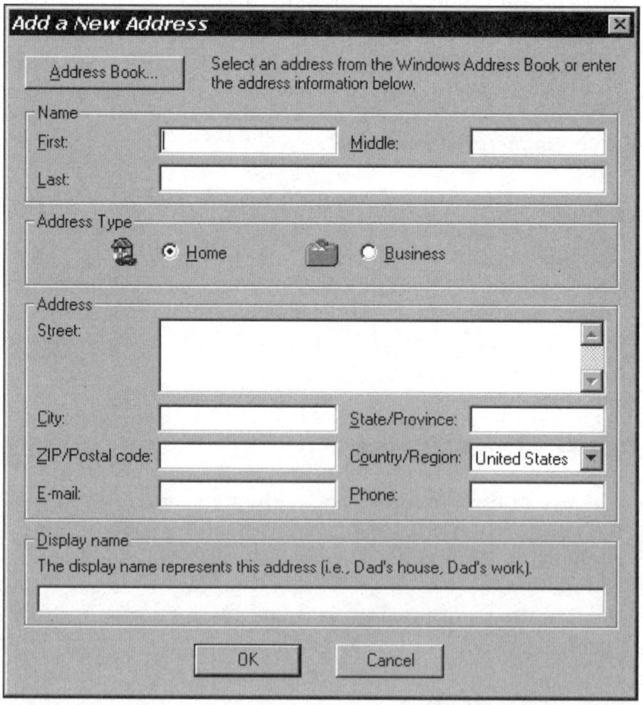

Once an address has been entered into the Address Selector, it will be displayed in it. If more than one address has been entered, we will be able to select a particular one by using the pull-down menu at the bottom of the Selector.

In principle, we should only have to enter an address in the Wallet once, and then reuse it the next time we visit the same store or another store that supports the plug-in – this is, after all, the product's main advantage. In practical terms, there is a particular instance in which the Windows Address Book can cause the Wallet to "forget" our addresses and require us to enter them every single time. This generally affects Outlook 98 users. Since this can be an annoying event for our customers, we should be aware of it and ready to recommend possible solutions, which Microsoft itself discusses in its Knowledge Base article number Q188215 that can be found by executing a search for the article number at the following address:

http://support.microsoft.com/support/search/

When we release our information in the shipping page – for example by clicking on the **Total** button – the Wallet will ask us whether we want to authorize the transfer of the information to the store. As much as this may seem a redundant step (after all, we had to select an address in the first place), it is designed to protect the customer from certain situations in which a malicious website could easily steal information.

Let's consider, for example, the following scenario – assume, for a moment, that the dialog doesn't exist or has been turned off: a site invokes the Wallet and then redirects the browser to another page (for example, by using some JavaScript code or special META tag), thus causing the data in the Address Selector to be sent over to the new script. Since the Selector automatically loads the first available address, the site would be able to collect information without the customer's consent.

Keep in mind that all this can still happen, because the user is given the possibility of turning off the dialog box that warns of the imminent release of information. The loss of address information, however important, is not as potentially damaging as the loss of payment information, and the Payment Selector is much stricter as to how its information is released.

The Payment Selector

Once we get to the payment page, we will meet the second facet of the Wallet, the Payment Selector. Once again, the Selector's interface (shown below) will be blank the first time we launch it, since it contains no payment information yet.

Similarly to what happened before, we can add a new set of payment data by clicking on the Add card button. In this case, however, you will notice that we have to select the type of card *before* we start editing the payment information. Clearly, the terminology used here is not accurate since we will not necessarily be adding a card, but possibly some other payment method.

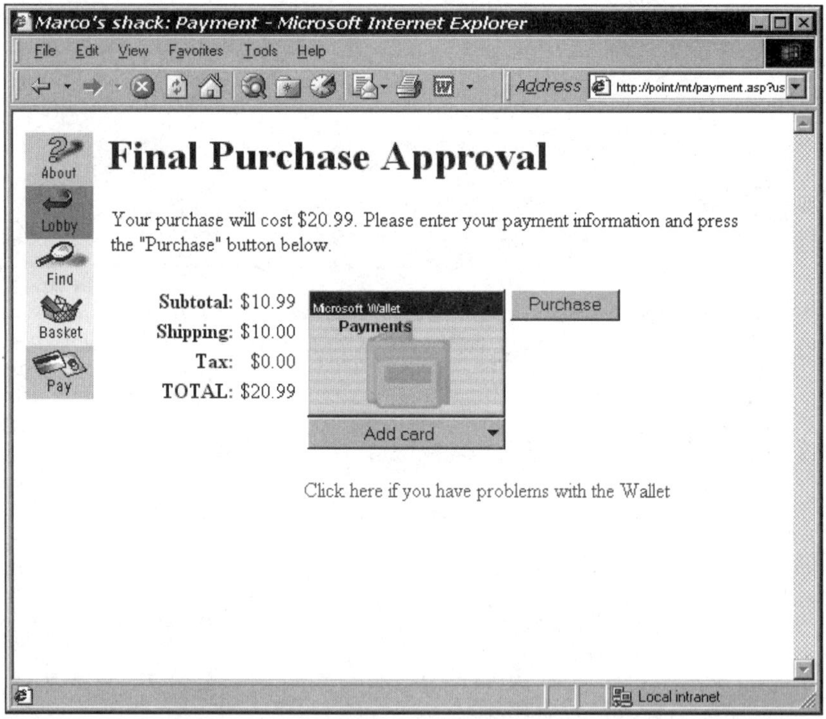

The Wallet comes with built-in support for the most common credit cards available internationally, such as VISA, MasterCard, American Express, and so on. In order to add a new card, the customer needs to go through a wizard, whose four steps are shown here (as is shown, I'm adding a VISA card). All the interfaces for the different type of credit cards supported look the same (and indeed use the same set of COM interfaces), and differ only minimally due to dissimilarities in details such as the number of digits in the credit card number. A different payment system, on the other hand, could present a completely different interface.

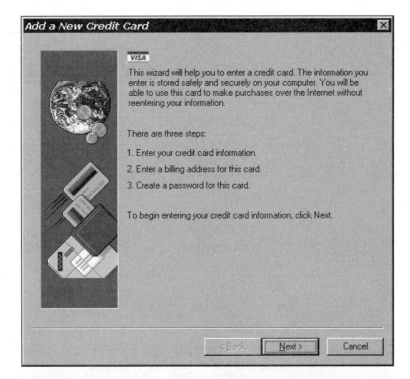

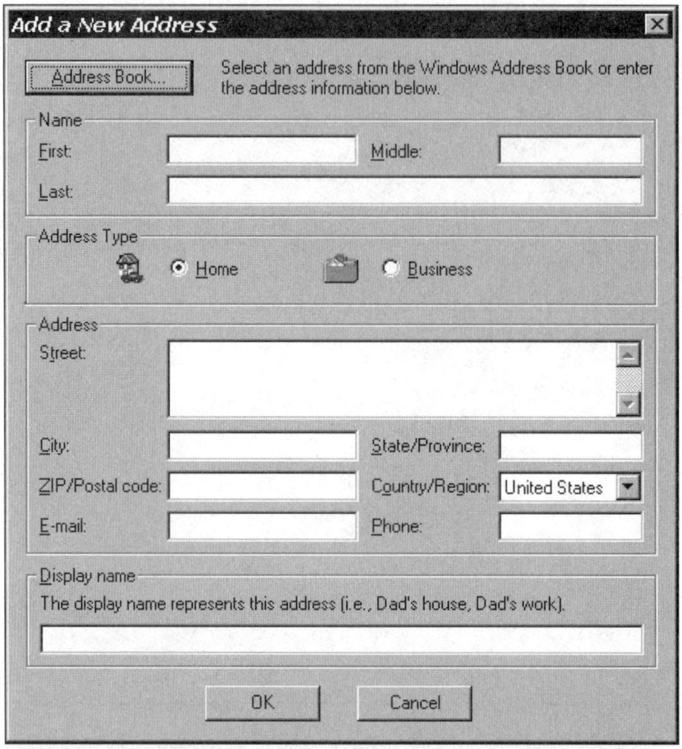

Add a New Address

[Address Book...] Select an address from the Windows Address Book or enter the address information below.

Name

First: [_____]   Middle: [_____]

Last: [_____]

Address Type

○ Home   ○ Business

Address

Street: [_____]

City: [_____]   State/Province: [_____]

ZIP/Postal code: [_____]   Country/Region: [United States ▼]

E-mail: [_____]   Phone: [_____]

Display name

The display name represents this address (i.e., Dad's house, Dad's work).

[_____]

[OK]   [Cancel]

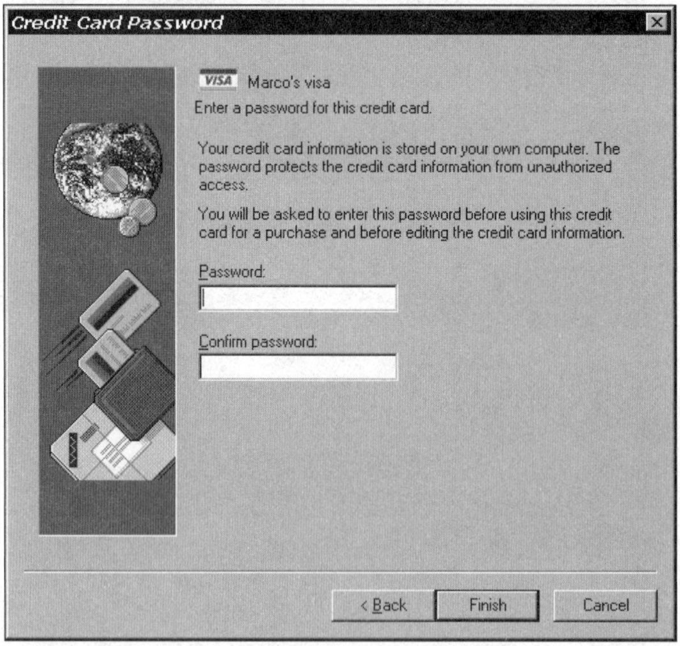

Credit Card Password

VISA Marco's visa

Enter a password for this credit card.

Your credit card information is stored on your own computer. The password protects the credit card information from unauthorized access.

You will be asked to enter this password before using this credit card for a purchase and before editing the credit card information.

Password:

[_____]

Confirm password:

[_____]

[< Back]   [Finish]   [Cancel]

As we can see, the last step of the wizard asks us for a password, which will be used by the Wallet to protect the credit card information – not only from unauthorized access by the stores, but also from unauthorized use by the users of the local computer. The latter protection accounts for those scenarios in which the same machine is shared among different users, or can potentially be used by somebody other than the owner.

Once the payment information has been entered, it will become visible in the payment page (shown below). Contrary to what happened with the Address Selector, however, the Payment Selector does not show any payment information other than the name we gave it during the configuration phase and the type of payment, by showing an appropriate logo (Visa, MasterCard etc.).

Clicking on the Purchase button in the page causes the Selector to display a confirmation dialog box, asking us for permission to send the information over to the site that is requesting it. As we can see from the screenshot under the following heading, the box not only shows us the amount that we are going to be charged for, but also requests a password (rather than a simple click) in order to authorize the data transfer. Also, there is no way to turn this window off, as we could with the Address Selector. The opposite is also true; that is, if we turned off Address Selector there is no way to fetch information directly from the Payment Selector on the client.

Configuring the Wallet

Internet Explorer users also have an additional way to get to the Wallet to change its configuration, by selecting Internet Options from the Tools menu. The Content tab, shown in the figure below, offers, amongst other things, a button that leads directly to the Wallet's configuration interface.

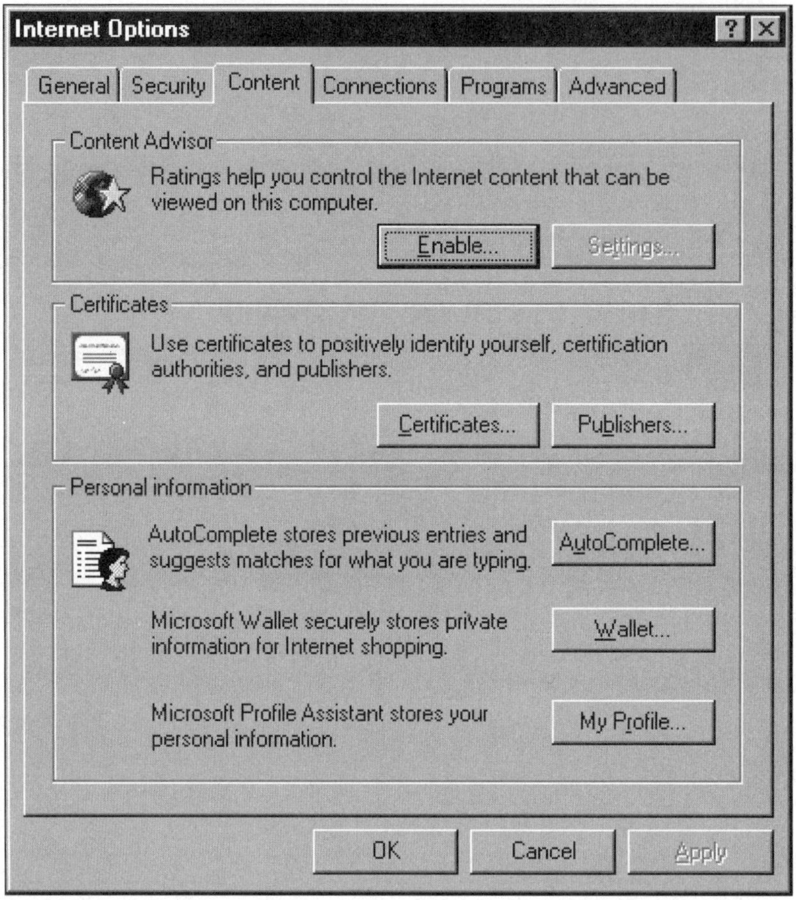

Navigator users, who do not enjoy built-in support for the Wallet in their browsers, can access the same interface once they have added at least one address to the Address Selector or one set of payment data to the Payment Selector. In that case, the drop-down menu at the bottom of the plug-in changes, and the new item Wallet Options... appears (shown below). If the user selects it, he or she will get to the very same configuration screen that can be reached from IE's menus.

There really isn't anything particularly complex about the configuration interface, so we won't talk too much about it. The one thing that is probably worth noticing, and that we haven't as yet discussed, is the third tab in the dialog box, which is shown here. It appears only in the latest versions of the Wallet (we'll talk more about how to get the latest version later on in the chapter), and contains a collection of the orders that have been completed by the user using the Wallet within a store that supports this particular feature of the plug-in.

Programming the Wallet

There are three distinct phases through which a site has to go in order to properly use Microsoft Wallet on its pages:

❑ **Browser identification**

As we mentioned earlier, since the Wallet only works with some browsers, it would be most inconvenient if we were to force customers whose browsers don't support them into using the Selectors. Therefore, we must first of all determine whether displaying the Wallet is possible, or whether plain old HTML forms should be used instead.

❑ **Plug-in display**

Next, we will display the appropriate Selector, which also must be initialized using the appropriate information from the store (for example, the correct properties must be set in order for the Payment Selector to be able to tell the user how much he or she is going to be charged).

❑ **Data collection and transmission**

Finally, once the user has entered all the information required by one of the Selectors, the information has to be collected and sent back to the store in a form suitable for processing. Although, as we will see, the process is quite straightforward, it does also require a little bit of scripting work, since the Selectors are plug-ins and they do not respond directly to the HTTP Submit command.

Browser Identification

Recognizing what browser software is at the other end of the wire is a misleadingly easy operation that can be done server-side with a little bit of ASP scripting. In fact, IIS comes with a built-in component, called MSWC.BrowserType, that makes it possible to identify the browser based on the "identification string" that is sent across when it requests any objects (for example, pages, images, sounds, and so on) from the server. There are other ways of doing this, though.

This string, however, can be confusing – particularly because it varies not only from browser to browser but also among different versions of the same browser. This means, for example, that the object might not be able to recognize a new or special version of a browser that it already knows (in particular, this was a vast problem between version 2 and 3 of both Netscape and Internet Explorer, because both technologies were still very much in their infancies, and developers kept on changing the format of the respective identification strings. These days, things are a little better, but we still have to keep our information up-to-date).

The BrowserType component makes its decision based on the contents of a text file, called browscap.ini and usually stored in the %windows%\system32\inetsrv\asp\cmpnts folder in our boot drive, that includes a list of sub-strings that can be matched against a part of the identification string sent from the browser. To better understand the way this works, we can take a look at our web server's log files; here's a line from one of mine:

```
18:26:11 206.47.244.94 - GET /Default.asp |25|800a01a8|Object_required:_'Sessions'
200 583 Mozilla/4.6+[en]+(Win98;+U) - -
```

As we can see, there's a lot of information here (ironically, this request generated an error), but the browser identification string is present, and is actually the third entry starting from the end:

```
Mozilla/4.6+[en]+(Win98;+U)
```

In this particular case, the browser was Netscape Navigator version 4.6 English, running on a Windows 98 machine. `BrowserType` can come to roughly the same conclusion by looking inside its INI file, where it will eventually find a section similar to the following:

```
;;;;;;;;;;;;;;;;;;;;;;;;;;;;;;;;;;;;;;;;;; Navigator 4.x
[Netscape 4.00]
browser=Netscape
version=4.00
majorver=4
minorver=00
frames=TRUE
tables=TRUE
cookies=TRUE
backgroundsounds=FALSE
vbscript=FALSE
javascript=TRUE
javaapplets=TRUE
ActiveXControls=FALSE
beta=True

[Mozilla/4.0b1 (Win95; I)]
parent=Netscape 4.00
platform=Win95

[Mozilla/4.0b1 (WinNT; I)]
parent=Netscape 4.00
platform=WinNT

[Mozilla/4.0b2 (Win95; I)]
parent=Netscape 4.00
platform=Win95

[Mozilla/4.0b2 (WinNT; I)]
parent=Netscape 4.00
platform=WinNT

;;;;;;;;;;;;;;;;;;;;;;;;;;;;;;;;;;;;;;;;;;; Navigator 4.x WILDCARD (IF ALL ABOVE
FAIL)
[Mozilla/4.0*]
parent=Netscape 4.00
```

The recognition engine will compare the string with each entry in the INI file, until a match is found. In this particular example, my INI file is out of date, because the last entry is in fact a fail-over arrangement to catch 4.x versions of the browser that weren't available when the INI file was first compiled. In fact, the only entry in that section is `parent=Netscape 4.00`, which simply redirects the engine to the main entry for Navigator 4.0. The latter also contains several important entries that are used to determine the browser's capabilities.

I'm sure that you can appreciate the importance of having an INI file that is up-to-date; although in this case I was lucky: if Navigator 5.0 (which is not yet available) was used, the engine wouldn't have been able to determine what the browser actually was and consequently, the site couldn't have risked using the Wallet because it might not have been supported by the client.

The maintenance of an up-to-date version of Browscap.ini used to be taken care of by Microsoft itself, but they have long turned it to a third-party organization, cyScape Inc., which still offers it for free to everybody. cyScape Inc. also has an interesting plug-in component for IIS that can recognize browser software with far greater accuracy, and in better detail, than the engine built into IIS. The latest INI file can be downloaded from cyScape's website at the following URL:

> http://www.cyscape.com/browscap

> **Even though using browscap.ini will help you – at least in most cases – to determine the type of browser that is knocking at your server's door, it will not tell you anything about how it has been configured. As a result, you will not be able to establish whether options such as scripting, ActiveX controls, and so on, are available.**

Inside the Code

The job of determining whether the client can support the Wallet is really not an easy task, since there are a number of variables to consider, including not only the brand of the browser, but also the underlying operating system. When we create a starter store using the SBW, the Shipping and Payment pages will already be able to do most of the work, as we have seen briefly in Chapter 11. For the sake of accuracy, all the Wallet-related operations are performed by two include files, I_mswallet.asp and I_selector.asp; the former simply sets a few global variables that are then used in the latter, which also contains all the detection, display and submission code.

Browser detection is performed at the beginning of the file with global scope – that is, as a direct consequence of the fact that the script is loaded and executed. After creating an instance of the MSWC.BrowserType component that will be used to perform most of the work, the code attempts to determine whether the browser is running on an Intel processor or some other CPU. This is done by looking at the HTTP_UA_CPU server variable, which is set by IE only (Navigator doesn't provide it):

```
' Browser Detection.
Set objBrowser = Server.CreateObject("MSWC.BrowserType")
strCPU = LCase(CStr(Request("HTTP_UA_CPU")))
                ' CPU is necessary to differentiate between alpha, x86 and
                ' other CPUs on NT.
                ' only set for IE, Nav doesn't set.

If strCPU = "alpha" Then
    fMSWltAlphaIE = true

Else
    fMSWltAlphaIE = false

End If
```

Next, a number of global variables are set by the script in response to the data retrieved by IIS's recognition engine. First of all, a test is made to determine three fundamental factors required to display the Wallet:

1. The browser supports JavaScript. This is necessary because a number of client-side scripts are required to collect and transmit Wallet data back to the store.

2. The user has not already requested that he or she be shown HTML forms and another script has not already determined that the browser is unable to display the Wallet. When either one of these conditions is true – or both are – the parameter `use_form=1` is passed as part of the URL query string. The parameter is blank or equal to zero otherwise.

3. The calling script has indeed requested a particular Selector (or both) to be shown to the user. The two global Boolean variables `fMSWltAddressSelector` and `fMSWltPaymentSelector` are reserved for this purpose, and at least one of them must be set to True.

If all the conditions are met, a number of tests are performed in order to determine several characteristics of the browser:

```
If Request.QueryString("use_form") = 0 And objBrowser.JavaScript = "True" _
    And (fMSWltAddressSelector Or fMSWltPaymentSelector) Then

    If objBrowser.ActiveXControls = "True" Then
        fMSWltActiveXBrowser = True
        fMSWltUplevelBrowser = True

    ElseIf objBrowser.Browser = "Netscape" _
        And (objBrowser.Platform = "Win95" Or objBrowser.Platform = "Win98" _
        Or ((objBrowser.Platform = "WinNT" Or objBrowser.Platform = "Win32") _
        And ((Len(strCPU) = 0) Or (strCPU = "x86")))) _
        And ((CInt(objBrowser.majorver) > 3) _
        Or ((CInt(objBrowser.majorver) = 3) And (objBrowser.beta = "False"))) _
    Then
        fMSWltLiveConnectBrowser = True
        fMSWltUplevelBrowser = True

    Else
        fMSWltActiveXBrowser = False
        fMSWltLiveConnectBrowser = False
        fMSWltUplevelBrowser = False

    End If

Else
    fMSWltActiveXBrowser = False
    fMSWltLiveConnectBrowser = False
    fMSWltUplevelBrowser = False

End If
```

Once this code has been executed, three variables are set:

Variable	Description
fMSWltLiveConnectBrowser	True if the browser supports LiveConnect, which is the standard used by Netscape browsers for their plug-ins.
fMSWltActiveXBrowser	True if the browser supports ActiveX components.
fMSWltUplevelBrowser	True if the browser supports either ActiveX or LiveConnect.

Displaying the Wallet

As part of the global code in I_selector.asp, a few more variables are set with the appropriate values; these include the Wallet's current version (strMSWltDwnldVer) and the download location for both the IE and Netscape versions (strMSWltIEDwnldLoc and strMSWltNavDwnldLoc). Each of these variables can also be set to a custom value *before* the script is included in our main file, in which case they won't be replaced with the standard values.

The shipping and payment pages contain very similar code that lets them display the appropriate Selector. First of all, at the beginning, they set either of the global variables that specify which selector should be displayed right before including I_mswallet.asp – which, in turn, includes I_selector.asp. For example, shipping.asp contains these two lines of code:

```
<% fMSWltAddressSelector = True %>
<!--#INCLUDE FILE="i_mswallet.asp" -->
```

Next, a decision is made on whether to use the Wallet by looking at the fMSWltUplevelBrowser variable; if that is set to True, the Wallet is displayed using the tag that is most appropriate for the user's browser:

```
<% if fMSWltUplevelBrowser then %>

    ...

    <% if fMSWltActiveXBrowser then %>
       <OBJECT
          ID="addrSelector"
          CLASSID="<% = MSWltIEAddrSelectorClassid() %>"
          CODEBASE="<% = MSWltIECodebase() %>"
          HEIGHT="123"
          WIDTH="154"
       >
       </OBJECT>

    <% elseif fMSWltLiveConnectBrowser then %>
       <EMBED
          NAME="addrSelector"
             TYPE="application/x-msaddr"
             PLUGINSPAGE="<%= MSWltNavDwnldURL("plginst.htm") %>"
             VERSION="<%= strMSWltDwnldVer %>"
          HEIGHT="123"
          WIDTH="154"
       >
```

```
        <% end if %>

    ...

  <% else %>

  ' Display HTML forms

  <% end if %>
```

As we can see, the `<OBJECT>` tag is used for IE browsers, while `<EMBED>` is chosen if the user is accessing the store using Navigator. In both cases, the code makes heavy use of several stock functions and global variables that are provided by `I_selector.asp`:

Variable	Description
MSWltIEAddrSelectorClassid()	A function that returns the ClassID of the Address Selector. Correspondingly, `MSWltIEPaySelectorClassid` is used to retrieve the Payment Selector's ClassID.
MSWltIECodebase()	Returns the correct location of the installation files for the Wallet's IE version.
MSWltNavDwnldURL(strInstructionsFileName)	Returns the URL that contains the instructions on how to download Navigator's version of the Wallet. `strInstructionsFileName` contains the name of the file that contains the instructions.
strMSWltDwnldVer	Returns the version number

A slightly different set of information is required for the Payment Selector, as we can see from this extract of the Payment page:

```
    <% if fMSWltActiveXBrowser then %>
      <OBJECT
        ID="paySelector"
        CLASSID="<% = MSWltIEPaySelectorClassid() %>"
        CODEBASE="<%= MSWltIECodebase() %>"
        HEIGHT="123"
        WIDTH="154">
        <PARAM NAME="AcceptedTypes" VALUE="<%= strMSWltAcceptedTypes %>">
        <PARAM NAME="Total" VALUE="<%= MSCSDataFunctions.Money(
                                    mscsOrderForm.[_total_total]) %>"

      >
      </OBJECT>
```

```
        <% elseif fMSWltLiveConnectBrowser then %>
            <EMBED
                NAME="paySelector"
                TYPE="application/x-mswallet"
                PLUGINSPAGE="<%= MSWltNavDwnldURL("plginst.htm") %>"
                VERSION="<%= strMSWltDwnldVer %>"
                HEIGHT="123"
                WIDTH="154"
                ACCEPTEDTYPES="<%= strMSWltAcceptedTypes %>"
                TOTAL="<%= MSCSDataFunctions.Money(mscsOrderForm.[_total_total]) %>"
            >

        <% end if %>
```

In both the IE and Navigator code portions, we will notice that two parameters have been added to the plug-in inclusion tags. `strMSWltAcceptedTypes` is a string that contains a comma-delimited list of the payment types accepted by the store, usually set in `I_mswallet.asp`:

```
strMSWltAcceptedTypes = "visa:clear;mastercard:clear;amex:clear;"
```

Its value is stored in the Selector's `AcceptedTypes` parameter. Similarly, the `Total` parameter is set to the total cost of the order for which payment is being authorized. Notice that the data is not stored in the format generally used by Commerce Server (in which currency values are multiplied by the value needed to convert them from the currency unit for this locale and expressed as integers), but rather as a string that is ready to be displayed and also expresses the currency: this makes it possible to use the Wallet with any currency worldwide.

Sending Back the Information

The action of collecting the information in a form suitable for HTTP posting operations also falls on the shoulders of `I_selector.asp`, which contains some JavaScript code for the purpose. A portion of this code is also called when either the Shipping or Payment page have finished loading, using the `OnLoad` event of the `<BODY>` tag:

```
<BODY
    BGCOLOR="#FFFFFF"
    TEXT=    "#000000"
    LINK=    "#FF0000"
    VLINK=   "#FF0000"
    ALINK=   "#FF0000"
    <% if fMSWltUplevelBrowser and CBool(nOrderItems > 0) then %>
    onLoad="<% = MSWltLoadDone(strDownlevelURL) %>"
    <% end if %>
>
```

The `MSWltLoadDone` function is used in Navigator to determine whether the Selector plug-in is available on the client machine or should be downloaded and installed. This is necessary because, unlike IE, Navigator does not provide automatic download and installation facilities. The function is quite long, and therefore we won't include it here, but its algorithm is quite easy to understand. One thing that we will want to notice is the `strDownlevelURL` parameter that is passed to `MSWltLoadDone` when the `OnLoad` event is raised.

This is the URL to a page that contains the plain-HTML version of the Shipping and Payment pages (it's actually the same file, but with the `use_form` URL parameter set to 1). `MSWltLoadDone` redirects the user to this URL if the Navigator version of the plug-in is not present on the machine and the user refuses to download and install it:

```
if (confirm("Click OK to install Microsoft Wallet Plugins."))
    <% ' open instructions page in a new window %>
    window.open("<% = MSWltNavDwnldURL("plginst.htm") %>")
else
    location = strDownlevelURL
return
```

The actual task of preparing the data for uploading to the server is taken care of in two steps. First of all, the main script contains an HTML form that includes a number of hidden parameters, one for each value that needs to be taken from the Wallet. For example, in `shipping.asp`, we find:

```
<FORM
    NAME="shipinfo"
    METHOD="POST"
    ACTION="<%= pageSURL("xt_orderform_prepare.asp") %>"
>

<INPUT TYPE="HIDDEN" NAME="ship_to_name">
<INPUT TYPE="HIDDEN" NAME="ship_to_street">
<INPUT TYPE="HIDDEN" NAME="ship_to_city">
<INPUT TYPE="HIDDEN" NAME="ship_to_state">
<INPUT TYPE="HIDDEN" NAME="ship_to_zip">
<INPUT TYPE="HIDDEN" NAME="ship_to_country">
<INPUT TYPE="HIDDEN" NAME="ship_to_phone">
<INPUT TYPE="HIDDEN" NAME="ship_to_email">

...

</FORM>
```

These parameters, as we can see, are initially empty of any value. They are filled by the `MSWltPrepareForm` function (always found in `I_selector.asp`), which is called when the user clicks on the submit button (which contains the text **Total** in the Shipping page and **Purchase** in `Payment.asp`), through a call to another function that takes care of setting the appropriate conditions. In the Shipping page, this function is called `submitShipToAddr`:

```
function submitShipToAddr()
{
    if (MSWltPrepareForm(document.shipinfo, 2)) {
        document.shipinfo.submit();}
}
```

As we can see, the code here simply calls `MSWltPrepareForm` with two parameters; the first one is a pointer to the form where the values must be written. The second one could be used in conjunction with a third optional parameter to indicate that a translation should occur between the way the parameters are called within the Selector and in the HTML form.

To better understand why this would be necessary, it's a good idea to take a look at how `MSWltPrepareForm` works. Its algorithm can be divided into three phases:

1. The raw information is retrieved from the Selector

2. The names of the raw parameters are translated into the same names as those used in the HTML form

3. The values of the raw parameters are copied to the parameters in the HTML form

Step 2 is meant to cover the scenario in which we need to send a value to the server using a specific name for the parameter that does not correspond to the name of any parameter available from the Selector. In practical terms, however, neither `Shipping.asp` or `payment.asp` make use of it.

The information is extracted from the plug-in using a combination of two methods. `GetValues` extracts a dictionary that contains all the values stored in the Wallet. This is then passed to the `GetValue` method, which proceeds to extract an individual parameter from the dictionary. This parameter, in turn, is transferred to the HTML form. `MSWltPrepareForm` returns `True` if it is successful, in which case the form is submitted using standard HTTP procedures.

The Microsoft Wallet Webmaster Kit

If you're craving more information about the Wallet – and if you're interested in getting the latest version, you can direct your attention, as well as your browser, to the following URL:

```
http://www.microsoft.com/wallet
```

This location contains a plethora of information about the Wallet, and includes two particularly interesting downloads. The first one, which we will examine in Chapter 15, is the Wallet SDK, which can be used to expand the Payment Selector in a variety of ways. The second one is the Microsoft Wallet Webmaster Kit (MSWWK), which includes all that a webmaster/web developer needs to include either Selector in his or her site.

In particular, you will find the latest version of the Wallet plug-in, and a number of documents and sample scripts that cover what we have illustrated so far in this chapter and add more information about the Wallet objects.

The Future of the Wallet

Things in our world move undoubtedly fast: technologies become obsolete, and are replaced by something more efficient and more practical. The Microsoft Wallet is certainly no exception, and has been continuously evolving since its inception a few years ago.

I hope that you'll agree with me when I say that, while the Wallet's technology provides an interesting solution to a rather important problem, it has a big shortfall that has so far hindered its diffusion across the Internet and that's its availability. Sure, Microsoft provides a version of the Wallet that works with IE and Netscape, but, let's face it, who wants to spend an hour (or even ten minutes) for it to download and install? What's more, the fact that it comes as an optional installation element with Internet Explorer 4 and 5 doesn't make things any easier, since most users will not have it on their machines.

Microsoft, ever sensitive to shifts in the marketplace, has obviously recognized this problem, and has evolved the concept behind the Wallet in a completely Internet-based system that doesn't require any plug-in to be installed on the user's machine called the **Microsoft Passport**. All the information is collected and stored by Microsoft, which releases it to sites who adhere to the program and receive a special certificate by a recognized authority. The functionality provided by the Passport is not yet complete while I'm writing this chapter (September 1999), but it should be ready by the 1999 holiday shopping season.

It's hard to predict whether the Passport will become popular – besides the obvious reluctance of people in releasing their information to some organization (even Microsoft) just for the sake of doing so, you should keep in mind that some of Microsoft's properties have already been the victims of well-targeted hacker attempts. However, to be fair, Microsoft does explain what level of security is involved in the Passport, and also recommends some ways for users to enhance their profile's security, such as choosing a good password, and so on.

You can find more information about the Passport at the following URL:

```
http://www.passport.com
```

Buy Now

In Chapter 4, while looking at the Volcano Coffee sample store, we encountered a rather unusual feature that we introduced as Buy Now. In short, this is used when the store is accessed from an entry point other than the main page with the intention of purchasing one specific item. As a result, it is displayed in a small pop-up window and, instead of providing the full feature set of the store, it offers an expedited check-out process consisting of four steps (product, shipping, payment, confirmation). At the end of the process, the pop-up window is closed and the user is free to continue browsing the original website.

Aside from the obvious advantages that we have already seen in Chapter 4, Buy Now can also be used internally to our site to capture the user's attention and facilitate "impulse" purchases. This way, we offer our customers a quick and easy way out if they decide they want something badly enough before they can really think too much about it.

How Buy Now Works

There is no particular technology behind Buy Now – nothing that could be compared to the plug-ins for the Wallet or the pipelines for the purchasing process. In the end, the Buy Now Wizard (BNW) is simply a set of ASP pages cleverly put together with the goal of providing a different way to look at how the purchase process can work.

The Ad

The first piece in the BNW puzzle is where the user comes from; in our case, it's a banner ad that is delivered using another product that ships with Commerce Server called the Ad Server (we'll talk more about it in Appendix E). For the moment, all that we should really worry about is what the banner's code looks like once it has been delivered to the user's browser. Here's the HTML code:

```
<SCRIPT language="JavaScript">
<!--
    function popUpWindow()
    {
        BuyNowWin = window.open
        ("../buynow/product.asp?pfid=5",
        "BuyNow",
        "width=400,height=525,scrollbars=yes");
    }
// -->
</SCRIPT>

<A HREF="javascript:popUpWindow()">
    <IMG SRC="../assets/images/buynow.gif" WIDTH=350 ALT="Link to Buy Now control">
</A>
```

As we can see, clicking on the banner triggers the execution of a short JavaScript function that simply instructs the browser application to open a new window (without address and status bars) and redirect it to the first page of the wizard.

The Buy Now Wizard

As we can see from the figure shown, the first page of the BNW, which is located in the /buynow folder of the Volcano Coffee main directory, is product.asp. This file does not differ much from its counterpart in the normal store, and essentially performs the same operations. First of all, a query is executed against the database to extract the particular item that must be shown to the user. The family ID of the object (remember that Volcano Coffee supports dynamic attributes) is retrieved from the pfid parameter in the SQL query.

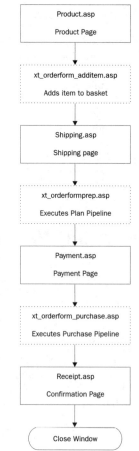

If we look at the script above, we will notice that, in the example, product.asp is invoked with the pfid=5 parameter. Incidentally, the query executed by the script to retrieve information about the product to be displayed is product, the same one used in the main store.

Aside from a simple check to determine whether the query execution has indeed returned one value, product.asp does not do anything particularly new for us. It's interesting to notice, however, that the query is executed by specifying the adOpenKeyset constant, which makes it possible to use the RecordCount property of the ADODB.Recordset object in order to determine whether the query returned one record.

Once the user clicks on the Next button from the product page, he or she is taken to xt_orderform_additem.asp, which takes care of creating an OrderForm object for the user and inserting the product into it. The functionality of this file can be fundamentally split into two parts: the first one retrieves and validates the information that was passed from the previous page (product family ID, quantity and attributes), while the second one creates a new OrderForm object (or retrieves an existing one if the user has visited the store before), and then adds the item to it.

All the utility functions are provided by two include files, `include/shop.asp` and `include/util.asp` that contain code which is essentially a duplicate of what is inside `I_shop.asp` and `I_util.asp`.

The next page in line is `shipping.asp`, which is exactly the same – at least code-wise – as its counterpart in the main store. Looking at the script, we will notice that the Microsoft Wallet is used as the primary payment method in the BNW as well. While the logic behind this decision is probably that the Wallet makes completing the purchase much quicker, we should keep in mind the considerations that we discussed earlier in the chapter: users who do not have the Wallet installed on their machines aren't going to benefit from having to download and install it.

`Shipping.asp` calls `xt_orderform_prepare.asp`, which executes the Plan pipeline. Once again, its functionality can be split into two portions: the first one collects and validates the data, while the other takes care of updating the `OrderForm` and running the pipeline. This script, as did the previous one, has a simple error-checking mechanism in place. If an error is detected, it is added to the `OrderForm`'s `purchase_errors` `SimpleList`. At the end of the execution, the script simply includes the file `include/error.asp` if it finds one or more element in the `SimpleList`.

`Error.asp` is a very simple script that generates a generic error message and redirects the user to the URL stored in the `errorBack` global variable. Clearly, the calling script must set that variable before `error.asp` is included. For example, `xt_orderform_prepare.asp` sets it to point to `shipping.asp`:

```
<%

...

if errorList.Count >0 then
    errorBack = mscsPage.SURL
    ("buynow/shipping.asp",
    "pfid",
    Request("pfid"),
    "use_form",
    Request("use_form"))
%>

    <!--#INCLUDE FILE="include/error.asp" -->

...
```

`Payment.asp`, the next step of the wizard, is in charge of collecting payment information. It prints out a detail of the order, including the usual shipping and tax fees, and then either displays the Wallet's Payment Selector or prints out the corresponding HTML forms. On the other hand, `xt_orderform_purchase.asp` takes care of executing the Purchase pipeline and reporting any errors using the same mechanism that we described a short time ago.

If all goes well, the user is redirected to `receipt.asp`. This simply prints out a confirmation that the order was successful, along with one of MS Commerce Server's own kilometric order IDs. The page also includes a **Finished** button, which executes the simple JavaScript statement `Window.Close` when it is clicked, thus closing the browser window and terminating the BNW.

Summary

The Microsoft Wallet is undoubtedly an interesting attempt at providing a tool to make it easier to shop online. Although it certainly solves a much-felt problem, it does come with a few strings attached. For one thing, the mere fact that it is not a consistent part of each Internet Explorer installation out there makes it difficult to offer it as the primary data collection method even for the users of that browser. Therefore, it can be used at best as a secondary system for gathering data from our customers.

Unfortunately, it's also true that the Wallet has not enjoyed too much success to this point. Even the section of the Microsoft website dedicated to the Wallet lists less than 25 sites that have been optimized for users of the technology. While that might not be a definitive list, it does not include any of the major international retail sites and serves as indication that the convenience of the Wallet is greatly limited by the comparatively little support that it has. In fact, there is little point in having a system designed to reduce the number of times one has to type information in if only a few sites support it!

In the last part of the chapter, we also examined the Buy Now feature of MS Commerce Server. *Feature* is probably the right term for it, since there is no particular technology behind it. This is not to say, however, that the Buy Now Wizard is not an interesting and useful tool. On the contrary, it can be of help, as we have seen, in a number of situations.

Writing Pipeline Components

Every animal leaves traces of what it was; man alone leaves traces of what he created.
— **Jacob Bronowski**, The Ascent of Man

Pipelines wouldn't be nearly as exciting a technology as they are if they couldn't be easily extended to support more functionality. In Chapter 10, we have already seen how it's possible to develop custom pipeline components using the `Scriptor` component; however, we also mentioned that `Scriptor` has its own limitations in terms of what can be done with it, if not for any other reason, then just because it's entirely based on the Windows Scripting Host.

If the capabilities of pipelines were to stop here, however, their usefulness would falter rapidly: the business processes they have been designed to deal with are so diverse – and so are the various scenarios to which they can be applied – that the built-in components would rapidly prove to be insufficient to handle them.

What Does This Chapter Talk About?

In this chapter, we will concentrate on how pipelines can be expanded through writing custom components using commonly available development tools, such as Visual C++ and Visual Basic. The goal of this chapter is not only to explain how these two languages can be used to create new components, but also to illustrate how they can be used together to fulfill a component's development and deployment cycle. We'll see that the simplicity and ease-of-use of Visual Basic makes it the perfect candidate for the trial-and-error process of writing a new component, while Visual C++ offers the performance and stability edge required in a production environment.

We will divide the chapter into two sections:

❑   **Writing a prototype using Visual Basic**

First, we'll take a look at how Visual Basic can be used to write a pipeline component. As we'll see, VB is at the same time easy and powerful to use, making it the perfect development tool for our goals. However, it's performance and stability in a production environment are not the best possible – which means that we'll have to resort to a different language once we decide to put our components online.

❑   **Finishing the job using Visual C++**

Next, we'll change the fruit of our initial labor – a fully functional pipeline component written in VB – to Visual C++, which, as we'll see, gives us a lot more performance and stability, but at the price of higher complexity of the code. Therefore, VC should only be used once the functionality of your VB prototype has been fleshed out completely.

Writing a Prototype using Visual Basic

There's no doubt that Visual Basic is the ideal environment for developing COM objects, since it's largely based on the Component Object Model to start with. As such, VB is an optimal platform for writing pipeline components, since it's much easier to manage in the development phase.

However, VB has also several limitations if you compare it to Visual C++, in particular the fact that it doesn't support the Free-Threaded threading model, the ideal model for pipeline components. In general, you will probably want to use VB for prototyping purposes – just because it's faster to write components with it – while VC should be your choice for production-grade code.

A Word of Warning

I should probably point out that you couldn't use just any version of Visual Basic component for developing pipeline components. In fact, the pipeline objects require every component to be based on the Apartment- or the Free-threading model, and neither model is supported by any versions of VB previous to 5.0 with SP1.

Therefore, you will need to either have installed Service Pack 1 for Visual Basic 5.0 (available for free from the Microsoft web site) or Visual Basic 6.0 and higher (available from Microsoft, alas not for free, I'm afraid) in order to write pipeline components that will actually work.

Using the Right Version of Visual Basic

In order to create a new pipeline component, you must first create a project of type `ActiveX DLL` or `ActiveX Control`. Next, you will need to create the actual component, which should either be a `User Control` or a `Class Module`. This choice depends largely on whether you expect to need one or more property pages, in which case you will need a `User Control`, or not, in which case either type will work for you.

In addition, you should check your project's properties to make sure that your component is being created using the Apartment threading model.

Starting Up

In order to make the component work, you will need, at a minimum, to implement the `IPipelineComponent` interface. In order to do so, you need to reference the **Pipeline 1.0 Type Library** from the **Project/References** dialog box. If that library doesn't appear in your list, you can include it by adding a reference to the `\bin\pipeline.dll` file in your Site Server installation folder.

The main interface that a pipeline component must implement provides two methods, one of which you are already familiar with since we illustrated it when we were discussing the `Scriptor` component.

`EnableDesign` is used to "prepare" the component for execution in one of two modes: *design mode*, which corresponds to the editing phase, and *execution mode*, which corresponds to the production phase. In principle, during the editing phase, the component should be more tolerant toward possible errors, while in execution mode it should report all the errors properly. The truth is, no component is ever executed in design mode – at least as far as I've been able to see – and the only errors that you normally report during the editing phase are those related to the validity of the properties that the user enters.

❑ **Syntax:**
   HRESULT IPipelineComponent::EnableDesign (BOOL fEnable // in);

```
Sub IPipelineComponent_EnableDesign(ByVal fEnable As Long)
```

❑ **Parameters:**
   fEnable   Specifies whether the component should be executed in design mode
                          (TRUE or <> 0) or in execution mode (FALSE or 0)

The implementation of `EnableDesign` is completely optional. In my personal experience of pipeline components, I have never found the need to use it.

One method that will be very useful is `Execute`, which we have already met while we were talking about `Scriptor`. `Execute` is called whenever the pipeline component is run from within a pipeline object.

❑ **Syntax:**
   HRESULT IPipelineComponent::Execute (IDispatch*   pDispOrder // in,
                                        IDispatch*   pDispContext // in
                                        long   lFlags // in
                                        long*   pErrorLevel //out, retval);

```
Function IPipelineComponent_Execute (ByVal pdispOrder As Object, ByVal
pdispContext As Object, ByVal lFlags As Long) As Long
```

❑ **Parameters:**
   pDispOrder   The pipeline's main dictionary
   pDispContext   The pipeline's context
   lFlags   Reserved value. Should always be zero
   pErrorLevel   A pointer to the return value for the function

In the case of Visual C++ implementations, the HRESULT function return value must be complemented by setting *pErrorLevel to the appropriate return code for the component's execution; Visual Basic implementations will simply use this as the return value for their function. The possible values for this variable are those we saw earlier for the pipeline objects, although a fourth one is also defined for "catastrophic failure" errors:

1	Success: the pipeline execution was successful
2	Warning: a non-fatal error was raised. The pipeline component may elect to continue the pipeline's execution. In a SSCE store, the Plan pipeline is designed to withstand this error level, while the Purchase pipeline terminates with an error. The error level withstood by a pipeline can be set in its properties when the Win32 editor is running in Expert Mode.
3	Failure: an error was raised. The pipeline execution should terminate immediately.
4	Fatal error: a fatal (catastrophic) error was raised. The pipeline execution should terminate immediately.

As a rule, level 2 errors are raised when the problems can be fixed with user interaction – for instance, re-entering a credit card number, and so on) – while level 3 errors represent user-independent issues, such as communication failures and inability to connect to a database. Level 4 is never used.

Writing the Code

Once you have added a reference to the pipeline library, you can tell VB that you intend to implement the IPipelineComponent interface in your component:

```
Implements IPipelineComponent
```

If you look at your editing window, you will notice that the Object list now contains the IPipelineComponent interface, which, in turn, provides you with the Execute and EnableDesign methods.

```
Private Sub IPipelineComponent_EnableDesign(ByVal fEnable As Long)

End Sub

Private Function IPipelineComponent_Execute(ByVal pdispOrder As Object, _
                ByVal pdispContext As Object, ByVal lFlags As Long) As Long

End Function
```

When the Execute method is called, you can access both the context and the main dictionary directly from the component, as you would from an ASP script – that's the beauty of a language so well integrated with COM!

Let's suppose, for example, that we want to write a component to handle a special promotion conceived by our marketing department that provides orders whose item count falls between two boundaries. For the moment, we'll store those boundaries in two private variables, called lLowerBound and lUpperBound, and the special shipping price in lShippingPrice. As you can see from the code below, we'll just go through all the items in the OrderForm using a simple For – Next loop:

```
Option Explicit

Implements IPipelineComponent
```

```
Private lLowerBound As Long
Private lUpperBound As Long
Private lShippingPrice As Long


'=======================
' Execute method of IPipelineComponent
'
' Called when the pipeline component is executed
'=======================

Private Function IPipelineComponent_Execute(ByVal pdispOrder As Object, _
                 ByVal pdispContext As Object, ByVal lFlags As Long) As Long

    Dim lTotalQuantity As Long
    Dim Item

    ' Only run if the shipping costs have not been set yet

    If Not IsNull(pdispOrder.[_shipping_total]) Then Exit Function

    lTotalQuantity = 0

    ' Calculate total number of items in the Orderform

    For Each Item In pdispOrder.Items
        lTotalQuantity = lTotalQuantity + Item.Quantity
    Next

    ' If total number of items within boundaries, apply special pricing

    If (lTotalQuantity > lLowerBound) And (lTotalQuantity < lUpperBound) Then
        pdispOrder.[_shipping_total] = lShippingPrice
    End If

    ' Return success value

    IPipelineComponent_Execute = 1
End Function
```

Creating the Component's Information Structures

In order to report the values read and written by our component, we'll need to implement the
IPipelineComponentDescription interface. To do so, however, you will need to have the Site
Server SDK, which comes with SSCE, installed on your computer. This will allow you to add a
reference to the pipecomplib.tlb object library, which is located in the lib_386 folder of the
SDK's main installation folder.

IPipelineComponentDescription is implemented to pass a list of the values that are accessed
by a component to the Win32 editor, which, in turn, displays them in the Properties dialog box for
that component. Each method in this interface returns a COM Variant variable that contains a
SafeArray of Variants, which are, in turn, initialized with wide-character string values.

> It's important to understand that, because they are entirely COM-based, pipeline components should store and retrieve all string values in wide-character (Unicode) format.

The list of values read from the pipeline's main dictionary is returned by the `ValuesRead` method:

❑ **Syntax:**
HRESULT IPipelineComponentDescription::ValuesRead (VARIANT*pVarRead // out);

```
Function IPipelineComponentDescription_ValuesRead() As Variant
```

❑ **Parameters:**
PVarRead   The return value of the function

Similarly, `ValuesWritten` and `ContextValuesRead` are used to report the Name/Value pairs that a component writes to the main dictionary and reads from the context respectively.

❑ **Syntax:**
HRESULT IPipelineComponentDescription::ValuesWritten (VARIANT *pVarRead // out);
HRESULT IPipelineComponentDescription::ContextValuesRead (VARIANT *pVarRead // out);

```
Function IPipelineComponentDescription_ValuesWritten() As Variant
Function IPipelineComponentDescription_ContextValuesRead() As Variant
```

❑ **Parameters:**
PVarRead   The return value of the function

Writing the Code

If we now add the following line to our component's source:

```
Implements IPipelineComponentDescription
```

this will let us add the code to support the interface's three methods. In our case, we are not reading any value from the context; however, we are reading and writing to the main dictionary:

Values Read	Item.Quantity_shipping_total
Values Written	(Optional)_shipping_total

As such, we'll have to return the appropriate Variant arrays to the editor:

```
' ========================
' IPipelineComponentDescription implementation
' Used to report the values read and written by the component
' ========================
```

```
Private Function IPipelineComponentDescription_ContextValuesRead() As Variant
    Dim ReturnValue(0) As Variant

    ReturnValue(0) = "[None]"

    IPipelineComponentDescription_ContextValuesRead = ReturnValue
End Function
```

```
Private Function IPipelineComponentDescription_ValuesRead() As Variant
    Dim ReturnValue(1) As Variant

    ReturnValue(0) = "Item.Quantity"
    ReturnValue(1) = "_shipping_total"

    IPipelineComponentDescription_ValuesRead = ReturnValue
End Function
```

```
Private Function IPipelineComponentDescription_ValuesWritten() As Variant
    Dim ReturnValue(0) As Variant

    ReturnValue(0) = "[Optional] _shipping_total"

    IPipelineComponentDescription_ValuesWritten = ReturnValue
End Function
```

Working with Properties

It's pretty obvious that our component uses three properties: the lower and upper boundaries, and the special shipping price. As such, we can start by implementing them using standard VB code:

```
'=======================
' Component properties, implemented using standard VB functionality
'=======================

Public Property Get LowerBound() As Variant
    LowerBound = lLowerBound
End Property

Public Property Let LowerBound(Value As Variant)
    lLowerBound = CLng(Value)
End Property

Public Property Get UpperBound() As Variant
    UpperBound = lUpperBound
End Property

Public Property Let UpperBound(Value As Variant)
    lUpperBound = CLng(Value)
End Property

Public Property Get ShippingPrice() As Variant
    ShippingPrice = lShippingPrice
End Property
```

```
Public Property Let ShippingPrice(Value As Variant)
    lShippingPrice = CLng(Value)
End Property
```

All we now need to do is create a property page for the component, adding to it the appropriate control and check logic: this is done by selecting Add **P**roperty Page... from the **P**roject menu. In general, the VB Property Page Wizard takes care automatically of creating a property page, so this is also an option. Whatever your choice, you will end up with something similar to what is shown in the following screenshot: make sure that your property page appears in the property page list for your components (accessible by selecting **Property Pages** from the component's properties).

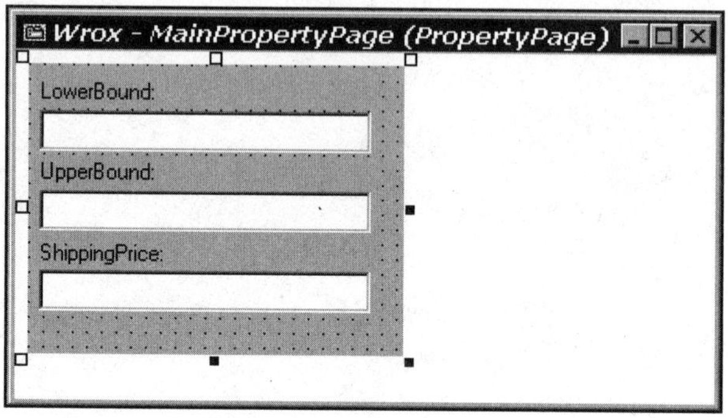

There needs to be at least some basic checks on the validity of the selection that the user makes for the property values, which can be performed by your property pages. In my case, I've added the code needed to make sure that all the values entered are valid positive integer numbers, and that the lower boundary is less than or equal to the upper boundary.

```
Private Sub txtShippingPrice_Change()
    Changed = True
End Sub

Private Sub txtShippingPrice_Validate(Cancel As Boolean)
    On Error Resume Next

    If CLng(txtShippingPrice.Text) < 0 Then
        Cancel = True
    End If

    ' if an error is detected the text entered cannot be converted to a long
    ' integer

    If Err.Number <> 0 Then
        Cancel = True
    End If
End Sub

Private Sub txtUpperBound_Change()
    Changed = True
End Sub

Private Sub txtUpperBound_Validate(Cancel As Boolean)
    On Error Resume Next
```

```
    If CLng(txtUpperBound.Text) < 0 Then
        Cancel = True
    End If

    ' if an error is detected the text entered cannot be converted to a long
    ' integer

    If Err.Number <> 0 Then
        Cancel = True
    End If
End Sub

Private Sub txtLowerBound_Change()
    Changed = True
End Sub

Private Sub txtLowerBound_Validate(Cancel As Boolean)
    On Error Resume Next

    If CLng(txtLowerBound.Text) < 0 Then
        Cancel = True
    End If

    ' if an error is detected the text entered cannot be converted to a long
    ' integer

    If Err.Number <> 0 Then
        Cancel = True
    End If
End Sub

Private Sub PropertyPage_ApplyChanges()
    SelectedControls(0).ShippingPrice = txtShippingPrice.Text
    SelectedControls(0).UpperBound = txtUpperBound.Text
    SelectedControls(0).LowerBound = txtLowerBound.Text
End Sub

Private Sub PropertyPage_SelectionChanged()
    txtShippingPrice.Text = SelectedControls(0).ShippingPrice
    txtUpperBound.Text = SelectedControls(0).UpperBound
    txtLowerBound.Text = SelectedControls(0).LowerBound
End Sub
```

IPipelineComponentAdmin

This interface is used to provide a means for ASP pages to directly access a component's properties. You will most likely implement this interface if you expect your component to be used for MicroPipe operations. In order for the properties to be passed along, you must include them in an instance of Dictionary.

`IPipelineComponentAdmin` provides two methods, one for loading the properties and the other for saving the properties. `GetConfigData` is used to return the configuration parameters:

❑ **Syntax:**
   HRESULT IPipelineComponentAdmin::GetConfigData (IDispatch **ppDict // out);

```
Function IPipelineComponentAdmin_GetConfigData() As Object
```

❑ **Parameters:**
   iDispatch   The return value of the function's C++ implementation

Even when your component's properties are not set, you should always return a complete `Dictionary` object when `GetConfigData` is called. This will allow whoever uses your component to find out what the correct name for the properties are, just like we did while looking at the `MicroPipe` component.

Properties are saved using the `SetConfigData` method, to which the caller passes a `Dictionary` object that contains all the appropriate Name/Value pairs:

❑ **Syntax:**
   HRESULT IPipelineComponentAdmin::SetConfigData (IDispatch *pDict // in);

```
Sub IPipelineComponentAdmin_SetConfigData(ByVal pDict As Object)
```

❑ **Parameters:**
   pDict   The Dictionary object that contains the Name/Value pairs of the properties to be set

Your implementation of `SetConfigData` should be flexible enough to recognize the scenario in which the caller has only set a few of the properties: in that case, only those properties that have been set in the `Dictionary` should be changed.

Writing the Code

Since our component already exposes all of its properties directly, there is very little point in implementing the `IPipelineComponentAdmin` interface; however, it is worth taking a look at it. In this case, we have already added a reference to the appropriate type library when we implemented `IPipelineComponentDescription`; therefore, we should be able to implement the interface right away. In fact, the addition of the following line:

```
Implements IPipelineComponentAdmin
```

allows us to insert the `GetConfigData` and `SetConfigData` members into our code. However, we're still unable to create the instance of the `Dictionary` object that we will need in order to return the properties to our callers. To make our component "Dictionary-aware", we can include a reference to the **Commerce – MSCSCore Type Library** that should be available on our computer. Note that the SSCE objects are available as part of the `MSCSCoreLib` group: for example, a `Dictionary` object is identified as `MSCSCoreLib.CDictionary`. Next, we are finally able to add the implementations of the `IPipelineComponentAdmin` interface:

```
'--------------------------
' GetConfigData/SetConfigData
'
' Implemented from IPipelineComponentAdmin
'=======================

Private Function IPipelineComponentAdmin_GetConfigData() As Object

    Dim dConfigData As MSCSCoreLib.CDictionary

    ' Create a dictionary object

    Set dConfigData = New MSCSCoreLib.CDictionary

    ' Fill it with the configuration data

    dConfigData.LowerBound = lLowerBound
    dConfigData.UpperBound = lUpperBound
    dConfigData.ShippingPrice = lShippingPrice

    Set IPipelineComponentAdmin_GetConfigData = dConfigData

End Function
```

```
Private Sub IPipelineComponentAdmin_SetConfigData(ByVal pDict As Object)

    ' Save values passed into properties

    lLowerBound = CLng(pDict.LowerBound)
    lUpperBound = CLng(pDict.UpperBound)
    lShippingPrice = CLng(pDict.ShippingPrice)

End Sub
```

The only thing missing, at this point, is support for loading and saving the component's properties from a storage medium. As mentioned earlier, Visual Basic provides all the functionality required through the ReadProperties and WriteProperties methods:

```
'=======================
' Persistency functions
'=======================

Private Sub UserControl_ReadProperties(PropBag As PropertyBag)
    lUpperBound = PropBag.ReadProperty("UBound", 0)
    lLowerBound = PropBag.ReadProperty("LBound", 0)
    lShippingPrice = PropBag.ReadProperty("ShippingPrice", 0)
End Sub
```

```
Private Sub UserControl_WriteProperties(PropBag As PropertyBag)
    PropBag.WriteProperty "UBound", lUpperBound, 0
    PropBag.WriteProperty "LBound", lLowerBound, 0
    PropBag.WriteProperty "ShippingPrice", lShippingPrice, 0
End Sub
```

Allowing the Editors to Recognize our Component

If you now go to the Win32 editor, you'll notice that the component we just created can't be seen anywhere! Don't worry, though: this happens because we haven't properly registered it.

In fact, in order for the editor to know that a COM component is really a pipeline object, a few extra entries must be added to its Registry key. This must also happen in order to declare the affinity of a component with one or more particular stages. If we open the Registry Editor and look for the component – assuming that you called it Wrox.ShippingSpecial – you'll find it under HKEY_CLASSES_ROOT/Wrox.ShippingSpecial. Inside, you will find a sub-key called CLSID, whose default value contains the Class ID for the component. Copying that sub-key into the clipboard, and then using it to make a search starting from the HKEY_CLASSES_ROOT/CLSID key, will enable us to find the component's main registry entries.

Another sub-key in the main entry is called Implemented Categories; this contains several other sub-keys that reference a number of Class IDs. Implemented Categories is used to express the kind of component described in the Registry: this is where the editor looks to see whether a COM object is indeed a pipeline component.

A pipeline component needs to implement the following category in order to be marked as a pipeline component:

{CF7536D0-43C5-11D0-B85D-00C04FD7A0FA}

It also needs to specify the stages with which it shows affinity. SSCE provides a different category for each possible stage, with a special category for those components that work in any stage. All components are listed in the C++ include file, Include\Microsoft Site Server\Commerce\Pipe_Stages.h. In our case, we will add the implemented category for the Shipping stage, which is {D82C349A-43C5-11D0-B85D-00C04FD7A0FA}.

We will see our component in the Win32-based editor once we have followed these steps and added the appropriate GUIDS to the Implemented Categories list for our component. We will also be able to see the relevant property page, as well as the values that our component will read and write.

Working with the Web-Based Editor

If you now try to add the component to a pipeline using the web-based editor, you will notice that it is unable to display a property page for it. That's because web editing works in a slightly different way to Win32 editing: you'll have to provide ASP-based property pages!

The editor will automatically recognize your property pages, as long as their names are constructed according to the following convention:

❑ The main property page must be called with the name of the component, taking care that any dots are turned into underscores. For example, the property page for Wrox.ShippingSpecial should be called Wrox_ShippingSpecial.ASP.

The "post" page, used to validate and save the values of the properties, should be called with the name of the main page, with the _Post suffix appended to it (for example, Wrox_ShippingSpecial_Post.ASP).

Both pages should be stored in the *SiteServer Root*\SiteServer\Admin\Commerce\Pipeline Configuration folder.

The main page should include two files provided by SSCE, which create the header and footer for the actual page displayed by the web browser: these files include all the structures required to access the component and post the newly entered values. The header include file is called `pe_3rd_party_edit_header.asp`, while the footer is called `pe_3rd_party_edit_footer.asp`. The header handles the component to be configured automatically, and makes it available in the `ComponentConfig` variable, so that all you have to do in the main page is add the proper HTML controls to display the properties and let the user change them. For example, here's a simple property page for our shipping control:

```
<%@ Language=VBScript %>

<!--#include file = "pe_3rd_party_edit_header.asp"-->

Lower boundary:
<INPUT TYPE="TEXT" NAME="LBound" Value="<% = ComponentConfig.LowerBound %>">
<BR>

Upper boundary:
<INPUT TYPE="TEXT" NAME="UBound" Value="<% = ComponentConfig.UpperBound %>">
<BR>

Shipping cost:
<INPUT TYPE="TEXT" NAME="SCost" Value="<% = ComponentConfig.ShippingPrice %>">
<BR>

<!--#include file = "pe_3rd_party_edit_footer.asp"-->
```

If you add this file to the editor's folder with the name Wrox_ShippingSpecial.ASP, you will notice that the property page will become visible, although you will not yet be able to save any information you type in. To be able to do so, you'll need to write the post script, which must include the `pe_3rd_party_post_header.asp` file at its beginning:

```
<%@ Language=VBScript %>

<!--#include file = "pe_3rd_party_post_header.asp"-->

<%
    ComponentConfig.LowerBound = Request ("LBound")
    ComponentConfig.UpperBound = Request ("UBound")
    ComponentConfig.ShippingPrice = Request ("SCost")
%>

<!--#include file = "pe_3rd_party_post_footer.asp"-->
```

In this case, we have used the properties that the component exposes directly – exactly like our VB property page does – but we could have just as well have used the configuration dictionary that we exposed as part of our implementation of `IPipelineComponentAdmin`.

Finishing the Job with Visual C++

The task of developing a pipeline component in Visual C++ is not an easy one, although it can be said that the tools provided by SSCE *do* help. The real challenge, unfortunately, is in the language itself, which is more complex than Visual Basic, but the results you can achieve are far better in terms of stability and performance.

As a result, I strongly recommend that you at least consider using VB for your development needs, unless there is a very good reason to do otherwise. When a component starts behaving erratically, you'll want to be able to fix it as quickly as possible, and not waste precious time digging into the realms of C++.

Before You Start...

I remember the first time I tried to write a pipeline component in VC – I ended the day feeling very desperate indeed! The documentation did offer some explanation, but dealing with all the problems of managing a COM component *plus* taking care of all the little idiosyncrasies of working with SSCE objects was a task too large to be undertaken by a mere mortal!

However, after some exploration into what SSCE had to offer, I found out that there is a built-in ATL Wizard, designed specifically for creating pipeline components. After cursing the injustice of all my hard work and struggles, I installed it and discovered a world in which developing a pipeline component didn't take away the best years of your life!

The ATL Wizard is the first thing that you have to install if you want to use VC for writing your components. You can find it in the SiteServer\Commerce\SDK\Commerce\Samples\ATLWizard subfolder in your SSCE installation's main directory. All you need to do is the following:

❑ **Register the Wizard's DLL**
This is located in the i386 directory and is called `CommerceDLG.dll`. You can register it by selecting Run from the Start menu, then typing in:

RegSvr32.exe SiteServer
Root\SiteServer\Commerce\SDK\Commerce\Samples\ATLWizard\i386\CommerceDlg.dll

where *SiteServer Root* is, as usual, the location where you installed SSCE. The COM server registration utility should pop up a dialog box similar to the one shown in the screenshot here, indicating that the dll was properly registered.

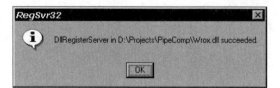

❑ **Copy the template files to the VC folder**
This will enable the Wizard to use certain files as templates for creating the component. You'll find the templates in the Template folder in the Wizard's directory. If you are running Visual C++ 5.0, you must copy them to the `C:\Program Files\DevStudio\SharedIDE\Template\ATL` folder, assuming that `C:\Program Files\DevStudio` is where you installed Visual Studio. If you're using VC 6.0, you should copy these files to the `C:\Program Files\Microsoft Visual Studio\Common\MSDev98\Template\ATL` directory, assuming, once again, that `C:\Program Files\Microsoft Visual Studio` is where you installed Visual Studio 98 in the first place.

Unfortunately, this will only work well if you run VC 5.0. If you're using version 6, moving the files to the right location will not suffice. In fact, you will have to download a file from Microsoft's technical support site, which is available by looking at the following Knowledge Base article:

http://support.microsoft.com/support/kb/articles/q214/8/32.asp

Once you have downloaded and unzipped the file, all you have to do is follow the instructions that come with it and you're ready to go!

Component Creation

In order to create a new pipeline component, you must first of all create a new project of type ATL COM AppWizard. In my case, I named it Wrox and chose it to be a DLL that supports neither MFC nor MTS.

Once the project is ready, you can create a pipeline component by selecting New ATL Object from the Insert menu, then double-clicking on the Commerce Component icon. This will cause the Pipeline Component ATL Wizard to pop up and ask you a few questions, such as what the component's name should be (I chose Wrox.VCShippingSpecial, as you can see) and, if you click on the Commerce Component tab, what additional SSCE interfaces you want the component to support. Our component will support all three available interfaces.

The good thing here is that the Wizard does almost all the work for you – to the point that you will only need to worry about actually implementing the component and its methods, rather than writing the code to declare its interface. You will notice that our newly created component already exposes all the methods required to implement `IPipelineComponent`, `IPipelineComponentDescription`, `ISpecifyPropertyPages` and `IPersistStreamInit`, although it doesn't (yet) support `IPipelineComponentAdmin`.

A Look at the Support Functionality

While accessing SSCE objects in VB was a relatively easy task – thanks, once again, to the language's built-in integration with COM – this time it's going to be a little more difficult, because VC won't know anything about them, nor does it provide easy-to-use functionality to handle Variants and Unicode strings.

Luckily, however, SSCE does that for us and, as part of the global methods of our project, it provides a wide variety of functions that can be used for many purposes, as we are about to see.

Dealing with SimpleList Objects

The manipulation of a `SimpleList` object begins with obtaining an instance of it. This can be done, as we have just seen, by extracting it from a `Dictionary` object, but the global functions also provide a method for extracting it directly from an instance of `IDispatch`:

❑ **Syntax:**
HRESULT GetSimpleListFromDispatch (IDispatch* pdisp,
                                          ISimpleList**   pplist);

❑ **Parameters:**
pdisp   The instance of `IDispatch` from which the `SimpleList` object will be instantiated
pplist   A pointer to the `ISimpleList` pointer that will receive the `SimpleList` object

Next, you can determine how many items are in the list by calling the `GetNumItems` function:

❑ **Syntax:**
HRESULT GetNumItems (ISimpleList*   plistItems,
                               long*   pcItems);

❑ **Parameters:**
ISimpleList   The `SimpleList` object whose item count must be retrieved
pcItems   A pointer to the long-typed variable that will receive the item count

Extracting items from a `SimpleList` is a relatively easy operation using its `get_Item` method, which corresponds to using the `Item` property in VBScript. However, since the only `SimpleList` that you will normally use in a pipeline component is the Items collection of the `OrderForm` object, you might find it convenient to use the `GetNthItem` function to retrieve a `Dictionary` object (corresponding to an individual product in the `OrderForm`) from it:

❑ **Syntax:**
HRESULT GetNthItem (ISimpleList*   plistItems
                             long   lItem
                             IDictionary**   ppdictItem);

❑ **Parameters:**
plistItems   The `SimpleList` object whose item must be retrieved
lItem   The number of the Item that should be retrieved
ppdictItem   A pointer to the `IDictionary` pointer that will receive the item

No global functions are provided for adding an item to a `SimpleList` (with the exception of certain "special" `SimpleList` objects, whose global functions are discussed in the *General Purpose* section). However, you can call its `put_Item` method, which corresponds to using the `Item` property in VBScript, to store any Variant variable in it.

To delete an item, you can call the `DeleteNthItem` function:

❏ **Syntax:**
HRESULT DeleteNthItem (ISimpleList*   plist
                    int*   lItem,);

❏ **Parameters:**
plist	The `SimpleList` object whose item must be deleted
lItem	The number of the item that has to be deleted

Manipulating Dictionaries

An instance of `IDictionary` can be extracted from an `IDispatch` pointer by calling `GetDictFromDispatch`:

❏ **Syntax:**
GetDictFromDispatch (IDispatch* pdisp
                    IDictionary**ppdict);

❏ **Parameters:**
pdisp	The instance of `IDispatch` from which the `Dictionary` object must be extracted
ppdict	A pointer to the `IDictionary` pointer that will receive the instance of `IDictionary`.

Once you've got an instance of `IDictionary`, you can use one of the `GetDictValue` functions to retrieve a value from it:

❏ **Syntax:**
HRESULT GetDictValue (IDictionary*   pdict,
                  LPCWSTR   name,
                  BSTR*   pvalue);
HRESULT GetDictValue (IDictionary*   pdict,
                  LPCWSTR   name,
                  VARIANT*   pvalue);
HRESULT GetDictValue (IDictionary*   pdict,
                  LPCWSTR   name,
                  int*   pvalue);

❏ **Parameters:**
pdict	The instance of `IDictionary` from which the value must be extracted
name	The name of the Name/Value pair that holds the value to be extracted. Must be a Unicode string
pvalue	Pointer to the variable that will receive the value extracted. The actual type depends on what version of the method is called.

Similarly, you can store a value in a Name/Value pair of a `Dictionary` object by using the `PutDictValue` method:

❑ **Syntax:**
```
HRESULT PutDictValue (IDictionary*    pdict,
                      LPCWSTR         name,
                      LPCWSTR         value);
HRESULT PutDictValue (IDictionary*    pdict,
                      LPCWSTR         name,
                      VARIANT&        value);
HRESULT GetDictValue (IDictionary*    pdict,
                      LPCWSTR         name,
                      int             value);
```

❑ **Parameters:**
Pdict	The instance of `IDictionary` to which the Name/Value pair must be written
Name	The name of the Name/Value pair that must be stored
Value	The value that must be stored. Its actual type depends on the version of the function that is being called.

You can also loop through the contents of a `Dictionary` object by using three functions that are used to extract the enumeration interface from it:

❑ **Syntax:**
```
HRESULT InitKeyEnumInDict (IDictionary*      pdict,
                           IEnumVARIANT**    ppenum);
```

❑ **Parameters:**
Pdict	The instance of `IDictionary` that must be enumerated
ppenum	A pointer to the `IEnumVARIANT` pointer that will receive the enumeration interface. `IEnumVARIANT` is a standard COM interface used for enumeration

❑ **Syntax:**
```
HRESULT GetNextKeyInDict (IEnumVARIANT*    penum,
                          BSTR*            pbstrkey);
```

❑ **Parameters:**
penum	The enumeration interface of the `Dictionary` object from which the
next	available key should be extracted
pbstrkey	A pointer to the **BSTR** variable that will receive the name of the next Name/Value pair in the `Dictionary`

❑ **Syntax:**
```
HRESULT DeInitKeyEnumInDict (IEnumVARIANT**          ppenum);
```

❑ **Parameters:**
ppenum	The enumeration interface that has to be released

As you may have imagined, in order to use the enumeration functions we must first of all obtain an enumeration interface by calling `InitKeyEnumInDict`, then we can start looping through the object's Name/Value pairs using `GetNextKeyInDict`. This function only changes the value of the `pbstrkey` parameter if the retrieval operation is successful; therefore, we can determine whether we are at the end of the list by initializing the parameter to NULL before calling the function. Once we're done with the enumeration, we *must* release the enumeration object by calling the `DeInitKeyEnumInDict` function.

Here's an example that goes through the entire main dictionary:

```
IDictionary      *dict;
IEnumVARIANT     *penum;
BSTR             pname;

// We'll assume that the dictionary is already loaded

// Get an enumeration interface for the dictionary

InitKeyEnumInDict (&dict, &penum);

// Now, start looping through the dictionary
// until GetNextKeyInDict stops changing the value or pname

do
{
   pname = NULL;
   GetNextKeyInDict (penum, &pname);

   // Use the pair here
}
while (pname);

// Release the enumeration object

DeInitKeyEnumInDict (&penum);
```

It's important to understand that `GetNextKeyInDict` does not return the actual values of the Name/Value pairs in the `Dictionary` object, but rather their name part. Therefore, you will still have to use either a `GetDictValue` or `PutDictValue` function in order to access the pairs.

Naturally, you can also extract a `SimpleList` object from within a `Dictionary`. There are two global functions for doing so: the first, `GetListFromDict`, is a generic function that can be used to extract a `SimpleList` if the name of the Name/Value pair that holds it inside the `Dictionary` object is known:

❑ **Syntax:**
```
HRESULT GetListFromDict (IDictionary*   pdict,
                         LPCWSTR          wszName,
                         ISimpleList**    pplist);
```

❑ **Parameters:**

pdict	The Dictionary object from which the SimpleList should be retrieved
wszName	The name of the Name/Value pair that holds the SimpleList object
pplist	A pointer to the ISimpleList pointer that will receive the SimpleList object

The second function provides us with a shortcut for retrieving the Items collection of an OrderForm object:

❑ **Syntax:**
```
HRESULT GetListItems (IDictionary*    pdict,
                      ISimpleList**    pplistItems);
```

❑ **Parameters:**

pdict	The OrderForm object from which the Items collection should be retrieved
pplistItems	A pointer to the ISimpleList pointer that will receive the Items collection

Other Functions

The global functions also include several general-purpose functions that can be used to carry out various tasks. For example, GenUniqueID is used to generate a unique ID based on a GUID plus an optional four-byte random value:

❑ **Syntax:**
```
HRESULT GenUniqueID (unsigned short* buf,
                     BOOL* fAddRandom,);
```

❑ **Parameters:**

buf	The buffer that will receive the unique ID
faddRandom	Specifies whether an optional 4-byte long random value should be appended to the GUID generated by the function

The unique ID is returned in base 32 as an array of Unicode characters (which means that the buffer passed on to the function must be at least 64 bytes long).

At times, you will need to extract text messages from the store's MessageManager object (which is located in the context dictionary). The GetMsgFromMsgMan function will help you do this:

❑ **Syntax:**
```
HRESULT GetMsgFromMsgMan (IDispatch*    pdispMsgMan,
                          LPCWSTR*      wszErrMsgName,
                          BSTR*         pbstrMessage);
```

❑ **Parameters:**

PdispMsgMan	The instance of IDispatch that points to the MessageManager object
WszErrMsgName	The name of the error message that has to be extracted
PbstrMessage	A pointer to the BSTR variable that will receive the error.

If you need to report an error into an OrderForm, however, you should usually both extract the message from the pipeline's context, and then store it into either _Purchase_Errors or _Basket_Errors. You can also use the AddErrToList global function, which will do all the work for you!

❏ **Syntax:**
HRESULT AddErrToList (IDictionary*   pdictOrder,
                                         LPCWSTR   wszErrListName,
                                         IDispatch*   pdispContext,
                                         LPCWSTR   wszErrMsgName);

❏ **Parameters:**

pdictOrder	The OrderForm object where the error will be stored
wszErrListName	The name of the error list to use
pdispContext	The pipeline's context, still in its IDispatch form, from whose MessageManager object the error message will extracted
wszErrMsgName	The name of the error message that should be extracted

The next two functions let us extract typed values from a Variant variable:

❏ **Syntax:**
HRESULT GetNumValueOfVariant (VARIANT*   pvar,
                                                int*   pvalue);

❏ **Parameters:**

pvar	A pointer to the Variant variable whose integer value must be extracted
pvalue	A pointer to the integer variable that will receive the value

❏ **Syntax:**
HRESULT GetStringValueOfVariant (VARIANT*   pvar,
                                                BSTR*   pvalue);

❏ **Parameters:**

pvar	A pointer to the Variant variable whose string value should be extracted
pvalue	A pointer to the string variable that will receive the value

Accessing the Registry

As we've had a chance to find out while developing our Visual Basic component, the Registry plays an important role in making a pipeline component work correctly. The problem with the VB component is that it won't be easy to deploy, since you will have to somehow force the user to add one or more Registry keys manually. You could, naturally, either write a Registry script or even an installation program to do so, but it would still be less practical than taking advantage of the fact that a COM dll must be able to register itself and, therefore, contain code to do so.

In VB, you do not have access to this code – and, even if you did, you wouldn't have the appropriate functions handy to use the Registry. In VC, however, the UpdateRegistry method of each component is promptly available to the developer. By default, they call the standard methods that register your object's main features, such as the ClassID, the threading model, and so on. However, nothing prevents you from adding your own code to them, and the pipeline component template provides three very helpful functions for doing so.

`RegisterCATID` can be used to add an entry to the **Implemented Category** key, and thus to mark a pipeline component as such, as well as specifying what stages it has affinity with:

- ❑ **Syntax:**
  HRESULT RegisterCATID (const CLSID&   clsid,
                               IID newCATID);

- ❑ **Parameters:**
clsid	The Class ID of the component
pvalue	The ID of the category that has to be added

The file `Pipe_Stages.h`, which we encountered while discussing the creation of a component in VB, can be included directly in our project, so that we will be able to use the symbols that have been defined for us by the SSCE team, rather than having to deal with GUIDs directly. For example, to register a pipeline component as such, we can use the symbol `CATID_MSCSPIPELINE_COMPONENT`, and so on.

You have probably noticed how the name displayed by the pipeline editor for the built-in components is not the same as the one that is stored as the component's main name in the Registry: for example, **DefaultShipping** is really called **Commerce.DefaultShipping**. Although the same doesn't happen with the components we create, this is not simply a consequence of the fact the editor already "knows" about the built-in components. In fact, the editor is looking at what is known as the "short display name" of the object, which VB sets normally to the Program ID of the object itself. The global function `RegisterName` lets us specify our own choice of name from within the component registration method:

- ❑ **Syntax:**
  HRESULT RegisterName (const CLSID & clsid,
                               LPCWSTR wszName);

- ❑ **Parameters:**
clsid	The Class ID of the component
wszName	The short display name for the component

If you are using your components within a transaction-enabled pipeline, you should specify what threading models they support by creating the **ThreadingModel** entry in the **InProcServer32** sub-key. As you may know, the possible threading models are the following:

Model	Value of ThreadingModel
Single	None (the entry should not be made)
Apartment	Apartment
Free	Free
Both	Both

The `RegisterThreadingModel` global function can be used to create the threading model entry from the component's registration methods:

❑ **Syntax:**
HRESULT RegisterThreadingModel (const CLSID&clsid,
LPCWSTR wszThreadingModel);

❑ **Parameters:**

Clsid	The Class ID of the component
WszThreadingModel	The string to store in the ThreadingModel entry

What's the Deal with HRESULT?

As you may have noticed, all the functions that we have seen so far return a value of type `HRESULT`. This is because often the functions they call do the same thing, and it's certainly more convenient to maintain this convention up to the highest level. The values returned by the functions can vary, although they are all documented in the MSDN library; in general, if a function succeeds, it returns `S_OK`, while any other value corresponds to some error condition. In particular, a return value equal to `E_INVALIDARG` means that at least one of the parameters you passed to the function is invalid. Common instances include passing a wrong type (for example, an `IDispatch` pointer where `IDictionary` was needed) and so on.

Getting Started with the Code

Similar to what happened for the VB component, the component is run by calling the `Execute` method that it inherits from `IPipelineComponent`. We will attempt to port the functionality of the VB component into VC (this might also be interesting if you want to run some performance comparisons between the two versions), so we'll start by defining the three global variables that we need as part of the public declarations of the component's class, `CVCShippingSpecial`. We'll do this in the `VCShippingSpecial.h` include file:

```
long    lLowerBound = 0;
long    lUpperBound = 0;
long    lShippingPrice = 0;
```

Next, we'll write the implementation of `Execute` so that it calculates the number of items in the `OrderForm` and, if appropriate, applies the correct discount.

```
STDMETHODIMP CVCShippingSpecial::Execute(
            IDispatch*  pdispOrder,
            IDispatch*  pdispContext,
            LONG        lFlags,
            LONG*       plErrorLevel)
{
    VARIANT             varDummy;
    IDictionary         *lpdictOrderform = NULL;

    ISimpleList         *lpItems = NULL;
    IDictionary         *lpItem = NULL;
    long                lItemCount;
    long                lProductCount;
```

```
   long              i;
   int               lItemQty;

   *plErrorLevel = OPPERRORLEV_SUCCESS // Let's be optimistic here!

   // First, let's get an IDictionary pointer to the Orderform

   if (GetDictFromDispatch (pdispOrder, &lpdictOrderform) != S_OK)
      goto labelError;

   // Next, check whether the shipping cost has already been set

   if (GetDictValue (lpdictOrderform, L"_shipping_total", &varDummy) != S_OK)
      goto labelError;

   if (!((varDummy.vt == VT_NULL) || (varDummy.vt == VT_EMPTY)))
      return S_OK;

   // Now, let's find out how many items are in the order

   lItemCount = 0;

   if (GetListItems (lpdictOrderform, &lpItems) != S_OK)
      goto labelError;

   if (GetNumItems (lpItems, &lProductCount) != S_OK)
   goto labelError;

   for (i = 0; i < lProductCount; i++)
   {
      if (GetNthItem (lpItems, i, &lpItem) != S_OK)
         goto labelError;

      if (GetDictValue (lpItem, L"Quantity", &lItemQty) != S_OK)
         goto labelError;

      lItemCount += lItemQty;

      lpItem->Release();
      lpItem = NULL;
   }

   lpItems->Release();
   lpItems = NULL;

   // Apply the discount, if appropriate

   if ((lItemCount > lLowerBound) && (lItemCount > lUpperBound))
      PutDictValue (lpdictOrderform, L"_shipping_total", (int) (lShippingPrice));

   // Exit (successful)

   lpdictOrderform->Release();
   lpdictOrderform = NULL;
```

```
        return S_OK;

    // Exit (unsuccessful)

labelError:

    if (lpItem)
    {
        lpItem->Release();
        lpItem = NULL;
    }

    if (lpItems)
    {
        lpItems->Release();
        lpItems = NULL;
    }

    if (lpdictOrderform)
    {
        lpdictOrderform->Release();
        lpdictOrderform = NULL;
    }

    // Return failure code

    *plErrorLevel = OPPERRORLEV_FAIL;
}
```

As you can see, the code is a little more complex than before. In particular, there are a number of checks that we must continuously perform in order to make sure that any call to global functions and methods of the various interfaces that we use are successful. In our case, we limit ourselves to returning a failure error code, although we could do exactly the same thing that VB does: raise a runtime error through normal COM mechanisms. Considering the errors that we were trying to trap, obviously, we couldn't use the error SimpleList objects within the OrderForm.

Providing the Component's Information Structures

If we take a look at our project, we will notice that the ATL wizard has already created all the methods we need to implement the IPipelineComponentDescription interface; as such, all we need to do is add the code!

C++ arrays are not good enough for us here, since COM uses SafeArray objects to store arrays, which we will have to use to pass along the values read and written by our component. Luckily, the template already contains most of the code needed to implement them. Therefore, making the changes needed to return the values that the component uses is a breeze:

```
//
// IPipelineComponentDescription Methods
//

STDMETHODIMP CVCShippingSpecial::ContextValuesRead(VARIANT *pVarRead)
```

```
{

    // allocate the safearray of VARIANTs

    SAFEARRAY*    psa = SafeArrayCreateVector(VT_VARIANT, 0, 0);

    // set up the return value to point to the safearray

    V_VT(pVarRead) = VT_ARRAY | VT_VARIANT;
    V_ARRAY(pVarRead) = psa;

    return S_OK;
}

STDMETHODIMP CVCShippingSpecial::ValuesRead(VARIANT *pVarRead)
{
    VARIANT        varElement;
    long           i;

    // allocate the safearray of VARIANTs

    SAFEARRAY*    psa = SafeArrayCreateVector(VT_VARIANT, 0, 2);

    // Populate the safearray variants

    i = 0;

    varElement.bstrVal = SysAllocString (L"Item.Quantity");
    varElement.vt = VT_BSTR;

    SafeArrayPutElement (psa, &i, &varElement);

    i = 1;

    varElement.bstrVal = SysAllocString (L"_shipping_total");
    varElement.vt = VT_BSTR;

    SafeArrayPutElement (psa, &i, &varElement);

    // set up the return value to point to the safearray

    V_VT(pVarRead) = VT_ARRAY | VT_VARIANT;
    V_ARRAY(pVarRead) = psa;

    return S_OK;
}

STDMETHODIMP CVCShippingSpecial::ValuesWritten(VARIANT *pVarWritten)
{
    // allocate the safearray of VARIANTs

    SAFEARRAY*    psa = SafeArrayCreateVector(VT_VARIANT, 0, 1);
```

```
        // Populate the safearray variants

        VARIANT* pvarT = (VARIANT*)psa->pvData;
        V_BSTR(pvarT) = SysAllocString(L"[Optional] _shipping_total");
        V_VT(pvarT) = VT_BSTR;

        // set up the return value to point to the safearray

        V_VT(pVarWritten) = VT_ARRAY | VT_VARIANT;
        V_ARRAY(pVarWritten) = psa;
        return S_OK;
}
```

These few lines of code demonstrate three possible approaches to creating the `SafeArray` objects that we need in order to return the values accessed by our component. The first method, `ContextValuesRead` returns an empty array. This is a slightly different approach from what we did in VB (where we passed an array that contained the string [None]). In VC, we can pass an empty array, and the editor automatically recognizes it.

The second approach uses the `SafeArrayPutElement` method to add the strings to the `SafeArray` object. As you can imagine, code like this works well only if you access only a few values (which is usually the case). For larger arrays, you might want to implement a loop that reads the values from a constant standard array defined globally.

The third approach, which is the one provided by the template, works well if you have to return only one value. In this case, the `pvData` member of the `SafeArray` structure can be used directly as the pointer to the only element of the array.

Working with Properties

As before, our first step in adding properties to our component is to expose them through normal COM mechanisms. To do so, all we have to do is right-click on `IVCShippingSpecial` in the project explorer and add three properties: `LowerBound`, `UpperBound` and `ShippingCost`. Next, we'll have to write their implementation, which, as you can see below, is not at all complex:

```
STDMETHODIMP CVCShippingSpecial::get_LowerBound(VARIANT *pVal)
{
    pVal->lVal = lLowerBound;
    pVal->vt = VT_I4;

    return S_OK;
}

STDMETHODIMP CVCShippingSpecial::put_LowerBound(VARIANT newVal)
{
    HRESULT hr;

    // Attempt to convert variant to long integer

    hr = VariantChangeType (&newVal, &newVal, 0, VT_I4);
```

```
    if (hr == S_OK)
        lLowerBound = newVal.lVal;

    return hr;
}

STDMETHODIMP CVCShippingSpecial::get_UpperBound(VARIANT *pVal)
{
    pVal->lVal = lUpperBound;
    pVal->vt = VT_I4;

    return S_OK;
}

STDMETHODIMP CVCShippingSpecial::put_UpperBound(VARIANT newVal)
{
    HRESULT hr;

    // Attempt to convert variant to long integer

    hr = VariantChangeType (&newVal, &newVal, 0, VT_I4);

    if (hr == S_OK)
        lUpperBound = newVal.lVal;

    return hr;
}

STDMETHODIMP CVCShippingSpecial::get_ShippingPrice(VARIANT *pVal)
{
    pVal->lVal = lShippingPrice;
    pVal->vt = VT_I4;

    return S_OK;
}

STDMETHODIMP CVCShippingSpecial::put_ShippingPrice(VARIANT newVal)
{
    HRESULT hr;

    // Attempt to convert variant to long integer

    hr = VariantChangeType (&newVal, &newVal, 0, VT_I4);

    if (hr == S_OK)
        lShippingPrice = newVal.lVal;

    return hr;
}
```

All three properties are exposed as Variants, because that's the native language used by VBScript (in fact, VBScript is only able to create Variants, and the only way to pass variables of a specific type is to typecast them). Obviously, this means that we'll have to handle all the conversion from Variant to long integer within the code, but even that is quite easy to do, thanks to the built-in Variant-manipulation function, `VariantChangeType`.

Next, we'll have to create and implement a property page. To do so, we'll use another ATL wizard, which we'll start by selecting New ATL Object... from the Insert menu, clicking on Controls and, finally, double-clicking on Property Page. I've called my property page Wrox.VCSSProp, and left all the other settings as they were. In your implementation, you might want to change the title of the property page from "Title" to something more significant, though!

When the property page is first displayed, its Activate method is called. We'll use it to load and convert the property values from our component:

```
STDMETHODIMP CVCSSProp::Activate (HWND hWndParent, LPCRECT pRect, BOOL fModal)
{
    VARIANT varPropValue;

    IPropertyPageImpl<CVCSSProp>::Activate(hWndParent, pRect, fModal);

    // First, retrieve a pointer to the component

    CComQIPtr<IVCShippingSpecial,
                        &IID_IVCShippingSpecial>pVCShippingSpecial(m_ppUnk[0]);

    // Next, retrieve all the properties and set the text boxes appropriately

    // ...Retrieve value

    pVCShippingSpecial->get_LowerBound (&varPropValue);

    // ...Convert to string

    VariantChangeType (&varPropValue, &varPropValue, 0, VT_BSTR);

    // ...Store in text box

    SetDlgItemText (IDC_LBOUND, varPropValue.bstrVal);

    // Now for the others

    pVCShippingSpecial->get_UpperBound (&varPropValue);
    VariantChangeType (&varPropValue, &varPropValue, 0, VT_BSTR);
    SetDlgItemText (IDC_UBOUND, varPropValue.bstrVal);

    pVCShippingSpecial->get_ShippingPrice (&varPropValue);
    VariantChangeType (&varPropValue, &varPropValue, 0, VT_BSTR);
    SetDlgItemText (IDC_SCOST, varPropValue.bstrVal);

    SetDirty (FALSE);

    return S_OK;
}
```

As you can see, we have to juggle a little bit with the fact that the properties are exposed as Variants, but, as you can see below, they come in pretty handy when we're going to respond to a request to apply the changes that the user has made to them in the `Apply` method:

```
STDMETHODIMP CVCSSProp::Apply(void)
    {
    VARIANT         varLBound;
    VARIANT         varUBound;
    VARIANT         varSPrice;
    CComBSTR    combstrTextboxValue;

    // Obtain a pointer to our pipeline object
    // We'll only have one object at a time, so we'll directly get the first
    // IUnknown interface

    CComQIPtr<IVCShippingSpecial,
                        &IID_IVCShippingSpecial>pVCShippingSpecial(m_ppUnk[0]);

    // Get the lower boundary, check it for validity

    GetDlgItemText (IDC_LBOUND, combstrTextboxValue.m_str);

    varLBound.vt = VT_BSTR;
    varLBound.bstrVal = SysAllocString (combstrTextboxValue);

    if (VariantChangeType (&varLBound, &varLBound, 0, VT_I4) != S_OK)
    {
        MessageBox (L"Lower bound must be a valid integer number", L"ERROR",
                                            MB_OK | MB_ICONEXCLAMATION);
        return E_UNEXPECTED;
    }

    if (varLBound.lVal < 0)
    {
        MessageBox (L"Lower bound must be greater then zero", L"ERROR",
                                            MB_OK | MB_ICONEXCLAMATION);
        return E_UNEXPECTED;
    }

    // Now, get the upper boundary, check it for validity

    GetDlgItemText (IDC_UBOUND, combstrTextboxValue.m_str);

    varUBound.vt = VT_BSTR;.
    varUBound.bstrVal = SysAllocString (combstrTextboxValue);

    if (VariantChangeType (&varUBound, &varUBound, 0, VT_I4) != S_OK)
    {
        MessageBox (L"Upper bound must be a valid integer number", L"ERROR",
                                            MB_OK | MB_ICONEXCLAMATION);
        return E_UNEXPECTED;
    }
```

```
    if (varUBound.lVal < 0)
    {
        MessageBox (L"Upper bound must be greater then zero", L"ERROR",
                                        MB_OK | MB_ICONEXCLAMATION);
        return E_UNEXPECTED;
    }

    // Finally, it's the shipping cost's turn

    GetDlgItemText (IDC_SCOST, combstrTextboxValue.m_str);

    varSPrice.vt = VT_BSTR;
    varSPrice.bstrVal = SysAllocString (combstrTextboxValue);

    if (VariantChangeType (&varSPrice, &varSPrice, 0, VT_I4) != S_OK)
    {
        MessageBox (L"Shipping cost must be a valid integer number", L"ERROR",
                                        MB_OK | MB_ICONEXCLAMATION);
        return E_UNEXPECTED;
    }

    if (varSPrice.lVal < 0)
    {
        MessageBox (L"Shipping must be greater then zero", L"ERROR",
                                        MB_OK | MB_ICONEXCLAMATION);
        return E_UNEXPECTED;
    }

    // If all values OK, then save them to our component

    pVCShippingSpecial->put_LowerBound (varLBound);
    pVCShippingSpecial->put_UpperBound (varUBound);
    pVCShippingSpecial->put_ShippingPrice (varSPrice);

    SetDirty (FALSE);
    return S_OK;
    }
```

In this code, we take full advantage of the `VariantChangeType` function to check whether the user has inserted a valid integer value. Variants also come in handy to manage all the text values that come from the input boxes, which are in wide-character format. Finally, you should be very careful (both in the `Activate` and `Apply` methods) to properly set the "dirty" flag so that the caller (that is, the editor) knows that any changes to the edit boxes have been properly taken care of.

The task is not yet complete, though. In fact, we're still missing a real-time response to the changes in our input boxes. You have probably noticed that the Apply button in the editor's properties dialog box is initially grayed, and that it becomes active as soon as one of the properties is changed. In order to do this, we should set the "dirty" flag to TRUE whenever we detect a change in our input boxes; we can do so by handling the `OnChange` method for all three of them:

```
LRESULT CVCSSProp::OnChangeLbound(WORD wNotifyCode, WORD wID, HWND hWndCtl, BOOL&
bHandled)
```

```
{
    if (wNotifyCode == EN_CHANGE)
        SetDirty (TRUE);
    return 0;
}

LRESULT CVCSSProp::OnChangeScost(WORD wNotifyCode, WORD wID, HWND hWndCtl,
                                                    BOOL& bHandled)
{
    if (wNotifyCode == EN_CHANGE)
        SetDirty (TRUE);
    return 0;
}

LRESULT CVCSSProp::OnChangeUbound(WORD wNotifyCode, WORD wID, HWND hWndCtl,
                                                    BOOL& bHandled)
{
    if (wNotifyCode == EN_CHANGE)
        SetDirty (TRUE);
    return 0;
}
```

> **When trying to compile the component after adding the property page, the linker might complain about being unable to find the _main entry point. This is caused by the fact that some of your functions now require the CRT library, which, by default, is excluded by an ATL project in order to save space. To eliminate this problem, just go to the project properties and remove the pre-processor directive called _ATL_MIN_CRT.**

We're still missing support for access to the properties through the configuration dictionary. Since our project does not yet support the IPipelineComponentAdmin interface, we'll have to implement it ourselves. We can do so by right-clicking on CVCShippingSpecial in the project explorer and selecting Implement Interface. In order for VC to recognize the interface, we'll have to point it to the right type library, located in the \lib_386\pipe_comp.tlb, by clicking on the Add typelib button.

Once the pipeline is implemented, the system will add the GetConfigData and SetConfigData members to our component, which we will implement with this simple code – similar, at least conceptually, to the code we wrote for the VB version of the component:

```
STDMETHODIMP CVCShippingSpecial::GetConfigData (IDispatch * * ppDict)
{
    IDictionary *dictCData;

    if (ppDict == NULL)
        return E_POINTER;

    if (CoCreateInstance (CLSID_CDictionary, NULL, CLSCTX_INPROC_SERVER,
                            IID_IDictionary, (void **) (&dictCData)) != S_OK)
        return E_UNEXPECTED;
```

```
        PutDictValue (dictCData, L"LowerBound", lLowerBound);
        PutDictValue (dictCData, L"UpperBound", lUpperBound);
        PutDictValue (dictCData, L"ShippingPrice", lShippingPrice);

        dictCData->QueryInterface (IID_IDispatch, (void **) ppDict);

        dictCData->Release();

        return S_OK;
    }

    STDMETHODIMP CVCShippingSpecial::SetConfigData (IDispatch * pDict)
    {
        IDictionary *dictCData;

        GetDictFromDispatch (pDict, &dictCData);

        GetDictValue (dictCData, L"LowerBound", (int *) &lLowerBound);
        GetDictValue (dictCData, L"UpperBound", (int *) &lUpperBound);
        GetDictValue (dictCData, L"ShippingPrice", (int *) &lShippingPrice);

        dictCData->Release();

        return E_NOTIMPL;
    }
```

Finally, we'll have to be able to read and write the properties to a pipeline configuration file. Visual C++ does not directly support the concept of "property bags" that we found in VB. Therefore, we'll have to resort to the mechanism that sits behind it from a low-level COM perspective.

Using IPersistStreamInit

`IPersistStreamInit` is a standard COM interface that is used to save data to and load data from a streaming storage medium, such as a file or a database field. A pipeline component needs to support it in order for the editor to load and save its configuration. Obviously, if the component does not expose any properties, it doesn't need to implement this interface, too. Also, you will only need to deal with this interface in Visual C++, since VB provides support for it through its property bags mechanism.

The `InitNew` method is called whenever a new instance of the component is created from scratch, rather than loaded from a storage medium:

❑ **Syntax:**
HRESULT IPersistStreamInit::InitNew (void);

Although you normally don't have to do much in this method, you must implement it, and you can use it to initialize the properties that your component exposes if necessary. When a component is instead loaded from a storage medium, the pipeline editor (or pipeline object) will call the `Load` method:

- **Syntax:**
  HRESULT IPersistStreamInit::Load (IStream *pStm // in);

- **Parameters:**
  PStm   An instance of `IStream` from which the component properties are to be read.

Reading from an instance of `IStream`, as we'll see later on, is not a very complex operation. All you have to do is use the `Read` method defined below:

- **Syntax:**
  HRESULT IStream::Read (void*   pv, // out
                                        ULONG   cb, // out
                                        ULONG*   pcbRead // in);

- **Parameters:**
  Pv   Pointer to a buffer that will receive the information read
  Cb   Number of bytes to read
  ocbRead   Number of bytes actually read

As for any streaming operation, you will have to save your data in a way that it will be possible to easily retrieve it from the stream. For example, if you decide to save a string, you must do so by making sure that the `Load` method will know how long the string is *before* reading the data from the stream. In general, you should use the built-in COM Variant variables available to an ATL VC++ project when developing your components, since they interface directly with `IPersistStreamInit`.

When it comes to saving a component's property to a stream, a particular sequence of events takes place. First of all, the editor will call the `IsDirty` method to establish whether the component has been saved since the last time it was recorded that it was saved.

- **Syntax:**
  HRESULT IPersistStreamInit::IsDirty (void);

`IsDirty` should return `S_OK` if the component's properties have been modified, and `S_FALSE` if it hasn't. It's a good idea to always return `S_OK`, so that there is never the possibility that certain information will not be saved.

If `IsDirty` indicates that the component's data should be saved, the editor calls the `GetSizeMax` method to determine how much space on the stream is required to save the information:

- **Syntax:**
  HRESULT IPersistStreamInit::GetSizeMax (ULARGE_INTEGER*   pcbSize // out);

- **Parameters:**
  pcbSize   A pointer to a 64-bit integer variable that receives the number of bytes required to save the object.

GetSizeMax should always return the upper bound of the possible space required to save the object, even though the actual requirements might end up being lower. This is because the stream that you might receive for saving the data could be limited in size to the amount returned by the method.

Finally, the data is saved to the stream using the Save method:

❑ **Syntax:**
HRESULT IPersistStreamInit::Save (IStream* pStm // out, BOOL fClearDirty);

❑ **Parameters:**

fClearDirty	A flag that indicates whether the dirty flag should be cleared.
pStm	An instance of IStream to which the component properties are to be written.

The "dirty" flag is simply an indication of whether the component has been modified or not since the last time it was saved

Similar to what happened for the Load method, the IStream interface provides us with the appropriate method for writing data to it:

❑ **Syntax:**
HRESULT IStream::Write (void const *   pv, // out
                        ULONG   cb, // out
                        ULONG*   pcbWritten // in);

❑ **Parameters:**

pv	Pointer to the buffer that holds the data to be written
cb	Number of bytes to write
pcbWritten	Number of bytes actually written to the stream

Writing the Code

The only trick with using IPersistInit in our component is to read and write data to the stream in the correct order:

```
STDMETHODIMP CVCShippingSpecial::Load(IStream *pStm)
{
    HRESULT hRes = S_OK;

    pStm->Read (&lLowerBound, sizeof (long), NULL);
    pStm->Read (&lUpperBound, sizeof (long), NULL);
    pStm->Read (&lShippingPrice, sizeof (long), NULL);

    return hRes;
}

STDMETHODIMP CVCShippingSpecial::Save(IStream *pStm, BOOL fClearDiry)
{
    HRESULT hRes = S_OK;
```

```
    pStm->Write (&lLowerBound, sizeof (long), NULL);
    pStm->Write (&lUpperBound, sizeof (long), NULL);
    pStm->Write (&lShippingPrice, sizeof (long), NULL);

    return hRes;
}

STDMETHODIMP CVCShippingSpecial::GetSizeMax(ULARGE_INTEGER *pcbSize)
{
    // TODO: Modify size to be the size of your data
    pcbSize->LowPart  = sizeof (long) * 3;
    pcbSize->HighPart = 0;
    return S_OK;
}

STDMETHODIMP CVCShippingSpecial::InitNew(void)
{
    // TODO: Add any component initialization

    lLowerBound = 0;
    lUpperBound = 0;
    lShippingPrice = 0;

    return S_OK;
}
```

You will have probably noticed that I have also implemented the `InitNew` method that we didn't take into account in the VB version of the component: this is because VB automatically initializes all long integer variables to zero, while VC doesn't do the same. Therefore, we'll have to manually force zero values on our properties.

The implementation of `GetSizeMax` is also included here – as mentioned earlier, it's necessary to implement it in order for the `IStream` object to be sized properly.

Allowing the Editors to Recognize our Component

Thanks to the global functions generated by the ATL wizard, creating the appropriate Registry entries to make the component visible in the editor is extremely easy. We'll even change the "short display name" to something more pleasing to the eye, while we will not worry about specifying a threading model because our component is not transaction-friendly. As discussed above, the right place all this can be done is the `UpdateRegistry` method, which we'll modify as follows:

```
static HRESULT WINAPI UpdateRegistry(BOOL bRegister)
{
    HRESULT hr = _Module.UpdateRegistryClass(GetObjectCLSID(),
            _T("Wrox.VCShippingSpecial.1"), _T("Wrox.VCShippingSpecial"),
            IDS_PROJNAME, THREADFLAGS_BOTH, bRegister);

    wchar_t wsName[50] = L"Wrox Shipping Special";

    if (SUCCEEDED(hr))
```

```
        {
            // TODO: Add stage affinities here
            hr = RegisterCATID(GetObjectCLSID(), CATID_MSCSPIPELINE_COMPONENT);
            hr = RegisterCATID(GetObjectCLSID(), CATID_MSCSPIPELINE_SHIPPING);
            hr = RegisterName (GetObjectCLSID(), &wsName[0]);
        }
        return hr;
    };
```

If we now try to add the component using the Win32 editor, it will show the short name – which is much easier to understand than the Program ID!

Summary

Well, that's all you need to know about writing pipeline components. The most important lesson that you should have learned from this chapter is that it's *not* a bad idea to try and take advantage of both VC and VB when developing pipeline components. I hope that you have found writing a component in VC complex (but not complicated) enough to make you think about using VB for your prototypes. At the same time, a few serious speed benchmark tests will convince you that VC is the ideal solution for a production environment.

A final note: because pipeline components are just another kind of COM object, your choice of programming language for developing new components is not limited to VB and VC. In fact, you can use just about any compiler that supports the COM standard, including Visual J++ or other third party tools, such as Borland C++ Builder, and so on. It might be an interesting exercise, if you are not familiar with VC, but are familiar with one of the other packages, to compare the performance of components written using the latter and VB – you might end up with something faster and more stable for your production environment.

Extending the Microsoft Wallet

*Our life is frittered away by
detail...Simplify, simplify.*
–Henry David Thoreau, *Walden*

In Chapter 13, we took a good look at how the Microsoft Wallet can be used to make the most of the shopping experience of our customers. As we have seen, there are a few special considerations that we have to make when deciding to include the Wallet in our own store, so that it doesn't become a nuisance rather than a help to our visitors.

If we're evaluating the Wallet for our own purposes – or for those of a client – one of the major points of concern will be the fact that it only supports a limited number of payment systems and, although all the most commonly used credit cards are supported, we might want to implement a custom payment method that is not already part of it.

The good news is, as mentioned earlier in the book, that the Wallet *can* be extended to include virtually any payment system that we can imagine, from private-label credit cards to innovative micro-payment systems specifically designed for use on the Internet. In addition, the Wallet can be used in special scenarios, such as a business-to-business application where Purchase Orders are used instead of credit cards and office numbers replace ship-to addresses.

What Does This Chapter Talk About?

Throughout Chapter 15, we will examine how the Microsoft Wallet can be extended, as well as what tools are needed to extend it. To better understand all of these concepts, we'll write a simple extension that will make it possible to enable the Wallet to support a new credit card type.

The chapter is divided into two parts:

❑ **Tools**
First of all, we'll take a look at the tools that we need to build extensions to the Wallet's architecture. It's very important that we examine these requirements carefully before we decide whether creating Wallet components is really for us.

❑ **Creating a new credit card type**
Next, we'll look at how it is possible to have the Wallet accept custom credit card types by simply extending the built-in interface that already supports all the major credit cards. Thanks to the tools available from Microsoft, writing the new component is as easy as modifying an existing Visual C++ template.

Tools

It's not particularly difficult to see how the Wallet must be a very secure application, since it has to handle such sensitive information as addresses and payment data. Even in its extensible architecture, therefore, one would expect to find a high level of security built-in.

As we have mentioned earlier, the Wallet is entirely based on the Microsoft COM technology; this is true regardless of whether we are running Internet Explorer or Netscape: in the latter case, although a different kind of interface is required for the Wallet to communicate with the browser, the architecture that allows us to write extensions will still be COM-based.

While COM gives us the advantage of a simplified approach to writing our own components, it also poses one big risk – virtually every site will be able to have a user download and install a new Wallet extension. Therefore, it's essential that the overall architecture be protected from malicious components that may compromise the user's information.

The Wallet solves this problem by requiring that all the components installed in it be digitally signed using a digital certificate that is recognized by the client computer, at least in the case of Internet Explorer. If a digital signature is not present or is corrupt, the Wallet will simply refuse to install the component, without even giving the user a choice (a wise decision to prevent inexperienced shoppers from inadvertently installing a Trojan horse). In Internet Explorer, however, the options presented to the user are based upon the security setting of low/medium/high which is set based on the location of the component to be downloaded (either from the Internet or an intranet).

As a result, if we are thinking about writing a Wallet extension, we must also consider that we will have to purchase a digital certificate from a recognized Certificate Authority (CA). VeriSign seems to be the only CA willing to release this kind of certificate, and they don't sell them cheap: one of them will cost $400 (US) for a two-year license. There are other CA providers mentioned in the Certificate Authority list in Internet Explorer, however, one of which you can find out more about at http://www.thawte.com/support/developer/contents.html.

Sure enough, once we acquire our certificate we can use it for as many applications as we want, but we will still have to buy it even if we're just planning to develop that one component. Bear in mind, though, that we only need a certificate if our extension is going into production – Microsoft provides a development certificate that can be used for development and unit testing.

For more information about VeriSign, visit their website at http://www.verisign.com

What Language Should You Use?

The fact that Wallet extensions are simply COM objects that implement a certain number of interfaces gives us an ample variety of languages to choose from for developing our components. However, a simple consideration effectively restricts the field to just one choice; because our customers will have to download the component (unless we can bundle it with Internet Explorer or Netscape, which is quite unlikely): we won't really be able to use either Visual Basic or Visual J++, since they both require a large amount of support code (the Visual Basic support DLL alone, called **Msvbvm60.dll**, is over 1.25MB!) and therefore would force terribly long installation time on our visitors.

Visual C++ is really the most suitable language from which we can expect the right amount of performance to produce code that is efficient and compact enough to allow for a decent download time on slower connections. Luckily, as much as writing C++ code is more difficult than doing the same in Visual Basic, Microsoft provides a number of tools that can help us out.

The Microsoft Wallet SDK

One of the good things about the Microsoft Wallet, at least from a developer's point of view, is that Microsoft has put a lot of support behind it, probably recognizing that many programmers would need to develop their Wallet-based solutions quickly and efficiently.

If we visit the section of the Microsoft Website dedicated to the Wallet, we will be able to download a tool called the Microsoft Wallet Software Development Kit, which contains plenty of information, samples and templates that will help us get going with the Wallet. The SDK can be downloaded from the same location as the Webmaster's Kit that we saw back in Chapter 13; the URL, once again, is:

http://www.microsoft.com/wallet

As we'll see later on in the chapter, the templates contained in the SDK make it a lot easier to create a new Wallet component, since the development process consists essentially of writing the appropriate code in several well-documented spots inside one of the templates. This should make extending the Wallet appealing even to those who are not very experienced in the use of VC++ and the Active Template Library (ATL), or who do not feel like starting a new COM project from ground zero.

Other Tools You'll Need

Although it was mentioned at the beginning of this section that we are going to have to digitally sign our components in order for our users to successfully install them, we didn't examine how that can actually be done.

The Microsoft Internet SDK (InetSDK), which is part of the Microsoft Web Workshop (found at http://msdn.microsoft.com/workshop), contains all the necessary tools for signing a component or an executable so that the browser and, indirectly, the Wallet will accept it as valid. Also in that package we will find a couple of utilities that will allow us to create our own test certificates; this will help us to maximize our two-year license from VeriSign by requesting the real certificate only when we need it because we are ready to distribute our component.

Another important element of the development process is distribution. In order for a COM object to work, it has to be registered within the System Registry. Although this task can be performed manually by using the `RegSvr32` utility that comes with Windows 9x and NT, a large majority of our users will not be able to do so, even if we explain it to them step-by-step.

Therefore, we will want our component to come with an installation process that is at the same time efficient and able to run without user intervention, and that does not add too much to the overall download time. The InetSDK contains the tools needed to create installation procedures using the "cabinet" technology developed by Microsoft.

Cabinet files, which end with the '.CAB' extension, are self-contained compressed archives that all the 32-bit versions of Windows support natively. A '.CAB' file can be automatically downloaded and decompressed when properly signed. It can optionally contain a digital signature – which is automatically verified by Internet Explorer – and an installation script that can take care of copying our component's file to the appropriate location and registering them with the Windows Registry.

Incidentally, the SDK also contains a '.CAB' template that has already been designed especially for installing Wallet components. Similar to what happens with the VC++ templates, this one, too, will help us make the development process simpler.

Creating a New Credit Card Type

Let's now take a look at how it is possible to create a component that will make the Wallet able to accept a new kind of credit card. The rest of the chapter assumes that we have installed both the Wallet SDK and the InetSDK on our machine, which will make it possible for us to complete the development of the component and prepare it for deployment to our users.

The MTcard Credit Card

Generally speaking, if we have been asked (or have decided) to implement a new credit card type, we will have received a series of instructions from the card issuing company that describes the information that characterizes a credit card, as well as any algorithms that should be used to validate the information passed along by the user.

For example, most credit cards have a **cardholder's name**, an **account number** and an **expiry date**. Usually, the account number is simply a sequence of numbers starting with a specific digit (for example, all VISA cards start with a 4), often computed using the Luhn algorithm that we saw back in Chapter 5. This combination of parameters represents a de-facto standard to which all issuers adhere so that it's easier for developers of credit card software and hardware to incorporate their cards into their system; this, in turn, translates into a lower price and larger acceptance for their cards.

Therefore, there's no reason why our credit card, which we'll call **MTCard**, should be any different. In fact, we'll have a cardholder's name, an account number that will be 12 digits long and will always start with 1, and an expiry date expressed as the last day of a particular month and year.

A Simple Luhn Checksum Calculator

The account numbers of our credit card type will contain a check digit (the last one) that will be calculated using the Luhn algorithm. The account number itself, therefore, will be actually 11 digits long, while the last one will be used to verify that the number as a whole represents a valid MTCard account.

If you remember from Chapter 5, the Luhn algorithm works by multiplying all the digits in the account number alternately by one and two (starting from the rightmost one, which is multiplied by two), then summing all the digits of the resulting numbers and calculating their modulus 10 complementary, which becomes the check digit. For example:

Account number	1	2	3	4	5	6	7	8	9	0	1		
Luhn calculations	2	1	2	1	2	1	2	1	2	1	2		
Results	2	2	6	4	10	6	14	8	18	0	2	(Totals)	45

The check digit, in this case, would be the modulus 10 complementary of 45, which is 5. Therefore, the complete account number as it would appear on a hypothetical plastic card would be 1234 5678 9015.

Calculating the Check Digit in C++

Let's now take a look at a simple C++ function that we can use to calculate the Luhn check digit for our credit card numbers. We'll make it adapt easily to any account number length, so that you'll be able to reuse it in your own projects.

One thing to keep in mind when working with COM objects is that we will be handling wide-character strings, in which a single character is represented by two bytes instead of one. However, all we will need to do will be add the _T prefix whenever we refer to a string and most of the code won't have to be different from what we'd write if we were using normal ASCII strings. Here's the function:

```
BOOL LuhnValid (BSTR wsAccountNumber)
{
    int wcTemp;         // temporary value
    int iLuhnCalc;      // Luhn calculation value holder
    int iStrLen;        // Length of account number
    int i;              // Counter

    iStrLen = SysStringLen (wsAccountNumber);
    iLuhnCalc = 0;

    // Loop through all characters in the string; verify they are digits
    // and calculate Luhn sum

    for (i = 0; i < iStrLen - 2; i++)
    {
        if ((wsAccountNumber [i] < _T ("0")) || (wsAccountNumber [i] > _T ("9")))
            return FALSE;
```

```
        if ((iStrLen % 2 == i % 2))
        {
            wcTemp = (wsAccountNumber [i] - _T("0")) * 2;
            wcTemp = (wcTemp > 9) ? wcTemp : wcTemp - 9;
        }
        else
            wcTemp = wsAccountNumber [i] - _T("0");

        iLuhnCalc += wcTemp;
    }

    // Calculate and compare check digit

    return (10 - (iLuhnCalc % 10) == wsAccountNumber [iStrLen - 1] - _T ("0")) ?
TRUE : FALSE;
}
```

As you can see from the listing, the algorithm is quite easy to understand. The only portion that might be a little obscure is the if-then-else condition in the middle of the for-next loop that is used to determine whether a digit in the string should be multiplied by one or by two.

The check that is performed originates from a simple observation of the fact that when the number of digits in the account number is even (that is its modulus 2 is 0), then all the even digits in the account are to be multiplied by two, as long as you count from left to right and start from 0:

Account	1	2	3	4	5	6
Multiplier	2	1	2	1	2	Check digit
Base-0 position	0	1	2	3	4	5

Conversely, when the number of digits is odd, all the odd digits in the account must be multiplied by 2:

Account	1	2	3	4	5
Multiplier	1	2	1	2	Check digit
Base-0 position	0	1	2	3	4

Thus, a multiplication by two should occur whenever the modulus 2 of both the account number length and the counter, i, have the same value.

Opening the Credit Card Component Template

Once we have installed the Microsoft Wallet SDK, we should be able to gain access to the template that can be used to create a new credit card component. This is located in the Samples\OtherCards\VolcanoCoffee folder, and is actually a sample that has been developed by Microsoft in order to demonstrate how the technology works. As such, it's a good idea for you to make a copy of the entire folder and leave the original untouched, so that you can reuse it for your next project.

Credit Card Extension Basics

The functionality required to create and edit credit cards is provided by what actually is already an extension to the Wallet, albeit of a different type to the one we are going to write (we'll take a look at this type of extension, called *payment method*, later on in the chapter). A dead giveaway of the fact that the underlying engine powering all the credit card functions in the Wallet is always the same is the fact that, as we have certainly noticed, the user interface for accessing our VISA account is essentially the same as the one we use for our American Express card.

The credit card payment system exposes two COM interfaces, `ICreditCardOtherCard` and `IPaymentCCTypeInstall` that our extension will have to fully implement in order to be compatible with the overall architecture. Although the template already implements most of the methods required, leaving us to simply fill the gaps, it's a good idea to take a quick look at both these interfaces to better understand how the whole system works.

IPaymentCCTypeInstall

This interface is called when the payment system needs to install or uninstall a new component. Whenever it is started, the Wallet itself scans the following Registry key:

HKEY_LOCAL_MACHINE\Software\Microsoft\Internet Shopper\InstallCreditCard

This key contains a list of all the Wallet components that were installed since the last time the Wallet was run. For each component, the Wallet calls the appropriate methods of `IPaymentCCTypeInstall`, thus causing the installation procedure to begin, and then deletes the entry from the Registry.

This means that a component only has one chance to install itself properly: if an error occurs, the Wallet will simply forget about it. Therefore, if the error is caused by a condition that is recoverable, the component itself should be able to rewrite its entry in the Registry as part of its failure handling procedure. The ability for the COM-based component we are developing to be able to recover from an error such as this, however, is something that should be tested quite extensively. Recovering from a failed installation process (for whatever reason) is something we will want to ensure our component will handle under all situations. If our component cannot recover, the result can be a complete lack of functionality, and it will probably cause Windows to produce some very cryptic error messages that a user will certainly not be able to understand.

`IPaymentCCTypeInstall` supports four different functions, which are used in a very specific order. The first one is `GetInstallInfo`, which is called by the Wallet when the DLL is first installed. Its goal is to return a few generic pieces of information about the component; in particular, `GetInstallInfo` is used to establish how many credit card types are supported by the component.

❑ **Syntax:**
```
HRESULT IPaymentCCTypeInstall.GetInstallInfo(long *plCount,
    BSTR *pbstrName, BSTR *pbstrSource);
```

❑ **Parameters:**

plCount	Pointer to a long integer that must be set to the number of credit card types that are supported by this component
pbstrName	Pointer to a wide-character string containing the name of the component
pbstrSource	Pointer to a wide-character string containing the name of the manufacturer of the component

The `GetTypeInfo` method is then called in a loop for each credit card type supported by the component, with the goal of retrieving additional information about it:

❑ **Syntax:**
```
HRESULT IPaymentCCTypeInstall.GetTypeInfo(long cIndex, BSTR *pbstrType,
    BSTR *pbstrFriendlyName);
```

❑ **Parameters:**

cIndex	Long integer value that identifies a particular credit card type.
pbstrType	Pointer to a wide-character string that will contain the "short name" of the credit card type, used for internal reference.
pbstrFriendlyName	Pointer to a wide-character string containing the name of the manufacturer of the component

As you can see, there are two strings that are used to identify a credit card type. The first one is employed internally by the system to refer to the credit card type during its calls to the component, while the other is shown to the user. It's a good idea to use a smaller string in the first case and a slightly more descriptive identifier in the second.

The uninstallation of the component also takes place in two different phases. First, the Wallet calls the `SelfUninstall`, which should take care of removing each of the types supported by the component from the credit card system:

❑ **Syntax:**
```
HRESULT IPaymentCCTypeInstall.SelfUninstall();
```

❑ **Parameters:**
None

Next, the `Uninstall` method is called, with the goal of removing any reference to the component from the System Registry and deleting any support files required by it that are not shared with other active programs in the system.

❑ **Syntax:**
```
HRESULT IPaymentCCTypeInstall.Uninstall();
```

❑ **Parameters:**
None

ICreditCardOtherCard

The `ICreditCardOtherCard` interface is where the real communication between the Wallet and the component takes place. Yet, even this interface only has three methods – a clear indication of how easy extending the credit card system is! The first method that we'll look at is `GetBitmap`, which the Wallet calls whenever it needs to retrieve the bitmap associated with a specific credit card type so that it can show it to the user.

❑ **Syntax:**
```
HRESULT ICreditCardOtherCard.GetBitmap(BSTR bstrType, long fType,
    long *hBitmap);
```

❑ **Parameters:**

bstrType	Wide-character string containing the short name of the credit card type for which the bitmap is being requested
fType	Long integer value indicating the bitmap being requested: 1: Small bitmap (30 x 18 pixels) 2: Large bitmap (120 x 79 pixels) All bitmaps must use the standard 16-color system palette
hBitmap	Pointer to a bitmap handle that must be set to the handle of the bitmap being returned. Can be set to zero if no bitmap exists, in which case the Wallet will display a default bitmap.

The `GetMask` method, on the other hand, is used to determine the format of the account numbers for a specific credit card type:

❑ **Syntax:**
```
HRESULT ICreditCardOtherCard.GetMask(BSTR bstrType, long *expDate,
    BSTR *bstrMask);
```

❑ **Parameters:**

bstrType	The short name of the credit card type for which the mask is being requested
expDate	Boolean value that expresses whether the credit card type has an expiry date. A value of FALSE (0) means that no expiration date should be asked, while TRUE (1) will cause a date to be requested from the user.
bstrMask	A string that expresses the mask to be used when requesting the credit card account from the user.

The `bstrMask` parameter is used to determine the format in which the credit card system will request the credit card number from the user. The mask string can contain a combination of *constants* and *placeholders*, which should not exceed 20 characters. Constants are values that help the user to understand the account number's format better, but they cannot be modified. For example, dashes or spaces can be inserted into the number to make it more readable, but they should never be substituted by anything else.

Placeholders are instead used to indicate a position in the string that should be substituted by user input. The credit card system supports three types of placeholders:

Character	Type
A	Alphabetic characters only
N	Numeric characters only
X	Alphanumeric characters

For example, a 16-digit VISA number could be formatted as follows:

```
NNNN-NNNN-NNNN-NNNN
```

It's important to understand that the credit card system does not have a default mask of its own. Therefore, if we return an empty string as the value of bstrMask, *we will cause an error to be displayed.*

This format indicates that the account number is identified by four groups of four digits separated by a hyphen. In our case, because of the way our Luhn check digit algorithm works, we'll simply use a straight sequence of digits:

NNNNNNNNNNNN

Finally, the IsValid method is called by the Wallet whenever the user enters a new account number or modifies an existing one with the purpose of determining whether the new number still satisfies the requirements for the credit card type.

❑ **Syntax:**
```
HRESULT ICreditCardOtherCard.IsValid (BSTR bstrType, BSTR bstrNumber,
long *fValid);
```

❑ **Parameters:**

bstrType	Wide-character string that identifies the short name of the credit card type for which the method is being called
bstrNumber	Wide-character string that contains the account number as it was entered by the user
fValid	Long integer value that must be set to TRUE if the account number is valid or FALSE otherwise.

Return Values

As you have probably noticed, all the methods that we have seen so far have a return value of type HRESULT. This is normal for COM applications, as the return value is used to indicate whether the function failed or was successfully executed.

In general if an error occurred and the method could not complete its execution successfully, a value of E_FAIL should be returned. If, on the other hand, everything went fine and the execution was completed with success, the return value should be set to S_OK.

For certain functions that involve memory manipulation, it is also possible to return the value E_OUTOFMEMORY, indicating specifically that the method ran out of memory and therefore could not complete its task. Similarly, it is also possible to return a value of E_INVALIDARG, indicating that one or more of the parameters passed to the method were invalid for some reason.

A Look at What the Template Does

As we mentioned at the beginning, the credit card extension template that comes with the Wallet SDK is actually a sample that was developed specifically for the Volcano Coffee store. Therefore, it has already been tailored to a specific need, although it can be changed easily enough to fit any purpose.

The template supports two types of credit card, called **Volcano Coffee Credit Card** and **Volcano Coffee Gold Credit Card**. This makes it possible to easily modify the template to support either an arbitrary number of cards (once we've got the code to handle two, a simple `switch` statement will let us control any number) or just one. No algorithm is used to check the validity of the credit card account numbers, which contain a combination of letters and numbers, but there is a simple verification of its length and of the first digit, which must be 2.

Installation

Upon registration, the template automatically creates an entry in the Registry that will force the Wallet to execute the installation procedure for the component. The program ID of the component is taken from the `OtherProgID` constant, which is declared in the `MyCard.h` file:

```
#define OtherProgID "VCCard.VCCard.1"
#define WideOtherProgID L"VCCard.VCCard.1"
```

The second constant, `WideOtherProgID`, is used in the component's code itself.

The template also provides standard implementations of the `IPaymentCCTypeInstall` interface. `GetInstallInfo`, in particular, returns the values of three variables that are defined at the beginning of the `MyCard.cpp` file: `cMaxCards` determines the number of card types supported by the component, while `wszAcceptName` contains the name of the component, and `wszSource` the name of the manufacturer.

`GetTypeInfo`, on the other hand, works by iterating through the `gCards` array, declared at the beginning of `MyCard.cpp`, which contains elements of type `CardDescription`, a simple collection containing the short and friendly names of each credit card type handled by the component.

Obviously, it is important that the number of elements in `gCards` is no less than the value of `cMaxCards`, or the method will return `E_OUTOFMEMORY`, indicating that it couldn't access one of the credit card types supported by the component.

Execution

The bitmaps used by each credit card type are loaded into the component when it is first instantiated. The constructor of the `MyCard` class, in fact, calls the built-in `Load256Bitmap` function to load all the bitmaps required by each credit card type. This function is required, because, while the bitmaps are stored using 256 colors in the component's resources, they need to be converted to 16 colors for the Wallet to display them properly.

Thus, when the `GetBitmap` function is called, the template's code simply returns the handle to one of the bitmaps that were loaded at the beginning.

Similarly, `GetMask` simply returns one of the masks that were defined at the beginning of `MyCard.cpp`. The variables that hold these masks have been given specific names (in the sample they are called `szVCName` and `szVCGName`), and therefore we'll have to change them when we get to developing our own component.

Finally, `IsValid` only performs two simple checks, as we mentioned above, aimed at determining whether the card number's length and its first digit are correct.

Uninstallation

The template's implementations of both `SelfUninstall` and `Uninstall` are completely hands-off and do not require any change regardless of how many cards your component needs to support.

`SelfUninstall` simply iterates through all the cards declared in `gCards` and calls the appropriate Wallet functions to remove them from the list of accepted credit cards. `Uninstall` simply calls the method of the '.DLL' in which the component is stored, which takes care of uninstalling itself and modifying the System Registry so that all references to it are removed.

Supporting the MTCard Credit Card

It's now time to modify the template so that it will support our own card. First of all, we'll need to copy the entire source code, including `Walletsdk.idl` to a different location. This will ensure that we'll be able to reuse it, untouched, for our next project – or for this one should we lose control of the code we write!

Preliminaries

Next, we'll start by modifying a few global parameters that are defined here and there:

Location	Name	Value
MyCard.h	OtherProgID	"MTCard.MTCard.1"
	WideOtherProdID	L"MTCard.MTCard.1"
MyCard.cpp	szVcName	L"MTCard"
	szVCFName	L"MT Card"
	szVCNameMask	L"nnnnnnnnnnnn"
	cVCCard	12
	wszAcceptName	L"MTCard Credit Card"
	wszSource	L"Wrox"
	cMaxCards	1
	gCards	{{szVCName, szVCFName}}

We'll also also have to modify the VC++ project so that it will create a component that is called `MTCard.MTCard` and has its own unique identifiers. This is a two-step process, which we'll begin in the `OtherCard.idl` file. This contains the directives that determine how the component is created and registered within the system. As you can see, the file contains an initial section where the main component's interface is defined:

```
[
    uuid(130AF030-E8B9-11d0-BB16-00AA00A13794),
    version(1.0),
    helpstring("VCCard 1.0 Type Library")
]
```

We'll need to change the GUID that is stored in the `uuid` parameter, which is used internally by Windows to uniquely identify our component. In order to obtain a new GUID, we can use the `uuidgen` utility that we can find in the **Common\Tools** folder of our Visual Studio 6.0 installation. If we run the program it will print out a UUID already properly formatted to be copied into the '.IDL' file, such as the following:

4866ca10–4206–11d3–9bfa–00107a901dd9

We will also need a new GUID for the type library section of the '.IDL' file:

```
library VCCardLib
{
    importlib("stdole32.tlb");

    [
        uuid(130AF031-E8B9-11d0-BB16-00AA00A13794),
        helpstring("VCCard Class")
    ]
    coclass VCCard
    {
        [default] interface ICreditCardOtherCard;
        interface IPaymentCCTypeInstall;
    };

};
```

Finally, we'll have to change the name of the library itself from the current `VCCardLib` to something representative of what our new component will contain, such as `MTCardLib`.

> You can also use the `GUIDGEN.EXE` program in the tools folder of your Visual Studio installation to create new GUIDs. `GUIDGEN` is a bit more user-friendly than `UUIDGEN`, since it has its own Windows GUID interface.

The last two files that we have to change before moving to the code itself are `MyCard.rgs` and `OtherCard.def`. The first one contains registry settings for the component. In it, we will need to replace all the references to `VCCard` with `MTCard`, and modify all the GUIDs to be the same as the first GUID we changed in the '.IDL' file. The second one contains instead the definitions that are used to create the '.DLL' in which the component will be stored. In it, we will need to change the name of the output file so that it will not conflict with any other '.DLL'. In our case, we'll use `MTCard.DLL`.

Execution

The only other change that we will need to make consists of modifying the `IsValid` method so that it performs a Luhn algorithm check on the account numbers entered by the user. All the other methods should work fine as they are, as long as we modify the bitmaps stored in the project's resources.

The new code for IsValid is very simple, thanks to the fact that we have already created a function that performs the Luhn check:

```
HRESULT CVCCard::IsValid(BSTR bstrType, BSTR bstrNumber, long *fValid)
{
    fValid =((SysStringLen(bstrNumber) == 12) && (LuhnValid(bstrNumber))) ? TRUE :
FALSE;
    return S_OK;
}
```

Digital Signature

Before being able to install our component onto a client machine, as we saw earlier, we'll have to digitally sign it. Since it's probably a good guess that we won't have a real digital certificate handy as soon as we have completed our component, we may want to create a "test" one that will make the component work at least on our machine.

To do so, we will need to use the InetSDK. In the \BIN\i386 folder, we will find a file called ROOT.CER. This is what is called a "root" certificate – that is, a certificate that has been "endorsed" by the very same organization that created it.

Endorsing is one of the fundamental concepts of digital signatures. We can imagine digital trust as a hierarchy, with at the top a "root organization" in which the program that has to verify a signature has "blind trust". This is generally a certificate authority of some kind, such as VeriSign. In other words, the software will "believe" everything that is "stated" by the root organization. Naturally, the identity of the root organization is embedded in the program when it's created – not just anybody who hands out self-endorsed certificates will be recognized as such.

A certificate authority has the option to "endorse" a certain digital certificate, which means that it has been created with its authorization and it is certified to be authentic. Endorsements can be nested, and can be limited to certain activities (for example: distribute content, distribute applications, sign other certificates, and so on).

The root certificate distributed with the InetSDK is a test certificate that will be recognized by the Wallet. We will, however, need to create the actual digital certificate that will be used to sign the component using the MAKECERT utility:

```
MAKECERT -n:"CN=Test Certificate" -k:MyPrivateKey MyCert.cer
```

This will cause the certificate to be created and stored in the MyCert.cer file. MAKECERT will also create a public key and store it in the system repository. Next, we will need to wrap the certificate in a PKCS#7 structure, which contains the entire hierarchy of all the certificates used to endorse a specific certificate. This can be done by using the CERT2SPC program:

```
CERT2SPC ROOT.CER MyCert.cer MyCert.spc
```

More information about the PKCS#7 structure can be found at the following:
http://www.microsoft.com/OpenType/otspec/DSIG.HTM

The output of this program, `MyCert.spc`, can be used to directly sign our component. This is done by using the `SIGNCODE` utility as follows:

```
SIGNCODE -spc MyCert.spc -pvk MyPrivateKey -prog your_dll_path
```

where `your_dll_path` is the complete path to the '`.DLL`' that contains the component. If the signing operation is successful, we should be able to register the '`.DLL`' with the system and later install it the next time that the Wallet is run. Keep in mind that we will have to re-sign the code every time we recompile the '`.DLL`'.

Summary

As we have seen in this chapter, extending the Wallet to accept other credit card types is not a particularly difficult task even if we are not very familiar with Visual C++, thanks to the fact that the Wallet SDK includes a template that can be easily modified.

Another interesting characteristic of this system is that our component is not required to store any information about the individual accounts that are entered by the user – the Wallet itself takes care of encrypting and saving them in the appropriate location. This avoids a number of problems connected with the fact that we'd have to find a secure way to store the data: the last thing we'd want is to make it possible for just anybody to open a file or the System Registry and read all the confidential information stored in them!

Improving Your Store's Performance

There's only one corner of the universe you can be certain of improving, and that's your own self.
—A. Huxley, Time Must Have a Stop

Now that our store is up and running, you may actually be wondering if there is any way for us to increase its efficiency. Many people tend to dismiss this thought as superfluous, their explanation being that computer hardware is so cheap these days that there's not much point in spending precious development time performing optimization procedures.

While this assumption is essentially correct, it's not complete. In fact, man-time is spent not only on the development of an application, but also on its maintenance. What's more, while the development can be a one-time effort, maintenance is generally ongoing, and therefore requires – at least in the long run – more manpower.

Thus, even though we may save a few hours of work by not optimizing our site, the higher number of machines required to eventually increase its performance will end up costing more in maintenance than what we would have spent in additional development time. Moreover, as we have discussed during the first few chapters of the book, employing a higher number of computers will also mean having to monitor a larger number of potential entry points for hackers and malicious users.

It's a good idea, therefore, to consider applying at least a certain degree of optimization to our site from the very beginning, while we're still in the design phase – this will make it easier to integrate all the code from the start.

Luckily, Microsoft has already performed a number of benchmarking tests and issued a series of recommendations on how to improve the performance of the basic store, therefore giving us the opportunity to make our own site faster even without having to spend many resources in research efforts aimed at identifying what the typical bottlenecks are.

What Does This Chapter Talk About?

In this chapter, we'll take a look at what steps we can take to improve the speed with which our SSCE store will process requests coming from its users, and consequently to increase its overall performance. We'll look at three ways to optimize a store:

❑ **The database**
   First of all, we'll look at how the use of stored procedures and smarter queries can speed up the site in a significant way, and also improve the performance on the DBMS's side.

❑ **The DBStorage object**
   Next we'll talk about the `DBStorage` object, which, as we already mentioned in Chapter 9, can represent a big bottleneck for your store, and how it can be removed from the site without giving up any functionality.

❑ **The pipeline**
   Finally, we'll examine how the pipeline can be optimized by having it perform only the operations that it needs to.

Know When to Draw the Line

It's important that we do not let ourselves get carried away by the improvement in speed that optimization can bring. In many cases, optimizing means having to make strategic decisions on the degree of functionality provided by a specific element of the site.

This means that we may have to trade in convenience and flexibility in order to achieve higher performance. While this is certainly a consideration that we should make, it's also important that we reach the appropriate balance between the two aspects of the situation.

Generally speaking, optimization should stop where it begins to hinder the fundamental ability of the store to react flexibly to changes in its environment: if implementing a certain optimization will limit the ease with which a store can be operated or extended, it probably isn't worth it.

As an example, it can be recommended that we refrain from using the store's Query Map and instead write the individual queries directly into the ASP scripts that make use of them. (Of course, this only applies to simplistic queries; otherwise we would be using stored queries anyway). While this will probably help us achieve at least a marginal performance improvement, the next time we change one of the tables in our database we will have to scan the entire store's source code in order to find where each of the queries is stored (and, almost certainly, we will forget one, go live with the site, and have to cope with the embarrassment of receiving customer complaints because the store isn't working properly).

Our first pass of optimization should instead focus on poorly written code, in which certain tasks are carried out using solutions more complex than needed. Poor code is not necessarily a sign of lesser programming ability, and therefore is likely to happen even if your developers are very experienced. Often, inefficient code is the result of a script being written in a hurry without the time, once it starts working, to make sure that it's as good as possible.

For example, let's take a look at the following snippet:

```
<%
   c = "SELECT * FROM ?"

   a = Replace (c, "?", "products") & " WHERE ID = 2"
   b = Replace (c, "?", "products") & " WHERE name LIKE %game%"
   c = Replace (c, "?", "products") & " WHERE price < 3300"
%>
```

As we can see, the `Replace` function is called several times in this script, resulting in a lot of computing time being wasted on useless calculations, particularly if this code belongs to a high-traffic page. The following might have been a little better:

```
<%
   c = "SELECT * FROM ?"
   d = Replace (c, "?", "products")

   a = d & " WHERE ID = 2"
   b = d & " WHERE name LIKE %game%"
   c = d & " WHERE price < 3300"
%>
```

If you think that it is unlikely that we will find mistakes like these in our store, I recommend that you take a look at its code. You will find that simple things like this are very common, and, although they will not compromise the functionality of the site, they will, on a large scale, cause a waste of computer processing time that could be used to assist more customers.

The Database

One of the most critical elements of our store is the database. The database server is also the only part of our network that we cannot easily expand in a server farm, and therefore any optimization that we can perform there will have a great impact on the total capacity of our store.

Writing Smarter Queries

One example of poorly written code of which everybody from the novice to the master can be a victim is the "select-star" syndrome, which tends to happen most often when the developer is in a hurry, but that can present itself in any circumstance.

The simplest way to write a SQL query consists of using the `*` wildcard in order to retrieve all the fields that are associated with the table, or tables, that we are accessing. Using the star is very convenient, and lets us focus on the more important task at hand, be it trying to write the correct selection parameters to obtain the data we are interested in, or actually going on to write the rest of the ASP script that will use the data our query is extracting.

When not all of the data that we extract is used, however, it's a mistake to leave the wildcard in place. In most cases, we will only require a smaller subset of the fields that are returned, and therefore we should limit the data extraction task to those. This will not only cause the DBMS to work less and return a smaller amount of data, but also all the drivers on our web server, from ODBC to OLE-DB, will create fewer structures, take up less memory and have an increased performance. Also, if the select columns are part of an index, optimization here can greatly reduce the cost of the query, which is definitely something to bear in mind.

Only Ask For What You Need

Another typical problem with database access is in the way data is extracted from a table. In many occasions throughout our store, we will need to somehow group the records we display to make them more accessible to our users. For example, product listings are often grouped in pages, with the goal of making them easier to read for our customers.

When the user requests a page in the listing that is not the first one, we will somehow have to position the cursor in the database so that the right record will be shown to him or her. It's not uncommon to see this task accomplished using a technique similar to the following:

```
<%
    FirstRecord = 144
    For i = 1 to FirstRecord
        rs.MoveNext
    Next
%>
```

If we're using an Oracle DBMS, this is our only choice, and therefore it would be justifiable to use this code in the store. If, on the other hand, we are using MS SQL Server, we should take advantage of the advanced functionality provided by the ODBC driver for this DBMS.

One possibility is using the Move ADO command to position the recordset's cursor at the appropriate record, and then start extracting the data from there:

```
<%
    FirstRecord = 144
    rs.Move FirstRecord
%>
```

However, as we are normally already on the first record of a recordset when we read it in, the previous piece of code would take us to record 145, as the cursor would move forward 144 records.

It is also possible to make ADO automatically divide the records into pages of the correct size and then jump between the pages without having to force SQL to transmit unnecessary data. This is done through the PageSize and AbsolutePage attributes of the Recordset object: while the former is used to set the dimension (in records) of a page, the latter makes it possible to jump to a specific page in the list. For example:

```
<%
    rs.PageSize = 20     ' 20 records per page
    rs.AbsolutePage = 2  ' Jumps to second page
%>
```

This would jump to the first record on page 2, which would be record 21.

Don't Create Too Many Objects

As we have seen in Chapter 11, in the starter store a new ADO connection and a command linked to it are created whenever a page is loaded. While we will need the connection in most cases (although probably not all of them), we can probably do without the command object.

Therefore, if we use the connection object's `Execute` method to run our queries, we will reduce the number of objects created for each page, and consequently increase its performance.

We should avoid the mistake of creating a single database connection to be shared by all the pages of the site: storing the connection in the `Application` object often creates this mistake. In fact, in order to prevent a page from interfering with another, we would need to continuously lock and unlock the `Application` object, with the disastrous result of effectively allowing only one page at a time to connect to the database.

In addition, this method would never increase the speed of our application because ADO already uses a *connection pooling* technique internally to speed up database access. Thanks to it, the system always maintains a certain number of open connections to the database, which are then assigned to individual objects as they are requested. Thus, keeping a single connection always active may even prevent other programs from gaining access to the database!

Using Stored Procedures

One of the things that many people find very surprising – at least when they finally come to understand it – is how database operations between the web servers and the DBMS work when we are using ADO. As we can see from the figure below, each query that we execute really follows a very complex path through five different software layers before being finally sent off to the database server:

❑ **ADO**
This is the object with which the script communicates directly. It provides an interface to OLE-DB, as well as several advanced functions.

❑ **OLE-DB**
OLE-DB is Microsoft's latest database technology, which is tipped to eventually supercede ODBC. It includes several high-level functions, and contains only 32-bit fully re-entrant and thread-safe code, which makes it perfect for COM applications. However, because it's so new, it must often rely on older ODBC drivers, with which it is compatible, in order to provide access to a wide variety of DBMS systems. However, there are drivers available for Oracle and SQL Server.

❑ **ODBC**
ODBC has been Microsoft's standard database access technology for several years now. Its goal is to provide an abstract API that can be used to access a variety of different DBMS systems. Even though its specifications have gradually become obsolete, its longevity still makes it the system with the highest number of drivers available. Chances are that you will be using ODBC to access your data.

❑ **ODBC Driver**
Where ODBC provides an abstract interface to any database, individual drivers are used to make access to specific DBMS systems possible. Therefore, once a request has been received from ODBC, it will be turned over to the appropriate driver, which, in turn, will translate into the correct commands for the DBMS it was designed for.

❑ **Network library**

Finally, SQL drivers in particular give their users the possibility of reaching the database server using any of a number of possible network protocols, such as NetBIOS, TCP/IP or Named Pipes. Each protocol is represented by a specific network library, which is used by the ODBC driver to open and maintain a communication channel between the client and the server.

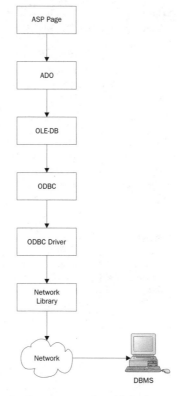

It's important to understand that, in the moment in which the query leaves the Network library and eventually reaches the database server, no execution has taken place. The DBMS still has to parse all the syntax, create a plan to access the data, extract the proper information from all the required tables and return it to the sender.

While there really isn't anything that we can do about the long way that our data has to travel before it can get to the database server, we can certainly try to reduce the amount of work that has to occur once it gets there. To do so, we need to consider that many of the queries that we run are similar. For example, all the product queries will only differ because of the different SKU used, while the product listings will almost always be the same, and so on.

The interesting part of all this is that the DBMS will always use the same sequence of operations, called a *plan*, in order to get to our data, even though different parameters are used. However, because it essentially behaves as a stateless machine, it will not remember that we have run a similar query before and therefore it will recalculate the same plan every time we execute that query. This is not true for SQL Server 7.0, which now features a Query Optimizer that will automatically create and maintain plans for us.

In order to reduce the time consumed by the database server when calculating the access plan for each query we send out, we should consider writing stored procedures. These are a sequence of SQL commands that are stored inside the DBMS's own cache and whose plan is only created once and then stored as well for one user connection.

When we run a stored procedure, as opposed to executing a query, we can save a lot of computing power for a number of reasons. First of all, as we just said, the database will already know how to access the data required by the operations that we need to perform. Moreover, we will not need to pass the entire SQL statement through the chain of software layers, but only the execution statement for the procedure; as a result, fewer bytes will need to be passed along and transmitted over our network (don't forget that we need to think on a larger scale: if we save ten bytes for each page, once we've served a million pages we will have saved almost 10MB of data!).

Take Advantage of What the DBMS Does Best

DBMS systems have been created with a single purpose in mind – organizing and manipulating data – and there is little doubt that they are very good at that. However, in many cases we seem to ignore this simple fact and choose to manipulate the data using more generic tools, like VBScript.

If we make the decision to implement stored procedures in our store, we should also consider moving at least part of the data manipulation logic to the procedures as well. For example, if we need to analyze a recordset to extract only a particular subset of the data it contains, it would be a good idea to do so with a stored procedure.

This would achieve two important goals: first, the data is manipulated directly inside the database *by* the database system, which was designed precisely for that purpose. Second, only the final data leaves the DBMS and travels back through the path that leads to ADO, leaving us with a faster execution process that will certainly improve the overall performance of the store.

Pros and Cons of Using Stored Procedures

With all the positive aspects of using stored procedures that we have considered, there are, of course, a few tradeoffs that we have to make. The biggest one is probably the fact that SQL Server in particular is not very good at maintaining the dependencies between tables and procedures.

This means that if we attempt to change a table on which a stored procedure is based, the DBMS will not make any modifications to any procedures. As a result, when we run the procedure the next time, we will get an error, or – in the best of cases – data access will be very slow as a result of the fact that the plan used by the server is now obsolete. This can also happen with queries built into the page, but the stored procedures that are querying the table are less scattered and easier to find. In this way, stored procedures force us to examine the dependencies in our database and make sure that everything will work accordingly.

Stored procedures are also somewhat complex to write, particularly if you do not have much familiarity with SQL, which has its oddities like any other language. Last but not least, there are certain things that simply cannot be done using a stored procedure and, unless you are well versed in SQL, you may spend a lot of time trying to figure something out only to find that you've hit a limit of the language itself.

While a tutorial on SQL stored procedures is outside the scope of this book, there are a lot of resources around: SQL has always been a very popular topic, even more so recently with the advent of the Internet and dynamic websites. If possible, try to purchase a book that covers the specific implementation of SQL that you will be using (for example: SQL Server, Oracle, and so on). Although all the major DBMS systems claim to be compatible with the current standard (called SQL-92), there are enough specific details that a general knowledge of SQL just won't make it possible for you to take advantage of the full power of your database server.

> **For a detailed reference on Microsoft SQL Server, check out Professional SQL Server 6.5 Administration published by Wrox Press, ISBN number 1-874416-49-4. Also, try the following URL for more information on ADO optimization: http://www.vbpj.com/upload/free/features/vbpj/1999/05may99/ds0599/ds0599 .asp**

The DBStorage Object

Back in Chapter 9, we mentioned how the DBStorage object is a mixed blessing for the store. On one hand, it certainly provides a very flexible storage medium that we can use for everything from basket contents to personalization data. On the other, it is cumbersome and slow, and makes it difficult to perform search operations on the database.

The reason why DBStorage is slow is not difficult to understand: whenever we load or store data, it has to be marshaled or un-marshaled. Depending on how much information is stored in the objects we are either writing or reading, this operation can take up a sizable amount of time, particularly if we consider that it is repeated indiscriminately in a number of oft-used pages, such as the basket.

Similarly, the fact that all the data is essentially compressed in an unreadable format makes it quite difficult to use simple SQL queries – by far the fastest data retrieval system around – to find specific information for a particular purpose. In fact, unless we have created separate structures in the table that holds the marshaled information (for example, the starter store does so with the order ID, which is stored in a field of its own) our only solution is to scan through the entire table, un-marshalling every record one by one and checking to see if the information we're looking for is there. Even trying that with a small table of say, 1,000 records, will require a couple of coffee breaks.

At First Sight

The obvious solution to the problem of marshalling is simply an extension of what already takes place inside the database used by the starter store. The use of DBStorage is completely eliminated from any part of the store (including receipt storage), and is substituted instead by a table that contains a well-defined set of information.

Typically, the data that you would need is that which is strictly necessary to complete a purchase, such as ship-to and bill-to information, a complete detail of each product that contains SKUs and quantities, shipping, handling, and tax information. Instead of using DBStorage, we will have to fill the OrderForm manually every time we need to run a pipeline, and then transfer the data back to the database with a similar process once the pipeline has finished executing.

As you can imagine, this involves a significant amount of change to the store's code, and therefore it's worth taking a good look to try and understand if it's the approach that provides the best balance between convenience and performance, which, as we said earlier, is what we are trying to achieve when applying optimizations to our site.

It's quite easy to see how our requirement is not fulfilled: by pre-defining the information that can be stored inside our database table, we automatically limit the amount of data that we have the possibility of saving. There go our personalization parameters, special order information, and any other custom value that were so easily added to the `OrderForm` and saved when `DBStorage` was around.

Even so, the gain in performance obtained through the introduction of fixed-field tables may justify the loss of flexibility, if we are willing to make that compromise *and* if no better solution can be found.

A Better Solution

A much better solution to the problem can be found by combining a set of tables with a fixed number of fields, with additional tables that hold dynamically definable information. This approach will, however, somewhat reduce any prospective performance gain, although the comparative difference will only be marginal if the system is properly designed and used in an appropriate manner.

First of all, let's analyze in detail how the system will work. We will keep the information that we know will always be required, such as ship-to and bill-to information, products and so on, in tables with well-defined fields. Since this will represent most of the data that needs to be used consistently throughout the store, it will enjoy the highest performance increase. The next figure shows the structure of the database tables used to handle this information.

We'll need to change several sections of the site in order for these two new tables to be integrated into the store. In order to maximize the performance, we'll write two stored procedures that we'll use to create the `OrderForm` containing the user's basket:

```
Create Proc ExtractBasketInfo (@ShopperID varchar (50)) as
    SELECT * FROM Baskets WHERE ShopperID = @ShopperID

Create Proc ExtractItemInfo (@ShopperID varchar (50)) as
    SELECT SKU, Quantity, Name, Placed_price FROM Items WHERE ShopperID =
@ShopperID
```

Note that we are using the star wildcard here because we do indeed need to use all the fields from the Baskets table. Next, we can write a simple piece of ASP code that loads the data from the database into the `OrderForm`, and use it inside `I_util.asp` in place of the `GetOrderform` function:

```
<%
    function GetOrderform (ShopperID)
        set Orderform = Server.CreateObject ("Commerce.Orderform")

        set rs = MSCS.Execute ("exec ExtractBasketInfo ('" & ShopperID & "')")

        if not rs.eof then

            for each Field in rs.Fields
                Orderform  (Field.Name) = Field.Value
            next

            rs.Close
            set rs = MSCS.Execute ("exec ExtractItemInfo ('" & ShopperID & "')")

            while not rs.eof
                Orderform.AddItem (rs ("SKU"), rs ("Quantity"), rs ("Placed_Price"))
                rs.MoveNext
            wend

        end if

        Set GetOrderform = Orderform
    end function
%>
```

Information is inserted back into the database in a similar way, keeping in mind, however, that the names of what is stored in the `OrderForm` may not be the same as what we have in the database. In particular, the `Placed_price` field in the `Items` table should be filled using the value of the `list_price` pair.

Handling Dynamic Data

Now for the fun part: how do we handle dynamic data? The answer is much simpler than you may think, and it comes from simply analyzing how a similar problem has been solved. In fact, all we have to do is observe how the need to store multiple items from the user's basket is handled in our solution: through a separate table that contains an individual record for each item and for each shopper.

If you think about it, there is not much difference between having to store an arbitrary number of items and an arbitrary number of custom values. The only significant distinction is in the fact that, while we know a priori what the data types of each field in the `Items` table is, we can't really say the same thing about our custom information.

Luckily, VBScript handles all variables as `Variants`, which means that if we store them as a string the system will be able to convert them to the appropriate type as needed. Naturally there are a few limitations: for one thing, we won't be able to store strings that are more than 255 characters long. If we did, we'd have to use `text` data fields, which are able to handle up to about 2GB of data but which always occupy a multiple of 2KB of space in the database, regardless of the actual amount of text stored in them; thus, a string 10 bytes long will still take up 2KB of disk space, and be a lot slower to index than a `varchar`.The situation gets even worse in SQL Server 7.0, where the page size of a `text` data field has been increased to 8Kb!

We also will not be able to save entire objects that may be stored in the `OrderForm`. We can, however, store their parameters and later use them to rebuild the object from VBScript. This also means that any dictionaries that may be stored in the `OrderForm` must be saved to the database using this technique.

The next figure contains a revised Entity/Relationship (E/R) diagram of our database, which now includes the `CustomData` table. As you can see, we will treat this table similar to a `Dictionary` object, with each of its records representing a Name/Value pair. The name of each parameter is unique to the individual shopper, so that duplicate parameters with the same name cannot be inserted.

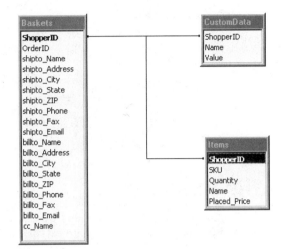

In order to extract and insert custom data into our table, we will write two very simple stored procedures:

```
Create Proc GetDatum (@ShopperID varchar (50),@Name varchar (20)) as
    SELECT Value FROM CustomData WHERE ShopperID = @ShopperID AND Name = @Name

Create Proc SetDatum (@ShopperID varchar (50),@Name varchar (20),@Value varchar
(255)) as
begin
    SELECT Value FROM CustomData WHERE ShopperID = @ShopperID AND Name = @Name

    if @@ROWCOUNT = 0
        INSERT INTO CustomData Values (@ShopperID, @Name, @Value)
    else
        UPDATE CustomData Set Value = @Value WHERE ShopperID = @ShopperID AND Name =
@Name
end
```

As you can see, in `SetDatum` we have to establish whether a record for the Name/Value pair we want to set already exists, in which case we only have to update it, or doesn't exist, in which case we have to create a new one.

We can now use these two simple queries to insert and retrieve data from the database. Even better, we may want to wrap a couple of VBScript functions around the code required to access the database and use them globally. Although doing so won't necessarily make our site faster, it will, at least, make it easier to read. Here's a quick example:

```
<%
   Function GetDatum (ShopperID, Name)
      set rs = MSCS.Execute ("Exec GetDatum ('" & ShopperID & "', '" & Name &
"')")

      if not rs.eof then
         GetDatum = rs ("Value")
      end if
   End Function

   Sub SetDatum (ShopperID, Name, Value)
      MSCS.Execute "Exec SetDatum ('" & ShopperID & "', '" & Name & "', '" & Value
"')"
   End Sub
%>
```

The Pipelines

The final elements of the store that we will talk about in this chapter are the pipelines. Similar to the database, these play a very important role in the store, and therefore should be the focus of some of our attention during the optimization phase.

For starters, we should make sure that we only use transaction-friendly pipelines when they are absolutely needed. As you can imagine, supporting MTS creates a lot of overheads and should be avoided when possible. The starter store already does a rather good job of this, since transactions are only used in the Payment pipeline; if we have used additional pipelines in our own store – for example for business-to-business transactions – we should review each one of them and determine if we really need to use transactions.

Use the Product Pipeline with Caution

By default, the starter store makes no use of the Product pipeline, which, as we have seen in Chapter 10, can be used to determine certain information, such as promotional prices, about an individual product.

Clearly, this pipeline can be of value if our store runs complex promotions and we want to make sure that each user always gets the best price upfront. At the same time, however, we should keep in mind that running a pipeline is always a time-consuming operation that can adversely affect the performance of our store.

If our store doesn't have complex promotions, then we should be able to extract all the information we need about a product directly from the database – possibly using a stored procedure – and therefore do not need to use the Product pipeline.

Component-Level Optimizations

Even if we do need to run a Product pipeline in our store, we should try to keep its contents to a minimum by eliminating all the superfluous components. For example, we don't really need an SQLItemAdo component to extract all the information available for each product in order to calculate promotion information. Running SQLItemAdo forces the system to load all the information into a data collection (handled by ADO) and then to copy it into another collection (the Dictionary inside the pipeline), where only a small part of it will actually be used.

`Scriptor` objects should also be used with extreme caution, because they are not very fast. In general, if we have to write a complex procedure, we should develop a custom component, possibly using Visual C++, which will give the highest possible performance. VB is another possibility, as we are developing COM components.

Adjust the Plan Pipeline

A number of similar considerations must be made for the Plan pipeline. We should take full advantage of the flexibility that the "expert" mode of the Win32-based pipeline editor provides and optimize the performance of the Plan pipeline, which is widely used in a number of pages throughout the store.

Eliminate Unnecessary Stages

While going through the editor, you will probably notice that there are certain stages that we have never used, such as Merchant Information or Order Check. Since chances are that we will never use them in the future as well, we might just as well get rid of them. This will prevent useless default components from running and wasting precious computing time.

Also, we may want to remove some of the components that perform queries against the database, such as `SQLItemADO`, and replace them by actually executing the query in the ASP code and copying the information directly into the `OrderForm`. The performance gain here will be caused by the fact that we will also be able to eliminate certain stages from the pipeline and therefore prevent the overheads caused by the end-of-stage logic used to validate the data.

Splitting the Pipeline

You have probably noticed that, most of the time, not all of the information produced by the Plan pipeline is actually used by the store. In particular, although at every execution it attempts to calculate shipping, handling and taxes for the order, these are not used until the shipping stage, to which probably only a smaller portion of our visitors – those who want to become customers – ever arrive.

Clearly, this means that all the CPU time required to run the Shipping, Handling, Tax and Total stages will be going to waste in a very large percentage of the cases. Therefore, we should consider splitting the Plan pipeline into two different custom pipelines.

The first one, to be used in all the pages up to the basket, will stop at the Order Subtotal stage, although we might want to include the Inventory stage in order to determine whether the items added by the user to his or her basket are out of stock. The second one, on the other hand, will be used from the execution of `xt_orderform_prepare.asp` onwards, when shipping, handling and tax costs will become relevant.

Summary

There are four important aspects of store optimization that we have discussed in this chapter:

❑ **The Code**
Time is our worst enemy when we are programming and, unfortunately, we know that, these days, competitiveness gives us less and less time that we can dedicate to writing good code. As a result, it's easy to make simple mistakes that, even without causing the store to malfunction, will reduce the overall performance of the system. Therefore, our first step in the world of optimization should consist of taking a good look at the code and trying to understand if there are areas that we can improve.

❑ **The Database**
Next, the database: as we have seen, we should start by making sure that our queries are not extracting information that the store doesn't use. Another good idea is to try and implement stored procedures, which eliminate some of the pre-processing operations that the DBMS must carry out before being able to return the appropriate information. Introducing the use of stored procedures also makes it possible to take advantage of SQL's advanced data manipulation functions, which are faster than what VBScript has to offer and let us control the data *before* it is transferred over to the web server.

❑ **The DBStorage object**
We should really try to avoid using DBStorage in our store: not using DBStorage will increase the overall performance of the site dramatically. During the course of this chapter, we looked at a simple way to get rid of DBStorage without removing most of its advantages; we even gained the possibility of searching for data using fast SQL queries!

❑ **The Pipelines**
Finally, we took a look at pipelines, and how they influence the speed of a store. The golden rule here is to always make sure that we are using only what we really need. This means using the expert mode of the Win32-based editor to remove unused stages and components; splitting complex pipelines into smaller pieces, if using them individually rather than all at the same time, makes more sense.

A while back, Microsoft released a very interesting white paper, which was distributed along with a "performance kit". This paper, which we also referenced in Chapter 9, contains a lot of useful information about the kind of performance that you can expect from a SSCE store, and illustrates a number of possible techniques that can be used to make a store faster. You can find the Site Server Commerce Edition Performance Kit at the following address:

http://www.microsoft.com/siteserver/commerce/DeployAdmin/VolcanoCoffee.htm

Case Study 1:
How to Run Commerce Server
in Batch Mode Using VB6

As you become more familiar with the various tools available within Microsoft's development environment, you will come to realize the pivotal role that Visual Basic (VB) plays. As VB continues to mature and gain acceptance as an enterprise-level development language, it is also enjoying widespread use in the Internet application development world.

Already within this book, we have seen that VB, and its variant VBScript, are the "glue" that enable the COM objects installed with Commerce Server to provide online storefront capabilities.

We have also seen that VB can be used to extend Commerce Server's middle tier pipeline environment through both Scriptor - and COM objects. These allow you to customize your storefront with your own business rules. When COM is combined with the Commerce Server pipeline, we are able to achieve true separation of business logic from the storefront's presentation layers. This is a crucial element toward the development of a highly robust, scalable, distributed application.

This case study pushes MS Commerce Server to a new level by running its environment in batch mode within VB. The term "batch mode" is used within this Case Study to refer to a computer's inherent capability to execute a software process without the need for human interaction. Unlike a service, which is started by the operating system, a batch processor is typically scheduled (via NT's or SQLServer's scheduler) and has a finite execution duration. Commerce Server's typical storefronts do not perform any processing without some form of human interaction (for example: HTML form submittal).

You will probably agree that this is a considerable departure from the traditional ASP approach to using Commerce Server. This does not mean that we will completely discard ASP: it is still an essential component of the overall e-commerce solution. Instead, I contend that this approach enables the order processing and fulfillment pieces of the store to be moved to a separate VB application. I will provide you with a batch processor template, which when leveraged with the Commerce Server pipeline technology, will enable you to satisfy a multitude of order processing tasks.

What Does This Case Study Talk About?

The aim of this case study is to give you a fully functional batch processor along with a working knowledge of its operation. We will do this by covering the following sections:

- ❑ **Why use batch processing?**
  We'll begin by taking a look at some of the advantages of the batch processing approach, these include both performance increases and greater control over your e-commerce system's reliability. At the same time, there are several disadvantages, which I will equally bring to your attention. Finally, I will try to convince you to use batch processing as part of your enterprise-level e-commerce application.

- ❑ **Design of the batch processor**
  Here we'll go over the logical design of the batch processor and explain how it is independent of the workflow tasks at hand.

- ❑ **Code review for the batch processor**
  This section gives a detailed review of the code available with the case study. This is probably the part to which you are all eager to advance. I would recommend reading through all of the sections before jumping to this one, as they provide the framework for the code presented here.

- ❑ **Installation procedure**
  Finally, we'll walk through the installation procedure that is provided for the download included in this case study.

Why Use Batch Processing?

Before I hype up batch processing too much, I would like to make it clear that this will not solve all of your e-commerce requirements: the scope of your problem will largely determine whether this is an appropriate solution. I will leave it for you to decide whether your individual requirements lend themselves to a solution using this approach.

Having said this, I would like to point out that I have already successfully deployed a batch store on several e-commerce projects. I have been able to take the code presented here, in its entirety, and use it as a foundation on which to build an entire order management system. This, when combined with an enhanced store manager (such as Administrative Intranet), has allowed me to build and deploy world-class e-commerce solutions.

Although the concept we are about to use has only been applied to the order processing piece of the store, it is intended for use across any part of the store that is able to take advantage of running in batch mode. Furthermore, you will find that by fully leveraging the Commerce Server pipeline technology, the potential the batch processor provides is limited only by your imagination.

Advantages of a Batch Store

What are the advantages of running the store in batch mode?

For one, it is highly educational, as you will get to experience the use of Commerce Server's objects outside of the ASP environment. While using Commerce Server within VB is obvious if you think about it and are familiar with both products, it might be a leap too big for the uninitiated. However, continuing on with the study of the provided code will help turn this leap into simple footsteps for you on your path to mastering how Microsoft satisfies the enterprise-level application needs by using COM as the foundation for their architecture.

However, and more importantly, your storefront's overall reliability can be improved by using a batch approach. A robust store developed around Commerce Server will probably leverage the services of many external providers (for example: Internet, payment processing, fulfillment managers, etc.) through the use of the Commerce Server *de facto* standard pipelines. While the inherent nature of the Internet provides a fairly reliable transport mechanism, the reliability of your whole system is a complex function of many variables. Since many of these variables are beyond your control, you should anticipate periods where access to your external service providers is unavailable. During these outage periods, should the store stop taking orders? If your clients are anything like mine, then the answer is "NO!".

Many of the COM objects written for the Commerce Server pipeline use a synchronous communication approach. This means that if you use the **out-of-the-box** pipelines, your consumer may have to wait for all of this synchronous communication to complete prior to getting confirmation that their order was collected. If an error occurs somewhere in the links to your external service providers, your customers are told that you are either experiencing technical difficulties or that the order could not be captured at this time. They are advised to revisit the store at a later time to try again. As you are aware, the longer your customer waits, the less they enjoy shopping at your storefront.

Without belaboring this point, could you imagine attempting to buy a pair of shoes at a department store, but you are unable to purchase them because of frequent problems with the store's registers? It wouldn't be long before the store received a bad reputation, and customers stopped going there.

Now, if we are able to perform this synchronous processing offline, then we can improve the quality of the consumer's shopping experience and help build customer acceptance to your storefront.

It is your responsibility as a developer to ensure a high level of availability and reliability. There are some deliberate design and architectural steps that can be taken to reach this point, and using batch processing is one such step.

One key area that batch processing can assist in is load balancing. Jobs can be scheduled during off-peak processing periods, thereby reducing the load on the application servers. I'm sure that this isn't a new concept to any of you, but it is definitely worth pointing out.

Disadvantages of Batching the Store

One of the biggest disadvantages to batch processing, and Commerce Server-based storefronts in general, is that the COM objects used within its pipeline must be written to provide the merchant with a certain level of feedback. For example, during a credit card authorization session the merchant will need to know if the component failed to return a valid authorization due to:

❑ **Customer errors**
For example, bad credit card / lack of sufficient funds

❑ **Network failures**
For example, link between merchant and payment processor down or link between payment processor and consumer bank down

❑ **Merchant errors**
For example, bad .pcf / .ini file for the pipeline component

❑ **General system errors**
For example, garbled data on transfer or processor timeout

As you are aware, error handling is crucial for any robust information system and we obviously want to use components that provide us with a high level of feedback. However, with that said, we have seen many market leaders in pipeline component development that do not provide this type of feedback. These vendors usually point you to their software development kit, which allows you to customize their **off-the-shelf** components to meet your needs.

I believe the reason for this is the myth that no flow control is possible within the pipeline. While it is true that you cannot branch within the pipeline, components should, at a minimum, communicate their internal errors to an OrderForm property prior to exiting the pipeline. Since the OrderForm object is passed by reference into the pipeline, these component specific error properties can then be examined for subsequent flow control either within your ASP or, as you will learn in this case study, VB's environment.

Another disadvantage is in the customer service area. Going back to the offline credit card processing example, customers may get the impression during the order collection at the storefront that everything was okay with their order. Sometime later, after the offline credit card processing is completed, the customer could receive an email alerting them that the store was unable to authorize payment on their credit card. Unlike the online approach, the customer's interest in purchasing the store's goods or services may have waned, and they may not wish to revisit the online store to remedy the problem.

Similarly, there are times when offline processing does not make sense. With respect to the credit card processing example, an offline approach totally eliminates online fulfillment of soft goods. So, you must apply some judgement as to what processing you move offline given your business concept.

An additional disadvantage to this approach is the increase in complexity of the store to the merchant. They will have to operate and maintain both online and offline code bases for the store. Not to mention that the offline store's business logic can be fairly complex to facilitate a revisit.

The e-mail, which facilitates a revisit, will have to contain a hyperlink directly to the contents of the customer's shopping cart. However, since the shopping cart is usually deleted upon checkout from the online store and archived within the receipt and line item tables within your database, the offline store will need to "unwind" this processing to return the order to its previous state.

So Should I Still Use a Batch Processor?

Yes!

I believe that the advantages offered to the merchant from a batch processing capability far outweigh its disadvantages. If you are like me, then you are probably always looking for ways to make your job easier, while still producing high quality code. You will be able to reach both of these goals, as code reuse, maintainability, and scalability are all achieved through this approach. As mentioned previously, I have been able to apply the enclosed batch processor to several e-commerce development initiatives with a minimal amount of code changes. As you become more familiar with it, you will gain an appreciation for its power as both a key component to your overall e-commerce solution and a generic development tool. Then, you will only be limited by your imagination as you proceed to expand its possibilities.

Are There Competing Architectures?

You may recall from reading Wrox's Professional Active Server Pages 2.0 that it covered MSMQ within the context of an Electronic Commerce application. Specifically, the case study presented an asynchronous communication approach that could be used by commerce developers to handle credit card processing.

While MSMQ is a superior architecture, its broad adoption by many of the external service providers has not yet been achieved. So, we decided to present this case study around offline credit card processing using a synchronous communication method to balance this shortfall.

With that said, it is important to note that the provided batch processor is not limited to a synchronous communication approach nor is it required that its pipeline be centered on credit card processing. Batch processing is a data- versus event- driven paradigm and there are times when both are required within an enterprise-level application.

Design of the Commerce Server Batch Processor Template

The main architectural requirements driving the Commerce Server Batch Processor template are:

1. retain the "look-and-feel" of a Commerce Server storefront

2. fully leverage the Commerce Server's Dictionary object by storing processor-unique context data

3. provide for robust error handling to facilitate "lights out" operation

4. record errors that occur when the batch processor runs (independent of those encountered within the pipeline) within the database in order to relieve any unnecessary administrative burden caused by flat files

5. isolate the workflow (that is, business process) within a customizable, transactional Commerce Server pipeline

6. provide for a generic "home" or interface for application-unique pre- and post-pipeline processing.

Depicted in the following figure is the logical design for the generic Commerce Server batch processor. The "guts" of the generic design are located within the last three stages of the order processing loop. These three stages, coupled with the customized components within the pipeline (whose order of execution is specified in its configuration file) are the "heart" of the design and the Commerce Server architecture.

Commerce Server really boils down to three basic concepts:

❑ the Commerce Dictionary or `OrderForm`

❑ the MTS-enabled transactional pipeline

❑ the mechanisms to move the `Dictionary` or `OrderForm` into and out of the database in binary form.

These three concepts are isolated to just three subroutines within the batch processor template. Since the pre- and post-pipe processors have referential access to all available objects and variables located within the main driver, code reuse is maximized as unique business requirements and their associated code changes are isolated to these routines. The third key component, the MTS pipeline, is completely isolated from the batch processor and is easily customizable through the Win32 Pipeline Editor.

Note that the processor is not completely isolated from one's business logic located in the pipeline, as it is responsible for overall flow control. However, it is as two tier as you can get with the majority of the business logic isolated within the Commerce Server pipeline.

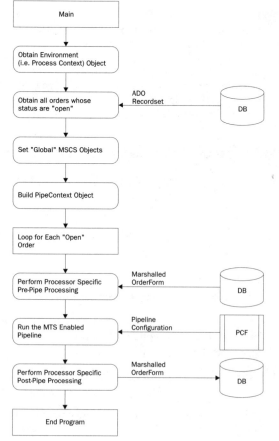

Code Review for the Batch Processor

Are you ready to roll up your sleeves and get dirty? We are now going to discuss the code provided for the batch processor template.

As you study the batch processor, it is important for you to realize that a VB application is very closely related to an ASP-based application. Within ASP you have a `global.asa` file that allows you to create objects and variables in global memory. This is similar to global objects and variables in a VB program or, as is the case with our batch processor, objects and variables with a local scope inside a main subroutine that are passed by reference to the subroutines with which they interact.

An additional analogy can be made to the relationship of VB subroutines to their ASP page counterparts. Each ASP page, like a VB subroutine, uses objects and variables of local scope that are isolated from their counterparts in `global.asa` or `Main`. Keep these thoughts in mind as you study the physical design for the batch processor.

You will also notice in reviewing the sample code that all Commerce Server objects are declared in their variant form and that late binding is used for their creation. The reason for this is that Commerce Server was designed to work within the constraints of VBScript and may expect to receive variant references to and from its objects. In the future, we will examine if early binding could work, as this will improve the overall performance of our batch processor.

> The sample code for this case study can be downloaded from the Wrox website at `http://www.wrox.com`. Guidelines on how to do this can be found at the end of this case study, under the section 'Installation Notes for the Code Sample'.

Main.bas

Like the ASP-based storefronts, the batch processor template is procedural in nature. A main subroutine that closely follows the logical design depicted in the previous figure drives it. Shown below is the entire code for the `Main()` subroutine.

```
Option Explicit

Public Sub Main()

' Error Handling
On Error GoTo ErrorTrap

    ' Begin Variable Declaration
' -----------------------------------------------------------------------------
-

    Dim bDebug As Boolean

    Dim oConn As ADODB.Connection

    Dim oFS As Scripting.FileSystemObject

    Dim oEnv As Object
    Dim oOrderDump As Object
    Dim oDbgFile As Object
    Dim oDBConn As Object
    Dim MSCSSite As Object
```

```
        Dim MSCSMessageManager As Object
        Dim PipeContext As Object
        Dim OrderForm As Object
        Dim UpdateStorage As Object

        Dim nCaseID As Long
        Dim I As Long
        Dim nErrNum As Long

        Dim sErrSrc As String
        Dim sErrDes As String
        Dim sTmpStr As String

        Dim aArrayData As Variant
        Dim errorStr As Variant

        ' End Variable Declaration
    ' -----------------------------------------------------------------------------
    -

        ' Turn on debug
        bDebug = True

        ' Obtain Environment Variables
        Call Set_Environment_Variables(oEnv)
        oEnv.bDebug = bDebug

        ' Obtain the Process Start Time and attach it to the environment object
        oEnv.Start = Format(Now, "mmddyyyyhhmmss")

        ' Set up debug files if in debug mode
        If bDebug Then
            Call Get_Debug_Files(oEnv, oFS, oOrderDump, oDbgFile)
            oDbgFile.WriteLine "Starting " & oEnv.sProcessName & " at " & oEnv.Start
        End If

        ' Open a Database Connection
        If bDebug Then oDbgFile.WriteLine "Opening a Database Connection"
        Set oConn = CreateObject("ADODB.Connection")
        oConn.Open oEnv.sConnectString

        ' Obtain array of order ids
        ' (Note:  Order GUIDs obtained from dbase are 26 chars)
        Call Get_Array_Data(oConn, CStr(oEnv.sOrderSPName), aArrayData)

        ' Check to see if array containing data is empty
        If Not IsEmpty(aArrayData) Then

            If bDebug Then
                sTmpStr = "Obtained a total of " & CStr(UBound(aArrayData, 2) + 1) & _
                          " order(s) requiring processing."
                oDbgFile.WriteLine sTmpStr
            End If
```

```vb
        ' Set up MSCS objects via Call to Global ASA
        If bDebug Then oDbgFile.WriteLine "Calling GLOBAL_ASA"
        Call GLOBAL_ASA(CStr(oEnv.sProcessName), CStr(oEnv.sConnectString), _
                    MSCSSite, MSCSMessageManager)

        ' Build Pipe Context Object
        If bDebug Then oDbgFile.WriteLine "Building Pipe Context"
        Call Build_PipeContext(MSCSSite, MSCSMessageManager, PipeContext)

    ' Loop for each Order
    For I = 0 To UBound(aArrayData, 2)

    ' On an error go to end of loop
    On Error GoTo EndofFor

        If bDebug Then
            sTmpStr = "Processing Order ID " & aArrayData(0, I)
            oDbgFile.WriteLine sTmpStr
        End If

    ' Perform Executable Specific "Pre-Pipe" Processing
        Call PrePipe_Processor(oEnv, oConn, I, aArrayData, MSCSSite, _
                            OrderForm, UpdateStorage, oDbgFile)

        ' Dump the OrderForm's contents prior to running the pipe
        If bDebug Then
            sTmpStr = "Contents of OrderForm prior to running the pipe:" & vbCrLf
            oOrderDump.WriteLine sTmpStr
            Call DumpOrderForm(OrderForm, oOrderDump)
        End If

        ' Run the transacted pipeline
        If bDebug Then
            sTmpStr = "Running Transacted " & oEnv.sPCFName & " Pipeline"
            oDbgFile.WriteLine sTmpStr
        End If

        Call Run_MTS_Pipeline(oEnv, OrderForm, PipeContext)

        ' Dump the OrderForm's contents after running the pipe
        If bDebug Then
            sTmpStr = vbCrLf & "Contents of OrderForm after running the pipe:"
            oOrderDump.WriteLine sTmpStr
            Call DumpOrderForm(OrderForm, oOrderDump)
        End If

        ' Perform Executable Specific "Post-Pipe" Processing
        Call PostPipe_Processor(oEnv, oConn, I, aArrayData, MSCSSite, _
                            OrderForm, UpdateStorage, oDbgFile)

EndofFor:
```

```
            If Err.Number Then
              nErrNum = Err.Number
              sErrSrc = Err.Source
             sErrDes = Err.Description
             Resume EndTrap

    EndTrap:
            On Error GoTo ErrorTrap

            sTmpStr = "Fatal Error Processing Order ID " & aArrayData(0, I)
            If bDebug Then oDbgFile.WriteLine sTmpStr
            Call InsertDBLogMsg(oConn, CStr(oEnv.sLogSPName), sTmpStr)

            If bDebug Then
                oDbgFile.WriteLine "  Error Number: " & nErrNum
                oDbgFile.WriteLine "  Error Source: " & sErrSrc
                oDbgFile.WriteLine "  Error Description: " & sErrDes
            End If

            Call InsertDBLogMsg(oConn, CStr(oEnv.sLogSPName), sErrDes, nErrNum, _
                           sErrSrc)

            sTmpStr = "Attempting to Continue onto Next Order"
            If bDebug Then oDbgFile.WriteLine sTmpStr
            Call InsertDBLogMsg(oConn, CStr(oEnv.sLogSPName), sTmpStr)
          End If

          If OrderForm.Value("_Purchase_Errors").Count > 0 Then
            sTmpStr = "Purchase Errors Processing Order ID " & _
                      CStr(aArrayData(0, I))
             If bDebug Then oDbgFile.WriteLine sTmpStr
             Call InsertDBLogMsg(oConn, CStr(oEnv.sLogSPName), sTmpStr)
             For Each errorStr In OrderForm.Value("_Purchase_Errors")
                If bDebug Then oDbgFile.WriteLine CStr(errorStr)
                Call InsertDBLogMsg(oConn, CStr(oEnv.sLogSPName), CStr (errorStr))
             Next
             sTmpStr = "Attempting to Continue onto Next Order"
             If bDebug Then oDbgFile.WriteLine sTmpStr
             Call InsertDBLogMsg(oConn, CStr(oEnv.sLogSPName), sTmpStr)
          End If

    '     Clear objects dependent on Loop
          Set OrderForm = Nothing
          Set UpdateStorage = Nothing

    '    Continue on with next Order
         Next
      Else
         If bDebug Then oDbgFile.WriteLine "No Orders Requiring Processing Found"
      End If

    '  Reset Error Trap
      On Error Resume Next
```

```
    If bDebug Then
        oEnv.End = Format(Now, "mmddyyyyhhmmss")
        oDbgFile.WriteLine "Ending " & oEnv.sProcessName & " at " & oEnv.End
        oOrderDump.Close
        oDbgFile.Close
    End If

    ' Close the connection to the database
    oConn.Close

    ' Clear objects dependent on Main
    Set oEnv = Nothing
    Set oFS = Nothing
    Set oOrderDump = Nothing
    Set oDbgFile = Nothing
    Set oConn = Nothing
    Set oDBConn = Nothing
    Set MSCSSite = Nothing
    Set MSCSMessageManager = Nothing
    Set PipeContext = Nothing
    Set OrderForm = Nothing
    Set UpdateStorage = Nothing

    ' Exit subroutine
    Exit Sub

' Trap an error
ErrorTrap:
    Set oEnv = Nothing
    Set oFS = Nothing
    Set oOrderDump = Nothing
    Set oDbgFile = Nothing
    Set oConn = Nothing
    Set oDBConn = Nothing
    Set MSCSSite = Nothing
    Set MSCSMessageManager = Nothing
    Set PipeContext = Nothing
    Set OrderForm = Nothing
    Set UpdateStorage = Nothing

End Sub
```

While the main subroutine looks overwhelming, it really isn't. Most of the code in the main subroutine is related to either debug statements or error handling.

We cannot emphasize enough how critical error handlers are for reliable operation. When in production, your code needs to be able to run in a "lights-out" environment. Should it encounter an error, it needs to be able to tell you why it failed. To satisfy this requirement, we have included two error handlers within the main subroutine.

`ErrorTrap` handles any errors that occur outside of the order loop. This is our weakest error handler as it currently does not provide any physical feedback. You will want to enhance this to either write to the NT Event Log or send your administrator an e-mail before you go into production.

EndofFor handles any errors that occur within the order loop. This one is probably most important as we wanted to ensure that if we encountered an error on a single order, we could write the error to a database log for future analysis and continue processing subsequent orders. We chose to write all errors to our database as its inherent services provide for easier administration of the error log than a flat file approach.

We have plenty of debug, all of which can be controlled by a single boolean switch. Debug exists for the purpose of understanding the state of the main subroutine, OrderForm, and pipeline. I suggest that you only use debugging for analyzing a single order's execution as the output is rather large.

You may notice that for debugging the OrderForm state we converted the Commerce Server-provided Scriptor, DumpOrder.vbs, to a single VB module, called Dump_OrderForm_Module.bas, and have altered it to write its output to a debug file.

You will also see that there are two types of errors that can occur within the order loop: those that are runtime errors, raised by the subroutines, and those that get appended to the OrderForm's "_Purchase_Errors" collection by the components found within the pipeline. In the post-pipe processor, we only commit changes to our OrderForm if this collection is empty. Depending on the error tolerance that you set the pipeline at, you could end up getting errors within this collection.

Our preference is to have the pipeline tolerate warnings and have the subsequent components bypass their processing under this scenario. Alternatively, you could only have your pipeline tolerate success. However, the pipeline will then raise a runtime error that will need to get caught within the subroutine Run_MTS_Pipeline(), which is in the Run_MTS_Pipeline_Module.bas file.

> **I recommend that you get into the habit of accessing the OrderForm's error collections using the syntax:**
>
> ```
> OrderForm.Value("_Purchase_Errors") or
> OrderForm.Value("_Basket_Errors")
> ```
>
> **within both the ASP/VBScript and VB environments in this form, as it is compatible in both.**

Supporting Subroutines for Main.bas

We will now take a closer look at the other modules included in our VB project.

Set_Environment_Variables_Module.bas

A Commerce Server Dictionary object is used to store the batch processor's context information. The Commerce Dictionary object was chosen, over a Scripting Dictionary, to illustrate its value and ease of use within VB's environment. It is easier to use than a Scripting Dictionary because properties can be added directly through assignment as opposed to a method call.

The following subroutine, Set_Environment_Variables(), was written to create the processor's environment object. You will need to customize some of these values for your machine.

```
Public Sub Set_Environment_Variables(oEnv As Object)
'   Purpose:
'   Loads commerce dictionary with global constants.
'   Note:   You may wish to populate this dictionary from an object that
'           extracts these strings from the registry.
'
'   Variable Definitions:
'   sPCFPath        - (String) Full path for the Pipeline Configuration File
'   sPCFName        - (String) Name of PCF file
'   sDbgPath        - (String) Full path for debug log output
'   sLogFilePrefix  - (String) Prefix for file containing debug
'   sLogSPName      - (String) Name of stored procedure used for error logging
'   sOrderSPName    - (String) Name of stored procedure used for obtaining order ids
'   sProcessName    - (String) Name of "batch" store
'   sConnectString  - (String) ODBC Connection String

'   Error Handling
    On Error GoTo ErrorTrap

'   Declare Variables
    Dim nIntErrNum As Long
    Dim sIntErrSrc As String

    Set oEnv = CreateObject("Commerce.Dictionary")

    With oEnv
      .sPCFPath = "D:\Wrox\Pipeline\"
      .sPCFName = "BatchStore.pcf"
      .sDbgPath = "D:\Wrox\Logs\"
      .sLogFilePrefix = "BATCH_AUTH_"
      .sLogSPName = "BATCH_insert_db_error_log"
      .sOrderSPName = "BATCH_get_open_orders"
      .sProcessName = "Batch Store"
      .sConnectString = "DSN=BatchStore;UID=sa;PWD=;"
    End With
    Exit Sub

'   Trap an error
ErrorTrap:
    nIntErrNum = Err.Number
    Set oEnv = Nothing
    Err.Raise Number:=nIntErrNum, Source:=sIntErrSrc

End Sub
```

Insert_Error_into_DB_Module.bas

Another feature provided in the sample batch processor is that any errors that occur within the order processing loop are "logged" into the database via the subroutine `InsertDBLogMsg()`. The code for this subroutine is shown as follows:

```
Public Sub InsertDBLogMsg(oDBConn As ADODB.Connection, _
                          sProcName As String, _
                          sMsgDes As String, _
                          Optional nMsgNum As Long, _
                          Optional sMsgSrc As String)

    ' Error Handling
    On Error GoTo ErrorTrap

    ' Declare Variables
    Dim oCmd As ADODB.Command
    Dim nIntErrNum As Long
    Dim sIntErrSrc As String

    ' Initialize the db_command object
    Set oCmd = CreateObject("ADODB.Command")
    Set oCmd.ActiveConnection = oDBConn
    oCmd.CommandText = sProcName
    oCmd.CommandType = adCmdStoredProc
    oCmd.Parameters.Refresh
    oCmd("@nMsgNum") = nMsgNum
    oCmd("@sMsgDes") = Mid(sMsgDes, 1, 1000)
    oCmd("@sMsgSrc") = Mid(sMsgSrc, 1, 100)
    oCmd.Execute
    Set oCmd = Nothing

    ' Exit Subroutine
    Exit Sub

' Trap an error
ErrorTrap:
    nIntErrNum = Err.Number
    sIntErrSrc = "InsertDBLogMessage"
    Set oCmd = Nothing
    Err.Raise Number:=nIntErrNum, Source:=sIntErrSrc

End Sub
```

This routine takes as input an open ADO connection, stored procedure name, and VB's native Error object properties, and calls the Transact-SQL stored procedure (provided with the database from the Wrox website download) `BATCH_insert_db_error_log.sql`, to insert the data into the database.

The code for this stored procedure is shown opposite.

```
Create PROCEDURE BATCH_insert_db_error_log
    ( @nMsgNum    INT=NULL,
      @sMsgDes    VARCHAR(1000)=NULL,
      @sMsgSrc    VARCHAR(100)=NULL
    )

AS

DECLARE @nErrorSave INT

SET NOCOUNT ON

SET @nErrorSave= 0
IF NOT EXISTS (SELECT * FROM sysobjects WHERE id =
OBJECT_ID(N'BATCH_STORE_ERROR_LOG') AND OBJECTPROPERTY(id, N'IsUserTable') = 1)
CREATE TABLE BATCH_STORE_ERROR_LOG
    (date_entered datetime NOT NULL,
     nMsgNum INT NULL,
     sMsgDes VARCHAR (1000) NULL,
     sMsgSrc VARCHAR (100) NULL)

INSERT INTO BATCH_STORE_ERROR_LOG
           (date_entered,nMsgNum,sMsgDes,sMsgSrc)

VALUES(GETDATE(),@nMsgNum,@sMsgDes,@sMsgSrc)

IF (@@ERROR <> 0) SET @nErrorSave= @@ERROR

RETURN @nErrorSave
```

We have it creating the error log table, BATCH_STORE_ERROR_LOG, because we found it easier during development and testing to delete the table in SQLServer's Enterprise Manager rather than issue a truncate statement via query interface.

Get_Debug_Files_Module.bas

The Get_Debug_Files() subroutine creates references to the Scripting Runtime's FileSystem and TextStream objects which perform the file I/O necessary to support the program's debug for recording the state of the OrderForm and Main subroutine. The code for this subroutine is as follows:

```
Public Sub Get_Debug_Files(oEnv As Object, _
                           oFS As Object, _
                           oOrderDump As Object, _
                           oDbgFile As Object)
' Error Handling
On Error GoTo ErrorTrap

    ' Declare Variables
    Dim nIntErrNum As Long
    Dim sIntErrSrc As String
    Dim sTmpStr As String
```

```
        Set oFS = CreateObject("Scripting.FileSystemObject")

        ' Construct full path name to debug the OrderForm object
        sTmpStr = CStr(oEnv.sDbgPath) & CStr(oEnv.sLogFilePrefix) & _
                 "ORDERFORM_" & CStr(oEnv.Start) & ".txt"

        Set oOrderDump = oFS.CreateTextFile(sTmpStr, True)

        ' Construct full path to debug the batch processor
        sTmpStr = CStr(oEnv.sDbgPath) & CStr(oEnv.sLogFilePrefix) & _
                 "PROCESS_" & CStr(oEnv.Start) & ".txt"

        Set oDbgFile = oFS.CreateTextFile(sTmpStr, True)

        Exit Sub

ErrorTrap:
    If Err.Number Then
        sIntErrSrc = "Get_Debug_Files"
        nIntErrNum = Err.Number
        Err.Raise Number:=nIntErrNum, Source:=sIntErrSrc
    End If

End Sub
```

It takes as input the environment object that stores the strings for building the debug file names.

Get_Array_Data_Module.bas

To determine if order IDs that need processing exist, the subroutine `Get_Array_Data()` was written to perform the database call via ADO and return the results within an array. Notice that, for performance reasons, we are passing ADO's Connection object in to the subroutine by reference and have declared all other ADO objects explicitly using VB's early binding technique.

```
Public Sub Get_Array_Data(oConn As ADODB.Connection, _
                         sProcName As String, _
                         aArrayData As Variant)

'  Error Handling
On Error GoTo ErrorTrap

    ' Declare Variables
    Dim oCmd As ADODB.Command
    Dim oRS As ADODB.Recordset
    Dim nIntErrNum As Long
    Dim sIntErrSrc As String

    ' Obtain the required ADODB Objects
    Set oCmd = New ADODB.Command
    Set oRS = New ADODB.Recordset

    ' Get the listing of order ids requiring processing
    oCmd.ActiveConnection = oConn
    oCmd.CommandType = adCmdStoredProc
    oCmd.CommandText = sProcName
    oCmd.Parameters.Refresh
```

```
    ' Get the recordset
    Set oRS = oCmd.Execute

    ' Place Returned Recordset into an array
    If Not oRS.EOF Then
      aArrayData = oRS.GetRows
    End If

    ' Close the recordset / Clear out objects
    oRS.Close
    Set oRS = Nothing
    Set oCmd = Nothing

    Exit Sub

' Trap an error
ErrorTrap:
    nIntErrNum = Err.Number
    sIntErrSrc = "Get_Array_Data"
    Set oCmd = Nothing
    Set oRS = Nothing
    Err.Raise Number:=nIntErrNum, Source:=sIntErrSrc

End Sub
```

This routine has been written to be independent of the stored procedure name. However, it will only support stored procedures that do not take input parameters.

For the sample batch processor, the stored procedure, BATCH_get_open_orders.sql was written. It implements a basic select statement for the order ids against the receipt table as follows:

```
Create PROCEDURE BATCH_get_open_orders

AS

SET NOCOUNT ON
SELECT order_id FROM receipt WHERE order_status = 'open'

RETURN
```

While this example mimics the code provided within the sample batch processor, you can make the selection criteria anything you want, depending on your needs.

GLOBAL_ASA_Module.bas

As long as orders requiring processing are found, `Main` continues to execute with a call to the subroutine, `GLOBAL_ASA()`. We stripped Commerce Server's typical `global.asa` file down to its essential elements required for batch processing and placed them into a subroutine as follows:

```
Public Sub GLOBAL_ASA(sStoreName As String, _
                      sConnectString As String, _
                      MSCSSite As Object, _
                      MSCSMessageManager As Object)

    On Error GoTo ErrorTrap

    Dim intErrNum

    ' Create the site dictionary
    Set MSCSSite = CreateObject("Commerce.Dictionary")

    With MSCSSite
      .DefaultConnectionString = sConnectString
      .DisplayName = sStoreName
    End With

    ' Create a message manager and initialize for rest of system
    Set MSCSMessageManager = CreateObject("Commerce.MessageManager")
    Call MSCSMessageManager.AddLanguage("usa", &H409)
    MSCSMessageManager.defaultLanguage = "usa"
    Call MSCSMessageManager.AddMessage("pur_out_of_stock", _
                                        "At least one item is out of stock.")
    Call MSCSMessageManager.AddMessage("pur_badsku", _
      "Products in your basket were deleted because they don't exist in this
store.")
    Call MSCSMessageManager.AddMessage("pur_badplacedprice", _
                            "Prices of products in your basket have been
updated.")
    Call MSCSMessageManager.AddMessage("pur_noitems", _
                                        "An order must have at least one item.")
    Call MSCSMessageManager.AddMessage("pur_badshipping", _
                        "Unable to complete order. Cannot compute shipping
cost.")
    Call MSCSMessageManager.AddMessage("pur_badtax", _
                                "Unable to complete order. Cannot compute
tax.")
    Call MSCSMessageManager.AddMessage("pur_badhandling", _
                        "Unable to complete order. Cannot compute handling
cost.")
    Call MSCSMessageManager.AddMessage("pur_badverify", _
                "Changes to the data require your review. Please review and
resubmit.")
    Call MSCSMessageManager.AddMessage("pur_badpayment", _
                                    "There was a problem authorizing your
credit.")
    Call MSCSMessageManager.AddMessage("pur_badcc", "Bad Credit Card Number.")
```

```
      Exit Sub

ErrorTrap:
    intErrNum = Err.Number
    Err.Raise Number:=intErrNum, Source:="GLOBAL_ASA"
End Sub
```

You will notice within the GLOBAL_ASA subroutine that all but two of the properties usually contained within the MSCSSite dictionary are not used and the call to read the storefront's site.csc file has been removed. This was done to eliminate an external file dependency. Since many of the properties obtained from this file are used to control a storefront's navigation, they are not applicable to a batch processor. We could have eliminated this entire subroutine, as it is only used to "wrap" the calls to the message manager and eliminate their "clutter" from the main program. However, we wanted to keep the "look-and-feel" of the batch processor consistent with what you would find in an ASP-based storefront.

Build_PipeContext_Module.bas

Following the typical execution found within Commerce Server's "out-of-the-box" storefronts, a call is made to the subroutine Build_PipeContext(), to build the context object used within the pipeline. The code within this subroutine is straightforward as it is used to pass the global Commerce Server objects into the pipeline, as shown below.

```
Public Sub Build_PipeContext(MSCSSite As Object, _
                             MSCSMessageManager As Object, _
                             PipeContext As Object)

    ' Error Handling
    On Error GoTo ErrorTrap

    ' Declare Variables
    Dim nIntErrNum As Long
    Dim sIntErrSrc As String

    Set PipeContext = CreateObject("Commerce.Dictionary")
    Set PipeContext("MessageManager") = MSCSMessageManager
    PipeContext("SiteName") = MSCSSite.DisplayName
    PipeContext("DefaultConnectionString") = MSCSSite.DefaultConnectionString
    PipeContext("Language") = MSCSMessageManager.defaultLanguage

    Exit Sub

' Trap an error
ErrorTrap:
    nIntErrNum = Err.Number
    sIntErrSrc = "Build_PipeContext"
    Set PipeContext = Nothing
    Err.Raise Number:=nIntErrNum, Source:=sIntErrSrc

End Sub
```

PrePipe_Processor_Module.bas

Once the pipeline's context object is established, we now need to obtain an OrderForm object. As mentioned previously, the main job of this subroutine, PrePipe_Processor(), is to obtain a complete OrderForm object. This can be accomplished by pulling a copy of an existing OrderForm from the database (in marshaled form) or through an ADO recordset that can then be used to populate an OrderForm object. For the sample batch processor, we chose to pull an existing OrderForm from the receipt table. The code is shown below.

```
Public Sub PrePipe_Processor(oEnv As Object, _
                              oConn As ADODB.Connection, _
                              I As Long, _
                              aArrayData As Variant, _
                              MSCSSite As Object, _
                              Receipt As Object, _
                              UpdateStorage As Object, _
                              oDbgFile As Object)


    ' Error Handling
    On Error GoTo ErrorTrap

    ' Declare Local Variables
    Dim nIntErrNum As Long
    Dim sIntErrSrc As String

    Dim sTmpStr As String
    Dim ReceiptStorage As Object

    sTmpStr = "Getting OrderForm Storage for Obtaining Receipt"
    If oEnv.bDebug Then oDbgFile.WriteLine sTmpStr

    ' Get the orderform storage object for extracting the receipt
    Call Get_OrderForm_Storage(MSCSSite, "receipt", "order_id", _
                            "marshalled_receipt", "date_changed",
ReceiptStorage)

    sTmpStr = "Getting OrderForm Storage for Updating Receipt"
    If oEnv.bDebug Then oDbgFile.WriteLine sTmpStr

    Call Get_OrderForm_Storage(MSCSSite, "receipt", "order_id", _
                            "marshalled_receipt", "date_changed", UpdateStorage)

    sTmpStr = "Getting OrderForm From Receipt Table"
    If oEnv.bDebug Then oDbgFile.WriteLine sTmpStr

    ' Lets get the receipt data from the receipt table
    Set Receipt = ReceiptStorage.GetData(Null, aArrayData(0, I))

    Set ReceiptStorage = Nothing

    ' Exit Subroutine
    Exit Sub
```

```
         ' Trap an error
   ErrorTrap:
      nIntErrNum = Err.Number
      sIntErrSrc = "PrePipe_Processor"
      Err.Raise Number:=nIntErrNum, Source:=sIntErrSrc

   End Sub
```

The sample code above shows that an `OrderForm` object is returned within the object named `Receipt`. It also returns an additional object, `UpdateStorage`, which can be used by the post-pipe processor for updating the receipt table. Please note that in this specific example, the redundant storage object `ReceiptStorage`, which is used for extracting the marshaled `OrderForm` from the receipt table, could be eliminated. Note also that this routine is dependent on the database (and schema) to which we are connected. While this is a limitation, it is the only routine in the batch processor that has such dependencies.

My intent is for you to retain this subroutine's calling interface, but place whatever pre-pipe processing logic you need within it to obtain the Commerce Dictionary object (for example, `OrderForm`), whether it be e-commerce related or not.

Get_OrderForm_Storage_Module.bas

As you have seen previously within this book, the `OrderFormStorage` object is used for moving the marshaled `OrderForm` into and out of the database. This object is obtained through the use of Commerce Server's `DBStorage` object as follows:

```
Public Sub Get_OrderForm_Storage(MSCSSite As Object, _
                         sTableName As Variant, _
                         sTableKey As Variant, _
                         sMarshalledColumn As Variant, _
                         sDateColumn As Variant, _
                         OrderFormStorage As Object)


'  Error Handling
On Error GoTo ErrorTrap

    ' Declare Variables
    Dim nIntErrNum As Long
    Dim sIntErrSrc As String

    Set OrderFormStorage = CreateObject("Commerce.DBStorage")
    Call OrderFormStorage.InitStorage(MSCSSite.DefaultConnectionString, _
        sTableName, sTableKey, "Commerce.OrderForm", sMarshalledColumn, sDateColumn)

    Exit Sub

' Trap an error
ErrorTrap:
    nIntErrNum = Err.Number
    sIntErrSrc = "Get_OrderForm_Storage"
    Set OrderFormStorage = Nothing
    Err.Raise Number:=nIntErrNum, Source:=sIntErrSrc


End Sub
```

As you can see in the sample code, this subroutine has been "hard-coded" to return Commerce Server's `OrderForm` object. You could generalize this routine further to return a plain, marshaled `OrderForm` instead.

Run_MTS_Pipeline_Module.bas

Now that we have the marshaled `OrderForm` object (that is, receipt), we can run the MTS-enabled, transactional pipeline against our customized components. This is achieved by calling the subroutine, `Run_MTS_Pipeline()`, given as follows:

```vb
Sub Run_MTS_Pipeline(oEnv As Object, _
                     OrderForm As Object, _
                     PipeContext As Object)

'   Error Handling
On Error GoTo ErrorTrap

    ' Declare Variables
    Dim nIntErrNum As Long
    Dim sIntErrSrc As String

    Dim sTmpStr As String
    Dim errorLevel As Long

    ' Get a Transacted Pipeline Object
    Set Pipeline = CreateObject("Commerce.MtsTxPipeline")

    If oEnv.bDebug Then
'       Build the debug file path
        sTmpStr = CStr(oEnv.sDbgPath) & CStr(oEnv.sLogFilePrefix) & "PIPE_" & _
                CStr(oEnv.Start) & ".txt"

        Call Pipeline.SetLogFile(sTmpStr)

    End If

    sTmpStr = CStr(oEnv.sPCFPath) & CStr(oEnv.sPCFName)

'   Load the PCF file
    Call Pipeline.LoadPipe(sTmpStr)

    ' Run the Pipeline
    errorLevel = Pipeline.Execute(1, OrderForm, PipeContext, 0)

    ' Place the errorlevel on the OrderForm for subsequent processing
    OrderForm.errorLevel = errorLevel

    ' Clear the object
    Set Pipeline = Nothing

    Exit Sub
```

```
'   Trap an error
ErrorTrap:
    nIntErrNum = Err.Number
    sIntErrSrc = "Run_MTS_Pipeline"
    Set Pipeline = Nothing
    Err.Raise Number:=nIntErrNum, Source:=sIntErrSrc

End Sub
```

This subroutine will optionally output to a debug file the results of the pipeline's execution. Again, debug is controlled via a single boolean switch in `Main`.

Wasn't the above subroutine easy? The pipeline, being a second tier, insulates our program from needing to know anything about our workflow. Imagine the possibilities of Commerce Server's technology beyond storefronts and transactions!

BatchStore.pcf

As you have learned in this book, our workflow, or business logic, is configured independent of the batch processor within an isolated tier. Commerce Server's Pipeline is the enabler of this capability.

We chose to execute the following sample pipeline, saved in the Pipeline folder from the Wrox download:

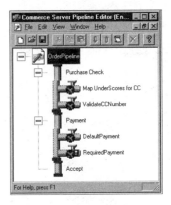

Given a receipt, the sample pipeline first executes the **Purchase Check** stage by mapping the archived credit card fields cc_expdate, cc_number, and cc_type to their underscored counterparts _cc_expdate, _cc_number, and _cc_type, using an internal commerce Scriptor written in VBScript. It does this so that the "out-of-the-box" component ValidateCC can be executed.

Assuming the credit card checks out, the pipeline continues to the **Payment** stage. Here the DefaultPayment component appends the code _payment_auth_code with the value "FAITH" preventing the RequiredPayment component from setting the pipeline error level to 2 (that is, completed with warnings) and appending the MSCSMessageManager's mnemonic, pur_badcc, to the _Purchase_Errors collection contained within the OrderForm object. See GLOBAL_ASA_Module.bas for the value contained for the mnemonic pur_badcc.

We chose this simply so that you can run several orders through the pipeline and gain an understanding of what is going on internally. We could just as easily have included a real life credit card component within the pipeline's payment stage instead of using DefaultPayment. Or we could have placed our own customized components within the pipeline.

557

Regarding the myth of flow control within the pipeline, you can build your own pipelines that provide for a more graceful exit during an error scenario rather than the current approach of raising an error to the caller. The Win32-based Pipeline Editor, when used in Enhanced Mode, allows you to specify the error level that a given stage within the pipeline will tolerate prior to raising an error to the caller. This feature, when combined with customized pipeline components that can skip processing based on "tolerable" pipeline error levels, allows for fairly robust flow control within the pipeline.

Within our sample database, all of the credit card numbers are successfully processed. We recommend that you alter the credit card numbers provided and see what happens to the "_Purchase_Errors" collection and pipeline error level values. You should also experiment with the "tolerable" error level within the pipeline and see what it does to the OrderForm and batch processor.

PostPipe_Processor_Module.bas

Now that the pipeline has been executed, we need to check the feedback reported by the various components and take appropriate action. To do this, we pass the OrderForm by reference, as the object Receipt, into the subroutine PostPipe_Processor() as follows:

```
Public Sub PostPipe_Processor(oEnv As Object, _
                    oConn As ADODB.Connection, _
                    I As Long, _
                    aArrayData As Variant, _
                    MSCSSite As Object, _
                    Receipt As Object, _
                    UpdateStorage As Object, _
                    oDbgFile As Object)

'  Error Handling
On Error GoTo ErrorTrap

    ' Declare Local Variables
    Dim nIntErrNum As Long
    Dim sIntErrSrc As String

    If Receipt.errorLevel = 1 And Receipt.Value("_Purchase_Errors").Count = 0 Then
        Receipt.errorLevel = Null
        Receipt.order_status = "authorized"
        Call UpdateStorage.CommitData(Null, Receipt)
    End If

    Exit Sub

'  Trap an error
ErrorTrap:
    nIntErrNum = Err.Number
    sIntErrSrc = "PostPipe_Processor"
    Err.Raise Number:=nIntErrNum, Source:=sIntErrSrc

End Sub
```

This sample routine ensures that the pipeline was completely successful by checking that the property `errorLevel`, appended to the Receipt by `Run_MTS_Pipeline`, is equal to one (1). If this property is equal to 1, we remove it from the `Receipt` by setting it to `Null`, set the `Receipt`'s (that is, `OrderForm` object) `order_status` to "`authorized`", and insert the marshaled `Receipt` back into the database via the `UpdateStorage` (that is, `DBStorage`) object's `CommitData` method.

Since the sample database table contains a field called `order_status`, the `DBStorage` object, while inserting the marshaled `OrderForm` back into the table, will update this field to the value stored within the similarly named `OrderForm` property. This process is known as "un-marshalling" the `OrderForm` data. This works in reverse as well. During extraction, the `DBStorage` object will compare the similarly named `OrderForm`'s properties to the un-marshaled data found in the table in which it resides. If it finds that the table's fields have been updated since prior insertion of the marshaled data, it will modify the marshaled data to reflect the updates.

> Note that the `DBStorage` object also provides methods for you to "map" dissimilar field names to any marshaled `OrderForm` property. We chose not to discuss this item as it creates additional dependencies for the batch processor on the database schema.

Installation Notes for the Code Sample

The entire code for this case study is available for free from the Wrox website.

Assumptions

The batch processor available for download assumes that:

- ❑ Its execution begins after orders are archived within the receipt table
- ❑ A "marshaled" `OrderForm` object is contained within the receipt table
- ❑ A column exists in the receipt table called `order_status` that is used to retain an order's state between successive runs
- ❑ Orders can only be extracted after subsequent sample runs once an update query is executed against the receipt table to change `order_status` to the value of "`open`".

Scope of the Sample Database

A sample database has been provided in the download. It is based on SQL Server 7.0 and contains: a receipt table with thirty three (33) marshaled `OrderForm` objects and two store procedures.

Installation Procedure

You can download the source code for the batch processor (`BatchStore.zip`) from the following URL:

```
http://www.wrox.com/
```

Follow these steps to complete the installation procedure once you have downloaded the zip file onto your computer:

- ❑ Unzip `BatchStore.zip` into a root level directory named **Wrox** on your local machine (you can choose a different directory if you want, but you will need to make the necessary modification to the code if this is the case).

- ❑ Physically copy the `Wrox.BAK` database backup device file from the `database` directory onto your database server machine.

- ❑ Use SQL Server to restore this device to a database named **Wrox**.

- ❑ Create a DSN named **BatchStore** that points to the restored **Wrox** database (the DSN should reside on your local machine).

- ❑ Open up `Batch_Store.vbp` from the **BatchStore** directory.

- ❑ Open up the `Set_Environment_Variables_Module` module and locate the following block of code:

```
With oEnv
  .sPCFPath = "D:\Wrox\Pipeline\"
  .sPCFName = "BatchStore.pcf"
  .sDbgPath = "D:\Wrox\Logs\"
  .sLogFilePrefix = "BATCH_AUTH_"
  .sLogSPName = "BATCH_insert_db_error_log"
  .sOrderSPName = "BATCH_get_open_orders"
  .sProcessName = "Batch Store"
  .sConnectString = "DSN=BatchStore;UID=sa;PWD=;"
End With
```

- ❑ Make sure that the hard-coded file paths for the `.sPCFPath` and `.sDbgPath` properties match the drive and directory that you unzipped the `BatchStore.zip` into (no modifications are required if you unzipped into the `D:\Wrox` directory).

- ❑ Finally, make sure that the database connection string, `.sConnectString`, has the appropriate UID and PWD to be able to access your database server (you should have already created the DSN).

And to test that the installation was successful, we can perform a test execution of the code:

- ❑ Start the batch processor by clicking on **Run** and **Start** ,while `Batch_Store.vbp` is still open in the Visual Basic development environment.

- ❑ The `BATCH_AUTH_PROCESS_mmddyyyyhhmmss.txt` log file should be created in the **Logs** directory, open up this file and you should notice log activity for the processing of 33 orders.

If you experience any problems, then check with the Wrox web site for any updates to this procedure.

Summary

Commerce Server is not just for storefronts! It is a simple, robust architecture that boils down to three basic concepts: the Commerce Dictionary or `OrderForm`; the MTS-enabled transactional pipeline; and mechanisms to move the `Dictionary` or `OrderForm` into and out of the database in binary form.

These three concepts have been covered through a fully functional, downloadable batch processor. You can use this proven batch processor template for future development, as it has previously been used to deploy world-class e-commerce solutions.

The benefits of the MTS-enabled transacted pipeline, and its power as an object request broker, creates a true enterprise-level foundation on which to build e-commerce applications.

I encourage you to study the template thoroughly and begin to think abstractly about applying Commerce Server's technology to other areas besides storefronts!

Case Study 2:
Report Emporium

This case study uses the features of Microsoft Site Server Commerce Edition to sell and distribute soft goods to customers. The actual products of the store, called Report Emporium, are Microsoft Excel spreadsheets and Microsoft Word documents that contain business analysis data.

The web site will demonstrate the use of several COM components to complete the task of providing security for the products and delivering the products to customers via the web browser for download. Some of the technologies used were covered previously in the book and only a short amount of time will be spent explaining their role in the operation of the site.

About the Company

Report Emporium's requirements are to fulfill product delivery electronically through download methods without allowing access to the actual product directly via the web server. The shoppers will have the option to download products for 30 days after purchase and the number of times the product has been downloaded by the shopper will be tracked and displayed on screen.

Report Emporium is essentially a Site Builder Wizard generated store with customizations to the pipeline and database schema, with additional ASP pages created to perform the specific functions of the web site. The site implements Site Server technology in a number of ways, ranging from product representation to the actual download of the product. By default, SSCE does not create pages to handle digital products or digital content as products. This functionality must be built into the pages using the basic store generated objects provided with Site Server.

The web site utilizes the AdminFiles object to access the product files, which reside outside of the web server directories. This is to ensure product security and to allow the product to be opened by the correct application using the MIME type of the file. This does not limit the product range to any specific file type. If the product file does not have an associated application, the user will be prompted to save the file to their hard drive or open the file. It is good practice to include instructions on your pages if you are not working with a widely used file type. This functionality allows the store to offer a wide range of products with any file type extension and cross browser support.

The ASP Response object is used to deliver the file to the shopper's computer. Working with digital products presents a challenge for security. We want to keep the user from actually browsing to a directory of products because they may try to modify the page url in their browser window. This would allow shoppers access to other products that have not been paid for, if they learn the file naming convention used for the products. Report Emporium keeps its product files outside of the web server directory, blocking users from directly browsing the directory. We will be using the BinaryWrite method of the object to achieve this functionality. The ASP page output at the time of download IS the product being delivered. The file path to be accessed by the AdminFiles object is passed in via the URL and no session variables are used. Session variables do not function correctly when the application is scaled to multiple web servers and were not an option to use when designing the web site. Session state is kept via callbacks to the database and through the transfer of data using the URL string.

> For a more detailed discussion of the Session object, we recommend Wrox's
> "Professional ASP 2.0"

The process for creating the site will be described as well as ASP code samples, code for pipeline changes, and the changes made to the database structure to support the site's needed capability.

Generating the Store

The Commerce Server wizards were used to create the foundation and the basic store. However, to prepare for running the wizard, a new database must be created.

Setting up the Database

You will need to create a database using the name dbEMP, with an initial size of 20 MB for the demo; this can change based on the needs of the site being created. Using the SQL Enterprise Manager, which is a snap-in for the MMC (Microsoft Management Console), this can be done by selecting the computer on which the database will reside, right clicking on the Databases folder and selecting New Database.

Then in Control Panel | ODBC Data Sources, create a System DSN on the server to point to this database. The DSN will be selected when creating the store through the Wizard process.

Using the Store Foundation Wizard

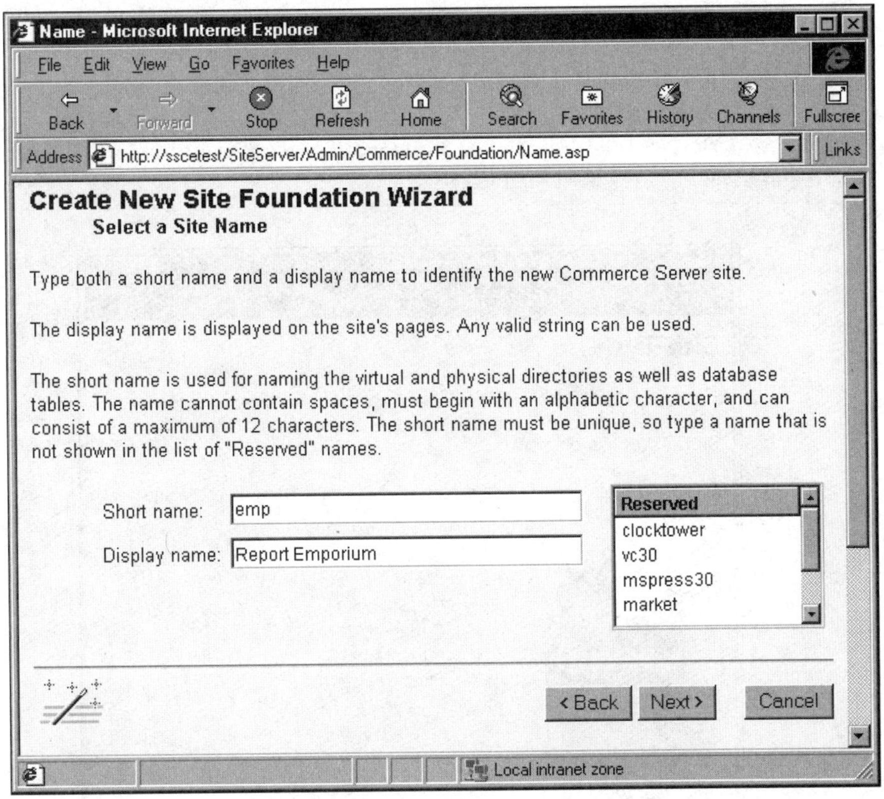

The Site Foundation Wizard has been discussed earlier in Chapter 5. Set the short name and display name as shown in the screenshot above and go through the steps using the default settings. Remember to formulate the database connection string to use our newly created DSN.

When you click the Finish button at the end of the wizard, the Site Server Foundation Wizard will create a directory using the "short name" specified within the web server root. It is important to note that Site Server 3.0 stores will only function as a directory under the wwwroot of the IIS server. A site.csc file has been created which holds the store name, database connection strings, the server's secure and non-secure path along with the path to the page you wish to have displayed if the store is closed. The wizard also generates pages that will prompt you to begin the Commerce Server Site Builder Wizard.

Using the Site Builder Wizard

This wizard actually builds the store pages, creates database tables and adds the pipelines customized for your store to the site. Click the link displayed on the page when the Foundation Wizard finished to start the Commerce Site Builder Wizard.

Site Type

Select Create a custom site since none of the sites used for starter stores meet the requirements for the site. This will allow us to choose which features we would like to implement and leave features we do not see a need for at the moment.

> **IMPORTANT NOTE: Running the Site Builder Wizard a second time will overwrite any changes you have made to the pages.**

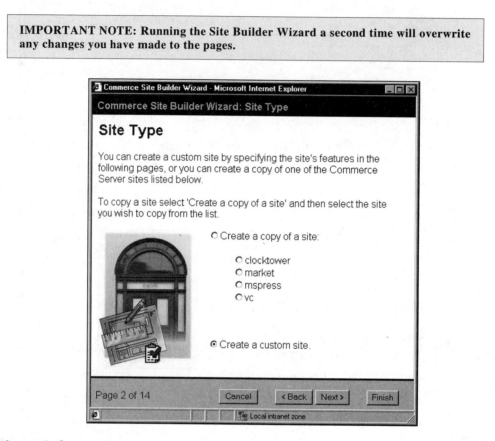

Merchant Information

The Merchant Information page of the wizard allows you to enter the name and company information of the merchant owning the site. The information is used to configure the Merchant Information stage of the plan pipeline. This can be useful if you are sending an e-mail confirmation out that is dynamically generated, if the merchant information changes you only need to update the component found in the pipeline.

For Report Emporium, the only information we use is the store name, which is pre-populated by the wizard.

Locale

Choose settings for English (United States).

Site Style

Keep the defaults chosen for these settings of the wizard.

Promotions

We want to keep this site simple and so chose not to set up any promotions during creation of this site.

Site Features

Select 'When Ordering' as the registration type. Report Emporium will deal with a type of "electronic" product so when a customer reaches shipping and handling, these do not apply to the type of product being sold unless we plan to ship out hard copies of each.

Departments should be set up as **Simple (single level)** since we are not using a complex product category scheme. Product Searching has been enabled.

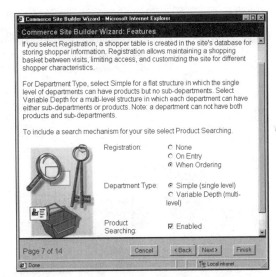

Product Attribute Type

Report Emporium's products share the same attributes. Because of this fact, 'Static Attributes' are chosen in the Wizard instead of the 'Dynamic Attribute' setting, which allows for more varying product types.

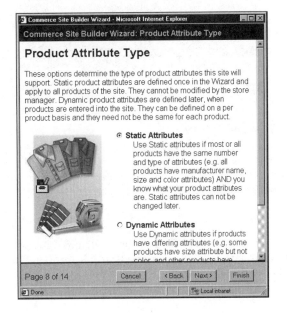

Product Structure

The product structure Wizard page allows us to pick from numerous attributes that are common within many products sold. If one is not found to fit the product of your store you have the option to create a new one. With Report Emporium we will be selecting 'Format' which is a multi-valued attribute. This will designate the product as being in Microsoft Excel format or Microsoft Word document format. This is needed since the product is offered in two different format types.

Shipping & Handling

The store does not deal with physical products; therefore these settings should be configured to zero and not enabled. If the store is later configured to handle physical products and these features are needed, they can easily be added by including the correct components in the plan pipeline using the Pipeline Editor included with Site Server.

Tax

Tax settings were not used with the demo of Report Emporium. Many different states have varying laws on how to charge tax on electronic or digital products sold. This is an area you might want to check with a tax attorney. There's no getting away from them!

Payment Methods

We will limit the types of credit cards processed to the standard default choices, so leave these unchanged (that is, all selected).

Order History

Storage of order history will be needed to meet the functional requirements of the site. This will allow us to relate product to shopper and give each person a review of what they have purchased. Therefore, check the 'Retain order history and receipt information' box.

Output Options

The output options required are basically the same as default. We do not want to load the database schema into the database at this time, so uncheck the 'Load Schema into Database' box. This will allow us to make the necessary changes to the table structure needed for the site's functionality. Do not load sample data either, as we will be adding our own products later.

Wizard Completion

Clicking the Finish button will give you a fully functional Site Server 3.0 Commerce Edition store. The site does not contain all of the functionality we require, however, so from this point on, we will make customizations to meet the requirements.

The Database

Due to the requirements of Report Emporium, some changes need to made to the standard database schema generated by the Site Builder Wizard. The SQL files would have been created in the folder `..\wwwroot\emp\Config\Sql\SQLSvr`. We will be storing the product path information so that the Excel and Word documents can be found and downloaded by the system.

We'll also need to change the `emp_variant` table to meet our needs. Open the `schema.sql` file using SQLServer's Query Tool, or in any text editor, and look for the section that creates the `emp_variant` table. Make the following changes to create another column called `path` in addition to the ones already being created:

```
CREATE TABLE emp_variant(
    sku         VARCHAR(100) NOT NULL,
    pf_id       VARCHAR(100) NOT NULL,
    attr_format INT NOT NULL,
    path        VARCHAR(255) NULL,
    PRIMARY KEY(sku),
    UNIQUE (pf_id, attr_format),
    FOREIGN KEY (pf_id) REFERENCES emp_product,
    FOREIGN KEY (attr_format) REFERENCES emp_attr_format(format_id)
)
GO
```

The next thing we need to do is create a table to store history information. We will create a column for `shopper_id`. We will also create a `pf_id` and `sku` column for product information, a `counter` so that we can tell how many times it is downloaded and finally a `date` column. Add the code below to the `schema.sql` file and execute it through the SQL Server query window.

```
CREATE TABLE dbo.emp_history(
    shopper_id CHAR(32) NOT NULL,
    pf_id       VARCHAR(100) NOT NULL,
    sku         VARCHAR(100) NOT NULL,
    counter     INT NULL,
    date        DATETIME NOT NULL CONSTRAINT DF_emp_history_date Default(getdate())
    PRIMARY KEY (shopper_id, pf_id, sku)
    FOREIGN KEY (shopper_id) REFERENCES emp_shopper,
    FOREIGN KEY (pf_id) REFERENCES emp_product,
    FOREIGN KEY (sku) REFERENCES emp_variant
)
GO
```

One problem that can occur with an e-commerce site requiring registration is that a user may register, add something to their shopping basket and never return to complete the purchase. Over a period of time this takes up space, if it occurs frequently enough. To counter this, we will create a stored procedure that checks the date of the basket entry and deletes those that are older than x number of days that we choose. You can schedule this to run nightly and it will keep orphaned orders out of your system.

We will create a stored procedure called sp_cleanbasket. This includes a DELETE statement to delete all rows that have a date_changed value that is greater than 24 hours from the time the stored procedure executes. The following will delete orders that have been orphaned for 24 hours:

```
CREATE PROCEDURE sp_cleanbasket
AS

DELETE emp_basket
WHERE date_changed < DATEADD(hh, - 24, GETDATE())

/* error checking */
IF @@Error <> 0
BEGIN
    return @@error
END

ELSE
BEGIN
    Return 0
END

GO
```

The Products

The products are the core reason the site exists. The site is built around supplying the customer with the products easily and conveniently. The products should be accessible from the web though the site download process but they cannot be allowed to be accessible by reverse engineering a URL; this is where someone, through knowing product file names, can access the products without an actual purchase taking place.

Each file will be stored on the server but will not be stored within directories located in or underneath the web server root directory. There are a few sample products used to demonstrate the functionality of Report Emporium and we will walk through the creation of these as well as enter them into the database using the Site Manager pages for Report Emporium.

The first step is to create a folder on the root of the C: drive called Product. (You do not have to select the C drive and you do not have to call the folder "Product" – the location and name are entirely up to you, but I will use this location and name for this case study). This will be the storage area for all products sold from the site. We will now need to create products to place within this storage area.

Create the following files and save them to the 'C:\Product' folder.

File name	File type
Sample1.doc	Word Document
Sample1.xls	Excel Spreadsheet
Sample2.doc	Word Document
Sample2.xls	Excel Spreadsheet

Note: You may want to add sample text within each file to distinguish the difference between the files to make sure that the correct file is being downloaded at the time of purchase.

Departments

Now, we will begin the process of entering the products via the Manager pages: the Store Manager can be found at http://yourhost/emp/manager/

Our first step is to set up "departments" so that we can categorize our products.
To do this, select Departments from the Manager page and create the following two departments with these attributes.

Department_ID	Department Name	Department Description
1	Sales Reports	Category contains reports on company sales figures.
2	Production Reports	Category contains reports on company production figures.

We can view each of the completed departments from the Manager Department page. This will list each department found within our store. The Manager page creates the necessary database entries for these to exist.

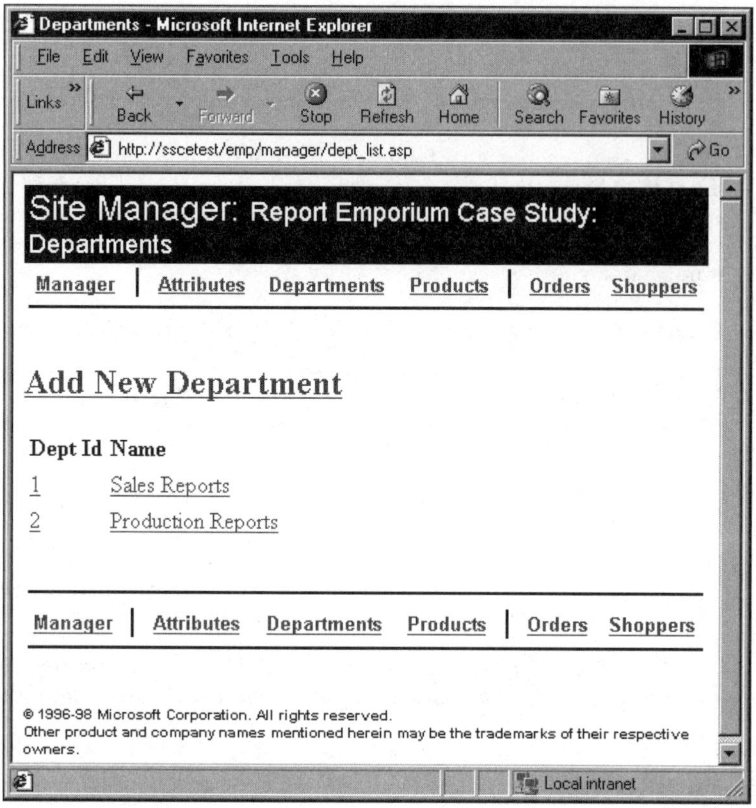

```
Departments - Microsoft Internet Explorer                    _ □ ×

 File   Edit   View   Favorites   Tools   Help

 Links  »    ↵         →        ⊗       ↻       ⌂        ◎       ▣        ◎       »
            Back    Forward    Stop    Refresh  Home    Search  Favorites History

 Address 🖺 http://sscetest/emp/manager/dept_list.asp         ▼    ⌐ Go

 Site Manager: Report Emporium Case Study:
 Departments

 Manager   |   Attributes   Departments   |   Products   |   Orders   Shoppers


 Add New Department

 Dept Id Name

 1       Sales Reports

 2       Production Reports


 Manager   |   Attributes   Departments   |   Products   |   Orders   Shoppers


 ® 1996-98 Microsoft Corporation. All rights reserved.
 Other product and company names mentioned herein may be the trademarks of their respective
 owners.

 🖺                                               🖳 Local intranet
```

Attributes

Now that we have our departments defined let's specify the values for the product attributes that we selected while using the Site Builder Wizard. On the menu, select Attributes and then choose the Format Attribute (it should be the only one in the list!).

Define the following values for the Format attribute, by clicking on Add New Format Value:

Format ID	Format Value
1	Excel Spreadsheet
2	Word Document

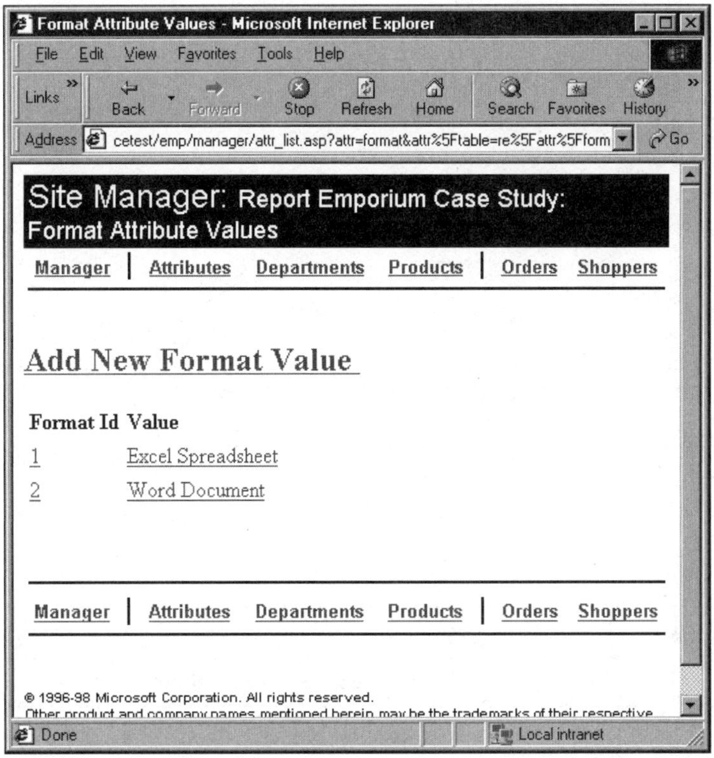

Site Manager: Report Emporium Case Study: Format Attribute Values

Manager | Attributes   Departments   Products   Orders   Shoppers

Add New Format Value

Format Id   Value

1   Excel Spreadsheet
2   Word Document

Manager | Attributes   Departments   Products   Orders   Shoppers

© 1996-98 Microsoft Corporation. All rights reserved.
Other product and company names mentioned herein may be the trademarks of their respective

Product

We will be selling two products from the site to begin with. Electronic products are treated in the same way as physical products by the site, because the store does not know the difference at this point. This knowledge is not required until the end of the purchase process. We are not mixing electronic and physical products; hence there is no attribute to assign the product type within this demo.

We will create two product families, each having two variants. The first product will contain the following information:

Product 1

Attribute	Value
PFID	001
Name	July Production Report
Description	Report detailing company production for the month of July
List Price	$10.00

Attribute	Value
Image File	<BLANK>
Image Width	0
Image Height	0
Sale Price	0
Sale Start	<BLANK>
Sale End	<BLANK>
Department	Production Reports

Product 1 Variant 1

SKU	Format
Doc	Microsoft Word Document

Product 1 Variant 2

SKU	Format
Xls	Microsoft Excel Spreadsheet

Product 2

Attribute	Value
PFID	002
Name	July Sales Report
Description	Report detailing company sales for the month of July
List Price	$10.00
Image File	<BLANK>
Image Width	0
Image Height	0
Sale Price	0
Sale Start	<BLANK>
Sale End	<BLANK>
Department	Sales Reports

Product 2 Variant 1

SKU	Format
Doc2	Microsoft Word Document

Product 2 Variant 2

SKU	Format
Xls2	Microsoft Excel Spreadsheet

Clicking on the product Name in the Products page will now show the details of your products with the specified variants – notice how Commerce Server changes the blank promotion start and end dates to a default value:

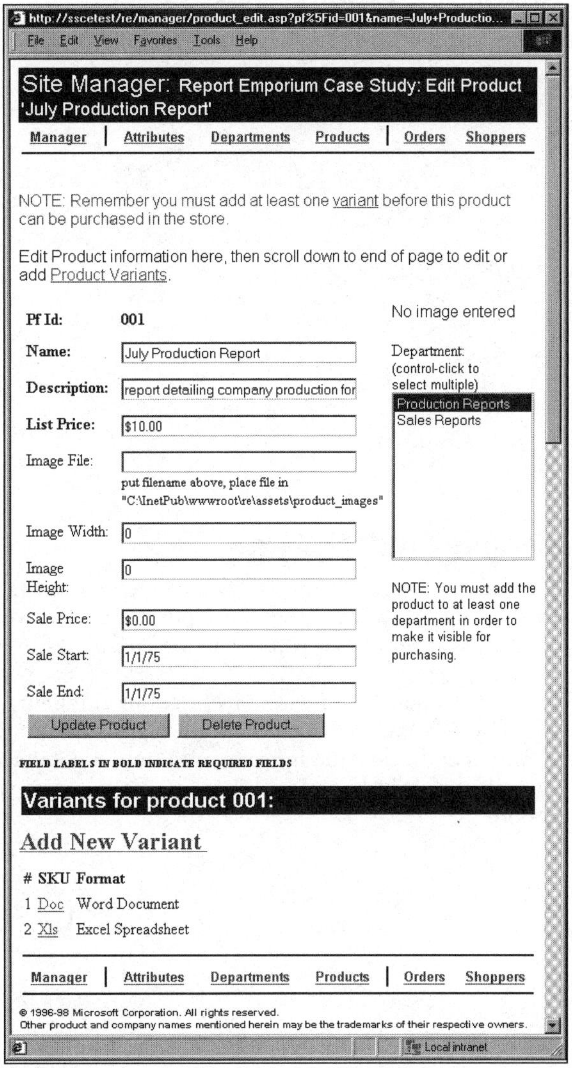

Now that the product information is located in the database, we need to add some more data specific to the functionality of the site. During the database setup we altered the `emp_variant` table to include a new column called `path`. This will relate the actual product's file path with the product information in the database. We can edit this either by using the database tools packaged with Visual Studio 97, Visual Studio 6.0 or by writing a SQL update statement to update the records in the database.

```
UPDATE emp_variant
SET path = 'c:\product\sample1.xls'
WHERE pf_id = '001' AND sku = 'Xls'
GO

UPDATE emp_variant
SET path = 'c:\product\sample1.doc'
WHERE pf_id = '001' AND sku = 'Doc'
GO

UPDATE emp_variant
SET path = 'c:\product\sample2.xls'
WHERE pf_id = '002' AND sku = 'Xls02'
GO

UPDATE emp_variant
SET path = 'c:\product\sample2.doc'
WHERE pf_id = '002' AND sku = 'Doc02'
GO

/* error checking */
...

GO
```

Recording Product Sales

For the required functionality to be met, we need to keep a record of which products were bought by the customer and when they were purchased. This will allow us to display the appropriate files available for download when the user completes the purchase.

There are a number of ways in which this can be implemented. In this case study we will use a Scriptor component, executing VBScript within the Purchase pipeline before the `SaveReceipt` component, to save the information into the database in Report Emporium. With the Pipeline Editor on Enhanced Mode, right click on the `SaveReceipt` component and select **Insert Component | Before...** :

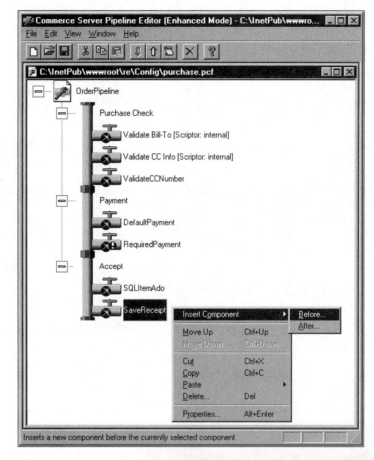

This will bring up the following dialog window:

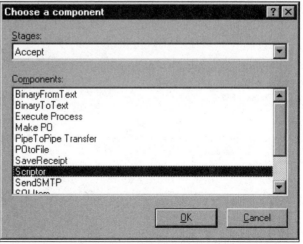

The script will be required to read values from the OrderForm for each product the customer is purchasing. Once these values are read, we then need to insert these into the emp_history table we created during the database setup.

The first thing we need to do is set up the objects we will be using.

```
' Setup objects
Set objConn  = CreateObject("ADODB.Connection")
Set items    = orderform.Items
```

Next, we write code to hold the values we need. The database connection string used by the site is accessible through the pipeline context using MSCSSite.DefaultConnectionString. Code can be written to change the pipeline context or add to the pipeline context within the ASP files of the web site. We also want to set a variable equal to the number of items (products) actually in the customer's shopping basket. We do this by looking at the Count property of the Items SimpleList object stored in the OrderForm. The shopper ID is important because it will relate our entries to the customer accessing the site. This can be read from the root OrderForm object: OrderForm.shopper_ID.

```
' Setup variables
ConnectString = Context.DefaultConnectionString
ShopperID     = OrderForm.shopper_id
nItems        = Items.count
```

The following step has the purpose of opening the connection to the database and executing the insert query to add the information to the appropriate table.

```
' Open database connection
objConn.Open ConnectString
```

We set up a For Next loop to retrieve the product information and set the values for our variables. Since the OrderForm is a collection of objects, the Set keyword is needed to get to the actual product line item's dictionary.

```
' Loop through products in OrderForm and execute insert query
For iLineItem = 0 to (nItems - 1)
Set lineItem = items(iLineItem)
    pfId = lineItem.[_product_pf_id]
    sku  = lineItem.sku
```

At this point it was necessary to dynamically build the query, filling in the values of the product just read. Our insert query will use placeholders for the values, similar to the way in which the Site Server Wizard-generated pages use placeholders. We will place this query in the query map found in the global.asa file of the store. In the global.asa file, the query map is initialized with a function called InitQueryMap.

```
sqlText = "INSERT INTO emp_history (shopper_id, pf_id, sku, date)"
sqlText = sqlText & " VALUES (':1',':2',':3',':4')"
Set MSCSQUeryMap.save_history = AddQuery(sqlText)
```

We then use VBScript's `Replace` function to dynamically set the values to be updated.

```
sqlText = MSCSQueryMap.save_history.SQLCommand
sqlText =    replace(sqlText,":1",shopperID)
sqlText =    replace(sqlText,":2",pfid)
sqlText =    replace(sqlText,":3",sku)
sqlText =    replace(sqlText,":4","DEFAULT")
```

The completed code with the query insert execution statement is as follows:

```
Function MSCSExecute(config, orderform, context, flags)

  ' Setup objects
  Set objConn  = CreateObject("ADODB.Connection")
  Set items    = orderform.Items

  ' Setup variables
  connectstring = context.defaultconnectionstring
  shopperID    = orderform.shopper_id
  nItems       = items.count

  ' Open Connection
  objConn.Open connectstring

  'Loop through products in OrderForm and execute insert query
  For iLineItem = 0 to (nItems - 1)
  Set lineItem = items(iLineItem)
    pfId = lineItem.[_product_pf_id]
    sku  = lineItem.sku
      sqlText = MSCSQueryMap.save_history.SQLCommand
      sqlText =    replace(sqlText,":1",shopperID)
      sqlText =    replace(sqlText,":2",pfid)
      sqlText =    replace(sqlText,":3",sku)
      sqlText =    replace(sqlText,":4","DEFAULT")

  objConn.Execute(sqlText)
  Next

  MSCSExecute = 1

/* error checking */


End Function
```

The Scriptor component will be inserted into the Accept stage of the purchase pipeline, just before the `Save Receipt` pipeline component. The purchase.`pcf` file used for the store is executed as a transacted pipeline through Microsoft Transaction Server. Scriptor Components do not allow access to the transaction context by nature. If access or control of the transaction is required from within component code, a pipeline component written in Visual Basic, C++ or with Java must be used.

Product Delivery

Report Emporium is designed to allow for electronic product delivery as well as securing the products from theft. Access to the products can only be achieved by an authenticated user who has previously purchased the product. The site allows users to download purchased reports within a period of 30 days. After this time, the product is no longer shown on the download screen.

There are two pages that provide the function of product delivery. The first of the pages, ProductView.asp retrieves a list of products the user has purchased that are available for download. These products are displayed on the page using an HTML link.

Our display criteria are based on information found in the emp_history table, which is updated by our custom script executed by the pipeline. Recall that we have a default value for the date column so that the date of purchase is recorded in the table. We will use this to determine if the product is within the 30 day allowed download timeframe. If it is not, we will not display the product. This ASP page returns the necessary information to complete the download process.

The next page in the process is called download.asp. The function of this page is for processing purposes only; it does not display data. The page uses information passed in via the hotlink to write to the purchased file. There are two very important objects used to provide this functionality. The first object is the Site Server AdminFiles object. The second is the ASP Response object, which will be discussed later in the case study.

Customizing Confirmed.asp

A small amount of editing is required to make confirmed.asp (found in the root of your site's directory) include the link to the product view page. The link passes in the shopper argument shopper_ID from its URL, by using URLShopperArgs, so it can be used by ProductView.asp:

```
Your order number is
<% order_id = mscsPage.HTMLEncode(Request("order_id")) %>

   <A HREF = "<% = baseURL("receipt.asp?") & mscsPage.URLShopperArgs("order_id", _
            Request("order_id")) %>"><STRONG><% = order_id %></STRONG></A>.
   <BR>
   <A HREF="<%= pageURL("productview.asp?") & mscsPage.URLShopperArgs()%>''>
      Download Products</A>
```

Building ProductView.asp

ProductView.asp is the page that is displayed at the end of the purchase process. It will be linked to the order confirmation page (confirmed.asp), which displays the order confirmation number. The page executes a query based on the shopper_ID and returns a list of products that have been purchased.

The code was written to create the ADO objects and set the database connection string.

```
<%


    'Create Objects
    Dim objConn
    Dim rs

    Set objConn = Server.CreateObject("ADODB.Connection")
    Set rs = Server.CreateObject("ADODB.Recordset")
    objConn.ConnectionString =MSCSSite.DefaultConnectionString


%>
```

Further down the page, we need to display the products. To do this we can write a query to return the product information needed based on the 30 day criteria and place it in the QueryMap located in the global.asa file of the store.

This is the query executed to return product download information (the lines with no shading are what we added earlier to the global.asa file):

```
sqlText = "INSERT INTO emp_history (shopper_id, pf_id, sku, date)"
sqlText = sqlText & " VALUES (':1',':2',':3',':4')"
sqlText = sqltext & "SELECT ev.sku, ev.pf_id,  ev.path, eh.date, eh.counter," & _
                    " ep.name"
sqlText = sqlText & " FROM emp_variant ev INNER JOIN emp_history eh ON"
sqlText = sqlText & " emp_variant.sku = emp_history.sku eh"
sqlText = sqlText & " AND emp_variant.sku = emp_history.sku"
sqlText = sqlText & " WHERE (emp_history.shopper_id = ':1') "
sqlText = sqlText & " AND (emp_history.date < DATEADD(DD, -30, GETDATE()))"
Set MSCSQueryMap.history_by_shopper = AddQuery(sqlText)
```

Note: The query written uses the :1 again as a placeholder for the probable value to be inserted into the query.

To display the products, we need to return the recordset and loop through each record writing out a link to download.asp with the appropriate product information.

```
<%
    objConn.Open
        sqlText = MSCSQueryMap.history_by_shopper.SQLCommand
        sqlText = replace(sqlText,":1",shopper_id)
    Set rs = objConn.Execute(sqlText)

    Do while not rs.EOF
%>
    <TR>
        <TD><A HREF="<%= baseURL("download.asp?") & _
            mscsPage.URLShopperArgs("pfId",rs("pf_id"),"sku",rs("sku"), _
            "path",rs("path"))%>" TARGET = "_blank"><%= rs("Name")%></A></TD>
```

```
       <TD><%= rs("counter")%></TD>
    </TR>
<%
    rs.MoveNext
    loop

    rs.Close
    objConn.Close
    Set rs = nothing
    Set objConn = nothing%>
```

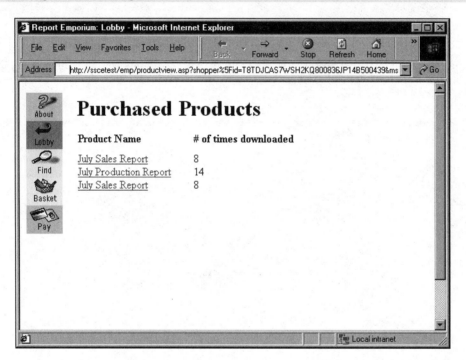

Building Download.asp

The final ASP page for delivering the order is a very simple processing page with a small amount of data access required. The page will not only deliver the product but it will also set a counter on the number of times the product has been downloaded by the customer. This can be useful in keeping track of how many documents were supplied during the 30-day download period.

First, we request the variables we have passed in. We also request the shopper_id from the URL so that we can validate the user as a shopper.

```
    ' Request variables
    path = request("path")
    sku  = request("sku")
```

Our validation code is a simple `If-Then-Else` statement to check the shopper_id variable for a null value. If there is no shopper_id present, we redirect the user to the home page.

```
' Validate user
If isNull(shopper_id) Then
    Response.Redirect("default.asp")
End If
```

The type of product must be determined at this point. The reason for this is that we later have to set the MIME type of the file as it is written out. This information is stored in our `emp_variant` table. The variables requested can be used in our `WHERE` clause to return the correct format. The query to retrieve this information is stored in the `global.asa` file for the site in the query map. We will also add the update query to update the history table to the query map.

```
' -- Query to select product information in history table by sku
sqlText = "SELECT ev.attr_format, eh.counter,"
sqlText = sqlText & " eh.sku FROM emp_variant ev INNER JOIN"
sqlText = sqlText & " emp_history eh ON emp_variant.sku = "
sqlText = sqlText & " emp_history.sku WHERE (emp_history.sku = ':1')"
Set MSCSQueryMap.history_by_sku = AddQuery(sqlText)

' - Update query to update the history table for each download
sqlText = "UPDATE emp_history SET counter = :1  "
sqlText = sqlText & "WHERE emp_history.shopper_id = ':2'"
sqlText = sqlText & " AND emp_history.sku = ':3'"
Set MSCSQueryMap.update_history = AddQuery(sqlText)
```

We then set the `sku` using the VBScript `Replace` function and execute the query using the `ADODB.Connection` object created in the `I_shop.asp` included file.

```
        sqlText = MSCSQueryMap.history_by_sku.SQLCommand
        sqlText = replace(sqlText,":1",sku)

    Set rs = MSCS.Execute(sqlText)
    format = Cint(rs("attr_format"))
```

Notice we are also retrieving the number of times the product has been downloaded. This will allow us to update the `emp_history` table with new information once the code is executed. To do this, we must execute an update query on the table using the appropriate values in the `WHERE` clause.

```
counter = rs("counter")
    rs.close
    Set rs  = nothing
    sqlText = MSCSQueryMap.update_history.SQLCommand
    sqlText = replace(sqlText,":3",sku)
    MSCS.Execute(sqlText)

    MSCS.Close
    Set MSCS = nothing
```

The code to track the download has been executed so we must now complete the delivery process and send the file to the user. We start by instantiating a `Commerce.AdminFiles` object. This will allow us to read the file in from any location on the server, not just the files under the web server directories. This is done using the `ReadFromBinaryFile()` method.

Once the file has been read, we must determine the correct format for output and set the MIME type accordingly. Report Emporium used a simple `Select Case` statement to differentiate between the two formats we use.

After the `ContentType` property of the Response object has been set we use the `BinaryWrite()` method of the Response object to send the file to the user.

```
'Create AdminFile object
    Set objAdminFile = Server.CreateObject("Commerce.AdminFiles")
    objFile = objAdminFile.ReadFromBinaryFile(path)

    Select Case format
    Case 1
        Response.ContentType = "application/vnd.ms-excel"
        Response.AddHeader "Content-Disposition", sku & ".xls"
    Case 2
        Response.ContentType = "application/msword"
        Response.AddHeader "Content-Disposition", sku & ".doc"
    End Select

    Response.BinaryWrite objFile
```

> **NOTE: At the beginning of the page, you must insert `<% response.buffer = true %>` so that the headers may be written dynamically.**

Download.asp

The complete code that we have just walked through is given below:

```
<%@ Language=VBScript %>
<% response.buffer=true %>
<!--#INCLUDE FILE="i_shop.asp" -->
<!--#INCLUDE FILE="i_util.asp" -->

<%
    'Request variables
    path = request("path")
    sku  = request("sku")

    'Validate user
    If isNull(shopper_id) Then
        Response.Redirect("default.asp")
    End If
```

```
        sqlText = MSCSQueryMap.history_by_sku.SQLCommand
        sqlText = replace(sqlText,":1",sku)
        Set rs = MCSC.Execute(sqlText)

        format = Cint(rs("attr_format"))
        counter = rs("counter")
        rs.close
        Set rs = nothing

    sqlText = MSCSQueryMap.update_history.SQLCommand
    sqlText = replace(sqlText ,":3",sku)
    MSCS.Execute(sqlText)
    MSCS.Close
    Set MSCS = nothing

    'Create AdminFile object
    Set objAdminFile = Server.CreateObject("Commerce.AdminFiles")
    objFile = objAdminFile.ReadFromBinaryFile(path)

    Select Case format

    Case 1
        Response.ContentType = "application/vnd.ms-excel"
        Response.AddHeader "Content-Disposition", sku & ".xls"
    Case 2
        Response.ContentType = "application/msword"
        Response.AddHeader "Content-Disposition", sku & ".doc"

    End Select

    Response.BinaryWrite objFile

%>
```

Report Emporium can now operate correctly meeting the functional requirements presented at the start of design.

Case Study 3:
The Wine Shop

Business Overview

Creating the Site

During this study, we'll assume a good background in setting up the Site Server commerce sites using the Site Foundation Wizard and the Site Builder Wizard as outlined in previous chapters. This case study has been designed around Microsoft SQL Server 7.0 although the principles are the same for Microsoft SQL Server 6.5.

Before We Start

Before we start configuration of our commerce site, the following should be set up:

- ❑ A DSN pointing to an database instance within SQL Server which you have set up previously
- ❑ A Web Site instance where you can create the commerce site

Keeping these details in mind, let's now configure our site.

The Basic Site

To begin with, fire up the Commerce Server MMC from Start | Programs | Microsoft Site Server | Administration | Site Server Service Admin (MMC) and expand the Commerce Host Administration entry. Now right-click on the server where you want to install the site and select New | Commerce Site Foundation which will start up Internet Explorer and take you to the Create New Site Foundation Wizard screen. Select the Web Site instance you want to install the site to and click Next. Enter both the Short name and Display name as **Cwine** and click Next. Select the desired directory location to install the site to (it will be similar to C:\InetPub\wwwroot\Cwine) and click Next. Select the DSN and login/password details for the database instance you created earlier and click Next. Choose an existing NT domain, click Next and then and choose account to administer the site – the local **Administrator** account allows you to create this commerce site without the worry about running into permission problems. However, when you go live with a store you should be sure to tighten security permissions. One way is to create a group that has access to the management interface scripts and then users can then be added to this group as necessary.

After clicking Next you should click Finish to create your site's foundation. After around 30 seconds your site foundation will have been created and a link to the manager page will be shown. Follow this link to start the Site Builder Wizard and a new window will open welcoming you to the wizard.

Configuring the Site

Click Next, click Create a Custom Site and Next again. Enter some Merchant Information details, as shown in the figure, and when complete click Next.

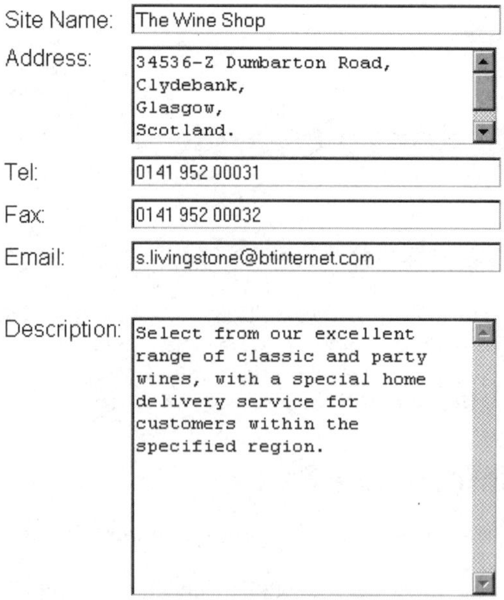

Site Name:	The Wine Shop
Address:	34536-Z Dumbarton Road, Clydebank, Glasgow, Scotland.
Tel:	0141 952 00031
Fax:	0141 952 00032
Email:	s.livingstone@btinternet.com
Description:	Select from our excellent range of classic and party wines, with a special home delivery service for customers within the specified region.

Set the Locale to English (United Kingdom) and click Next. Choose a look for the site and click the Next button. Check both Price Promotions and Cross-Sell promotions and click Next. Set the Registration radio button to When Ordering and leave the Department Type at the default Simple (single level) selection and enable Product Searching. Click Next and leave Static Attributes selected and click Next again. On the screen that appears, create the following custom attributes:

Name	Type	Purpose
volume	Single Valued	The alcoholic level of the wine
country	Single Valued	The country of origin of the wine
winecase	Single Valued	The cost of a case (12 bottles) of this wine (in pence)
bottlesize	Single Valued	The size of the bottle in liters

Click **Next** when complete. Now follow the steps below :

❑   On the Shipping and Handling screen uncheck the first two checked entries (Overnight and 2nd Day)

❑   Check the 3rd entry and enter **Delivery** as the **Method Name**, with a **Cost** of £4.00

❑   Click **Next**

❑   Enter a TAX rate of 17.5%

❑   Click **Next**

❑   Click **Next** again.

❑   Check **Retain order history and receipt information**

❑   Click **Next**

❑   Check **Load Schema into Database**

❑   Click the **Finish** button

The Site Builder Wizard will now create the pages and database tables for the new commerce site.

Populating the Site

There are two options for populating the commerce site and databases. The first (and simplest) is to use a set of SQL scripts which are available from the Wrox website at http://www.wrox.com, and this procedure is described below. The second method is to create the tables and enter the data manually. An example of this is given at the end of this section, and more explanation is given as you work through the relevant sections of the case study, so don't worry – you won't miss anything !!

Using the Data Population Script

The following scripts can be run to populate the commerce site and databases. The method of running the scripts differs slightly between SQL Server 6.5 and SQL Server 7, as described below. We also need to add a column to our Product table, for when we implement special offers.

SQL Server 7

Departments and Products

Launch the Query Analyser from Start I Programs I Microsoft SQL Server 7.0 and connect to the server where you created your commerce database. From the databases list shown, select the database where your commerce table is stored (you would have used this when setting up your DSN for creating the commerce site). Select File I Open and browse to the `dept_products.sql` file and click Open.

When this file has been open, either press *F5* or select Query I Execute to insert all of the product and department information into your database.

Cross-Sell Data Construction

The next SQL Script is called `cross_sell.sql` and should be run as described for the Departments and Products script. Alternatively, you can create the table manually, which is outlined in the Cross-Sell section below.

Predictor Data

Running the `predict.sql` script creates the prediction table we will be using later in the chapter, and populates it with some data. It should be run as described above. Again, you can create the table manually.

Delivery Data

The final SQL Script is called `delivery.sql`. It creates a table containing information about the cost of delivery to certain postcodes. Once again, manual creation of this table is described later.

The Special Offer Column

Fire up the SQL Server MMC (Start I Programs I Microsoft SQL Server 7.0 I Enterprise Manager) and navigate to the Commerce database and click Tables and right-click on the `cwine_product` table and choose the Design Table option. Enter a new column called `special_offer` of type `tinyint`, which should be set to allow NULLS and have a default value of 0. Save and close the design window.

SQL Server 6.5

SQL Server 6.5 has a query tool as part of SQL Server Enterprise Manager, and the above scripts can be executed through this, taking care to run them on the database where our commerce table is stored. The Enterprise Manager can also be used to add the `special_offer` column to the Product table, by choosing the Manage I Tables menu option.

Example of Manually Entering Data

Navigate to the manager site at http://servername/cwine/manager/default.asp and click on the Departments button and click the Add New Department link. Add the two departments in turn by entering the following details to the text boxes shown.

Dept ID	Name	Description
1	Red Wines	Come and look at our selection of Red Wines.
2	White Wines	See our range of White wines ideal for parties and functions.

Finally, click the **Products** link at the top of the page and then the **Add New Product** link. Add the following details to the New Product screen (the others are boxes not important to the study):

SKU
R010
Name
Le Saint-Auriol Vin de Pays de L'Aude Red
Description
1996/7. Made from a blend of Portan and Grenache grapes. Supple and full-bodied.
List_Price
3.25
Volume
12%
Country
French
Winecase
3900
Bottlesize
75cl

Installing the Site Files

Now that you have created the framework of the site, you need to install the case study file available from http://www.wrox.com. This is a zip file and should be expanded to a temporary directory. A directory called `Files` will be exist with the Commerce files – copy all of the files and directories within this directory to the directory where you installed the commerce files earlier in the chapter (it will be similar to C:\InetPub\wwwroot\Cwine). Ensure that you overwrite any files when prompted. When you have done this, you will have installed all of the files necessary to view the commerce site. The modifications to the code of our site described in the rest of this chapter have already been made to the files in the download. The changes are clearly commented in the code so you can see where the modifications have been made.

Customizing the Products Page For Our New Product Attributes

We want to modify the `products.asp` page so that we can display more information on each of the products that the user could buy. We need to also modify the `global.asa` to retrieve the necessary information.

Product attributes are obtained from the `cwine_product` table and following the attributes we selected to add earlier in the chapter, it looks as shown here:

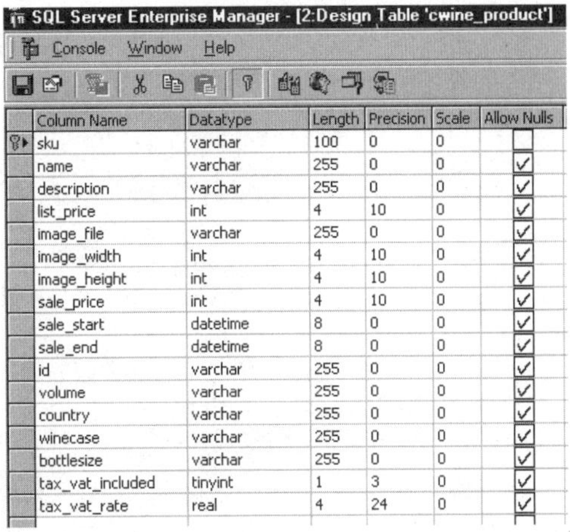

SQL Server Enterprise Manager - [2:Design Table 'cwine_product']

Console   Window   Help

Column Name	Datatype	Length	Precision	Scale	Allow Nulls
sku	varchar	100	0	0	
name	varchar	255	0	0	✓
description	varchar	255	0	0	✓
list_price	int	4	10	0	✓
image_file	varchar	255	0	0	✓
image_width	int	4	10	0	✓
image_height	int	4	10	0	✓
sale_price	int	4	10	0	✓
sale_start	datetime	8	0	0	✓
sale_end	datetime	8	0	0	✓
id	varchar	255	0	0	✓
volume	varchar	255	0	0	✓
country	varchar	255	0	0	✓
winecase	varchar	255	0	0	✓
bottlesize	varchar	255	0	0	✓
tax_vat_included	tinyint	1	3	0	✓
tax_vat_rate	real	4	24	0	✓

In the wizard, we defined the product attributes:

- **winecase**, specifying the cost for a case of 12 bottles of the same wine
- **bottlesize**, defining the amount of wine that the bottle holds
- **country**, specifying the country the wine originates from
- **volume**, indicating the alcoholic volume of the wine

The query defined in the `global.asa` QueryMap does not get these values by default, so we must modify this query. The query before the modification is:

```
Set MSCSQueryMap.product_by_sku = AddQuery("SELECT pf.sku, pf.name,
pf.description, pf.list_price, pf.sale_price, pf.sale_start, pf.sale_end,
pf.image_file, pf.image_width, pf.image_height, dept.dept_id,
dept.dept_name FROM cwine_product pf, cwine_dept_prod deptprod,
cwine_dept dept WHERE pf.sku = :1 and pf.sku = deptprod.sku and
dept.dept_id = deptprod.dept_id and dept.dept_id = :2")
```

We have to modify the code as shown below (the additions are highlighted in bold):

```
Set MSCSQueryMap.product_by_sku = AddQuery("SELECT pf.sku, pf.name,
pf.description, pf.list_price, pf.sale_price, pf.sale_start, pf.sale_end,
pf.image_file, pf.image_width, pf.image_height, dept.dept_id, dept.dept_name,
pf.winecase, pf.bottlesize, pf.country, pf.volume
FROM cwine_product pf, cwine_dept_prod deptprod, cwine_dept dept WHERE pf.sku = :1
and pf.sku = deptprod.sku and dept.dept_id = deptprod.dept_id and dept.dept_id =
:2")
```

You can see in the modified query that we also select the extra attributes.

We now need to display these new product attributes to the customer when he (she) arrives at the product page, by modifying the `product.asp` page. Near the top of the page we execute the MSCSQueryMap query and the product information is returned as a recordset. We must therefore add a section that gets these values from the RecordSet and assigns them to variables, as shown below:

```
winecase = rsProduct("winecase").value
bottlesize = rsProduct("bottlesize").value
country = rsProduct("country").value
volume = rsProduct("volume").value
```

Now that we have them as variables, we can use them to customize the description of each product that the customer will see. The code below illustrates this:

```
At <%= mscsPage.HTMLEncode(volume) %> volume, this
<%= mscsPage.HTMLEncode(country) %> wine comes in a bottle of size
<%= mscsPage.HTMLEncode(bottlesize) %>.

<P>If you purchase a case of 12 bottles of this wine, you will pay only
£<%= (mscsPage.HTMLEncode(winecase))/100 %>.
```

Implementing Simple Cross-Selling Promotions

We have a range of wines which we wish to cross-sell to customers, based on a knowledge of wines which the user may be currently viewing. These selections of wines are those that the owner of the site wishes to sell in relation to those wines being viewed.

The cross-sell shall have the default fields, along with another 3 fields which contain "selling point" comments which can be used to sell the product further. Examples of these may be "sold over 50 bottles last month", or "our most favored dinner white wine", and so on. One of these comments will be randomly displayed when a user happens across a product which has a cross sell.

Modifying the Product Cross-Sell Database

If you ran the data scripts as requested earlier, then now we should have the `cwine_promo_cross` table and the added three fields *sell1*, *sell2* and *sell3* as text descriptions, as shown in the diagram below:

> Note that the SQL script for creating this table is found in the downloads. The SQL Script is called `cross_sell.sql` and should be run as described earlier for the site population script. Alternatively, you can create the table manually.

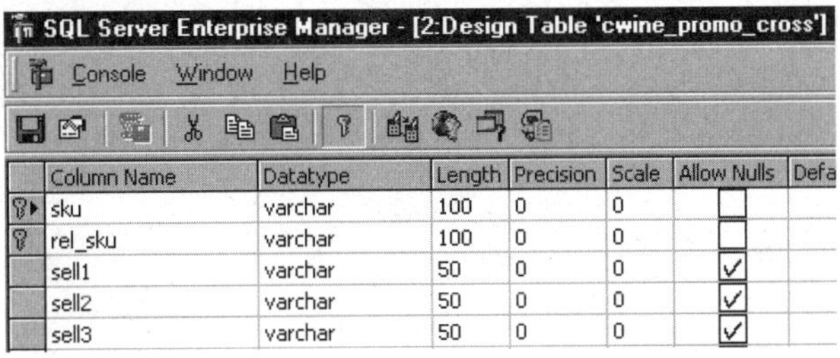

Modifying the Script

The script below shows how the `product.asp` page has been customized as information is retrieved from the database and one of the three selling tips are displayed at random.

Modifying our query in the global.asa

We must first add an SQL statement to the MSCSQueryMap in the `global.asa` which can be called to retain the information about the potential products we may wish to cross promote. The statement is shown below:

```
Set MSCSQueryMap.related_products_with_dept = AddQuery("SELECT prod.sku,
prod.name, deptprod.dept_id, promo_cross.sell1, promo_cross.sell2,
promo_cross.sell3 FROM cwine_promo_cross promo_cross, cwine_product prod,
cwine_dept_prod deptprod WHERE promo_cross.sku = :1 and prod.sku = deptprod.sku
and promo_cross.rel_sku = prod.sku")
```

Displaying the Cross-Sell product information

We must then generate the SQL text we will use which we have just defined in the MSCSQueryMap object in the `global.asa`, setting the SKU for the product the customer is currently viewing, and setting the text we are going to be using. So, we have the following code in `product.asp`:

```
<%
REM get related products (if any):
sqlText = MSCSQueryMap.related_products_with_dept.SQLCommand
sqlText = Replace(sqlText, ":1", quoted_sku)
cmdTemp.CommandText = sqlText

Set rsRelated = Server.CreateObject("ADODB.Recordset")
rsRelated.Open cmdTemp, , adOpenForwardOnly, adLockReadOnly

REM display up to 5 related products:
if Not rsRelated.EOF then
%>
    <BR>
    <B>See Also</B>
    <%
    nRelated = 0
    set skuField = rsRelated("sku")
    set nameField = rsRelated("name")
```

When we have the product information returned as a recordset we have to select a 'random' quotation from our selling point quotations a product manager will define in the database. We do this by creating an array containing each of the returned quotations, which would consist of a maximum of three elements. We follow this up by generating a number at random between 0 and 2 and using this value to return one of the quotations from the array.

```
Dim arrSells(3)

arrSells(0) = rsRelated("sell1")
arrSells(1) = rsRelated("sell2")
arrSells(2) = rsRelated("sell3")

SellingPointIndex=Second(Time()) Mod 3

sellString=arrSells(SellingPointIndex)
```

Finally, we have to write out each of the products that have been returned and at the end of each product, we employ our quotation, giving a touch of personalized information on each individual bottle.

```
    set dept_idField = rsRelated("dept_id")

    do while Not (rsRelated.EOF OR nRelated >= 5)%>
    <BR>

    <A HREF="<% = baseURL("product.asp") _
    & mscsPage.URLShopperArgs("sku",skuField.value, _
    & "dept_id", dept_idField.value) %>">
    <% = mscsPage.HTMLEncode(nameField.value) %>
    </A>
    - <I><%=sellString%></I>
    <%
            nRelated = nRelated + 1
            rsRelated.MoveNext
        loop %>
    <% end if %>
```

Adding Our Products to the Database

Now that we have created the script to display products which we want to cross-sell, we need to add some product information to the database. **Click Start | Programs | Microsoft SQL Server 7.0 | Enterprise Manager** and navigate to the **Commerce** database and click **Tables** and right-click on `cwine_promo_cross` and select Open Table | Return all Rows. Enter the following details under the columns defined on the left:

Sku	R011
Rel_sku	R019
Sell1	One of our best selling red wines !!
Sell2	A bottle with every meal.
Sell3	Try our fruity and rich red wine.

If you now navigate to the site at http://servername/cwine/default.asp and navigate to the **Red Wines** department and click on the *Bell Sud Cabernet Sauvignon* product link, you will see the *Dom Brial Le Vin D'Ici* product advertised as a potential cross sell, as shown here:

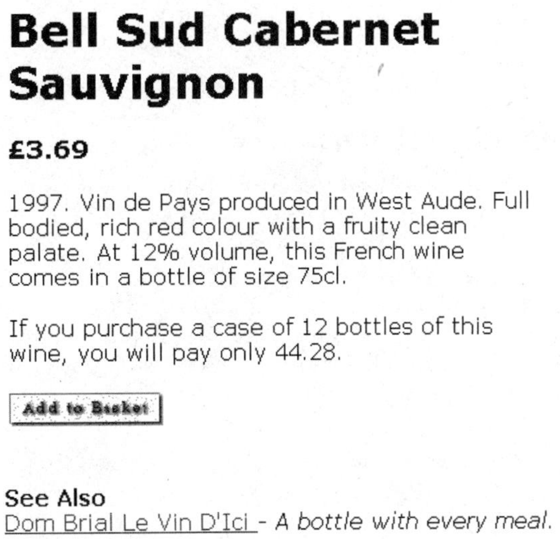

Bell Sud Cabernet Sauvignon

£3.69

1997. Vin de Pays produced in West Aude. Full bodied, rich red colour with a fruity clean palate. At 12% volume, this French wine comes in a bottle of size 75cl.

If you purchase a case of 12 bottles of this wine, you will pay only 44.28.

Add to Basket

See Also
Dom Brial Le Vin D'Ici - *A bottle with every meal.*

595

Refreshing the page a few times will show different quotations from the database. Go ahead and add more product relationships to cross-sell and quotations to display with them.

Intelligent Cross-Selling

Creating the Predictions Table

If you ran the scripts described at the start of the chapter, you would have created a table that we can use to store information we want to use in predictions. If not, you will need to create the table by hand. The table is called `cwine_predictor_data` and the following columns and constraints are applied:

Column name	Datatype	Length	Precision
shopper_id	varchar	32	0
sku	varchar	30	0
quantity	int	4	10
date_purchased	datetime	8	0

Beyond the table being created, some data was also entered into this table. This is because in order for Site Server commerce to make predictions to consumers, there has to be some history on which it can base these predictions. It is suggested that when applying this feature, that you either your own intelligent data as we have done here, or turn it off until a "reasonable" amount of data has been collected. Obviously, the more data you have, the better your predictions will become.

Modifying the Script

Now that we have created the table to store the Predictor data, we must modify several of the pages within our site to record and utilize predictor data. The pages within our site that will be key to the predictor object are `global.asa`, `product.asp`, `basket.asp` and `xt_orderform_purchase.asp`.

Modifying the global.asa

The first scripting we need to perform, is to modify the `global.asa` and add statements to perform the SQL queries which will be necessary, as well as create and initialize the Predictor object.

In the `InitQueryMap` function, we first add a SQL command to the QueryMap to insert predictive data to the predictor table in the `InitQueryMap` function. This function will insert the shopperID, SKU of the product the shopper has bought and quantity of the product requested (each being represented by one of the '?'s in the query), along with the data and time when purchased (defined using the `Now` function).

```
Set MSCSQueryMap.insert_predictor_data = AddQuery("insert into " _
    & "cwine_predictor_data values (?, ?, ?, {fn Now()})")
```

When the application starts for the first time, we need to call the `InitPredictor` method of the Predictor object to build our knowledge base of customer preferences. A function, `InitPredictorObject` has been added to the `global.asa`. This function creates an instance of the Predictor object and passes the default data connection string, the name of the column holding our shopper id's ("`shopper_id`"), the name of the column containing our stock-keeping unit ("`sku`"), the column containing the quantity of the sku ordered ("`quantity`") and a suggestion of the memory requirement of the Predictor.

```
Function InitPredictorObject
  Set MSCSPredictor = Server.CreateObject("Commerce.Predictor")
  call MSCSPredictor.InitPredictor(MSCSSite.DefaultConnectionString," _
    "cwine_predictor_data", "shopper_id", "sku", "quantity", 1500)
  Set InitPredictorObject = MSCSPredictor
End Function
```

Consulting the Site Server Commerce documentation, we have suggested a memory requirement of 1500Kb as we won't have more than 100 unique SKUs in our receipt database (we only have around 50 products) and we will have around 12 SKU's per customer.

We now add a call to this function in the `Application_OnStart` Sub procedure,

```
  Set MSCSPredictor = InitPredictorObject
```

and assign our Predictor object to an application variable so that it can be used throughout our application without having to be reloaded each time (which can be resource intensive).

```
  Set Application("MSCSPredictor")    = MSCSPredictor
```

Now that we have created and initialized our site's Predictor object, we need to configure the application to populate the tables it uses when a customer buys a product.

Inserting the Predictive Data

The best place to insert product information into the predictor tables is at the purchase pipeline, in the Accept stage, when you know that the customer has definitely selected the products. This gives the best data on products which customers follow through and buy. To complete this task, we use the `SQLItemADO` pipeline component, which uses the `insert_predictor_data` SQL command we defined in the `global.asa` earlier.

Navigate to the manager page http://servername/CWine/manager/default.asp and select the `purchase.pcf` entry, from the drop down in the system row and click the **Edit Pipeline** button and scroll down to the Accept stage:

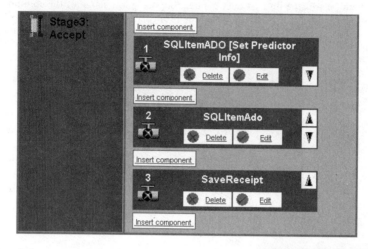

We can see a list of the components that may be inserted by clicking on the **Insert Component** in Stage 3.

#	Component
1	BinaryFromText
2	BinaryToText
3	Execute Process
4	Make PO
5	PipeToPipe Transfer
6	POtoFile
7	SaveReceipt
8	Scriptor
9	SendSMTP
10	SQLItem
11	SQLItemADO
12	SQLOrder
13	SQLOrderADO

We have used the `SQLItemADO` component – click Cancel as we already have our component added. Within the first `SQLItemADO` entry, select the **Edit** link and this takes you to a screen that allows you to modify the configuration of the component. Modify the **Label** to read **SQLItemAdo [Set Predictor Info]**, leaving the **Connection String** blank, as the default connection string is used in this event.

The **Query** setting defines the SQL text used to insert the predictor data. We defined this earlier in the `global.asa` MSCSQueryMap object and we reference the command defined by inserting the following into the text box:

```
insert_predictor_data
```

This has the same effect as setting the **Query** to be:

```
insert into cwine_predictor_data values (?, ?, ?, {fn Now()})
```

To complete the configuration of the component, we must specify the **Parameter List** to pass to the query (specified by the ?'s in the SQL query), namely the shopper ID, SKU, quantity and purchase date, as written below:

```
order.shopper_id item.sku item.quantity
```

Click the update button and you will be returned to the pipeline display. You must commit the update to the pipeline by clicking the **Save** button at the top of the page.

If you want, you can test that data is being entered into your predictor table. Simply purchase some of the products from the site and look at the `cwine_predictor_data` table and you will see entries for each of the products you have purchased.

Now that we have a way of recording data, we need to implement methods to predict the products that users may be interested in.

Displaying Product Predictions

The best areas to advance products to customers is when they are viewing a particular product range, viewing a specific product or preparing to purchase their products. This corresponds to the following two pages:

❑   **Product.asp**
The SKU of the product being viewed is the minimum information needed for a prediction and this is combined with the OrderForm products if any are present.

❑   **Basket.asp**
The SKU of the product being viewed is the minimum information needed for a prediction and this is combined with the OrderForm products available.

A function to generate predictions

A general function has been written which can be included in all pages where you wish to use the predictor object and has the ability to cater for all scenarios. In our case, the include file, `i_util.asp` located in the root directory, contains a function which is used in all of the above files to create our predictions. We will now walk through the `ShowPredictions` function that provides this functionality.

The function can accept three parameters, namely the collection of order items from the OrderForm object used in the pipeline, the SKU of a particular product and the quantity of a particular SKU.

```
Function ShowPredictions(objOrderItems,strSku,intQuantity)
```

We then get a reference to the Predictor object, which is initialized in the `global.asa`.

```
Dim strProducts
strProducts=""

predictor = NULL
set predictor = Application("MSCSPredictor")
```

It is possible that when a customer enters a particular page that he has not yet had an `OrderForm` created (for example, the first time he enters), so to cater for this, we allow the calling page to specify a particular product SKU and quantity combination to be specified, rather than an `OrderFormItems` collection. So, after ensuring that the Predictor object is valid (that is, has been initialized and contains merged baskets), we check if an SKU has been passed. We create a list and dictionary object and assign the SKU and quantity parameters to the dictionary object, which is assigned to the list object we have created.

```
If Not IsNull(predictor) and Not IsEmpty(predictor) then

    If NOT strSKU="" Then
    Set objOrderItems = Server.CreateObject("Commerce.SimpleList")
    set thisitem = Server.CreateObject("Commerce.Dictionary")

    thisitem.sku = CStr(strSKU)
    thisitem.quantity = CInt(intQuantity)

    objOrderItems.add(thisitem)
```

We retrieve an `OrderForm` object containing any existing data which may be present from current orders for the specific `ShopperID` and we iterate through each order present, adding the `sku` and `quantity` values to the Dictionary object we have created above. This combination will give us an `OrderForm` object with at least one entry.

```
    set orderformstorage = UtilGetOrderFormStorage()
    set orderForm = UtilGetOrderForm(orderformstorage, created)
    set OrderItem = orderform.items

    For i = 0 to OrderItem.Count - 1
        set thisitem = Server.CreateObject("Commerce.Dictionary")
        thisitem.quantity = OrderItem(i).quantity
        thisitem.sku = OrderItem(i).sku
        objOrderItems.add(thisitem)
    Next
End If
```

At this point, we have a collection of `OrderItems` for our `OrderForm`, either created within this function, or passed in directly from the calling page. We can now use this collection within the `GetPredictions` method to generate a range of products that the users may potentially be interested in. We want a maximum of 6 products to be returned and use a value of 0.4 as the item filter, giving a bias towards predictions based on customers with similar tastes in wines. We use a value of 4 to get reasonable predictions when at least 4 customers have bought similar wines.

```
    set predictions = predictor.GetPredictions(objOrderItems, 6, 0.4, 4)
```

We continue by checking that we have some suggestions returned and if we do, we create a table and use the prediction product SKU for each product which has been suggested to execute a SQL query to obtain name and department information about the product.

```
If predictions.Count > 0 Then

header = 0
strProducts=strProducts & "<TABLE CLASS='TableStyle' " _
    & "BORDER=0 CELLSPACING=0 CELLPADDING=1>"
strBG="CLASS='CellHigh'"

For i = 0 To predictions.Count - 1
 cmdTemp.commandText = "select cwine_product.sku, cwine_product.name," _
    & "cwine_dept_prod.dept_id from cwine_product, cwine_dept_prod where " _
    & "cwine_product.sku = '" & Replace(predictions(i).sku, "'", "''") _
    & "' AND cwine_dept_prod.sku=cwine_product.sku"

Set rsProduct = Server.CreateObject("ADODB.RecordSet")
rsProduct.Open cmdTemp, , adOpenKeyset, adLockReadOnly
```

Finally, we ensure that we have some records returned about the product and create a styled table displaying a link to the `product.asp` and the necessary values in the query string along with displaying the name of the wine. Rather than writing the results directly out, we build up a string variable containing all of the product information.

```
If rsProduct.RecordCount > 0 Then
    If header = 0 Then
        strProducts=strProducts & "<TR CLASS='RowHead'><TD>"
        strProducts=strProducts & "<B>People with similar tastes have" _
            & " also bought the following wines :</B><P>"
        strProducts=strProducts & "</TD></TR>"
        header = 1
    End If

    'rotate colors
    If strBG="CLASS='RowHigh'" Then
            strBG="CLASS='RowLow'"
    Else
            strBG="CLASS='RowHigh'"
    End If

    strProducts=strProducts & "<TR " &  strBG & "><TD>"
    strProducts=strProducts & "<A HREF=" & mscsPage.URL("product.asp", _
        "sku", rsProduct("sku").Value,"dept_id",rsProduct("dept_id")) _
        & " STYLE='TEXT-DECORATION:none'>"

    strProducts=strProducts & rsProduct("name").Value & "</a>"
    strProducts=strProducts & "</TD></TR>"
  End If
 Next
 strProducts=strProducts & "</TABLE>"
 End If
End If
```

We then return the variable containing the HTML to write out back to the page:

```
    ShowPredictions=strProducts
End Function
```

Now that the general function has been written, we need to ensure that each of the calling pages includes the i_util.asp file and also calls the ShowPredictions function with the correct parameters.

Displaying predictions in product.asp

When viewing a particular product for a particular department, the customer is in the product.asp page. At this point, there may not yet be any products added to the basket and therefore we can only base our prediction on the product currently being viewed. Before we can use the function to give us some predictions, we must add a reference to the i_util.asp file.

```
<!--#INCLUDE FILE="i_util.asp" -->
```

We then call the ShowPredictions function to generate our predictions, passing the SKU of the product we are currently viewing (which has already been defined further up in the page) and a quantity of 12, as this is the number of items the average user will purchase (1 case of wine = 12 bottles).

```
<%=ShowPredictions("",sku,"12")%>
```

This generates a list of suggested products as shown:

Le Saint-Auriol Vin de Pays de L'Aude Red

Image not available

£3.25

1996/7. Made from a blend of Portan and Grenache grapes. Supple and full-bodied. At 12% volume, this French wine comes in a bottle of size 75cl.

If you purchase a case of 12 bottles of this wine, you will pay only 39.00.

| Add to Basket |

People with similar tastes have also bought the following wines :

Dom Brial Le Vin D'Ici
Medi Montepulciano D'Abruzzo DOC
Poderj Montepulciano D'Abruzzo
Fontauriol Cotes de Malepere

Displaying predictions in basket.asp

In contrast to product.asp, when the customer is viewing basket.asp, she will already have a populated OrderForm object, so we can pass the collection of items from this to the ShowPredictions function.

```
<%=ShowPredictions(orderFormItems,"","")%><hr>
```

This will give the customer a suggestion of some items she may be interested in.

Shopping Basket

You have 1 item in your shopping basket:

To change an item's quantity, edit the number and press "Update Basket".

| | Purchase | | Empty Basket | | Update Basket | |

Label	Name	Unit Price	Today's Price	Qty	Extra Disc.	Total Price	
R011	Bell Sud Cabernet Sauvignon	£3.69	£3.69	1	£0.00	£3.69	Remove Item
					Subtotal:	£3.69	

People with similar tastes have also bought the following wines :

Le Saint-Auriol Vin de Pays de L'Aude Red
Fontauriol Cotes de Malepere
Dom Brial Le Vin D'Ici
Medi Montepulciano D'Abruzzo DOC
Poderj Montepulciano D'Abruzzo

Our site can now make purchase suggestions to customers (based on the buying patterns of other customers), which adds a touch of personalization to it.

Delivery Charges

The delivery of wine cases can have a charge associated with it if the delivery area is outside a range specified by the owner. Within this range, the goods are delivered free of charge. The cost associated with a delivery is determined by the postcode/zipcode that the user specifies, with a default delivery charge for postcodes that are not recognized. This obviously requires some kind of postcode look-up when the shipping charges are determined. To implement this functionality, we are going to use the `TableShippingADO` pipeline component.

Creating the Table Structure

To implement the `postcode` to `shipping_cost` information, we need to create a table within our database to hold the lookup information. This table will have already been created and populated if you used the scripts at the start of the study, but the following paragraph explains how this could be done manually.

Start up Enterprise Manager (**Start** | **Programs** | **Microsoft SQL Server 7.0** | **Enterprise Manager**) and navigate to the **Commerce** database which contains our commerce tables. Right-Click on the **Tables** entry and choose the **New Table** option. Call your table cwine_delivery_costs and click the **OK** button. Add the entries as shown below :

Column Name	Datatype	Length	Precision	Scale	Allow Nulls
postcode	varchar	15	0	0	
shipping_cost	int	4	10	0	✓

Save the table, close it and open it up for data entry (right-click and **Open Tables | Return All Rows**). The postcode column should have some postcodes entered into it, and the shipping cost contains the cost of delivery in pence (or cents). Enter the following information into the table:

postcode	shipping_cost
B8 U98	400
BR5 YY6	0
L45 2S3	200
L45 A43	200
BR5 YY9	0
BR5 YJ7	0
L45 JJ7	200
L45 OP9	200
L45 HH6	200
G13 4JA	1000

We have now set up the database to determine shipping costs, and now need to configure the site to make use of these costs in calculating total delivery costs.

Configuring the Web Pages

Shipping.asp

The shipping page is where the customer enters his address details, but the default site does not have a field to enter postcode information, so we must include an entry for this, for the `ship_to_zip` `OrderForm` attribute. The average UK postcode is 7 characters (including the space) and we will set a maximum length of 15 characters.

```
<TR>
    <TD ALIGN="RIGHT">
        <B>Postcode :</B>
    </TD>
    <TD COLSPAN="3">
    <INPUT TYPE="text"
        NAME="ship_to_zip"
        SIZE="6"
        MAXLENGTH="15"
        VALUE="<%= mscsPage.HTMLEncode(mscsOrderForm.ship_to_zip) %>">
    </TD>
</TR>
```

> Note that if we want users to be able to use the Microsoft Wallet with this system, then we must append a hidden INPUT element to those currently listed within `shipping.asp` for the Wallet scenario as shown below.
>
> ```
> <INPUT TYPE="HIDDEN" NAME="ship_to_zip">
> ```
>
> This information should be put within the FORM element named "shipinfo". If you choose not to do this, you will get an error with the postcode validation, as this information is not being posted.

Adding the Query to global.asa

A query has to be used to get back the delivery information from our database, and the best place to add this query is to the QueryMap in the `global.asa`. The statement should query the `cwine_delivery_costs` table and get the shipping cost for a particular postcode. The query as defined in the `global.asa` is now given.

```
Set MSCSQueryMap.shipping_cost = AddQuery("SELECT shipping_cost FROM " _
    & "cwine_delivery_costs WHERE postcode = ?")
```

Determining Charges

We now need to be able to calculate the delivery cost based on the postcode the user has entered. The most effective way to do this is in the **Shipping** section of the `plan.pcf` pipeline. We can use the `TableShippingADO` component which returns a cost based on a select from a database table and based on the `OrderForm` criteria you provide and sets the `_shipping_total` value of the `OrderForm`. There are two business rules, which this component must fulfill to be useful in our application:

1. To provide a cost for delivery to a specified postcode and set the `OrderForm`'s `_shipping_total` attribute

2. To set `Orderform`'s `_shipping_total` attribute to a default charge of the maximum £10.00 when a postcode is unknown. When the customer's order is processed, a sales assistant will contact him and reduce the amount if it is too high and the new postcode and delivery cost will be added to the database.

To provide point one, we will make direct use of the `TableShippingADO` pipeline component. Firstly, start the Commerce Server Pipeline Editor from http://servername/cwine/manager/default.asp and open the `plan.pcf` file for this site.

> To add the component to the pipeline as we have done in the case study, go to the **Shipping** stage and remove the **LinearShipping** component (or any other component which happens to be in that stage) and when this is done, right-click on the **Shipping** stage and select the **Insert Component** option. A list of components is now displayed and you should select the TableShippingADO component from the list, which will then be added to the pipeline.

Go to the Shipping stage, right-click on the `TableShippingADO` entry and select **Properties**. The values have been entered as shown on the screenshot adjacent (you will have a different view for a SQL 6.5 Database, but the same concept applies to the delivery component):

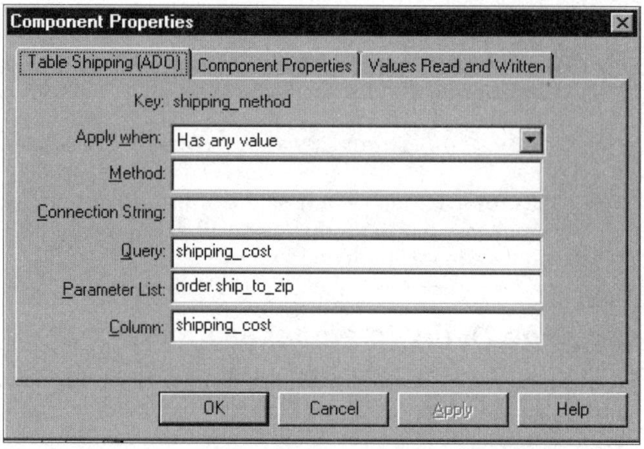

We set the **Apply when** entry to `Has any value`, as we want to ensure that a shipping calculation is made only when we have a postcode to act upon and the Connection String should be left blank, ensuring that the default connection string is used. We specify `shipping_cost` as the **Query**, indicting the string that is to be executed as defined in the QueryMap in the `global.asa`. The Parameter List defines the values that are to be passed to the query (defined by the '?' in the QueryMap string) and so we specify that the customer zip code should be used. Finally, the Column value should define the database column containing the cost of the shipping, which is `shipping_cost` in our case.

Click the OK button to close the dialog and complete the requirements for step 1.

Now, although we have added a component to satisfy the first of the business rules described above, that is not true for the second – no value would be set for an unknown postcode and would cause problems for the rest of the calculation. We will add a simple implementation of a Scriptor component to do this. Right-Click on the `TableShippingADO` component and select **Insert Component | After...** and from the component list which appears, select the `Scriptor` component and click **OK**. The MSCSExecute function is as shown below:

```
function MSCSExecute(config, orderform, context, flags)
    If IsNull(orderform.[_shipping_total]) OR _
IsEmpty(orderform.[_shipping_total]) Then
        Rem If no _shipping_total, set default
        orderform.[_shipping_total]=1000
    End If

    MSCSExecute = 1
end function
```

Notice that we check if the shipping total has a value and set the default to be £10.00 if this is not the case. We have now satisfied requirements of the second point. Close down the Pipeline editor.

We can now order some wine. The three examples here show the result for the same case of wine for delivery to a different location. The first is for a local customer (postcode BR5 YY6), the second is for a customer a medium distance away (postcode B8 U98), and the final one is for a customer with an unknown postcode (SW13 4JJ).

Subtotal: £44.28
Shipping: £0.00
Tax: £0.00
TOTAL: £44.28

Subtotal: £44.28
Shipping: £4.00
Tax: £0.00
TOTAL: £48.28

Subtotal: £44.28
Shipping: £10.00
Tax: £0.00
TOTAL: £54.28

We have now implemented shipping, and this should be an ongoing process, with new postcode information being added as required. We could even build on this further by using the country *and* postcode/zipcode information to generate costs for international shipping charges.

Managing Product Order Integrity

When a customer makes an order, the number of bottles ordered must be in multiples of 12, with 12 being the minimal amount allowed in a single order. This is an important business rule which we must now look at. In English, we can state the rule as:

A customer may order a minimum of 12 bottles of wine, or one case, consisting of either the same type of wine or mixed bottles. Further bottles must add up to a multiple of 12.

To implement these rules we will use a combination of script and the Scriptor pipeline component.

Displaying Order Messages to the Customer

When the user has either ordered less than 12 items, or a multiple of items not divisible by 12, we need to give him an appropriate message and ask him to rectify the problem. The two obvious pieces of information we must give the customer are that he has not ordered at least 12 products or that he has not bought in multiples of 12.

We can add these messages to the MessageManager in the `global.asa` and access them when necessary by a variable name. The following code is in the `global.asa` and defines these messages:

```
call MSCSMessageManager.AddMessage("val_notenoughitems", _
    "You must enter at least 12 items")

call MSCSMessageManager.AddMessage("val_moreitems", _
    "Purchases must be in multiple of 12 - please add " _
    & "the following number of items to your order : ")
```

607

We can call these by their names - `val_notenoughitems` or `val_moreitems` when we want to access the message string.

When to actually check the order and display these messages is carried out when processing the `basket.asp` page, before the customer has started the process of purchasing the goods. We are actually going to carry out the processing in the pipeline, but if we want to be able to display the messages we defined to the user without causing an error (as an error has not actually occurred) then we need some attribute within the `OrderForm` to store this in. In fact we use a `SimpleList` object within the `UtilRunPlan` function of the `i_util.asp` include file as shown below :

```
Set mscsOrderForm("_OrderItemsMessage") = _
Server.CreateObject("Commerce.SimpleList")
```

This allows us to use `_OrderItemsMessage` to store our messages from the `OrderForm` object that is passed into the pipeline. We will now look at how the business rules are carried out and how messages are returned to the user, using the pipeline Scriptor component.

Checking the order

To ensure that the customer has entered a valid order, we need to use a Scriptor component in the pipeline editor, so fire up http://servrname/cwine/manager/default.asp and choose the `plan.pcf` pipeline from the dropdown menu and then click the **Edit Pipeline** button.

> **The component was added by right clicking on the Order Check stage and choosing Insert Component and select Scriptor from the list and clicking OK.**

Scroll to the **Order Check** stage and within this stage, a Scriptor is the first component – click the **Edit** link. Let's run through the code within the `MSCSExecute` function of the Scriptor.

We first get a reference to the MessageManager containing the text we may want to display to a customer. This will allow us to access the two messages we added in the last section.

```
function MSCSExecute(config, orderform, context, flags)
    set errors = orderform.[_Purchase_Errors]
    set msg_mgr = context.messagemanager
    result = 1
```

We then initialize a counter variable and set the value of this counter to hold the number of items the customer is ordering for all products. Notice that a product may contain a specified quantity and so we can't just assume the value of the number of items in the `OrderForm`. Finally, we set the value of `orderdiff` to the number of items in excess of a multiple of 12 (that is, the modulus)

```
ordercount=0
for i=0 to orderform.items.count-1
    ordercount = ordercount + orderform.items(i).[Quantity]
next

orderdiff = ordercount mod 12
```

Now we validate these values against our business rules, which are that if the number of items in the order is less than 12 or the total value is not an exact multiple of 12 (i.e. orderdiff is not zero). In the first case, we simply reference the SimpleList object we created in i_util.asp and add to it our message defined in the MessageManager for too few items (val_notenoughitems). The latter case is similar, except that we tell the user how many items they are short of a full case (the difference between 12 and the number left over in orderdiff).

```
'now make sure that at least 12 items have been ordered
    if ordercount < 12 Then
        set tempMessageDict = orderform.[_OrderItemsMessage]
        tempMessageDict.Add msg_mgr.GetMessage("val_notenoughitems")
    else if (orderdiff) <> 0 Then
        set tempMessageDict = orderform.[_OrderItemsMessage]
        tempMessageDict.Add msg_mgr.GetMessage("val_moreitems") _
        & 12 - orderdiff
        end if

    end if

    MSCSExecute = result
end function
```

When user messages are passed back to the calling page, we need to display them to the customer in a fashion that lets them understand why they may not yet have a valid purchase. The file basket.asp does this with the following code that is styled to highlight each of the messages which may have returned.

```
<DIV STYLE="BACKGROUND-COLOR:RED;color:white;font-weight:bold;width:86%;">
<%
    For i=0 To mscsOrderForm("_OrderItemsMessage").Count-1
        Response.Write mscsOrderForm("_OrderItemsMessage")(i) & "<BR>"
        i=i+1
    Next
%>
</DIV>
```

We could implement this part of the site as it is just now, but we could improve the user interface by not showing purchase buttons when the business criteria have not yet been fulfilled. We will now look at this.

Improving the Site Display

To prevent the user from having access to purchase buttons before satisfying the sites order business rules, we should modify both the basket.asp and i_header.asp pages. Within basket.asp, we only display the purchase button when no messages have been returned by the pipeline.

```
<%   If mscsOrderForm("_OrderItemsMessage").Count = 0 Then %>

<input TYPE="Image" VALUE="Purchase" SRC="<%= "/" &
siteRoot%>/manager/MSCS_Images/buttons/btnpurchase2.gif"
WIDTH="116" HEIGHT="25" BORDER="0" ALT="Purchase">

<%End If%>
```

The include file `i_header.asp` has been modified in a similar fashion, with the exception that we first have to ensure that an `OrderForm` item is present, before we ask for a count of how many items it may be holding.

```
If IsObject(mscsOrderForm) Then
  If mscsOrderForm("_OrderItemsMessage").Count = 0 Then %>
    <% if Not IsNull(mscsShopperID) then %>
    <a HREF="<%= pageSURL("shipping.asp") %>">
    <img SRC="<%= "/" & siteRoot %>/manager/MSCS_Images/navbar/btnpay.gif"
    WIDTH="53" HEIGHT="41" BORDER="0" ALT="Pay" ALIGN="TOP"></a>

    <% else %>

    <a HREF="<%= baseSURL("shopper_lookup.asp") &
      mscsPage.URLShopperArgs("target","shipping.asp") %>">
    <img SRC="<%= "/" & siteRoot %>/manager/MSCS_Images/navbar/btnpay.gif"
    WIDTH="53" HEIGHT="41" BORDER="0" ALT="Pay" ALIGN="TOP"></a>
    <% end if
  End If
End If
```

The following diagram shows what happens when a user enters an unacceptable value for a number of wine bottles. In this case we have tried to order 8 bottles of one wine and 8 bottles of another. This gives a total of 16 items (I knew that Calculator in Accessories would come in handy one day!!). We know that we must have multiples of 12 and so the next multiple is 24, therefore we are short by another 8 bottles (24 - 16) and advise the consumer about this.

Shopping Basket

You have 2 items in your shopping basket:

To change an item's quantity, edit the number and press "Update Basket".

| Empty Basket | Update Basket |

Purchases must be in multiple of 12 - please add the following number of bottles to your order : 8

Label	Name	Unit Price	Today's Price	Qty	Extra Disc.	Total Price	
R033	Poderj Montepulciano D'Abruzzo	£3.29	£3.29	8	£0.00	£26.32	Remove Item
W097	Lambrusco Di Bianco	£2.35	£2.35	8	£0.00	£18.80	Remove Item
						Subtotal:	£45.12

This Month's Special Offer

It is quite common to have a special offer available to customers and in this case each month a new offer is available. This should be available to all visitors and displayed as soon as the customer enter the site.

To indicate which product is on special offer we need to add a column to the product table in our Commerce database.

Creating the Special Offer Column

If you did not create the `special_offer` column as described at the start of the chapter, then you must add a new column called `special_offer` to the `cwine_product` table as described below.

Fire up the SQL Server MMC (Start | Programs | Microsoft SQL Server 7.0 | Enterprise Manager) and navigate to the **Commerce** database and click **Tables** and right-click on the `cwine_product` table and choose the Design Table option. Enter a new column called `special_offer` of type `tinyint`, which should be set to allow NULLS and have a default value of 0. Save and close the design window.

Putting a product on Special Offer

Within SQL Server 7 Enterprise Manager, if you want to make a particular product available on special offer, then right-click on the `cwine_product` table. Enter a value of 1 into the `special_offer` column of any products you wish to be on special offer and close the window.

A Monthly Special Offer

To get the information, a SQL query has been added to the QueryMap in the `global.asa` as shown below. This query gets the SKU, department ID and name of the product on offer.

```
Set MSCSQueryMap.special_offer = AddQuery("SELECT cwine_product.sku," _
   & "cwine_dept_prod.dept_id,cwine_product.name FROM cwine_product," _
   & "cwine_dept_prod WHERE special_offer=1 AND" _
   & " cwine_product.sku=cwine_dept_prod.sku")
```

We then display the product on offer by executing this query and creating a link to the products page passing the SKU and department ID.

```
<P>
<i>or choose from one of this months special offers ... </I><BR>
<%

   sqlText = MSCSQueryMap.special_offer.SQLCommand
   cmdTemp.CommandText = sqlText

Set rsRelated = Server.CreateObject("ADODB.Recordset")
rsRelated.Open cmdTemp, , adOpenForwardOnly, adLockReadOnly

if Not rsRelated.EOF then
    Do While NOT rsRelated.EOF%>
        <A HREF="<% Response.Write baseURL("product.asp") & _
            mscsPage.URLShopperArgs("sku", rsRelated("sku"), _
            "dept_id", rsRelated("dept_id")) %>">
        <% = mscsPage.HTMLEncode(rsRelated("name")) %> </A><BR>
<%   rsRelated.MoveNext
    Loop
End If

MSCS.Close%>
```

> Note that we could further optimize looping through the RecordSet by using the
> `GetString()` **method of ADO.**

When a customer views the site, he would see
something like the following.

The Wine Shop

Welcome to our shop. We have a broad range of
products you can choose from.

Select a department below:

Red Wines

*or choose from one of this months special
offers ...*
Le Saint-Auriol Vin de Pays de L'Aude Red
Poderj Montepulciano D'Abruzzo

If you have been here before please login.

Conclusion

We have now completed the creation of our commerce site. Although there are some areas where we
would enhance and secure such a site, the business processes would remain the same and we would
have an effective commerce site, which can be easily re-used.

We have looked at the effectiveness of the pipeline using both the Scriptor component for
customizing other components according to our sites requirements, as well as providing stand alone
business processes.

The cross-selling features and predictor component can be extended to provide for better predictions
by removing the predictive information from older product orders. You may monitor how effective
you predictive methods are by recording statistics on how many product predictions are followed and
this may give you an insight into improving your product advertising.

Why not have a go at extending the features outlined in the study, such as adding VAT to an order.
Also, why not try to replace the order integrity Scriptor pipeline component with a custom
component using some of the methods outlined elsewhere in this book. Finally, there are many ways
in which you could use and improve on the predictions made to users as described in the previous
paragraph – why not try extending the current application to consider some of these points.

Microsoft Commerce Server Object Model Quick Reference

Configuration components

AdminFile

Member	Method/Property	Description
ReadFromBinaryFile	Method	Reads an entire file in binary format into memory
ReadFromFile	Method	Reads an entire file in ASCII format into memory

AdminWebServer

Member	Method/Property	Description
GetWebSites	Method	Enumerates all the instances of IIS running on a server
GetWebSiteProperties	Method	Retrieves the IIS metabase for a specific instance of IIS
GetCommerceSites	Method	Enumerates all the MSCS stores installed on a server

AdminSite

Member	Method/Property	Description
Create	Method	Creates a new store foundation
Initialize	Method	Initializes an instance of AdminSite
Delete	Method	Deletes a store
InitializeFromMDPath	Method	Initializes an instance of AdminSite using an IIS metabase path
ReadDefaultProperties	Method	Reads the Store Dictionary for a particular store
WriteDefaultProperties	Method	Writes the Store Dictionary for a particular store
ReadManagerProperties	Method	Reads the Store Dictionary used in the Store Manager of a particular store
WriteManagerProperties	Method	Writes the Store Dictionary used in the Store Manager of a particular store
Status	Property	Reads/Sets the status of a store (open or closed)
IsValidName	Property	Determines whether a store with a particular name exists on a specific instance of IIS

Storage components

SimpleList

Member	Method/Property	Description
Add	Method	Adds an entry to the list
Delete	Method	Deletes an entry from the list
Count	Property	Returns the number of entries in the list
Item	Property	(Default property) Returns a particular entry in the list

Dictionary

Member	Method/Property	Description
Prefix	Property	Causes the object to filter its name/value pairs during persistency operations
Count	Property	Returns the number of name/value pairs in the dictionary
Value	Property	(Default property) Sets or returns a particular name/value pair in the list

FileDocument

Member	Method/Property	Description
WriteToFile	Method	Persists a particular object to a file
ReadFromFile	Method	Creates a copy of a persisted object
ReadDictionaryFromFile	Method	Loads the data of a persisted Dictionary object into another Dictionary object that was previously created

Orderform

Member	Method/Property	Description
Items	Property	List of products in the object
Items.SKU	Property	SKU of a particular product
Items.Quantity	Property	Quantity of a particular product in the Orderform
Items.Name	Property	Name of the product
Items.List_price	Property	List price of the product
Items._product_x	Property	Product-specific information retrieved from the database
Items._n_unadjusted	Property	Unadjusted number of items available to the user
Items._oadjust_ adjustedprice	Property	Total cost of all the items of a specific product available for purchase by the user
Items._iadjust_ regularprice	Property	The base price of a product
Items._iadjust_ currentprice	Property	The current price of the product, considering only product-wide modifiers
Items.placed_price	Property	The final price of the product, considering all product- and order-wide modifiers
Items._tax_total	Property	Total tax paid on the product
Items._tax_included	Property	Tax actually included in the product's price
Shopper_ID	Property	ID of the shopper who owns this Orderform
Ship_to_x	Property	Shipping information
Bill_to_x	Property	Billing information
_Basket_errors	Property	SimpleList containing all errors generated in the Plan pipeline
_Purchase_errors	Property	SimpleList containing all errors generated in the Purchase pipeline
Cc_x	Property	Credit card fields

Member	Method/Property	Description
Order_id	Property	Pipeline-generated, unique ID of the order
_total_total	Property	Total cost of the order
_oadjust_subtotal	Property	Subtotal of the order, not counting shipping, handling and taxes
Shipping_method	Property	Name of the shipping method used to complete the order
_shipping_total	Property	Total cost of shipping
_tax_total	Property	Total cost of taxes
_handling_total	Property	Total cost of handling
_tax_included	Property	Amount of tax included in _oadjust_subtotal
_verify_with	Property	Dictionary object used to determine when the basket's contents have changed without the user being informed.
_payment_auth_code	Property	The authorization code released by the organization that processed the order
Value	Property	(Default property) Sets or returns a name/value pair in the object
AddItem	Method	Adds one product to the Orderform
ClearItems	Method	Empties the Items SimpleList
ClearOrderForm	Method	Completely clear all entries in the object

DBStorage

Member	Method/Property	Description
InitStorage	Method	Initializes the object to point to a specific database
GetData	Method	Reads data from a database
LookupMultipleData	Method	Retrieves multiple instances of the same object from the database
LookupData	Method	Retrieves data from the database based on the value of a specific column

Table Continued on Following Page

Member	Method/Property	Description
InsertData	Method	Writes data to the database
CommitData	Method	Updates data already in the database
DeleteData	Method	Deletes data from the database
Mapping	Property	Establishes how data that is persisted through the object is mapped to the database

User Interface Components

DataFunctions

Member	Method/Property	Description
Locale	Property	Determines the locale used to interpret and format data
ConvertXY	Method	Convert data from type X to type Y, where X or Y can be any of: - String - Date - Time
ConvertZ	Method	Converts a string from a specific locale into a numeric value of type Z, where Z can be any of: - Integer - Float - Money (in ConvertMoneyStringToNumber)
Date	Method	Converts a date value into a string formatted appropriately for the selected locale
Time	Method	Converts a time value into a string formatted appropriately for the selected locale
DateTime	Method	Converts a datetime value into a string formatted appropriately for the selected locale

Member	Method/Property	Description
Number	Method	Converts an integer numeric value into a string properly formatted for the selected locale
Float	Method	Converts a floating-point value into a string properly formatted for the selected locale
Money	Method	Converts an integer numeric value into a currency representation properly formatted for the selected locale
CleanString	Method	Removes unwanted characters from a string
ValidateK	Method	Validate a value of type *K*, where *K* is one of the following:
		- Number
		- Float
		- DateTime

MessageManager

Member	Method/Property	Description
AddLanguage	Method	Adds an additional language to the object
DefaultLanguage	Method	Sets the default language for the object
GetLocale	Method	Returns the locale for a particular language
AddMessage	Method	Adds a new message for a particular language
GetMessage	Method	Retrieves a message for a particular language

StandardSManager

Member	Method/Property	Description
InitManager	Method	Initializes the object
CreateShopperID	Method	Creates a new shopper ID

Page

Member	Method/Property	Description
GetShopperID	Method	Retrieves the shopper ID for the current user
PutShopperID	Method	Saves the shopper ID for the current user so that a session can be maintained
Check	Method	Creates an HTML checkbox control
Option	Method	Creates an entry of an HTML listbox
RequestX	Method	Retrieves a value of type *X* from the HTTP parameter list. *X* can be one of the following: - Date - Datetime - Default (defaults to the optimal type given the data's format) - Float - MoneyAsNumber - Number - String - Time
SURLPrefix	Property	Sets/Retrieves the prefix to use in building secure URLs
SURL	Method	Constructs a secure URL
URLPrefix	Property	Sets/Retrieves the prefix to use in building URLs
URL	Method	Constructs an URL
URLArgs	Method	Constructs the query portion of an URL
URLShopperArgs	Property	Returns an URL query parameter that contains the shopper ID for the current user
VirtualDirectory	Property	Returns the name of the virtual directory where the current store resides

Member	Method/Property	Description
VerifyWith	Method	Creates a digest of the user's basket used by the ProcessVerifyWith method
ProcessVerifyWith	Method	Determines whether the contents of the user's basket have changed without the user knowing about it
HTMLEncode	Method	Converts an ASCII string to HTML
URLEncode	Method	Converts an ASCII or HTML string in a format suitable for usage in the URL query string

Predictor

Member	Method/Property	Description
InitPredictor	Method	Initializes the object
GetPredictions	Method	Returns one or more predictions

Pipeline MS Commerce Server Objects

MtsPipeline and MtsTxPipeline

Member	Method/Property	Description
LoadPipe	Method	Loads a pipeline configuration file
Execute	Method	Executes a pipeline
SetLogFiles	Method	Turns on logging and sets the pathname of the log file

ConfigurationCacheHelper

Member	Method/Property	Description
SaveToCache	Method	Saves a pipeline configuration file in the object's internal cache
LoadFromCache	Method	Loads a pipeline configuration file from the object's internal cache
DeleteFromCache	Method	Deletes a pipeline configuration file from the object's internal cache

Micropipe

Member	Method/Property	Description
SetComponent	Method	Sets the component that the object will execute
Execute	Method	Executes the micropipe
SetLogFile	Method	Turns logging on and sets the pathname of the log file

Pipeline Components Quick Reference

The Order Processing Pipeline

Stage	Name	Description
Any	Scriptor	Executes a script using the Windows Scripting Host
Product Info	QueryProdInfoAdo	Extracts product information from the database
Shopper Info	DefaultShopperInfo	Sets the shopper information to the default values
Item Price	DefaultItemPrice	Sets the item price information to the default values
Item Adjust	SaleAdjust	Determines whether one or more products in the Orderform are on sale
	ItemPromo	Applies sale prices to one or more products in the Orderform

Table Continued on Following Page

Stage	Name	Description
Order Adjust	DBOrderPromoADO	Applies price promotions to the order
Order Subtotal	DefaultOrderSubtotal	Sets the order subtotal information to the default values
Shipping	FixedShipping	Applies a fixed shipping cost for the entire order
	LinearShipping	Applies a shipping cost that depends on the number of items in the order
	TableShippingADO	Calculates the shipping costs based on the values extracted from a database
	DefaultShipping	Sets the shipping information to its default values
Handling	DefaultHandling	Sets the handling information to its default values
	FixedHandling	Applies a fixed handling cost to the entire store
	LinearHandling	Applies a handling costs that depends on the number of items in the order
	TableHandlingADO	Calculates the handling costs based on the values extracted from a database
Tax	DefaultTax	Sets the tax information to its default values
	SimpleUSTax	Calculates tax based on US rules
	SimpleCanadaTax	Calculates tax based on Canadian rules
	SimpleJapanTax	Calculates tax based on Japanese rules
	SimpleVATTax	Calculates tax based on European rules
Order total	DefaultOrderTotal	Sets the order total information to its default values
Inventory	LocalInventory	Determines whether one or more products are out of stock
	FlagInventory	Marks products that are out of stock
Purchase Check	ValidateCCNumber	Validates a credit card number
Payment	DefaultPayment	Sets the payment information to its default values

Stage	Name	Description
Accept	SQLOrderADO	Executes a query whose parameters are taken from the Orderform
	MakePO	Creates a Purchase Order using a template written in VBScript that retrieves data from the Orderform
	POToFile	Saves a Purchase Order to a text file
	ExecuteProcess	Runs an executable program on the hard disk
	SaveReceipts	Saves receipt information to the database
	PipeToPipeTransfer	Executes a new pipeline

The Commerce Interchange Pipeline

Transmit pipelines

Stage	Name	Description
Map	MapToXML	Maps the Dictionary's contents to XML format
Add Header	AddHeader	Adds a standard header to the interchange
	EncodeMime	Encodes the interchange using the MIME protocol
Digitally sign	DigitalSig	Digitally signs the interchange
	EncodeSMime	Encodes the interchange using the SMIME protocol
Encrypt	EncryptPKCS	Encrypts the interchange using one of the algorithms supported by Microsoft's CryptoAPI
Audit	Audit	Creates an audit record of the interchange
Transport	SendSMTP	Sends the interchange using the SMTP protocol
	SendHTTP	Sends the interchange using the HTTP protocol
	SendDCOM	Sends the interchange through a DCOM component

Receive pipeline

Stage	Name	Description
Decrypt	DecryptPKCS	Decrypts the interchange using one of the algorithms supported by Microsoft's CryptoAPI
	DecodeSMIME	Decodes an interchange sent in SMIME format
Verify Digital Signature	VerifyDigitalSig	Verifies the digital signature attached to an interchange
Open Header	OpenHeader	Retrieves and interprets the header associated with an interchange
	DecodeMime	Decodes an interchange sent in MIME format
Generate Receipt	GenerateReceipt	Generates and sends a receipt for the interchange
Map	MapFromXML	Maps the interchange from XML into a Dictionary object
Audit	AuditReceipt	Updates log information if the interchange is a receipt

ISO Country Codes

Whenever MS Commerce Server refers to a particular country, it uses well-known three-letter country codes that have been developed by the International Standards Organization (ISO), which resides in Zurich. It's always a good idea to adhere to this standard, which is very practical and recognized worldwide (almost everybody knows the code of their own country: for example, the United States have the code USA, while Canada has CAN and Italy has ITA).

> Keep in mind that the postal service (or any courier, for that matter) does not deliver mail in all the countries listed below. Check with your shipment service provider to find out a list of reachable countries!

Afghanistan	AFG	Albania	ALB
Algeria	DZA	American Samoa	ASM
Andorra	AND	Angola	AGO
Anguilla	AIA	Antarctica	ATA
Antigua and Barbuda	ATG	Argentina	ARG
Aruba	ABW	Australia	AUS
Austria	AUT	Bahamas	BHS

Bahrain	BHR	Bangladesh	BGD
Barbados	BRB	Belgium	BEL
Belize	BLZ	Benin	BEN
Bermuda	BMU	Bhutan	BTN
Bolivia	BOL	Botswana	BWA
Bouvet Island	BVT	Brazil	BRA
British Indian Ocean Territory	IOT	Brunei Darussalam	BRN
Bulgaria	BGR	Burkina Faso	BFA
Burma	BUR	Burundi	BDI
Byelorussian	BYS	Cameroon	CMR
Canada	CAN	Cape Verde	CPV
Cayman Islands	CYM	Central African Republic	CAF
Chad	TCD	Chile	CHL
China	CHN	Christmas Island	CXR
Cocos (Keeling) Islands	CCK	Colombia	COL
Comoros	COM	Congo	COG
Cook Islands	COK	Costa Rica	CRI
Cote D'Ivoire	CIV	Cuba	CUB
Cyprus	CYP	Czechoslovakia	CSK
Denmark	DNK	Djibouti	DJI
Dominica	DMA	Dominican Republic	DOM
East Timor	TMP	Ecuador	ECU
Egypt	EGY	El Salvador	SLV
Equatorial Guinea	GNQ	Ethiopia	ETH
Falkland Islands	FLK	Faroe Islands	FRO
Fiji	FJI	Finland	FIN
France	FRA	French Guiana	GUF
French Polynesia	PYF	French Southern Territories	ATF
Gabon	GAB	Gambia	GMB
German Democratic Republic	DDR	Germany, Federal Republic of	DEU
Ghana	GHA	Gibraltar	GIB

Greece	GRC	Greenland	GRL
Grenada	GRD	Guadeloupe	GLP
Guam	GUM	Guatemala	GTM
Guinea	GIN	Guinea-Bissau	GNB
Guyana	GUY	Haiti	HTI
Heard and McDonald Islands	HMD	Honduras	HND
Hong Kong	HKG	Hungary	HUN
Iceland	ISL	India	IND
Indonesia	IDN	Iran	IRN
Iraq	IRQ	Ireland	IRL
Israel	ISR	Italy	ITA
Jamaica	JAM	Japan	JPN
Jordan	JOR	Kampuchea Democratic	KHM
Kenya	KEN	Kiribati	KIR
Korea Democratic People's Republic	PRK	Korea Republic of	KOR
Kuwait	KWT	Lao People's Democratic Republic	LAO
Lebanon	LBN	Lesotho	LSO
Liberia	LBR	Libyan Arab Jamahiriya	LBY
Liechtenstein	LIE	Luxembourg	LUX
Macau	MAC	Madagascar	MDG
Malawi	MWI	Malaysia	MYS
Maldives	MDV	Mali	MLI
Malta	MLT	Marshall Islands	MHL
Martinique	MTQ	Mauritania	MRT
Mauritius	MUS	Mexico	MEX
Micronesia	FSM	Monaco	MCO
Mongolia	MNG	Montserrat	MSR
Morocco	MAR	Mozambique	MOZ
Namibia	NAM	Nauru	NRU
Nepal	NPL	Netherlands	NLD

Netherlands Antilles	ANT	Neutral Zone	NTZ
New Caledonia	NCL	New Zealand	NZL
Nicaragua	NIC	Niger	NER
Nigeria	NGA	Niue	NIU
Norfolk Island	NFK	Northern Mariana Islands	MNP
Norway	NOR	Oman	OMN
Pakistan	PAK	Palau	PLW
Panama	PAN	Papua New Guinea	PNG
Paraguay	PRY	Peru	PER
Philippines	PHL	Pitcairn Island	PCN
Poland	POL	Portugal	PRT
Puerto Rico	PRI	Qatar	QAT
Reunion	REU	Romania	ROM
Rwanda	RWA	St. Helena	SHN
Saint Kitts and Nevis	KNA	Saint Lucia	LCA
St. Pierre and Miquelon	SPM	Saint Vincent and the Grenadines	VCT
Samoa	WSM	San Marino	SMR
Sao Tome and Principe	STP	Saudi Arabia	SAU
Senegal	SEN	Seychelles	SYC
Sierra Leones	SLE	Singapore	SGP
Solomon Islands	SLB	Somalia	SOM
South Africa	ZAF	Spain	ESP
Sri Lanka	LKA	Sudan	SDN
Suriname	SUR	Svalbard and Jan Mayen Islands	SJM
Swaziland	SWZ	Sweden	SWE
Switzerland	CHE	Syrian Arab Republic	SYR
Taiwan Province of China	TWN	Tanzania United Republic of	TZA
Thailand	THA	Togo	TGO
Tokelau	TKL	Tonga	TON
Trinidad and Tobago	TTO	Tunisia	TUN

Turkey	TUR	Turks and Caicos Islands	TCA
Tuvalu	TUV	Uganda	UGA
Ukranian SSR	UKR	United Arab Emirates	ARE
United Kingdom	GBR	United States	USA
US Minor Outlying Islands	UMI	Uruguay	URY
USSR	SUN	Vanuatu	VUT
Vatican City State	VAT	Venezuela	VEN
Vietnam	VNM	Virgin Islands (British)	VGB
Virgin Islands (U.S.)	VIR	Wallis and Futuna Islands	WLF
Western Sahara	ESH	Yemen	YEM
Yemen Democratic	YMD	Yugoslavia	YUG
Zaire	ZAR	Zambia	ZMB
Zimbabwe	ZWE		

Active Server Pages Object Model

This appendix offers a handy reference to the Active Server Pages **object model**, and in each case provides the properties, methods and events for the object, along with their collections.

The Request Object

Together, the `Request` object and the `Response` object form the 'conversational mechanism' of ASP. The `Request` object is responsible for controlling how the user sends information to the server. Using the `Request` object, the server can obtain information about what the user wants – either explicitly (for example, through programmed ASP code) or implicitly (for example, through the HTTP headers).

Collections	Description
ClientCertificate	Client certificate values sent from the browser. Read Only
Cookies	Values of cookies sent from the browser. Read Only
Form	Values of form elements sent from the browser. Read Only
QueryString	Values of variables in the HTTP query string. Read Only
ServerVariables	Values of the HTTP and environment variables. Read Only

Property	Description
TotalBytes	Specifies the number of bytes the client is sending in the body of the request. Read Only

Method	Description
BinaryRead	Used to retrieve data sent to the server as part of the POST request

The Response Object

The Response object is responsible for sending the server's output to the client. In this sense, the Response object is the counterpart to the Request object: the Request object gathers information from both the client and the server, and the Response object sends, or resends, the information to the client by writing to the HTTP data stream.

Collection	Description
Cookies	Values of all the cookies to send to the browser.

Properties	Description
Buffer	Determines whether the page is to be buffered until complete
CacheControl	Determines whether proxy servers are allowed to cache the output generated by ASP
Charset	Appends the name of the character set to the content-type header
ContentType	HTTP content type (e.g. "Text/HTML") for the response
Expires	Number of minutes between caching and expiry, for a page cached on the browser
ExpiresAbsolute	Explicit date and/or time of expiry for a page cached on a browser
IsClientConnected	Indicates whether the client has disconnected from the server
PICS	Adds the value of a PICS label to the pics-label field of the response header
Status	Value of the HTTP status line returned by the server

Methods	Description
AddHeader	Adds or changes a value in the HTML header
AppendToLog	Adds text to the web server log entry for this request
BinaryWrite	Sends text to the browser without character-set conversion
Clear	Erases any buffered HTML output
End	Stops processing the page and returns the current result
Flush	Sends buffered output immediately
Redirect	Instructs the browser to connect to a different URL
Write	Writes variable values, strings etc. to the current page as a string

The Response interface elements can be divided into groups, like this:

Response Items	Description
Write, BinaryWrite	Inserts information into a page
Cookies	Sends cookies to the browser
Redirect	Redirects the browser
Buffer, Flush, Clear, End	Buffers the page as it is created
Expires, ExpiresAbsolute, ContentType, AddHeader, Status, CacheContol, PICS, Charset	Sets the properties of a page
IsClientConnected	Checks the client connection

The Application Object

Each application is represented by an instance of the Application object. This object stores variables and objects for application-scope usage. It also holds information about any currently-active sessions.

Collections	Description
Contents	Contains all of the items added to the application through script commands
StaticObjects	Contains all of the objects added to the application with the <OBJECT> tag

Methods	Description
Lock	Prevents other clients from modifying application properties
Unlock	Allows other clients to modify application properties

Events	Description
OnStart	Occurs when a page in the application is first referenced
OnEnd	Occurs when the application ends, that is, when the web server is stopped

The Session Object

The Session object is used to keep track of an individual browser as it navigates through your web site.

Collections	Description
Contents	Contains all of the items added to the session through script commands
StaticObjects	Contains all of the objects added to the session with the <OBJECT> tag

Method	Description
Abandon	Destroys a Session object and releases its resources

Properties	Description
CodePage	Sets the codepage that will be used for symbol mapping
LCID	Sets the locale identifier
SessionID	Returns the session identification for this user
Timeout	Sets the timeout period for the session state for this application, in minutes

Events	Description
OnStart	Occurs when the server creates a new session
OnEnd	Occurs when a session is abandoned or times out

The Server Object

The main use of the `Server` object is to create components.

Property	Description
ScriptTimeout	Length of time a script can run before an error occurs

Methods	Description
CreateObject	Creates an instance of an object or server component
HTMLEncode	Applies HTML encoding to the specified string
MapPath	Converts a virtual path into a physical path
URLEncode	Applies URL encoding including escape chars to a string

The ObjectContext Object

When we use MTS (Microsoft Transaction Server) to manage a transaction, we have the functionality within our script to commit (or to abort) the transaction. This functionality is provided by the `ObjectContext` object.

Methods	Description
SetComplete	Declares that the script knows no reason for the transaction not to complete. If all participating components call `SetComplete` then the transaction will complete. `SetComplete` overrides any previous `SetAbort` method that has been called in the script
SetAbort	Aborts a transaction initiated by an ASP

Events	Description
OnTransactionCommit	Occurs after a transacted script's transaction commits
OnTransactionAbort	Occurs if the transaction is aborted

Introducing the Ad Server

There is an example that I always make when I'm writing about the Ad Server component of SSCE. Invariably, I get all sorts of comments about how good or bad a comparison it represents. Soon enough, people will also start complaining that I always reuse the same story, too, but for the moment I'm content to have found the archetype of online advertising, and therefore shall employ it again here.

There is a simple parallel that can be made between online advertising and the history of television commercials. Even though time is measured in weeks in one case and in decades in the other, they both started out as "undiscovered lands" for the people who wanted to make money out of them. Very much like the example of whoever first started selling online, the pioneers of advertising had to understand what could be made out of these new media they had to deal with *before* they could actually take advantage of their full potential.

Since an experimental approach often yields excellent results (unless human beings or animals are involved!), their only way was to try, and try again until they had reached their goals. As a result, the first TV commercials in the early fifties were essentially radio adverts in which it was possible to actually see the person who was making the announcement (at least until they discovered the beauty of lip synch). Naturally, that must have been quite astonishing for the people who lived in the Fifties, but as time went on, new technologies became available and more creative thinkers began to better understand what television could do; the face of commercials changed dramatically, to the point that their importance is paramount in our economy.

From this point of view, the Internet is very much still in its infancy. I think it's fair to say that nobody has yet truly understood what the future of online advertising is, but the good thing is that they're trying. The real problem is in the fact that it's difficult to guess what one can expect from the Internet – with TV, it's easy: you send a picture signal, everyone gets it the same, whether they have a three-inch black-and-white Zenith dinosaur or the latest drive-in-into-your-dining room thingy. The experience will be different, but people will *understand* – if you have a small receiver, you won't be blown away by the 3-D sound, but hey, it's smaller, right? With the Internet, it's a lot more difficult – the box for an 8086 is dangerously similar to the latest Pentium III chip (and the similarities don't stop there, sadly), and many people are not experienced enough to tell that the reason why it takes thirty minutes to download an animated GIF is simply that their connection is not fast enough, or maybe that they don't have enough RAM in their system, and so on.

On the other hand, even experienced users – or, at least, one of them – have similar problems. I use a decent system and have a fast connection coming into my home, but I often find myself annoyed by the fact that it takes ten seconds to download a file, or wondering whether the OS was really slower with my older PC. I'm not trying to show off my equipment (any of it), or be snobbish – these things *do* really happen. So, what do I do? I watch TV. At least I know what I'm getting.

The Ad Server

With all the problems of a newborn communication medium, the good news is that a few serious players have begun to create a set of standardized tools for the delivery of online advertisement. Since there are only a few players who are as serious about the Internet as Microsoft is, it's really not a surprise that we find a complete ad delivery system inside Site Server. The pleasant surprise, considering that it is part of such a large package, is what great things it does and how much performance it delivers.

Compared to Commerce Server, P&M and many of the other components of SSCE, the Ad Server (AS for brevity) is less evident, and also more "compact" than its counterparts. By this, I mean that its code is based much less on ASP and more on a well-written (at least judging from how it works) and efficiently compiled language. There are a number of good reasons for this: first of all, the Ad Server must readily provide its functions whenever it has to provide an ad. It's all right if the user has to wait a couple more seconds to get to a page in a store, but such a delay in delivering a banner ad could mean a lost impression if the user has already left the page. Also, the functionality that the Ad Server provides hardly requires as much expansion as an online store or a P&M implementation; thus, the core (compiled) code of the AS works as a great advertisement selection engine, and any other operation can be taken care of through normal ASP scripts.

A Few Terms to Remember

Before getting into more detail, we should get acquainted with some of the terms that are often used in the online advertising industry, which is young, but not young enough to be free from having its own jargon. We'll start by examining in what formats ads are delivered online, and then quickly go through how they are kept track of and sold.

Common Ad Delivery Formats

The most common format for delivery ads is the **banner ad**, often referred to simply as a "banner". A banner is simply an image, usually 468 pixels wide and 68 pixels high, that is delivered to the user's browser through normal HTML commands. In most cases, the banner is in either JPG or GIF format, and in the latter case can also contain short animations. Most recently, however, a few software developers have come out with new proprietary formats that deliver a "richer" experience by integrating sounds, longer animations and a higher degree of interactivity with the user. A typical example of this is the Enliven format, based on the Java language and available from the Enliven web site (http://www.enliven.com). The problem with these formats is that they often require special software or browser capabilities that not all users will have, and therefore are precluded to at least a portion of the total Internet audience.

Finally, a banner can also be a simple HTML table, formatted so that it will fit in the space otherwise dedicated to a simple image. Well-designed HTML banners give most Internet users the possibility of truly interacting with the advertisement they carry, and therefore represent a good balance between usability and functionality. Unfortunately, in the beginning most ad delivery systems were unable to offer anything beyond the simple image, and therefore this type of banner is still not very much in use to this day.

Another common format for delivering ads over the Internet is the **button**, which is simply a picture whose size is not standardized, even though it's smaller than that of a banner.

Delivery Mechanisms

The delivery of a single ad on a web page is called an **impression**. As you can imagine, the impression is the unit of measurement used in advertising campaigns. The cost of a single impression, however, is very small since the rate of return on Internet advertising, as we'll see shortly, is rather minuscule. As a result, the actual measurement of campaign costs is done in *thousands* of impressions, or CPM (cost per mil). Thus, when an advertising campaign is set up, its cost is determined by multiplying the number of thousand impressions that have to be delivered by the *CPM rate* of the site or network on which they are being delivered.

The success of a banner ad is determined by measuring how many people "click" on it. Every time a user clicks on the link associated with a particular banner, his or her browser actually goes through a "redirection URL" – a simple script that counts the click and redirects the browser to its final destination. The ratio between the number of clicks and the number of impressions, called *click-through rate* and expressed in percentile points, determines the success of the banner. Non-targeted ads – those who are delivered to anybody, regardless of their preferences or behavior on a particular site – usually have very low click-through rates (a banner that scores between 2% and 5% is usually considered a success), while targeted ads can yield much better results, since there is a greater possibility that whoever sees them will be interested in finding out where they will take them.

> **Sometimes ad campaigns are scheduled by the number of clicks rather than by the number of impressions.**

So, What Can This Ad Server Do?

The Ad Server is capable of handling all the specifications that we have just given, plus some more that we'll find out later on – which makes it quite a flexible piece of software. In particular, it supports just about any delivery format that you can think of, with the added bonus of letting us specify any additional number of arbitrary formats. In addition, it will let us organize our ad delivery system by campaign, and the campaigns by customer. Thanks to this, managing our entire network of ad deliveries will be a breeze.

What's more, the Ad Server makes it possible to *target* the delivery of ads so that they reach a specific category of users. This means that it will be possible to integrate the AS with other Site Server components, such as P&M, and truly deliver a superior web-browsing experience. Naturally, that is not to say that integration is easy to perform, nor that the AS is already well integrated with the other components of SSCE – unfortunately, that seems to be a recurring problem with most of the package! However, the targeting feature of the AS gives us at least the basic tools, if not exactly the means, to create a fully integrated and targeted delivery system.

A target is simply a keyword that is defined for the location where an ad has to be delivered. For example, a banner that appears in the soccer section of your local newspaper might have the targets "sport" and "soccer". When an ad has to be delivered, the AS makes its decision based on the relationships that each banner declares with the particular targets that belong to the location. There are three types of relationships that can be declared by a banner:

❑ **Required**
Indicates that, in order for the ad to be delivered, the target must be present in the location.

❑ **Exclude**
Indicates that, in order for the ad to be delivered, the target must *not* be present in the location

❑ **Target**
Indicates an affinity between the banner and the target that will influence the delivery decision. It corresponds to something like "the banner should preferentially be delivered where this target is present".

Thus, a banner that has the relationships (Required, Sports), (Target, Soccer) would be likely to be displayed in the location we just mentioned, while another one with the relationship (Exclude, Sports) would never be displayed there.

When no other ad can be delivered, the AS delivers a "standard" or "default" banner – which is much better than producing an error.

The Ad Manager

Let's now move on to take a quick look at the Ad Manager (AM from now on, lest we kill too many trees), which is the Ad Server's primary management platform. The Ad Manager is a completely web-based application (in fact, it's written in ASP and takes advantage of the same COM object used to deliver the ads!) that lets us administer all the aspects of the ad server, with the exception, obviously, of the ASP code that we need to write in order to deliver the ads themselves!

The AM, whose main page is shown in the following figure, is divided into four distinct sections: Customers, Performance, Ad Sizes and Refresh. With the exception of Customers, the other three perform simple functions. The Performance section gives a real-time report regarding the status of each campaign and ad that is being delivered to the users. The Ad Sizes, on the other hand, lets us specify new ad sizes or modify existing ones. Clicking on Refresh, on the other hand, lets us regenerate the internal cache in which the AS keeps all its data. This is necessary because, for performance reasons, the COM object that takes care of the delivery only reads and writes to its database at pre-defined intervals (refresh rate).

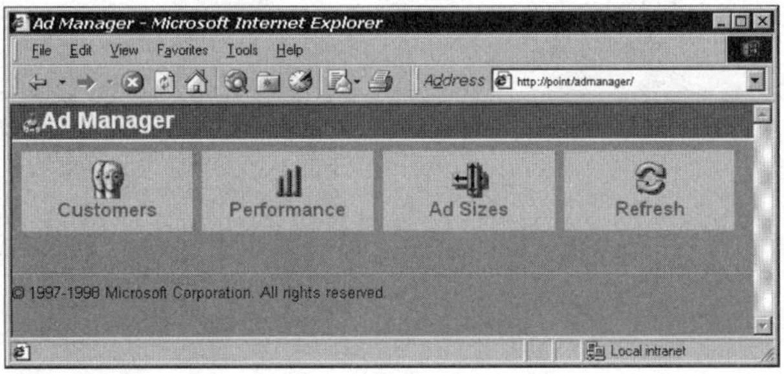

Customers, Campaigns and Items

After a minimal setup process – which is barely necessary given the completeness in which the AS will be installed on your machine – the Customers section of the AM will be the most accessed portion of the management site; if you could, you would definitely wear the link that leads to it!

The first page that appears once you click on the Customers link (seen in the next figure) includes a list of all the customers that you have in your database. A customer represents the highest-level logical grouping in the Ad Server's structure, and it's there simply to help you organize your ads better, since the AS doesn't really make any significant use of it. As you can see, you can specify a number of useful information bits for any given customer that will be useful when you need to get in touch with them (hopefully to tell them how well their campaign went!)

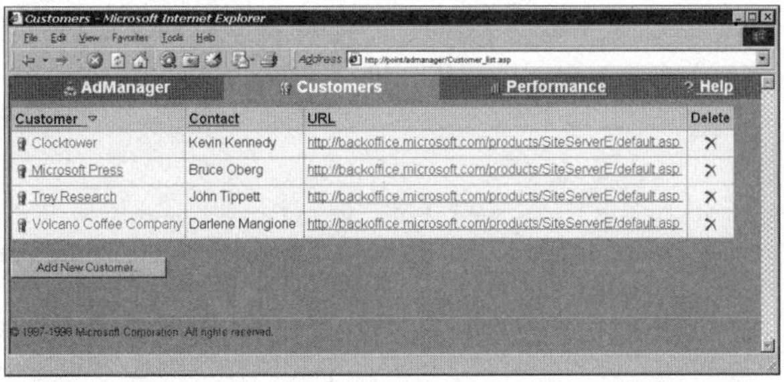

Each customer can contain zero or more **campaigns**, as shown in the first of the following figures. A campaign, as you can imagine, is essentially a group of ads that share the same delivery method (that is, by clicks or by impressions). As with Customers, Campaigns are also logical groupings that are part of the system to make the organization of the entire delivery schedule a little easier.

Finally, a campaign contains zero or more **campaign items**. A campaign item is, essentially, the definition of a single ad, complete with its delivery method, number of impressions or clicks, start and end date, targeting and so on. As you can see from the second of the following figures, all these parameters can be specified when the item is being created.

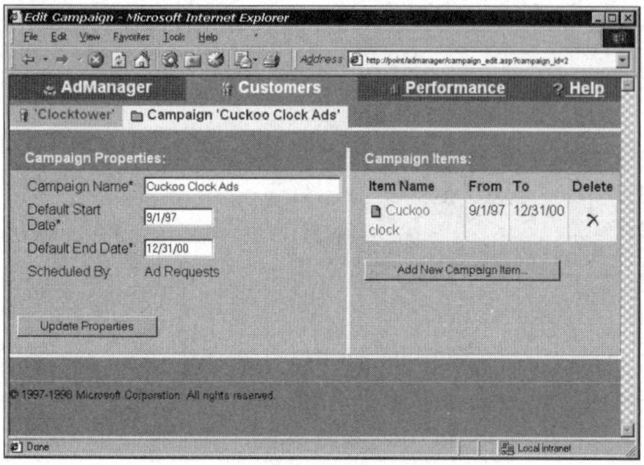

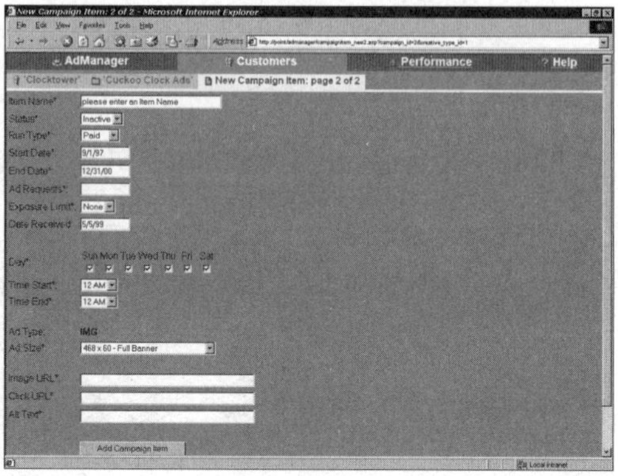

Using the Ad Server

In order to deliver ads in your site, you will need to follow a three-step process:

1. Create a redirection URL

2. Modify `global.asa` to start up the AS

3. Write the delivery code

The first part can be easily undertaken by creating a new ASP script and making sure that it contains the following two lines of code:

```
<%
Application ("AS").RecordEvent (Application, Request ("CIID"), "CLICK")
Response.Redirect (Request ("URL"))
%>
```

The first line calls a method of the delivery COM object (we'll see how it ends up in the `Application` object in a few lines) that "records" an event – a click-through in this case. As you can see, `RecordEvent` needs a pointer to the `Application` object, the `CIID` parameter, which contains the internal identifier of the ad that was clicked on, and the type of event to record (`CLICK` in our case).

Setting up `global.asa` is by no means a complex operation, although you should pay attention to two details: first, you must have a database that the AS can use to store its internal information; second, make sure that you write your code in the right place. In fact, for performance reasons, the delivery COM object is loaded into memory once at the beginning of the ASP application and then used throughout the site (that's how it ends up in the `Application` object, in case you were wondering). A very common error is to place the code to create and load the ad in the `Session_OnStart` method rather than the `Application_OnStart` one. As a result, a new instance of the COM object is created every time a user enters the site, and your server runs out of memory at a rapid rate.

Thus, your `global.asa` will contain something similar to the following in the `Application_OnStart` subroutine:

```
Set ASobj = Server.CreateObject ("Commerce.AdServer")
Set Application ("AS") = ASobj

ASobj.ConnectionString = MSCSSite.DefaultConnectionString
Asobj.RedirectURL = "http://www.myserver.com/redirect/click.asp"
ASobj.RefreshInterval = 240
Asobj.Application = "MyApp"
```

The first two lines simply create an instance of the AS object and store it in the `Application` intrinsic ASP object. Next, we assign a connection string that the object can use to access the database. In this case, we're assuming that the site is a Commerce Server store, but you can specify anything in here, as long as it's a working ODBC string, and you *don't* need Commerce Server to run the AS.

Next, we indicate the address of the redirection URL, which is also the location of the small script that we just saw a few paragraphs back. The last two lines of code determine respectively how often (in seconds) the system will refresh its data, updating the database with the latest performance information and loading in the most recent campaign schedule, and what the name of our application in the Ad Manager will be.

Delivering Ads

Ad delivery is usually a relatively easy task performed directly from within your ASP scripts. The first step consists of creating a "list of targets", which is an array of strings that contains all the targets declared by the location where the ad will be delivered. The AS predefines six different targets, indicating the position, size or border size of the location, but an arbitrary number of additional targets can be specified. For example:

```
TargetList = Array ("Soccer", "Sports", "_top")
```

Next, we'll have to generate an "Impression History", which is simply a list, stored in a string, of all the ads that have been delivered to a particular user during the current session. The AS object automatically updates and interprets this string, so we don't have to worry about its contents, with the exception that it has to be passed along from page to page. If you have sessions enabled, you can use them; otherwise you can take advantage of the `OrderForm` object of a Commerce Server store. If all else fails, you can still pass it along in the URL query.

Finally, the ad can be delivered by calling the `GetAd` method of the delivery COM object. For example:

```
<%
    TargetList = Array ("Sports", "Soccer")
    HistoryString = Session ("HistoryString")
    Response.Write As.GetAd (Response, TargetList, HistoryString)
%>
```

Where To Find More Information

The information in this Appendix should be enough to get you started, particularly considering that the AS is very intuitive and well documented. The first place I would therefore recommend that you look for more information is the documentation that comes with Site Server. You'll find answers to most of your questions there.

Eventually, however, you'll begin to find certain shortcomings in the system. One of them, for example, is that since the delivery COM object has to reside on the machine where the ad has to be delivered, it's impossible to display ads on another site. This is a bit of a problem, particularly if you consider that being able to build an "advertisement network" is a major feature in an ad delivery system. Here's another one: since the AM is such a beautiful web-based application, it would be great if you could have your customers access it and therefore allow them to view real-time performance data of their ads. The major stumbling block, however, is that you can't limit access to just *their* ads – they would be able to see everyone else's as well.

Naturally, Microsoft has already thought about this – and more. The second problem has been solved with a patch to the system that makes it possible to regulate the access to the AM so that a customer can only see his or her account's information. The first one is a bit more complex to solve, although some have been known to overcome it completely; Microsoft has indeed published a small whitepaper that illustrates several possible solutions to it. The locations of these files on the Microsoft website changes frequently, but a good starting point is the following URL:

http://www.microsoft.com/commerce

Look for the Deployment section and check out the availability of downloadable files.

F

Support and Errata

One of the most irritating things about any programming book is when you find that bit of code you've just spent an hour typing simply doesn't work. You check it a hundred times to see if you've set it up correctly and then you notice the spelling mistake in the variable name on the book page. Of course, you can blame the authors for not taking enough care and testing the code, the editors for not doing their job properly, or the proofreaders for not being eagle-eyed enough, but this doesn't get around the fact that mistakes do happen.

We try hard to ensure no mistakes sneak out into the real world, but we can't promise that this book is 100% error free. What we can do is offer the next best thing by providing you with immediate support and feedback from experts who have worked on the book and try to ensure that future editions eliminate these gremlins. The following section will take you step by step through the process of posting errata to our web site to get that help. The sections that follow, therefore, are:

❑ Wrox Developers Membership
❑ Finding a list of existing errata on the web site

There is also a section covering how to e-mail a question for technical support. This comprises:

❑ What your e-mail should include
❑ What happens to your e-mail once it has been received by us

So that you only need view information relevant to yourself, we ask that you register as a Wrox Developer Member. This is a quick and easy process, that will save you time in the long run. If you are already a member, just update membership to include this book.

Wrox Developer Membership

To get your FREE Wrox Developer Membership click on Membership in the navigation bar of our home site – `http://www.wrox.com`. This is shown in the following screenshot:

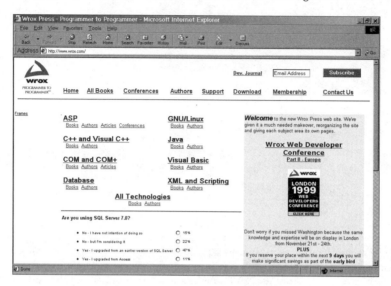

Then, on the next screen (not shown), click on New User. This will display a form. Fill in the details on the form and submit the details using the Register button at the bottom. Go back to the main Membership page, enter your details and select Logon. Before you can say 'The best read books come in Wrox Red' you will get the following screen:

Finding an Errata on the Web Site

Before you send in a query, you might be able to save time by finding the answer to your problem on our web site – http:\\www.wrox.com.

Each book we publish has its own page and its own errata sheet. You can get to any book's page by clicking on Support from the top navigation bar.

From this page you can locate any book's errata page on our site. Select your book from the pop-up menu and click on it.

Then click on Errata. This will take you to the errata page for the book. Select the criteria by which you want to view the errata, and click the Apply criteria... button. This will provide you with links to specific errata. For an initial search, you are advised to view the errata by page numbers. If you have looked for an error previously, then you may wish to limit your search using dates. We update these pages daily to ensure that you have the latest information on bugs and errors.

E-mail Support

If you wish to directly query a problem in the book with an expert who knows the book in detail then e-mail support@wrox.com, with the title of the book and the last four numbers of the ISBN in the subject field of the e-mail. A typical email should include the following things:

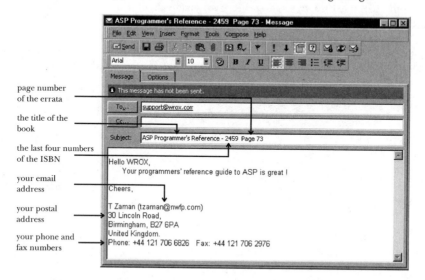

We won't send you junk mail. We need the details to save your time and ours. If we need to replace a disk or CD we'll be able to get it to you straight away. When you send an e-mail it will go through the following chain of support:

Customer Support

Your message is delivered to one of our customer support staff who are the first people to read it. They have files on most frequently asked questions and will answer anything general immediately. They answer general questions about the book and the web site.

Editorial

Deeper queries are forwarded to the technical editor responsible for that book. They have experience with the programming language or particular product and are able to answer detailed technical questions on the subject. Once an issue has been resolved, the editor can post the errata to the web site.

The Authors

Finally, in the unlikely event that the editor can't answer your problem, s/he will forward the request to the author. We try to protect the author from any distractions from writing. However, we are quite happy to forward specific requests to them. All Wrox authors help with the support on their books. They'll mail the customer and the editor with their response, and again all readers should benefit.

What We Can't Answer

Obviously with an ever-growing range of books and an ever-changing technology base, there is an increasing volume of data requiring support. While we endeavor to answer all questions about the book, we can't answer bugs in your own programs that you've adapted from our code. So, while you might have loved the help desk systems in our Active Server Pages book, don't expect too much sympathy if you cripple your company with a live adaptation you customized from Chapter 12. However, do tell us if you're especially pleased with the routine you developed with our help.

How to Tell Us Exactly What You Think

We understand that errors can destroy the enjoyment of a book and can cause many wasted and frustrated hours, so we seek to minimize the distress that they can cause.

You might just wish to tell us how much you liked or loathed the book in question. Or you might have ideas about how this whole process could be improved, in which case you should e-mail feedback@wrox.com. You'll always find a sympathetic ear, no matter what the problem is. Above all you should remember that we do care about what you have to say and we will do our utmost to act upon it.

Index

B